Java Development with Ant

Java Development with Ant

ERIK HATCHER
STEVE LOUGHRAN

MANNING

Greenwich
(74° w. long.)

For online information and ordering of this and other Manning books,
go to www.manning.com. The publisher offers discounts on this book
when ordered in quantity. For more information, please contact:

Special Sales Department
Manning Publications Co.
209 Bruce Park Avenue   Fax: (203) 661-9018
Greenwich, CT 06830   email: orders@manning.com

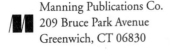
Manning Publications Co.   Copyeditor: Maarten Reilingh
209 Bruce Park Avenue   Typesetter: Martine Maguire-Weltecke
Greenwich, CT 06830   Cover designer: Leslie Haimes

ISBN 1930110588
Printed in the United States of America
3 4 5 6 7 8 9 10 – VHG – 06 05 04 03 02

To my wife Carole and our two sons, Jakob and Ethan.
Thank you for taking care of me while I took care of this book.
Erik

To Bina and Alexander.
Thank you for being so patient during the long hours of this project.
Steve

brief contents

Part 1 Learning Ant 1

    1 Introducing Ant 3

    2 Getting started with Ant 23

    3 Understanding Ant datatypes and properties 47

    4 Testing with JUnit 85

    5 Executing programs 111

    6 Packaging projects 134

    7 Deployment 163

    8 Putting it all together 188

Part 2 Applying Ant 203

    9 Using Ant in your development projects 205

    10 Beyond Ant's core tasks 234

    11 XDoclet 260

12 Developing for the web   278

13 Working with XML   317

14 Enterprise JavaBeans   333

15 Working with web services   355

16 Continuous integration   386

17 Developing native code   407

18 Production deployment   431

Part 3   Extending Ant 465

19 Writing Ant tasks   467

20 Extending Ant further   498

Appendices

A Installation   523

B XML primer as it applies to Ant   532

C IDE integration   536

D The elements of Ant style   544

E Ant task reference   561

contents

foreword   xxv

preface   xxvii

acknowledgments   xxix

about this book   xxxi

about the authors   xxxvi

about the cover illustration   xxxvii

Part 1   Learning Ant 1

1   Introducing Ant   3

1.1   What is Ant?   3
What is a build process and why do you need one?   4
Why do we think Ant makes a great build tool?   4

1.2   The core concepts of Ant   5
An example project   7

1.3   Why use Ant?   10
Integrated development environments   10
Make   11   ✦   Other build tools   13
Up and running, in no time   14

1.4   The evolution of Ant   14

1.5   Ant and software development methodologies   16
eXtreme Programming   16
Rational Unified Process   17

1.6   Our example project   17
Documentation search engine—example Ant project   18

1.7   Yeah, but can Ant…   19

1.8   Beyond Java development   21
Web publishing engine   21   ✦   Simple workflow engine   21
Microsoft .NET and other languages   21

1.9   Summary   22

2   *Getting started with Ant*   23

2.1   Defining our first project   23

2.2   Step one: verifying the tools are in place   24

2.3   Step two: writing your first Ant build file   24
      Examining the build file   25

2.4   Step three: running your first build   26
      If the build fails   27   ✦   Looking at the build in more detail   29

2.5   Step four: imposing structure   31
      Laying out the source directories   32   ✦   Laying out the
      build directories   33   ✦   Laying out the dist directories   34
      Creating the build file   35   ✦   Target dependencies   35
      Running the new build file   36   ✦   Rerunning the build   37
      How Ant handles multiple targets on the command line   38

2.6   Step five: running our program   39
      Why execute from inside Ant   39
      Adding an execute target   40   ✦   Running the new target   40

2.7   Ant command line options   41
      Specifying which build file to run   42
      Controlling the amount of information provided   42
      Getting information about a project   44

2.8   The final build file   44

2.9   Summary   46

3   *Understanding Ant datatypes and properties*   47

3.1   Preliminaries   48
      Datatype overview   48   ✦   Property overview   48

3.2   Introducing datatypes and properties with <javac>   49

3.3   Paths   51

3.4   Filesets   52
      Fileset examples   53   ✦   Default excludes   53

3.5   Patternsets   54

3.6   Selectors   56

3.7   Datatype element naming   57

3.8   Filterset   58
      Inserting date stamps in files at build-time   58

3.9   FilterChains and FilterReaders   59

3.10   Mappers   61
       Identity mapper   61   ✦   Flatten mapper   62
       Merge mapper   62   ✦   Glob mapper   63
       Regexp mapper   63   ✦   Package mapper   64

3.11 Additional Ant datatypes   65
ZipFileset   65   ✦   Dirset   65
Filelist   65   ✦   ClassFileset   66

3.12 Properties   66
Setting properties with the <property> task   67
How the <property> task is different   70
Checking for the availability of resources: <available>   70
Saving time by skipping unnecessary steps: <uptodate>   72
Testing conditions with <condition>   72
Setting properties from the command-line   74
Creating a build timestamp with <tstamp>   75
Loading properties from an XML file   76

3.13 Controlling Ant with properties   77
Conditional target execution   77
Conditional patternset inclusion/exclusion   78
Conditional build failure   78

3.14 References   79
Properties and references   80
Using references for nested patternsets   81

3.15 Best practices   82

3.16 Summary   83

4   *Testing with JUnit*   85

4.1   Refactoring   86

4.2   Java main() testing   86

4.3   JUnit primer   87
Writing a test case   88   ✦   Running a test case   88
Asserting desired results   88   ✦   TestCase lifecycle   90
Writing a TestSuite   90   ✦   Obtaining and installing JUnit   91
Extensions to JUnit   91

4.4   Applying unit tests to our application   92
Writing the test first   92
Dealing with external resources during testing   93

4.5   The JUnit task—<junit>   94
Structure directories to accommodate testing   94
Fitting JUnit into the build process   95

4.6   Test failures are build failures   97
Capturing test results   97   ✦   Running multiple tests   99
Creating your own results formatter   100

4.7   Generating test result reports   100
Generate reports and allow test failures to fail the build   102
Run a single test case from the command-line   103
Initializing the test environment   103   ✦   Other test issues   104

4.8 Short-circuiting tests   105
Dealing with large number of tests   108

4.9 Best practices   109

4.10 Summary   110

5   Executing programs   111

5.1 Why you need to run external programs   111

5.2 Running Java programs   112
Introducing the <java> task   113 ✦ Setting the classpath   114
Arguments   115 ✦ Defining system properties   116
Running the program in a new JVM   117
Setting environment variables   118 ✦ Controlling the
new JVM   118 ✦ Handling errors with failonerror   119
Executing JAR files   120 ✦ Calling third-party programs   121
Probing for a Java program before calling it   123
Setting a timeout   124

5.3 Starting native programs with <exec>   124
Setting environment variables   126 ✦ Handling errors   126
Handling timeouts   127 ✦ Making and executing
shell commands   127 ✦ Probing for a program before calling it   129

5.4 Bulk execution with <apply>   130

5.5 Processing output   131

5.6 Limitations on execution   132

5.7 Best practices   132

5.8 Summary   133

6   Packaging projects   134

6.1 Moving, copying, and deleting files   135
How to delete files   135 ✦ How to copy files   136
How to move files   137 ✦ Filtering   138

6.2 Preparing to package   139
Building and documenting release code   139
Adding data files   141 ✦ Preparing documentation   142
Preparing install scripts and documents   143
Preparing libraries for redistribution   145

6.3 Creating archive files   146
JAR files   148 ✦ Creating a JAR file   148
Testing the JAR file   149 ✦ Creating JAR manifests   150
Adding extra metadata to the JAR   152
JAR file best practices   152 ✦ Signing JAR files   152

6.4 Creating Zip files 154
Creating a binary distribution 154 ✦ Creating a
source distribution 156 ✦ Merging Zip files 157
Zip file best practices 157

6.5 Creating tar files 158

6.6 Creating web applications with WAR files 160

6.7 Testing packaging 161

6.8 Summary 162

7   Deployment 163

7.1 Example deployment problems 164
Reviewing the tasks 164 ✦ Tools for deployment 164

7.2 Tasks for deployment 165
File transfer with <ftp> 166 ✦ Probing for server availability 166
Inserting pauses into the build with <sleep> ·168
Ant's email task 169 ✦ Fetching remote files with <get> 170
Using the tasks to deploy 171

7.3 FTP-based distribution of a packaged application 171
Asking for information with the <input> task 172

7.4 Email-based distribution of a packaged application 173

7.5 Local deployment to Tomcat 4.x 174
The Tomcat management servlet API 175
Deploying to Tomcat with Ant 176

7.6 Remote deployment to Tomcat 181
Interlude: calling targets with <antcall> 182
Using <antcall> in deployment 185

7.7 Testing deployment 187

7.8 Summary 187

8   Putting it all together 188

8.1 Our application thus far 188

8.2 Building the custom Ant task library 189

8.3 Loading common properties across multiple projects 194

8.4 Handling versioned dependencies 196
Installing a new library version 198

8.5 Build file philosophy 200
Begin with the end in mind 200 ✦ Integrate tests with
the build 200 ✦ Support automated deployment 200
Make it portable 200 ✦ Allow for customizations 201

8.6 Summary 201

Part 2 Applying Ant 203

9 Using Ant in your development projects 205

9.1 Designing an Ant-based build process 206
Analyzing your project 206 ✦ Creating the core build file 208
Evolve the build file 208

9.2 Migrating to Ant 209

9.3 The ten steps of migration 210
Migrating from Make-based projects 211
Migrating from IDE-based projects 211

9.4 Master builds: managing large projects 212
Refactoring build files 212 ✦ Introducing the <ant> task 213
Example: a basic master build file 213
Designing a scalable, flexible master build file 215

9.5 Managing child project builds 221
How to control properties of child projects 221
Inheriting properties and references from a master build file 223
Declaring properties and references in <ant> 224
Sharing properties via XML file fragments 225
Sharing targets with XML file fragments 227

9.6 Creating reusable library build files 228

9.7 Looking ahead: large project support evolution 230

9.8 Ant project best practices 231
Managing libraries 232 ✦ Implementing processes 232

9.9 Summary 233

10 Beyond Ant's core tasks 234

10.1 Understanding types of tasks 235
So, what is an "optional" task? 235 ✦ Ant's major
optional tasks 236 ✦ Why third-party tasks? 237

10.2 Optional tasks in action 237
Manipulating property files 237
Adding audio and visual feedback during a build 239
Adding dependency checks 241 ✦ Grammar parsing
with JavaCC 243 ✦ Regular expression replacement 244

10.3 Using software configuration management tasks 245
CVS 245 ✦ ClearCase 246

10.4 Using third-party tasks 247
Defining tasks with <taskdef> 247

10.5 Notable third-party tasks 248
Checkstyle 248 ✦ Torque–object-relational mapping 250

10.6 The ant-contrib tasks 253

10.7 Sharing task definitions among projects 258

10.8 Best practices 258

10.9 Summary 259

11 *XDoclet* *260*

11.1 Installing XDoclet 261

11.2 To-do list generation 261

11.3 XDoclet architecture 262
XDoclet's Ant tasks 263 ✦ Templating 264
How XDoclet works 265

11.4 Writing your own XDoclet template 265
Code generation 267 ✦ Per-class versus single-file
generation 272 ✦ Filtering classes processed 273

11.5 Advanced XDoclet 273
Custom subtasks 274
Creating a custom tag handler 274

11.6 The direction of XDoclet 275
XDoclet versus C# 275
Looking into Java's future: JSR 175 and 181 276

11.7 XDoclet best practices 276
Dependency checking 276

11.8 Summary 277

12 *Developing for the web* *278*

12.1 How are web applications different? 279

12.2 Working with tag libraries 280
Creating a tag library 280 ✦ Integrating tag libraries 286
Summary of taglib development with Ant 287

12.3 Compiling JSP pages 288
Installing the <jspc> task 289 ✦ Using the <jspc> task 289
JSP compilation for deployment 291
Other JSP compilation tasks 292

12.4 Customizing web applications 292
Filterset-based customization 292
Customizing deployment descriptors with XDoclet 294
Customizing libraries in the WAR file 297

12.5 Generating static content 297
Generating new content 297 ✦ Creating new files 298
Modifying existing files 299

12.6 Testing web applications with HttpUnit   299
Writing HttpUnit tests   300 ✦ Compiling the tests   302
Preparing to run HttpUnit tests from Ant   303
Running the HttpUnit tests   303 ✦ Integrating the tests   304
Limitations of HttpUnit   306 ✦ Canoo WebTest   306

12.7 Server-side testing with Cactus   310
Cactus from Ant's perspective   311 ✦ How Cactus works   313
And now our test case   314 ✦ Cactus summary   314

12.8 Summary   315

13 Working with XML   317

13.1 Preamble: all about XML libraries   318

13.2 Validating XML   319
When a file isn't validated   320 ✦ Resolving XML DTDs   321
Supporting alternative XML validation mechanisms   322

13.3 Transforming XML with XSLT   323
Using the XMLCatalog datatype   325
Generating PDF files from XML source   327
Styler–a third-party transformation task   327

13.4 Generating an XML build log   327
Stylesheets   328 ✦ Output files   329
Postprocessing the build log   330

13.5 Loading XML data into Ant properties   331

13.6 Next steps in XML processing   332

13.7 Summary   332

14 Enterprise JavaBeans   333

14.1 EJB overview   333
The many types of Enterprise JavaBeans   334
EJB JAR   334 ✦ Vendor-specific situations   335

14.2 A simple EJB build   335

14.3 Using Ant's EJB tasks   336

14.4 Using <ejbjar>   337
Vendor-specific <ejbjar> processing   339

14.5 Using XDoclet for EJB development   340
XDoclet subtasks   341 ✦ XDoclet's @tags   342
Supporting different application servers with XDoclet   343
Ant property substitution   343

14.6 Middlegen   345

14.7 Deploying to J2EE application servers   348

14.8 A complete EJB example   349

14.9 Best practices in EJB projects   354

14.10 Summary   354

15   *Working with web services*   *355*

15.1 What are web services and what is SOAP?   356
The SOAP API   357 ✦ Adding web services to Java   357

15.2 Creating a SOAP client application with Ant   357
Preparing our build file   358 ✦ Creating the proxy classes   359
Using the SOAP proxy classes   361 ✦ Compiling the
SOAP client   361 ✦ Running the SOAP service   362
Reviewing SOAP client creation   363

15.3 Creating a SOAP service with Axis and Ant   363
The simple way to build a web service   364

15.4 Adding web services to an existing web application   367
Configuring the web application   367
Adding the libraries   368
Including SOAP services in the build   368
Testing the server for needed classes   369
Implementing the SOAP endpoint   370
Deploying our web service   370

15.5 Writing a client for our SOAP service   371
Importing the WSDL   371 ✦ Implementing the tests   372
Writing the Java client   375

15.6 What is interoperability, and why is it a problem?   376

15.7 Building a C# client   376
Probing for the classes   377 ✦ Importing the WSDL
in C#   378 ✦ Writing the C# client class   379
Building the C# client   379 ✦ Running the C# client   380
Review of the C# client build process   381

15.8 The rigorous way to build a web service   381

15.9 Reviewing web service development   382

15.10 Calling Ant via SOAP   383

15.11 Summary   384

16   *Continuous integration*   *386*

16.1 Scheduling Ant builds with the operating system   387
The Windows way   387 ✦ The Unix version   388
Making use of scripting   388

16.2 CruiseControl   388
How it works   389 ✦ It's all about the cruise—getting the
build runner working   389 ✦ Build log reporting   395
Email notifications and build labeling   396
CruiseControl summary   396 ✦ Tips and tricks   396
Pros and cons to CruiseControl   396

16.3 Anthill   397
Getting Anthill working   398 ✦ How Anthill works   399
Anthill summary   400

16.4 Gump   401
Installing and running Gump   401
How Gump works   403 ✦ Summary of Gump   404

16.5 Comparison of continuous integration tools   405

16.6 Summary   406

17   *Developing native code*   *407*

17.1 The challenge of native code   407

17.2 Using existing build tools   408
Delegating to an IDE   408 ✦ Using Make   409

17.3 Introducing the <cc> task   410
Installing the tasks   410 ✦ Adding a compiler   411
A quick introduction to the <cc> task   411

17.4 Building a JNI library in Ant   412
Steps to building a JNI library   413 ✦ Writing the Java stub   414
Writing the C++ class   415 ✦ Compiling the C++ source   416
Deploying and testing the library   419

17.5 Going cross-platform   422
Migrating the C++ source   422 ✦ Extending the build file   423
Testing the migration   424 ✦ Porting the code   424

17.6 Looking at <cc> in more detail   425
Defining preprocessor macros   425 ✦ Linking to libraries
with <libset>   426 ✦ Configuring compilers and linkers   427
Customizing linkers   428

17.7 Distributing native libraries   429

17.8 Summary   430

18   *Production deployment*   *431*

18.1 The challenge of different application servers   432
Fundamentally different underlying behaviors   432
Different Java run-time behavior   433
Coping with different API implementations   434

Vendor-specific libraries   436   ✦   Deployment descriptors   436
Server-specific deployment processes   436
Server-specific management   436

18.2   Working with operations   437
Operations use cases   437   ✦   Operations tests   437
Operations defect tracking   438   ✦   Integrating operations
with the build process   438

18.3   Addressing the deployment challenge with Ant   440
Have a single source tree   440   ✦   Have a unified target
for creating the archive files   440   ✦   Run Ant server-side
to deploy   441   ✦   Automate the upload and
deployment process   442

18.4   Introducing Ant's deployment power tools   442
The <copy> task   442   ✦   The <serverdeploy> task   443
Remote control with <telnet>   443

18.5   Building a production deployment process   446
The plan   446   ✦   The directory structure   447
The configuration files   447   ✦   The build files   447
The remote build.xml build file   447
Writing the build file for installing to a server   449
Uploading to the remote server   450
The remote deployment in action   454
Reviewing the deployment process   455

18.6   Deploying to specific application servers   456
Tomcat 4.0 and 4.1   456   ✦   BEA WebLogic   458
HP Bluestone application server   458   ✦   Other servers   459

18.7   Verifying deployment   459
Creating the timestamp file   460
Adding the timestamp file to the application   460
Testing the timestamp   462

18.8   Best practices   462

18.9   Summary   463

Part 3   Extending Ant   465

19   Writing Ant tasks   467

19.1   What exactly is an Ant task?   468
The world's simplest Ant task   468   ✦   Compiling and using
a task in the same build   469   ✦   Task lifecycle   469

19.2   Ant API primer   470
Task   470   ✦   Project   471   ✦   Path   472   ✦   FileSet   472
DirectoryScanner   472   ✦   EnumeratedAttribute   473   ✦   FileUtils   473

19.3 How tasks get data   474
Setting attributes   474 ✦ Supporting nested elements   480
Supporting datatypes   481 ✦ Allowing free-form body text   482

19.4 Creating a basic Ant Task subclass   483
Adding an attribute to a task   483 ✦ Handling element text   484

19.5 Operating on a fileset   485

19.6 Error handling   486

19.7 Testing Ant tasks   487

19.8 Executing external programs   487
Dealing with process output   490 ✦ Summary of native execution   490

19.9 Executing a Java program within a task   490
Example task to execute a forked Java program   490

19.10 Supporting arbitrarily named elements and attributes   493

19.11 Building a task library   495

19.12 Supporting multiple versions of Ant   497

19.13 Summary   497

20 Extending Ant further   498

20.1 Scripting within Ant   499
Implicit objects provided to <script>   500
Scripting summary   501

20.2 Listeners and loggers   502
Writing a custom listener   503 ✦ Using Log4j logging capabilities   506
Writing a custom logger   509 ✦ Using the MailLogger   513

20.3 Developing a custom mapper   514

20.4 Creating custom selectors   515
Using a custom selector in a build   516

20.5 Implementing a custom filter   517
Coding a custom filter reader   519

20.6 Summary   520

A Installation   523

B XML primer as it applies to Ant   532

C IDE integration   536

D The elements of Ant style   544

E Ant task reference   561

resources   621
index   625
license   635

foreword

Ant started its life on a plane ride, as a quick little hack. Its inventor was Apache member, James Duncan Davidson. It joined Apache as a minor adjunct—almost an afterthought, really—to the codebase contributed by Sun that later became the foundation of the Tomcat 3.0 series. The reason it was invented was simple: it was needed to build Tomcat.

Despite these rather inauspicious beginnings, Ant found a good home in Apache Jakarta, and in a few short years it has become the *de facto* standard not only for open source Java projects, but also as part of a large number of commercial products. It even has a thriving clone targeting .NET.

In my mind four factors are key to Ant's success: its extensible architecture, performance, community, and backward compatibility.

The first two—extensibility and performance—derive directly from James's original efforts. The dynamic XML binding approach described in section 19.3 of this book was controversial at the time, but as Stefano Mazzocchi later said, it has proven to be a "viral design pattern": Ant's XML binding made it very simple to define new tasks, and therefore many tasks were written. I played a minor role in this as I (along with Costin Manolache) introduced the notion of nested elements discussed in section 19.3.2. As each task ran in the same JVM and allowed batch requests, tasks that often took several minutes using make could complete in seconds using Ant.

Ant's biggest strength is its active development community, originally fostered by Stefano and myself. Stefano acted as a Johnny Appleseed, creating build.xml files for numerous Apache projects. Many projects, both Apache and non-Apache, base their Ant build definitions on this early work. My own focus was on applying fixes from any source I could find, and recruiting new developers. Nearly three dozen developers have become Ant "committers," with just over a dozen being active at any point in time. Two are the authors of this book.

Much of the early work was experimental, and the rate of change initially affected the user community. Efforts like Gump, described in section 16.4, sprang up to track the changes, and have resulted in a project that now has quite stable interfaces.

The combination of these four factors has made Ant the success that it is today. Most people have learned Ant by reading build definitions that had evolved over time and were largely developed when Ant's functionality and set of tasks were not as rich as they are today. You have the opportunity to learn Ant from two of the people who know it best and who teach it the way it should be taught—by starting with a simple build definition and then showing you how to add in just those functions that are required by your project.

You should find much to like in Ant. And if you find things that you feel need improving, then I encourage you to join Erik, Steve, and the rest of us and get involved!

—SAM RUBY
Director, Apache Software Foundation

preface

In early 2000, Steve took a sabbatical from HP Laboratories, taking a break from research into such areas as adaptive, context-aware laptops to build web services, a concept that was very much in its infancy at the time.

He soon discovered that he had entered a world of chaos. Business plans, organizations, underlying technologies—all could be changed at a moment's notice. One technology that remained consistent from that year was Ant. In the Spring of 2000, it was being whispered that a "makefile killer" was being quietly built under the auspices of the Apache project: a new way to build Java code. Ant was already in use outside the Apache Tomcat group, its users finding that what was being whispered *was* true: it was a new way to develop with Java. Steve started exploring how to use it in web service projects, starting small and slowly expanding as his experience grew and as the tool itself added more functionality. Nothing he wrote that year ever got past the prototype stage; probably the sole successful deliverable of that period was the "Ant in Anger" paper included with Ant distributions.

In 2001, Steve and his colleagues did finally go into production. Their project—to aggressive deadlines—was to build an image processing web service using both Java and VB/ASP. From the outset, all the lessons of the previous year were applied, not just in architecture and implementation of the service, but in how to use Ant to manage the build process. As the project continued, the problems expanded to cover deployment to remote servers, load testing, and many other challenges related to realizing the web service concept. It turned out that with planning and effort, Ant could rise to the challenges.

Meanwhile, Erik was working at eBlox, a Tucson, Arizona, consulting company specializing in promotional item industry e-business. By early 2001, Erik had come to Ant to get control over a build process that involved a set of Perl scripts crafted by the sysadmin wizard. Erik was looking for a way that did not require sysadmin effort to modify the build process; for example, when adding a new JAR dependency. Ant solved this problem very well, and in the area of building customized releases for each of eBlox's clients from a common codebase. One of the first documents Erik encountered on Ant was the infamous "Ant in Anger" paper written by Steve; this document was used as the guideline for crafting a new build process using Ant at eBlox.

At the same time, eBlox began exploring Extreme Programming and the JUnit unit testing framework. While working on JUnit and Ant integration, Erik dug under the covers of Ant to see what made it tick. To get JUnit reports emailed automatically from an Ant build, Erik pulled together pieces of a MIME mail task submitted to the ant-dev team. After many dumb-question emails to the Ant developers asking such things as "How do I build Ant myself?" and with the help of Steve and other Ant developers, his first contributions to Ant were accepted and shipped with the Ant 1.4 release.

In the middle of 2001, Erik proposed the addition of an Ant Forum and FAQ to jGuru, an elegant and top-quality Java-related search engine. From this point, Erik's Ant knowledge accelerated rapidly, primarily as a consequence of having to field tough Ant questions. Soon after that, Erik watched his peers at eBlox develop the well-received *Java Tools for Extreme Programming* book. Erik began tossing around the idea of penning his own book on Ant, when Dan Barthel, formerly of Manning, contacted him. Erik announced his book idea to the Ant community email lists and received very positive feedback, including from Steve who had been contacted about writing a book for Manning. They discussed it, and decided that neither of them could reasonably do it alone and would instead tackle it together. Not to make matters any easier on himself, Erik accepted a new job, and relocated his family across the country while putting together the book proposal. The new job gave Erik more opportunities to explore how to use Ant in advanced J2EE projects, learning lessons in how to use Ant with Struts and EJB that readers of this book can pick up without enduring the same experience. In December of 2001, after having already written a third of this book, Erik was honored to be voted in as an Ant committer, a position of great responsibility, as changes made to Ant affect the majority of Java developers around the world.

Steve, meanwhile, already an Ant committer, was getting more widely known as a web service developer, publishing papers and giving talks on the subject, while exploring how to embed web services into devices and use them in a LAN-wide, campus-wide, or Internet-wide environment. His beliefs that deployment and integration are some of the key issues with the web service development process, and that Ant can help address them, are prevalent in his professional work and in the chapters of this book that touch on such areas. Steve is now also a committer on Axis, the Apache project's leading-edge SOAP implementation, so we can expect to see better integration between Axis and Ant in the future.

Together, in their "copious free time," Erik and Steve coauthored this book on how to use Ant in Java software projects. They combined their past experience with research into side areas, worked with Ant 1.5 as it took shape—and indeed helped shape this version of Ant while considering it for this book. They hope that you will find Ant 1.5 to be useful—and that *Java Development with Ant* will provide the solution to your build, test, and deployment problems, whatever they may be.

acknowledgments

When we used to visit a bookstore or library, we saw nothing but the learning of the authors we enjoyed. Now we also see the collective and professional efforts of many people. This book simply could not have been written had not so many fine people supported us.

First comes each of *our families*. We could not have done this without their support and understanding. Steve and Erik's wives both gave birth to sons as we labored with this book.

The wonderful people at Manning made writing this book as pleasurable as possible. The folks that we interacted with most often were Lianna Wlasiuk, Susan Capparelle, Ted Kennedy, Helen Trimes, Mary Piergies, Chris Hillman, Laura Lewin, Maarten Reilingh, Elizabeth Martin, Martine Maguire-Weltecke, and publisher Marjan Bace.

Our many reviewers kept us on our toes, and gave us very beneficial feedback and fixes. Special thanks go to Jon Skeet for his technical reviewing efforts. Not only did Jon carefully check our Ant code, his expert Java knowledge also helped to refine our Java code and related commentary. Our reviewers included Ara Abrahamian, Scott Ambler, Shawn Bayern, Armin Begtrup, Cos Difazio, Gabe Beged-Dov, Rick Hightower, Sally Kaneshiro, Nick Lesiecki, Max Loukianov, Ted Neward, Michael Oliver, Toby Perkins, Tim Rapp, and Tom Valesky.

We also thank Aslak Hellesøy for his review of the XDoclet and Middlegen pieces, Bobby Woolf and Jonathan Newbrough especially for their input on the EJB chapter. Otis Gospodnetic found and fixed an issue in our HTML parser example code. David Eric Pugh built the Torque piece of our sample application, and spent many hours refining it and teaching it to us. Curt Arnold deserves credit, not just for reviewing our chapter on native code generation, but for coauthoring the <cc> task that we cover in that chapter.

Erik gives special thanks to eBlox, which is where his Ant learning started. Rick Hightower and Nick Lesiecki gave Erik prods to write his own book, and they deserve extra mention for this. The jGuru folks provided not only a forum for Erik to practice and learn Ant in more detail, it also gave us access to the sharpest Java developers in the world. Many ideas were bounced around with John Mitchell. Drew Davidson provided insight into Ant's limitations and the types of problems he has encountered while developing a highly sophisticated multitiered Java build process. Ted Neward was always an email away, giving us much needed moral and technical support, as well as harassment and Ant bug reports.

Steve would like to thank Gabe Beged-Dov for pointing him to Ant back in April 2000, and Sally Kaneshiro for tolerating his development of a web service deployment process on a schedule that didn't have room for failures. Sally, and the rest of the Evergreen team, chapters 12, 15, and 18 were born from the experiences we got from that death march; next time we will be in control.

Key to the success of Ant—and this book—are all the great people at Apache, especially the Ant development and user communities. Without these dedicated developers, Ant would not be the award-winning Java build tool that it is. Specifically we'd like to thank some committers by name: Stefan Bodewig, Conor MacNeill, Peter Donald, Diane Holt, Sam Ruby, and Stephane Bailliez. Magesh Umasankar, also an Ant committer, was the release manager for Ant 1.5. He did a superb job of getting the releases built (which is no small feat for Ant) and distributed, and he dealt with our patching Ant's Javadoc comments for use in generating the task reference in appendix E. Our patches added a lot of work for him during some of the beta releases, because of the merging in CVS that was required. Magesh, here's to you: +1.

Finally, we want to thank James Duncan Davidson for coming up with Ant in the first place. Ant's come a long way since then, but we know you still recognize it, and are proud of its success.

about this book

This book is about Ant, the award-winning Java build tool. Ant has become the centerpiece of so many projects' build processes because it is easy to use, is platform independent, and addresses the needs of today's projects to automate testing and deployment. From its beginnings as a helper application to compile Tomcat, Sun's (now Apache's) Java web server, it has grown to be a stand-alone tool adopted by all major open source Java projects, and has changed people's expectations of their development tools.

If you have never before used Ant, this book will introduce you to it, taking you systematically through the core stages of most Java projects: compilation, testing, execution, packaging, and delivery. If you are an experienced Ant user, we will show you how to "push the envelope" in using Ant. Indeed, we believe that some of the things shown in this book were never before done with Ant. We also place an emphasis on how to use Ant as part of a large project, drawing out best practices from our own experiences.

Whatever your experience with Ant, we believe that you will learn a lot from this book, and that your software projects will benefit from using Ant as a foundation of their build process.

WHO SHOULD READ THIS BOOK

This book is for all Java developers working on software projects ranging from the simple personal project to the enterprise-wide team effort. We assume no prior experience of Ant, although even experienced Ant users should find much to interest them in the later chapters. We do expect our readers to have basic knowledge of Java, although the novice Java developer will benefit from learning Ant in conjunction with Java. Some of the more advanced Ant projects, such as building Enterprise Java applications and web services, are going to be of interest primarily to those people working in those areas. We will introduce these technology areas, but will defer to other books to cover them fully.

HOW THIS BOOK IS ORGANIZED

We divided this book into three parts. Part 1 is designed to be read from start to finish, providing the fundamentals of Ant and its capabilities. Part 2 covers specialized topics for each chapter. The relevance of each of the part 2 chapters depends on the needs of your projects. We have covered the many types of projects we are personally familiar with, and how Ant plays a crucial role in each of them. Part 3 is short, but it is rich with content for the power users of Ant that need to extend it beyond its out-of-the-box capabilities.

Part 1

In chapter 1, we first provide a gentle introduction to what Ant is, what it is not, and what makes Ant the best build tool for Java projects. We also introduce the example application we will build during the development of this book in order to showcase Ant's capabilities in a variety of situations.

Chapter 2 digs into Ant's syntax and mechanics, starting with a simple project to compile a single Java file and evolving it into an Ant build process, which compiles, packages, and executes a Java application.

To go further with Ant beyond the basic project shown in chapter 2, Ant's abstraction mechanisms need defining. Chapter 3 introduces properties, which is Ant's way of parameterization. Ant's datatypes provide a high-level domain-specific language that build file writers use to easily reuse common pieces among several steps. This is a key chapter for the understanding of what makes Ant shine.

Before jumping into executing and deploying software, we want to ensure that our build process integrates testing first. Ant works nicely with the JUnit framework, providing fine-grained control on the execution of test cases and very attractive and configurable reporting. With automated testing in place, Ant makes it easy to write and run test cases. By reducing the effort needed for constant testing, Ant is an enabler of such agile methodologies as Extreme Programming. Chapter 4 covers testing with JUnit from within Ant.

After showing how Ant can launch Java or native programs in chapter 5, we address the challenges of delivering the software, covering packaging in chapter 6 and deployment in chapter 7.

It's often difficult to envision the full picture when looking at fragments of code in a book. In chapter 8, we show you a moderately complex build file, tying it back to what was learned in the earlier chapters. We also discuss a method to deal with library dependencies. Using this scheme, projects can reuse a common set of libraries and be customized to depend on different versions of each library.

Part 2

The first chapter in this section, chapter 9, discusses the issues involved in migrating to Ant, configuring a sensible directory structure, and other general topics related to managing a project with Ant.

Ant ships with many built-in capabilities, but often needs arise that require using third-party Ant tasks or using some of Ant's optional tasks that require the installation of their dependencies. Chapter 10 covers the different types of Ant tasks, providing examples of many, including the infamous ant-contrib tasks at SourceForge.

Chapter 11 gives special attention to XDoclet's incredible third-party Ant tasks. XDoclet can generate artifacts from source code metadata, reducing double-maintenance on deployment descriptors, Enterprise JavaBeans, and many other time-saving benefits.

Web development is where many Java developers spend their time these days. Chapter 12 addresses issues such as build-time customizations of deployment descriptors, JavaServer Page taglibs, and HttpUnit and Cactus testing.

Chapter 13 discusses a topic that touches almost all Java developers, XML. Whether you are using XML simply for deployment descriptors, or transforming documentation files into presentation format during a build process, this chapter covers it.

Chapter 14 is for the developers working with Enterprise JavaBeans. Ant provides several tasks for automating EJB development. Two other third-party tools are covered that make EJB development much easier. XDoclet was originally designed for EJB development, so it shines in this area. Middlegen is a front-end tool to reverse engineer databases into XDoclet-friendly code.

The buzzword of the day: web services. In chapter 15, we build web service clients in both Java and C# and perform test cases against a web service using Ant.

Extreme programmer or not, we all benefit from continuous integration by having our systems built, tested, and even deployed on an hourly basis to ensure quality is never sacrificed. Chapter 16 covers several techniques and tools used for implementing a continuous integration process using Ant.

Chapter 17 discusses the issues and challenges faced when developing native code. The highlight of this chapter is the coverage of the C/C++ compilation Ant task that is emerging.

We close part 2 with rigorous discussions on the complex issues of production deployment. This is a topic that many developers neglect for one reason or another, but it typically ends up coming back to haunt us. Starting with a production deployment plan, and building it into an automated build process can save many headaches later.

Part 3

The final part of our book is about extending Ant beyond its built-in capabilities. Ant is designed to be extensible in a number ways.

Chapter 19 provides all the information needed to write sophisticated custom Ant tasks, with many examples. Wrapping native executable calls within an Ant task is a popular reason for writing a custom task, and this is covered explicitly in detail.

Beyond custom tasks, Ant is extensible in several other ways such as executing scripting languages and adding FilterReaders and Selectors. Monitoring or logging the build process is easy to customize too, and all of these techniques are covered in detail in chapter 20.

At the back

Last but not least are five appendices. Appendix A is for new Ant users, and explains how to install Ant on Windows and Unix platforms and covers common installation problems and solutions. Because Ant uses XML files to describe build processes, appendix B is an introduction to XML for those unfamiliar with it. All modern Java integrated development environments now tie in to Ant. Using an Ant-enabled IDE allows you to have the best of both worlds. Appendix C details the integration available in several of the popular IDEs.

One of the items we're most proud of in this book is appendix D, "The elements of Ant style." This appendix provides guidelines to make writing build files consistent, maintainable, and extensible. There are several nice tidbits of trivia. This appendix will be best understood after understanding the fundamentals of Ant covered in part 1.

We leave you with an Ant task reference at the end to easily look up those attribute names you've forgotten, or to remind yourself of the datatypes or possible values allowed. We recommend scanning the list of available tasks and their descriptions to get an idea of what Ant has to offer.

ONLINE RESOURCES

All the source code and Ant build files accompanying this book can be downloaded from the book's web site at http://www.manning.com/antbook.

You can also download some quick start build files that you can use in your own projects with minimal customization; these will let you get up and running with Ant as quickly as possible. There is also a discussion forum on the web site, where you can discuss the book.

The other key web site for Ant users is its Apache home page at http://jakarta. apache.org/ant/. Ant, and its online documentation, can be found here, while this book's authors can be found in the Ant developer and Ant user mailing lists, alongside many other Ant experts. If you have questions about Ant, or want to make it better, the mailing lists are where to go.

CODE CONVENTIONS

Courier typeface is used to denote Java code and Ant build files. **Bold Courier** typeface is used in some code listings to highlight important or changed sections.

Code annotations accompany many segments of code. Certain annotations are marked with numbered bullets. These annotations have further explanations that follow the code.

ON VERSIONS OF ANT AND OTHER PROJECTS

This book is written for Ant 1.5 and later. We started writing the book just as Ant 1.4 shipped, in Fall 2001, and finished it just as Ant 1.5 was released. There are many changes between Ant 1.4 and Ant 1.5, changes that make Ant easier to use and more flexible. There were also several fixes made to Ant as we discovered issues and inconsistencies in the process of writing the book. It is often easier to fix the source than explain why something does not always work. Because of all the changes, this book is not targeted at Ant 1.4 or earlier. If you do have a pre-1.5 version of Ant, now is the time to upgrade.

Ant tries hard to retain backwards compatibility, so as Ant 1.6 and successors are developed, everything in this book should still work. However, later versions of the product may provide easier means to accomplish tasks. Check with the documentation that comes with later versions of Ant to see what has changed.

In part 2 of the book, we work with third-party projects, such as XDoclet and Apache Axis. These open source projects are currently less stable than Ant, and within a few months of publishing, we fear that what we wrote about these projects may be incorrect. Check at our web site to see if we have any additions to the book on these topics.

Finally, one of the fun things about open source is that the user can become the developer. We would encourage the reader to not merely view Ant and the other open source projects in the book as sources of binaries, but as communities of developers that welcome more people to help with the code, the documentation, and even the artwork. If you think the products are great, come and make them greater!

AUTHOR ONLINE

Purchase of *Java Development with Ant* includes free access to a private web forum run by Manning Publications where you can make comments about the book, ask technical questions, and receive help from the authors and from other users. To access the forum and subscribe to it, point your web browser to www.manning.com/antbook. This page provides information on how to get on the forum once you are registered, what kind of help is available, and the rules of conduct on the forum.

Manning's commitment to our readers is to provide a venue where a meaningful dialog between individual readers and between readers and the authors can take place. It is not a commitment to any specific amount of participation on the part of the authors, whose contribution to the AO remains voluntary (and unpaid). We suggest you try asking the authors some challenging questions lest their interest stray!

The Author Online forum and the archives of previous discussions will be accessible from the publisher's web site as long as the book is in print.

about the authors

ERIK HATCHER, an Ant project committer, has written popular articles on Ant's JUnit integration. He maintains jGuru's Ant FAQ where he answers the world's toughest Ant questions. Erik is both a Sun Certified Java Programmer and a Microsoft Certified Solution Developer. He has written several articles for IBM developerWorks, most notably about, and improving upon, Ant's JUnit integration. He lives in Charlottesville, Virginia, where he works as a Senior Java Architect by day, and enjoys spending time with his beautiful wife, Carole, and two wonderful sons, Jakob and Ethan. See him on the Web at http://erik.hatcher.net/.

STEVE LOUGHRAN works for Hewlett Packard, where he develops imaging and printing web services that fuse Java and Ant. He is also a committer on the Ant and Axis projects at Apache. Prior to this, he was a research scientist in HP Laboratories in Bristol, England, dabbling in areas from distributed systems to context aware laptops. He holds a first-class honors degree in Computer Science from Edinburgh University. He lives in Corvallis, Oregon, with his wife Bina, and son, Alexander. For entertainment he enjoys Alpine-style mountaineering, saying "it's all about risk management." See him on the Web at http://www.iseran.com/Steve.

about the cover illustration

The figure on the cover of *Java Development with Ant* is an "Yndiano de Goa," an inhabitant of Goa, which is a region on the western coast of India, south of Bombay. The illustration is taken from a Spanish compendium of regional dress customs first published in Madrid in 1799. The book's title page states:

> *Coleccion general de los Trages que usan actualmente todas las Nacionas del Mundo desubierto, dibujados y grabados con la mayor exactitud por R.M.V.A.R. Obra muy util y en special para los que tienen la del viajero universal*

which we translate, as literally as possible, thus:

> *General collection of costumes currently used in the nations of the known world, designed and printed with great exactitude by R.M.V.A.R. This work is very useful especially for those who hold themselves to be universal travelers*

Although nothing is known of the designers, engravers, and workers who colored this illustration by hand, the exactitude of their execution is evident in this drawing. The "Yndiano de Goa" is just one of many figures in this colorful collection. Their diversity speaks vividly of the uniqueness and individuality of the world's towns and regions just 200 years ago. This was a time when the dress codes of two regions separated by a few dozen miles identified people uniquely as belonging to one or the other. The collection brings to life a sense of isolation and distance of that period—and of every other historic period except our own hyperkinetic present.

Dress codes have changed since then and the diversity by region, so rich at the time, has faded away. It is now often hard to tell the inhabitant of one continent from another. Perhaps, trying to view it optimistically, we have traded a cultural and visual diversity for a more varied personal life. Or a more varied and interesting intellectual and technical life.

We at Manning celebrate the inventiveness, the initiative, and the fun of the computer business with book covers based on the rich diversity of regional life of two centuries ago brought back to life by the pictures from this collection.

PART 1

Learning Ant

Chapters 1 through 8 lay the foundation for using Ant. In this section, you learn the fundamentals of Java build processes—including compilation, packaging, testing, and deployment—and how Ant facilitates each step. Ant's reusable datatypes and properties play an important role in writing maintainable and extensible build files. After digesting the material in this section, you are ready to use Ant in your projects.

C H A P T E R   1

Introducing Ant

1.1 What is Ant?   3
1.2 The core concepts of Ant   5
1.3 Why use Ant?   10
1.4 The evolution of Ant   14
1.5 Ant and software development
     methodologies   16
1.6 Our example project   17
1.7 Yeah, but can Ant...   19
1.8 Beyond Java development   21
1.9 Summary   22

Welcome to the future of your build process.

This is a book about Ant. But much more than a reference book for Ant syntax, it is a collection of best practices demonstrating how to use Ant to its greatest potential in real-world situations. If used well, you can develop and deliver your software projects better than you have done before.

We begin by exploring what Ant is, its history, and its core concepts. Ant is not the only build tool available, so we will also compare it to the alternatives and explain how Ant can fit in to whatever formal or informal development methodologies you may encounter. Finally, we'll introduce the sample application we developed for this book that demonstrates much of Ant's capabilities.

1.1   WHAT IS ANT?

We certainly don't want bugs in our software! However, this industrious creature called Ant is just what we need to get control of our Java build process. While the term Ant was coined by the original author to mean Another Neat Tool, this acronym meaning has faded and the analogy to the actual ant insect has taken precedence. Here are some insightful comparisons:

- Ants find the shortest distance around obstacles ("Behavior of Real Ants").
- Ants can carry 50 times their own weight.
- Ants work around the clock; they do rest, but they work in shifts (*Ant Colony FAQs*).

Ant is a *Java-based build tool* designed to be cross-platform, easy to use, extensible, and scalable. It can be used in a small personal project, or it can be used in a large, multiteam software project.

1.1.1 What is a build process and why do you need one?

Think of your source code as raw materials that you are sending into a factory for processing and assembly into a product, say an automobile. These raw materials must be cut, molded, welded, glued, assembled, tested for quality assurance, labeled, packaged, and shipped. This process and these steps are so analogous to how software products are constructed that it's well worth keeping these similarities in mind throughout this book and beyond. It's our job as software, build, or QA engineers to construct the "factory." People made cars long before factory automation entered the scene. Even after some forms of automation came about, things were still tough and required much manual labor. The motor vehicle industry has come a long way in its relatively brief existence. It is an interesting intellectual exercise to attempt matching up the progress of both industries, and it's likely that factory automation has us beat because of its longer history. However, software is much more malleable than steel, so with a bit of automation we can do amazing things with it in only a matter of seconds.

In order to build a software product, we manipulate our source code in various ways: we compile, generate documentation, unit test, package, deploy, and even dynamically generate more source code that feeds back into the previous steps. Not unlike the auto industry, these steps are initially done manually, and when we tire from doing the repetitive, we look for existing tools—or create our own—that can ease the burden of repetition. Source code is the raw material; Ant is the factory floor with all the whiz-bang gizmos.

1.1.2 Why do we think Ant makes a great build tool?

We have been working with Ant for a long time and are convinced that it is a great build tool. Here are some of the reasons:

- It has a very simple syntax, which is easy to learn, especially if you have used XML before.
- It is easy to use, eliminating the full-time makefile engineer common on large Make-based software projects.
- It is cross-platform, handling Java classpaths and file directory structures in a portable manner.

- It is very fast. Java routines such as the Java compiler or the code to make a JAR file can all start inside the Ant JVM, reducing process startup delays. Ant tasks are also designed to do dependency checking to avoid doing any more work than necessary.
- It integrates tightly with the JUnit test framework for XP-style unit testing.
- It is easily extensible using Java.
- It has built-in support for J2EE development, such as EJB compilation and packaging.
- It addresses the deployment problems of Java projects: FTP, Telnet, application servers, SQL commands; all can be used for automated deployment
- It is the de facto standard for most open source Java projects, such as Apache Tomcat and Apache Xerces. Many application servers even ship with embedded versions of Ant for deployment.

Because Ant understands testing and deployment, it can be used for a unified build-test-deploy process, either from a single command on the command-line or a button press on an Ant-aware Java IDE, such as NetBeans, Eclipse, IDEA, and jEdit.

In a software project experiencing constant change, an automated build can provide a foundation of stability. Even as requirements change and developers struggle to catch up, having a build process that needs little maintenance and remembers to test everything can take a lot of housekeeping off developers' shoulders. Ant can be the means of controlling the building and deployment of Java software projects that would otherwise overwhelm a team.

1.2   THE CORE CONCEPTS OF ANT

To understand Ant, you need to understand the core concepts of Ant build files. The overall design goals aimed at meeting the core need—a portable tool for building and deploying Java projects—are as follows:

- *Simplicity*—Ant should be simple for a competent programmer to use.
- *Understandability*—Ant should be easy for new users to understand.
- *Extensibility*—Ant should be easy to extend.

Ant mostly meets these goals. A complex build process may still look complicated, but it will be manageable. The use of XML as a file format can be intimidating to anyone who has limited experience with XML. Once you have crossed that hurdle, however, an Ant build file is easy to work with. Having the build process described in a portable text file format allows your build process to be easily communicated and shared with others.

Ant meets the design goals in two key ways. First, Ant is Java-based and tries to hide all the platform details it can. It is also highly extensible in Java itself. This makes it easy to extend Ant through Java code, with all the functionality of the Java platform and third party libraries available. It also makes the build very fast, as you can run Java programs from inside the same Java virtual machine as Ant itself.

Putting Ant extensions aside until much later, here are the core concepts of Ant as seen by a user of the tool.

XML format

Ant uses XML files called *build files* to describe how to build, test, and deploy an application. Using XML enables developers to edit files directly, or in any XML editor, and facilitates parsing the build file at run time. Using XML as the format also allows enables developers to create templates easily and to generate build files dynamically.

Declarative syntax

Ant is declarative. Rather than spelling out the details of every stage in the build process, developers list the high-level stages of the build, leaving Ant and its tasks to execute the high-level declaration. This keeps the build files short and understandable, and lets the Ant developers change implementation details without breaking your build files.

A build file contains one project

Each XML build file includes how to build, test, and deploy one *project*. Very large projects may be composed of multiple smaller projects, each with its own build file. A higher-level build file can coordinate the builds of the subprojects.

Each project contains multiple targets

Within the single project of a build file, you declare the different *targets* for the build process. These targets may represent actual outputs of the build, such as a redistributable file, or stages in the build process, such as compiling source or deploying the redistributable file to a remote server.

Targets can have dependencies on other targets

When declaring a target, you can declare which targets have to be built first. This ensures that the source gets compiled before the redistributables are built, and that the redistributable is built before the remote deployment.

Targets contain tasks

Inside targets you declare what actual work is needed to complete that stage of the build process. You do this by listing the *tasks* that constitute each stage. Each task is actually a reference to a Java class, built into Ant or an extension library, that understands the parameters in the build file and can execute the task based upon the parameters. These tasks are expected to be smart—to handle much of their own argument validation, dependency checking, and error reporting.

New tasks can easily be added in Java

The fact that it is easy to extend Ant with new classes is one of its core strengths. Often, someone will have encountered the same build step that you have and will have written the task to perform it, so you can just use their work.

1.2.1 An example project

Figure 1.1 shows the conceptual view of an Ant build file as a graph of targets, each target containing the tasks. When the project is built, the Ant run time determines which targets need to be executed, and chooses an order for the execution that guarantees a target is executed after all those targets it depends on. If a task somehow fails, it signals this to the run time, which halts the build. This lets simple rules such as "deploy after compiling" be described, as well as more complex ones such as "deploy only after the unit tests and JSP compilation have succeeded."

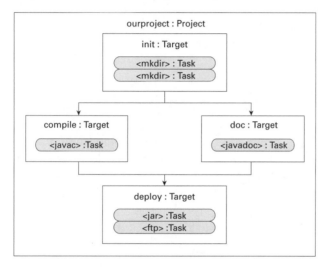

Figure 1.1   Conceptual view of a build file. The project encompasses a collection of targets. Inside each target are task declarations, which are statements of the actions Ant must take to build that target. Targets can state their dependencies on other targets, producing a graph of dependencies. When executing a target, all its dependents must execute first.

Listing 1.1 shows the build file for this typical build process.

Listing 1.1   A typical scenario: compile, document, package, and deploy

```xml
<?xml version="1.0" ?>
<project name="OurProject" default="deploy">

  <target name="init">
    <mkdir dir="build/classes" />
    <mkdir dir="dist" />
  </target>
```

```
<target name="compile" depends="init" >
  <javac srcdir="src"
    destdir="build/classes"/>
</target>

<target name="doc" depends="init" >
  <javadoc destdir="build/classes"
         sourcepath="src"
         packagenames="org.*" />
</target>

<target name="deploy" depends="compile,doc" >
  <jar destfile="dist/project.jar"
      basedir="build/classes"/>
  <ftp server="${server.name}"
      userid="${ftp.username}"
      password="${ftp.password}">
    <fileset dir="dist"/>
  </ftp>
</target>

</project>
```

While listing 1.1 is likely to have some confusing pieces to it,[1] it should be mostly comprehensible to the Java-experienced Ant newbie; for example, deployment (`target name="deploy"`) depends on the successful compilation and generation of documentation (`depends="compile,doc"`). Perhaps the most confusing piece is the `${...}` notation used in the FTP task (`<ftp>`). These are Ant *properties*, which we introduce in chapter 3. The output of our build is

```
> ant -propertyfile ftp.properties
Buildfile: build.xml

init:
    [mkdir] Created dir: /home/ant/Projects/OurProject/build/classes
    [mkdir] Created dir: /home/ant/Projects/OurProject/dist

compile:
    [javac] Compiling 1 source file to /home/ant/Projects/OurProject/build/
classes

doc:
  [javadoc] Generating Javadoc
  [javadoc] Javadoc execution
  [javadoc] Loading source files for package org.example.antbook.lesson1...
  [javadoc] Constructing Javadoc information...
  [javadoc] Building tree for all the packages and classes...
  [javadoc] Building index for all the packages and classes...
  [javadoc] Building index for all classes...
```

---

[1] Hey, this is only chapter 1 after all!

```
deploy:
      [jar] Building jar: /home/ant/Projects/OurProject/dist/project.jar
      [ftp] sending files
      [ftp] 1 files sent

BUILD SUCCESSFUL
Total time: 5 seconds.
```

Why did we invoke Ant with -propertyfile ftp.properties? The ftp.proper-
ties file contains the three properties server.name, ftp.username, and
ftp.password. The property handling mechanism allows parameterization and
reusability of our build file. This particular example, while certainly demonstrative, is
minimal and gives only a hint of things to follow. In this build, we tell Ant to place
the generated documentation alongside the compiled classes, which is not a typical
distribution layout but allows this example to be abbreviated. Using the property-
file command-line option is also atypical and used in situations where forced override control is desired, such as forcing a build to deploy to a server other than the
default. One final note is that a typical distributable is not a JAR file; more likely it
would be a tar, Zip, WAR, or EAR. Caveats aside, the example shows Ant's basics
well: target dependencies, use of properties, compiling, documenting, JAR'ing, and
finally deploying. To jump ahead, here are pointers to more information on the technical specifics: chapter 2 covers build file syntax, target dependencies, and <javac> in
more detail; chapter 3 explains Ant properties including -propertyfile; chapter 6
delves into <jar> and <javadoc>; and finally, <ftp> is covered in chapter 7.

   Because Ant tasks are Java classes, the overhead of invoking each task is quite small.
Ant instantiates a Java object, sets some parameters, then tells it to perform its work.
A simple task such as <mkdir> would call a Java library package to execute the function. A more complex task such as <ftp> would invoke a third-party FTP library to
talk to the remote server, and optionally perform dependency checking to only upload
files that were newer than those at the destination. A very complex task such as
<javac> not only uses dependency checking to decide which files to compile, it sup-
ports multiple compiler back ends, calling Sun's Java compiler in the same VM, or executing IBM's Jikes compiler as an external executable.

   These are implementation details. Simply ask Ant to compile some files with the
debug flag turned on; how Ant decides which compiler to use and how to translate
the debug flag into a compiler specific option are issues that you rarely need to worry
about. It just works.

   That is the beauty of Ant: it just works. Specify the build file correctly and Ant will
work out target dependencies and call the targets in the right order. The targets run
through their tasks in order, and the tasks themselves deal with file dependencies and
the actual execution of the appropriate Java package calls or external commands
needed to perform the work. Because each task is usually declared at a high level, one
or two lines of XML is often enough to describe what you want a task to do. Five or
six lines might be needed for something as complex as Enterprise JavaBean (EJB)

deployment. With only a few lines needed per task, you can keep each build target small, and keep the build file itself under control.

Build file maintenance is simple, eliminating the need to have one person in charge of the build; it can be left to the team as a whole to expand the build process as the project progresses. It also becomes very easy to add new features to the build. Suddenly the notion of automated FTP deployment—maybe even remote installation followed by deployment testing—is not so far-fetched. In a recent project one of the authors worked on, the development team managed to automate deployment to multiple remote test systems through separate Ant targets. They then added keyboard shortcuts in the IDE to compile, unit test, archive, and finally deploy to these servers. This reduced the time from editing code to deploying the changes on an application server to one and a half minutes, a time that included regression tests on the core functionality.

1.3 WHY USE ANT?

Ant is not the only build solution available. How does it fare in comparison to its competition and predecessors? We'll compare Ant to its most widely used competitors: IDEs and Make.

1.3.1 Integrated development environments

The integrated development environment, or IDE, is the common development system for small projects. IDEs are great for editing, compiling, and debugging code, and are easy to use. It is hard to convince a user of a good IDE that they should abandon it for a build process based on a text file and a command line prompt. There are, in fact, many good reasons to supplement an IDE with an Ant build process, extending rather than abandoning their existing development tools.

Several limitations of IDEs only become apparent as a project proceeds and grows. First, the functionality of IDEs is limited: although they can compile and package code, it is hard to include testing and deployment into an IDE process. This limits how much of the build process can be automated. Second, it is hard to transfer one person's IDE settings to another user. Settings can end up tied to an individual's environment. You can take someone's project and tweak it to work on your own system, but then it usually does not work on the original system. Finally, IDE-based build processes do not scale. If a project has a single deliverable, then an IDE can build it. However, if the project consists of many different subcomponents, you need to build each project as its own IDE project. Producing replicable builds is an important part of most projects, and it's risky to use manual IDE builds to do so. Replication is difficult because of the multiple steps involved in pulling a tagged version of code from the repository and ensuring that the build environment is the same as it was for previous builds that may have been done by a different team member on a different machine. It is not uncommon for such teams to dedicate a machine solely for the purpose of generating builds, often with yellow sticky notes around the monitor describing the steps! This scalability issue gradually becomes apparent as a project progresses.

The IDE build works at the beginning, but by the end someone is manually triggering multiple IDE builds, or struggling to put together a shell script or batch file wrapper, or a makefile.

Ant does not supplant much of the functionality of an IDE; a good editor with debugging and even refactoring facilities is an invaluable tool to have and use. Ant just takes control of compilation, packaging, testing, and deployment stages of the build process in a way that is portable, scalable, and often reusable. As such, it complements IDEs. In fact, the latest generation of Java IDEs usually provides support for Ant-based builds in some form or other, a topic we look at in chapter 10.

1.3.2 Make

Make is the definitive automated build tool in widespread use; variants of it are used in nearly every large C or C++ project. In Make, you list targets, their dependencies, and the actions to bring each target up to date.

The tool is inherently file-centric. Each target in a makefile is either the name of a file to bring up-to-date or what, in make terminology, is called a *phony* target. A named target triggers some actions when invoked. Make targets can be dependent upon files or other targets. Phony targets have names like "clean" or "all" and can have no dependencies (that is, they always execute their commands) or can be dependent upon real targets. All the actual build stages that Make invokes are actually external functions. Besides explicit build steps to produce one file from another, Make supports pattern rules that it can use to determine how to build targets from the available inputs.

Here is an example of a very simple makefile (for GNU make) to compile two Java classes and archive them into a JAR file:

```
all: project.jar

project.jar: Main.class XmlStuff.class
        jar -cvf $@ $<

%.class: %.java
        javac $<
```

The makefile has a phony target, `all`, which, by virtue of being first in the file, is the default. The real target is `project.jar`, which depends on two compiled Java files. The final rule states how to build class (`.class`) files from Java (`.java`) files. In Make, you list the file dependencies, and the run time determines which rules to apply and in what sequence, while the developer is left tracking down bugs related to the need for invisible tab characters rather than spaces at the start of each action.

Make works well on a platform in which the underlying tools are good at performing the different tasks of the build process (which is why it excels on a Unix system) and when all dependencies are quite simple. It is language-independent, flexible, and widely understood.

When the build stages do not generate local files but issue commands to SQL databases or deploy software to remote servers, the simple dependency checking of Make does not work so well. It is possible to execute these tasks, but the makefile gets more and more complex, making maintenance of the build a full-time operation.

How Ant is not Make

Besides learning the core concepts of Ant, it is important to forget preconceptions that come with extensive use of Make. The two tools have the same role: they automate a build process by taking a specification file and performing a sequence of operations based on the content of that file and the state of the file system. Even ignoring operational details such as the different syntax and means of executing targets, Ant and Make have some fundamentally different views of how the build process should work.

With Ant, you list sequences of operations and dependencies between them, and let file dependencies sort themselves out through code that understands each operation in the build process. The only targets that Ant supports are those like Make's phony targets: targets that are not files and exist only in the build file. The dependencies of these targets are other targets. You omit file dependencies, along with any file conversion rules. Instead, the Ant build file states the stages used in the process, and while you may name the input or output files often you can use a wild card or even a default wild card to specify the source files. For example, here the `<javac>` task automatically includes all Java files in all subdirectories below the source directory:

```
<?xml version="1.0" ?>
<project name="makefile" default="all">
  <target name="all">
    <javac srcdir="."/>
    <jar destfile="project.jar" includes="*.class" />
  </target>
</project>
```

Both the `<javac>` and `<jar>` tasks will compare the sources and the destinations and decide which to compile or add to the archive. Ant must call every task in the target-derived order, and the tasks can choose whether or not to do work. The advantage of this approach is that the tasks can contain more domain-specific knowledge than the build tool, such as performing directory hierarchy-aware dependency checking, or even addressing dependency issues across a network: Ant's FTP and HTTP tasks can use dependency checking to manage their downloads or uploads. The other subtlety of using wildcards to describe source files, JAR files on the classpath, and the like is that you can add new files without having to edit the build file. This is nice when projects start to grow—it keeps build file maintenance to a minimum.

It may seem that invoking tasks to check dependencies adds overhead to the execution, but because most tasks are just Java classes that are loaded into the current JVM, there is little overhead compared to having the run time do any file dependency checking. Even when a task works by executing a native application, the Java code can perform the task-specific dependency checking before calling that native program.

Make's related tools

Because makefiles are inherently nonportable, several tools exist to ease the burden of creating them. Automake and imake are makefile generators, which build off of a file describing the build process in a more general way than the resultant makefiles. The Automake tool generates the appropriate makefile for the platform based upon the results of the probes and a template makefile. There is also a tool called Autoconf which produces `configure` shell scripts that adapt source code packages to their environment, adjusting for all the various platform and environment differences. Other tools, like CLAM, provide macros and rules to control GNU make (Koeritz 2001).

If you think this all sounds too messy to deal with, you are in the right place. Some readers will come here with expert-level knowledge of Make, others will come here with absolutely no knowledge of it. Knowledge of Make is not a prerequisite for this text. We only mention it here for purposes of comparison, and later in discussions of integrating Ant with Make in mixed-language environments. While we certainly tout the benefits of Ant over Make in building pure Java projects, Ant is not necessarily the right tool (yet) for building C/C++ applications. Ant plays well with spawning to Make, and Make can execute Ant easily. Chapters 10 and 17 look at Ant and Make integration in both directions.

1.3.3   Other build tools

Ant and Make are the two most popular build tools, but there are others worth mentioning.

Jam

Jam provides a simpler alternative to Make's complexity. Its syntax is very similar to Make, yet simpler. Jam is written in C and, with built-in handling of cross-platform paths, is designed to be more cross-platform friendly than Make.

Amber

Differences of opinion led the original architect of Ant to leave the Ant community and develop a build tool based on his architectural vision. This project is called Amber. It currently appears to be stalled in development, but is worth keeping an eye on. It is entirely Java-based.

Cons

Cons is a Perl-based build system. It is cross-platform and very powerful because you can use any Perl command in the Conscript file used to build the project. The language of Ant build files is not as powerful, and although you can embed scripts inside the files, Ant is regularly extended in Java instead. Cons is good at Perl, C, and C++ projects as it can scan inside source files for dependency information, but it does not work well with Java.

1.3.4 Up and running, in no time

One of the benefits of using Ant comes when a new developer joins a team. With a nicely crafted build process, the new developer can be shown how to get code from the source code repository, including the build file and library dependencies. Even Ant itself could (and likely should) be stored in the repository for a truly repeatable build process. The new developer then runs the build, which would build, test, deploy, and perhaps even run a demo of the system.

We have seen environments where bringing up a new build environment takes hours to configure and is prone to not being quite like the other build environments in the group. With Ant and some planning, these types of problems can be alleviated. Being capable of quickly getting a new development environment up and running is a sign that your project is on the right track.

1.4 THE EVOLUTION OF ANT

Ant is still evolving, in the semistructured yet open process under which open-source projects normally operate. As an Apache project, Ant is controlled by the Apache bylaws, which cover decision making and write access to the source tree. Those with write access to Ant's source code repository are called *committers*, because they are allowed to commit code changes directly. Both authors are privileged and honored to be among the few in the world known as Ant committers. Anyone is allowed— indeed encouraged—to make changes to the code, to extend Ant to meet their needs, and to return those changes to the Ant community. Returning such changes and extensions is entirely optional, yet doing so is beneficial not just for the author who offloads the maintenance workload, but for all the other Ant users who benefit from the improvements.

Ant is therefore under continuous change as people regularly submit improvements and modifications to the system, some of which are accepted, others rejected. As table 1.1 shows, the team releases a new version of Ant on a regular basis. When this happens, the code is frozen for a few weeks with only bug fixes and documentation changes accepted, and more rigorous testing is applied, including a brief beta release program. The result of this process is that, while changes may "break" things in Ant's nightly build, point or milestone releases are stable and usable for a long period.

Table 1.1 The release history of Ant. Unless you are working on a short project, there will be a new version during the life of your project.

Date	Ant version	Notes
March 2000	Ant 1.0	Really Ant 0.9; with Tomcat 3.1
July 2000	Ant 1.1	First stand-alone Ant release
October 2000	Ant 1.2	
March 2001	Ant 1.3	
September 2001	Ant 1.4	Followed by Ant 1.4.1 in October
July 2002	Ant 1.5	

With a new release every six months or so, it is likely that a new version will emerge during the lifetime of any significant project. This may seem like a risk, but really is an opportunity: if the current version does not meet all your needs, then filing bug reports or submitting changes may ensure that the next official version of Ant will meet your needs. If the current version of Ant does work fine, then there is no need to upgrade until you feel it is necessary; and there is nothing to stop you from keeping the version used in your project under source code management, to ensure that it will still build many years into the future.

One area where the evolution of Ant does create problems is in the documentation, both online and printed. Although the core Ant manual pages are kept up to date, referenced articles and presentations on other sites may be out of date. This book has the same problem. We started writing this just as Ant 1.4.1 came out, yet we targeted the forthcoming version, Ant 1.5. If we had only covered Ant 1.4.1, readers would have missed out on all the improvements that are already in the pipeline. Even the act of writing this book has a side effect on the next version of Ant: rather than explain why things do not always work as expected, sometimes it is easier to fix them. Consequently, much of what we describe does not work on older versions. We have targeted Ant 1.5 and successors with this book, because even if you were using an older version, it costs you nothing but the time to download a new version from jakarta.apache.org. If we had tried to be compatible with older versions of Ant, it would have been much harder to explain and demonstrate many things.

Because new versions of Ant come out so regularly, this book will slowly become less accurate. Nothing in the book should actually break with future versions of Ant; the Ant team strives to maintain backwards compatibility with existing builds. But easier ways of doing things will emerge. We strongly recommend that you consult the latest Ant online documentation as well as our book.

At some point, Ant 2.0 will come out. This new version of Ant will break many things, probably including builds and plug-in tasks. We do not cover Ant 2.0 at all, as we do not know what it will be, exactly. We do know what the feature requirements are, and that one of them will be an automated means of migrating Ant 1.x builds to Ant 2.0. So do not worry about Ant 2.0 making all your work obsolete. There could even be a means of calling Ant 1.x builds from Ant 2.0, so old build code and new build code can live side by side.

Because Ant's change is so public and frequent, it may seem less stable than existing products. However, every night, one person's computer attempts to build the planet's most popular open-source Java projects from their latest source, using the latest version of Ant as the foundation. When that build breaks because of a change in Ant, the owner of that computer, Sam Ruby, lets the Ant development team know. Because of that nightly build (known as Gump[2]), changes to Ant rarely break other people's projects, which is good news for everyone who relies on Ant as their build tool.

---

[2] See http://jakarta.apache.org/gump/

1.5 ANT AND SOFTWARE DEVELOPMENT METHODOLOGIES

Ant plays well on any platform that supports Java, but it also plays well with any software development methodology in use. Regardless of the higher level processes in place, we all, as Java developers, need a tool that facilitates the mundane error-prone tasks involved in building a Java project from source code to end product. Two such popular methodologies are eXtreme Programming and the Rational Unified Process, and there are several other variants of these. How does Ant fit into these methodologies?

1.5.1 eXtreme Programming

At a business level, eXtreme Programming (XP) is about flattening the cost-of-change curve so that it is no more costly to add a feature later in the development cycle than early on. Viewed from traditional methodologies such as the waterfall methodology, this seems insane. How can change have such little effect? The idea is that change is embraced; it is planned for and expected. The software is continually *refactored* during development to keep it simple, clean, and *agile* at all times. Change occurs in small incremental steps when using XP, leaving the system ever in a production-ready state. Feedback is rapid, with end-users ideally on site during development to provide immediate answers.

Testing is the key to agility

Quality is the one inflexible variable of the four variables in a software project: cost, time, quality, and scope. Quality is usually the one to focus on, because anything else just delays problems until they cost more to fix. (Scope is the ideal adjustable parameter, with the others being more or less constrained outside of the development team.) Quality is obtained by testing. Unit tests are developed before production code is even written. Continuous testing and integration are crucial to obtaining agility in adaptation to change. Keeping code simple and clean is tough as it evolves and as cruft forms, but having test suites in place gives developers the courage to undertake massive refactorings to simplify things once again. Run the tests successfully, make some code changes, and run the tests again. If the tests break, you know precisely what just changed to cause the breakage.

Ant and XP

Ant fits beautifully into an XP process! Automation is mandatory in XP processes. Ant is all about automating build processes, including testing. Advanced uses for Ant could include a continuous integration process, in which a server continually checks out the source and builds and tests the system. Continuous integration is easily realized using an Ant container tool such as CruiseControl or AntHill. We will cover how to do this in chapter 16.

1.5.2 Rational Unified Process

The Rational Unified Process (RUP, from Rational Software Corporation) is an iterative, prescriptive, architecture-centric process in which the code is merely one of the artifacts delivered by iterations of the project; design models and code documentation are usually other key artifacts. *Use cases*—the intended uses of the system—direct the design and development of the system. These provide insight into the problem domain, and a focus for development.

The RUP divides the software process into four phases (inception, elaboration, construction, and transition), whereas different tasks (business modeling, analyzing and designing requirements, implementing, testing, and deploying) consume different resources in the different phases. There can be a number of iterations in each phase, and even in later phases, the high-level tasks in the process, such as analyzing and designing requirements, still take place. This enables yet controls change.

Rational provides a large and integrated suite of products to automate the different stages of the software process. Their modeling tool, Rational Rose, and configuration management tool, ClearCase, are probably the most well known.

Where we have personally found the RUP weak is that it delays deployment until the end of development. For large web or enterprise applications, deployment is one of the difficult and risky parts of the process. So, it should be emphasized sooner and fed into the basic architecture (Loughran 2002a), as well as into every iteration. This does not mean that RUP is unnecessary for such projects, merely insufficient. Scott Ambler, a leading proponent of the Agile Software movement, has proposed that developers explicitly include production as a new phase for the RUP, and operations and infrastructure management as new tasks in a project (Ambler 2001). This revised model aligns better with our experience, and enables Ant to act as the core of a continuous deployment system.

Ant integrates with the Unified Process as a means of automating the compilation and deployment stages. It also supports the Rational ClearCase revision control tool with tasks to check files in and out. Ant does not integrate with Rational's testing product family, such as Visual Test or Purify; the latter code analysis tool would be a valuable task to be able to run from a build. The Rational TestSuite is more of a higher level test system than the JUnit tests, and would be hard to integrate unless the Rational product family actually hosted Ant itself.

1.6 OUR EXAMPLE PROJECT

This book covers how to use Ant, starting with first principles and finishing with large projects complete with complex deployment, testing challenges, and extensions of Ant's capabilities. We also develop a Java application as we go along, because without a project there is no need for a build process. We base most of our examples on this project; although for some of the side topics, such as native code integration, we include stand-alone examples.

1.6.1 Documentation search engine—example Ant project

The example project is a text search engine for indexing and searching through HTML documentation files—such as the Ant documentation itself. This will work from the command line, and on an application server. To avoid having to write most of the search engine ourselves, we chose to use the Lucene search engine, which is another subproject of the Apache Jakarta group. It is Java-based, fast, and flexible. We also will integrate with Struts to provide a model/view/controller framework, and a data tier that can easily switch between a simple object-relational (O/R) framework and EJB to provide data persistence. For the complete source code of this application, visit the companion Manning web site.

Our example project consists of several components designed for generalized reuse and illustrates how Ant not only automates mundane tasks, but adds tremendous value by accomplishing tasks that are simply not possible without it. Here are details of our project with chapter cross-references:

- We wrote a custom Ant task to create a Lucene index at build time. We are currently indexing Ant's own documentation, but it can index any set of HTML or text files. Chapter 19 covers creating custom Ant tasks and the Ant API.

- Incorporating custom Ant tasks into a build file becomes much easier if a task-name/classname-mapping properties file is included with the custom task distributable. We accomplish the automatic generation of this mapping file using XDoclet templates and custom tags. This eliminates the need for a possibly missed manual step, retains metadata in a single place, and reduces duplication. We introduce XDoclet in chapter 11.

- We developed stand-alone command-line tools to allow indexing and searching. Executing Java programs from within Ant is one topic of chapter 5.

- We wrote a web application incorporating a build-time generated index. The web application uses Struts, and later Apache Axis for its Web Service entry point. We start building a WAR file in chapter 6, and deploy it in chapter 7. Incorporating third-party (or internally versioned) libraries takes the spotlight in chapter 10. Chapter 12 goes into detail on customizing and testing web applications, and chapter 15 adds SOAP support to the build.

- We developed a common component to be the Lucene liaison used by the command-line applications and web application. This allows a level of abstraction so that our applications do not directly know that Lucene is the search engine. Our search engine could theoretically be replaced without affecting any code in any of the applications. This common component is in its own Ant build, the control of which we cover in chapter 9.

- Each of our individual builds reuses common pieces such as library mapping properties, directory naming conventions, and general build settings. XML entity references are detailed in appendix B.

- Unit testing was performed at every step of our application development, generating detailed HTML reports of failures and (optionally) preventing our build from proceeding until unit tests pass. Testing gets full attention in chapter 4.

- Documenting our application's API using Javadoc occurs as an integral part of our distribution process. Packaging files and purposing them for proper platform line endings also occurs during distribution. We maintain our user manual in XML format; Ant transforms it into web-based documentation using XSLT and incorporates it into the web application. We can also generate PDF files for more printer-friendly use. Packaging and documentation are covered in chapter 6. Chapter 13 describes XML manipulation and XSL transformations.

- In-container testing (testing the web application and EJB layers through their own containers) ensures that our Struts actions and session beans are performing their job as expected. We explore in-container testing via Cactus in chapter 12.

- Automated deployment to Tomcat and other application servers, locally and remotely, is an integral part of the process. Testing even occurs after deployment to ensure that our application is alive and well. Deployment merits two whole chapters, 7 and 18.

- Continuous integration via CruiseControl provides automated builds of our system as code is being checked into our CVS server, notifying the relevant developers upon failure and providing customizable intranet web reporting capability. CruiseControl is covered in chapter 16.

1.7   YEAH, BUT CAN ANT…

…help with database driven applications?

Code generation from an initially developed schema can generate many artifacts, such as code and documentation. Tools such as Torque and Middlegen facilitate this process. Chapter 10 introduces Torque and chapter 14 describes Middlegen.

…take care of J2EE deployment descriptor issues?

Generating configuration data such as EJB deployment descriptors, EJB JAR files, web.xml, and struts-config.xml are done with relative ease using XDoclet, the `<ejb-jar>` task, and Ant techniques such as build-time textual replacement configuration. Having the initial code generation generate extensible Javadoc-like tags allows tools such as Torque and XDoclet to chain off the output. Chapter 11 demonstrates XDoclet's non-EJB capabilities, while chapter 14 expands on its EJB features as well as the use of `<ejbjar>`.

…allow developers to use the IDE of their choice?

Building with Ant, rather than using proprietary IDE builds, minimizes IDE configuration pain. Developers would be free to choose any IDE. Building a new development environment would consist of only a few steps: install Ant, install the development application server (which could be the IDE), pull the source code and build file from the source code repository, and execute Ant from within the IDE or from a command prompt. Ant works with relative paths, so each developer could store local source code in any directory of their choosing without affecting the build.

...enhance deployment quality?

Compilation errors halt the build process. As a result, developers take great pains to avoid "breaking the build." It is our philosophy that compilation errors are indeed showstoppers and should be addressed immediately. Chapter 2 introduces Java compilation with Ant. Chapter 12 shows how to compile JSP pages at build time, which catches JSP errors early.

Incorporating unit tests into an Ant build is easy, and with a few timesaving dependency tricks shown in chapter 4, having every build perform unit tests (if necessary) ensures that the only code that breaks tests is the code just touched. Tracking down the cause in such situations is typically trivial. Chapter 4 goes into detail on JUnit incorporation into a build process.

...deploy directly to production systems?

Deployments would be a matter of typing `ant deploy` at the command-line and could be done by any developer (or routinely via time-scheduled jobs) any time in an automated, repeatable manner. This would allow anyone (with proper permission, of course!) to build—and even deploy—a live production system. We introduce deployment in chapter 7, and explore it further in chapter 17.

...provide flexible development environments?

Even with a unified Ant build process, each developer can have individual settings that override the project defaults. Usually server passwords and switches to choose a debug over a release build of the software are set on a per-developer basis. Ant provides a number of ways for user and system settings to override project defaults in a clean, flexible, and safe manner. We discuss using Ant properties to accomplish this in chapter 3.

...provide for build-time parameterization and customization?

Using the same mechanisms that enable developer customizations, end-user customizations can be easily accomplished with Ant in ways that are impossible with typical IDE build processes. For example, a web interface can be customized on a per-client basis, allowing for client-specific text, graphics, and styles. With some naming conventions for the customized files, a common base system can be overlaid, at build time, with client-specific files and settings.

...automate it all?

Crafting an interactive build process lends itself directly (and without much additional effort) to waking up in the morning with an e-mail informing you that your system built successfully overnight, or having a build run on an integration server immediately upon code being committed to the source code repository. We show how to set up a continuous integration system with Ant in chapter 16.

1.8   BEYOND JAVA DEVELOPMENT

Not only is Ant the ideal build tool for routine Java development needs such as compiling, packaging, documenting, and deploying, but there are many other uses besides these. Ant is a task engine that automates routine chores. For example, we used Ant to publish drafts of this book to Manning's review web site via FTP. There were many large files, and with Ant's FTP dependency checking, we only uploaded the files that had changed on our local system, saving lots of time and bandwidth.

1.8.1   Web publishing engine

Both of the authors have used Ant for personal web-site maintenance. Erik created an XML file with information about his employment history, published articles, and other professional data. Using Ant, he builds HTML files using XSL transformations, and uploads them automatically. Steve has a similar process where he calls a command-line Win32 application to build HTML files from an Access database and then uploads only the files that have changed.

Our good friend Ted Neward uses Ant to transform his XML-formatted white papers using XSL:FO, into PDF files that he uploads with Ant. During the development of this book, we became Ted's personal Ant support hotline and fixed a bug in Ant's FTP task that he reported to us. He has even written a white paper describing this process (Neward 2001).

1.8.2   Simple workflow engine

Ant plays well with other tools natively, or through custom Ant wrapper tasks that can provide dependency checking and other benefits that native tools do not provide. Ant can serve as a simple workflow engine that automates many routine computer processes. Integrating your own custom Ant tasks into an Ant build file allows you to focus on the task at hand, inheriting an execution infrastructure that provides many useful facilities such as datatypes and parameterization.

1.8.3   Microsoft .NET and other languages

Certainly Ant was built to be a Java language build tool, but it is moderately adept at building software in other languages. There are .NET tasks within Ant's distribution to wrap Microsoft's C# compiler, for example. Efforts are under way to more tightly integrate C/C++ compilation and linking into Ant's framework.

1.9 SUMMARY

To summarize Ant briefly, it is a Java-based tool that can build, test, and deploy Java projects ranging in size from the very small to the very large. Ant uses XML *build files* to describe what to build. Each file covers one Ant *project*; a project is divided into *targets*; targets contain *tasks*. These tasks are the Java classes that actually perform the construction work. Targets can depend on other targets. Ant orders the execution so they execute in the correct order. Unlike Make, which is driven by file dependencies and derivation rules, Ant lets the tasks worry about file dependencies; the build file author merely lists the sequence of steps.

One of the most important points we want to get across in this book is that Ant itself does not make a successful Java project; rather the use of best practices learned from the cumulative experience of decades of software engineering is necessary for projects to succeed. Ant itself does not organize your project's directory tree in a normalized manner. Ant does not write your business logic code for you. Ant is a tool and, like any tool, provides greatest benefit when used properly. Sure, you could build a house with the traditional hammer, a box of nails, and a stack of wood, but why do things the harder way when you've got a cordless framing nailer handy?[3]

Ant is not only a Java build tool, but also an extensible simple workflow engine enabling the automation of almost any routine set of tasks and steps. While this book's focus is primarily the use of Ant within the Java development world, its tasks and extensibility allow it to go beyond this. And yet, the benefits Ant brings to Java projects cannot be overstated.

---

[3]   And safety goggles!

C H A P T E R 2

Getting started with Ant

2.1 Defining our first project 23
2.2 Step one: verifying the tools are in place 24
2.3 Step two: writing your first Ant build file 24
2.4 Step three: running your first build 26
2.5 Step four: imposing structure 31
2.6 Step five: running our program 39
2.7 Ant command line options 41
2.8 The final build file 44
2.9 Summary 46

Let's start a gentle introduction to Ant with a demonstration of what it can do. The first chapter describes how Ant views a project: a project contains targets, targets contain tasks and can depend on other targets, and all of these are declared in an XML file. The simplest project is one that contains one target, so that is where we will begin.

2.1 DEFINING OUR FIRST PROJECT

We obviously need a reason to use Ant, and we will use the reason that is common to almost all Java development projects: compiling Java source. We begin by creating an empty directory, called GettingStarted, which will be the base directory of our first project. We then create some real Java source to compile. In the new directory, we create a file called Main.java, containing the following minimal Java program:

```
public class Main {

    public static void main(String args[]) {
        for(int i=0;i<args.length;i++) {
            System.out.println(args[i]);
        }
    }
}
```

The fact that this program does nothing but print the argument list is unimportant; it is still Java code that we need to build, package, and execute—work we will delegate to Ant.

2.2   STEP ONE: VERIFYING THE TOOLS ARE IN PLACE

First, ensure that Ant is installed and ready to run. You will also need a properly installed Java development kit appropriate for your platform. Appendix A describes how to set up an Ant development system on both Unix and Windows.

After having installed everything, at a command prompt type

```
ant -version
```

A good response would be something listing a recent version of Ant, ideally 1.5 or later:

```
Apache Ant version 1.5 compiled on May 1 2002
```

A bad response would be any error message saying Ant was a not a recognized command, such as this one on a Unix system:

```
bash: ant: command not found
```

On Windows, the response will be less terse, but contains the same underlying message:

```
'ant' is not recognized as an internal or external command,
operable program or batch file.
```

Any such response indicates you have not installed or configured Ant yet, so turn to appendix A: Installation and follow the instructions there on setting up and testing the system. The rest of this chapter, and indeed the entire book, assumes that Ant is installed and working.

2.3   STEP TWO: WRITING YOUR FIRST ANT BUILD FILE

With Ant installed, and the source file created, it is time for Ant to compile our project.

Ant is controlled by providing a text file that tells how to perform all the stages of building, testing, and deploying a project. These files are *build files*, and every project that uses Ant must have at least one. The most minimal build file useful in Java development is one that builds all Java source in and below the current directory:

```xml
<?xml version="1.0"?>
<project name="firstbuild" default="compile" >
  <target name="compile">
    <javac srcdir="." />
    <echo>compilation complete!</echo>
  </target>
</project>
```

This is a piece of XML text, which we save to a file called build.xml. It is not actually a very good build file. We would not recommend you use it in a real project, for reasons revealed later, but it does do something useful.

It is almost impossible for a Java developer to be unaware of XML, but editing it may be a new experience. Don't worry. While XML may seem a bit hard to read at first, and it can be an unforgiving language, it is not very complex. If you really need to understand XML in all its gory details, the *Annotated XML Reference* (Bray 1998) is a good reference on the subject (online at http://www.xml.com/axml/testaxml.htm). We briefly skim over the surface of a subset of XML as it applies to Ant files in appendix B. If you know XML already, the most unusual point about Ant's use of XML is that it cannot have a DTD, because it is entirely possible to extend the tags Ant supports during a build.[1]

2.3.1 Examining the build file

Let us look at that first build file from the perspective of XML format rules. The <project> element is always the *root* element in Ant build files, in this case containing two attributes, name and default. The <target> element is a child of <project>. The <target> element contains two child elements: <javac> and <echo>.

This file could be represented as a tree, which is how XML parsers represent XML content when a program asks the parser for a Document Object Model (DOM) of the file. Figure 2.1 shows the tree representation.

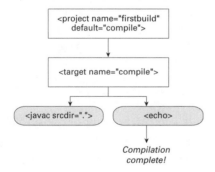

Figure 2.1
The XML representation of a build file is a tree: the project at the root contains one target, which contains two tasks. This matches with the Ant conceptual model: projects contain targets, targets contain tasks.

The graphical view of the XML tree makes it easier to look at a build file, and so the structure of the build file should become a bit clearer. At the top of the tree is a node project, which has a name and another attribute, default. All Ant build files must contain a single project as the root node.

---

[1] Ant actually can dynamically generate its DTD using <antstructure>, although it is not perfect. Most IDE plug-ins have their own DTDs to validate against.

Underneath the project is a node called `<target>` with the name `compile`. In Ant, a target is a single stage in the build process. It can be explicitly invoked from the command line or it can be used internally. A build file can have many targets, each of which must have a unique name that can be any arbitrary string. Note that a target that contains spaces or begins with a hyphen is very hard to call from the command line, so we recommended avoiding such situations.

The build file's `compile` target contains two XML elements, one called `<javac>` and one called `<echo>`. The names of these elements should hint as to their function: one calls the `javac` compiler to compile Java source, the other echoes a message to the screen. These are the *tasks* that do the work of this build. The compilation task has one attribute, `srcdir`, which is set to `"."`. This tells the task to look for source files from the current directory downward. The second task, `<echo>`, has a text child node which will be printed when the build reaches that far. If the compilation fails then the build will fail before the message gets printed.

In this example, we configured the `<javac>` task with attributes of the task: we have told it to compile files in the current directory. Here, the `<echo>` task relies on the text element inside it to determine its behavior. Attributes describe simple options and settings that are only set once in a task. Elements can specify multiple entries simultaneously, such as a list of files to delete, or of commands to send to a remote server over a network connection. All tasks list the attributes and elements they support in the online documentation. This documentation is worth bookmarking, as you will use it regularly when creating Ant build files. In the documentation, all "parameters" are XML attributes, and all "parameters specified as nested elements" are exactly that: nested XML elements that configure the task. Usually the examples shown on each task's page provide handy examples of how to use the tasks, and can be cut, pasted, and customized to your own needs.

2.4 STEP THREE: RUNNING YOUR FIRST BUILD

We've just covered the basic theory of Ant: an XML build file can describe targets to build and the tasks used to build them. You have just created your first build file, so let's try it out. With the Java source and build file in the same directory, Ant should be ready to build the project. At the command prompt type:

```
ant
```

If the build file has been typed in correctly, then you should see the following response:

```
Buildfile: build.xml

compile:
    [javac] Compiling 1 source file
    [echo] compilation complete!

BUILD SUCCESSFUL

Total time: 2 seconds
```

There it is. Ant has compiled all the Java source in the current directory (one file) and printed a success message afterwards. This is the core build step of all Ant projects that work with Java source. It may seem strange at first to have an XML file telling a tool how to compile a single file, but it will soon become familiar. Note that we did not have to name the source files; Ant just worked it out "somehow." We will spend time in chapter 3 covering how Ant decides which files to work on. For now, you just need to know that the <javac> will compile any and all Java files in the current directory and any subdirectories. If that is all you need to do, then this build file is adequate for your project: you can just add more files and Ant will find them and compile them.

Of course, a modern project has to do much more than just compile files, which is where the rest of Ant's capabilities, and the rest of this book, come in to play.

2.4.1 If the build fails

When you are learning any new computer language, it is easy to overlook mistakes that cause the compiler or interpreter to generate error messages that do not make much sense. Imagine if somehow the XML was mistyped so that the line calling the <javac> task was misspelled:

```
<javaac srcdir="." />
```

With this task in the target, the output will look something like

```
Buildfile: build.xml

compile:    <——  Target executed

BUILD FAILED

C:\AntBook\gettingstarted\build.xml:4:    <—— File and line where the build failed
   Could not create task of type: javaac.

Ant could not find the task or a class this task relies upon.

This is common and has a number of causes; the usual
solutions are to read the manual pages then download and
install needed JAR files, or fix the build file:
 - You have misspelt 'javaac'.   <——————————————————————— The problem:
   Fix: check your spelling.                                "javac" was
 - The task needs an external JAR file to execute           misspelled
   and this is not found at the right place in the classpath.
   Fix: check the documentation for dependencies.
   Fix: declare the task.
 - The task is an Ant optional task and optional.jar is absent
   Fix: look for optional.jar in ANT_HOME/lib, download if needed
 - The task was not built into optional.jar as dependent
   libraries were not found at build time.
   Fix: look in the JAR to verify, then rebuild with the needed
   libraries, or download a release version from apache.org
```

```
 - The build file was written for a later version of Ant
   Fix: upgrade to at least the latest release version of Ant
 - The task is not an Ant core or optional task
   and needs to be declared using <taskdef>.
Remember that for JAR files to be visible to ant tasks implemented
in ANT_HOME/lib, the files must be in the same directory or on the
classpath

Please do not file bug reports on this problem, nor email the
ant mailing lists, until all of these causes have been explored,
as this is not an Ant bug.
```

Whenever Ant fails to build, the BUILD FAILED message appears—a message that will hopefully not be too familiar. Usually it is associated with Java source errors or unit test failures, but build file syntax problems result in the same failure message, accompanied by some informative text.

If you do get an error, don't worry. Nothing drastic will happen, files won't be deleted (not in this example, anyway!) and you can try to correct the error by looking at the line of XML named, as well as the lines on either side of the error. If your editor has good XML support, the editor itself will point out any XML language errors, leaving the command line to find only Ant-specific errors. Editors that are Ant-aware or validate against an Ant DTD will also catch many Ant-specific syntax errors. An XML editor would also catch the omission of an ending tag from an XML element, such as forgetting to terminate the target element:

```
<?xml version="1.0"?>
<project name="firstbuild" default="compile" >
  <target name="compile">
    <javac srcdir="." />
    <echo>compilation complete!</echo>
</project>
```

The error here would come from the XML parser:

```
C:\AntBook\gettingstarted\xml-error.xml:6:
  Expected "</target>" to terminate element starting on line 3.
```

Well laid out build files, formatted for readability, help to make such errors visible.

One error we still encounter regularly comes from having an attribute that isn't valid for that task. Spelling the srcdir attribute as sourcedir is an example of this:

```
    <javac sourcedir="." />
```

If the build file contains that line, you would see this error message:

```
compile:

BUILD FAILED

C:\AntBook\gettingstarted\build.xml:4:
 The <javac> task doesn't support the "sourcedir" attribute.
```

This message indicates that the task description contained an invalid attribute. Usually this means whoever created the build file typed something wrong, but could mean that the file's author wrote it for a later version of Ant, one with newer attributes or tasks than the version doing the build. That can be hard to fix without upgrading; sometimes a workaround isn't always possible. It is rare that an upgrade would be incompatible or detrimental to your existing build file; such an upgrade is not anything to fear, since the Ant 1.x product line maintains strict backwards compatibility.

The error you are likely to see often in Ant is not caused by an error in the build file; rather, it is the build halting after the compiler failed to compile your code. If, for example, someone forgot the semicolon after the `println` call, a compiler error message would appear, followed by build failure information:

```
Buildfile: build.xml
compile:
 [javac] Compiling 1 source file
 [javac] /home/ant/Projects/firstbuild/Main.java:5: ';' expected
 [javac] System.out.println("hello, world")
 [javac]                                                    ^
 [javac] 1 error

BUILD FAILED
/home/ant/Projects/firstbuild/build.xml:4: Compile failed, messages should
have been provided.

Total time: 4 seconds
```

The build failed on the same line as the previous example error, line four, but this time it did the correct action. The compiler found something wrong, printed out its messages, and notified Ant of the error, which promptly stopped the build. When you get compiler error messages, the line of the XML file is usually unimportant. The name of the Java file and the location within it, along with the compiler error, are the messages that matter.

The key point to note is that failure of a task will usually result in the build itself failing. This is essential for a successful build process: there is no point packaging or delivering a project if it did not compile. Ant enforces the rule that failure of a single task halts the entire build.[2]

2.4.2 Looking at the build in more detail

If the build does actually succeed, then the only evidence of this is the message that compilation was successful. Let's run the task again, this time in verbose mode, to see what happens. Ant produces a verbose log when invoked with the `-verbose` parameter. This is a very useful feature when figuring out what a build file does. For our simple build file, it doubles the amount of text printed:

---

[2] Some tasks allow for internal failure to be ignored and for the build to continue.

```
> ant -verbose
Apache Ant version 1.5alpha compiled on February 1 2002
Buildfile: build.xml
Detected Java version: 1.4 in: /usr/java/j2sdk1.4.0/jre
Detected OS: Linux
parsing buildfile /home/ant/Projects/firstbuild/build.xml with
 URI = file:/home/ant/Projects/firstbuild/build.xml
Project base dir set to: /home/ant/Projects/firstbuild
Build sequence for target `compile' is [compile]
Complete build sequence is [compile]

compile:
    [javac] Main.java omitted as
            /home/ant/Projects/firstbuild/Main.class is up to date.
    [javac] build.xml skipped - don't know how to handle it
    [javac] Main.class skipped - don't know how to handle it
     [echo] compilation complete!

BUILD SUCCESSFUL

Total time: 1 second
```

For this build, the most interesting lines are those generated by the <javac> task. It shows two things. First, the task has decided not to recompile Main.java, because it has determined that the destination class is up to date. The task not only includes source files without needing to know their names, it can determine the name and location of the generated class file and, based on simple timestamp checking, decide whether or not to recompile the files. All this is provided in the single line of the build file, <javac srcdir="." />, which is a lot of functionality for twenty characters.

The second finding is that the task explicitly skipped the build file, and the generated Main.class bytecode file. This shows that the task looks at all files in the current directory, but because it only knows how to compile Java source files, files without a .java extension are ignored.

What is the login verbose mode if Ant compiled the source file? Delete Main.class then run Ant again to see. The core part of the output provides detail on the compilation process:

```
compile:
    [javac] Main.java added as
            /home/ant/Projects/firstbuild/Main.class doesn't exist.
    [javac] build.xml skipped—don't know how to handle it
    [javac] Compiling 1 source file
    [javac] Using modern compiler
    [javac] Compilation args: -classpath
            /home/ant/Java/jakarta-ant/lib/jaxp.jar:
            /home/ant/Java/jakarta-ant/lib/crimson.jar:
            /home/ant/Java/jakarta-ant/lib/ant.jar:
            /usr/java/j2sdk1.4.0/lib/tools.jar
            -sourcepath /home/ant/Projects/firstbuild -g:none
```

```
[javac] File to be compiled:
        /home/ant/Projects/firstbuild/Main.java
[echo] compilation complete!
```

BUILD SUCCESSFUL

This time the `<javac>` task does need to compile the source file, a fact it prints to the log. It still skips the build.xml file, printing this fact out before it actually compiles any Java source. This provides a bit more insight into the workings of the task: it builds a list of files to compile before it sends the set to the compiler. Actually, as you can discover by looking at the Ant source, it hands off this entire list of Java files to the compiler in one go. By default the Java-based compiler that came with the JDK is used, from inside the same JVM as Ant itself. This makes the build fast, even though it is all written in Java and has to parse an XML file before it even begins to do any work.

A final point of interest from these verbose runs is that we are clearly running under Linux, while the earlier examples were clearly running on a Windows PC. We decided to test the build on a different computer. Ant does not care what platform you are running on, as long as it is one of the many it supports. The same build file can compile, package, test, and deliver the same source files on whatever platform it is executed on, which helps unify a development team where multiple system types are used for development and deployment.

Don't worry yet about running the program we compiled. We need to get the compilation process under control before actually running it.

2.5   STEP FOUR: IMPOSING STRUCTURE

The build file is now compiling Java files, but the build process is messy. Source files, output files, the build file: they are all in the same directory. If this project gets any bigger, things will get out of hand. Before that happens, we must impose some structure. The structure we are going to impose is the de facto standard in Ant, but it is imposed for a reason, a reason driven by the three changes we want to make to the project.

- We want to automate the cleanup in Ant. If done wrong, this could accidentally delete source files. To minimize that risk, you should always cleanly separate source and generated files into different directories.

- We want to place the Java source file into a Java package.

- We want to create a JAR file containing the compiled code. This should be placed somewhere that can also be cleaned up by Ant.

To add packaging and clean-build support to the build, we have to isolate the source, intermediate, and final files. Once you have separated source and generated files, it is easy and safe to automate cleanup of the latter, making it easy to perform clean builds. A clean build is always preferable to an incremental build as there is no chance of old classes sneaking into the build with out-of-date constants or method declarations. It is good to get into the habit of doing clean builds. Do this not just when you know something like a constant or compiler option has changed. Do it whenever you are going to release code, or first thing after a big update from the source code repository, and do it when the build just seems "odd."

The structure we are going to use is a subset of the standard structure we use throughout this book, and which we encourage you to adopt—or at least ignore from a position of knowledge. We list the structure in table 2.1.

Table 2.1   An Ant project should split source files, intermediate files, and distribution packages into separate directories. This makes them much easier to manage during the build process. The directories are a de facto standard in Ant projects. If you use them it will be easier to integrate your build files with those of others.

Directory name	Function
src	source files
build/classes	intermediate output (created; cleanable)
dist	distributable files (created; cleanable)

2.5.1   Laying out the source directories

The first directory, src, contains the source and is the most important. The other two contain files that are created during the build. To clean these directories up, these entire directory trees can be deleted. Of course, this means the build file may need to recreate the directories if they are not already present.

We want to move the Java source into the src directory and extend the build file to create and use the other directories. Before moving the Java file, it needs a package name; we have chosen org.example.antbook.lesson1. Add this at the top of the source file in a package declaration:

```
package org.example.antbook.lesson1;
public class Main {

    public static void main(String args[]) {
        for(int i=0;i<args.length;i++) {
            System.out.println(args[i]);
        }
    }
}
```

You must then save the file in a directory tree beneath the source directory that matches that package hierarchy: src/org/example/antbook/lesson1. This is because the dependency checking code in <javac> relies on the source files being laid out this way. When the Java compiler compiles the files, it always places the output files in a directory tree that matches the package declaration. The next time the <javac> task runs, its dependency checking code looks at the tree of generated class files and compares it to the source files. It does not look inside the source files to find their package declarations; it relies on the source tree being laid out to match the destination tree.

NOTE For Java source dependency checking to work, you *must* lay out source in a directory tree that matches the package declarations in the source.

Only when the source is not in any package can you place it in the base of the source tree and expect <javac> to track dependencies properly, which is what we have been doing up until now. If Ant keeps on recompiling your Java files every time you do a build, it is probably because you have not placed them correctly in the package hierarchy.

It may seem inconvenient having to rearrange your files to suit the build tool, but the benefits become clear over time. On a large project, such a layout is critical to separating and organizing classes. If you start with it from the outset, even on a small project, you can grow more gently from a small project to a larger one. Modern IDEs also prefer this layout structure, as does the underlying Java compiler.

Be aware that dependency checking of <javac> is simply limited to comparing the dates on the source and destination files. There is a secondary task to do more advanced dependency checking, which is covered in chapter 10. Even then, a regular a clean build is a good practice.

2.5.2 Laying out the build directories

We want to configure Ant to put all intermediate files—those files generated by any step in the build process that are not directly delivered or deployed—into the build directory tree. A large project can use Ant to generate many kinds of intermediate files: HTML pages from XML source, Java source files from JSP source, even text or data files generated by running programs that Ant compiles and executes during the build.

The simple project being developed in this chapter has none of these needs, but we will plan ahead by putting the compiled files into a subdirectory of build, a directory called classes. Different intermediate output types can have their own directories alongside this one.

As we mentioned in section 2.4.1, the Java compiler lays out packaged files into a directory structure that matches the package declarations in the source files. The compiler will create the appropriate subdirectories on demand, so we do not need to create them by hand. What we need to create is the top-level build directory, and the classes subdirectory. We do this with the Ant task <mkdir>, which, like the shell command of the same name, creates a directory. In fact, it creates parent directories, too, if needed:

```
<mkdir dir="build/classes">
```

This call is all that is needed to create the two levels of intermediate output. To actually place the output of Ant tasks into the build directory, we need to use whichever attribute specifies a destination directory, and set it to a location in the build subdirectories. For the <javac> task, as with many other Ant tasks, the appropriate attribute is destdir.

2.5.3   Laying out the dist directories

The dist directories are usually much simpler than the intermediate file directories, because one of the common stages in a build process is to package files up, placing the packaged file into the dist directory. There may be different types of packaging: JAR, Zip, tar, and WAR, for example, and so a subdirectory is needed to keep all of these files in a place where they can be identified and deleted for a clean build. To create the distribution directory, we insert another call to `<mkdir>`:

```
<mkdir dir="dist">
```

To create the JAR file, we are going to use an Ant task called, appropriately, `<jar>`. We have dedicated a whole chapter, chapter 6, to this and the other tasks used in the packaging process. For this introductory tour of Ant we use the task at its simplest, when it can be configured to make a named JAR file out of a directory tree:

```
<jar destfile="dist/project.jar" basedir="build/classes" />
```

This shows the advantage of placing intermediate code into the build directory: you can build a JAR file from it without having to list what files are included, because all files in the directory tree should go in, which, conveniently, is the default behavior of the `<jar>` task.

With the destination directories defined, we now have completed the directory structure of the project, which looks like the illustration in figure 2.2. When the build is executed, a hierarchy of folders will be created in the class directory to match the source tree, but as these are automatically created we are not worrying about them.

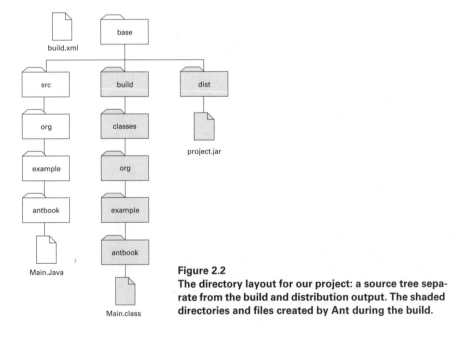

Figure 2.2
The directory layout for our project: a source tree separate from the build and distribution output. The shaded directories and files created by Ant during the build.

2.5.4 Creating the build file

Now that we have the files in the right places, and we know what we want to do, the build file needs to be rewritten. Rather than glue all the tasks together in one long list of actions, we have broken the separate stages—directory creation, compilation, packaging, and cleanup—into four separate targets inside the build file.

```
<?xml version="1.0" ?>
<project name="structured" default="archive" >

  <target name="init">
    <mkdir dir="build/classes" />        Creates the output
    <mkdir dir="dist" />                  directories
  </target>

  <target name="compile" depends="init" >
    <javac srcdir="src"
      destdir="build/classes"     ◁——— Compiles into the
      />                               output directories
  </target>

  <target name="archive" depends="compile" >
    <jar destfile="dist/project.jar"           Creates the
      basedir="build/classes" />               archive
  </target>

  <target name="clean" depends="init">
    <delete dir="build" />               Cleans the
    <delete dir="dist"  />               output
  </target>                             directories

</project>
```

This build file adds an init target to do initialization work, which means creating directories. We've also added two other new targets, clean and archive. The archive target uses the <jar> task to create the JAR file containing all files in and below the build/classes directory, which in this case means all .class files created by the compile target. One target has a dependency upon another, a dependency that Ant needs to know about. The clean target cleans up the output directories by deleting them. It uses the <delete> task to do this. We have also changed the default target to archive, so this will be the target that Ant executes when you run it.

2.5.5 Target dependencies

We need a way of ensuring that Ant runs some targets before other targets that depend on their outputs.

In our current project, for the archive to be up to date, all the source files must be compiled, which means the archive target must come after the compilation target. Likewise, compile needs the directories created in init, so Ant must execute it after the init task. These are dependencies that we need to communicate to Ant. We do this as the targets are declared, listing the dependencies in their depends attributes:

```
<target name="compile" depends="init" >
<target name="archive" depends="compile" >
<target name="clean" depends="init">
```

If a target directly depends on more than one predecessor target, then you should list both dependencies in the dependency attribute, for example depends="compile,test". In our example build, the archive task does depend upon both init and compile, but we do not bother to state the dependency upon init because the compile target depends upon it. If Ant must execute init before compile, and archive depends upon compile then Ant must run init before archive. Put formally, dependencies are transitive. They are not however reflexive: the compile target does not know or care about the archive target. Another useful fact is that the order of targets inside the build file is not important: Ant reads in the whole file before it builds the dependency tree and executes targets. There is no need to worry about forward references.

If you look at the dependency tree of targets in the current example, it looks like figure 2.3. Before Ant executes any target, all the predecessor targets must already have been executed. If these predecessors depend on targets themselves, the execution order will also consider those and produce an order that satisfies all dependencies. If two targets in this execution order share a common dependency, then that predecessor will only execute once.

Experienced makefile editors will recognize that Ant targets resemble Make's pseudotargets—targets in a makefile that you refer to by name in the dependencies of other makefile targets. Usually in Make, you name the source files that a target depends on, and the build tool itself works out what to do to create the target file from the source files. In Ant, you name stages of work as targets, and the tasks inside each target work out for themselves what their dependencies are.

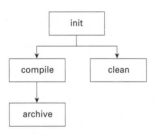

Figure 2.3
**Once you add dependencies,
the graph of targets gets more
complex. Here clean depends
upon init; archive depends on
compile directly and init
indirectly. All of a target's
dependencies will be executed
ahead of the target itself.**

2.5.6 Running the new build file

Now that there are multiple targets in the build file, we need a way of specifying which to run. You can simply list one or more targets on the command line, so all of the following are valid, as are other combinations:

```
ant
ant init
ant clean
```

```
ant compile
ant archive
ant clean archive
```

Calling Ant with no target is the same as calling the default target named in the project. In this example, it is the `archive` target:

```
init:
    [mkdir] Created dir: C:\AntBook\secondbuild\build
    [mkdir] Created dir: C:\AntBook\secondbuild\dist

compile:
    [javac] Compiling 1 source file to C:\AntBook\secondbuild\build

archive:
      [jar] Building jar: C:\AntBook\secondbuild\dist\project.jar

BUILD SUCCESSFUL
Total time: 2 seconds
```

This demonstrates that Ant has determined execution order of tasks. When you invoke a target with dependencies, all their dependencies execute first. As both the `compile` and `archive` targets depend upon the `init` target, Ant must call `init` before it executes either of those targets. It orders the targets so that first the directories get created, then the source compiled, and finally the JAR archive built.

2.5.7 Rerunning the build

What happens when the build is run a second time? Let's try it and see:

```
init:

compile:

archive:

BUILD SUCCESSFUL

Total time: 1 second
```

We go through all the targets, but none of the tasks say that they are doing any work. Here's why: all of these tasks check their dependencies, `<mkdir>` does not create directories that already exist, `<javac>` compares source and class file timestamps, and the `<jar>` task compares the time of all files to be added to the archive with the time of the file itself. Only if a source file is newer than the generated archive file does the task rebuild the JAR file.

If you add the `-verbose` flag to the command line you will get more detail on what did or, in this case, did not take place.

```
>ant -verbose

Apache Ant version 1.5alpha compiled on February 1 2002
Buildfile: build.xml
Detected Java version: 1.3 in: D:\Java\jdk13\jre
Detected OS: Windows 2000
parsing buildfile C:\AntBook\secondbuild\build.xml with
```

```
        URI = file:C:/AntBook/secondbuild/build.xml
Project base dir set to: C:\AntBook\secondbuild
Build sequence for target `archive' is [init, compile, archive]
Complete build sequence is [init, compile, archive, clean]

init:

compile:
    [javac] org\example\antbook\lesson1\Main.java omitted as
            C:\AntBook\secondbuild\build\org\example\antbook\
                lesson1\Main.class is up to date.

archive:
     [jar] org\example\antbook\lesson1\Main.class omitted as
            C:\AntBook\secondbuild\dist\project.jar is up to date.

BUILD SUCCESSFUL
Total time: 2 seconds
```

The verbose run provides a lot of information, much of which may seem distracting. When a build is working well, you do not need it, but it is invaluable while developing that file.

> **TIP**   If ever you are unsure why a build is not behaving as expected, run Ant with the -verbose option to get lots more information.

2.5.8   How Ant handles multiple targets on the command line

Here is an interesting question which expert users of Make will usually get wrong: what happens when you type ant compile archive at the command line? Many people would expect Ant to pick an order that executes each target and its dependencies once only: init, compile, archive. Make would certainly do that, but Ant does not. Instead, it executes each target and dependents in turn, so the actual sequence is init, compile, then init, compile, archive:

```
C:\AntBook\secondbuild>ant compile archive
Buildfile: build.xml

init:
    [mkdir] Created dir: C:\AntBook\secondbuild\build
    [mkdir] Created dir: C:\AntBook\secondbuild\dist

compile:
    [javac] Compiling 1 source file to C:\AntBook\secondbuild\build

init:

compile:

archive:
     [jar] Building jar: C:\AntBook\secondbuild\dist\project.jar

BUILD SUCCESSFUL
Total time: 2 seconds
```

This behavior can be unexpected to anyone experienced in other build tools, as it seems to add extra work rather than save work by sharing dependencies. However, if you look closely, the second time Ant executes the `compile` target it does no work; the tasks get executed but their dependency checking stops existing outputs being rebuilt.

Our next question is this: when a target lists multiple dependencies, does Ant execute them in the order listed? The answer is yes, unless other dependency rules prevent it. Imagine if we modified the `archive` target with the dependency attribute `depends="compile,init"`. A simple left-to-right execution order would run the `compile` target before it was initialized. Ant would try to execute the targets in this order, but because the `compile` target depends upon `init`, Ant will call `init` first. This subtle detail can catch you out. If you try to control the execution order by listing targets in order, you may not get the results you expect as explicit dependencies always take priority.

2.6   STEP FIVE: RUNNING OUR PROGRAM

We now have a structured build process that creates the JAR file from the Java source. At this point the next steps could be to run tests on the code, distribute it, or deploy it. We shall be covering how to do all these things in the following chapters. For now, we just want to run the program.

2.6.1   Why execute from inside Ant

We could just call our program from the command line, stating the classpath, the name of the entry point and the arguments:

```
>java -cp build/classes org.example.antbook.lesson1.Main a b .
a
b
.
```

If the classpath is not complex and the arguments to the application are simple, calling Java programs from the command line is not particularly hard, just a manual process. We still want to run our program from the build file, not just to show it is possible, but because it provides some tangible benefits the moment we do so:

- A target to run the program can depend upon the compilation target, so we know we are always running the latest version of the code.
- It is easy to pass complex arguments to the program.
- It is easier to set up the classpath.
- The program can run inside Ant's own JVM; so it loads faster.
- You can halt a build if the return code of the program is not zero.

The fact that the execute target can be made to depend on the compile target is one of the key benefits during development. There is simply no need to split program compilation from execution.

2.6.2 Adding an execute target

To call the program from inside Ant, we merely add a new target, execute, which we make dependent upon compile. It contains one task, <java>, that runs our Main.class using the interim build/classes directory tree as our classpath:

```
<target name="execute" depends="compile">
  <java
    classname="org.example.antbook.lesson1.Main"
    classpath="build/classes">
    <arg value="a"/>
    <arg value="b"/>
    <arg file="."/>
  </java>
</target>
```

We have three <arg> tags inside the <java> task; each tag contains one of the arguments to the program: "a", "b", and ".", as with the command line version. Note, however, that the final argument, <arg file="."/>, is different from the other two. The first two arguments use the value attribute of the <arg> tag, which passes the value straight down to the program. The final argument uses the file attribute, which tells Ant to resolve that attribute to an absolute file location before calling the program.

2.6.3 Running the new target

What does the output of the run look like? First, let's it run it on Windows:

```
C:\AntBook\secondbuild>ant execute
Buildfile: build.xml

init:

compile:

execute:
     [java] a
     [java] b
     [java] C:\AntBook\secondbuild
```

The compile task didn't need to do any recompilation, and the execute task called our program. Ant has prefixed every line of output with the name of the task currently running, showing here that this is the output of an invoked Java application. The first two arguments went straight to our application, while the third argument was resolved to the current directory; Ant turned "." into an absolute file reference. Next, let's try the same program on Linux:

```
[secondbuild]$ ant execute
Buildfile: build.xml

init:

compile:

execute:
     [java] a
     [java] b
     [java] /home/ant/Projects/secondbuild
```

Everything is identical, apart from the final argument, which has been resolved to a different location, the current directory in the Unix path syntax, rather than the DOS one. This shows another benefit of starting programs from Ant rather than any batch file or shell script: a single build file can start the same program on multiple platforms, transforming file names and file paths into the appropriate values for the target platform.

This is a very brief demonstration of how and why to call programs from inside Ant; enough to round off this little project. We have dedicated an entire chapter to the subject of calling Java and native programs from Ant during a build process. Chapter 5 explores the options and issues of the topic in detail.

2.7   ANT COMMAND LINE OPTIONS

We have nearly finished our quick look at some of what Ant can do, but we have one more little foundational topic to cover: how to call Ant. We have already shown that Ant is a command-line program, and that you can specify multiple targets as parameters, and we have introduced the -verbose option to get more information on a build. We want to do some more with Ant's command line to run our program. First, we want to remove the [java] prefixes, then we will run the build without any output at all unless something goes wrong. Ant command line options can do this.

Ant can take a number of options, which it lists if you ask for them with ant -help. The current set of options is listed in table 2.2.

Table 2.2   Ant command line options

Option	Meaning
-help	List the options Ant supports and exit
-version	Print the version information and exit
-buildfile *file*	Use the named buildfile, use -f as a shortcut
-find *file*	Search for the named buildfile up the tree
-projecthelp	Print information about the current project
-verbose	Be extra verbose
-quiet	Be extra quiet
-debug	Print debugging information
-emacs	Produce logging information without adornments
-D*property*=*value*	Set a property to a value
-propertyfile file	Load all properties from file
-logfile *file*	Use given file for log
-listener *classname*	Add a project listener
-logger *classname*	Name a different logger
-inputhandler *classname*	The name of a class to respond to <input> requests
-diagnostics	Print information that might be helpful to diagnose or report problems.

Some options require more explanation of Ant before they make sense. In particular, the two options related to properties are not relevant until we explore Ant's properties in chapter 3. Likewise, we don't introduce listeners and loggers until chapter 13, so let's ignore those options for now. Just keep in mind that it is possible to write Java classes that get told when targets are executed, or that get fed all the output from the tasks as they execute, a feature that is the basis for integrating Ant into IDEs.

2.7.1 Specifying which build file to run

Perhaps the most important option for Ant is -buildfile. This option lets you control which build file Ant uses, allowing you to divide the targets of a project into multiple files, and select the appropriate build file depending on your actions. A shortcut to -buildfile is -f. To invoke our existing project, we just name it immediately after the -f or -buildfile argument:

```
ant -buildfile build.xml compile
```

This is exactly equivalent to calling ant compile with no file specified. If for some reason the current directory was somewhere in the source tree, which is sometimes the case when you are editing text from a console application such as vi, emacs, or even edit, then you can refer to a build file by passing in the appropriate relative file name for your platform, such as ../../../build.xml or ..\..\..\build.xml. This is fiddly. It is better to use the -find option, which must be followed by the name of a build file. This variant does something very special: it searches up the directory tree to find the first build file in a parent directory of that name, and invokes it. With this option, when you are deep down the source tree editing files, you can easily invoke the project build with the simple command:

```
ant -find build.xml
```

2.7.2 Controlling the amount of information provided

We stated that we want to reduce the amount of information provided when we invoke Ant. Getting rid of the [java] prefix is easy: we run the build file with the -emacs option; this omits the task-name prefix from all lines printed. The option is called -emacs because the output is now in the emacs format for invoked tools, which enables that and other editors to locate the lines on which errors occurred. When calling Ant from any IDE that lacks built-in support, the -emacs option may tighten the integration.

For our exercise, we only want to change the presentation from the command line, which is simple enough:

```
[secondbuild]$ ant -emacs execute
Buildfile: build.xml

init:

compile:

execute:
```

```
a
b
/home/ant/Projects/secondbuild
```
```
BUILD SUCCESSFUL
Total time: 2 seconds.
```

This leaves the next half of the problem, hiding all the output entirely. Three of the Ant options control how much information is output when Ant runs. Two of these (-verbose and -debug) progressively increase the amount. The verbose option is useful when you are curious about how Ant works, or why a build isn't behaving. The debug option includes all the normal and verbose output, and much more low level information, primarily only of interest to Ant developers. The -quiet option reduces the amount of information to a success message or errors:

```
[secondbuild]$ ant -quiet execute
```
```
BUILD SUCCESSFUL
Total time: 2 seconds
```

This leaves us with no way of telling if the program worked, unless we can infer it from the time to execute. Would adding an <echo> statement in the execute target help? Not by default. One of the attributes of echo is the level attribute: error, warning, info, verbose, and debug control the amount of information that appears. The default value info ensures that echoed messages appear in normal builds, or the two levels of even more information, verbose and debug. By inserting an echo statement into our execute target with the level set to warning, we ensure that even when the build is running in quiet mode the output appears. The Ant task declaration

```
<echo level="warning" message="running" />
```

results in the following output:

```
>ant -quiet
    [echo] running
```

To eliminate the [echo] prefix, we add the -emacs option again, calling

```
>ant -quiet -emacs
```

to get the following output:

```
running
```
```
BUILD SUCCESSFUL
Total time: 2 seconds.
```

Controlling the output level of programs is not only useful when debugging, but when trying to run a large build that has worked in the past; only errors and occasional progress messages matter. A quiet build with a few manual <echo level= "warning"> tags is ideal for a bulk build. Likewise, some <echo level="verbose"> tags can provide extra trace information when more detail is required.

2.7.3　Getting information about a project

The final option of immediate relevance is -projecthelp. It lists the main targets in a project, and is invaluable whenever you need to know what targets a build file provides. Ant only lists targets containing the optional description attribute, as these are the targets intended for public consumption.

```
>ant -projecthelp
Buildfile: build.xml
Main targets:

Subtargets:

 archive
 clean
 compile
 execute
 init

Default target: archive
```

This is not very informative, which is our fault for not documenting the file thoroughly enough. If we add a description attribute to each target, such as description="Compiles the source code" for the compile target, and a <description> tag right after the project declaration, then the target listing includes these descriptions, marks all the described targets as "main targets," and hides all sub targets from view:

```
Buildfile: build.xml
Compiles and runs a simple program
Main targets:

 archive  Creates the JAR file
 clean    Removes the temporary directories used
 compile  Compiles the source code
 execute  Runs the program

Default target: archive
```

To see both main and sub targets in a project, you must call Ant with the options -projecthelp and -verbose. The more complex a project is, the more useful the -projecthelp feature becomes. We strongly recommend providing description strings for every target intended to act as an entry point to external callers, and a line or two at the top of each build file describing what it does.

2.8　*THE FINAL BUILD FILE*

We close with the complete listing of the final build file, listing 2.1. As well as adding the description tags, we decided to change the default target to run the program, rather than just create the archive. We have marked the major changes in bold, to show where this build file differs from the build files and build file fragments shown earlier.

```xml
<?xml version="1.0" ?>
<project name="secondbuild" default="execute" >
<description>Compiles and runs a simple program</description>

  <target name="init">
    <mkdir dir="build/classes" />
    <mkdir dir="dist" />
  </target>

  <target name="compile" depends="init"
      description="Compiles the source code">
    <javac srcdir="src"
      destdir="build/classes"
      />
  </target>

  <target name="archive" depends="compile"
      description="Creates the JAR file">
    <jar destfile="dist/project.jar"
      basedir="build/classes"
      />
  </target>

  <target name="clean" depends="init"
      description="Removes the temporary directories used">
    <delete dir="build" />
    <delete dir="dist" />
  </target>

  <target name="execute" depends="compile"
      description="Runs the program">
    <echo level="warning" message="running" />
    <java
      classname="org.example.antbook.lesson1.Main"
      classpath="build/classes">
      <arg value="a"/>
      <arg value="b"/>
      <arg file="."/>
    </java>
  </target>

</project>
```

It seems somewhat disproportionate, forty-some lines of Ant build file to compile a ten-line program, but think of what those lines of build file do: they compile the program, package it, run it, and can even clean up afterwards. More importantly, if we added a second Java file to the program, how many lines of code need to change in the build file? Zero. As long as the build process does not change, you can now add

Java classes and packages to the source tree to build a larger JAR file and perform more useful work on the execution parameters, yet you don't have to make any changes to the build file itself. That is one of the nice features of Ant: you don't need to modify your build files whenever a new source file is added to the build process. It all just works.

2.9   SUMMARY

Ant is a command-line tool that takes a build file describing how to build and deploy Java software projects.

The tool uses XML as the file format, with the root element of a *build file* representing an Ant *project*. This project contains one or more *targets*, which represent stages of the project, or actual outputs. Each target can be dependent upon one or more other targets, which creates a graph-like structure representing the processing stages in a project.

A target can contain *tasks*, which perform the actual steps in the build process. These tasks themselves implement dependency checking and execute actions.

Some of the basic Ant tasks are <echo>, which simply prints a message, <delete>, which deletes files, <mkdir>, which creates directories, <javac>, which compiles Java source, and <jar> to create an archive of the binaries. The first three of these tasks look like XML versions of shell commands, which is roughly what they are, but the latter two demonstrate the power of Ant. They are aware of dependency rules, so that <javac> will only compile those source files for which the destination binary is missing or out of date, and <jar> will only create a JAR file if its input files are newer than the output.

Running Ant is called *building*; a build either succeeds or fails. Builds fail when there is an error in the build file, or when a task fails by throwing an exception. In either case, Ant lists the line of the build file where the error occurred. Rerunning the build with the -verbose option may provide more information as to why the failure occurred. Alternatively, the -quiet option runs a build nearly silently.

Now that you have sampled this powerful build tool called Ant, we'll plant some seeds for effective use before you get too carried away. We recommend separating source files from generated output files. This keeps valuable source code safely isolated from the generated files. Also remember that the Java source must be stored in a directory hierarchy that matches the package naming hierarchy; the <javac> dependency checking relies on this layout.

Another best practice we strongly encourage including description attributes for all targets, and a <description> tag for the project as a whole. These help make a build file self-documenting, as the -projecthelp option to Ant will list the targets that have descriptions. By explaining what targets do, you not only provide an explanation for the reader of the build file, you show the user which targets they should call and what they can do.

C H A P T E R   3

Understanding Ant datatypes and properties

3.1   Preliminaries   48
3.2   Introducing datatypes and
      properties with <javac>   49
3.3   Paths   51
3.4   Filesets   52
3.5   Patternsets   54
3.6   Selectors   56
3.7   Datatype element naming   57
3.8   Filterset   58

3.9   FilterChains and FilterReaders   59
3.10 Mappers   61
3.11 Additional Ant datatypes   65
3.12 Properties   66
3.13 Controlling Ant with properties   77
3.14 References   79
3.15 Best practices   82
3.16 Summary   83

Reusability is often a primary goal as developers, and Ant gives us this capability. This chapter is foundational. Understanding the concepts presented here is crucial to crafting build files that are adaptable, maintainable, reusable, and controllable. This chapter contains a lot of material that can't be digested in one reading. Read this chapter completely to understand how Ant operates and about the facilities it provides to make your build life easier, and then use this chapter later as a reference to pick up the syntax details when you begin incorporating datatypes and properties into your build files.

3.1 PRELIMINARIES

There are two fundamental concepts at the core of Ant's capabilities: properties and datatypes. Let's start with a gentle overview of them both.

3.1.1 Datatype overview

One of the great advantages Ant has over the alternatives to building and packaging Java applications is that it understands the primary problem domain, that of building Java projects. Most steps to build a typical Java project deal with files and paths (such as classpaths). Ant provides *datatypes* to handle these two concepts natively. You can think of an Ant datatype as similar to Java's own built-in core classes: data that can be passed around and provided to tasks. The *fileset* and *path* datatypes, and several others, form the basic building blocks of Ant build files.

Classpath-related headaches are commonplace in Java development. Ant makes dealing with classpaths much more natural and pleasant than the command-line manual alternative, and provides for the reuse of defined classpaths wherever needed. For example, compiling source code requires that referenced classes be in the classpath. A path can be defined once for compilation with `<javac>`, and reused for execution (via `<java>`, covered in chapter 5). One of the consequences of classpaths being specified inside the build file is that Ant can be invoked without an explicitly defined system classpath, making it easy to install Ant and build a project with little or no environmental configuration.[1] Another no less important consequence is that classpaths can be easily and tightly controlled. This reduces CLASSPATH configuration problems, both for compilation and execution.

A set of files is a common entity to manipulate for such tasks as compiling, packaging, copying, deleting, and documenting. Defining a fileset of all .java files, for example, is straightforward:

```
<fileset dir="src" includes="**/*.java" id="source.fileset"/>
```

By providing an `id` attribute, we are defining a *reference*. This reference name can be used later wherever a fileset is expected. For example, copying our source code to another directory using the previously defined `source.fileset` is

```
<copy todir="backup">
  <fileset refid="source.fileset"/>
</copy>
```

3.1.2 Property overview

Ant's *property* handling mechanism allows for build file extensibility and reusability by parameterizing any string-specified item. The control users get over build files can be dramatically increased with the techniques shown in this chapter. For example,

---

[1] This is somewhat oversimplified, as Ant's wrapper scripts do build a system classpath before invoking Ant. It is also, unfortunately, necessary to add dependent JAR files to ANT_HOME/lib to utilize some tasks.

changing a build to use a different version of a third-party library, perhaps for testing purposes, can be made as trivial as this:

```
ant -Dstruts.jar=/home/ant/newstruts/struts.jar
```

In this case, `struts.jar` represents an Ant property, and in our build file, we refer to it with special syntax: `${struts.jar}`.

A key feature of an Ant property is its *immutability;* it resists change once set.[2] The interesting and powerful consequence of properties retaining their first set value is that build files can be coded to load property files in a specific order to allow user-, project-, or environment-controlled overrides.

3.2 INTRODUCING DATATYPES AND PROPERTIES WITH <JAVAC>

Compiling Java source is the most fundamental task during a build. Ant provides Java compilation using the `<javac>` task. The `<javac>` task provides a façade over Java source compilation by wrapping many different Java compilers and their associated switches behind a generalized task definition. A *façade* is a design pattern that provides an interface to a system of classes, hiding the implementation details of those classes behind a common interface. The `<javac>` task is the common interface to JDK 1.1 and up, Jikes, and several other Java compilers.

There is much more to Java compilation than just specifying a source directory and destination directory. A comparison of Sun's JDK 1.3.1 `javac` command-line compiler switches to Ant's `<javac>` task is shown in table 3.1.

Table 3.1   Sun's JDK 1.3.1 javac compared to Ant's wrapper <javac> task. Note the similarities between all of the parameters. Also note Ant's way of using domain-specific terminology for concepts such as classpath. This fundamental concept of specifying a build in a higher-level "language" is one of Ant's greatest benefits over any other alternative to building Java projects.

Option Name	JDK's javac switch	Ant's <javac> syntax
Debugging info	`-g` (generate all debugging info)	`debug="yes"`
	`-g:none` (generate no debugging info)	`debug="no"`
	`-g:{lines,vars,source}` (generate only some debugging info)	`debug="yes"` `debuglevel="lines,vars,source"`
Optimize	`-O`	`optimize="yes"`
Generate no warnings	`-nowarn`	`nowarn="true"`
Output messages about what the compiler is doing	`-verbose`	`verbose="true"`
Output source locations where deprecated APIs are used	`-deprecation`	`deprecation="on"`

continued on next page

---

[2] There are exceptions to this rule, but properties generally are immutable.

Table 3.1 Sun's JDK 1.3.1 javac compared to Ant's wrapper <javac> task. Note the similarities between all of the parameters. Also note Ant's way of using domain-specific terminology for concepts such as classpath. This fundamental concept of specifying a build in a higher-level "language" is one of Ant's greatest benefits over any other alternative to building Java projects. *(continued)*

Option Name	JDK's javac switch	Ant's <javac> syntax

Specify where to find referenced class files and libraries	`-classpath <path>`	`<classpath>`
		`  <pathelement`
		`     location="lib/some.jar"/>`
		`</classpath>`

Specify where to find input source files	`-sourcepath <path>`	`<src path="src"/>`
Override location of bootstrap class files	`-bootclasspath <path>`	`<bootclasspath …/>`
Override location of installed extensions	`-extdirs <dirs>`	`<extdirs …/>`
Specify where to place generated class files	`-d <directory>`	`destdir="build"`
Specify character encoding used by source files	`-encoding <encoding>`	`encoding="…"`
Generate class files for specific VM version	`-target 1.1`	`target="1.1"`
Enable JDK 1.4 assertions	`-source 1.4`	`source="1.4"`

NOTE   Ant itself is *not* a Java compiler; it simply contains a façade over compilers such as Sun's `javac`. You need a Java compiler such as the JDK javac compiler. See appendix A for installation and configuration information in order to use `<javac>`.

The `<javac>` syntax shown in table 3.1 introduces several new attributes, as well as several new subelements of `<javac>`. Most of these attributes are Boolean in nature—debug, optimize, nowarn, verbose, and deprecation. Ant allows flexibility in how Booleans can be specified with *on*, *true*, and *yes* all representing true, and any other value mapping to false. The elements `<classpath>`, `<src>`, `<bootclasspath>`, and `<extdirs>` introduce one of Ant's greatest assets—its path and file handling capability. Each of these elements represents a *path*.

For comparisons sake, to compile the code for our projects-indexing Ant task using Sun's JDK 1.3.1 `javac` compiler, the following command line is used:

```
javac -d build\classes
      -classpath lib\lucene-1.2-rc3\lucene-1.2-rc3.jar;
                 lib\jtidy-04aug2000r7-dev\build\Tidy.jar;
                 C:\AntBook\jakarta-ant-1.5\lib\ant.jar;
      -sourcepath src
      -g
      src\org\example\antbook\ant\lucene\*.java
```

The following Java compilation with Ant, utilizing Ant's datatypes and properties, shows the equivalent Ant task declaration in our build file.

```
<javac destdir="${build.classes.dir}"
        debug="${build.debug}"
        includeAntRuntime="yes"
        srcdir="${src.dir}">
  <classpath refid="compile.classpath"/>
  <include name="**/*.java"/>
</javac>
```

In this build file, we have already defined the path `compile.classpath` as

```
<path id="compile.classpath">
  <pathelement location="${lucene.jar}"/>
  <pathelement location="${jtidy.jar}"/>
</path>
```

This `<javac>` example is dramatically more sophisticated than shown in the previous chapter. Each of these new concepts will be covered in detail in this chapter. Here is a quick roadmap of what is to follow:

- The "`${...}`" notation denotes an Ant *property*, which is simply a mapping from a name to a string value, in this case referring to the source directory, the destination directory, what debug mode to use, and JAR locations.

- The subelement `<classpath>` specifies a *path* using a *reference* (indicating which previously defined path to use). The previously defined `<path>` indicates which JAR files to use, which here are specified by the use of properties within the `location` attribute.

- The `srcdir` attribute implicitly defines a *fileset* containing all files in the specified directory tree, and the nested `<include>` specifies a *patternset* used to constrain the files to only Java source files.

We have set the `includeAntRuntime` attribute because we are compiling a custom Ant task; this flag tells the task to add ant.jar to the classpath as well as the rest of Ant's classpath.

3.3   PATHS

A path, sometimes called a "path-like structure" in Ant's documentation, is an ordered list of path elements. It is analogous to the Java CLASSPATH, for example, where each element in the list could be a file or directory separated by a delimiter. An example of a path definition is:

```
<classpath>
  <pathelement location="lib/some.jar"/>
</classpath>
```

The `location` attribute lets you specify a single file or directory. You can also extend a path with another path, using `path` instead of `location`:

```
<classpath>
  <pathelement path="build/classes;lib/some.jar"/>
</classpath>
```

The path specified can have its elements separated by either a semicolon (;) or colon (:) and directories separated by either forward-slash (/) or back-slash (\),[3] regardless of operating system, making it extremely friendly for cross-platform use. If a path structure only consists of a single path or location, it can be specified using a shortcut form as in `<classpath location="lib/some.jar"/>` or `<classpath path="build/classes;lib/some.jar"/>`.

Paths can also include a set of files:

```
<classpath>
  <fileset dir="lib">
    <include name="*.jar"/>
  </fileset>
</classpath>
```

It is important to note that Ant guarantees no order within a `<fileset>`. Each element in a path is ordered from the top and down so that all files within a fileset would be grouped together in a path. However, the order within that fileset is not guaranteed.

3.4   FILESETS

Implicitly, all build processes will operate on sets of files, either to compile, copy, delete, or operate on them in any number of other ways. Ant provides the fileset as a native datatype. It is difficult to imagine any useful build that does not use a fileset. Some tasks support paths, which implicitly support filesets, while other tasks support filesets directly—and this distinction should be made clear in each task's documentation.

A fileset is a set of files rooted from a single directory. By default, a fileset specified with only a root directory will include all the files in that entire directory tree, including files in all subdirectories recursively. For a concrete running example that will demonstrate fileset features as we discuss them, let's copy files from one directory to another:

```
<copy todir="new_web">
  <fileset dir="web"/>
</copy>
```

In its current form, all files from the web directory are copied to the new_web directory. This example will evolve into copying only specific files, altering them during the copy with token replacement, and flattening the directory hierarchy in the new_web directory.

---

[3]   Ant is not at all ashamed to be bi-slashual, and is actually quite proud of it!

3.4.1 Fileset examples

During a build, you often need to build a fileset by including or excluding sets of files. A few examples of typical filesets follow.

Include all JAR files in the lib directory (nonrecursive, no subdirectories are considered):

```
<fileset dir="lib">
  <include name="*.jar"/>
</fileset>
```

Include all .java files below the test directory that end with the word "Test" (Chapter 4 will elaborate on this particular usage.):

```
<fileset dir="test">
  <include="**/*Test.java"/>
</fileset>
```

All non-JSP pages in the web directory and below:

```
<fileset dir="web">
  <exclude name="**/*.jsp"/>
</fileset>
```

By default, includes and excludes are case-sensitive, but this can be disabled by specifying `casesensitive="false"`. The `<include>` and `<exclude>` elements are called *patternsets*.

3.4.2 Default excludes

In many cases, special or temporary files end up in your source tree from IDEs and source code management (SCM) systems like CVS. In order to avoid the unpleasant situation of always specifying exclude clauses in each fileset, exclude patterns are enabled by default for many of these special patterns. The default exclude patterns are shown in table 3.2.

Table 3.2 Default exclude patterns, and the typical reason for their existence.

Pattern	Typical program that creates and uses these files
`**/*~`	jEdit and many other editors use this as previous version backup
`**/#*#`	editors
`**/.#*`	editors
`**/%*%`	editors
`**/CVS`	CVS (Concurrent Version System) metadata directory
`**/CVS/**`	CVS, metadata files
`**/.cvsignore`	CVS, contains exclusion patterns for CVS to ignore during routine operations
`**/SCCS`	SCCS metadata directory
`**/SCCS/**`	SCCS metadata files
`**/vssver.scc`	Microsoft Visual SourceSafe metadata file
`**/._*`	Mac OS/X resource fork files

Table 3.2 Default exclude patterns, and the typical reason for their existence. *(continued)*

Pattern	Typical program that creates and uses these files
`**/.svn`	Subversion SCM files
`**/.svn/**`	Subversion SCM files

The `**` is a pattern to match multiple directories in a hierarchy. (These patterns are discussed in more detail in the Patternset section.) Many users have been bitten by the confusion caused when a fileset does not include every file that was intended because it matches one of these default exclude patterns. The `<fileset>` element has a `defaultexcludes` attribute for turning off this behavior. Simply use `defaultexcludes="no"` to turn off the automatic exclusions. Unfortunately, these default exclude patterns are hard-coded and not extensible, but in most cases using the default excludes is the desired behavior and rarely becomes an issue.

> **NOTE** Filesets resolve their files when the declaration is encountered during execution. This is important to know when referring to a previously defined fileset later, as new files and directories matching the patterns may have appeared between the resolution and reference—these new files would *not* be seen by tasks operating upon that fileset.

3.5 PATTERNSETS

Filesets accomplish the include/exclude capability by utilizing another of Ant's core datatypes: the patternset. A patternset is a collection of file matching patterns. A patternset itself does not refer to any actual files until it is nested in a fileset and therefore rooted at a specific directory. A pattern is a path-matching specification similar to Unix- and MS-DOS-based file matching. Examples of this have already been shown with `*.jar` used to represent all files with the .jar extension in the top directory and `**/*.jsp` to represent all files in the entire directory tree with the .jsp extension. The pattern matching features are as follows:

- `*` matches zero or more characters.
- `?` matches a single character.
- `**`, used as the name of a directory, represents matching of all directories from that point down, matching zero or more directories.
- A pattern ending with a trailing / or \ implies a trailing `**`.

Implicitly a `<fileset>` holds a patternset, but patternsets can also be specified independently, allowing for the reuse of patternsets in multiple filesets. (See section 3.14.) Table 3.3 lists the attributes available on the `<patternset>` element.

Table 3.3 Patternset attributes. Including and excluding patterns allows filesets to be defined precisely to encompass only the files desired. The includesfile and excludesfile adds a level of indirection and external customization.

Attribute	Description
includes	Comma-separated list of patterns of files that must be included. All files are included when omitted.
excludes	Comma-separated list of patterns of files that must be excluded. No files (except default excludes) are excluded when omitted.
includesfile	The name of a file; each line of this file is taken to be an include pattern. You can specify more than one include file by using nested includesfile elements.
excludesfile	The name of a file; each line of this file is taken to be an exclude pattern. You can specify more than one exclude file by using nested excludesfile elements.

Excludes take precedence, so that if a file matched both an include and exclude pattern the file would be excluded. Elements corresponding to these attributes are also available as child elements of <patternset> for increased flexibility and control. The elements are <include>, <exclude>, <includesfile>, and <excludesfile>. Each of these elements has a name attribute. For <include> and <exclude>, the name attribute specifies the pattern to be included or excluded, respectively. For the <includesfile> and <excludesfile> elements, the name attribute represents a file name. Each of these elements has if/unless attributes, which are covered in the conditional patternset section later in this chapter Here are some examples of patternsets:

```
<patternset>
  <include name="*.jsp"/>
</patternset>
```

The <patternset> element is not always explicitly specified when used within a fileset. A fileset implicitly contains patternsets. Our running copy example is shown again using a patternset to include all JSP files:

```
<copy todir="new_web">
  <fileset dir="web" includes="**/*.jsp"/>
</copy>
```

This is equivalent to

```
<copy todir="new_web">
  <fileset dir="web">
    <include name="**/*.jsp"/>
  </fileset>
</copy>
```

Had we specified just *.jsp, only the JSP files in the web directory would have been copied, but no files in its subdirectories.

Patternsets may be nested within one another, such as

```
<patternset>
  <include name="**/*.gif,**/*.jpg"/>
  <patternset>
    <exclude name="**/*.txt,**/*.xml"/>
  </patternset>
</patternset>
```

This is a contrived example simply demonstrating the nesting capability. This nesting is unnecessary in this example, but datatype references make the nesting capability powerful. Patternset nesting is a feature introduced with Ant 1.5. This example is shown again using references in section 3.14.2

3.6 SELECTORS

Ant 1.5 includes a sophisticated new feature, called *selectors*, for selecting the files included in a fileset. The selectors are listed in table 3.4.

Table 3.4 Ant's built-in selectors

Selector	Description
`<filename>`	Works like a patternset `<include>` or `<exclude>` element to match files based on a pattern.
`<depth>`	Selects files based on a directory depth range.
`<size>`	Selects files that are less, equal, or more than a specified size.
`<date>`	Selects files (and optionally directories) that have been last modified before, after, or on a specified date.
`<present>`	Selects files if they exist in another directory tree.
`<depend>`	Selects files that are newer than corresponding ones in another directory tree.
`<contains>`	Selects files that contain a string.

These selectors can be combined inside *selector containers* to provide grouping and logic. The containers are `<and>`, `<or>`, `<not>`, `<none>`, and `<majority>`. Containers may be nested inside containers, allowing for the construction of complex selection logic. Rather than detailing every available selector, container, and their options, we refer you to Ant's documentation for this information. We will, however, provide a couple of examples showing how selectors work.

To compare two directory trees and copy the files that exist in one tree but not another we use a combination of `<not>` and `<present>`:

```
<copy todir="newfiles" includeemptydirs="false">
  <fileset dir="web">
    <not>
      <present targetdir="currentfiles"/>
    </not>
  </fileset>
</copy>
```

The `<copy>` task is copying only the files from the web directory that do not exist in the currentfiles directory. Using the `<contains>` selector, we can choose only the files that contain a certain string:

```
<copy todir="currentfiles" includeemptydirs="false">
  <fileset dir="web">
    <contains text="System"/>
  </fileset>
</copy>
```

Only the files containing the text "System" in the web directory are copied to the currentfiles directory. By default `<contains>` is case-sensitive, but can be changed using `casesensitive="no"`.

All rules must be satisfied before a file is considered part of a fileset, so when using selectors in conjunction with patternsets, the file must match the include patterns, must not match any exclude patterns, and the selector rules must test positively. A `<custom>` selector enables you to write your own selector logic in a Java class. (See chapter 20 for more details on writing a custom selector.)

3.7 DATATYPE ELEMENT NAMING

Ant exposes the patternset, path, and fileset datatypes (and some others) in its API so, for example, task writers have the luxury of implementing tasks to operate on a set of files very easily. The framework does not force these datatypes to have specific element names and tasks can support these datatypes without the need to explicitly specify `<fileset>`.

`<javac>` is an example of a task implicitly encompassing a fileset, with `includes`, `excludes`, `includesfile`, and `excludesfile` attributes as well as nested `<include>`, `<exclude>`, `<includesfile>`, and `<excludesfile>` elements. Note that a `<fileset>` has a mandatory root `dir` attribute, and in the case of `<javac>` this is specified with the `srcdir` attribute. Confusing? Yes. However, it was done this way in order to remove ambiguity for build file writers. Would a `dir` attribute on `<javac>` have represented a source directory or a destination directory?

The `<javac>` task is also an example of a task allowing paths as nested elements. Different types of paths may be specified (`<src>`, `<classpath>`, `<bootclasspath>`, and `<extdirs>`); and they may be combined in any way. For example, you could use two `<src>` tags to compile two directory trees of source code into a single output directory:

```
<javac destdir="build/classes">
  <src path="src"/>
  <src path="test/junit"/>
</javac>
```

The `<javac>` task aggregates all `<src>` paths for compilation. There are lots of permutations of all the ways in which these fileset and path capabilities can work together to accomplish choosing precisely the files desired. You will be exposed to some of these variations throughout this book.

3.8   FILTERSET

During the build process, it is common to encounter situations that require simple text substitutions in files based on dynamic build information or state. The two primary tasks that support filterset functionality are `<copy>` and `<move>`. Two situations typically take advantage of filtered copy:

- Putting the current date or version information into files bundled with a build, such as documentation.
- Conditionally "commenting out" pieces of configuration files.

A filter operation replaces tokenized text in source files during either a `<move>` or `<copy>` to a destination file. In a filtered `<copy>`, the source file is not altered. A token is defined as text surrounded by beginning and ending token delimiters. These delimiters default to the at-sign character (@), but can be altered using the `<filterset>` `begintoken` and `endtoken` attributes.

3.8.1   Inserting date stamps in files at build-time

Returning to our running copy example, we will now enhance the copy to substitute a date and time stamp tokens with the actual build date and time into the resultant files, leaving the original files unaltered. An example JSP file including the tokens is:

```
<html>
  <head><title>Ant Book</title></head>
  <body>
    System build time: @DATE@ @ @TIME@
  </body>
</html>
```

Here `@DATE@` and `@TIME@` will be replaced during the copy:

```
<tstamp/>
<copy todir="new_web" overwrite="true">
  <fileset dir="web" includes="**/*.jsp"/>
  <filterset>
    <filter token="DATE" value="${DSTAMP}"/>
    <filter token="TIME" value="${TSTAMP}"/>
  </filterset>
</copy>
```

There are a few new features introduced here. The `<tstamp>` task creates the DSTAMP and TSTAMP Ant properties. Ant properties get covered extensively in section 3.12, but, for our purposes, the values of `${DSTAMP}` and `${TSTAMP}` contain the date and time stamps respectively. The `<copy>` task has dependency checking so that it does not copy files if the source file's modification timestamp is earlier than the destination file's. Because our filtered copy should always replace the destination files, we disable the dependency checking with `overwrite="true"`. Applying this filtered copy on the templated JSP file shown produces the following:

```html
<html>
  <head><title>Ant Book</title></head>
  <body>
    System build time: 20020207 @ 1501
  </body>
</html>
```

NOTE   Do not try to filter binary files as they may be corrupted in the process.

A `<filter>` task creates a globally defined filterset. Because this filter applies on all `<copy>` or `<move>` tasks that are then executed, it can be dangerous, unexpectedly transforming binary files. We recommend, therefore, that filtered `<copy>` or `<move>` tasks individually specify their own filterset. If a filterset needs to be reused for several instances within a build, it can be defined globally using the `<filterset id="global.filterset">` syntax and referenced where needed. (See section 3.14.)

3.9   FILTERCHAINS AND FILTERREADERS

Processing text files has never been so easy with Ant until the introduction, in version 1.5, of *FilterChains* and *FilterReaders*. A FilterReader is a simple filter of text input that can remove or modify the text before it is output. A FilterChain is an ordered group of one or more FilterReaders. A FilterChain is analogous to piping output from one command to another in Unix, with the output of one command being the input to the next, and so on.

There are a number built-in FilterReaders, as shown in table 3.5.

Table 3.5   Ant's built-in FilterReaders

FilterReader	Description
`<classconstants>`.	Generates "name=value" lines for basic and String datatype constants found in a class file.
`<expandproperties>`	Replaces Ant property values. (See section 3.12 for property discussion.)
`<headfilter>`	Extracts the first specified number of lines.
`<linecontains>`	Only lines containing the specified string are passed through.
`<linecontainsregexp>`	Only lines matching specified regular expression(s) are passed through.
`<prefixlines>`	All lines have a prefix prepended.
`<replacetokens>`	Performs token substitution, just as filtersets do.
`<stripjavacomments>`	Removes Java style comments.
`<striplinebreaks>`	Removes line breaks, defaulting to "\r" and "\n" but characters stripped can be specified.
`<striplinecomments>`	Removes lines beginning with a specified set of characters.
`<tabstospaces>`	Replaces tabs with a specified number of spaces.
`<tailfilter>`	Extracts the last specified number of lines.

Four of Ant's tasks support FilterChains: `<copy>`, `<move>`, `<loadfile>`, and `<loadproperties>`. Stripping comments out of a Java properties file, perhaps to ship without comments and keep comments in developer files, is a simply matter of using the `<striplinecomments>` FilterReader within a `<copy>`.

Our properties file contains

```
# <Internal developer info>
config.parameter=47
```

We copy our original properties file to our build directory.

```
<copy file="config.properties" todir="build">
  <filterchain>
    <striplinecomments>
      <comment value="#"/>
    </striplinecomments>
  </filterchain>
</copy>
```

The resultant build/config.properties file will not have the comment line, only config.parameter=47.

Pulling class constants from Java class files is an even more spectacular display of the power of FilterReaders. Using the <loadproperties> task, which is getting a bit ahead of ourselves because Ant properties are not introduced until section 3.10, we are able to pull values from Java code into Ant as parameters. Take an interface that defines a constant:

```
package org.example.antbook;

public interface Constants {
    public static final String VERSION ="1.7";
}
```

Our build compiles the code into the build directory. Using the <classconstants> and <prefixlines> FilterReaders in a <loadproperties> task, we can now give Ant access to the VERSION constant.

```
<loadproperties srcfile="build/org/example/antbook/Constants.class">
  <filterchain>
    <classconstants/>
    <prefixlines prefix="Constants."/>
  </filterchain>
</loadproperties>

<echo>Constants.VERSION = ${Constants.VERSION}</echo>
```

This results in the following output:

```
[echo] Constants.VERSION = 1.7
```

NOTE   <classcontants> operates on .class files rather than .java files. This FilterReader uses the Byte Code Engineering Library (BCEL) API to directly access the byte code information rather than parsing Java source code. The Jakarta BCEL JAR is required in ANT_HOME/lib for this FilterReader to work.

This is only scratching the surface of the FilterChain/FilterReader capability. It is even possible to use a generic `<filterreader>` FilterReader to provide your own Java implementation. It is beyond the scope of this chapter to provide extensive detail on all of the FilterReaders and their options. See chapter 20 for details on writing custom FilterReaders. The capabilities that FilterReaders provide are astounding! Pulling actual constants from our Java code to parameterize our build process gives us the flexibility to store values where it makes the most sense, either as part of the build process or within our source code.

3.10 MAPPERS

Ant's mapper datatype is used to match sets of files with one another. There are several built-in mapper types as shown in table 3.6. Mappers are used by `<uptodate>`, `<move>`, `<copy>`, and `<apply>` and several other tasks. Depending on the mapper type, `to` and `from` attributes may be required.

Table 3.6 Mapper types. Mappers are used to flatten a directory tree during a `<copy>`, or check all files mapped into an archive against the archives modification date.

Type	Description
identity	The target is identical to the source file name.
flatten	Source and target file names are identical, with the target file name having all leading directory path stripped.
merge	All source files are mapped to a single target file specified in the `to` attribute.
glob	A single asterisk (*) used in the `from` pattern is substituted into the `to` pattern. Only files matching the `from` pattern are considered.
package	A subclass of the `glob` mapper, it functions similarly except replaces path separators with the dot character (`.`) so that a file with the hierarchical package directory structure can be mapped to a flattened directory structure retaining the package structure in the file name.
regexp	Both the `from` and `to` patterns define regular expressions. Only files matching the `from` expression are considered.

3.10.1 Identity mapper

The target file name maps exactly to the source file name. The `to` and `from` attributes are not used by the `identity` mapper.

```
<mapper type="identity"/>
```

By default, the `<copy>` task uses the `identity` mapper. The following two `<copy>` tasks have the same effect:

```
<copy todir="new_web">
  <fileset dir="web" includes="**/*.jsp"/>
  <mapper type="identity"/>
</copy>

<copy todir="new_web">
  <fileset dir="web" includes="**/*.jsp"/>
</copy>
```

3.10.2 Flatten mapper

The `flatten` mapper removes all directory path information from the source file name to map to the target file name. The `to` and `from` attributes are not used. The `flatten` mapper is useful in copying files from a nested directory structure into a single directory eliminating the hierarchy.

To copy all JSP pages from the web directory hierarchy into a single flat directory, the `flatten` mapper is used in this manner:

```
<copy todir="new_web">
  <fileset dir="web" includes="**/*.jsp"/>
  <mapper type="flatten"/>
</copy>
```

Note that if multiple files have the same name in the source fileset, regardless of directory, only one of them will make it to the destination directory; it is unspecified which one it will be.

3.10.3 Merge mapper

The target file name remains fixed to the `to` attribute specified. All source file names map to the single target.

```
<mapper type="merge" to="archive.zip"/>
```

The `merge` mapper is used with `<uptodate>` in cases where many files map to a single destination. For example, many files are bundled together into a single Zip file. A property can be set if the Zip contains all the latest sources:

```
<uptodate property="zip.notRequired">
  <srcfiles dir="src" includes="**/*.java"/>
  <mapper type="merge" to="${dist.dir}/src.zip"/>
</uptodate>
```

The `<uptodate>` task is covered in section 3.12.4.

The `merge` mapper in `<copy>` is not extremely useful since all files get copied to the same file, with the last unpredictable file becoming the sole new file. There is one interesting case, however, that is worthy of mention. If, for example, you have a directory containing a single file whose name is not precisely known (perhaps with a timestamp suffix), you can copy this file to a known file name using the `merge` mapper:

```
<copy todir="output">
  <fileset dir="data"/>
  <mapper type="merge" to="data.dat"/>
</copy>
```

Assume that there is a single file in the data directory called data_20020202.dat, yet this file name is dynamically generated. The use of the `merge` mapper will copy it to the output directory with the name data.dat. This particular technique, remember, is only useful with filesets containing a single file.

3.10.4 Glob mapper

The glob mapper uses both the to and from attributes, each allowing a single asterisk (*) pattern. The text matched by the pattern in the from attribute is substituted into the to pattern.

```
<mapper type="glob" from="*.jsp" to="*.jsp.bak"/>
```

The glob mapper is useful for making backup copies of files by copying them to new names as shown in the example. Files not matching the from pattern are ignored.

```
<copy todir="new_web">
  <fileset dir="web" includes="**/*.jsp"/>
  <mapper type="glob" from="*.jsp" to="*.jsp.bak" />
</copy>
```

All JSP pages are copied from the web directory to the new_web directory with the directory hierarchy preserved, but each source .jsp is renamed with the .jsp.bak extension in the new_web directory.

3.10.5 Regexp mapper

The king of all mappers, but overkill for most cases, is regexp. The from attribute specifies a regular expression. Only source files matching the from pattern are considered. The target file name is built using the to pattern with pattern substitutions from the from pattern, including \0 for the full matched source file name and \1 through \9 for patterns matched with enclosing parenthesis in the from pattern.

In order to use the regexp mapper, a regular expression library is needed. The Ant documentation refers to several implementations. We recommend Jakarta ORO, although JDK 1.4 comes with an implementation as well and is used by default if present. Simply drop the JAR file for the regular expression implementation into ANT_HOME/lib to have it automatically recognized by Ant. Here's a simple example having the same effect as the glob mapper example to map all .java files to .java.bak files:

```
<mapper type="regexp" from="^(.*)\.java$" to="\1.java.bak"/>
```

The <copy> example shown for the glob mapper can be replicated using the regexp mapper:

```
<copy todir="new_web">
  <fileset dir="web" includes="**/*.jsp"/>
  <mapper type="regexp" from="^(.*)\.jsp$" to="\1.jsp.bak" />
</copy>
```

Quite sophisticated mappings can occur with the regexp mapper, such as removing a middle piece of a directory hierarchy and other wacky tricks. This can be just the technique for complex situations, but think twice before using this mapper, as it usually means you're making life much too complicated and doing unnecessarily complex operations. Neither of the authors have found a need to use it thus far in our extensive Ant usage.

3.10.6 Package mapper

The `package` mapper is a specialized form of the `glob` mapper that transforms the matching piece of the `from` pattern into a dotted package string in the `to` pattern. The transformation simply replaces each directory separator (forward or back slashes) with a dot (.). The result is a flattening of the directory hierarchy for scenarios where Java files need to be matched against data files that have the fully qualified class name embedded in the file name. More specifically, this mapper was developed for use with the data files generated by the `<junit>` task.

The data files written out from running a test case with `<junit>` are written to a single directory with the filenames TEST-*fully qualified classname*.xml. In order to determine if the test case data file is no older than its corresponding Java class file, the `<uptodate>` task is used with the `package` mapper.

```
<property name="results.dir" location="test_results"/>
<uptodate property="tests.uptodate">
  <srcfiles dir="src" includes="**/*.java"/>
  <mapper type="package" from="*.java" to="${results.dir}/TEST-*.xml" />
</uptodate>
```

One of the tricky aspects of using the `package` mapper with `<uptodate>` is that the `to` path is relative to the `<srcfiles>` dir. This is resolved by ensuring that the `<mapper>` to attribute contains an absolute path. The absolute path can be obtained by using the `location` variant of `<property>`, which is covered in section 3.12.1. When using the `<copy>` task, the `to` mapper pattern is relative to the `<copy>` `todir` attribute, so converting to an absolute path is not necessary. If this example is a bit too esoteric, don't worry, as we will explain the `<uptodate>` in section 3.12.4, and the rationale for this particular mapping in chapter 4.

A simpler yet perhaps marginally useful example is creating a flat directory tree of your source code:

```
<copy todir="flat_source">
  <fileset dir="src" includes="**/*.java"/>
  <mapper type="package" from="*.java" to="*.java" />
</copy>
```

For example, the file `src/org/example/antbook/ant/lucene/HtmlDocumentTest.java` is copied to `output/org.example.antbook.ant.lucene.HtmlDocumentTest.java`. The resulting file, of course, will not compile properly because `<javac>` expects classes to be in a directory hierarchy matching the package name, but it will present a different view of all of your source code.

3.11 ADDITIONAL ANT DATATYPES

We have covered the Ant datatypes that are frequently used by Ant tasks, but there are several other datatypes that are used by a smaller number of tasks. These datatypes are no less important, of course, when you need them for your build. Rather than provide detailed discussion of these types here, we show them with the appropriate tasks elsewhere in this book.

3.11.1 ZipFileset

Building an archive that contains the contents of other archive files can be accomplished using the <zipfileset> datatype. A <zipfileset> not only allows putting the contents of one archive inside another, it also provides the capability to prefix an archives contents within another. For example, when building the WAR file for our search engine application, we incorporate the Javadoc HTML in an api subdirectory and our documentation under the help directory. These were not the directory names used during our build process, yet the WAR file will have these names in its structure.

```
<war destfile="dist/antbook.war" webxml="web.xml">
  <classes dir="${build.classes.dir}"/>

                .
                .
                .

  <fileset dir="web"/>

  <zipfileset dir="${javadoc.dir}" prefix="api" />
  <zipfileset dir="${build.dir}/webdocs" prefix="help"/>
</war>
```

The tasks that support the ZipFileset datatype are <zip>, <jar>, <war>, and <ear>.

3.11.2 Dirset

The fileset datatype incorporates both files and directories, but some tasks prefer to only operate on directories. The <dirset> datatype is used in only the <javadoc> and <pathconvert> tasks. The path datatype also supports a nested <dirset>, which allows for easier construction of classpath elements for multiple directories.

3.11.3 Filelist

Recall that a fileset is an unordered collection of files and directories. When concatenating files or doing other operations that require a specific order, the filelist datatype comes in handy. The filelist datatype is supported in the <concat>, <dependset>, and <pathconvert> tasks, as well as a nested element within the <path> datatype.

3.11.4 ClassFileset

The ClassFileset datatype can be used by reference wherever a fileset is used. It provides only the .class files that are explicitly referenced by a set of specified classes. This can be important when constructing a minimal archive, for example, and ship only the classes used. It is important to note, however, that classes referenced via reflection will not be considered dependencies, and therefore overlooked by ClassFileset.

3.12 PROPERTIES

Perhaps the most important concept to fully understand in Ant is its notion of *properties*. Properties are loosely analogous to variables in that they are mappings between names and values and, not coincidentally, are very similar conceptually to `java.util.Properties`. Ant provides the built-in properties listed in table 3.7.

Table 3.7 Built-in properties

Name	Definition
ant.file	The absolute path of the build file.
ant.home	The path to executing version of Ant's root directory.
ant.java.version	The JVM version Ant detected; currently it can hold the values 1.1, 1.2, 1.3, and 1.4.
ant.project.name	The name of the project that is currently executing; it is set in the name attribute of <project>.
ant.version	The version of Ant.
basedir	The absolute path of the project's basedir (as set with the basedir attribute of <project>).

Ant properties are typically, depending on the context of their use, denoted by ${*property.name*} within the build file. To examine the properties provided in table 3.7, we can use the <echo> task:

```
<target name="echo">
  <echo message="ant.file = ${ant.file}"/>
  <echo message="ant.home = ${ant.home}"/>
  <echo message="ant.java.version = ${ant.java.version}"/>
  <echo message="ant.version = ${ant.version}"/>
  <echo message="basedir = ${basedir}"/>
</target>
```

This generates output similar to this:

```
echo:
     [echo] ant.file = C:\AntBook\Sections\Learning\datatypes\properties.xml
     [echo] ant.home = c:\AntBook\jakarta-ant-1.5Beta1
     [echo] ant.java.version = 1.3
     [echo] ant.version = Apache Ant version 1.5Beta1 compiled on April 30 2002
     [echo] basedir = C:\AntBook\Sections\Learning\datatypes
```

This example was run with the -f command-line option to specify a different build file name as shown in ant.file. By the time of publication, many of us will probably see 1.4 for ant.java.version. The latest release version of Ant at the time of writing was version 1.5 Beta, but it will be an official release by the time of publication. The basedir property defaults to the path of the current build file, and can be changed by specifying basedir on the <project> element or controlled externally using property overrides as discussed shortly.

Implicitly, all JVM system properties are provided as Ant properties, allowing valuable information such as the users home directory path and the current username to be utilized as desired. The JVM system properties will vary from platform-to-platform, but there are many that you can rely on, for example

```
<echo message="user.name = ${user.name}"/>
<echo message="user.home = ${user.home}"/>
<echo message="java.home = ${java.home}"/>
```

Here are sample results from running this code on a Windows machine:

```
[echo] user.name = erik
[echo] user.home = C:\Documents and Settings\erik
[echo] java.home = c:\jdk1.3.1\jre
```

3.12.1 Setting properties with the <property> task

The <property> task allows build files to define their own sets of custom properties. The most common variants of creating properties are

- Name/value attributes
- Load a set of properties from a properties file
- Load environment variables

Setting and using a simple property

A typical development-versus-production build difference is in the enabling or disabling of debug mode on compilation. Since we want a single build file with a single <javac> task, we use a property to parameterize it. We define a property named build.debug and set its value to on (the value that <javac> uses on its debug attribute).

```
<property name="build.debug" value="on"/>
```

Enhancing the <javac> example from the previous chapter, we now have this:

```
<javac srcdir="src" debug="${build.debug}"/>
```

The obvious next step is to vary that property value; to begin, let's load properties from a file.

Loading properties from a properties file

A useful method to provide configuration and settings information to a build process is to load all name/value pairs from a properties file that creates internal Ant properties for each one. To demonstrate: we create a file named `build.properties` in the root directory of our project, where our build file lives. This file has the following contents:

```
build.debug=off
```

To load it we use one of the variants of the `<property>` task:

```
<property file="build.properties"/>
```

Property values in the properties file may also contain property references. For example, consider a properties file containing these lines:

```
build.dir=build
output.dir=${build.dir}/output
```

When loaded, `output.dir` will have the value `build/output`. Forward-referencing property values may be used in a single properties file as well; if the previous lines had been in opposite order, the same results would be obtained. Circular definitions will cause a build failure.

> **NOTE** Properties that refer to relative paths are best set using the `location` variant. See "Fixing properties to absolute path locations." Properties set from a properties file are set as a simple values.

Since properties are immutable, you may want to load properties from a file and prefix their name. In the last example, had we used `prefix="temp"`, the properties created would have been `temp.build.dir` and `temp.output.dir`. This is a nice trick to load two property files that may have the same named property, yet ensure that you have access to both values.

Overriding a property

First, a little pop-quiz—examine the following code lines and guess their output given the properties file just defined:

```
<target name="override">
  <property file="build.properties"/>
  <property name="build.debug" value="on"/>
  <echo message="debugging is turned ${build.debug}"/>
</target>
```

As you may have guessed, we would not have asked this question had it been completely straightforward. The result is

```
[echo] debugging is turned off
```

A property's value does not change once set: *properties are immutable*. Let's explore what this mechanism gives us in terms of control and flexibility. What if our properties file had not contained the line defining `build.debug`, or what if `build.properties` had not existed? The `<property file="...">` task simply does nothing but warn in verbose mode when the specified property file does not exist. Only properties listed in an existing properties file are loaded, so in the case where `build.debug` is not present in the properties file, its value would not be set until it is defined in the build file itself, in the line `<property name="build.debug" value="on"/>`.

> **NOTE** Once a property has been set, either in the build file or on the command line, it cannot be changed. Whoever sets a property first fixes its value. This is the direct opposite of variables in a program, where the last assignment becomes its value.

You have just witnessed the mechanism that will bring your build files to life: allowing them to adapt to user preferences, environment conditions, provide mapping indirections, and scaling to large multi-build-file processes.

> **NOTE** There are ways to break the immutability of properties using `<ant>`, `<antcall>`, `<available>`, and the `-D` command-line option. Most of the reasons for these exceptions are logically legitimate, yet certainly an area of confusion and concern.

Loading environment variables

Another important variant of `<property>` allows environment variables to be pulled into Ant properties. In order to avoid inadvertent collision with existing Ant properties (in other words: what would happen if an environment variable was named `build.debug`?), environment variables are loaded with a name prefix. Consider the following example:

```
<property environment="env"/>
```

All environment variables are loaded into Ant's internal properties with the prefix `env.` (including the trailing period). This gives us properties like `env.CATALINA_HOME`, which we can then use in tasks related to deployment, for example. Although you can use any prefix for environment variables, it is customary to use `env.` as the prefix. For consistency, we shall use this convention in the book and build files, and we recommend that readers do the same.

Fixing properties to absolute path locations

One of the key uses of properties is to abstract file system paths so that tasks deal only with the property names, and the concrete definition is defined, or more likely built up, elsewhere. To craft build files without absolute paths is easy; simply define paths relative from the base directory of the project. Relative paths work great in most cases, but can cause confusion and problems when passed to a subbuild or handed to a task or another executable that is expecting an absolute path. The <property> task has yet another variation that sets a property to the absolute path of the path specified:

```
<property name="build.dir" location="build"/>
```

The build.dir property is not simply set to the string build. The current project base directory (typically the directory where build.xml resides) is used as the root for relative references and the full path resolved to /home/erik/AntBook/Sections/ Learning/datatypes/build. We recommend that you use direct references to files or directories by using the location feature to lock logically relative paths to absolute paths.

A useful analogy for defining properties for directories is the Unix concept of mount points. Logically the root directory / has several underlying top-level directories, yet /usr or /home do not have to physically reside under /. Setting properties to mirror this concept allows, for example, the distribution directory of a build to be lifted up and placed elsewhere by simply overriding a single property value. Building directory paths up from root directories (i.e., the "mount" points) allows for this capability. The crafting of properties in this hierarchical and loosely bound way is crucial in allowing a build to be easily integrated into other build files.

3.12.2 How the <property> task is different

The <property> task is special in that it has the special right to function outside of a <target>: it is allowed to stand alone directly as a child element of <project>. All tasks that appear outside of targets are evaluated before any target is executed. We recommend that you to put all such "nontarget declarations" of <project> before any target declarations, to avoid confusion.

3.12.3 Checking for the availability of resources: <available>

The <available> task will set a property value if a specified resource exists. It has the capability to check for

- Existence of a class in a classpath
- Existence of a file or directory
- Existence of a JVM system resource

Checking for the existence of a class in a classpath

It can be quite useful to craft your build file to adapt to the existence or nonexistence of a particular class in a classpath. For example, Ant can omit steps from a build if a dependency is missing and still allow the build to proceed successfully. Conditional targets are discussed in section 3.13.1; first let's find out how to set a property conditionally. The variant of <available> to check a classpath for a class is

```
<available property="xdoclet.present"
        classname="xdoclet.doc.DocumentDocletTask"
        classpath="${xdoclet.jar}"/>
<echo message="xdoclet.present = ${xdoclet.present}"/>
```

If the class xdoclet.doc.DocumentDocletTask is found, xdoclet.present is set to true. If it is not present in the classpath, the property is not touched and hence has no value whatsoever. The output will either be xdoclet.present = true or xdoclet.present = ${xdoclet.present}. Optionally, the value set to the property in the true case can be specified using the value attribute of <available>, with true being the default value.

NOTE   An undefined property will not be expanded, and the string ${<property.name>} will be used literally.

At the time of this writing, several holes in Ant's property immutability rule were being patched. In the spirit of backwards compatibility the hole in <available> is being left—but deprecated—so that build files relying on this undocumented "feature" do not break. While we would rather not have to write about this anomaly, it deserves mention so that it is not stumbled upon inadvertently, causing unexpected behavior. Here is an example:

```
<property name="xdoclet.present" value="maybe"/>
<available property="xdoclet.present"
        classname="xdoclet.doc.DocumentDocletTask"
        classpath="${xdoclet.jar}"/>
<echo message="xdoclet.present = ${xdoclet.present}"/>
```

If xdoclet.present were truly immutable once set, then the value displayed should be maybe after executing <available>. If XDoclet is present, the output is:

```
[available] DEPRECATED - <available> used to overide an existing property.
 Build writer should not reuse the same property name for different values.
    [echo] xdoclet.present = true
```

Had XDoclet not been present the warning would not have appeared and xdoclet.present = maybe would have displayed. The deprecation warning is saying that the <available> task is breaking the rules by using a deprecated method in Ant's API, but also saying that we, as build file writers, should carefully use unique property names for each situation rather than attempting to reuse them for other purposes. We recommend you avoid writing build files to take advantage of this property immutability loophole, as one day it may be closed off completely.

Checking for the existence of a file or directory

A property can be set, using a variant of <available>, if a file or directory exists. This is useful in allowing the build process to adapt, for example, to existence of a different Java compiler as you will see in chapter 4. An example of its usage is:

```
<available property="lib.properties.present"
           file="${lib.dir}/lib.properties"
           type="file"/>
```

The `file` attribute specifies the file or directory to locate. The `type` attribute determines whether the file should be a `file` or `directory` specifically. The default behavior, without a `type` attribute, is to indicate success if the `file` exists as either a file or directory.

Checking for the existence of a JVM system resource

The final availability check is for a resource, which is any file that can be found on the classpath. This is usually used to check for the availability of configuration files:

```
<available property="resource.exists" resource="org/example/etc/struts.xml" />
```

3.12.4 Saving time by skipping unnecessary steps: <uptodate>

To determine if target files are up-to-date with source files, Ant provides the `<uptodate>` task. Most tasks (such as `<javac>`) deal with source/target out-of-date checking internally, but there are cases where it is necessary to do this yourself. For example, the JUnit test (see chapter 4 for in-depth coverage) task does no dependency checking and simply runs all tests regardless of whether or not any .class files were modified. Skipping the unit test target if all the test related files are up-to-date dramatically improves build time without sacrificing integrated testing:

```
<uptodate property="tests.unnecessary">
  <srcfiles dir="src" includes="**/*.java"/>
  <mapper type="glob" from="*.java" to="${build.dir}/classes/*.class" />
</uptodate>
```

Deferring the discussion of the `<mapper>` element for just a moment, this example is setting the property `tests.unnecessary` to `true` if each module from the source tree is not newer than its corresponding .class file. (This default is changed by specifying a `value` attribute.) This example is showing a one-to-one mapping from source file to target file, also ignoring any non-.java files in the source tree. Other scenarios take advantage of many-to-one mappings or other more complex mappings available with the mappers. Combining the use of `<uptodate>` and conditional targets is a useful technique to allow your build file to handle some dependency checking that tasks do not.

3.12.5 Testing conditions with <condition>

For Ant old-timers, the introduction of `<condition>` in Ant 1.4 was a real treat—previously build files that required checking of multiple properties required several dummy targets to accomplish some simple property-based logic. The `<condition>` task provides property setting capability using logical operators `<and>`, `<or>`, and `<not>`.

Within the logical elements, the Boolean conditions shown in table 3.8 are available.

Table 3.8   Conditions available within <condition>

Element	Definition
`<available>`	Exactly the same semantics and syntax as the `<available>` task, except `property` and `value` are ignored. Evaluates to `true` if the resource is available.
`<uptodate>`	Exactly the same semantics and syntax as the `<uptodate>` task, except `property` and `value` are ignored. Evaluates to `true` if file(s) are up-to-date.
`<os>`	Evaluates to `true` if the O/S family (`mac`, `windows`, `dos`, `netware`, `os/2`, or `unix`), name, architecture, and version match.
`<equals>`	Evaluates to `true` if both properties have the same value.
`<isset>`	Evaluates to `true` if the property exists.
`<checksum>`	Uses the same syntax as the `<checksum>` task, evaluating to true if the checksum of the file(s) match.
`<http>`	Checks for a status code < 500 from a URL.
`<socket>`	Checks for a socket listener on a specified port and host.
`<filesmatch>`	Byte-for-byte file comparison between two files.
`<contains>`	Tests whether one string contains another, optionally case-sensitive.
`<istrue>`	True if the value is `on`, `true`, or `yes`.
`<isfalse>`	The negation of `<istrue>`.

Some examples of complex conditions will be shown in chapter 4, as tests for the availability of classes and programs are made. Here is the partial example of `<condition>` usage from our sample application:

```
<condition property="tests.unnecessary">
  <and>
    <uptodate>
      <srcfiles dir="src" includes="**/*.java"/>
      <mapper type="glob" from="*.java" to="${build.dir}/classes/*.class" />
    </uptodate>
    <uptodate>
      <srcfiles dir="test" includes="**/*.java"/>
      <mapper type="glob" from="*.java" to="${test.dir}/*.class" />
    </uptodate>
    <uptodate>
      <srcfiles dir="test" excludes="**/*.java"/>
      <mapper type="glob" from="*" to="${test.dir}/*" />
    </uptodate>
  </and>
</condition>
```

It sets the property `tests.unnecessary` to `true` if all files relating to testing are up-to-date. The .class files of both the production code (`src`) and testing code (`test`) are checked, as well as non-.java files. Chapter 4 will explain the use of the non-.java files used during testing. Using a `<condition>` to check for available dependencies and failing the build if necessary components are not present is also another useful technique using `<condition>`. Refer to Ant's documentation for syntax details of the conditions.

3.12.6   Setting properties from the command-line

Controlling the build process can be accomplished on a per-build basis by setting an Ant property from the command line. For example, if you want to use a new library version for a single build to ensure that it passes all the test cases, or if you want to supply a password to a deploy process. There are two command-line switches used to set properties: -D and -propertyfile.

A property set from the command line cannot be overridden, even using <available> or <condition>. There are two classes of properties, *user* properties and *standard* properties. User properties consist of system properties and command-line defined properties, as well as properties overridden using <ant>. Properties defined on the command line get set as user properties and are truly immutable, ignoring even the immutability exceptions noted earlier.

Building with a different library version

In our project, we use Ant properties to represent the absolute paths to all the JAR files we use. These absolute paths are determined by using something like

```
<property name="${lucene.jar}" location="lib/lucene/lucene.jar"/>⁴
```

We use `${lucene.jar}` wherever needed for classpath definitions and incorporating into a WAR file. When the Lucene development team announced a new version release, as occurred more than once while writing this book, we upgraded to it to stay as up-to-date as possible. Before involving the entire development team on our project (the pair of us!) by converting the build to use the new version, a single developer ensured the builds and test cases ran successfully. Our build files were designed to be adaptable and controllable by using properties for JAR file location indirection. Running a full build/test/deploy with a new local library is as simple as running the following from the command line:

```
ant -Dlucene.jar=c:/dev/lucene-dev.jar clean dist
```

Properties defined with -D are defined before any processing of the build file occurs. The -propertyfile switch defines all properties from the specified property file exactly as if each were individually specified with -D. Properties specified from -D take precedence over -propertyfile-defined ones to allow for individual override control. For example, suppose lucene.jar had been defined in newlibraries.properties:

```
lucene.jar=lib/lucene/lucene-recent.jar
```

If the following command line is executed

```
ant -propertyfile newlibraries.properties -Dlucene.jar=c:/dev/lucene-dev.jar
```

the value from the -D switch would be used, in this case `lucene.jar` would have the value `c:/dev/lucene-dev.jar`.

---

⁴ There is actually a bit more indirection than this in our build files, as explained in chapter 8.

3.12.7 Creating a build timestamp with <tstamp>

The `<tstamp>` task in its simplest form

```
<tstamp/>
```

sets three properties automatically based on the current date/time. These properties are listed in table 3.9.

Table 3.9 Properties set by the <tstamp/> task

Property	Value format (based on current date/time)
DSTAMP	"yyyymmdd"
TSTAMP	"hhmm"
TODAY	"month day year"

The `<tstamp/>` task also allows any number of nested `<format>` elements, which define properties given a format specification. For example, to create a property with only the day of the week, use `<format property="..." pattern="...">`:

```
<tstamp>
  <format property="dayofweek" pattern="EEEE"/>
</tstamp>
<echo message="It is ${dayofweek}"/>
```

This results in the following:

```
[echo] It is Monday
```

The `pattern` is specified using the format described in Javadoc for `java.text.SimpleDateFormat`. `<format>` also supports locale and offsets—refer to the task reference for these specifics.

Creating ISO 8601 timestamp

Creating a timestamp in a recognized standard format is important. We use it in our application to embed into a properties file. This build-time–generated properties file is embedded into our distributables such as the web applications WAR file. The `<tstamp>` task can create an ISO timestamp:

```
<tstamp>
  <format property="buildtime"
          pattern="yyyy-MM-dd'T'HH:mm:ss" />
</tstamp>
<echo message="buildtime = ${buildtime}"/>
```

This produces output similar to

```
[echo] buildtime = 2002-02-09T17:17:21
```

Prefixing timestamps

The `<tstamp>` task supports an optional `prefix` attribute to allow setting unique property names and avoid clashing with already-set property names. The immutability rules of Ant properties prevent overwriting the value of an already-set property, including the ones `<tstamp>` sets.

```
<tstamp prefix="start"/>
```

This sets three properties—`start.DSTAMP`, `start.TSTAMP`, and `start.TODAY`—with the same formats as the default `<tstamp>` usage.

3.12.8 Loading properties from an XML file

Ant 1.5 includes a handy new task that pulls in properties from an XML file. Hierarchy of the XML file is preserved using dotted property notation. Here is an example of a build scenario in which our build is designed to handle customization for customers. Each customer has a corresponding XML file with specific information, such as a name and possibly some specific implementation details like a custom class name used to override default behavior. For example, Acme, Inc.'s definition file, acme.xml, is

```
<customer name="Acme, Inc.">
  <settings>
    <impl>org.example.antbook.acme.SomeClass</impl>
  </settings>
</customer>
```

The `<xmlproperty>` traverses the XML file, creating properties for element and attribute data as it goes. Our build file can use this information easily:

```
<project name="xmlprops" default="main">
  <target name="main">
    <property name="customer" value="acme"/>
    <xmlproperty file="${customer}.xml"/>
    <echo message="Building for ${customer(name)}..."/>
    <echo level="verbose">
      classname = ${customer.settings.impl}
    </echo>
  </target>
</project>
```

First, we use a property, `customer`, to define the customer nickname which defaults to `acme`. The output of our build, using verbose mode, is

```
main:
     [echo] Building for Acme, Inc....
     [echo]          classname = org.example.antbook.acme.SomeClass
```

This indirection allows us to build for any customer by overriding the value of customer. For example, we could use

```
ant -Dcustomer=joes_garage
```

The `<xmlproperty>` task has a few notable options. Like loading a properties file, it has a `prefix` option that prepends a prefix to all properties created. By default the XML file is not validated, but setting `validate="true"` enables validation. If the root element in your XML file is simply a placeholder, `keeproot="false"` can be used to skip its processing; in our example it would have omitted setting `customer(name)` and the classname property would be named `settings.impl` instead. The final option for `<xmlproperty>` controls how XML attributes are named as properties. Normally attributes are assigned to Ant properties using parenthesis notation, such as `customer(name)`. Using `collapseAttributes="true"`, dotted syntax is used instead and would result in the `name` attribute being mapped to a `customer.name` property.

A limitation exists with `<xmlproperty>` in how it handles multiple sibling elements with the same name. Only the first of duplicate named sibling elements is processed; there is no indexing.

3.13 CONTROLLING ANT WITH PROPERTIES

Utilizing Ant's properties wisely can give a build file a highly dynamic nature, allowing it to easily adjust to its operating environment and user preferences. Here are some of the many ways in which properties can help control builds.

> **NOTE** The value of a property is not always important. In several contexts, simply the existence of a property is relevant and its actual value not.

3.13.1 Conditional target execution

Properties are the mechanism used to provide conditional target execution. A target definition can include optional `if` and/or `unless` attributes.

> **NOTE** Property names are left unadorned in target `if`/`unless` clauses. In other words, you can simply specify the property name with no `${ }`. Only the existence of a property, regardless of value, is taken into consideration for `if`/`unless`.

The following lines demonstrate the use of the `if` attribute to conditionally include source code in a JAR file built:

```
<target name="init">
  <mkdir dir="build/classes"/>
  <mkdir dir="dist"/>
</target>

<target name="compile" depends="init">
  <javac srcdir="src" destdir="build/classes"/>
</target>

<target name="copysource" depends="init" if="copy.source">
  <copy todir="build/classes">
    <fileset dir="src"/>
```

```
    </copy>
  </target>

  <target name="jar" depends="compile,copysource">
    <jar basedir="build/classes" jarfile="dist/our.jar">
  </target>
```

The target conditions are evaluated just prior to the execution of each target. This allows dependent targets to set properties influencing future target execution dynamically. In this little demonstration, the copysource target could be enabled by setting copy.source, the value is irrelevant. (Even "false" would enable it.) This could be done from the command line:

```
ant -Dcopy.source=true jar
```

Alternatively, the copy.source property could be defined using one of the many variants of <property>.

3.13.2 Conditional patternset inclusion/exclusion

As mentioned in section 3.5, patternsets have an if and unless property on the <include> and <exclude> elements. This is a useful feature for including or excluding files from compilation depending on the existence of libraries.

```
<javac srcdir="src"
       destdir="${build.dir}/classes"
  <exclude name="org/example/antbook/xdoclet/*.java"
           unless="xdoclet.present" />
</javac>
```

This example takes advantage of <javac> acting as an implicit fileset, but the if/unless technique works for any patternset.

3.13.3 Conditional build failure

An enhancement from Ant 1.4.1 to Ant 1.5 is the addition of the if/unless construct to the <fail> task. The <fail> task forces the failure of a build with an optional message (similar to <echo>). In versions prior to 1.5 conditionally failing a build required several dummy targets with the one containing <fail> having a condition on it. Using the example shown for <condition> to set a property if all dependencies are present along with the conditional <fail>, a build can exit alerting the user of missing dependencies:

```
<target name="init">
  <condition property="all.dependencies.present">
    <and>
      <available classname="xdoclet.doc.DocumentDocletTask" />
      <available classname="junit.framework.TestCase" />
    </and>
  </condition>

  <fail message="Missing dependencies" unless="all.dependencies.present"/>
</target>
```

In chapter 4, we use a conditional `<fail>` to exit a build when the unit tests fail. Because you may encounter Ant 1.4.1 or earlier build files, we should mention the technique used to accomplish conditional failure pre-Ant 1.5 is a build-file construct like

```
<project name="fail" default="dist">

  <target name="compile"/>

  <target name="check-tests-failed" if="tests.failed">
    <fail>Tests failed</fail>
  </target>

  <target name="test">
    <property name="tests.failed" value="true"/>
  </target>

  <target name="dist" depends="compile,test,check-tests-failed"/>

</project>
```

The `dist` target specifies its dependencies, and they execute in the order shown: `compile`, `test`, and then `check-tests-failed`. Note that the `test` target has not been implemented yet; our mock implementation sets a property to indicate a failure. Use of the conditional `<fail>` attributes eliminates this complexity.

3.14 REFERENCES

Ant provides rich datatypes to work with, and it also provides the ability to reuse these datatype definitions. Each Ant datatype declaration allows an optional unique identifier, which you can refer to elsewhere—these are called *references*. Our sample application takes full advantage of references, particularly with paths. Many tasks accept a classpath, defaulting to the one used by the executing virtual machine if one is not specified. We recommend specifying classpaths explicitly as this provides the greatest amount of control and reproducibility. We define our compile classpath with an `id="compile.classpath"` in this fashion:

```
<path id="compile.classpath">
  <pathelement location="${lucene.jar}"/>
  <pathelement location="${tidy.jar}"/>
</path>
```

There is a level of indirection going on in this example that will be explained later, but each of the properties used in `<pathelement location=?...?>` refer to the full path of the corresponding JAR file. This is the complete set of dependencies needed to compile our main production code. This, however, is not the full set of dependencies required for compiling and running our test code. To ensure that we compile and run against the minimum dependencies necessary, we craft several `<path>` declarations for use in different situations. The classpath used for testing is a superset of the one used for compilation; references allow us to reuse `compile.classpath`'s definition in this manner:

```
<path id="test.classpath">
  <path refid="compile.classpath"/>
  <pathelement location="${junit.jar}"/>
  <pathelement location="${build.dir}/classes"/>
  <pathelement location="${build.dir}/test"/>
</path>
```

The `refid` and `id` attributes are available on all datatypes, which include the ones discussed in this chapter: path, fileset, patternset, filterset, and mapper. Anywhere a datatype is declared, it can have an `id` associated with it, even when used inside a task. It is recommended, however, that datatypes that will be reused with `refid` be declared as stand-alone datatypes for readability and clarity.

3.14.1 Properties and references

In the Ant conceptual model, a property is not a datatype but is implicitly reusable by its name, such as `${build.dir}`. While users can view properties, datatypes, and their references as independent from one another for most practical purposes, there are a couple of interesting intersections between them. Another variant of the `<property>` task converts a reference to its string representation.

Obtaining a string representation of a path

If a `<path>` has been dynamically constructed, being built from `<pathelement location="..."/>` or `<path refid="..."/>` nested elements, you can get its string representation. This can be used for displaying or passing to a spawned command through `<exec>` or `<apply>`. Here is an example of displaying:

```
<path id="the.path">
  <pathelement path="some.jar;another.jar"/>
</path>

<property name="path.string" refid="the.path"/>
<echo message="path = ${path.string}"/>
```

The `<path>` datatype resolves all relative items to their absolute paths and converts all file and path separators to the local platform, and so the result is

```
[echo] path = /home/ant/some.jar: /home/ant/another.jar
```

Dereferencing properties

Makefile experts, and others desiring tricky variable dereferencing may be disappointed to find that Ant does not have advanced evaluation of properties. They are simply string substitutions and nesting properties does not accomplish what some may expect. For example

```
<property name="X" value="Y"/>
<property name="Y" value="Z"/>
<property name="A" value="${${X}}"/>
<property name="B" value="$${${X}}"/>    ◁——— The "$$" is replaced by "$"
```

```
<echo message="A = ${A}"/>
<echo message="B = ${B}"/>
```

The output of the above is

```
[echo] A = ${${X}}
[echo] B = ${Y}
```

It is possible, however, to accomplish this, though rarely, if ever, would this particular technique be needed in a build file. Make has a feature called "computed variable names," which is similar to our first attempts at dereferencing, yet with different results. (In other words, A would have equaled Z.) Using an additional property is required as a `selector`:

```
<property name="X" value="Y" id="X.prop"/>
<property name="Y" value="Z" id="Y.prop"/>
<property name="selector" value="${X}"/>
<property name="A" refid="${selector}.prop"/>
<echo message="A = ${A}"/>
```

While this appears fairly straightforward, it is actually taking advantage of some fairly complex capability of Ant, that of assigning an `id` to a task (in this case `<property>`). The value of `selector` becomes Y, and the assignment of A uses the value of the referenced "object" (in this case a task) by the name of Y.prop. Avoid this kind of wackiness at almost all costs because there are much more standard and clearer ways to choose a different set of properties, such as

```
<property name="props" value="default"/>
<property file="${props}.properties"/>
```

In this case, we load `default.properties` unless the property `props` has been overridden previously, perhaps with

```
ant -Dprops=my
```

This would load `my.properties` instead, thanks to property immutability and -D setting `props` first.

> **NOTE** There is a third-party task `<propertycopy>` provided at the Source-forge ant-contrib project that more cleanly accomplishes property dereferencing. We recommend using this task instead of the craziness shown here. See section 10.6 for details on `<propertycopy>`.

3.14.2 Using references for nested patternsets

Patternsets provide a nice abstraction for file and directory name matching for use inside of filesets. Defining a patternset only once with an `id` allows it to be reused in any number of filesets. Nesting patternsets allows for patternset grouping. Here's an example:

```
<patternset id="image.files" includes="**/*.gif,**/*.jpg"/>
```

```
<patternset id="binary.files">
  <exclude name="**/*.txt"/>
  <exclude name="**/*.xml"/>
  <patternset refid="image.files"/>
</patternset>

<property name="binary.files.debug" refid="binary.files"/>
<echo level="verbose">
  binary.files.debug = ${binary.files.debug}
</echo>
```

The `binary.files` patternset excludes both .txt and .xml files, and the files included or excluded by the `image.files` patternset. In this case, `binary.files` will also include .jpg and .gif files. The string representation of a patternset is useful for debugging purposes, so defining a property using the patternset `refid` yields these results:

```
[echo]       binary.files.debug = patternSet{ includes: [**/*.gif, **/
*.jpg] excludes: [**/*.txt, **/*.xml] }
```

3.15 BEST PRACTICES

While it is necessary to understand the correct syntax and rules for utilizing Ant's datatypes and properties, this is only scratching the surface. There are several practices that we recommend in order to realize far greater benefit from these abstractions:

- Use `<property location="..."/>` to define file and paths. Use the `value` variant for other string values, including file name fragments if needed.

- Nest path definitions. For example, our application has a `<path id="compile.classpath">` defined, and that same path along with some other dependencies are needed in our testing compilation and execution. Our `<path id="test.classpath">` is defined as including `<path refid="compile.classpath"/>`. This is to eliminate duplication and increases maintainability and reusability.

- Using `<filterset>` to perform simple text substitutions during a build can accomplish powerful things like inserting dates or other dynamic build-time information. Be careful not to use it on binary files, however.

- Take advantage of conditional target execution and conditional patternset capabilities to allow your build to adapt to its environment. Perhaps it is acceptable if a dependency is not present, and its absence will simply omit some classes from compilation, testing, packaging, and deployment. For example, Ant's very own build makes extensive use of conditional patternsets to exclude compilation of the many optional tasks if their dependencies are not present; this allows Ant to be easily built with no configuration changes or need to install dependencies for unused tasks.

- Carefully consider the directory structure of your project, including how properties will map to top-level or subordinate directories. By planning this well, a parent build can easily control where it receives the output of the child build. View properties that refer to directories as Unix-like mounted directories—they reside logically as a rooted tree from the base build directory, yet physically do not necessarily reside in that hierarchy.

3.16 SUMMARY

The purpose of this chapter is to introduce the foundational Ant concepts of paths, filesets, patternsets, filtersets, properties, and references. Let's now take a look at how these concepts are used in practice with an example straight from our sample application build file. Our compilation step shown in section 3.2 utilizes all of these facilities, either directly or indirectly.

```
<target name="compile" depends="init">
  <javac destdir="${build.dir}"
         debug="${build.debug}"
         includeAntRuntime="yes"
         srcdir="src">
    <classpath refid="compile.classpath"/>
  </javac>
</target>
```

We use a property, build.debug, to control whether compilation is performed with debug on or off. Typically, the includeAntRuntime value should be set to no, but our compilation is building a custom Ant task and requires ant.jar. The <javac> task acts as an implicit fileset, with srcdir mapping to <fileset>'s dir attribute. All files in the src tree are considered for compilation because no excludes or explicit includes were specified. A reference to a previously defined path, compile.classpath, is used to define our compilation classpath.

From this chapter, several important facts about Ant should stick with you throughout this book and on into your build file writing:

- Ant uses *datatypes* to provide rich reusable parameters to tasks.
- <javac> is a task utilizing most of Ant's datatypes.
- Paths represent an ordered list of files and directories. Many tasks can accept a classpath, which is an Ant *path*. Paths can be specified in a cross platform manner, using the MS-DOS conventions of semicolon (;) and slash mark (/) or the Unix conventions of colon (:) and backslash (\); Ant sorts it all out at run time.
- Filesets represent a collection of files rooted from a specified directory. Tasks that operate on sets of files often use Ant's fileset datatype. Filesets are resolved when they are encountered by the build process and therefore do not take into account files that are added or removed afterwards.

- Patternsets represent a collection of file matching patterns. Patternsets can be defined and applied to any number of filesets.

- The actual element names used for datatypes within a task may vary, and a task may have several different elements all using the same datatype. Some tasks even implicitly represent a path or fileset. Ant's documentation clearly defines the types each attribute and element represent, and is the best reference for such details.

- Properties are the heart of Ant's extensibility and flexibility. They provide a mechanism to store variables and load them from external resources including the environment. The rules governing properties, such as immutability, are critical to understand in designing build files.

- Wisely utilizing the features presented in this chapter gives the build file elegance, structure, reusability, extensibility, and control. The rest of the book—including our sample application's build process—will take full advantage of each of these facilities, and so should yours!

Several additional datatypes have been introduced, yet not much detail provided yet. The XMLCatalog datatype, for example, is best covered with the XML tasks that utilize it in chapter 13. To reiterate—an underlying theme of our book is Ant best practices and effective use of Ant for real-world build situations. We refrained from making this book too much of a reference-only type of text because Ant's documentation serves this purpose, and as such the details and syntax of some datatypes is not explicitly provided here. You now have a solid general overview of Ant's abstractions, which enable you to define your build process at a higher level than otherwise possible with shell scripting or other build tools.

C H A P T E R   4

Testing with JUnit

4.1   Refactoring   86
4.2   Java main() testing   86
4.3   JUnit primer   87
4.4   Applying unit tests to our application   92
4.5   The JUnit task—<junit>   94

4.6   Test failures are build failures   97
4.7   Generating test result reports   100
4.8   Short-circuiting tests   105
4.9   Best practices   109
4.10 Summary   110

"Any program feature without an automated test simply doesn't exist." [1]

Software bugs have enormous costs: time, money, frustrations, and even lives. How do we alleviate as much of these pains as possible? Creating and continuously executing test cases for our software is a practical and common approach to address software bugs before they make it past our local development environment.

The JUnit testing framework is now the de facto standard unit testing API for Java development. Ant integrates with JUnit to allow executing test suites as part of the build process, capturing their output, and generating rich color enhanced reports. In this chapter, we cover in more detail what testing can give us beyond knowing that our code is working well within some boundaries, then we cover the primary alternative to JUnit testing and why it is insufficient. The bulk remainder of the chapter, the largest part, is devoted to Ant's JUnit integration: how to use it, its limitations, and the techniques to make seamless integrated testing part of every build.

---

[1]   *Extreme Programming Explained,* Kent Beck, page 57

4.1 REFACTORING

Assuming we accept the statement that all software systems must and will change over time, and also assuming that we all want our code to remain crisp, clean, and uncluttered of quick-and-dirty patches to accommodate the customer request du jour, how do we reconcile these conflicting requirements? Refactoring is the answer! Refactoring, as defined by Fowler, is the restructuring of software by applying a series of internal changes that do not affect its observable behavior (Fowler 1999).

Refactoring is one of the primary duties in agile methodologies such as eXtreme Programming. How can we facilitate constant refactoring of our code? Some of the key ways this can become easier is to have coding standards, simple design, a solid suite of tests, and a continuous integration process (Beck 1999). In an eXtreme Programming team, the names of the refactorings "replace type code with strategy" can become as commonplace as design patterns such as "the strategy pattern." Fowler's definitive *Refactoring* book provides a catalog of refactorings and when and how to apply them, just as the "Gang of Four" book (Gamma et al. 1995) is the definitive guide to design patterns.

We are not going to tell you how you should write your Java programs; instead, we refer you to some of the books in the Bibliography, such as *The Elements of Java Style* (Vermeulen et al. 2000) and Bloch's *Effective Java* (2001). These should be on the desk of every Java developer. We address Ant coding standards in appendix D. Just as good Java code should be simple, testable, and readable, your build file should be simple, testable, and follow coding standards; the XP methodology applies to build files and processes as much as to the Java source.

The remainder of this chapter is all about how to use Ant for testing. Continuous integration is a topic that will be touched upon in this chapter, but covered in more detail in chapter 16.

4.2 JAVA MAIN() TESTING

A common way that many Java developers exercise objects is to create a `main` method that instantiates an instance of the class, and performs a series of checks to ensure that the object is behaving as desired. For example, in our `HtmlDocument` class we define a `main` method as

```
public static void main(String args[]) throws Exception {
    HtmlDocument doc = new HtmlDocument(new File(args[0]));
    System.out.println("Title = " + doc.getTitle());
    System.out.println("Body = " + doc.getBodyText());
}
```

We are then able to run the program from the command-line, with the proper classpath set:

```
java org.example.antbook.ant.lucene.HtmlDocument
        test/org/example/antbook/ant/lucene/test.html
```

Using Ant as a Java program launcher, we can run it with the `<java>` task:

```
<java classname="org.example.antbook.ant.lucene.HtmlDocument">
  <arg value="test/org/example/antbook/ant/lucene/test.html"/>
  <classpath refid="test.classpath"/>
</java>
```

Writing `main` method checks is convenient because all Java IDEs provide the ability to compile and run the class in the current buffer, and certainly have their place for exercising an object's capability. There are, however, some issues with this approach that make it ineffective as a comprehensive test framework:

- There is no explicit concept of a test passing or failing. Typically, the program outputs messages simply with `System.out.println`; the user has to look at this and decide if it is correct.

- `main` has access to `protected` and `private` members and methods. While you may want to test the inner workings of a class may be desired, many tests are really about testing an object's interface to the outside world.

- There is no mechanism to collect results in a structured fashion.

- There is no replicability. After each test run, a person has to examine and interpret the results.

The JUnit framework addresses these issues, and more.

4.3   JUNIT PRIMER

JUnit is a member of the xUnit testing framework family and now the de facto standard testing framework for Java development. JUnit, originally created by Kent Beck and Erich Gamma, is an API that enables developers to easily create Java test cases. It provides a comprehensive assertion facility to verify expected versus actual results. For those interested in design patterns, JUnit is also a great case study because it is very pattern-dense. Figure 4.1 shows the UML model. The abstract `TestCase` class is of most interest to us.

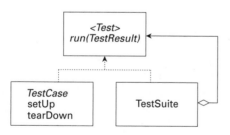

Figure 4.1
JUnit UML diagram depicting the composite pattern utilized by TestCase and TestSuite. A TestSuite contains a collection of tests, which could be either more TestSuites or TestCases, or even classes simply implementing the test interface.

4.3.1 Writing a test case

One of the primary XP tenets is that writing and running tests should be *easy*. Writing a JUnit test case is intentionally designed to be as easy as possible. For a simple test case, you follow three simple steps:

1 Create a subclass of `junit.framework.TestCase`.

2 Provide a constructor, accepting a single String `name` parameter, which calls `super(name)`.

3 Implement one or more no-argument void methods prefixed by the word `test`.

An example is shown in the `SimpleTest` class code:

```
package org.example.antbook.junit;

import junit.framework.TestCase;

public class SimpleTest extends TestCase
{
    public SimpleTest (String name) {
        super(name);
    }

    public void testSomething() {
        assertTrue(4 == (2 * 2));
    }
}
```

4.3.2 Running a test case

`TestRunner` classes provided by JUnit are used to execute all tests prefixed by the word "test." The two most popular test runners are a text-based one, `junit.textui.TestRunner`, and an attractive Swing-based one, `junit.swingui.TestRunner`. From the command line, the result of running the text `TestRunner` is

```
java junit.textui.TestRunner org.example.antbook.junit.SimpleTest
.
Time: 0.01

OK (1 tests)
```

The dot character (.) indicates a test case being run, and in this example only one exists, `testSomething`. The Swing `TestRunner` displays success as green and failure as red, has a feature to reload classes dynamically so that it can remain open while code is recompiled, and will pick up the latest test case class each time. For this same test case, its display appears in figure 4.2.

4.3.3 Asserting desired results

The mechanism by which JUnit determines the success or failure of a test is via assertion statements. An *assert* is simply a comparison between an expected value and an

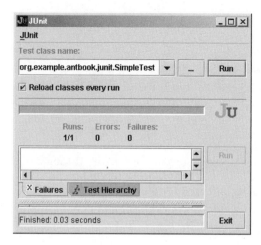

Figure 4.2
JUnit's Swing TestRunner

actual value. There are variants of the assert methods for each primitive datatype and for `java.lang.String` and `java.lang.Object`, each with the following signatures:

```
assertEquals(expected, actual)
```

```
assertEquals(String message, expected, actual)
```

The second signature for each datatype allows a message to be inserted into the results, which makes clear identification of which assertion failed. There are several other assertion methods:

- `assertEquals(expected, actual)`
  `assertEquals(String message, expected, actual)`
  This assertion states that the test `expected.equals(actual)` returns true, or both objects are null. The equality test for a `double` also lets you specify a range, to cope with floating point errors better. There are overloaded versions of this method for all Java's primitive types.

- `assertNull(Object object)`,
  `assertNull(String message, Object object)`
  This asserts that an object reference equals null.

- `assertNotNull(Object object)`,
  `assertNotNull(String message, Object)`
  This asserts that an object reference is not null.

- `assertSame(Object expected, Object actual)`,
  `assertSame(String message, Object expected, Object actual)`
  Asserts that the two objects are the same. This is a stricter condition than simple equality, as it compares the object identities using `expected == actual`.

- `assertTrue(boolean condition)`,
  `assertTrue(String message, boolean condition)`
  This assertion fails if the condition is false, printing a message string if supplied. The `assertTrue` methods were previously named simply `assert`, but JDK 1.4 introduces a new assert keyword. You may encounter source using the older method names and receive deprecation warnings during compilation.

- `fail()`,
  `fail(String message)`
  This forces a failure. This is useful to close off paths through the code that should not be reached.

JUnit uses the term *failure* for a test that fails expectedly, meaning that an assertion was not valid or a `fail` was encountered. The term *error* refers to an unexpected error (such as a `NullPointerException`). We will use the term *failure* typically to represent both conditions as they both carry the same show-stopping weight when encountered during a build.

4.3.4 TestCase lifecycle

The lifecycle of a `TestCase` used by the JUnit framework is as follows:

1 Execute `public void setUp()`.

2 Call a `test`-prefixed method.

3 Execute `public void tearDown()`.

4 Repeat these steps for each test method.

Any number of test methods can be added to a `TestCase`, all beginning with the prefix `test`. The goal is for each test to be small and simple, and tests will usually require instantiating objects. In order to create some objects and preconfigure their state prior to running each individual test method, override the empty `TestCase.setUp` method, and store state as member variables to your test case class. Use the `TestCase.tearDown` method to close any open connections or in some way reset state. Our `HtmlDocumentTest` takes advantage of `setUp` and `tearDown` (see later this chapter) so that all test methods will have implicit access to an `HtmlDocument`.

NOTE The `setUp` and `tearDown` methods are called before and after every test method is invoked, preventing one test from affecting the behavior of another. Tests should never make assumptions about the order in which they are called.

4.3.5 Writing a TestSuite

With JUnit's API, tests can be grouped into a *suite* by using the `TestSuite` class. Grouping tests may be a benefit to let you build several individual test cases for a particular subsystem and write an all-inclusive `TestSuite` that runs them all. A `TestSuite` also allows specific ordering of tests, which may be important—

although ideally the order of tests should not be relevant as each should be able to stand alone. Here is an example of a test suite:

```
public class AllTests extends TestSuite {
  static public Test suite() {
    TestSuite suite = new TestSuite();
    suite.addTestSuite(SimpleTest.class);
    return suite;
  }
}
```

You don't need to bother with test suites when running JUnit tests using Ant, because you can list a group of `TestCase` classes to run as a batch from the build file itself. (See section 4.6.2 for discussion of `<batchtest>`.) However, running a single `TestSuite` using the "running a single test case" trick in section 4.7.2 gives you flexibility in the grouping and granularity of test cases. Remember that a `TestCase` is a `Test`, and a `TestSuite` is also a `Test`, so the two can be used interchangeably in most instances.

4.3.6 Obtaining and installing JUnit

JUnit is just a download away at http://www.junit.org. After downloading the Zip or tar file, extract the junit.jar file. You must put junit.jar into ANT_HOME/lib so that Ant can find it. Because of Ant class loader issues, you must have junit.jar in the system classpath or ANT_HOME/lib; our recommendation is to keep your system classpath empty by placing such Ant dependencies in its lib directory.

Many IDEs can create JUnit test cases automatically from an existing Java class—refer to the documentation of your IDE for details. Be careful, however, not to let the habit of automatic test generation deter you from writing the tests first! We also encourage the exploration of the many great resources also found at the JUnit web site.

4.3.7 Extensions to JUnit

Because of its architecture, it is easy to build extensions on top of JUnit. There are many freely available extensions and companions for JUnit. Table 4.1 shows a few.

Table 4.1 A few notable companions to enhance the capabilities of JUnit testing

Name	Description
HttpUnit	A test framework that could be embedded in JUnit tests to perform automated web site testing.
JUnitPerf	JUnit test decorators to perform scalability and performance testing.
Mock Objects	Allows testing of code that accesses resources such as database connections and servlet containers without the need of the actual resources.
Cactus	In-container unit testing. Covered in detail in chapter 12.
DBUnit	Sets up databases in a known state for repeatable DB testing.

4.4 APPLYING UNIT TESTS TO OUR APPLICATION

This is the first place in our book where we delve into the application built to accompany this text. We could have written the book without a sample application and contrived the examples, but we felt that to have a common theme throughout the book would give you the benefit of seeing how all the pieces fit together.

Without a doubt, one of the key points we want to emphasize is the importance of testing. Sure, this book is about Ant, yet Ant exists as a tool for assisting with the development of software and does not stand alone. To reiterate: "any program feature without an automated test simply doesn't exist." For developers to embrace testing as a routine, and even *enjoyable*, part of life, it must be easy. Ant facilitates this for us nicely with the ability to run JUnit test cases as an integral part of the build.

Why is the "Testing" chapter the right place to start seriously delving into our application? Because the tests were written first, our application did not exist until there was an automated test in place.

4.4.1 Writing the test first

At the lowest level of our application is the capability to index text files, including HTML files. The Jakarta Project's Lucene tool provides fantastic capabilities for indexing and searching for text. Indexing a document is simply a matter of instantiating an instance of `org.apache.lucene.document.Document` and adding *fields*. For text file indexing, our application loads the contents of the file into a field called *contents*. Our HTML document handling is a bit more involved as it parses the HTML and indexes the title (`<title>`) as a title field, and the body, excluding HTML tags, as a contents field. Our design calls for an abstraction of an HTML document, which we implement as an `HtmlDocument` class. One of our design decisions is that content will be indexed from filesystem files, so we will build our `HtmlDocument` class with constructor accepting a `java.io.File` as a parameter.

What benefit do we get from testing `HtmlDocument`? We want to know that JTidy, the HTML parser used, and the code wrapped around it is doing its job. Perhaps we want to upgrade to a newer version of JTidy, or perhaps we want to replace it entirely with another method of parsing HTML. Any of those potential scenarios make `HtmlDocument` an ideal candidate for a test case. Writing the test case first, we have

```
package org.example.antbook.ant.lucene;
import java.io.IOException;
import junit.framework.TestCase;

public class HtmlDocumentTest extends DocumentTestCase
{
    public HtmlDocumentTest (String name) {
        super(name);
    }

    HtmlDocument doc;
```

```
    public void setUp() throws IOException {
        doc = new HtmlDocument(getFile("test.html"));
    }

    public void testDoc() {
        assertEquals("Title", "Test Title", doc.getTitle());
        assertEquals("Body", "This is some test", doc.getBodyText());
    }

    public void tearDown() {
        doc = null;
    }
}
```

To make the compiler happy, we create a stub `HtmlDocument` adhering to the signatures defined by the test case. Take note that the test case is driving how we create our production class—this is an important distinction to make; test cases are not written after the code development, instead the production code is driven by the uses our test cases make of it. We start with a stub implementation:

```
package org.example.antbook.ant.lucene;
import java.io.File;

public class HtmlDocument {
    public HtmlDocument(File file) { }
    public String getTitle() { return null; }
    public String getBodyText() { return null; }
}
```

Running the unit test now will fail on `HtmlDocumentTest.testDoc()`, until we provide the implementation needed to successfully parse the HTML file into its component title and body. We are omitting the implementation details of how we do this, as this is beyond the scope of the testing chapter.

4.4.2 Dealing with external resources during testing

As you may have noticed, our test case extends from `DocumentTestCase` rather than JUnit's `TestCase` class. Since our application has the capability to index HTML files and text files, we will have an individual test case for each document type. Each document type class operates on a `java.io.File`, and obtaining the full path to a test file is functionality we consolidate at the parent class in the `getFile` method. Creating parent class `TestCase` extensions is a very common technique for wrapping common test case needs, and keeps the writing of test cases easy.

Our base `DocumentTestCase` class finds the desired file in the classpath and returns it as a `java.io.File`. It is worth a look at this simple code as this is a valuable technique for writing test cases:

```
package org.example.antbook.ant.lucene;
import java.io.File;
import java.io.IOException;
import junit.framework.TestCase;
```

```
public abstract class DocumentTestCase extends TestCase
{
    public DocumentTestCase(String name) {
        super(name);
    }

    protected File getFile(String filename) throws IOException {
        String fullname =
                    this.getClass().getResource(filename).getFile();
        File file = new File(fullname);
        return file;
    }
}
```

Before implementing the `HtmlDocument` code that will make our test case succeed, our build must be modified to include testing as part of its routine process. We will return to complete the test cases after adding testing to our Ant build process.

4.5   THE JUNIT TASK—<JUNIT>

One of Ant's many "optional"[2] tasks is the `<junit>` task. This task runs one or more JUnit tests, then collects and displays results in one or more formats. It also provides a way to fail or continue a build when a test fails.

In order to execute the test case that we have just written via Ant, we can declare the task with the name of the test and its classpath:

```
<junit>
  <classpath refid="test.classpath"/>
  <test name="org.example.antbook.ant.lucene.HtmlDocumentTest"/>
</junit>
```

And, oddly, the following is displayed:

```
    [junit] TEST org.example.antbook.ant.lucene.HtmlDocumentTest FAILED
BUILD SUCCESSFUL
```

There are two issues to note about these results: no details were provided about which test failed or why, and the build completed successfully despite the test failure. First let's get our directory structure and Ant build file refactored to accommodate further refinements easily, and we will return in section 4.6 to address these issues.

4.5.1   Structure directories to accommodate testing

A well-organized directory structure is a key factor in build file and project management simplicity and sanity. Test code should be separate from production code, under unique directory trees. This keeps the test code out of the production binary distributions, and lets you build the tests and source separately. You should use a package hierarchy as usual. You can either have a new package for your tests, or

---

[2] See chapter 10 for a discussion on Ant's task types

mimic the same package structure that the production classes use. This tactic makes it obvious which tests are associated with which classes, and gives the test package-level access privileges to the code being tested. There are, of course, situations where this recommendation should not be followed (verifying package scoping, for example), but typically mirroring package names works well.

> **NOTE**   A peer of one of the authors prefers a different and interesting technique for organizing test cases. Test cases are written as public nested static classes of the production code. The advantage is that it keeps the production and test code in very close proximity. In order to prohibit packaging and deploying test cases, he takes advantage of the $ that is part of a nested class filename and excludes them. We mention this as an alternative, but do not use this technique ourselves.

During the build, Ant compiles production code to the build/classes directory. To separate test and production code, all test-generated artifacts go into `build/test`, with classes into `build/test/classes`. The other products of the testing process will be result data and reports generated from that data. Figure 4.3 shows the relevant structure of our project directory tree.

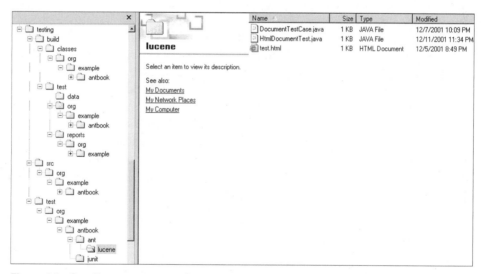

Figure 4.3   Our directory structure for unit test source code and corresponding compiled code and test results

4.5.2   Fitting JUnit into the build process

Adding testing into our build process is straightforward: simply add a few additional targets to initialize the testing directory structure, compile the test code, and then execute the tests and generate the reports. Figure 4.4 illustrates the target dependency graph of the build file.

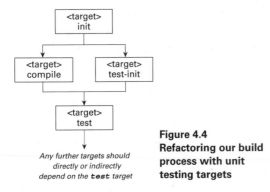

Figure 4.4
Refactoring our build
process with unit
testing targets

Any further targets should
directly or indirectly
*depend on the **test** target*

We use several build file properties and datatypes to make writing our test targets cleaner, to avoid hard-coded paths, and to allow flexible control of the testing process. First, we assign properties to the various directories used by our test targets:

```
<property name="test.dir" location="${build.dir}/test"/>
<property name="test.data.dir" location="${test.dir}/data"/>
<property name="test.reports.dir" location="${test.dir}/reports"/>
```

As we stated in chapter 3, when constructing subdirectories, like `test.data.dir` and `test.reports.dir`, of a root directory, you should define a property referring to the root directory and build the subdirectory paths from the root-referring property. If, for example, we had defined `test.data.dir` as `${build.dir}/test/data`, then it would not be possible to relocate the entire test output directory structure easily. With `test.dir` used to define the subdirectory paths, it is straightforward to override the `test.dir` property and move the entire tree. Another benefit could be to individually control where Ant places test reports (overriding `test.reports.dir`), so that we could place them in a directory served by a web server.

Compiling and running tests requires a different classpath than the classpath used in building our production compilation. We need JUnit's JAR file compilation and execution, and the test/classes directory for execution. We construct a single `<path>` that covers both situations:

```
<path id="test.classpath">
  <path refid="compile.classpath"/>
  <pathelement location="${junit.jar}"/>
  <pathelement location="${build.dir}/classes"/>
  <pathelement location="${build.dir}/test"/>
</path>
```

We originally defined the `compile.classpath` path in chapter 3; we reference it here because our test code is likely to have the same dependencies as our production code. The `test-compile` target utilizes `test.classpath` as well as `test.dir`:

```
<target name="test-compile" depends="compile,test-init">
  <javac destdir="${test.dir}"
         debug="${build.debug}"
         includeAntRuntime="true"
         srcdir="test">
    <classpath refid="test.classpath"/>
  </javac>

  <copy todir="${test.dir}">
    <fileset dir="test" excludes="**/*.java"/>
  </copy>
</target>
```

Note that in this particular example we are planning on building a custom Ant task so we set the includeAntRuntime attribute. Typically, you should set this attribute to false, to control your classpaths better. We follow the compilation with a <copy> task to bring over all non-.java resources into the testing classpath, which will allow our tests to access test data easily. Because of dependency checking, the <copy> task does not impact incremental build times until those files change.

4.6   TEST FAILURES ARE BUILD FAILURES

By default, failing test cases run with <junit> do not fail the build process. The authors believe that this behavior is somewhat backwards and the default should be to fail the build: you can set the haltonfailure attribute to true to achieve this result.[3] Developers must treat test failures in the same urgent regard as compilation errors, and give them the same show-stopping attention.

Adding both haltonfailure="true" and printsummary="true" to our <junit> element attributes, we now get the following output:

```
    [junit] Running org.example.antbook.ant.lucene.HtmlDocumentTest
    [junit] Tests run: 1, Failures: 1, Errors: 0, Time elapsed: 0.01 sec
BUILD FAILED
```

Our build has failed because our test case failed, exactly as desired. The summary output provides slightly more details: how many tests run, how many failed, and how many had errors. We still are in the dark about what caused the failure, but not for long.

4.6.1   Capturing test results

The JUnit task provides several options for collecting test result data by using *formatters*. One or more <formatter> tags can be nested either directly under <junit> or under the <test> (and <batchtest>, which we will explore shortly). Ant includes three types of formatters shown in table 4.2.

---

[3] The authors do not recommend haltonfailure to be enabled either. Read on for why.

Table 4.2   Ant JUnit task result formatter types.

<formatter> type	Description
brief	Provides details of test failures in text format.
plain	Provides details of test failures and statistics of each test run in text format.
xml	Provides an extensive amount of detail in XML format including Ant's properties at the time of testing, system out, and system error output of each test case.

By default, <formatter> output is directed to files, but can be directed to Ant's console output instead. Updating our single test case run to include both the build failure upon test failure and detailed console output, we use this task declaration:

```
<junit printsummary="false" haltonfailure="true">
  <classpath refid="test.classpath"/>
  <formatter type="brief" usefile="false"/>
  <test name="org.example.antbook.ant.lucene.HtmlDocumentTest"/>
</junit>
```

This produces the following output:

```
[junit] Testsuite: org.example.antbook.ant.lucene.HtmlDocumentTest
[junit] Tests run: 1, Failures: 1, Errors: 0, Time elapsed: 0.01 sec
[junit]
[junit] Testcase: testDoc(org.example.antbook.ant.lucene
                .HtmlDocumentTest):FAILED
[junit] Title expected:<Test Title> but was:<null>
[junit] junit.framework.AssertionFailedError:
        Title expected:<Test Title> but was:<null>
[junit]     at org.example.antbook.ant.lucene
                .HtmlDocumentTest.testDoc(HtmlDocumentTest.java:20)
[junit]
[junit]
```

```
BUILD FAILED
```

Now we're getting somewhere. Tests run as part of our regular build, test failures cause our build to fail, and we get enough information to see what is going on. By default, formatters write their output to files in the directory specified by the <test> or <batchtest> elements, but usefile="false" causes the formatters to write to the Ant console instead. It's worth noting that the stack trace shown is abbreviated by the formatter, showing only the most important pieces rather than line numbers tracing back into JUnit's classes. Also, we turned off the printsummary option as it duplicates and interferes with the output from the brief formatter.

XML formatter

Using the brief formatter directed to Ant's console is very useful, and definitely recommended to allow quick inspection of the results and details of any failures. The <junit> task allows more than one formatter, so you can direct results toward several formatters at a time. Saving the results to XML files lets you process them in a number of ways. Our testing task now evolves to this:

```
<junit printsummary="false" haltonfailure="true">
  <classpath refid="test.classpath"/>
  <formatter type="brief" usefile="false"/>
  <formatter type="xml"/>
  <test todir="${test.data.dir}"
        name="org.example.antbook.ant.lucene.HtmlDocumentTest"/>
</junit>
```

The effect of this is to create an XML file for each test case run in the ${test.data.dir} directory. In this example, the file name will be TEST-org. example.antbook.ant.lucene.HtmlDocumentTest.xml.

Viewing System.out and System.err output

While it is typically unnecessary to have test cases write to standard output or standard error, it might be helpful in troubleshooting. With no formatters specified and printsummary either on or off, the <junit> task swallows the output. A special value of printsummary lets you pass this output through back to Ant's output: printsummary="withOutAndErr". The plain, brief, and xml formatters capture both output streams, so in our example printsummary is disabled because we use the brief formatter to output to the console instead.

With a System.out.println("Hi from inside System.out.println") inside a testOutput method of SimpleTest, our output is

```
test:
    [junit] Testsuite: org.example.antbook.junit.SimpleTest
    [junit] Tests run: 2, Failures: 0, Errors: 0, Time elapsed: 0.09 sec
    [junit] ------------- Standard Output ---------------
    [junit] Hi from inside System.out.println
    [junit] ------------- ---------------- ---------------
    [junit]
    [junit] Testcase: testSomething took 0.01 sec
    [junit] Testcase: testOutput took 0 sec
[junitreport] Using Xalan version: 2.1.0
[junitreport] Transform time: 932ms

BUILD SUCCESSFUL
Total time: 2 seconds.
```

Note that it does not identify the test method, testOutput in this case, which generated the output.

4.6.2 Running multiple tests

So far, we've only run a single test case using the <test> tag. You can specify any number of <test> elements but that is still time consuming. Developers should not have to edit the build file when adding new test cases. Enter <batchtest>. You can nest filesets within <batchtest> to include all your test cases.

TIP Standardize the naming scheme of your test cases classes for easy fileset inclusions, while excluding helper classes or base test case classes. The normal convention-naming scheme calls for test cases, and only test cases, to end with the word "Test." For example, `HtmlDocumentTest` is our test case, and `DocumentTestCase` is the abstract base class. We use "TestCase" as the suffix for our abstract test cases.

The `<junit>` task has now morphed into

```
<junit printsummary="true" haltonfailure="true">
  <classpath refid="test.classpath"/>
  <formatter type="brief" usefile="false"/>
  <formatter type="xml"/>
  <batchtest todir="${test.data.dir}">
    <fileset dir="${test.dir}" includes="**/*Test.class"/>
  </batchtest>
</junit>
```

The `includes` clause ensures that only our concrete test cases are considered, and not our abstract `DocumentTestCase` class. Handing non-JUnit, or abstract, classes to `<junit>` results in an error.

4.6.3 Creating your own results formatter

The authors of the JUnit task framework wisely foresaw the need to provide extensibility for handling unit test results. The `<formatter>` element has an optional `classname` attribute, which you can specify instead of `type`. You must specify a fully qualified name of a class that implements the `org.apache.tools.ant.taskdefs.optional.junit.JUnitResultFormatter` interface. Given that the XML format is already provided, there is probably little need to write a custom formatter, but it is nice that the option is present. Examine the code of the existing formatters to learn how to develop your own.

4.7 GENERATING TEST RESULT REPORTS

With test results written to XML files, it's a straightforward exercise to generate HTML reports using XSLT. The `<junitreport>` task does exactly this, and even allows you to use your own XSL files if you need to. This task works by aggregating all of the individual XML files generated from `<test>`/`<batchtest>` into a single XML file and then running an XSL transformation on it. This aggregated file is named, by default, `TESTS-TestSuites.xml`.

Adding the reporting to our routine is simply a matter of placing the `<junit-report>` task immediately following the `<junit>` task:

```
<junitreport todir="${test.data.dir}">
  <fileset dir="${test.data.dir}">
    <include name="TEST-*.xml"/>
  </fileset>
  <report format="frames" todir="${test.reports.dir}"/>
</junitreport>
```

The <fileset> is necessary, and typically will be specified using an include pattern of "TEST-*.xml" since that is the default naming convention used by the XML formatter of <junit>. The <report> element instructs the transformation to use either frames or noframes Javadoc-like formatting, with the results written to the todir directory. Figure 4.5 shows the frames report of this example.

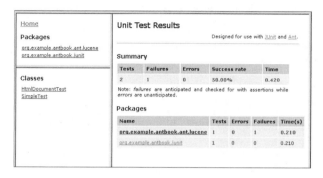

Figure 4.5
The main page, index.html, of the default frames <junitreport>. It summarizes the test statistics and hyperlinks to test case details.

Navigating to a specific test case displays results like figure 4.6.

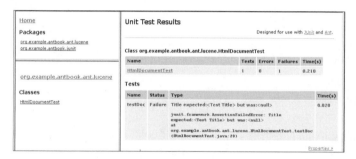

Figure 4.6
Test case results. The specific assertion that failed is clearly shown.

Clicking the Properties » hyperlink pops up a window displaying all of Ant's properties at the time the tests were run, which can be handy for troubleshooting failures caused by environmental or configuration issues.

NOTE There are a couple of issues with <junit> and <junitreport>. First, <junit> does not have any dependency checking logic; it always runs all tests. Second, <junitreport> simply aggregates XML files without any knowledge of whether the files it is using have any relation to the tests just run. A technique using <uptodate> takes care of ensuring tests only run if things have changed. Cleaning up the old test results before running tests gives you better reports.

Requirements of <junitreport>

The <junitreport> task requires an XSLT processor to do its thing. We recommend Xalan 2.x. You can obtain Xalan from http://xml.apache.org/xalan-j/. As with other dependencies, place xalan.jar into ANT_HOME/lib.

4.7.1   Generate reports and allow test failures to fail the build

We run into a dilemma with `<junitreport>` though. We've instructed `<junit>` to halt the build when a test fails. If the build fails, Ant won't create the reports. The last thing we want to do is have our build succeed when tests fail, but we must turn off `haltonfailure` in order for the reports to generate. As a solution, we make the `<junit>` task set specified properties upon a test failure or error, using the `failure-Property` and `errorProperty` attributes respectively.

Using the properties set by `<junit>`, we can generate the reports before we fail the build. Here is how this works:

```
<target name="test" depends="test-compile">
  <junit printsummary="false"
         errorProperty="test.failed"
         failureProperty="test.failed">      <──── haltonfailure has been removed
    <classpath refid="test.classpath"/>
    <formatter type="brief" usefile="false"/>
    <formatter type="xml"/>
    <batchtest todir="${test.data.dir}">
      <fileset dir="${test.dir}" includes="**/*Test.class"/>
    </batchtest>
  </junit>

  <junitreport todir="${test.data.dir}">
    <fileset dir="${test.data.dir}">
      <include name="TEST-*.xml"/>
    </fileset>
    <report format="frames"
      todir="${test.reports.dir}"/>
  </junitreport>

  <fail message="Tests failed. Check log and/or reports."
        if="test.failed"/>      <──┐
</target>                           │  Conditional <fail> task-based
```

> **NOTE**   *Remember that properties are immutable.* Use a unique previously undefined property name for `failureProperty` and `errorProperty`. (Both may be the same property name.) As for immutability, here is one of the holes in its rules. The value of these properties will be overwritten if an error or failure occurs with the value `true`. See chapter 3 for more information on properties.

Customizing the JUnit reports

If the default HTML generated by `<junitreport>` does not suit your needs, the output can be customized easily using different XSL files. The XSL files used by the task are embedded in Ant's `optional.jar`, and ship in the etc directory of the installation for customization use. To customize, either copy the existing `junit-frames.xsl` and `junit-noframes.xsl` files to another directory or create new ones—you do need to use these exact file names. To use your custom XSL files, simply point the `styledir` attribute of the `<report>` element at them. Here we have a property `junit.style.dir` that is set to the directory where the XSL files exist:

```
<junitreport todir="${test.data.dir}">
  <fileset dir="${test.data.dir}">
    <include name="TEST-*.xml"/>
  </fileset>
  <report format="frames"
      styledir="${junit.style.dir}"
      todir="${test.reports.dir}"/>
</junitreport>
```

4.7.2 Run a single test case from the command-line

Once your project has a sufficiently large number of test cases, you may need to isolate a single test case to run when ironing out a particular issue. This feat can be accomplished using the `if`/`unless` clauses on `<test>` and `<batchtest>`. Our `<junit>` task evolves again:

```
<junit printsummary="false"
       errorProperty="test.failed"
       failureProperty="test.failed">
  <classpath refid="test.classpath"/>
  <formatter type="brief" usefile="false"/>
  <formatter type="xml"/>
  <test name="${testcase}" todir="${test.data.dir}" if="testcase"/>
  <batchtest todir="${test.data.dir}" unless="testcase">
    <fileset dir="${test.dir}" includes="**/*Test.class"/>
  </batchtest>
</junit>
```

By default, `testcase` will not be defined, the `<test>` will be ignored, and `<batchtest>` will execute all of the test cases. In order to run a single test case, run Ant using a command line like

```
ant test -Dtestcase=<fully qualified classname>
```

4.7.3 Initializing the test environment

There are a few steps typically required before running `<junit>`:

- Create the directories where the test cases will compile to, results data will be gathered, and reports will be generated.
- Place any external resources used by tests into the classpath.
- Clear out previously generated data files and reports.

Because of the nature of the `<junit>` task, old data files should be removed prior to running the tests. If a test case is renamed or removed, its results may still be present. The `<junit>` task simply generates results from the tests being run and does not concern itself with previously generated data files.

Our `test-init` target is defined as:

```
<target name="test-init">
  <mkdir dir="${test.dir}"/>

  <delete dir="${test.data.dir}"/>
  <delete dir="${test.reports.dir}"/>
  <mkdir dir="${test.data.dir}"/>
  <mkdir dir="${test.reports.dir}"/>
</target>
```

4.7.4   Other test issues

Forking

The `<junit>` task, by default, runs within Ant's JVM. There could be VM conflicts, such as static variables remaining defined, so the attribute `fork="true"` can be added to run in a separate JVM. The `fork` attribute applies to the `<junit>` level affecting all test cases, and it also applies to `<test>` and `<batchtest>`, overriding the fork setting of `<junit>`. Forking unit tests can enable the following (among others):

- Use a different JVM than the one used to run Ant (`jvm` attribute)
- Set timeout limitations to prevent tests from running too long (`timeout` attribute)
- Resolve conflicts with different versions of classes loaded by Ant than needed by test cases
- Test different instantiations of a singleton or other situations where an object may remain in memory and adversely affect clean testing

Forking tests into a separate JVM presents some issues as well, because the classes needed by the formatters and the test cases themselves must be in the classpath. The nested classpath will likely need to be adjusted to account for this:

```
<classpath>
  <path refid="test.classpath"/>
  <pathelement path="${java.class.path}"/>
</classpath>
```

The JVM provided property `java.class.path` is handy to make sure the spawned process includes the same classpath used by the original Ant JVM.

Configuring test cases dynamically

Test cases ideally are stateless and can work without any external information, but this is not always realistic. Tests may require the creation of temporary files or some external information in order to configure themselves properly. For example, the test case for our custom Ant task, `IndexTask`, requires a directory of documents to index and a location to place the generated index. The details of this task and its test case are not covered here, but how those parameters are passed to our test case is relevant.

The nested `<sysproperty>` element of `<junit>` provides a system property to the executing test cases, the equivalent of a –D argument to a Java command-line program:

```
<junit printsummary="false"
       errorProperty="test.failed"
       failureProperty="test.failed">
  <classpath refid="test.classpath"/>
  <sysproperty key="docs.dir" value="${test.dir}/org"/>
  <sysproperty key="index.dir" value="${test.dir}/index"/>
  <formatter type="xml"/>
  <formatter type="brief" usefile="false"/>
  <test name="${testcase}" if="testcase"/>
  <batchtest todir="${test.data.dir}" unless="testcase">
    <fileset dir="${test.dir}" includes="**/*Test.class"/>
  </batchtest>
</junit>
```

The `docs.dir` property refers to the `org` subdirectory so that only the non-.java files copied from our source tree to our build tree during `test-init` are seen by `IndexTask`. Remember that our test reports are also generated under `test.dir`, and having those in the mix during testing adds unknowns to our test case. Our `IndexTaskTest` obtains these values using `System.getProperty`:

```
private String docsDir = System.getProperty("docs.dir");
private String indexDir = System.getProperty("index.dir");
```

Testing database-related code and other dynamic information

When crafting test cases, it is important to design tests that verify expected results against actual results. Code that pulls information from a database or other dynamic sources can be troublesome because the expected results vary depending on the state of things outside our test cases' control. Using mock objects is one way to test database-dependent code. Refactoring is useful to isolate external dependencies to their own layer so that you can test business logic independently of database access, for example.

Ant's `<sql>` task can preconfigure a database with known test data prior to running unit tests. The DBUnit framework (http://dbunit.sourceforge.net/) is also a handy way to ensure known database state for test cases.

4.8   SHORT-CIRCUITING TESTS

The ultimate build goal is to have unit tests run as often as possible. Yet running tests takes time—time that developers need to spend developing. The `<junit>` task performs no dependency checking; it runs all specified tests each time the task is encountered. A common practice is to have a distribution target that does not depend on the testing target. This enables quick distribution builds and maintains a separate target that performs tests. There is certainly merit to this approach, but here is an alternative.

In order for us to have run our tests and have build speed too, we need to perform our own dependency checking. First, we must determine the situations where we can skip tests. If all of the following conditions are true, then we can consider skipping the tests:

- Production code is up-to-date.

- Test code is up-to-date.

- Data files used during testing are up-to-date.

- Test results are up-to-date with the test case classes.

Unfortunately, these checks are not enough. If tests failed in one build, the next build would skip the tests since all the code, results, and data files would be up-to-date; a flag will be set if a previous build's tests fail, allowing that to be taken into consideration for the next build. In addition, since we employ the single-test case technique shown in section 4.7.2, we will force this test to run if specifically requested.

Using <uptodate>, clever use of mappers, and conditional targets, we will achieve the desired results. Listing 4.1 shows the extensive <condition> we use to accomplish these up-to-date checks.

Listing 4.1   Conditions to ensure unit tests are only run when needed

```
<condition property="tests.uptodate">
  <and>
    <uptodate>
      <srcfiles dir="${src.dir}" includes="**/*.java"/>        ❶
      <mapper type="glob"
              from="*.java"
              to="${build.classes.dir}/*.class" />
    </uptodate>

    <uptodate>
      <srcfiles dir="${test.src.dir}" includes="**/*.java"/>   ❷
      <mapper type="glob"
              from="*.java"
              to="${test.classes.dir}/*.class" />
    </uptodate>

    <uptodate>
      <srcfiles dir="${test.src.dir}" excludes="**/*.java"/>   ❸
      <mapper type="glob"
              from="*"
              to="${test.classes.dir}/*" />
    </uptodate>

    <not>                                                       ❹
      <available file="${test.last.failed.file}"/>
    </not>

    <not>                                                       ❺
      <isset property="testcase"/>
    </not>
```

```
        <uptodate>
          <srcfiles dir="${test.src.dir}" includes="**/*.java"/>
          <mapper type="package"⁴
                  from="*Test.java"
                  to="${test.data.dir}/TEST-*Test.xml"/>
        </uptodate>
      </and>
    </condition>
```
❻

Let's step back and explain what is going on in this `<condition>` in detail.

❶ Has production code changed? This expression evaluates to true if production class files in `${build.classes.dir}` have later dates than the corresponding .java files in `${src.dir}`.

❷ Has test code changed? This expression is equivalent to the first, except that it's comparing that our test classes are newer than the test .java files.

❸ Has test data changed? Our tests rely on HTML files to parse and index. We maintain these files alongside our testing code and copy them to the test classpath. This expression ensures that the data files in our classpath are current with respect to the corresponding files in our test source tree.

❹ Did last build fail? We use a temporary marker file to flag if tests ran but failed. If the tests succeed, the marker file is removed. This technique is shown next.

❺ Single test case run? If the user is running the build with the `testcase` property set we want to always run the test target even if everything is up to date. The conditions on `<test>` and `<batchtest>` in our "test" target ensure that we only run the one test case requested.

❻ Test results current? The final check compares the test cases to their corresponding XML data files generated by the "xml" `<formatter>`.

Our test target, incorporating the last build test failure flag, is now

```
<property name="test.last.failed.file"
          location="${build.dir}/.lasttestsfailed"/>

<target name="test" depends="test-compile"
        unless="tests.uptodate">

  <junit printsummary="false"
         errorProperty="test.failed"
         failureProperty="test.failed"
         fork="${junit.fork}">
    <!-- . . . -->
  </junit>
```

----

⁴ The `package` mapper was conceived and implemented by Erik while writing this chapter.

```
<junitreport todir="${test.data.dir}">
  <!-- . . . -->
</junitreport>

<echo message="last build failed tests"
      file="${test.last.failed.file}"/>
<fail if="test.failed">
  Unit tests failed.  Check log or reports for details
</fail>

<!-- Remove test failed file, as these tests succeeded -->
<delete file="${test.last.failed.file}"/>
</target>
```

The marker file `${build.dir}/.lasttestsfailed` is created using `<echo>`'s file creation capability and then removed if it makes it past the `<fail>`, indicating that all tests succeeded.

While the use of this long `<condition>` may seem extreme, it accomplishes an important goal: tests integrated directly in the dependency graph won't run if everything is up-to-date.

Even with such an elaborate up-to-date check to avoid running unit tests, some conditions are still not considered. What if the build file itself is modified, perhaps adjusting the unit test parameters? What if an external resource, such as a database, changes? As you can see, it's a complex problem and one that is best solved by deciding which factors are important to your builds. Such complexity also reinforces the importance of doing regular clean builds to ensure that you're always building and testing fully against the most current source code.

This type of up-to-date checking technique is useful in multiple component/build-file environments. In a single build-file environment, if the build is being run then chances are that something in that environment has changed and unit tests should be run. Our build files should be crafted so that they play nicely as subcomponent builds in a larger system though, and this is where the savings become apparent. A master build file delegates builds of subcomponents to subcomponent-specific build files. If every subcomponent build runs unit tests even when everything is up-to-date, then our build time increases dramatically. The `<condition>` example shown here is an example of the likely dependencies and solutions available, but we concede that it is not simple, foolproof, or necessary. Your mileage is likely to vary.

4.8.1 Dealing with large number of tests

This technique goes a long way in improving build efficiency and making it even more pleasant to keep tests running as part of every build. In larger systems, the number of unit tests is substantial, and even the slightest change to a single unit test will still cause the entire batch to be run. While it is a great feeling to know there are a large number of unit tests keeping the system running cleanly, it can also be a build burden. Tests must run quickly if developers are to run them every build. There is no single solution for this situation, but here are some techniques that can be utilized:

- You can use conditional patternset includes and excludes. Ant properties can be used to turn off tests that are not directly relevant to a developer's work.
- Developers could construct their own JUnit `TestSuite` (perhaps exercising each particular subsystem), compiling just the test cases of interest and use the single test case method.

4.9   BEST PRACTICES

This chapter has shown that writing test cases is important. Ant makes unit testing simple by running them, capturing the results, and failing a build if a test fails. Ant's datatypes and properties allow the classpath to be tightly controlled, directory mappings to be overridden, and test cases to be easily isolated and run individually. This leaves one hard problem: designing realistic tests.

We recommend the following practices:

- Test *everything* that could possibly break. This is an XP maxim and it holds.
- A well-written test is hard to pass. If all your tests pass the first time, you are probably not testing vigorously enough.
- Add a new test case for every bug you find.
- When a test case fails, track down the problem by writing more tests, before going to the debugger. The more tests you have, the better.
- Test invalid parameters to every method, rather than just valid data. Robust software needs to recognize and handle invalid data, and the tests that pass using incorrect data are often the most informative.
- Clear previous test results before running new tests; delete and recreate the test results and reports directories.
- Set `haltonfailure="false"` on `<junit>` to allow reporting or other steps to occur before the build fails. Capture the failure/error status in a single Ant property using `errorProperty` and `failureProperty`.
- Pick a unique naming convention for test cases: *Test.java. Then you can use `<batchtest>` with Ant's pattern matching facility to run only the files that match the naming convention. This helps you avoid attempting to run helper or base classes.
- Separate test code from production code. Give them each their own unique directory tree with the same package naming structure. This lets tests live in the same package as the objects they test, while still keeping them separate during a build.
- Capture results using the XML formatter: `<formatter type="xml"/>`.
- Use `<junitreport>`, which generates fantastic color enhanced reports to quickly access detailed failure information.
- Fail the build if an error or failure occurred: `<fail if="test.failed"/>`.

- Use informative names for tests. It is better to know that `testDocumentLoad` failed, rather than `test17` failed, especially when the test suddenly breaks four months after someone in the team wrote it.

- Try to test only one thing per test method. If `testDocumentLoad` fails and this test method contains only one possible point of failure, it is easier to track down the bug than to try and find out which one line out of twenty the failure occurred on.

- Utilize the testing up-to-date technique shown in section 4.8. Design builds to work as subcomponents, and be sensitive to build inefficiencies doing unnecessary work.

Writing test cases changes how we implement the code we're trying to test, perhaps by refactoring our methods to be more easily isolated. This often leads to developing software that plays well with other modules because it is designed to work with the test case. This is effective particularly with database and container dependencies because it forces us to decouple core business logic from that of a database, a web container, or other frameworks. Writing test cases may actually improve the design of our production code. In particular, if you cannot write a test case for a class, you have a serious problem, as it means you have written untestable code.

Hope is not lost if you are attempting to add testing to a large system that was built without unit tests in place. Do not attempt to retrofit test cases for the existing code in one big go. Before adding new code, write tests to validate the current behavior and verify that the new code does not break this behavior. When a bug is found, write a test case to identify it clearly, then fix the bug and watch the test pass. While some testing is better than no testing, a critical mass of tests needs to be in place to truly realize such XP benefits as fearless and confident refactoring. Keep at it and the tests will accumulate allowing the project to realize these and other benefits.

4.10   SUMMARY

Unit testing makes the world a better place because it gives us the knowledge of a change's impact and the confidence to refactor without fear of breaking code unknowingly. Here are some key points to keep in mind:

- JUnit is Java's de facto testing framework; it integrates tightly with Ant.
- `<junit>` runs tests cases, captures results, and can set a property if tests fail.
- Information can be passed from Ant to test cases via `<sysproperty>`.
- `<junitreport>` generates HTML test results reports, and allows for customization of the reports generated via XSLT.

Now that you've gotten Ant fundamentals down for compiling, using datatypes and properties, and testing, we move to executing Java and native programs from within Ant.

CHAPTER 5

Executing programs

5.1 Why you need to run external programs 111

5.2 Running Java programs 112

5.3 Starting native programs with <exec> 124

5.4 Bulk execution with <apply> 130

5.5 Processing output 131

5.6 Limitations on execution 132

5.7 Best practices 132

5.8 Summary 133

We now have a build process that compiles and tests our Java source. The tests say the code is good, so it is time to run it. This means that it is time for us to explore the capabilities of Ant to execute external programs, both Java and native.

5.1 WHY YOU NEED TO RUN EXTERNAL PROGRAMS

In the Make tool, all the real functionality of the build comes from external programs. Ant, with its built-in tasks, accomplishes much without having to resort to external code. Yet most large projects soon discover that they need to use external programs, be they native code or Java applications.

The most common program to run from inside Ant is the one you are actually building, or test applications whose role is to perform unit, system, or load tests on the main program. The other common class of external program is the "legacy build step": some part of your software needs to use a native compiler, a Perl script, or just some local utility program you need in your build.

When you need to run programs from inside Ant, there are two solutions. One option, worthwhile if you need the external program in many build files, is to write a custom Ant task to invoke the program. We will show you how to do this in chapter 19. It is no harder than writing any other Java class, but it does involve programming, testing, and documentation. This is the most powerful and flexible means of integrating external code with Ant, and the effort is usually justified on a long project. We have often written Ant task wrappers to our projects, simply because for an experienced Ant developer, this is a great way of making our programs easier to use from a build file.

The alternative to writing a new Ant task is simply to invoke the program from the build file. This is the best approach if reuse is unlikely, your use of it is highly non-standard, or you are in a hurry. Ant lets you invoke Java and native programs with relative ease. Not only can it run both types of applications as separate processes, Java programs can run inside Ant's own JVM for higher performance. Figure 5.1 illustrates the basic conceptual model for this execution. Interestingly enough, many Ant tasks work by calling native programs or Java programs. Calling the programs directly from the build file is a simple first step toward writing custom tasks.

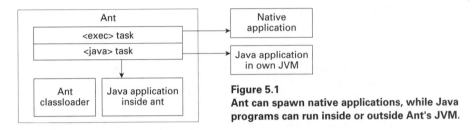

Figure 5.1
Ant can spawn native applications, while Java programs can run inside or outside Ant's JVM.

Whatever type of program you execute, and however you run it, Ant halts the build until the program has completed. All console output from the program goes to the Ant logger, where it usually goes to the screen. The spawned program cannot read in input from the console, so programs that prompt the user for input cannot run. This may seem inconvenient, but remember the purpose of Ant: manual and automated builds. If user input is required, builds could not be automated. You can specify a file that acts as input for native applications, although this feature is currently missing from the Java execution path.

5.2   RUNNING JAVA PROGRAMS

As you would expect, Ant is good at starting Java programs. One of the best features is the way that classpath specification is so easy. It is much easier than trying to write your own batch file or shell script with every library manually specified; being able to include all files in `lib/**/*.jar` in the classpath is a lot simpler.

The other way that Ant is good at Java execution is that it can run programs inside the current JVM. It does this even if you specify a classpath through the provision of custom classloaders. An in-JVM program has reduced startup delays; only the time to load the new classes is consumed, and so helps keep the build fast. However, there are a number of reasons why executing the code in a new JVM, "forking" as it is known in Unix and Ant terminology, is better in some situations:

- If you do not fork, you cannot specify a new working directory.
- If you get weird errors relating to classloaders or security violations that go away when you fork, it is probably because you have loaded the same class in two

classloaders: the original Ant classloader and the new one. Either fork or track down the errant JAR in the parent or child classloader and remove it.

- You cannot execute a JAR in the same JVM; you must fork instead. Alternatively, you can specify the actual class inside to run, although then any JAR files referenced in the manifest will not be loaded automatically.

- Memory hungry or leaky Java programs should run in their own JVM with an appropriate memory size defined.

- Forking also lets you run code in a version of Java that is different from the one you started with.

With all these reasons to fork, you might feel that it is not worth trying to run in the same JVM, but there is no need to worry. Most programs run perfectly well inside the Ant JVM, so well that it soon becomes a more convenient way of starting Java programs than shell scripts or batch files, primarily because it makes setting up the classpath so easy. It also only takes one attribute setting to move a program into its own JVM.

5.2.1 Introducing the <java> task

The name of the task to start Java programs is, not very surprisingly, <java>. It has many options, and is well worth studying. We demonstrated it briefly in our introductory build file in chapter 2. Now it is time to study it in-depth. First, let's look at running our own code, by calling a routine to search over the index files we have somehow created. The Java class to do this is simple, taking two arguments: the name of an index directory and the search term. It then searches the index for all entries containing the term. Listing 5.1 shows the entry point.

Listing 5.1   A Java main entry point to search an index for a search term

```java
package org.example.antbook;

import org.example.antbook.common.Document;
import org.example.antbook.common.SearchUtil;

public class Search {

    public static void main(String args[]) throws Exception {
        if(args.length!=2) {
            System.out.println("search: index searchterm");
            System.exit(-1);
        }
        SearchUtil.init(args[0]);
        Document[] docs = SearchUtil.findDocuments(args[1]);
        for (int i=0; i < docs.length; ++i) {
            System.out.println((i + 1) + ": "
                            + docs[i].getField("path"));
        }
        System.out.println("files found: "+docs.length);
    }
}
```

This program is a typical Java entry point class. We validate our arguments, exiting with an error code if they are invalid, and can throw an Exception for the run time itself to handle. So let's run it against an existing index:

```
<target name="run-search" depends="compile">
  <echo>running a search</echo>
  <java classname="org.example.antbook.Search">
    <arg file="${index.dir}"/>
    <arg value="WAR"/>
  </java>
</target>
```

We call the task with the name of the class we want to run. What is the output? First, there is the whole compilation process, bringing the classes up to date when needed. Then Ant reaches the target itself:

```
[echo] running a search
```

```
BUILD FAILED
build.xml:504: Could not find org.example.antbook.Search.
    Make sure you have it in your classpath
```

We left out the classpath, and so nothing works. Let's fix that now.

5.2.2 Setting the classpath

The <java> task runs with Ant's classpath, in the absence of any specified classpath; that of ant.jar and any other libraries in the ANT_HOME/lib directory, plus anything in the CLASSPATH environment variable. For almost any use of the <java> task, you should specify an alternate classpath. When you do so, the contents of the existing classpath other than the java and javax packages are immediately off-limits. This is very different from <javac>, where the Ant run-time classpath is included unless the build file says otherwise.

Adding classpaths is easy: you just fill out the <classpath> element with a path or the classpath attribute with a simple path in a string. If you are going to use the same classpath in more than one place, it is always better to set the classpath first and then refer to it using the classpathref attribute. This is simple and convenient to do. One common practice is to extend the compile time classpath with a second classpath that includes the newly built classes, either in archive form or as a directory tree of .class files. This is what we do, declaring two classpaths, one for compilation, the other for execution:

```
<path id="compile.classpath">
  <pathelement location="${antbook-common.jar}"/>
  <pathelement location="${lucene.jar}"/>
</path>

<path id="run.classpath">
  <path refid="compile.classpath"/>
```

```
  <pathelement location="${build.dir}/classes"/>
</path>
```

The first classpath includes the libraries we depend upon to build, and the second appends the code just written. The advantage of this approach is ease of maintenance; any new library needed at compile time automatically propagates to the run time classpath.

With the new classpath defined, we can modify the <java> task and run our program:

```
<java
  classname="org.example.antbook.Search"
  classpathref="run.classpath"
  >
  <arg file="${index.dir}"/>
  <arg value="WAR"/>
</java>
```

The successful output of this task delivers the results we want: all references to the word "WAR" in the Ant documentation.

```
run-search:
    [echo] running a search
    [java] 1: C:\jakarta-ant\docs\manual\CoreTasks\war.html
    [java] 2: C:\jakarta-ant\docs\manual\coretasklist.html
    [java] 3: C:\jakarta-ant\docs\manual\CoreTasks\unzip.html
    [java] 4: C:\jakarta-ant\docs\manual\CoreTasks\ear.html
    [java] 5: C:\jakarta-ant\docs\manual\OptionalTasks\jspc.html
    [java] 6: C:\jakarta-ant\docs\manual\CoreTasks\overview.html
    [java] 7: C:\jakarta-ant\docs\ant_in_anger.html
    [java] 8: C:\jakarta-ant\docs\external.html
    [java] files found: 8

BUILD SUCCESSFUL
Total time: 7 seconds.
```

5.2.3   Arguments

The most important optional parameter of the <java> task is the nested argument list. You can name arguments by a single value, a line of text, a file to resolve prior to use in the argument list, or a path. You specify these in the <arg> element of the task, which supports the four attributes listed in table 5.1. Ant passes the arguments to the Java program in the order they are declared.

Table 5.1   The attributes of Java's <arg> element. Each <arg> may use only one at a time.

<arg> attribute	Meaning
value	String value
file	File or directory to resolve to an absolute location before invocation
line	Complete line to pass to the program
path	A string containing files or directories separated by colons or semicolons

We have used the first two of these already, one to provide a string to search on:

```
<arg value="WAR"/>
```

This is the simplest argument passing. Any string can be passed in; the task will forward the final string to the invoked class. Remember to escape XML's special symbols, such as > with > and other special characters with their numeric equivalents, such as
 for the newline character.

The other argument option we used specified the name of the index directory:

```
<arg file="${index.dir}"/>
```

As with `<property location>` assignments, this attribute can take an absolute or relative path. Ant will resolve it to an absolute location before passing it down.

An alternative approach would have been to create the entire argument list as a single string, then pass this to the task

```
<arg line="${index.dir} WAR" />
```

This would have let us pass an arbitrary number of arguments to the program. However the file arguments would not have been resolved and it would have been impossible to use a search term containing a space without surrounding it by single quote characters:

```
<arg line="${index.dir} 'search term'" />
```

For these reasons, we do not encourage its use in normal situations. Certainly using the `<arg line>` option for specifying arguments is risky. The argument-by-argument specification is more detailed, providing more information about the type of arguments to Ant, and to readers.

The final option, `path`, takes a path parameter, generating a single argument from the comma- or colon-separated file path elements passed in

```
<arg path="${env.ProgramFiles};../bin" />
```

As with other paths in Ant, relative locations are resolved and Unix or MS-DOS directory and path separators can be used. The invoked program will receive a path as a single argument containing resolved file names with the directory and path separators appropriate to the platform.

5.2.4 Defining system properties

System properties are those definitions passed to the Java command line as `-Dproperty=value` arguments. The nested `<sysproperty>` element lets you define properties to pass in. At its simplest, it can be used as a more verbose equivalent of the command line declaration, such as when defining the socks server and port used to get through a firewall:

```
<sysproperty key="socksProxyHost" value="socks-server"/>
<sysproperty key="socksProxyPort" value="1080"/>
```

There are two alternate options instead of the `value` parameter: `file` and `path`. Just as with arguments, the `file` attribute lets you name a file; Ant resolves relative references to pass in an absolute file name, and convert file separators to the native platform. The `path` attribute is similar, except that you can list multiple files

```
<sysproperty key="configuration.file" file="./config.properties"/>
<sysproperty key="searchpath"
    path="build/classes:lib/j2ee.jar" />
```

5.2.5 Running the program in a new JVM

As we stated at the beginning of section 5.1, the `<java>` task runs the program inside the current JVM unless the `fork` attribute is set to true. This can reduce the startup time of the program. As an experiment, we can run the search in a new JVM:

```
<target name="run-search-fork" depends="create-jar">
  <echo>running a search</echo>
  <java
    classname="org.example.antbook.Search"
    classpathref="run.classpath"
    fork="true">
    <arg file="${index.dir}"/>
    <arg value="WAR"/>
  </java>
</target>
```

What difference does it make to the performance? None that we can measure:

```
run-search-fork:
     [echo] running a search
     [java] 1: C:\jakarta-ant\docs\manual\CoreTasks\war.html
     [java] 2: C:\jakarta-ant\docs\manual\coretasklist.html
     [java] 3: C:\jakarta-ant\docs\manual\CoreTasks\unzip.html
     [java] 4: C:\jakarta-ant\docs\manual\CoreTasks\ear.html
     [java] 5: C:\jakarta-ant\docs\manual\OptionalTasks\jspc.html
     [java] 6: C:\jakarta-ant\docs\manual\CoreTasks\overview.html
     [java] 7: C:\jakarta-ant\docs\ant_in_anger.html
     [java] 8: C:\jakarta-ant\docs\external.html
     [java] files found: 8

BUILD SUCCESSFUL
Total time: 7 seconds.
```

We repeated this experiment a few times; while there was no apparent difference in overall build file execution time between the forked and unforked options, rerunning the build itself did speed the process up by a second or so. We conclude that for this problem, on the test system having data files in file system cache mattered more than whether we chose to run in the same or a different JVM. The limited granularity of the timer, one second, will hide small differences in this particular example. Different programs with different uses may not behave the same, and even our search example will have different times on another platform.

Based on this test, we don't see a compelling reason not to fork Java programs inside a build file. If you are concerned with the performance of your own build files, you will have to conduct a test and make up your own mind. A good strategy could be to always fork unless you are trying to shave off a few seconds from a long build process, or when you are running many Java programs in your build.

5.2.6 Setting environment variables

You can set environment variables in a forked JVM, using the nested element <env>. The syntax of this element is identical to that of the <sysproperty> element introduced in section 5.1.4.

Because it is so hard to examine environment variables in Java, they are rarely used inside a pure Java application. Unless you are using environment variables to control the Java run time itself or configure a native program started by the Java program you are forking, there is no real reason to use this element.

5.2.7 Controlling the new JVM

You can actually choose a Java run time that is different from the one hosting Ant by setting the command of the JVM with the jvm attribute. This is useful if you need to run a program under an older JVM, such as a test run on a Java 1.1 system, or perhaps a beta version of a future Java release. One JVM not well supported is Microsoft's jview.exe, as this one has different command parameters from the standard run times. However, nobody has found this much of a limitation, judging by the complete absence of bug reports on the matter.

As well as specifying the JVM, it is also possible to declare parameters to control it. The most commonly used option is the amount of memory to be used, which is so common that it has its own attribute, the maxmemory attribute, and some behind-the-scenes intelligence to generate the appropriate command for Java1.1 and Java1.2 systems. The memory option, as per the java command, takes a string listing the number of bytes (4096), kilobytes (64), or megabytes (512) to use. Usually the megabyte option is the one to supply.

Other JVM options are specific to individual JVM implementations. A call to java -X will list the ones on your local machine. Although nominally subject to change without notice, some of the -X options are universal across all current JVMs. The memory size parameter is one example. Incremental garbage collection (-Xincgc) is another one you can expect to find on all of Sun's recent Java run times. When you start using more advanced options (such as selecting the HotSpot server VM with -server and adding more server specific commands), JVM portability is at risk. If you are setting JVM options, make sure to put the JVM argument assignment into a property so that it can be overridden easily:

```
<target name="run-search-jvmargs" depends="create-jar">
  <property name="Search.JVM.extra.args" value="-Xincgc"/>
  <java
```

```
        classname="org.example.antbook.Search"
        classpathref="run.classpath"
        fork="true"
        maxmemory="64m">
        <jvmarg line="${Search.JVM.extra.args}"/>
        <arg file="${index.dir}"/>
        <arg value="WAR"/>
    </java>
</target>
```

You supply generic JVM arguments using <jvmarg> elements nested inside the <java> task. The exact syntax of these arguments is the same as for the <arg> elements. We set the line in the previous example, as that makes it possible for a single property to contain a list of arguments; if the build file is explicitly setting many JVM arguments, then the alternate means of providing individual arguments is probably better.

The final option is to specify the starting directory. This lets you use relative file references in your code, and have them resolved correctly when running. It is usually a bad thing for programs to be so dependent on their location. If only the location of files passed in as arguments needs to be specified, then the <arg file> element lets you specify relative files for resolution by Ant itself. If the program uses relative file access to load configuration data, then you have no such workaround, especially if the code is not yours. If it is your program, then consider adding a directory argument to control the directory to load configuration information, or store data within the classpath instead, and use getClass.getResourceAsStream to read in configuration data from the classpath.

None of the JVM options has any effect when fork="false"; only a warning message is printed. So if any attempt to change them does not seem to work, look closely at the task declaration and see if forking needs to be turned on. Using Ant's -verbose flag can be helpful to see more details as well.

5.2.8   Handling errors with failonerror

Although the core build steps such as compile and JAR must complete for a build to be viewed as successful, there are other tasks in the build process whose failure is non-critical. As an example, emailing a progress report does not have to break the build just because the mail server is missing, nor should many aspects of deployment, such as stopping a web server.

Several Ant tasks have a common attribute, failonerror, which lets you control whether the failure of a task should break the build. Most tasks have a default of failonerror="true", meaning any failure of the task is signalled as a failure to the Ant run time, resulting in the BUILD FAILED message which all Ant users know so well.

The <java> task supports this attribute, in a new JVM only, to halt the build if the return value of the Java program is non-zero. When an in-JVM program calls System.exit(), the whole build stops suddenly with no BUILDFAILED message because Java has stopped running: the call exits Ant as well as the program. There is no clear solution for this in the Ant 1.x codebase. If you use a security manager to intercept the API call, other parts of the program will behave oddly, as the `java.*` and `javax.*` packages will be running under a different security manager.

To return to our example, we can not only set the `failonerror` flag, we can generate an error by sending an incorrect number of arguments to the program, for example by removing the search term:

```
<target name="run-search-invalid" depends="compile">
  <echo>running a search</echo>
  <java
    classname="org.example.antbook.Search"
    classpathref="run.classpath"
    failonerror="true"
    fork="true">
    <arg file="${index.dir}"/>
  </java>
</target>
```

The result of calling this target is an error message from our program followed by failure of the build:

```
run-search-invalid:
     [echo] running a search
     [java] search: index searchterm
BUILD FAILED
C:\AntBook\app\tools\build.xml:532: Java returned: -1
```

Handling error failures, as opposed to ignoring them, is a complex problem. This is because Ant was designed to build programs, where either the build succeeded or it failed completely. Recovery from partial failure becomes important when dealing with deployment and installation, which are areas that Ant has grown to cover only over time. We will review some of the details of logging and reporting errors in chapter 20.

5.2.9   Executing JAR files

As most Java developers know, a JAR file can list in its manifest the name of a class to use as an entry point when the JAR is started with `java -jar` on the command line. Ant can run JAR files similarly, but only in a forked JVM. This is because the process of executing a JAR file also loads files listed on the classpath in the manifest, and other details related to Java "extensions." To tell the task to run a JAR file, set the `jar` attribute to the location of the file. For example, to run the search against a jar, use

```
<target name="run-search-jar" depends="create-jar">
  <echo>running a search</echo>
  <java
    jar="${jarfile.path}"
    classpathref="run.classpath"
    failonerror="true"
    fork="true">
```

```
      <arg file="${index.dir}"/>
      <arg value="WAR"/>
   </java>
</target>
```

This example target does not actually work, because we have not set the manifest up correctly:

```
run-search-jar:
     [echo] running a search
     [java] Failed to load Main-Class manifest attribute from
     [java] C:\AntBook\app\tools\dist\antbook-tools-1.1.jar
BUILD FAILED
C:\AntBook\app\tools\build.xml:548: Java returned: 1
```

At least we can see that failure to run a Java program raises an error that the failon-error attribute causes Ant to pick up. We will have to wait until we explore the <jar> task in chapter 6 to create a JAR file with a manifest which enables the JAR to be run this way.

5.2.10   Calling third-party programs

You can, of course, use the task to run programs supplied by third parties. For example, imagine that part of our deployment process consists of stopping the web server, specifically Jakarta Tomcat 3.x. This is quite a common action during deployment; to deploy from the build file we must automate every step of deployment. Fortunately, most web servers provide some means or other to do this. We have extracted the Tomcat commands from its startup scripts and made a <java> task from it:

```
<property environment="env"/>    ◁——  Get the environment variables

<target name="stop-tomcat"
    description="stop tomcat if it is running">
  <java
    classname="org.apache.tomcat.startup.Tomcat">
    <classpath>
      <fileset dir="${env.TOMCAT_HOME}/lib">
        <include name="**/*.jar"/>                          Pass the Tomcat
      </fileset>                                        home directory down
    </classpath>
    <arg value="-stop"/>
    <sysproperty key="tomcat.home" value="${env.TOMCAT_HOME}"/>   ◁
  </java>
</target>
```

To run this task, we must not only name the entry point, we must set up the classpath to include everything in the applications library directory, and name its home directory in a system property that we pass down. We do that by turning all the environment variables into Ant properties and then extracting the one we need.

When running the target, Ant will stop Tomcat if it is present and the library files are where they are supposed to be. The output of this revised build should be one of three responses. The first indicates that the Tomcat stopped successfully:

```
[java] Stopping Tomcat.
[java] Stopping tomcat on :8007 null
```

BUILD SUCCESSFUL

The second displays a message that means that there was no version of Tomcat running locally to stop. This is not an error as far as the build is concerned.

```
[java] Stopping Tomcat.
[java] Stopping tomcat on :8007 null
[java] Error stopping Tomcat with Ajp12 on
       nordwand/192.168.1.2:8007
       java.net.ConnectException: Connection refused: connect
```

BUILD SUCCESSFUL

A third message is possible, one that indicates that even though the classpath was set, because Tomcat is not installed, or because its environment variable is not configured correctly, the classpath could not be created as the lib directory was missing:

BUILD FAILED

```
C:\AntBook\callingotherprograms\java.xml:52:
   C:\AntBook\callingotherprograms\${env.TOMCAT_HOME}\lib not found.
```

To have a more robust build process, the build file needs to be resistant to such non-critical failures. In this particular example, the simplest method is to check that the environment variable is set before running the task. We do this by making the target conditional.

As covered in section 3.13.1, Ant skips conditional targets if its condition is not satisfied, yet it still executes predecessors and dependents. To make the Tomcat stop target conditional on Tomcat being present, we check for property env. TOMCAT_HOME.

Figure 5.2 shows how conditional targets can be included in a build process. The project loads the current environment variables, so any task can declare that they are conditional on an environment variable being present or absent. The conditional build-and-deploy target depends on the copy-to-tomcat target, which depends on the unconditional build target and the conditional stop-tomcat target. If Tomcat is present, all targets execute in the order determined by their dependencies, probably build, stop-tomcat, copy-to-tomcat, build-and-deploy. If env.TOMCAT_HOME is undefined, then Ant skips the conditional tasks to produce an execution order of build, build-and-deploy. This stops the build from breaking just because that system lacks a web server.

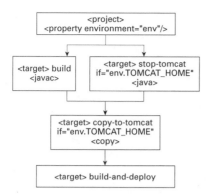

Figure 5.2
How to combine conditional deployment tasks into a build and deploy process. The `<property declarations>` in the build file at the same level as the the `<target>` declarations beneath project are evaluated before any target, so all targets are implictly dependent upon them. Here that ensures that the environment has been copied to properties before any target is executed.

5.2.11   Probing for a Java program before calling it

It is easy to look for a Java class on the classpath before attempting to call it. Doing so makes it possible to print a warning message or even fetch a JAR file from a remote server. For the Tomcat problem, we could use the <available> task, or better yet, the <condition> task, which can combine an <available> test with a check for the environment variable:

```
<target name="validate-tomcat"
  <condition property="tomcat.available">
    <and>
      <isset property="env.TOMCAT_HOME"/>
      <available
        classname="org.apache.tomcat.startup.Tomcat">
        <classpath>
          <fileset dir="${env.TOMCAT_HOME}/lib">
            <include name="**/*.jar"/>
          </fileset>
        </classpath>
      </available>
    </and>
  </condition>
  <echo>tomcat.available=${tomcat.available}</echo>
</target>
```

Here we have specified that the property tomcat.available must be set to true only if the env.TOMCAT_HOME is defined, and the class we intend to call, org.apache.tomcat.startup.Tomcat is on the classpath under the TOMCAT directory. Because the <and> element of the <condition> task is short-cutting, it does not run the second test if the first one fails, which is good, as the classpath is not going to be valid when env.TOMCAT_HOME is undefined.

The test can be used for a conditional task, or, if a program must be present, the conditional <fail> task can be used to halt the build immediately. For the target in section 5.1.10, we choose simply to skip the process if Tomcat is missing, by making the target depend upon the validation target, and conditional on the tomcat.available property:

```
<target name="stop-tomcat"
    if="tomcat.available"
    depends="validate-tomcat"
    description="stop tomcat if it is running">
  <java
    classname="org.apache.tomcat.startup.Tomcat">
    <classpath>
      <fileset dir="${env.TOMCAT_HOME}/lib">
        <include name="**/*.jar"/>
      </fileset>
    </classpath>
    <arg value="-stop"/>
    <sysproperty key="tomcat.home" value="${env.TOMCAT_HOME}"/>
  </java>
</target>
```

This practice of probing for classes and making parts of the build process conditional on their presence is very powerful: it helps you write a build file that integrates with components that are not guaranteed to be on all developers' desks.

5.2.12 Setting a timeout

Ant 1.5 extended the <java> task with a timeout attribute that lets you specify the maximum time in milliseconds that a spawned Java application can run. Only use this attribute in a forked JVM, as the stability of Ant itself may be at risk after it forcibly terminates the timed out <java> thread.

We will look at timeouts shortly in section 5.3.2, in connection with <exec>.

5.3 STARTING NATIVE PROGRAMS WITH <EXEC>

Java execution does not give a build file access to the full capabilities of the underlying OS, or native platform build steps, unless the Java program calls a native program. Actually, almost all the Ant source code control tasks do this, as do some others. You can call native programs from inside Ant, although in our personal experience, this is less common than running Java programs. Native programs are less portable, so to support in a cross-platform manner custom tasks can provide a portable wrapper. Yet, there are many commands that can be useful in a small project, from mounting a shared drive to running a native installer program. Ant can call these with the parameters you desire.

Ant lets you execute native programs through a task that is very similar to the <java> task. The moment you do so, you are going to create portability problems. If the command is something built into the operating system, such as the call ln -s to create a symbolic link, then the execution stage is bound to an operating system family, in this case Unix. If the native program is portable, but requires manual installation, then the build may be cross-platform, though it needs to handle the case that the native program is missing. At the very least, you should document these requirements, so that whoever tries to build your program without you can find out what they need. It is possible to go one step further and have the build file probe for the existence of the program before running it. This is a powerful trick that, like most maintenance-related coding, gets most appreciated long after the effort has been expended.

To run an external program in Ant, use the <exec> task. It lets you perform the following actions:

- Specify the name of the program and arguments to pass in.
- Name the directory in which it runs. There is a lot of platform-specific work behind the scenes here to support Java 1.2 and earlier.
- Use the failonerror flag to control whether application failure halts the build.
- Specify a maximum program duration, after which a watchdog timer will kill the program. The task is deemed to have failed at this point, but at least the build will terminate, rather than hang. This is critical for automated builds.
- Store the output into a file or a property.
- Specify environment variables that will be set prior to calling the program from Java.

One thing that the task does not do that would be convenient is to use an OsFamily flag to restrict operation to an operating system family, such as Windows or Unix. Instead, you have to name every platform supported, which does not work so well for targeting Unix. The <condition> task does have an OsFamily test that you can use for clearer operating system tests, but then the whole target needs to be made conditional.

It is somewhat bad practice to tie an <exec> call to a particular operating system, unless the call is definitely an underlying operating system feature. The flaw in tying a call to an operating system is that if a different platform implements the appropriate functionality, the os attribute will stop it from being called. It is much better to probe for the program and call it, if it exists. We will cover that technique shortly.

To run a program with <exec>, the syntax is similar to <java>, except that you name an executable rather than a Java classname. For example, one use of the task would be to create a symbolic link to a file, for which there is no intrinsic Java command:

```
<exec executable="ln">
  <arg value="-s"/>
  <arg location="execution.xml"/>
  <arg location="symlink.xml"/>
</exec>
```

You do not need to supply the full path to the executable if it is on the current path. You can use all the options for the <arg> nested element as with the <java> task, as covered in section 5.3.1.

5.3.1   Setting environment variables

Just as the `<java>` task supported system properties as nested elements, the `<exec>` task allows environment variables to be set, using the `<env>` child element. This has syntax identical to that of the `<sysproperty>` element of `<java>`, apart from the different element name. One extra feature of `<exec>` is that you can also choose whether or not the program inherits the current environment. Usually it makes sense to pass down all current environment settings, such as PATH and TEMP, but sometimes you may want absolute control over the parameters:

```
<exec executable="preprocess"
  newenvironment="true" >
  <env key="PATH" path="${dist.dir}/win32;${env.PATH}"/>
  <env key="TEMPLATE" file="${src.dir}/include/template.html"/>
  <env key="USER" value="self"/>
</exec>
```

Even if the existing environment is passed down, with `newenvironment="false"` (which is the default) any environment variables that are explicitly defined will override those passed in. In this example, there was no real need to request a new environment unless some other environment variable could have affected the behavior of the executable.

5.3.2   Handling errors

The `<exec>` task is another of the Ant tasks which has `failonerror="false"` by default. This is one of those historical accidents: there was no return value checking originally, so when someone implemented it, the check had to be left as false to avoid breaking existing builds. At least the Java and native execution tasks have a consistent default, even if it is different from most other tasks.

It is important when using `<exec>` to state when you want failure on an error, and to avoid confusing future readers of your build file, it is wise to declare when you don't want to fail on an error. You should always declare `failonerror` as true or false, ignoring the default value entirely.

The `failonerror` parameter does not control how the system reacts to a failure to execute the program, which is a different problem. In Ant 1.5, `<exec>` added a second failure test, `failIfExecuteFails`, which controls whether or not actual execution failures are ignored. If this seems confusing, it is for those historical reasons again. After someone[1] noticed that the `failonerror` flag did not catch execution failures, he wrote a patch. Because the default of `failonerror` was false, it was suddenly likely that existing builds would get into trouble if they did not want to process the return value of the program, but did need to know if the program failed. Hence, the new attribute.

---

[1] Steve says: I was the one who noticed it and put the patch in. This bit is my fault.

5.3.3 Handling timeouts

Suppose your external program sometimes hangs, perhaps when talking to a remote site, and you don't want your build to hang forever as a result. You may want it to fail explicitly, or perhaps you can even recover from the failed execution. Either way, you need to kill the task after it runs out of time. To solve this problem, the <exec> task supports a timeout attribute, which takes a number in milliseconds. It's easy to forget the unit and assume that it takes seconds: if your <exec> times out every run, you may have made the same mistake.

If this timeout attribute is set, then a watchdog timer starts running, which kills the external program if it takes longer than the timeout. The watchdog does not explicitly tell the run time that the timeout occurred, but then the return code of the execution is set to the value "1". If failonerror is set, then this will break the build; if not, it will be silently ignored.

```
<target name="sleep-fifteen-seconds" >
  <echo message="sleeping for 15 seconds" />
  <exec executable="sleep"
    failonerror="true"
    timeout="2000">
    <arg value="15" />
  </exec>
</target>
```

Running this target produces an error when the timeout engages:

```
sleep-fifteen-seconds:
     [echo] sleeping for 15 seconds
     [exec] Timeout: killed the sub-process


BUILD FAILED

execution.xml:18: exec returned: 1
```

If your external program is set to pass its result into a property and failonerror is off, then there is no way of differentiating between a legitimate result of value 1 and a timeout. Be careful when using this combination of options.

Note that if you really need to insert a pause into a build, the <sleep> task works across all platforms.

5.3.4 Making and executing shell commands

A common problem for an Ant beginner is that their build file issues a native command that works on the console but not in the build file. This can happen whenever the command only works if it is processed by the current command line interpreter: the current shell on Unix, and usually CMD.EXE or COMMAND.COM on Windows. This means that it contains shell-specific wild cards or a sequence of one or more shell or native commands glued together using shell parameters, such as the pipe (|), the angle bracket (>), double angle brackets (>>), and the ampersand (&).

For example, one might naively try to list the running Java processes and save them to a file by building a shell string, and use this in <exec> as a single command, via the deprecated command attribute:

```
<exec command="ps -ef | grep java &gt; processes.txt"
  failonerror="false"/>
```

This will not work. As well as getting a warning for the use of the command attribute, the whole line needs to be interpreted by a shell. Instead, you will probably see a usage error from the first program on the line:

```
[exec] The command attribute is deprecated.
       Please use the executable attribute and nested
       arg elements.
[exec] ps: error: Garbage option.
[exec] usage: ps -[Unix98 options]
[exec]         ps [BSD-style options]
[exec]         ps --[GNU-style long options]
[exec]         ps --help for a command summary
[exec] Result: 1
```

You could set vmlauncher="false" to ensure that the program is executed through the Ant support scripts, rather than any launcher code built directly into the Java libraries. This *may* work. However, the method that really works is to start the shell as the command, and pass in a string containing the parameters. The Unix sh program does let you do this with its -c command but it wants the commands it has to interpret to follow in a quoted string. XML does not permit double quotes inside a double quote–delimited literal, so you must use single quotes, or delimit the whole string in the XML file with single quotes:

```
<exec executable="sh"
  failonerror="true"/>
  <arg line="-c 'ps -ef | grep java &gt; processes.txt'"
    />
</exec>
```

A command that uses both single and double quotes needs to use the " notation instead of the double quote. The simple example shown does not have this problem.

The Windows NT command shell CMD behaves moderately the same as the Unix one, except there is no ps command installed by default, so a more contrived example will be used:

```
<exec executable="cmd"
  failonerror="true"/>
  <arg line="/c echo hello &gt; hello.txt"
    />
</exec>
```

For Windows NT and successors, including Windows XP, you do not usually need to quote the command passed to the shell. The NT command line interpreter has some complex rules about quotes, which you can see if you type help cmd. In particular, there is one option /s to turn on a behavior which matches the Unix style more. If you do want to get into handing off commands to the Windows shell on a regular basis, it probably merits reading this help page and experimenting to understand its exact behavior.

Windows 9x, from Windows 95 to Windows Me, uses command.com as the command interpreter. It has the same basic syntax as the NT cmd shell, so you can switch from one to the other using a <condition> test prior to calling the shell. Alternatively, and relying on the fact that Windows 2000 and Windows XP both ship with a version of command.com for backwards compatibility support, you could write a shell command that works under that shell for both the NT and 9x branches of windows, and not bother with testing. There is still the risk that the different platforms will behave differently.

Another tactic for supporting not just Windows 9x and NT in a uniform manner, but also to unify the build file with the Unix support, is to use the cygwin port of the GNU command line tools to Win32. This gives the Win32 platforms a Unix-like shell and the programs to accompany it.

Finally, remember that Ant runs on many other platforms, each with its own native code model and shell equivalent. Targeting Windows NT and Unix covers a lot of developer platforms, but not all. If the build file is robust and fails gracefully in the absence of native applications and shells, then people will be able to use those portions that still work on their system.

5.3.5 Probing for a program before calling it

Sometimes if a program is not available, you can skip a step in the build or fail with a helpful error. If you know where the program must be, then an <available> call can test for it. But what if the only requirement is that is must be on the path? The <available> task can search a whole file path for a named file, so probing for a program's existence is a simple matter of searching for its name down the environment variable PATH. Of course, in a cross-platform manner, nothing is ever simple; MS-DOS and Unix systems name executables differently, and sometimes even the path variable. Taking these into account, a probe for a file becomes a multicondition test. The test needs to look for the executable with and without the .exe extension, and the MS-DOS/Windows executable must be searched across two options for the environment variable, Path and PATH:

```
<target name="probe_for_gcc" >
 <condition property="found.gcc">
   <or>
     <available file="gcc"     filepath="${env.PATH}" />
     <available file="gcc.exe" filepath="${env.PATH}" />
     <available file="gcc.exe" filepath="${env.Path}" />
   </or>
  </condition>
</target>
```

You can then write dependent targets that fail if the program is missing, using the `<fail>` task, or merely bypass an execution stage:

```
<target name="compile_cpp" depends="verify_gcc" if="found.gcc">
  <exec executable="gcc" ... />
</target>
```

We sometimes use this in our build files to probe for programs. In chapter 15, for example, we will look for the C# compiler, CSC.EXE before trying to compile a C# program.

5.4   BULK EXECUTION WITH <APPLY>

What if you have a set of files that you want to pass in as parameters to some native program? How can you do it? If you know in advance the list of files, you can just repeat the task, but that makes maintenance worse. You could use a special task `<antcall>` to call targets dynamically; this complex task has not been covered yet because it has many subtle issues. For the special problem of passing a list of files to an external executable, there is a better solution: `<apply>`. This task takes a fileset and hands it off to the named application, either in one go or one at a time.

Apply is implemented as a subclass of `<exec>`, so all the attributes of that task can be used with `<apply>`, with the additional feature of bulk execution. Let's start with an example. Suppose we have a native program that converts XML files to PDF, which takes two command-line parameters: the path to an XML file, and a path to the resultant PDF file. Before we go crazy and accidentally run our program destructively, let's first just have it output to the screen what it would do. This is a nice way to develop the use of `<apply>` in your build files so that you can see what it's going to, giving you the chance to tweak the parameters.

```
<apply executable="cmd"
       dest="docs">
  <arg line="/c echo"/>
  <arg value="convert"/>
  <srcfile/>
  <targetfile/>
  <fileset dir ="." includes="*.xml"/>
  <mapper type="glob" from="*.xml" to="*.pdf"/>
</apply>
```

We are running on a Windows platform, and use the built-in `echo` command. We must set our executable to `cmd` for echo to work properly, and the `/c` switch causes the command shell to exit after echo completes. Our output, run on a directory with several XML files, is:

```
    [apply] convert C:\AntBook\Sections\Learning\callingotherprograms\apply.xml
C:\AntBook\Sections\Learning\callingotherprograms\docs\apply.pdf
    [apply] convert C:\AntBook\Sections\Learning\callingotherprograms\execution.
xml C:\AntBook\Sections\Learning\callingotherprograms\docs\execution.pdf
    [apply] convert C:\AntBook\Sections\Learning\callingotherprograms\java.xml C
```

```
:\AntBook\Sections\Learning\callingotherprograms\docs\java.pdf
    [apply] convert C:\AntBook\Sections\Learning\callingotherprograms\probes.xml
C:\AntBook\Sections\Learning\callingotherprograms\docs\probes.pdf
    [apply] convert C:\AntBook\Sections\Learning\callingotherprograms\shells.xml
C:\AntBook\Sections\Learning\callingotherprograms\docs\shells.pdf
```

For now, all it did was display the command that we want executed, but did not actually execute it. We used a nested `<mapper>` to specify the name conversion from source to target. The `<srcfile>` and `<targetfile>` elements are placeholders that define where in the argument list the source and target names should appear. All the standard `<exec>` `<arg>` variants are allowed. The `dest` attribute defines the directory used for generating the mapped target file name. The nice thing about `<apply>` is its implicit dependency checking. If the target file is newer than the source file, then it is skipped. This is roughly equivalent to Make's dependency checking behavior. If you do not want this dependency checking, you must delete the target files first, or simply not provide a mapper.

Once we are satisfied with the echo output and see that it will be executing the desired command line for each file, we move the `convert` to the `executable` attribute and remove the `/c echo` argument and we are in business.

Note that the `parallel` option of this task means "pass all files in one go," rather than "execute this task many times in parallel." There is a difference: only one copy of the program will be called in parallel mode. In that case the created command would be one `convert` call, with all the source XML files listed first, followed by all the target PDF files.

5.5   PROCESSING OUTPUT

All three of the execution tasks, `<java>`, `<exec>`, and `<apply>`, let you save the output of the execution to a file, using the `output` parameter. You can feed this file into another program, or an Ant task. Two of the tasks, `<exec>` and `<apply>`, can also save the value of the call to a property, which can then be used for expansion into other task parameters. This is a powerful facility, if used sparingly. For example, you could email the results of a build stage to somebody:

```
<exec executable="unregbean" output="beans.txt" >
  <arg value="-d"/>
</exec>
<mail from="build" tolist="operations"
    subject="list of installed beans for ${user.name}"
    failonerror="false"
    files="beans.txt"/>
```

Such emailing of generated files and reports is a common feature of automated build and test systems, as only the salient points of the build success or where and how it failed need to be reported.

5.6 LIMITATIONS ON EXECUTION

You cannot (currently) spawn an application that outlives Ant, although a spawned process can start a new program that can then outlive the build. This is an ongoing issue related to JVM implementations.

All console output in a subprocess goes to the Ant logging system; all console input is also subverted. For Java applications, this means System.out, System.in, and System.err are under Ant's control, as are stdin, stdout, and stderr for native applications. You cannot handle prompts for input at the console. If the application is waiting for user input, Ant just hangs.

Finally, there is currently no Java equivalent of <apply>. This is a sensitive issue: it is mostly deliberate; the intent is to force you to write your own task instead.

5.7 BEST PRACTICES

This chapter has demonstrated that while it is simple to call other programs from Ant, it soon gets complicated as you try to produce a robust, portable means of executing external applications as part of the build process.

Java programs are easy to work with, as the classpath specification and JVM options make controlling the execution straightforward. In-JVM execution has a faster startup, but external execution is more trouble-free, which makes it the wise choice for any complex program.

For Java programs to be callable from Ant, they should be well documented. Ideally, they should have a library API as well as a main entry point. The API enables Java programs to use the external program as a set of classes to use, rather than just as something to run once. This makes migration to a custom task much easier. The programs should let you set the base directory for reading in relative information, or have parameters setting the full paths of any input and output files used. One feature that Ant does not support in a Java or native program is user input. If a program needs any user intervention then it does not work in an automated build process.

When calling a Java program, we recommend that you:

- Set the arguments using one <arg> entry per parameter, instead of one entry for the whole line
- Use <arg file> whenever you pass in a file parameter, for better portability
- Explicitly state the classpath, rather than rely on the Ant classpath
- Explicitly state the failonerror behavior when fork is set
- Consider probing for classes being present using the <available> task
- Implement a custom task if the integration with Ant is getting very complex

Using <exec> to call external applications or glue together commands in the local shell is a more complex undertaking, as you are vulnerable to all the behavior of the underlying operating system. It is very hard to write a portable build file that uses native programs. Our recommendations for native programs are very similar to those of the Java recommendations:

- Set the arguments using one <arg> entry per parameter, instead of one entry for the whole line.
- Use <arg file> whenever you pass in a file parameter.
- Explicitly state the failonerror behavior.
- Probe for programs using a <condition> task.
- Test on more than one platform to see what breaks.
- Test on a system that does not have the program to see what happens. This can be your own system if you just rename the native program or change the path.
- Implement a custom task if the integration with Ant is getting very complex.

The final recommendation is to remember that Ant is not a scripting language. Calling external programs and processing the results through chained input and output files is not its strength. Ant expects tasks that do their own dependency checking and hide all the low-level details of program invocation from the user. If you find yourself using many <exec> and <java> calls, then maybe you are working against Ant, rather than with it.

5.8   SUMMARY

The <java> and <exec> tasks let you invoke external Java and native programs from a build; both have many similarities in function and parameters.

The <java> task lets you start any Java program, using the current classpath, or, through the <classpath> element, any new classpath. You will likely find this task an essential tool in executing your newly written software, and in integrating existing code with your Ant-based development process. By default, Java programs run inside the current JVM, which is faster, although the forked version is more controllable and robust. If ever anything does not work under Ant, set fork="true" to see if this fixes the problem.

The <exec> task is the native program equivalent. This gives Ant the ability to integrate with existing code and with existing development tools, though the moment you do so, you sacrifice a lot of portability.

For either task, you can probe for the availability of the program before you attempt to call it. This lets you skip targets that are not available on the current system, or fail with an informative error message. We strongly advise you do this, even for small projects, as over time you forget what external programs you depend upon. Documenting these dependencies in any build process documentation is also a good counterpart to a robust build file.

C H A P T E R   6

Packaging projects

6.1   Moving, copying, and deleting files   135
6.2   Preparing to package   139
6.3   Creating archive files   146
6.4   Creating Zip files   154
6.5   Creating tar files   158
6.6   Creating web applications
       with WAR files   160
6.7   Testing packaging   161
6.8   Summary   162

So far in this book we have created a build process that now compiles, tests, and executes the Java programs being developed in our software project. It is now time to start thinking about packaging the software for distribution and delivery to its destination. This does not mean the software is ready for release yet, just that the software is ready to deploy to local client and server test systems. The same targets used for the development phase work are used for the final release process, so the build process will not only generate packages for testing, it will verify that the packaging process itself is working correctly.

The steps that a team needs to cover when preparing a release usually include:

1　Writing the documentation

2　Writing any platform-specific bootstrap scripts, batch files, or programs

3　Writing any installer scripts, using installation tools

4　Checking all the source, documentation, and sundries into the source repository

5　Labeling the source in the source code repository

6　Running a clean build directly off the source repository image

7　Running the complete test suite

8　Packaging the software in a form suitable for distribution and installation

For early internal package builds, you can omit the documentation if it is incomplete. Even internal builds will benefit from a change log and a build version number, so start adding documentation like this as early as possible.

The steps in the production process that Ant can handle are shown in figure 6.1; the Java source, data files, documentation, and shell scripts all need to be taken and transformed into Zip and tar files containing the software packages for execution and the documentation to accompany them.

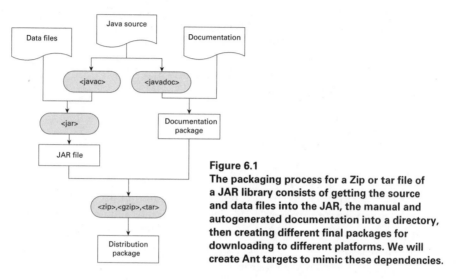

Figure 6.1
The packaging process for a Zip or tar file of a JAR library consists of getting the source and data files into the JAR, the manual and autogenerated documentation into a directory, then creating different final packages for downloading to different platforms. We will create Ant targets to mimic these dependencies.

6.1 MOVING, COPYING, AND DELETING FILES

A general part of the packaging and deployment process is simply copying and moving files around. Before we get any deeper into the processes, it is important to introduce the three main tasks used for package and deploy applications.

6.1.1 How to delete files

We have been deleting files since chapter 2, but now is a good time to look more closely at the tool we have been using, the `<delete>` task. To date we have either deleted individual files `<delete file="somefile" />` or a whole directory `<delete dir="somedir" />`. Some other options are useful during installation and deployment. The most important feature is that the task takes a fileset as a nested element, so you can specify a more detailed pattern, such as all backup files in the source directories:

```
<delete>
  <fileset dir="${src.dir}"
           includes="*~"
           defaultexcludes="false"
  />
</delete>
```

Here, as well as providing a pattern to delete, we have told the task to ignore the default exclusion patterns. We introduced these patterns in section 3.4.2. Usually, automatically omitting editor- and SCM-generated backup files is useful, but when trying to delete such files you need to turn this filtering off. Setting the default-excludes attribute to false has this effect.

There are two Boolean attributes, quiet and failonerror, that tell the task how to behave when something can't be deleted. This happens quite often if a program has a lock on a file, such as when a JAR is loaded into an application server. It also happens when Windows Explorer has a directory listed in a window, preventing Ant from deleting the directory. When the failonerror flag is set, as it is by default, Ant reports the error and the build breaks. If the flag is false, then Ant reports the error before it continues to delete the remaining the files. You can tell that something went wrong, but the build continues:

```
<delete defaultexcludes="false"
  failonerror="false" >
  <fileset dir="${src.dir}" includes="*.~"/>
</delete>
```

The quiet option is nearly the exact opposite of failonerror. When quiet="true", errors are not reported and the build continues. Setting this flag implies you don't care whether the deletion worked, and don't want any information if it doesn't. It is the equivalent of rm -q in Unix.

There is also a verbose flag that causes the task to list all the files as it goes. This can be useful for verifying that it does clean up:

```
<delete failonerror="false"
  verbose="true">
  <fileset dir="${src.dir}" includes="*.bak"/>
</delete>
```

Using this combination of verbose output with errors logged but ignored makes it easy to notice when a file was not deleted, and which files were. This is useful if you can delete the file by hand afterward, or just rerun the task a second time with more windows and applications closed.

We should warn that the <delete dir> option is unforgiving, as it can silently delete everything in the specified directory and those below it. If you have accidentally set the directory attribute to the current directory (dir="."), then the entire project will be destroyed. This will happen regardless of any settings in nested filesets. Setting the directory to root, (dir="/"), would be even more destructive.

6.1.2   How to copy files

The task to copy files is, of course, <copy>. At its simplest, you can copy files from somewhere, to somewhere else. You can specify the destination directory, which the task creates if it is not already present:

```
<copy file="readme.txt" todir="doc"/>
```

You can also give the complete destination file name, which renames the file during the copy:

```
<copy file="readme.txt" tofile="doc/README"/>
```

The task performs bulk copies when you specify a fileset inside the copy task; you must also specify the destination directory with the todir attribute and omit the tofile attribute:

```
<copy todir="${dist.bin.dir}">
  <fileset dir="src/scripts" >
    <include name="**/*.*"/>
  </fileset>
</copy>
```

Be aware that <copy> is timestamp-aware by default; sometimes that can catch you out. One of the authors used Ant to install a web application off a CD onto a server, but one system wouldn't upgrade because the CD file was older than the dates of the file installed on the server. A build file that had worked for months suddenly broke. The solution to such a problem is to set overwrite="true", which tells Ant to overwrite the file regardless of timestamp differences.

Another point to note is <copy> gives the file a timestamp of the current time. You can request that the date of the original file is propagated to the new file, by setting preservelastmodified="true". This may be useful, even though we have not used it ourselves.

If you want to change the names of files when copying or moving them, or change the directory layout as you do so, you can specify a <mapper> as a nested element of the task. We introduced mappers in chapter 3; packaging is one of the times where you may want to make use of them.

6.1.3   How to move files

To move files around, use the <move> task. It first tries to rename the file or directory; if this fails then it copies the files and deletes the originals. Note that this is a change in Ant 1.5; previous versions always copied files, even when a rename was possible.

The syntax of this task is nearly identical to <copy>, as it is a direct subclass of the <copy> task, so any of the examples listed in section 6.1.2 can be renamed and used to move files:

```
<move file="readme.txt" todir="doc"/>
```

As with <copy>, this task uses timestamps unless overwrite is set to true.

Although the task supports the preservelastmodified attribute, it is undocumented and has no effect upon the task itself: it is simply a vestigial attribute of the parent class. When the task *copies* a file, it gets a new timestamp; when the task *renames* a file, it retains the original timestamp unless the operating system prevents this.

6.1.4 Filtering

We introduced Ant's filtering feature in section 3.8. Both the `<move>` and `<copy>` tasks can be set up to act as token filters for files. When filtering, the tasks replace tokens in the file with absolute values. This is sometimes useful in documentation; you can enter timestamps and URLs into the pages. You do this by nesting a `<filterset>` element inside the `<copy>` task. For example, we can set a property to current time. Then, when Ant copies our text file, the `<filterset>` instructs it to replace all references to the token TIMESTAMP with the property:

```
<tstamp>
  <format property="timestamp.isoformat"
    pattern="yyyy-mm-dd'T'HH:mm:ss" locale="en"/>
</tstamp>
<copy file="${readme.file}"
  tofile="${doc.dir}/readme.txt">
  <filterset>
    <filter token="TIMESTAMP" value="${timestamp.isoformat}"/>
  </filterset>
</copy>
```

Replacing text in a file can be tricky, which is why the filter token specified in the filter set is searched for within delimiters. The default token prefix and suffix is the at sign (@), so the filterset will only replace occurrences of @TIMESTAMP@ in the file. If for some reason that prefix string is not appropriate, you can supply a new prefix and suffix in the filterset declaration. For example, to replace the string [[TIMESTAMP]] the declaration would be

```
<filterset begintoken="[[" endtoken ="]]">
  <filter token="TIMESTAMP" value="${timestamp.isoformat}"/>
</filterset>
```

Although it is possible to manipulate Java files prior to compilation in a similar manner, we strongly advise against it. If you do want to do this, only filter a simple source file, such as a class containing nothing but `static final` declarations of constants. Have the `<copy>` task place it somewhere under the build directory, for example as build/generated, and then include an extra `<src>` element in `<javac>` to include it in the build.

We have used a similar service provided by the `<replace>` task to modify ASP and HTML pages before deployment; it was the best way to configure the pages automatically. Another common use is to modify template deployment descriptors, such as web.xml and application.xml, with per-system configuration options. This lets you easily build different WAR or EAR files for different installations, each with its own custom settings such as database URLs and passwords. The easiest way to do this is to use `<filtersfile>`, which is another child element of `<filterset>` that you point at a Java properties file to act as the source of filter tokens. Each name=value assignment in the file declares a token and its value. You can then use a different properties file for each server:

```
<copy file="web/WEB-INF/web.xml"
  tofile="${dist.dir}/web.xml">
  <filterset>
    <filtersfile file="${targetname}.properties"/>
  </filterset>
</copy>
```

Note that Ant properties are not resolved from inside the filter file itself, in contrast to the system's behavior when loading a property with `<property file="...">`, where properties used inside the file are expanded.

You may also notice the `<filter>` task in Ant, which lets you specify a default filter for *every* move and copy that follows, but only with @ as a token prefix and suffix. This is dangerous; using an explicit filter for every copy where you need it is extra work, but is much less dangerous. Once set, global filtering remains set for the rest of the build. Do not use the `<filter>` task unless you really, really want to make life hard for yourself and the rest of the team.

6.2 PREPARING TO PACKAGE

Although our source is written and tested, you must take additional steps before the program can be packaged.

6.2.1 Building and documenting release code

When preparing to distribute code, always do a clean build first, regardless whether it is a release build or a debug build. It is important to ensure that you build all classes with the same compiler flags.

You should usually make sure that release code includes some debug information, at the very least line numbers, which help to track down exceptions. If you are deploying to a trusted destination, or redistributing open source software, including complete symbol information is useful to the recipients. If you want to keep code private, then Java bytecode obfuscation is needed along with line-number removal. Including debugging information does not have a direct effect on performance, merely JAR file size.

> **NOTE**   In Ant 1.3, setting `debug="false"` in `<javac>` defaulted to generating line-number data from the Sun compilers; in Ant 1.4 this option really does mean "generate no debug information." Ant 1.5 added the `debuglevel` attribute, which gives you complete control.

Although the Java compiler has a flag to enable source optimization, and the Ant `<javac>` task has a matching attribute, we choose to remain with the default of an unoptimized compile. The flag only tells the Java compilers of Java 1.1 and 1.2 to inline some methods, which the hotspot JVM can do automatically when it sees the need (Shirazi 2000). By not optimizing the source, we keep our binaries smaller and let the JVM do the inlining when and where appropriate. This has an added benefit:

we don't run the risk of optimizing compiler bugs, a risk large enough in C++ development to mandate running all tests on release builds.[1]

Ideally, the release code build sequence should be `clean`, `build`, `test`, `package`. You can do this by making the package task dependencies include `clean` and `test` in that order; the `test` target should be dependent upon the build itself. If some of the tests take a long time, it may make sense to split the tests into two targets by adding a `full-test` target that thoroughly tests everything. You or an automated process can run this target sporadically, and still run the core tests before packaging.

The first step in adding a release build is to provide property-based control of the parameters of the `<javac>` task by defining the default values and using them in the task declaration. Here is our modified `compile` target.

```
<target name="compile" depends="init,release-settings">
  <property name="build.debug" value="true"/>
  <property name="build.debuglevel" value="lines,vars,source"/>
  <echo>debug level=${build.debuglevel}</echo>
  <javac destdir="${build.dir}/classes"
         debug="${build.debug}"
         debuglevel="${build.debuglevel}"
         includeAntRuntime="no"
         srcdir="src">
    <classpath refid="compile.classpath"/>
  </javac>
</target>
```

Now that properties control the generation of debug information, we can override them. We add another target to do this, one that we schedule before the compile target but whose condition prevents it from being run unless the property `release.build` is defined:

```
<target name="release-settings" if="release.build">
  <property name="build.debuglevel" value="lines"/>
</target>
```

We can now enable a release build by defining the `release.build` on the command line:

```
ant clean compile -Drelease.build=true
```

If you have a dedicated machine for release builds, it could have a default properties file that sets the flag for a release option, or the ANT_ARGS environment variable could define it. We do not like the latter approach as it can lead to confusion; it's better to write your own wrapper script to call Ant with the property defined for clarity. That approach is convenient when the release process gets more complicated.

---

[1] Different compilers may provide optimizations worth enabling, but Jikes does not, and it is the main alternative to javac in widespread use in Ant projects. Neither Sun's nor IBM's compiler needs the optimization flag.

When setting up the release process it is useful to see what the compile options are; this is what the `<echo>` task in the compile target does. Downgrading the level of this message to verbose (with `level="verbose"`) might be worthwhile once the build is working.

6.2.2 Adding data files

Any complex program needs to store some data with the code: initialization and configuration files, XML files and schemas, or simply localized text messages. The ideal way to transport such static content with a JAR file is inside the file, on the classpath. It can then be retrieved using the current classloader with a call to `this.get-Class().getResource()` or `getResourceAsStream()` to retrieve the data. The Java program can reference resources using a directory pattern. For example, xml/manifest.xml finds the resource in the package `data` below that of the package containing the class whose classloader is being loaded. Absolute references can be resolved by starting the path with a forward slash, such as /org/example/xml/manifest.xml. Alternatively, you can use the `getResourceAsStream()` method in the `java.lang.Classloader` class. If you do this, then you must *not* use a forward slash at the beginning of the resource name, here org/example/xml/manifest.xml. Even if the data files are in the source tree, you need to pull them in the package. You can do this in two ways. One is to copy the selected files into `build/classes`, the other is to import the files explicitly when creating the JAR.

We recommend the first approach, as it ensures that the data is available during unit tests, and it makes it easier to verify that Ant copied the files. The mechanism for getting the files into the location is the ubiquitous `<copy>` task. Whenever we build, we tack in to the compile target a quick recursive copy of other file types we need.

```
<copy todir="${build.dir}/classes">
  <fileset dir="src"
    includes="**/*.properties,**/*.dtd,**/*.xml,**/*.xsd"/>
</copy>
```

Very old Ant versions (e.g., Ant 1.1) had a version of the `<java>` task that automatically copied everything it found in its source path that was not a Java file into the destination tree, pulling in data files without extra coding. This may seem like a good feature, but it tended to pull too much cruft, backup files for example, into the build file. If you come across an old build file that produces code that fails with errors about missing files, it may be expecting Ant to copy the files over implicitly; you need to add a `<copy>` task to fix this.

Some developers keep their resources in a parallel tree to the source, because this lets them keep different configurations from different customers. Their build files have to copy in the appropriate resources for each customer when creating the customer-specific JAR file.

6.2.3   Preparing documentation

This is a good time to start creating the Javadoc web pages from the code. If you and the rest of the team have been thorough in creating the documentation, you can do this simply by using the `<javadoc>` task. The task provides complete control of the normal `javadoc` program. For example, it enables custom doclets to generate customized documentation files and provides control over the generated HTML.

Its basic use is quite straightforward:

```
<target name="javadocs" depends="compile" description="make the java docs" >
    <mkdir dir="${javadoc.dir}"/>
    <javadoc author="true"
             destdir="${javadoc.dir}"
             packagenames="org.example.antbook.*"
             sourcepath="src"
             use="true"
             version="true"
             windowtitle="documentation"
             private="true">
        <classpath refid="compile.classpath"/>
    </javadoc>
</target>
```

We aren't going to cover how to use the `<javadoc>` task because it would take far too long. It has 50-some parameters and over a dozen nested elements that show how complex creating the documentation can be. The underlying `javadoc` program has about 25 arguments; the complexity in the task is mainly to provide detailed control as to what that program does. Fortunately, only three arguments are required: the source and destination directories, and a list of files to document. The `source` attribute and `<source>` nested element let you name the Java files to document, but specifying packages is usually much easier, especially when you can give a wildcard to import an entire tree. There are three ways to specify a package, as listed in table 6.1. For any complex project, the standard tactic is to list the packages to compile with nested `<package>` elements, using wild cards to keep the number of declarations to a minimum.

Table 6.1 Ways to specify packages to include. The final option, packagelist is not usually used; it exists to make it easier to migrate from Ant.

Attribute/element	Specification	Example
packagenames	List of packages, wildcards OK	packagenames="org.*,edu.*,com.*"
<package>	One package, wildcards OK	<package name="org.example.antbook.*"/>
packagelist	File listing the packages to import. This is handed directly to the javadoc program using the @ command.	packagelist="packages.txt" packages.txt= org.example. org.example.antbook

As well as declaring the packages or files to document, you must point to the source and provide a classpath to the libraries used in the application. If the task cannot resolve references to objects used by classes it documents, it prints out warnings and the documentation ends up incomplete. To avoid this, we pass the task the same classpath as we used for the compilation, using the `classpathref` attribute. By placing the `<javadoc>` task in a target that depends upon the compilation succeeding, we know this classpath is valid and all the source actually compiles.

If you are making a public release that doesn't expose all the internal methods of a library or application, a separate documentation build could be made that only includes the public methods and hides the author details. For open source development, we advise against including author information, as it only encourages direct email of support questions to the authors. By hiding the names in the source, you ensure that the person sending the email has to put in some effort to fix the problem before mailing the individuals.

If the distribution package includes the javadoc documentation, then you could make the task that creates the package explicitly dependent upon the `<javadoc>` task. Doing that, however, runs the risk of significantly extending the build time, as the task takes much longer than compiling the code, perhaps even longer than testing it. We are going to do exactly that in the rest of this chapter, but advise developers to avoid generating the documentation for any internal build that is rebuilt many times an hour, as it slows down the whole build process.

You need a more complex documentation process if the base format of the rest of the documentation is in XML, such as the DocBook format, and if the distribution process consists of generating HTML or even PDF from the base files. Ant can do this, but it is an advanced technique covered in chapter 13. We are also going to introduce the XDoclet task, which uses Javadoc comments to generate deployment descriptors, to-do lists, and many other useful artifacts of a project, in chapter 11.

6.2.4 Preparing install scripts and documents

Preparing documentation for packaging is mostly a matter of copying files into place for incorporating into the archive file used for redistribution.

There is one extra step for scripts and some documentation: the lines need the appropriate line endings for the target platform. Files intended for use on Windows should have \r\n line endings, and Unix files have \n terminators. This is usually needed just for plain text files, not HTML or XML files.

Batch files and shell scripts *must* have the correct line endings or they will not work. It is very frustrating when building and deploying a complex system to a remote site only to discover that the line endings on the Perl scripts are wrong. The task for adjusting line endings is `<fixcrlf>`; this can be set to convert to the Unix (\n), MS-DOS (\r\n), or MacOS (\r) line endings, depending on the setting of the `eol` option. If that option is not set, the task defaults to setting the line ending of the local system:

```
<fixcrlf srcdir="${dist.bin}" eol="crlf"
    includes="*.bat" />
<fixcrlf srcdir="${dist.bin}" eol="lf" includes="*.sh" />
<fixcrlf srcdir="${dist.bin}" includes="*.pl" />
<fixcrlf srcdir="${dist.bin}" includes="*.txt" />
```

The `<fixcrlf>` task is a MatchingTask. Like many other Ant tasks it has an implicit fileset and attributes such as `includes` and `excludes`. By default, it overwrites the source files; if the `destdir` attribute is set to a directory, then the task makes copies of the original files.

One problem is that the appropriate line ending for the build system may not be that of the end user, so using local file options can introduce intermittent defects. Depending upon who releases the project, different files will be usable by different people.

The trick is to take the same source file and generate multiple output files, such as one with the Unix title README and Unix line endings, and another nearly identical copy called README.TXT with MS-DOS line endings. Listing 6.1 shows a target that does this. It also uses another service provided by the task, the conversion of tabs to spaces. This avoids layout surprises when the recipient views a file in an editor with different tab spacing parameters than normal.

Listing 6.1 Example target to generate Unix and Windows Readme files from the same original

```
<target name="prepare-docs" depends="init">
  <property name="readme.file"
    location="xdocs/readme.txt" />

  <copy file="${readme.file}" todir="${doc.dir}"/>

  <copy file="${readme.file}"
    tofile="${doc.dir}/README"/>

  <fixcrlf srcdir="${doc.dir}"
    tab="remove" tablength="8"
    eol="crlf"
    includes="**/readme.txt" />

  <fixcrlf srcdir="${doc.dir}"
    tab="remove" tablength="8"
    eol="lf"
    includes="**/README" />
</target>
```

Shell scripts and executables for Unix also need to have their execute bit set, so that the OS will run them. There is a `<chmod>` task in Ant that can be used to set the permissions for files, using the standard Unix permissions syntax. Continuing our example, after setting the file line endings, the permissions can follow.

```
<patternset id="unix.script.patterns">
  <include name="**/*.sh"/>            Define a reusable
  <include name="**/*.pl"/>            patternset
</patternset>

<target name="prepare-scripts" depends="init">
  <copy todir="${dist.bin.dir}">
    <fileset dir="src/scripts" >
      <include name="**/*.*"/>                   Batch files
    </fileset>                                   need crlf
  </copy>                                        endings

  <fixcrlf srcdir="${dist.bin.dir}" eol="crlf" includes="*.bat" />

  <fixcrlf srcdir="${dist.bin.dir}" eol="lf">
    <patternset refid="unix.script.patterns"/>   The rest get
  </fixcrlf>                                      Unix endings

  <chmod perm="ugo+rx" type="file">
    <fileset dir="${dist.bin.dir}">
      <patternset refid="unix.script.patterns"/> Set the permissions
    </fileset>                                   for the Unix files
  </chmod>
</target>
```

This <chmod> declaration requests that read and execute permissions be added to the user, the user's group, and the "other" users on the system for the shell and Perl files in the distribution directory. The task only works on Unix; on other systems, it is silently skipped. Thus, you can use the task in targets that are called on any platform. Unfortunately, file permissions are lost when <copy> copies a file or <tar> tars it. The reason for this is simple: there is no way in Java to read or set file permissions. Until this is possible in Java, you need to set the permissions after moving or copying files. You also need to set the permissions in the <tar> task, which is equally unable to pick up any file permissions. Effectively the <chmod> task is only of use to set the permissions on files you intend to use immediately, without doing any copying or packaging.

6.2.5   Preparing libraries for redistribution

What versions of dependent libraries are you going to ship? How are you going to ensure that the correct dependent versions are shipped? WAR and EAR files can include dependent JAR files inside themselves; JAR files do not have this option. You can specify dependencies in the manifest, or document the needs, and/or include the JARs in the main distribution.

To build your classes you often need more libraries under your lib directory than you actually need at run time, especially when writing code to run under an application server. Such server applications will need j2ee.jar or servlet.jar to build, but neither of these should be included in the distribution. More problematic is the question of what to do about XML parsers. Should you redistribute XML and XSLT support libraries, and if so, which versions?

XML parser versioning issues, especially of jaxp.jar and parser implementations, cause inordinate amounts of grief. Java 1.4 and its built-in XML libraries may simplify the process, or make it worse over time if updates to the run time are needed to run applications. The whole endorsed directory mechanism complicates things further: if you are planning to redistribute libraries that implement javax.* packages, you need to understand this mechanism and its implications, which is beyond the scope of our book. Consult the section "Endorsed Standards Override Mechanism" in the Java1.4 documentation.

For a web application, first try deploying without including any XML parsers in your distribution, to see if it works. This will give you whichever parser the application server chooses to supply. Attempting to replace this with your own choice can often prevent the server or application from working.

Another potential issue is that you compile against j2ee.jar but deploy to a web server such as Tomcat, instead of a full J2EE engine, some services may be missing or need to be implemented by other means. For example, you can add the mail support of J2EE to Tomcat by adding Sun's activation.jar and mail.jar libraries.

The final application server issue is that each one may have different requirements of libraries to include. For our example program, we are going to target Tomcat 4.x. We recommend that you develop against the same server that you finally intend to deploy to; if you are targeting different servers for production, start working with them as early as possible.

6.3   CREATING ARCHIVE FILES

In many ways, Java simplifies the software development process, and makes cross-platform development significantly easier than almost all predecessor technology. But, the problem of producing software that installs and runs across multiple platforms is still a major issue in any large client-side software project. Originally, Java applications were distributed with a directory tree full of the class files. The arrival in Java 1.1 of the JAR file format containing the same tree inside a single file significantly improved the deployment process. As they stand, JAR files still contain weaknesses.

First, they are not treated as executables by the different platforms; usually to start the JAR file, helper scripts are used to call java -jar against the file, setting up environment variables and generally providing an easier interface to the program. Sometimes native binaries provide this service, but the functionality is the same. A more insidious problem with the JAR file has been that few modern Java program is stand-alone. Most Java programs have dependencies outside the core Java library, usually to packages such as an XML parser, and sometimes to native libraries that also need to be on the execution path. The JAR file has historically not completely addressed these issues, which frequently lead to CLASSPATH-related installation problems. The Java versioning and extension mechanisms have started to address these issues, but they are not yet trouble free. If you ever have to field support calls, you will know that "What is on your CLASSPATH?" comes just after asking what version of Java and what application they have, and usually just before "what version of Crimson/Xerces is that?"

Server-side development has been reasonably tractable since the WAR and EAR files were standardized. WAR files are JAR files for web applications, combining the Java code with web content such as images, HTML, and JSP pages. The WAR file also added an innovation: all dependent libraries other than those provided by the web application server could actually be included inside the WAR file. This simplifies deployment significantly; the WAR file should nominally be stand-alone. The WAR file also contained a new feature, an XML file declaring many of the operational parameters of the service. An application server could read this file and configure itself. That said, because each application server bundles a different set of extra packages, different WAR files are often needed for different servers; the XML parser is a core source of problems, and the configuration file is another focal point for customization. If you are only developing for one application server, this is not an issue, but for generally reusable web applications, each application server is likely to need its own WAR file, testing, and installation notes.

EAR files are the archive files for J2EE applications; they can contain JAR library files, EJB beans as JAR files, web application WAR files, and a deployment descriptor to describe the entire application. This makes them a superset of WAR files— more powerful and more complex.

While the server-side deployment process has been evolving, client-side deployment has remained somewhat stagnant—until the emergence of Java Web Start. This is a radical improvement in client-side software; now you can publish your components on a web server, along with a descriptor of the components and invocation details of the application. With this new service, which is bundled with Java1.4SE, client deployment may actually be almost as easy as server-side deployment.

Regardless of the ultimate packaging format, JAR files are the foundation, and the successor formats are primarily JAR files with extensions. All the packaging tasks have roughly the same parameters; learn one and you can configure the others by cut-and-paste coding (figure 6.2).

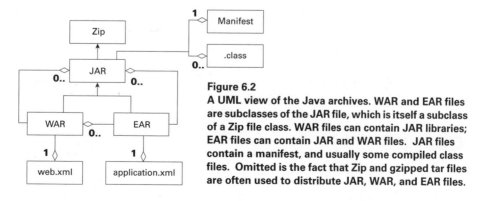

Figure 6.2
A UML view of the Java archives. WAR and EAR files are subclasses of the JAR file, which is itself a subclass of a Zip file class. WAR files can contain JAR libraries; EAR files can contain JAR and WAR files. JAR files contain a manifest, and usually some compiled class files. Omitted is the fact that Zip and gzipped tar files are often used to distribute JAR, WAR, and EAR files.

The Ant tasks that provide the packaging services all have a class hierarchy similar to the archive class model (see figure 6.3).

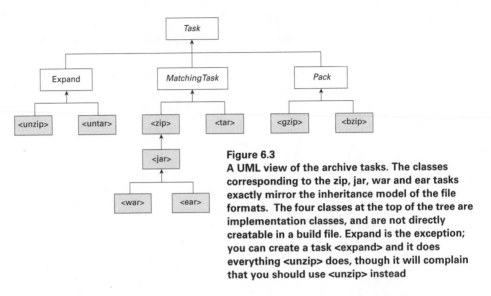

Figure 6.3
A UML view of the archive tasks. The classes corresponding to the zip, jar, war and ear tasks exactly mirror the inheritance model of the file formats. The four classes at the top of the tree are implementation classes, and are not directly creatable in a build file. Expand is the exception; you can create a task <expand> and it does everything <unzip> does, though it will complain that you should use <unzip> instead

6.3.1 JAR files

A normal JAR file stores classes in a simple tree, resembling a package hierarchy, with any metadata added to the META-INF directory. This directory should contain at least the manifest file MANIFEST.MF, which describes the JAR file to the classloader.

6.3.2 Creating a JAR file

We have been generating JAR files since chapter 2 with the <jar> task. At its simplest, it compiles an entire tree of files, usually the output of the build.

```
<target name="dist" depends="compile">
  <jar destfile="${dist.dir}/antbook-tools.jar"
       compress="true">
    <fileset dir="${build.dir}/classes"/>
  </jar>
</target>
```

The task will automatically create a manifest file inside the archive, unless one is explicitly provided. The compress attribute controls whether or not the archive is compressed. By default compress="true", but for loading speed an uncompressed archive may be faster to load. We will opt to compress all our files as the benefits for storage and downloads can be significant.

One good practice is to create the archive filename from a project name and a predefined version number, with some property definitions ahead of the <jar> task to build a customized short filename, and the full path to the soon-to-be-created file.

```xml
<property name="project.name" value="${ant.project.name}"/>
<property name="project.version" value="1.1"/>
<property name="jarfile.name"
  value="${project.name}-${project.version}.jar" />
<property name="jarfile.path"
  location="${dist.dir}/${jarfile.name}"/>
```

These declarations should all go at the top of the project. Remember that Ant automatically defines the property ant.project.name from the <project> declaration in the build file; we reassign this to a new property to give people (and their property files) the opportunity to pick a different name. The targets to create output file names, and the target to generate the archive, are both now highly reusable, provided you use a consistent naming scheme across projects. To create the JAR file, simply use the property to specify its name:

```xml
<target name="dist" depends="compile"
    description="make the distribution" >
  <jar destfile="${jarfile.path}"
       index="true">
    <fileset dir="${build.dir}/classes"/>
  </jar>
</target>
```

This invocation adds one new unrelated option, the index flag, which is a new attribute in Ant 1.5 that controls whether it creates an index file. Java 1.3 added a little speedup to JAR file processing in the classloader: if it finds the file META-INF/INDEX.LIST in the archive, it uses it to construct a hash table of files in the archive. This apparently speeds up classloading on applets and other network-launched programs, as the class hierarchy can be built up from a few selective downloads, without downloading the contents of all the files. We suspect that the Web Start library uses this, as one really needs an API with a consistent partial archive download mechanism; HTTP1.1 with byte ranges is a crude alternative. Provided nobody changes the JAR file by adding or removing files, requesting an index file on the off-chance it may deliver a speedup in some use cases seems worth the effort. If one line in the build file may deliver a speedup on network application loading, why not use it?

Before closing our coverage of the <jar> task, we should mention the update attribute. This mimics the -u option of the jar command-line tool; it adds files to an existing JAR file. This enables a very large project to incrementally create a single big JAR, or to edit an existing JAR as part of some very complex deployment process, for example, injecting classes into an existing (unsigned) JAR file.

6.3.3 Testing the JAR file

Just as there is a <jar> task, there is an <unjar> task to expand a JAR. This enables you to expand a file into a directory tree, where you can then verify that files and directories are in place either manually, or within the build file using the <available> and <filesmatch> tests. Graphical tools may be easier to use, but they have a habit of changing the case of directories for usability, which can cause confusion. Thus,

```
<target name="unjar" depends="dist" >
  <unjar
    src="${jarfile.path}"
    dest="${build.dir}/unjar"/>
</target>
```

The task takes a source file, specified by `src`, and a destination directory, `dest`, and unzips the file into the directory, preserving the hierarchy. It is dependency-aware; files will not be overwritten if they are newer, and the timestamp of the files in the archive is propagated to the unzipped files, except on Java 1.1.

You can selectively unzip parts of the archive, which may save time when the file is large. To use the task to validate the build process, after the archive has been unzipped, you should check for the existence of needed files, or perhaps even their values:

```
<target name="test-dist" depends="dist" >
  <unjar
    src="${antbook-ant.jar}"
    dest="${build.dir}/unjar">
    <patternset>
      <include name="org/**"/>
    </patternset>
  </unjar>
  <condition property="jar.uptodate">
    <filesmatch
    file1="${build.dir}/classes/org/example/antbook/Search.class"
    file2="${build.dir}/unjar/org/example/antbook/Search.class"
    />
  </condition>
  <fail unless="jar.uptodate" message="file mismatch in JAR"/>
</target>
```

Here we expand classes in the archive and then verify that a file in the expanded directory tree matches that in the tree of compiled classes. Binary file comparison is a highly rigorous form of validation, which works well for comparing files downloaded from web sites, making it ideal for validating upload processes.

6.3.4 Creating JAR manifests

JAR files are required to contain a manifest. The `<jar>` task will create one if needed; it contains the manifest version and the version of Ant used to build the file:

```
Manifest-Version: 1.0
Created-By: Apache Ant 1.5
```

Sometimes this is not enough, such as when you want to specify the default entry point of the JAR, or add version information to the manifest, as is covered in the JDK document "Java Product Versioning Specification." You also need to provide a manifest if you want to add extension libraries, following the even more complex Java extension specification "Extension Mechanism Architecture." Extension libraries aren't so much a complex specification, as they are a complex implementation.

They have historically caused trouble; see *Understanding Class.forName()* in the Bibliography for details (Neward 2000).

Adding a manifest to the JAR file is trivial; set the manifest parameter of the task to a predefined manifest file:

```
<target name="dist-with-manifest"
  depends="compile"
    description="make the distribution" >
    <jar destfile="${jarfile.path}"
        index="true"
      manifest="src/META-INF/MANIFEST.MF">
      <fileset dir="${build.dir}/classes"/>
    </jar>
</target>
```

This target needs a manifest file, here in src/META-INF/MANIFEST.MF

```
Manifest-Version: 1.0
Created-By: Apache Ant 1.5alpha
Sealed: false
Main-Class: org.example.antbook.Search
```

This manifest reinforces that our package is not sealed; the classloader should not throw an exception if it finds any classes in these packages outside the JAR, and that our default entry point is to our Search class.

This process has one weakness: someone has to create the manifest first. Why not create it during the build process, enabling us to use Ant properties inside the manifest? This is where the <manifest> task comes in.

```
<target name="create-manifest"
    depends="init"
    description="make the manifest" >
  <manifest file="${build.dir}/MANIFEST.MF">
    <attribute name="Built-By" value="${user.name}"/>
    <attribute name="Built-On" value="${timestamp.isoformat}"/>
    <attribute name="Main-Class" value="org.example.antbook.Search"/>
  </manifest>
</target>
```

The outcome of this task will be something like the following manifest, although the exact details depend on who created the file, when they created it, and the version of Ant:

```
Manifest-Version: 1.0
Built-By: slo
Main-Class: org.example.antbook.Search
Built-On: 2002-02-15T23:22:33
Created-By: Apache Ant 1.5alpha
```

For complex manifests the task can create manifest sections, using the <section name="..."> nested element, which can contain attributes and values to be defined in that section. The task also acts as an element inside the <jar> task, avoiding the need to save the manifest to a temporary file. We prefer the stand-alone action, as it is easier to examine the generated content.

6.3.5 Adding extra metadata to the JAR

Sometimes you may need to add extra content to the META-INF directory, alongside the manifest, such as when providing extra declarative data for use in applications that use JAR files for plug-in code. There is a nested fileset element, `<metainf>`, which lets you specify the metadata files to add to the JAR. To avoid seeing a warning message, do not refer to the manifest file in this fileset. Either keep the files in separate locations, or exclude the manifest from the fileset:

```
<target name="dist-with-meta-inf"
        depends="compile,create-manifest"
        description="make the distribution">
  <jar destfile="${jarfile.path}"
       index="true"
       manifest="${build.dir}/MANIFEST.MF">
    <fileset dir="${build.dir}/classes"/>
    <metainf dir="src/META-INF/"/>
  </jar>
</target>
```

This may seem quite a complex task, but provided the same layout patterns are used across projects, the same tasks can be copied into new build files and tuned to individual projects.

6.3.6 JAR file best practices

There are two tricks to consider for better `<jar>` tasks. First, copy all the files you want to include in the JAR into one place before building. This makes it easier to test that the needed files have been copied.

Second, create your own manifest so you can be sure what is going in there. If you leave it to the `<jar>` task, you get a very minimal manifest.

6.3.7 Signing JAR files

If you need to sign a JAR file, such as for use in the Java Web Start system, or to create a signed applet with extra rights in the web browser, then the `<signjar>` task is for you. The task can sign a JAR with a certificate that, for proper authentication, you should buy from one of the appropriate certificate vendors. For testing purposes, you can generate a self-signed certificate using Sun's Keytool tool, which is wrapped up by the `<genkey>` task. This task adds a key into a Keystore, creating the store if needed:

```
<target name="create-signing-key">
  <genkey
    alias="autosigner"
    keystore="local.keystore"
    storepass=".oO0OOo." >
    <dname>
      <param name="CN" value="autosigner"/>
      <param name="OU" value="Erik Hatcher"/>
      <param name="O"  value="Eric Conspiracy"/>
```

```
        <param name="C"  value="US"/>
      </dname>
    </genkey>
</target>
```

Remember, self-generated certificates cannot sign production code. Even though the generated keys are cryptographically sound, tools such as the applet loader do not trust self-generated keys, and make a point of expressing their concern at load time. Developers are supposed to pay the annual premium for a commercial certificate, which for a commercial application is not much of an outlay. For open source development, the outlay is significant, and the whole signing process is more tortuous. Anyone with commit rights can release a version of the code. You can authenticate a <genkey> generated key by signing it with your PGP/GPG key to authenticate the key yourself, but the classic certification authority-based mechanism of the Java classloaders and Web Start will not use that information.

To sign the JAR file, use the <signjar> task after generating it. This will add signature information to the META-INF directory of the JAR, and add signatures to the manifest. The task needs to be given the location and the password of the Keystore file, and the alias and any optional extra password for the signature itself. It will then modify the JAR file in place, by invoking the Jarsigner tool in the JDK:

```
<target name="sign-jar"
  depends="dist-with-meta-inf">
  <signjar jar="${jarfile.path}"
    alias="autosigner"
    keystore="local.keystore"
    storepass=".oO0OOo."
    verbose="true"
    />
</target>
```

Our manifest now contains digest signatures of the classes inside the JAR:

```
Manifest-Version: 1.0
Built-By: slo
Main-Class: org.example.antbook.Search
Built-On: 2002-02-15T23:51:51
Created-By: Apache Ant 1.5alpha

Name: org/example/antbook/Index.class
SHA1-Digest: dnjKU+kElUammJHy1kq7SOYM4Pg=

Name: org/example/antbook/Search.class
SHA1-Digest: 1y52Hx31qHqJSXxvYXpMJoLwwVM=
```

The <signjar> task can bulk sign a set of JAR files, using a nested fileset element. It also performs basic dependency checking, by not attempting to sign any files that are already signed by the identity in the task. It does not check to see if the file has changed since the last signing.

Signing JAR files adds extra complexity to a build, especially to perform it securely. The passwords should not be kept in the build file; a personal properties file with tightened access controls may be acceptable. With the `<input>` task you can ask for user input during the build, so perhaps you could avoid keeping the key on the computer, but then automated processes and GUI-based execution are not possible. A better solution may be to keep the Keystore on a physically removable object, such as a CD-ROM disc, and only insert it when needed.

6.4   CREATING ZIP FILES

Ant creates Zip files as easily as it creates JAR files, using the `<zip>` task. The most complex part is deciding which files to include and where to put them. The task is the parent class of `<jar>`. All attributes and elements of `<zip>` can be used in `<jar>`, but the JAR-specific extras (the manifest and the metadata fileset) are not supported. What is useful in the `<zip>` task and its subclasses, is the `<zipfileset>` element. This extends the normal fileset with some extra parameters, as listed in table 6.2. This fileset lets you include the contents of one Zip file into another, expanding it in the directory tree where you choose, and it lets you place files imported from the file system into chosen places in the Zip file. This obviates the need to create a complete directory tree on the local disk before creating the archive.

Table 6.2   Extra attributes in `<zipfileset>` compared to a `<fileset>`

Attribute	Meaning
prefix	A directory prefix to use in the Zip file
fullpath	The full path to place the single file in archive
src	The name of a Zip file to include in the archive

To include the Zip file creation in the delivery process we are putting together, the first step is to define the names of the new output files. We use the plural as we plan to create two files for distribution: a binary redistributable and a source edition. We do this by adding four properties to the start of the project, declaring the name and full path of each Zip file.

```
<property name="zipfile.name"
  value="${project.name}-${project.version}.zip" />
<property name="zipfile.path"
  location="${dist.dir}/${zipfile.name}"/>
<property name="srczipfile.name"
  value="${project.name}-${project.version}-src.zip" />
<property name="srczipfile.path"
  location="${dist.dir}/${srczipfile.name}"/>
```

6.4.1   Creating a binary distribution

To create a binary distribution, use a `<zip>` task in a target that depends upon the JAR file, and other targets that prepare artifacts for the binary, such as the documentation and script preparation tasks. These files are to be included in the file: simple documentation and JAR file at the base, scripts in the bin directory. Here is how we create the binary Zip file:

```
<target name="create-bin-zipfile"
  depends="dist-with-meta-inf,prepare-docs,prepare-scripts">
  <zip destfile="${zipfile.path}">
    <fileset dir="${dist.dir}"
      includes="${jarfile.name}"/>
    <fileset dir="${doc.dir}"
       includes="README,readme.txt"/>
    <zipfileset dir="${dist.bin.dir}"
      prefix="bin">
      <include name="**/*.sh"/>
      <include name="**/*.pl"/>
      <include name="**/*.bat"/>
    </zipfileset>
  </zip>
</target>
```

The first two filesets used to create the Zip file are quite straightforward: the JAR file and the two README files are included by name. Because the filesets are based in the directory where these files are stored, and the `<zip>` task stores all path information from the base of the fileset onward, these files are all imported to the base directory of the archive. The final fileset is for files we want placed into the bin directory, files created in the directory named in the property `dist.bin.dir`. It would be possible to rely on the fact that the name of this directory is really dist/bin and use a fileset one directory up, asking for files in the bin subdirectory:

```
<fileset dir="${dist.bin.dir}/..">
  <include name="bin/*.sh"/>
  <include name="bin/*.pl"/>
  <include name="bin/*.bat"/>
</fileset>
```

This does work today, but there is no guarantee that it will work tomorrow; it is too brittle. Because we use a property to name the directory, we can never be sure what the property will be in future. If the name is changed, the files will not be included. Using the `<zipfileset>` element makes it possible to produce a build file that is more robust, which means it needs less maintenance.

You can manually test the task by expanding the archive. The JDK jar tool can do this, giving a log of its actions:

```
>jar xvf antbook-tools-1.1.zip

extracted: antbook-tools-1.1.jar
extracted: README
extracted: readme.txt
  created: bin/
extracted: bin/indexer.bat
extracted: bin/indexer.pl
extracted: bin/indexer.sh
```

This is exactly what is wanted. You can make a manual check to verify that the line endings are correct for the file types by opening the files in a text editor, then this Zip file is ready to distribute. Well almost; there is still the need to pull in the javadoc documentation. With the target to generate the documentation written, we need only a new dependency and another `<zipfileset>`:

```
<target name="create-bin-zipfile"
  depends="dist-with-meta-inf,prepare-docs,prepare-scripts,javadocs">
  <zip destfile="${zipfile.path}">
    <fileset dir="${dist.dir}"
      includes="${jarfile.name}"/>
    <fileset dir="${doc.dir}"
      includes="README,readme.txt"/>
    <fileset dir="${dist.bin.dir}/..">
      <include name="bin/*.sh"/>
      <include name="bin/*.pl"/>
      <include name="bin/*.bat"/>
    </fileset>
    <zipfileset dir="${dist.bin.dir}"
      prefix="bin">
      <include name="**/*.sh"/>
      <include name="**/*.pl"/>
      <include name="**/*.bat"/>
    </zipfileset>
    <zipfileset dir="${javadoc.dir}"
      prefix="doc/javadocs"/>
  </zip>
</target>
```

With these changes, the Zip file of the application binary is ready for redistribution. There is the small issue of dependent libraries; we are not redistributing them. In this particular build process, we are creating and distributing them separately, though we may write a master build file to include all libraries and documentation in one unified package. If you need to bundle JAR files in the distribution, the common practice is to include them in the lib subdirectory of the Zip file, then write launcher scripts to include these files in the classpath.

6.4.2 Creating a source distribution

Hand in hand with the binary distribution goes the source distribution. In the open source world there is often little difference between the two. In commercial closed-source software there is, but the source is still regularly archived and emailed around.

There seem to be two types of source distribution in common circulation. First, there is the pure source distribution, containing the source tree and the build file(s); the recipient has to compile everything. At the other extreme is the binary distribution with the source and build files included. In between are distributions that omit some of the generated files, such as the javadoc pages, for brevity. Pure source distribution is common for C++ projects where everyone's platform and compiler are different. Because Java is so portable, and because JAR files are relatively compact, we prefer source distributions that also include the binaries. This lets users get started faster, and if they don't want to build the code immediately, they can get working now and fix things later.

Having made the decision to include the binaries of the project, the components for the source build file become clear. They are: the source tree, the build file, and the binary Zip file itself. Remember how we mentioned `<zipfileset>` could import one Zip file into another? That is what we are going to do:

```
<target name="create-src-zipfile"
  depends="create-bin-zipfile">
  <zip destfile="${srczipfile.path}">
    <zipfileset src ="${zipfile.path}"
      excludes="doc/javadocs/**" />
    <fileset dir="." includes="src/**" />
    <fileset dir="." includes="xdocs/**" />
    <fileset dir="." includes="*.xml" />
  </zip>
</target>
```

The target to create the source archive reuses most of the work the binary Zip file target has performed. It depends on the `create-bin-zipfile` target, and uses `<zipfileset>` to import all the content of the first Zip file *except for the javadocs*. Even when importing the contents of one Zip file into another, the fileset patterns can control what to import or omit. Alongside the binary files, we include the source, the documents in the xdocs directory, and any XML files in the base directory—which means the build.xml file itself. The result is a file that runs out the box, but which contains the entire source and, of course, the build file.

6.4.3 Merging Zip files

One addition to the `<zip>` task in Ant 1.5 is the `<zipgroupfileset>`. This is a nested fileset element that lets you list one or more Zip files whose entire contents will get pulled into the current Zip file. This could be useful when creating JAR files, as well as pure Zip files:

```
<jar destFile="everything.jar">
  <zipgroupfileset dir="lib" includes="**/*.jar" />
</jar>
```

6.4.4 Zip file best practices

Here are some tips to make creating Zip files easier:

- Copy all files you want to include in the JAR into one place before building. This makes it easier to test that the needed files have been copied.

- Leave compression enabled unless you have a particular reason not to.

- Don't distribute JAR files with a .zip extension. Some software publishers still do this, but it is an outdated approach and not entirely compatible with Ant's classloader policies.

- Use the `<zipfileset>` element to produce a more robust build file.
- Remember that Unix file permissions are not retained: this needs to be documented on your download page.

Our final observation is that many people can use the Zip format for Unix installations too, so you should include the Unix documents and scripts alongside the Windows ones, with a note listing all scripts that need to have their execute bit set.

6.5 CREATING TAR FILES

Tar files are the best format for the Unix platform, as the format includes not only the folder hierarchy, but also the file permissions, permissions Ant can set when it creates a tar file, regardless of the platform it runs on. A version of the tar program can be found on every Unix platform, and even cross-compiled for Windows. To create a tar file in Ant, use the `<tar>` task. This task takes an implicit fileset; with attributes such as `includes` and `excludes` to control which files to include. We prefer a more verbose and explicit policy of listing filesets as nested elements. This task is more than simply a style policy for better maintenance, it is a way of having more control over the build. Listing 6.2 shows our tar target to create the archive of source with binaries, including scripts with read permissions.

Listing 6.2 A target to create a tar archive of the source and binaries

```xml
<property name="tarfile.name"
          value="${project.name}-${project.version}.tar" />
<property name="tarfile.path"
          location="${dist.dir}/${tarfile.name}"/>

<target name="create-tarfile"
  depends="dist-with-meta-inf,prepare-docs,prepare-scripts,javadocs">

  <tar destfile="${tarfile.path}"
    longfile="warn">
    <tarfileset dir="${dist.dir}"
      includes="${jarfile.name}"/>
    <tarfileset dir="${doc.dir}"
      includes="README,readme.txt"/>
    <tarfileset dir="." >
      <include name="src/**"/>
      <include name="xdocs/**"/>
      <include name="doc/javadocs/**"/>
    </tarfileset>
    <tarfileset dir="${dist.dir}"
                mode="755" >
      <include name="bin/*.sh"/ >
      <include name="bin/*.pl"/ >
      <include name="bin/*.bat"/>
    </tarfileset>
  </tar>

</target>
```

This task extends the usual <fileset> element to produce the <tarfileset>: a fileset with Unix user and group identity and Unix file permissions. Users and groups are simply strings: user="root", group="system". The file permission is in the low-level octal permission format used in the UMASK environment variable and in Unix API calls. The default permission is 644 (read/write to the owner, read to everyone else) and the default identity is simply the empty string. A mask of 755 adds an executable flag to this, whereas 777 grants read, write, and execution access to all. The <tarfileset> element also supports the prefix element found in <zipfileset>, which lets you place files into the archive in a different directory from their origin. This is a new addition in Ant 1.5; previously you had to create the final structure with <copy> tasks before creating the archive.

One major problem with the tar format is that the original file format does not handle very long path names; there is a hundred-character limit, which is easily exceeded in any Java source tree. However, the GNU implementation of tar does support longer file names. You can tell the <tar> task what to do when it encounters this situation with its longfile attribute, which takes any of the values listed in table 6.3.

Table 6.3   Values for the longfile attribute. Although optional, setting it shows that you have chosen an explicit policy. Of the options, fail, gnu and warn make the most sense.

Longfile value	Meaning
fail	Fail the build
gnu	Save long pathnames in the gnu format
omit	Skip files with long pathnames
truncate	Truncate long pathnames to 100 characters
warn	Save long pathnames in the gnu format, and print a warning message [default]

If you choose to use the GNU format, add a warning note in the documentation about using GNU tar to expand the library. Also, tell whoever deals with support calls about the issue, because not enough people read the documentation.

After making the archive, use the <gzip> task to compress it. This task takes a source file and a destination filename and generates the output file. We place this in the create-tarfile target immediately after we create the tar file, first defining the name of the output as the name of the tar archive with a .gz file ending appended. This is the convention of the gzip process; the standard gunzip program expects this and uses it to determine the name of the unzipped file. First, we add the appropriate properties at the top of the file:

```
<property name="tarfile.gz.name"
  value="${tarfile.name}.gz" />
<property name="tarfile.gz.path"
  location="${dist.dir}/${tarfile.gz.name}"/>
```

Then we append the <gzip> task to the create-tarfile target:

```
<gzip
    src ="${tarfile.path}"
    zipfile="${tarfile.gz.path}"/>
```

The result of this is that whenever Ant creates the tar file, it builds a gzipped copy of the file.

At the time of writing, this task does not perform any dependency checking, which means it always creates the .gz file. Someone really needs to fix this. Maybe by the time you read this document someone may have done so; check the online documentation.

6.6 CREATING WEB APPLICATIONS WITH WAR FILES

As stated earlier WAR files are JAR files with an extended format, a WEB-INF folder containing classes and a `lib` folder containing libraries. A web.xml file in the WEB-INF directory describes the application to the web server; if this file is missing or invalid the WAR file does not contain a web application. Figure 6.4 shows an example WAR file layout.

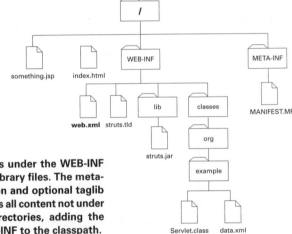

Figure 6.4
A WAR file pushes the class files under the WEB-INF directory, along with imported library files. The metadata includes the web application and optional taglib descriptors. The web server serves all content not under the META-INF and WEB-INF directories, adding the classes and libraries under WEB-INF to the classpath.

Sometimes, and especially when developing under an IDE, it may be useful to actually mimic the same layout in the directory structure of the code under development. Ant does not require this, letting you use a directory structure that is independent of the actual distribution layout. There is still merit in keeping metadata files such as web.xml in the directory under src/WEB-INF, because the <jspc> task to compile JSP pages prefers it.

To generate WAR files in Ant, there are two strategies. The first is to create the WAR folder tree manually, using <copy>, then <jar> the output. The second is to use the <war> task to generate the layout as class, web, and library files are built up. This is simpler, but there is one key advantage of the first approach: if your web server can run from a directory, rather than a web file, then building up the directory by hand

gives you a directory tree to point the server to. If the <war> task is used, the
<unwar> task can create the same effect.

```
<war
  destfile="${dist.dir}/antbook.war"
  webxml="web/WEB-INF/web.xml">
  <classes dir="${build.dir}/classes"/>
  <webinf dir="${struts.dir}/lib" includes="*.tld,*.dtd"/>
  <fileset dir="web" excludes="WEB-INF/web.xml"/>
  <lib dir="${struts.dir}/lib" includes="struts.jar"/>
</war>
```

This looks like a complex task, but it is not really. You specify different fileset elements of content to include in the WAR file, just as for the <zip> and <jar> tasks.
Here you have to declare what they are: library files, classes, WEB-INF files, or simply web content to serve up. The task then places these files in their appropriate places. You could just use the <jar> task and <zipfileset> elements with the prefix attribute to achieve the same effect. Then there would be no need to explicitly include the web.xml file at the start and exclude it later from the web content fileset.
So why use it? It is simpler and stops you having to know so much about the file layouts inside a WAR file.

Because the <war> task is a subclass of the <jar> task, it also supports all of the parent task's attributes and elements. In particular, you can specify the manifest for the archive with the manifest attribute, or create it with the <manifest> element.
You can also sign the <war> file afterwards, for an authenticated binary.

6.7   TESTING PACKAGING

There is no easy automated mechanism for completely testing redistribution packages, short of redistributing them, installing them, and testing the installations.

What you can do is expand the archive into a directory and verify that everything is in place. This is important when tasks such as <war> create a complex archive file from a number of sources, or just when creating a complex tar or Zip file. You can do this by using multiple <available> tests inside a <condition> task and then using <fail> to halt the build if any of the files are missing.

It is also possible to use native tools such as tar and gzip to verify that they can process the data correctly. It is conceivable that Ant tasks somehow create content that cannot be recognized by the native tools. This should not be the case for the JAR file and its derivatives, as they use the same Java packages as the command line tools, but it may be true for the other file formats. A manual check here may be sufficient; an <exec> to expand the files using the native program is an option if you really feel this is an issue. Be cautious when using WinZip and similar graphical tools to view archives; they often prettify the file names by changing the display case, which can cause confusion.

6.8 SUMMARY

Ant provides a multitude of tasks for packaging up your Java code for redistribution. The basic <jar> task generates a JAR archive, with extended tasks <war> and <ear> for special derivatives of the JAR file.

After generating the JAR file, it is usually common to generate a redistribution package to include the archive and any documentation and startup scripts. The <zip> and <tar> tasks are the foundation for this, <tar> being preferred for Unix as you can state the permissions of files and mark executable files as executable.

Before creating the distribution packages, there are often preparation tasks such as setting the line endings on text files to the appropriate form for the target platform, creating the Javadoc documentation, and including data files with the binary. There are tasks in Ant to meet all these needs, including <fixcrlf>, <javadoc>, and <move>, <copy>, and <delete>.

Ant also contains special tasks to create WAR and EAR files, which you can use to create deployment packages for application servers. These are helpful for the server applications, but not essential, as <jar> can do everything that is required.

C H A P T E R   7

Deployment

7.1 Example deployment problems   164
7.2 Tasks for deployment   165
7.3 FTP-based distribution of
     a packaged application   171
7.4 Email-based distribution of
     a packaged application   173

7.5 Local deployment to
     Tomcat 4.x   174
7.6 Remote deployment to
     Tomcat   181
7.7 Testing deployment   187
7.8 Summary   187

Deployment covers the process of getting Java client code out the door. For client code, this usually involves email or uploading to a redistribution site, such as an FTP server. For server code, deployment means getting it actually executed on a server. This is one area where older build tools and applications are weak, and where Ant is relatively strong. This does not mean that Ant makes deployment easy, it merely makes it possible. The more complex your deployment problem, the harder it is to automate.

Many deployment processes are manual, especially on production systems where you have to test on a staging server before deploying over a secure channel to the remote production server. Ant can help with such a process by reducing the number of manual steps, and thus reducing the likelihood of something going wrong after someone leaves a step out or performs two steps in the wrong order. Ant is best, however, at the fully automated deployment, where invoking "ant stack-a" will trigger a rebuild, a rerun of the JUnit test suite, followed by an upload to and restart of the application on a remote web application server.

With such a broad spread of deployment problems, covering how to automate the tasks in Ant will be a long task. We are going to start with a short chapter on basic deployment, covering two use cases of deployment to a web server, and two use cases of redistributing a binary package. We are also going to cover only one server: Jakarta Tomcat, version 4, also known as Catalina. This is the Apache project's own Java web application server. As it is free, robust, and easy to install and use there is almost no reason not to have a copy installed on your system. The only argument against using it for any servlet development project is that to minimize problems, you should always use the same application server in production as development. If you plan to use a different server in production, start with that product from the outset.

7.1 EXAMPLE DEPLOYMENT PROBLEMS

We are going to use four deployment problems as "stories" to explore what Ant can do in deployment terms. All these deployment options are being used in the application we are writing for the book. The great thing about deployment is that there are so many ways to deploy a single project. These include:

- *FTP-based distribution of a packaged application*
  An application has been packaged up into source and binary distributions, with Windows Zip and Unix gzip packages to redistribute. The distribution files are to be uploaded to a remote server such as SourceForge.

- *Email-based distribution of a packaged application*
  The application is to be distributed to multiple recipients by email. Recipients will receive the source distribution in Zip or gzip format. The recipient list will be manually updated, but it must be kept separate from the build file for easy editing.

- *Local deployment to Tomcat*
  Tomcat 4.x is installed into a directory pointed to by CATALINA_HOME. Ant must deploy the web application as a WAR file into CATALINA_HOME /webapps and restart Tomcat or get the site updated by some other means.

- *Remote deployment to Tomcat*
  Tomcat 4.x is installed on a remote server. The build file must deploy the WAR file it creates to this server.

7.1.1 Reviewing the tasks

Looking at these tasks, they represent the two alternate ways of delivering software: redistributing for other people to install and use, or deploying to a server for use as an executing program. Complex projects blur the distinction: people can redistribute a server program, giving the recipient their own server deployment challenges. To keep our examples tractable we will split the two delivery routes cleanly. See figure 7.1.

7.1.2 Tools for deployment

We are going to use Ant to deploy everything, but because we are using optional tasks with dependencies upon external libraries, you need the libraries listed in table 7.1 in your ANT_HOME/lib directory. We list the location to download these libraries in

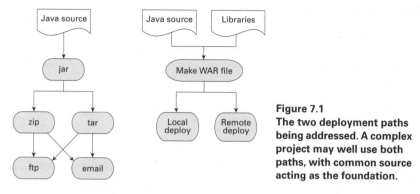

Figure 7.1
The two deployment paths being addressed. A complex project may well use both paths, with common source acting as the foundation.

our installation guide; the online Ant documentation contains live links to the most up-to-date locations.

Table 7.1 Libraries you need for deployment. If you get an error using these tasks, make sure these files are found.

Library	Comment
optional.jar	May have a name such as jakarta-ant-1.4.1-optional.jar
netcomponents.jar	Needed for `<ftp>` and `<telnet>`
activation.jar	Needed for `<mail>`
mail.jar	Needed for `<mail>`

The other tool for deployment is, of course, Tomcat, which you should have installed and running before trying to deploy to it from Ant. For remote deployment, the remote server should support FTP and perhaps Telnet. This is pretty much standard for Unix systems; for Windows systems it is not. Microsoft supplies an FTP server as part of IIS[1]: you can install it from the Add/Remove Windows Components section of the control panel.

An email server is also useful. We are assuming that the local system is running an SMTP server of some kind, but use a property to define the mail server for easy overriding.

7.2   *TASKS FOR DEPLOYMENT*

We have covered the basic deployment tasks already: `<copy>`, `<delete>`, `<java>`. These are the foundation for local server deployment. For remote deployment, we need to introduce a few more tasks.

---

[1] Just be sure to stay on top of Microsoft security bulletins and be aware of all the services your Windows system is running. In a former life, Erik was an NT security "expert" having co-authored award-winning NT security analysis software. Long live NtSpectre!

7.2.1 File transfer with `<ftp>`

If you have a development server's file system mounted on your own machine, such as with NFS or LAN Manager, then you can deploy files to a remote server using `<copy>`. If you cannot do this, then you need to resort to `<ftp>`. The `<ftp>` task is very powerful; it lets you perform the following tasks in a build file:

- Connect to a remote server using a specified username and password.
- Control the port of the server and whether passive mode is used for better firewall pass-through.
- Upload files to a remote server using timestamp-based dependency checking.
- Download files from a remote server using timestamp-based dependency checking.
- Delete remote files.
- Save a listing of a directory to a file.
- Create remote directories.

For deployment, we are only concerned with connecting to a server and uploading changed files. The remaining functionality may be of use in more complex deployment situations, and for automating other parts of the build process, such as fetching updated libraries and data files from a central server.

One important point to note is that for Ant to work with Windows' FTP server, you should configure the server to provide Unix, not MS-DOS, directory listings. If this is not done, then some commands won't work.

7.2.2 Probing for server availability

The `<condition>` task can contain a few tests that probe to see whether remote systems are available.

The `<http>` test can probe for a remote page on a local or remote web server. The test only succeeds if the server responds to the request with an HTTP status code below 400. Missing pages, error code 401, and access-denied pages, error code 403, both fail the test. With the condition we can test for local or remote web servers:

```
<http url="http://127.0.0.1/"/>
<http url="http://127.0.0.1:8080/"/>
<http url="http://eiger:8080/antbook/happy.jsp"/>
<http url="http://jakarta.apache.org/ant/"/>
```

You can use the command to fetch a JSP page, forcing its compilation. Web application containers generate an error code of 500 when the page won't compile, breaking the build.

A sibling test, `<socket>`, probes for a local or remote TCP socket being reachable. This can be used to test for any well-known port being available, including telnet (23), SMTP (25), and HTTP (80, sometimes 8080 and 8088):

CHAPTER 7   DEPLOYMENT

```
<socket port="8080" server="127.0.0.1"/>
<socket port="23"   server="${deployment.server}"/>
<socket port="25"   server="${mail.server}"/>
<socket port="2401" server="${cvs.server}"/>
```

Using these tests in a <condition> statement lets you control actions that could otherwise fail. For example, you could send email if the local mail server is running, or deploy to a server if it was accessible, but skip that part of the build process if it was not reachable. What if you have just restarted a server and want to wait for a service to become available?

There is another task in which the tests can be used, called <waitfor>. Any test, complex or simple, that you can use in <condition>, you can also use in <waitfor>. While <condition> evaluates a test once, then sets a property, <waitfor> evaluates a test repeatedly until it succeeds or the time limit is reached, sleeping between each test. You can specify the maximum wait and sleep times in units ranging from milliseconds to weeks. To an extent, the <waitfor> task represents the fundamental difference between a declarative language and a procedural one. To implement the same behavior as <waitfor> in Java you would have to implement some while() loop, testing for the condition, and having a sleep and a timeout test in the body of the loop. In Ant, you just state the time to loop and the sleep interval and let it choose its own implementation. Listing 7.1 demonstrates using the task to wait for a local server to become available; to probe a remote server simply change the server attribute to a different machine.

Listing 7.1 Waiting for a local web server to appear

```
<target name="wait-for-server">
  <waitfor maxwait="30" maxwaitunit="second"
    timeoutproperty="server.missing">
    <socket port="8080" server="127.0.0.1"/>
  </waitfor>
  <fail if="server.missing">No server found</fail>
</target>
```

The <waitfor> task has five attributes, listed in table 7.2. You can specify how long to wait, how often to poll for changes, and what property to set if the condition timed out. There is no explicit property to set on success: if the condition is successful, the containing target continues executing, perhaps long before the timeout was reached. The timeoutproperty names the property to be set to "true" if timeout occurred; a conditional <fail> task can be set to break the build if probe timed out, or conditional targets can be used to control build actions.

Table 7.2 Attributes for the <waitfor> task. Usually the polling interval of every half a second is adequate, but the maximum wait time needs tuning for the particular problem. Too short and the task fails prematurely, too long and the build takes too long before giving up.

Attribute	Description
timeoutproperty	A property to set if the task times out
maxwait	How long to keep waiting. Defaults to 180000 `maxwaitunits`; usually 180 seconds.
checkevery	How often to check. By default, 500 `checkeveryunits`; effectively twice a second.
maxwaitunit	The time unit used by the `maxwait` attribute, a millisecond by default. One of millisecond, second, minute, hour, day, or week.
checkeveryunit	The time unit used by the `checkevery` attribute, a millisecond by default. This takes the same options as the `maxwaitunit`.

It is tempting to use these network probes as a preamble to performing arbitrary network operations, the aim being to degrade when off line, such as on a notebook or home system with a dial-up connection. Even a DNS lookup can trigger a network connection attempt, and in areas such as Europe or with paid wireless connectivity, this may incur costs of some sort. If you use this test to set a property such as network.unavailable for tasks to use as a condition, then make the probe task conditional on this property not being already set. This enables a notebook or home computer to run the build with the property set from the command line, disabling all network connection attempts.

7.2.3 Inserting pauses into the build with <sleep>

One of this book's authors wrote <sleep> explicitly to deal with a deployment problem. Our team needed to completely delete the directory tree of an expanded WAR file on a server, yet when we tried this with <delete> the files would still be in use. We added the failonerror attribute to the task so that a failed deletion would not break the build, but it did not solve the fundamental problem. A short bit of coding later and we had a sleep task that could wait for thirty seconds before we tried to delete things. Contributing the task back to Ant, it has found many more uses; deployment is where it tends to crop up.

The task has four time attributes: hours, minutes, seconds, and milliseconds. You can specify any or all of them and the total time to sleep is the sum of the values. In fact, you can specify negative values to any of the attributes; provided the total time is positive, this is not an error. A simple sleep for deployment usually only has one time attribute specified:

```
<sleep seconds="15"/>
```

The multiple attribute specification permits more in obscure timeouts:

```
<sleep minutes="5" seconds="-15"/>
```

Such a declaration sleeps for four minutes and forty-five seconds, give or take a few tens of milliseconds, which is a level of precision rarely needed in a build file. You can use <sleep> to delay after starting or stopping a web server before doing other work, although wherever possible we prefer the <waitfor> test. Subtle changes in system configuration can cause a <sleep> to be too short; <waitfor> uses testing to wait for as long as required, which makes it much less brittle.

7.2.4 Ant's email task

Prior to version 1.4, Ant had a <mail> task that could send plain text emails. Ant 1.4 added the <mimemail> task that added MIME and attachment capabilities. Ant 1.5 brings these two tasks together under the <mail> façade. In order to take advantage of the more sophisticated MIME and attachment features, the JavaMail libraries (mail.jar and activation.jar) must be on the classpath or in ANT_HOME/lib. If they are not there, the task falls back to plain text mode. See table 7.3.

Table 7.3 <mail> task attributes

Attribute	Description	Required?
from	Sender	Yes
tolist	Recipient list	Yes
subject	Subject of message	No
message	Text of the email	Yes, unless included elsewhere
mailhost	Mail server host name	No, default to localhost
failonerror	Stops the build if an error occurs sending the email	No, default to true
files	A list of files	Yes, if message is not set
includefilenames	Flag to include the names of included files in the next	No, default to false
mailport	Port number of the server	No, default to 25
messageFile	File to use as the text of the message	No, but a message or attachment is needed somehow
messageMimeType	Mime type to use for message body	No, default to text/plain
cclist	CC: recipient list	No
bcclist	BCC: recipient list	No

It needs an available SMTP server; the default is localhost; this usually works on a Unix system, but not a Windows box. When declaring the task, always specify the mailhost attribute from a property, even if the default is simply localhost, so that other users can override it. Also, unless delivery of the message is central to the build process, set failonerror="false" to keep the build alive if a mail server is not available.

The simplest use of the <mail> task is to send notification messages:

```
<mail
  from="ant@example.org"
  tolist="team@example.org"
  mailhost="${deploy.mail.server}"
  subject="new build ready"
  message="build ${build.version} is on the server"  />
```

You can send binaries by nesting one or more `<fileset>` elements inside. To send HTML text messages, simply state the MIME type of the message body to be `text/html`:

```
<mail
  from="ant@example.org"
  tolist="team@example.org"
  mailhost="${deploy.mail.server}"
  subject="new build test results"
  messageFile="build/tests/junit.html"
  messageMimeType="text/html" />
```

7.2.5 Fetching remote files with <get>

Once Ant has deployed something to a remote web or FTP server, the `<get>` task can be used to retrieve it. This task has very few parameters, as shown in table 7.4.

Table 7.4 The attributes of the `<get>` command. The usetimestamp attribute for dependency based downloads is only valid with HTTP.

Attribute	Description	Required?
src	The source URL	Yes
dest	The local destination file	Yes
verbose	Print a "." every 100KB of download	No, default to `false`
ignoreerrors	Don't fail on errors	No, default to `false`
password	Password	No, unless username is set
username	Username for 'BASIC' http authentication	No, unless password is set
usetimestamp	Download an HTTP file only if it is newer than the local copy	No, default to `false`

Any URL schema the run time supports is valid here, even though the task contains biases towards HTTP. If the Java Secure Socket Extension package is added to the Java run time, the task also supports HTTPS; you must add JSSE by hand for versions of Java prior to version 1.4.

You specify the download destination in the `dest` attribute; you must specify this even if all you want to do is probe for a URL being valid. When using HTTP or HTTPS, you can apply version-based checking to the download by using the `usetimestamp` attribute, so that it sends the `If-Modified-Since` header to the web server. The web server may then reply, stating that the file is unmodified, in which case the task does not download the file again.

The fundamental flaw with the `<get>` task is that it is based on the `java.net` implementation of the HTTP client, a portion of the Java run time that is not only quirky, but the quirks vary from version to version. This means it is impossible to write code that works consistently across all implementations. In the <get> task, these platform differences surface in two places. First, the task will not necessarily detect an incomplete download. Second, if the remote page, say application.jsp, returns an error code, such as 501 and detailed exception information, *that information cannot be read from all versions of Java.* If the task ran on Java 1.2, it may be able to get the information, but not on Java 1.3, and this behavior depends on the value of the file extension of the remote URL. This is sometimes problematic when attempting to test JSP page installation. There are even other quirks of the java.net.HttpURLConnection class that you probably will not encounter when using this task. These issues have stopped the Ant team from releasing a reworked and more powerful HTTP support framework of <httpget>, <httppost>, and <httphead>, pending someone refactoring an existing prototype implementation to use the Jakarta project's own HttpClient library. When it does see the light of day, Ant will be able to POST files and forms, which could be of use in many deployment processes.

7.2.6 Using the tasks to deploy

Having run through the tasks for deployment, and having the repertoire of other tasks, such as <exec> and <java>, plus all the packaging we have just covered in chapter 6, we are ready to sit down and solve those distribution problems. We are presenting the tasks in XP style, each with a story card stating what we need. Where we have diverted from the XP ethos is in testing, as some of these problems are hard to test. We will do the best we can with automated testing, but these tasks force you to check inboxes and the like, to verify complete functionality.

7.3 *FTP*-BASED DISTRIBUTION OF A PACKAGED APPLICATION

An application has been packaged up into source and binary distributions, with Windows Zip and Unix gzip packages to redistribute. The distribution files are to be uploaded to a remote server such as SourceForge.

We created the distribution packages in chapter 6, so they are ready to go. All that we need is the <ftp> task. There is one little detail, however. If you put the password to the server into the build file, everyone who gets a copy of the source can log in to the server. You have to pull the password out into a properties file that you keep private and secure.

SourceForge is such a popular target for deployment that we want to show how to deploy to it. The current process is that you FTP up the distribution, using anonymous FTP, then go to the project web page where a logged-in project administrator can add a new package or release an update to an existing package in the project administration section, under "edit/release packages."

Ant can perform the upload, leaving the web page work to the developers. Listing 7.2 shows the basic upload target.

Listing 7.2   FTP upload to SourceForge

```
<target name="ftp-to-sourceforge"
    depends="create-tarfile,create-src-zipfile">
  <ftp server="upload.sourceforge.net"
    remotedir="incoming"
    userid="ftp"
    password="nobody@"
    depends="true"
    binary="true"
    verbose="true"
    >
  <fileset dir="${dist.dir}"
    includes="${tarfile.gz.name},${srczipfile.name}"
  />
  </ftp>
  <echo>go to
    https://sourceforge.net/projects/YOUR-PROJECT
    and make a new release </echo>
</target>
```

This target depends upon the `create-tarfile` and `create-src-zipfile` targets of chapter 6, so the distribution packages are all ready to go. Following the SourceForge rules, we upload the file to the directory `incoming` on the server `upload.sourceforge.net`. We use the anonymous account `ftp` and a password of nobody@, which SourceForge accepts.

We explicitly state that we want binary upload, with `binary="yes"`; with that as the default we are just being cautious. We do override a default where we ask for dependency checking on the upload, by declaring `depends="true"`. The effect of this is that the task only uploads changed files.

The build file selects files to upload by declaring a simple fileset of two files. The `<ftp>` task can take a complex fileset, such as a tree of directories and files, in which case the task replicates the tree at the destination, creating directories as needed. In such a bulk upload the dependency checking makes deployment significantly faster. After uploading the files, the target prints a message out, telling the user what to do next.

Deploying to any other site is just as simple. For example, the task could upload a tree full of web content served up by a static web server, only uploading changed files and images. Selecting text upload (`binary="false"`) is useful to upload files used in the deployment process or by the server, such as shell scripts to go into a cgi-bin directory.

7.3.1   Asking for information with the <input> task

To allow people to ask for a password, or other user input, there is a little task called `<input>`. This displays a message and asks for a response:

```
<target name="get-input">
  <input
```

```
    message="what is the password for SourceForge?"
    addproperty="sf.password"
    />
  <echo message="sf.password=${sf.password}"/>
</target>
```

We could insert this task in the above, and use the property sf.password in the password attribute of the <ftp> task. However, the password is then visible on the screen, as the user types it:

```
    [input] what is the password for SourceForge?
who knows
     [echo] sf.password=who knows
```

The input task also adds complications in an automated build, or in IDEs. You can specify a class that implements the InputHandler interface, a class that returns the values in a property file, using the request message as the property name to search for. To use this new property handler is complex: you must select the class on the command line with the -inputhandler PropertyFileInputHandler options, and name the file to hold the inputs, as a Java property defined with a -D definition in ANT_OPTS, not as a Java property. In this use case, it's a lot easier to place the password in a private properties file with very tight access controls and omit the <input> task. You may find the task useful in other situations, such as when you use <ant> as a way of running Java programs from the command line.

7.4   *EMAIL-BASED DISTRIBUTION OF A PACKAGED APPLICATION*

The application is to be distributed to multiple recipients as email. Recipients will receive the source distribution in Zip or gzip format. The recipient list will be manually updated, but it must be kept separate from the build file for easy editing.

This is not a hard problem; it is a simple application of the <mail> task with the JavaMail libraries present. Maintaining the recipient list and mapping it to the task could be complex. We shall keep the recipients in a separate file and load them in. We use a property file, in this case one called "recipients.properties":

```
deploy.mail.ziprecipients=steve
deploy.mail.gziprecipients=erik
```

There is a task called <loadfile>, to load an entire file into a single property. This could be a better way of storing the recipient names. If you were mailing to many recipients, having a text file per distribution would be a good idea.

To send the mail, we simply read in the recipient list using the <property file> task to load a list of properties from a file, and then use <mail> to send the two messages, as shown in listing 7.3. This sends the different packages to different distribution lists.

Listing 7.3 Delivering by email

```
<property name="deploy.projectname" value="antbook" />
<property name="deploy.mail.server" value="localhost" />
<property name="deploy.mail.sender"
    value="support-never-reads-this@example.org" />

<target name="deploy-to-mail"
  depends="create-tarfile,create-src-zipfile">
  <property file="recipients.properties" />
  <mail
    from="${deploy.mail.sender}"
    bcclist="${deploy.mail.ziprecipients}"
    mailhost="${deploy.mail.server}"
    subject="new source distribution"
    >
  <fileset dir="${dist.dir}"
    includes="${srczipfile.name}"
   />
  </mail>
  <mail
    from="${deploy.mail.sender}"
    bcclist="${deploy.mail.gziprecipients}"
    mailhost="${deploy.mail.server}"
    subject="new source distribution"
    >
  <fileset dir="${dist.dir}"
    includes="${tarfile.gz.name}"
   />
  </mail>
```

We send the mail using the BCC: field, to prevent others from finding out who else is on the list, and use localhost as a mail server by default. Some of the systems on which we run the build file override this value, as they have a different mail server. This is very common in distributed development; in a single site project you can nominate a single mail server.

The first <mail> task sends the Zip file; the second dispatches the gzip file to the Unix users. We use an invalid sender address in the example: any real user must use a valid sender address, not just to field user queries or delivery failure messages, but also to ensure that any SMTP server that performs address validation through DNS lookup will accept the messages. The domain we used, example.org, is one of the official "can never exist" domains, so will automatically fail such tests.

7.5 LOCAL DEPLOYMENT TO TOMCAT 4.x

Tomcat 4.x is installed into a directory pointed to by CATALINA_HOME. Ant must deploy the web application as a WAR file into CATALINA_HOME/webapps and restart Tomcat or get the site updated in some other means.

Before describing how we can do this, we should observe that it is possible to configure Tomcat to treat a directory tree as a WAR file and to poll for updated JSP and .class pages, dynamically updating a running application. If this works for your project, then Ant can just use <copy> to create the appropriate directory structure and Tomcat will pick up the changes automatically. Be warned, however, that sometimes behavior can be unpredictable when you change parts of the system. A full deployment is cleaner and more reliable, even if it takes slightly longer.

7.5.1   The Tomcat management servlet API

Tomcat 4.x lets you perform a hot update on a running server. That is, without restarting the web server you can remove a running instance of your application and upload a new version, which is ideal for busy servers or simply fast turnaround development cycles. The secret to doing this is to use the web interface that the server provides for local or remote management. This management interface exports a number of commands, all described in the Tomcat documentation. Table 7.5 lists the commands that HTTP clients can issue as GET requests. Most commands take a path as a parameter; this is the path to the web application under the root of the server, not a physical path on the disk. The `install` command also takes a URL to content, which is of major importance to us.

Table 7.5   The Tomcat deployment commands, which are all password-protected endpoints under the manager servlet. Enabling this feature on a production system is somewhat dangerous, even if convenient.

Command	Function	Parameters
install	Install an application	Path to application and URL to WAR file contents
list	List all running applications	N/A
reload	Reload an application from disk	Path to application
remove	Stop and unload an application	Path to application
sessions	Provide session information	Path to application
start	Start an application	Path to application
stop	Stop an application	Path to application

To use these commands, you must first create a Tomcat user with administration rights. Do this by adding a user entry in the file CATALINA_HOME/conf/tomcat-users.xml with the role of manager.

```
<tomcat-users>
  <user name="admin" password="password" roles="manager" />
  ...
</tomcat-users>
```

The same user name and password will be used in <get> tasks to access the pages, so if you change these values, as would seem prudent, the build file or the property files it uses will need changing. After saving the users file and restarting the server, a simple test of it running is to have a task to list running applications and print them out:

```
<target name="list-catalina-apps">
 <get src="http://localhost:8080/manager/list"
   dest="status.txt"
   username="admin"
   password="password" />
 <loadfile property="catalina.applist" srcFile="status.txt"/>
 <echo>${catalina.applist}</echo>
</target>
```

This target saves the list of running applications to a file, and then loads this file to a property, which <echo> can then display. There is a <concat> task that combines the latter two actions; our approach of loading it into a property gives us the option of adding a <condition> test to look for the word OK in the response, to verify the request. We have not exercised this option, but it is there if we need to debug deployment more thoroughly.

The output when the server is running should look something like:

```
list-catalina-apps:
      [get] Getting: http://localhost:8080/manager/list
      [echo] OK - Listed applications for virtual host localhost
/examples:running:0
/webdav:running:0
/tomcat-docs:running:0
/manager:running:0
/:running:0
```

If a significantly different message appears, something is wrong. If the build fails with a java.net.ConnectException error, then no web server is running at that port. Other failures, such as a FileNotFoundException, are likely due to username and password being incorrect, or it may not be Catalina running on that port. Restart the server, then try fetching the same URL with a web browser to see what is wrong with the port or authentication settings.

7.5.2 Deploying to Tomcat with Ant

To deploy to Tomcat, Ant checks that the server is running, and then issues a command to the server to force it to load a web application. The first step in this process is to set the CATALINA_HOME environment variable to the location of the tool; this has to be done by hand after installing the server. The Ant build file will use the environment variable to determine where to copy files. Ant uses this to verify that the server is installed; we use a <fail unless> test to enforce this. Making the targets conditional on the env.CATALINA_HOME property would create a more flexible build file.

To deploy locally you need to provide two things. The first is the path to the application you want; we are using "/antbook" for our web application. The second piece of information is more complex: a URL to the WAR file containing the web application, and which is accessible to the server application.

If the WAR file is expanded into a directory tree, you can supply the name of this directory with a "file:" URL, and it will be treated as a single WAR file. Clearly, this file path must be visible to the management servlet, which is trivial on a local system, but harder for remote deployment, as we must copy the files over or use a shared file system.

The alternative URL style is to pass in the name of a single WAR file using the "jar:" URL schema. This is a cascading schema that must be followed by a real URL to the WAR file, and contain an exclamation mark to indicate where in this path the WAR file ends and the path inside it begins. The resultant URL would look something like `jar:http://stelvio:8080/redist/antbook.war!/`, which could be readily included in a complete deployment request:

```
http://remote-server:8080/manager/install?
            path=/antbook&
            war=jar:http://stelvio:8080/redist/antbook.war!/
```

With this mechanism, you could serve the WAR file from your local web server, then point remote servers at the file for a live remote deployment, with no need to worry about how the files are copied over; all the low-level work is done for you. This would make it easy to update remote systems without needing login access, only an account on the web server with management rights.

Unfortunately, we found out it does not work properly. To be precise, on the version of Tomcat we were using (Tomcat 4.02), the deployment worked once, but then the server needed to be restarted before the WAR file can be updated. The server needs to clean out its cached and expanded copy of the WAR file when told to `remove` an application. It did not do this, and the second time Ant sent an `install` request, it discovered the local copy and ran with that. It is exactly this kind of deployment subtlety that developers need to look out for. It works the first time, but then you change your code, the build runs happily, and nothing has changed at the server.[2]

Given that we cannot upload a WAR file in one go to the server, we need to resort to the "point the server at an expanded archive in the file system" alternative, of which the first step is to create an expanded WAR file. This could be done by following up the `<war>` task with an `<unzip>` task, thereby handing off path layout work to the built in task. We are going to eschew that approach and create the complete directory tree using `<copy>`, and then `<zip>` it up afterwards, if a WAR file is needed for other deployment targets. This approach requires more thinking, but has two benefits. First, it makes it easy to see what is being included in the WAR file, which aids testing. Second, it is faster. The war/unzip pair of tasks has to create the Zip file and then expand it, whereas the copy/zip combination only requires one Zip stage, and the copy process can all be driven off file timestamps, keeping work to a minimum. The larger the WAR file, in particular the more JAR files included in it, the more the speed difference of the two approaches becomes apparent.

---

[2] Later versions apparently fix this. We are sticking with our approach as it works better for remote deployment.

Our original target to create the WAR file was eleven lines long:

```
<war destfile="${warfile}"
  webxml="web/WEB-INF/web.xml">
  <classes dir="${build.classes.dir}"/>
  <webinf dir="${build.dir}" includes="index/**"/>
  <webinf dir="${struts.dir}/lib" includes="*.tld,*.dtd"/>
  <fileset dir="web" excludes="WEB-INF/web.xml"/>
  <fileset dir="${build.dir}" includes="${buildinfo.filename}"/>
  <lib dir="${struts.dir}/lib" includes="*.jar"/>
  <lib dir="${lucene.dir}" includes="${lucene.map}.jar"/>
  <lib dir="${build.dir}" includes="antbook-common.jar"/>
</war>
```

The roll-your-own equivalent is more than double this length, being built out of five
<copy> tasks, each for a different destination in the archive, a manifest creation, and
finally the zip-up of the tree:

```
<property name="warfile.asdir"
  location="${dist.dir}/antbook" />

<target name="makewar"
    depends="compile,webdocs">

  <copy todir="${warfile.asdir}/WEB-INF/classes"
      preservelastmodified="true" >
    <fileset dir="${build.classes.dir}"/>
    <fileset dir="${struts.dir}/lib" includes="*.tld,*.dtd"/>
  </copy>

  <copy todir="${warfile.asdir}/WEB-INF/lib"
      preservelastmodified="true" >
    <fileset dir="${struts.dir}/lib" includes="*.jar"/>
    <fileset dir="${lucene.dir}" includes="${lucene.map}.jar"/>
    <fileset dir="${build.dir}" includes="antbook-common.jar"/>
  </copy>

  <copy todir="${warfile.asdir}/WEB-INF"
      preservelastmodified="true" >
    <fileset dir="${build.dir}" includes="index/**"/>
    <fileset dir="${struts.dir}/lib" includes="*.tld,*.dtd"/>
  </copy>

  <copy todir="${warfile.asdir}" preservelastmodified="true" >
    <fileset dir="web"/>
  </copy>

  <mkdir dir="${warfile.asdir}/META-INF"/>
  <manifest file="${warfile.asdir}/META-INF/MANIFEST.MF"/>
  <zip destfile="${warfile}">
   <fileset dir="${warfile.asdir}"/>
  </zip>
</target>
```

None of the `<copy>` task declarations are particularly complex, but they do add up. With the WAR file now available as a directory, all we need to do to deploy to the server is:

- Unload any existing version of the application.
- Point the application at the new one.

Once Tomcat has installed the application, it should keep an eye on the file time-stamps and reload things if they change, but we prefer to restart applications for a more rigorous process. A clean restart is, well, cleaner. We could actually issue the `reload` command to the management servlet and have the reload done, but we are choosing to not differentiate between the "application not installed" and "application already installed" states, and always force the installation of our application. This keeps the build file simpler.

First, a few up-front definitions are needed, such as the name of the web application, the port the server is running on, and the logon details:

```
<property name="webapp.name" value="antbook"/>
<property name="catalina.port" value="8080" />
<property name="catalina.username" value="admin" />
<property name="catalina.password" value="password" />
```

We should really keep the passwords outside the build file; we certainly will for more sensitive boxes. The `remove-local-catalina` target uninstalls the existing copy by sending the application path to the management servlet:

```
<target name="remove-local-catalina">
  <fail unless="env.CATALINA_HOME"
    message="Tomcat 4 not found" />

  <property name="deploy.local.remove.url" value=
    "http://localhost:${catalina.port}/manager/remove"     <─── The removal
    />                                                            command

  <get
    src="${deploy.local.remove.url}?path=/${webapp.name}"  <─── The complete
    dest="deploy-local-remove.txt"                               URL to get
    username="admin"
    password="password" />

  <loadfile property="deploy.local.remove.result"
    srcFile="deploy-local-remove.txt"/>
  <echo>${deploy.local.remove.result}</echo>
</target>
```

Running this target produces the message that Tomcat removed the application, after which a new installation succeeds:

```
remove-local-catalina:
     [get] Getting: http://localhost:8080/manager/remove?path=/antbook
     [echo] OK - Removed application at context path /antbook
```

Calling the target twice in a row reveals that a second call generates a FAIL message, but as Ant does not interpret the response, the build continues. Only if the local server is not running, or the username or password is incorrect, does the <get> request break the build. This means that the deployment target can depend on removing the web application without a <condition> test to see if the web application is actually there and hence in need of removal.

Once the old version is unloaded, it is time to install the new application. We do this with a target that calls management servlet's "install" URL:

```
<target name="deploy-local-catalina"
  depends="makewar,remove-local-catalina" >
  <property name="deploy.local.urlpath"
   value="file:///${ warfile.asdir}/" />

  <property name="deploy.local.url.params" value=
    "path=/${webapp.name}&amp;war=${deploy.local.urlpath}"
    />

  <property name="deploy.local.url" value=
    "http://localhost:${catalina.port}/manager/install"
    />

  <get src="${deploy.local.url}?${deploy.local.url.params}"
    dest="deploy-local.txt"
    username="${catalina.username}"
    password="${catalina.password}" />

  <loadfile property="deploy.local.result"
    srcFile="deploy-local.txt"/>
  <echo>${deploy.local.result}</echo>
</target>
```

Because of its predecessors, invoking this target will create the WAR file image and remove any existing application instance, before installing the new version:

```
makewar:
     [copy] Copying 1 file to C:\AntBook\app\webapp\dist\antbook
      [zip] Building zip: C:\AntBook\app\webapp\dist\antbook.war

remove-local-catalina:
      [get] Getting: http://localhost:8080/manager/remove?
              path=/antbook
     [echo] FAIL - No context exists for path /antbook

deploy-local-catalina:
      [get] Getting: http://localhost:8080/manager/install?
              path=/antbook
              &war=file:///C:\AntBook\app\webapp\dist\antbook/
     [echo] OK - Installed application at context path /antbook

BUILD SUCCESSFUL
```

In three targets, we have live deployment to a local Tomcat server. This allows us to check this deployment problem off as complete.

7.6 REMOTE DEPLOYMENT TO TOMCAT

Tomcat 4.x is installed on a remote server. The build file must deploy the WAR file it creates to this server.

This is simply an extension of the previous problem. If you can deploy locally, then you can deploy remotely; all you need is a bit of remote access. The management interface of Tomcat works remotely, so the only extra work is the file copy to the server. This can be done with `<ftp>`, or by using `<copy>` if the client can mount the remote server's disk drive. Using FTP, the expanded WAR file can be copied up in one task declaration:

```
<target name="ftp-warfile"
    depends="makewar" if="ftp.login" >          ◁—— This target depends
  <ftp server="${target.server}"                     upon makewar
    remotedir="${ftp.remotedir}"
    userid="${ftp.login}"
    password="${ftp.password}"
    depends="true"
    binary="true"
    verbose="true"
    ignoreNoncriticalErrors="true"
    >
    <fileset dir="${warfile.asdir}" />          ◁—— Upload the
  </ftp>                                              expanded
</target>                                             WAR file
```

This target needs a login account and password on the server, which must be kept out the build file. We will store it in a property file and fetch it in on demand. The `<ftp>` task has set the `ignoreNonCriticalErrors` to avoid warnings that the destination directory already exists; the standard Linux FTP server, wu-ftpd, has a habit of doing this. The flag tells the task to ignore all error responses received when creating a directory, on the basis that if something really has gone wrong, the following file uploads will break. Note that we have made the `<ftp>` task conditional on a login being defined; this lets us bypass the target on a local deployment.

Once `<ftp>` has uploaded the files, the build file needs to repeat the two steps of removing and installing the application. This time we have refactored the targets to define common URLs as properties, producing the code in listing 7.4.

Listing 7.4 The targets to deploy to a remote Tomcat server

```
<target name="build-remote-urls" >
  <property name="target.port" value="8080" />
  <property name="target.base.url"                      Define the base
    value="http://${target.server}:${target.port}" />  URL properties
  <property name="target.manager.url"
    value="${target.base.url}/manager" />
```

```
  </target>

  <target name="remove-remote-app" depends="build-remote-urls">
    <property name="status.file"
      location="deploy-${target.server}.txt" />
    <get
      src="${target.manager.url}/remove?path=/${webapp.name}"
      dest="${status.file}"                                        Remove the
      username="${target.username}"                                old copy
      password="${target.password}" />
    <loadfile property="deploy.result" srcFile="${status.file}"/>
    <echo>${deploy.result}</echo>
  </target>

  <target name="deploy-remote-server"
      depends="build-remote-urls,remove-remote-app,ftp-warfile">
    <property name="redist.url"                                    Create a URL to
      value="file://${target.directory}" />                       the uploaded files
    <property name="target.url.params"
      value="path=/${target.appname}&amp;war=${redist.url}" />
    <get
      src="${target.manager.url}/install?${target.url.params}"
      dest="deploy-remote-install.txt"                             Install the
      username="${target.username}"                                application
      password="${target.password}"
      />
    <loadfile property="deploy.remote.result"
      srcFile="deploy-remote-install.txt"/>
    <echo>${deploy.remote.result}</echo>
  </target>
```

The most significant change is that all the targets use properties; there is no hard coding of machine names or other details in the targets. These properties have to be set in a properties file or passed in on the command line. The deployment task also needs to know the absolute directory into which FTP-uploaded files go, as seen by the web server. Usually it is a subdirectory of the account used to upload the files.

The targets to deploy to the remote server are all in place. All that remains is to execute them with the appropriate properties predefined. We are going to do this, but we plan to deploy to more than one server and do not want to cut and paste targets, or invoke Ant with different command line properties. Instead, we want a single build run to be able to deploy to multiple destinations, all using the same basic targets. This means we need to be able to reuse the targets with different parameters, a bit like calling a subroutine. We need <antcall>.

7.6.1 Interlude: calling targets with <antcall>

The <antcall> task is somewhat controversial: excessive use of this task usually means someone has not fully understood how Ant works. As long as you use it with restraint, it is a powerful task. The task lets you call any target in the build file, with any property settings you choose. This makes it equivalent to a subroutine call, except that instead of passing parameters as arguments, you have to define "well known properties" instead. Furthermore, any properties that the called target sets will not be remembered when the call completes.

A better way to view the behavior of <antcall> is as if you are actually starting a new version of Ant, setting the target and some properties on the command line. When you use this as a model of the task's behavior, it makes more sense that when you call a target, *its dependent targets are also called.* This fact causes confusion when people try to control their entire build with <antcall>. Although it is nominally possible to do this with high-level tasks which invoke the build, test, package, and deploy targets, this is the wrong way to use Ant. Usually, declaring target dependencies and leaving the run time to sort out the target execution order is the best thing to do. Our deployment task in listing 7.5 is the exception to this practice. This target can deploy to multiple remote servers, simply by invoking it with <antcall> with the appropriate property settings for that destination. That is why we left out any target dependencies: to avoid extra work when a build deploys to a sequence of targets.

To illustrate the behavior, let's use a project containing a target that prints out some properties potentially defined by its predecessors, do-echo:

```
<project name="antcall" default="do-echo">
  <target name="init">
    <property name="arg3" value="original arg3" />
  </target>

  <target name="do-echo" depends="init">
   <echo>${arg1} -- ${arg2} -- ${arg3}</echo>
  </target>
</project>
```

When you call the do-echo target directly, the output should be predictable:

```
init:
do-echo:
     [echo] ${arg1} -- ${arg2} -- original arg3
```

Now let's add a new target, which invokes the target via <antcall>:

```
<target name="call-echo" depends="init">
  <property name="arg1" value="original arg1" />
  <property name="arg2" value="original arg2" />
  <echo>calling...</echo>
  <antcall target="do-echo">
   <param name="arg1" value="overridden"/>
  </antcall>
  <echo>...returned</echo>
</target>
```

This target defines some properties and then calls the do-echo target with one of the parameters overridden. The <param> element inside the <antcall> target is a direct equivalent of the <property> task: all named parameters become properties in the called target's context, and all methods of assigning properties in that method (value, file, available, resource, location, and refid) can be used. In this declaration, we have used the simple, value-based assignment.

The output of running Ant against that target is:

```
init:
call-echo:
     [echo] calling...
init:
do-echo:
     [echo] overridden -- original arg2 -- original arg3
     [echo] ...returned
```

The first point to notice is that the init target has been called twice, once because call-echo depended upon it, the second time because do-echo depended upon it; the second time both init and call-echo were called, it was in the context of the <antcall>. The second point to notice is that now the previously undefined properties, arg1 and arg2, have been set. The arg1 parameter was set by the <param> element inside the <antcall> declaration; the arg2 parameter was inherited from the current context. The final observation is that the final trace message in the call-echo target only appears after the echo call has finished. Ant has executed the entire dependency graph of the do-echo target as a subbuild within the new context of the defined properties.

The task has one mandatory attribute, target, which names the target to call, and two optional Boolean attributes, inheritall and inheritrefs. The inheritall flag controls whether the task passes all existing properties down to the invoke target, which is the default behavior. If the attribute is set to "false", only those defined in the task declaration are passed down. To demonstrate this, we add another calling target:

```
<target name="call-echo2" depends="init">
  <property name="arg1" value="original arg1" />
  <property name="arg2" value="original arg2" />
  <echo>calling...</echo>
  <antcall target="do-echo"
      inheritall="false">
   <param name="arg1" value="newarg1"/>
  </antcall>
  <echo>...returned</echo>
</target>
```

When you execute this target the log showed that do-echo did not know the definition of arg2, as it was not passed down:

```
[echo] newarg1 -- ${arg2} -- original arg3
```

Note that arg3 is still defined, because the second invocation of the init target will have set it; all dependent tasks are executed in an <antcall>. Effectively, arg3 has been redefined to the same value it held before.

Regardless of the inheritance flag setting, Ant always passes down any properties explicitly set on the command line. This ensures that anything manually overridden on the command line stays overridden, regardless of how you invoke a target. Take, for example, the command line

```
ant -f antcall.xml call-echo2 -Darg2=predefined -Darg1=defined
```

This results in an output message of

```
[echo] defined  -- predefined -- original arg3
```

This clearly demonstrates that any properties defined on the command line override anything set in the program, no matter how hard the program tries to avoid it. This is actually very useful when you do want to control a complex build process from the command line.

You can also pass references down to the invoked target. If you set `inheritrefs="true"`, all existing references are defined in the new "context". You can create new references from existing ones by including a `<reference>` element in the `<antcall>` declaration, stating the name of a new reference to be created using the value of an existing path or other reference:

```
<reference refid="compile.classpath" torefid="execution.classpath" />
```

This is useful if the invoked target needs to use some path or patternset as one of its customizable parameters.

Now that we have revealed how to rearrange the order and context of target execution, we want to state that you should avoid getting into the habit of using `<antcall>` everywhere, which some Ant beginners do. The Ant run time makes good decisions about the order in which to execute tasks; a target containing nothing but a list of `<antcall>` tasks is a poor substitute.

7.6.2 Using <antcall> in deployment

Our first invocation of the deployment target will be to deploy to our local machine, using the remote deployment target. This acts as a stand-alone test of the deployment target, and if it works, it eliminates the need to have a separate target for remote deployment. It relies on the fact that Ant bypasses the FTP target if the property `ftp.login` is undefined; instead of uploading the files, we simply set the `target.directory` property to the location of the expanded WAR file:

```
<target name="deploy-localhost-remotely"
    depends="dist">
  <antcall target="deploy-and-verify">
    <param name="target.server" value="127.0.0.1"/>
    <param name="target.appname" value="antbook"/>
    <param name="target.username" value="admin"/>
    <param name="target.password" value="password"/>
    <param name="target.directory" value="${warfile.asdir}"/>
  </antcall>
</target>
```

Running this target deploys to the server, uninstalling the old application and uploading a new version, building the WAR package in the process. This enables us to remove the targets written only to deploy to the local server. The same build file target can be used for remote and local deployment.

To justify that claim we need to demonstrate remote deployment. First, we create a properties file called deploy.eiger.properties which contains the sensitive deployment information:

```
target.server=eiger
target.appname=antbook
target.username=admin
target.password=password
ftp.login=tomcat
ftp.password=.oO00Oo.
ftp.remotedir=warfile
target.directory=/home/tomcat/warfile
```

We do not add this to the SCM system, and we alter its file permissions to be readable only by the owner. We now want a target to load the named file into a set of properties and deploy to the named server. We do this through the `<property file>` technique, this time to a `<param>` element inside the `<antcall>`:

```
<target name="deploy-to-eiger">
  <antcall target="deploy-remote-server">
    <param file="deploy.eiger.properties" />
  </antcall>
</target>
```

That is all we need. A run of this target shows a long trace finishing in the lines:

```
    [get] Getting: http://eiger:8080/manager/install?
                    path=/antbook&war=file:///home/tomcat/warfile
    [echo] OK - Installed application at context path /antbook
BUILD SUCCESSFUL
Total time: 28 seconds
```

That is it: twenty-eight seconds to build and deploy. Admittedly, we had just built and deployed to the local system, but we do now have an automated deployment process. As a finale, we write a target to deploy to both servers one after the other:

```
<target name="deploy-all"
  depends="deploy-localhost-remotely,deploy-to-eiger" />
```

This target does work, but it demonstrates the trouble with `<antcall>`: dependency re-execution. All the predecessors of the deployment targets to make the WAR file are called again, even though there is nothing new to compile. With good dependency checking this is not necessarily a major delay; our combined build time is thirty-eight seconds, which is fast enough for a rapid edit-and-deploy cycle.

7.7 TESTING DEPLOYMENT

How can you verify that the deployment process worked?

If you are redistributing the files by email or FTP, then all you can do is verify that files that come through the appropriate download mechanism can be unzipped and then used. Ant does let you fetch the file with `<get>`; it can expand the downloaded files with the appropriate tasks or with the native applications. For rigorous testing, the latter are better, even if they are harder to work with.

A build file can test Web server content more automatically, and more rigorously, by probing pages written specifically to act as deployment tests. A simple `<get>` call will fetch a page; a `<waitfor>` test can spin for a number of seconds until the server finally becomes available.

We want to cover this process in detail, as deployment can be unreliable, and a good test target to follow the deployment target can reduce a lot of confusion. However, we don't want to cover the gory details in this chapter, as it would put everyone off using Ant to deploy their code. Rest assured, however, that in chapter 18, when we get into the techniques and problems of production deployment, we will show you how to verify that the version of the code you just built is the version the users see.

7.8 SUMMARY

Deployment is the follow-on step of packaging an application for redistribution. It may be as simple as uploading the file to an FTP site or emailing it to a mailing list. It may be as complex as updating a remote web server while it is running. Ant can address all such deployment problems, and more advanced ones. The `<get>` task can fetch content after deployment, but for a web server with a web-based management interface, you can use it for deployment itself. The Tomcat 4 web server is well suited to this deployment mechanism.

The key to successful deployment, in our experience, is to keep the process simple and to include automated tests for successful deployment. Another success factor is to use the same targets for local and remote deployment, on the basis that it simplifies debugging of the deployment process, and reduces engineering overhead: only one target needs maintenance. The `<antcall>` task lets you call targets with different properties predefined, which is exactly what you need for reusable targets within the same build file.

One of the other best practices in deployment is to make the targets conditional on any probes you can make for the presence of a server. It is very easy to forget that a build file deploys to two server types until someone else tries to run the build and it does not work for them. The `<condition>` task lets you probe for server availability, while the `<waitfor>` task lets the build spin until a condition is met. This can be used when waiting for a server to start, for it to stop, or to see if a web server exists at that location at all.

This chapter is not our last word in Ant deployment. Chapter 18 is dedicated to the subject. We also have a chapter on web applications (chapter 12), where we explore running functional tests against a newly deployed application.

C H A P T E R   8

Putting it all together

8.1 Our application thus far 188
8.2 Building the custom Ant task library 189
8.3 Loading common properties across multiple projects 194

8.4 Handling versioned dependencies 196
8.5 Build file philosophy 200
8.6 Summary 201

In the previous chapters, we introduced the basic concepts and tasks of Ant. You should now be able to create build files to accomplish many of the most common build-related tasks. What we have not shown you is a single build file that incorporates these.

It is easier to explain concepts piece by piece, yet it is difficult to get the full scope and rationale for each element of the build process when you only see it in little fragments. This chapter provides a higher-level view of our sample application's build process, glossing over the details that we have already presented, and introducing new some new concepts. We have not covered all of the techniques shown in the sample build files; these will be noted with references to later chapters.

8.1   OUR APPLICATION THUS FAR

Our application consists of a custom Ant task that indexes documents at build time, uses a command-line tool to search an existing index, and contains an interface to allow searching the index and retrieving the results through a web application. In order to maximize reusability of our components and minimize the coupling between them, we split each into its own stand-alone build. Note:

- The custom Ant task to build a Lucene index (IndexTask) is useful in many projects and its only dependencies are the Lucene and JTidy libraries.

188

- A common component that hides the Lucene API details is used in both the command-line search tool and the web application.
- The command-line search tool only relies on the shared common component and is used to demonstrate running a Java application from Ant.
- The web application has the same dependencies as the command-line search tool, as well as the Struts web framework.

In an effort to demonstrate as much of Ant's capabilities as possible within the context of our documentation search engine application's build process, we have used a number of techniques and tasks that may be overkill or unnecessary in your particular situation. Ant often provides more than one way to accomplish things, and it is our job to describe these ways and the pros/cons.

8.2 BUILDING THE CUSTOM ANT TASK LIBRARY

Without further ado, let's jump right into listing 8.1, which is the build file for our custom Ant task library.

Listing 8.1 Build.xml for our custom Ant task library

```xml
<?xml version="1.0"?>
<!DOCTYPE project [                                              Declare include
    <!ENTITY properties SYSTEM "file:../properties.xml">                files
    <!ENTITY tests_uptodate SYSTEM "file:../tests_uptodate.xml">
    <!ENTITY taskdef SYSTEM "file:../taskdef.xml">
    <!ENTITY targets SYSTEM "file:../targets.xml">
]>
<project name="AntBook - Custom Ant Tasks" default="default">

  <description>
    Custom Ant task to index text and HTML documents
  </description>

  <!-- import external XML fragments -->
  &properties;                              Include project-
  &taskdef;                                 wide pieces
  &targets;

    <!-- For XDoclet usage -->
  <property name="template.dir" location="templates"/>
  <property name="taskdef.template"                    XDoclet
          location="${template.dir}/taskdef.xdt"/>    properties
  <property name="taskdef.properties" value="taskdef.properties"/>

  <!-- ========================================================= -->
  <!-- Datatype declarations                                     -->
  <!-- ========================================================= -->
  <path id="compile.classpath">
    <pathelement location="${lucene.jar}"/>    Define compile
    <pathelement location="${jtidy.jar}"/>     path
  </path>
```

```xml
<path id="test.classpath">
  <path refid="compile.classpath"/>
  <pathelement location="${junit.jar}"/>
  <pathelement location="${build.classes.dir}"/>
  <pathelement location="${test.classes.dir}"/>
</path>
```

Nest compile path in test path

```xml
<!-- ========================================================= -->
<!-- Public targets                                            -->
<!-- ========================================================= -->

<target name="default" depends="dist"
  description="default: build verything" />
<target name="all" depends="test,dist"
  description="build and test everything"/>
<target name="test" depends="run-tests"
  description="run tests" />
<target name="docs" depends="javadocs"
  description="generate documentation" />

<target name="clean"
        description="Deletes all previous build artifacts">
  <delete dir="${build.dir}"/>
  <delete dir="${build.classes.dir}"/>
  <delete dir="${dist.dir}"/>

  <delete dir="${test.dir}"/>
  <delete dir="${test.classes.dir}"/>
  <delete dir="${test.data.dir}"/>
  <delete dir="${test.reports.dir}"/>
</target>
```

Remove build artifacts

```xml
<target name="dist" depends="taskdef,compile"
        description="Create JAR">
  <jar destfile="${antbook-ant.jar}"
       basedir="${build.classes.dir}"/>
</target>
```

Build JAR

```xml
<!-- ========================================================= -->
<!-- Private targets                                           -->
<!-- ========================================================= -->

<target name="release-settings" if="release.build">
  <property name="build.debuglevel" value="lines"/>
</target>

<!-- compile the java sources using the compilation classpath -->
<target name="compile" depends="init,release-settings">
  <property name="build.optimize" value="false"/>
  <property name="build.debuglevel" value="lines,vars,source"/>
  <echo>debug level=${build.debuglevel}</echo>
  <javac destdir="${build.classes.dir}"
         debug="${build.debug}"
         includeAntRuntime="yes"
         srcdir="${src.dir}">
    <classpath refid="compile.classpath"/>
    <include name="**/*.java"/>
```

⟵ **Atypical—our code uses Ant's API**

```
    </javac>
  </target>

  <target name="javadocs" depends="compile"          <—— Generate API docs
<mkdir dir="${javadoc.dir}"/>
    <javadoc author="true"
             destdir="${javadoc.dir}"
             packagenames="org.example.antbook.*"
             sourcepath="${src.dir}"
             use="true"
             version="true"
             windowtitle="ant book task"
             private="true"
             >
      <classpath refid="compile.classpath"/>
    </javadoc>
  </target>


  <target name="test-compile" depends="compile"
          unless="tests.uptodate">
    <javac destdir="${test.classes.dir}"
           debug="${build.debug}"                       Compile
           includeAntRuntime="yes"                       test code
           srcdir="${test.src.dir}">
      <classpath refid="test.classpath"/>
    </javac>
                                                              Copy
    <!-- copy resources to be in classpath -->            resources
    <copy todir="${test.classes.dir}">                         ❶
      <fileset dir="${test.src.dir}" excludes="**/*.java"/>
    </copy>
  </target>


  <target name="run-tests" depends="test-compile"       <—— TEST!
          unless="tests.uptodate">
    <junit printsummary="no"
           errorProperty="test.failed"
           failureProperty="test.failed"
           fork="${junit.fork}">
      <classpath refid="test.classpath"/>                 Pass params to
                                                            test cases
      <sysproperty key="docs.dir" value="${test.classes.dir}"/>
      <sysproperty key="index.dir" value="${test.dir}/index"/>

      <formatter type="xml"/>
      <formatter type="brief" usefile="false"/>

      <test name="${testcase}" if="testcase"/>
      <batchtest todir="${test.data.dir}" unless="testcase">
        <fileset dir="${test.classes.dir}"
                 includes="**/*Test.class"/>              Run single test
      </batchtest>                                        technique
    </junit>
```

```
  <junitreport todir="${test.data.dir}">
    <fileset dir="${test.data.dir}">
      <include name="TEST-*.xml"/>
    </fileset>
    <report format="frames" todir="${test.reports.dir}"/>
  </junitreport>
```
Generate test reports

```
  <!-- create temporary file indicating these tests failed -->
  <echo message="last build failed tests"
        file="${test.last.failed.file}"/>
  <fail if="test.failed">
    Unit tests failed.  Check log or reports for details
  </fail>
```
Last tests failed check trick

```
  <!-- Remove test failed file, as these tests succeeded -->
  <delete file="${test.last.failed.file}"/>
</target>

<target name="todo" depends="init">
  <mkdir dir="${build.dir}/todo"/>
  <document sourcepath="${src.dir}"
            destdir="${build.dir}/todo"
            classpathref="xdoclet.classpath">
    <fileset dir="${src.dir}">
      <include name="**/*.java" />
    </fileset>
    <info header="Todo list"
          tag="todo"/>
  </document>
</target>
```
❷ Generate to-do list from source

```
<target name="taskdef" depends="init" unless="taskdef.uptodate">
  <echo message="Building taskdef descriptors"/>
  <property name="xdoclet.classpath.value"
    refid="xdoclet.classpath"/>
  <xdoclet sourcepath="${src.dir}"
            destdir="${build.classes.dir}"
            classpathref="xdoclet.classpath">
    <fileset dir="${src.dir}">
      <include name="**/*.java" />
    </fileset>
    <template templateFile="${taskdef.template}"
              destinationfile="${taskdef.properties}">
      <configParam name="date" value="${DSTAMP} @ ${TSTAMP}"/>
    </template>
  </xdoclet>
</target>
```
❸ Generate descriptor from source

```
<target name="init">
  <echo message="Building ${ant.project.name}"/>
  <tstamp/>

  <!-- create directories used for building -->
```

```
    <mkdir dir="${build.dir}"/>
    <mkdir dir="${build.classes.dir}"/>
    <mkdir dir="${dist.dir}"/>

    <!-- create directories used for testing -->
    <mkdir dir="${test.dir}"/>
    <mkdir dir="${test.classes.dir}"/>
    <mkdir dir="${test.data.dir}"/>
    <mkdir dir="${test.reports.dir}"/>

    <!-- Include common test bypass check condition -->
    &tests_uptodate;

    <!-- Check taskdef.properties dependency to speed up build -->
    <uptodate property="taskdef.uptodate"
              targetfile="${build.classes.dir}/${taskdef.properties}">
      <srcfiles dir="${src.dir}" includes="**/*.java"/>
      <srcfiles dir="${template.dir}" includes="taskdef.xdt"/>
    </uptodate>
  </target>

</project>
```

④ **Create directories**

Some items in listing 8.1 deserve explanation in greater detail. At the beginning of the build file we take advantage of XML entity references to share build file fragments with other build files. Entity reference includes are covered in more detail in chapter 9.

All temporary build directories are deleted, even if they default to being physically under one another. We cannot assume that this default configuration is always the case. A user could override test.reports.dir, for example, to generate test reports to a different directory tree, perhaps under an intranet site.

❶ Copying of non-.java files from the source tree to the compiled class directory is a common practice. Often property files or other metadata files live alongside source code. In our case, we have test cases that need known test data files. We keep them tightly coupled with our JUnit test case source code.

❷, ❸ XDoclet is used to generate a to-do list from @todo Javadoc comments and to dynamically construct a descriptor file making our custom tasks easier to integrate into build files. We cover these techniques in chapter 11.

❹ For the same reason we delete all temporary directories explicitly in our "clean" target, we create them individually here.

8.3 LOADING COMMON PROPERTIES ACROSS MULTIPLE PROJECTS ⟍

Our project consists of multiple components, as shown in listing 8.2.

Listing 8.2   Properties.xml—an include file that all subcomponent build files use

```xml
<property environment="env"/>     <---- Load environment variables as properties

<property name="env.COMPUTERNAME" value="${env.HOSTNAME}"/>   <------

<!-- ========================================================= -->        Cross-
<!-- Load property files                               -->                platform
<!--   Note: the ordering is VERY important.           -->                machine
<!-- ========================================================= -->        name
<property name="user.properties.file"                     Allow user      trick
        location="${user.home}/.build.properties"/>      properties to
                                                         be relocated
<!-- Load the application specific settings -->
<property file="build.properties"/>

<!-- Load user specific settings -->
<property file="${user.properties.file}"/>     <---- Load user properties


<!-- ========================================================= -->
<!-- Directory mappings                                -->
<!-- ========================================================= -->
<property name="root.dir" location="${basedir}"/>
<property name="masterbuild.dir" location="${root.dir}/.."/>

<property file="${masterbuild.dir}/build.properties"/>    <---- Application-wide
                                                                properties
<property name="src.dir" location="${root.dir}/src"/>

<property name="build.dir" location="build"/>
<property name="build.classes.dir"
  location="${build.dir}/classes"/>
<property name="dist.dir" location="dist"/>
<property name="dist.bin.dir" location="${dist.dir}/bin"/>
<property name="doc.dir" location="doc"/>
<property name="javadoc.dir" location="${doc.dir}/javadoc"/>
property name="lib.dir" location="${masterbuild.dir}/lib"/>


<!-- ========================================================= -->
<!-- Compile settings                                  -->
<!-- ========================================================= -->
<property name="build.debug" value="on"/>              Default compile settings
<property name="build.optimize" value="off"/>


<!-- ========================================================= -->
<!-- Test settings                                     -->
<!-- ========================================================= -->
```

```
<property name="test.dir" location="${build.dir}/test"/>
<property name="test.classes.dir" location="${test.dir}/classes"/>
<property name="test.data.dir" location="${test.dir}/data"/>
<property name="test.reports.dir" location="${test.dir}/reports"/>
<property name="test.src.dir" location="${root.dir}/test"/>
<property name="test.last.failed.file"
  location="${build.dir}/.lasttestsfailed"/>


<!-- ============================================================ -->
<!-- Library dependency settings                                  -->
<!-- ============================================================ -->
<property name="lib.properties.file"
  location="${lib.dir}/lib.properties"/>          Library mappings section

<!-- lib.properties.file contains .version props -->
<property file="${lib.properties.file}"/>

<!-- library directory mappings -->
<!-- . . . others omitted -->
<property name="lucene.dir"
  location="${lib.dir}/lucene-${lucene.version}"/>    Library .dir mappings
<property name="struts.dir"
  location="${lib.dir}/jakarta-struts-${struts.version}"/>

<!-- each library has its own unique directory structure -->
<!-- . . . others omitted -->
<property name="lucene.subdir" value=""/>    <——— Library .subdir mappings
<property name="struts.subdir" value="lib"/>

<!-- JAR file mappings -->
<!-- . . . others omitted -->
<property name="lucene.dist.dir"
  location="${lucene.dir}/${lucene.subdir}"/>    Library .dist.dir mappings

<property name="lucene.jarname"
  value="lucene-${lucene.version}.jar"/>

<property name="lucene.jar"
  location="${lucene.dist.dir}/${lucene.jarname}"/>    .jar mappings

<property name="struts.dist.dir"
  location="${struts.dir}/${struts.subdir}"/>
<property name="struts.jar"
  location="${struts.dist.dir}/struts.jar"/>
<!-- ============================================================ -->
<!-- index info                                                   -->
<!-- ============================================================ -->
<property name="index.dir"
  location="${masterbuild.dir}/index/build/index"/>

<property name="docstoindex.dir" value="${ant.home}/docs"/>

<fileset dir="${docstoindex.dir}" id="indexed.files"/>
```

```
<!-- ============================================================ -->
<!-- generated output                                             -->
<!-- ============================================================ -->
<property name="antbook-ant.dist.dir"
  location="${masterbuild.dir}/ant/dist/"/>

<property name="antbook-ant.jar"
  location="${antbook-ant.dist.dir}/antbook-ant.jar"/>

<property name="antbook-common.dist.dir"
  location="${masterbuild.dir}/common/dist/"/>

<property name="antbook-common.jar"
  location="${antbook-common.dist.dir}/antbook-common.jar"/>

<property name="antbook-webapp.name"
  value="antbook.war" />
<property name="antbook-webapp.dist.dir"
  location="${masterbuild.dir}/webapp/dist/"/>
<property name="antbook-webapp.war"
  location="${antbook-webapp.dist.dir}/${antbook-webapp.name}"/>

<property name="warfile"
  location="${antbook-webapp.war}" />

<property name="war.expanded.dir"
  location="${masterbuild.dir}/webapp/build/war" />
```

8.4 HANDLING VERSIONED DEPENDENCIES

The many Ant properties shown in listing 8.2 that are used to handle our library dependency mappings is arguably overkill for our needs, but it illustrates the power of Ant's property mechanisms quite well. We do not necessarily recommend this particular scheme for your project, but certainly a subset of this type of mapping indirection will add greater adaptability to your build process.

The whole purpose of the build file is to let individual build files refer to a library by a short name, such as ${struts.jar}, provide a single place where these libraries are named, and provide a way for subprojects to override the supplied library versions on a case-by-case basis. It certainly seems easier just to place all the JAR files in a single lib directory, but this does not scale to large projects. Using an indirection mechanism gives you the control that large projects need. Figure 8.1 shows our library directory structure.

There are some important goals for our library layout and Ant property mappings:

- Make it easy to introduce a new version of a library alongside an existing one.

- Give a single place to upgrade the system as a whole to a new version.

- Let different users, projects, and builds override the default version.

- Allow ability to override on a per-user, per-project, or per-build level.

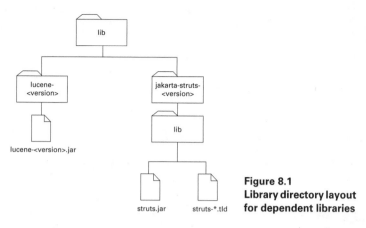

**Figure 8.1
Library directory layout
for dependent libraries**

Our properties.xml file, by default, points to a lib/lib.properties file, the location of which users can override. This properties file contains simply the version number (or label) of all of our dependencies. A snapshot of our file contains:

```
checkstyle.version = 2.1
j2ee.version       = 1.3
jtidy.version      = 04aug2000r7-dev
log4j.version      = 1.1.3
lucene.version     = 1.2-rc3
struts.version     = 20011223
xdoclet.version    = dev
xalan.version      = 2.2
hsqldb.version     = 1.61
torque.version     = 3.0-dev
httpunit.version   = 1.4
axis.version       = beta-2
```

Not only does this give an example to fit into our discussion about dependency property mappings, it is also illustrative of the versions of software that we used for our project, many of which put us on the bleeding edge.[1]

Figure 8.2 shows how the version number property works in conjunction with the directory property mappings.

We minimize the effort to install a new version of, say, Lucene, by placing full distributions into our lib directory, in their normal directory structure. Figure 8.2 shows the standard distribution directory structures of both Lucene and Struts. They differ; we account for this with our .subdir property. Table 8.1 describes each of these propeties.

With these properties, build files do not need to know the directory structure of a library distribution. This defends our projects against products which change packaging from version to version: we can just change a property or two and everything works again.

---

[1] And we in fact did bleed profusely! We really tried to only use released versions of libraries, but in several cases, we found bugs, fixed them, and sent patches back to the appropriate developer communities.

Table 8.1 The different properties used to reference a library. The path to the JAR file, here ${struts.jar}, is the most important, though we use the distribution directory when we create the WAR file.

Property	Description
struts.version	Version label. By default, it is defined in lib.properties.
struts.dir	Top-level directory to the specified version of Struts.
struts.subdir	The name of the subdirectory (no path included, just the name) where the libraries are stored. This value may be blank if the libraries are in the top-level directory, as in the case of Lucene.
struts.dist.dir	The complete path to the directory containing the Struts libraries.
struts.jar	Mapping to the full path of the actual JAR file.

8.4.1 Installing a new library version

All that work and indirection for what benefit? What if we want to upgrade to a new version of Struts or Lucene? It's easy! We simply drop the new version of a product into a new subdirectory of lib, named with the new library version number, and then change the version label in our lib.properties—that's it. The next time the build runs, it pulls the version number from the properties file, and binds to the new version. It's that simple, but it is also only one of the numerous ways we can control our dependencies. There are a number of different scenarios that illustrate the flexibility we've added.

Switching versions on a per-component basis

Each component in our application may have its own build.properties file, and the order in which it is loaded allows for it to take precedence over user and application-wide properties. The idea is that if a project has overridden something, it has done so for a very good reason and it should be one of the higher priority places to pick up such settings. For example, one of our components could specify an exception to the project suite's standard library versions by specifying a new version it its build.properties file (figure 8.2).

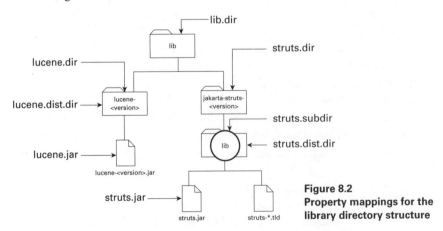

Figure 8.2 Property mappings for the library directory structure

```
lucene.version = 1.2
```

For maximum flexibility, any of the properties shown in table 8.1 could be overridden, though that is rarely, if ever, needed.

Allowing user-specific overrides

In our property loading hierarchy, user-specific properties are loaded after the component-specific properties, allowing per-user overrides for settings that are not hardcoded for a component. The user.home property is supplied by the JVM system properties, which Ant automatically provides, and refers to the current users operating system defined home directory. The properties file we load from the users home directory is named .build.properties, with the preceding dot (.) used to hide the file on Unix systems so the home directory doesn't look cluttered with preference files strewn about. If a user wanted to make sure their builds used a special version of a library, their ${user.home}/.build.properties file could say:

```
lucene.jar = c:/lucene-special/lucene.jar
```

It's important to note that in the case of a dependency like Struts, there is more to it than its single JAR file. While overriding the struts.jar property could be handy, care must be taken because our web application build file not only uses the struts.jar property, it uses struts.dist.dir to get at other pieces such as tag library descriptor (TLD) files. In order to override the full directory of a Struts installation, you should really set struts.dir; the other properties will be adjusted accordingly by default.

Controlling properties for a single build

As we discussed in chapter 3, a property takes on the first value that sets it, and is immutable from then on. The first possible place that a property can be set is from the command line. Why would we want to do such a thing? Suppose the Lucene team releases a new version of Lucene. Before upgrading our source code repository to rely on the new version, potentially breaking everyone's builds, we want to ensure that our code compiles, and our tests run successfully.

We would install the new library in a directory of our choosing, probably under our standard lib directory using its unique version-labeled directory. From the command line we run:

```
ant test -Dlucene.version=1.2
```

If we had not installed the new version under our lib directory, we could instead override lucene.dir, or even lucene.jar.

Using a different set of dependencies

This is by far on the extreme edge of use cases, but with the property mappings we have created, it is possible even to point lib.dir at a different directory altogether. This would have the effect of shifting all dependencies to that directory tree, unless otherwise individually overridden. The main idea to take away from these examples is that by making logically organized hierarchical properties that are constructed from one another, entire directory trees can be redirected easily.

8.5   BUILD FILE PHILOSOPHY

There are several key ideas that we want to convey with our build file examples:

- Begin with the end in mind.
- Integrate tests with the build.
- Support automated deployment.
- Make it portable.
- Allow for customizations.

We achieve each of these by using features such as properties, datatypes, and target dependencies.

8.5.1   Begin with the end in mind

Your build file exists to build something. Start with that end result and work backwards as you write your targets. The goal of our Ant task build file is to build a distributable JAR library that we can use in other build files. We started with the dist target of listing 8.1 and created its dependent targets such as compile. We want the JAR to contain a dynamically built taskdef.properties file, so we also depend on a target that creates it using XDoclet.

8.5.2   Integrate tests with the build

We cannot overemphasize the importance of integrated and automated testing. By putting testing into your build processes early, developers can write and execute tests without having to worry about the mechanics of how to run them. The easier you make testing, the more tests get written, and the more tests get run. The result is that your project will be of higher quality.

8.5.3   Support automated deployment

Automating deployment early in the project is as important as being test-centric. By ensuring your code goes from source to deployment server at all stages of the project you can rest easy that on the delivery date, your project will deploy successfully. Why wouldn't it? With continuous deployment, you have been deploying your application since you wrote the first line of code.

8.5.4   Make it portable

We're writing Java code, and as such we want to make sure our code and builds work in other environments from the start. Ant runs on many platforms, but be wary of using tasks, such as <exec>, that can prevent your build files from running on other platforms. Not only is it a good idea to make sure your builds work cross-platform, it is probably a good idea for you to make sure your tests and deployments work well in other environments. Portability can also mean that your code deploys successfully on multiple application servers. With a little up-front attention to portability, there will be fewer headaches when you need to migrate from, say, WebSphere to JBoss.

8.5.5 Allow for customizations

We've shown how Ant properties allow for user, project, and per-build overrides for settings. You can use build files to allow them to adapt well to their environment. Basing parameters on environment variables is another way to ensure build files work well when moved from machine to machine. For example, by basing its deployment location off the CATALINA_HOME environment variable, our deployment targets deploy to Tomcat, wherever it lives.

Per-user customizations give developers build-specific options. For example, a developer may want to deploy the application locally with full debugging enabled; a production build from the same source and same build file should disable it. You can accomplish this by taking advantage of Ant properties, understanding their rules, and always loading in user-specific properties files at the start of every build.

8.6 SUMMARY

This chapter demonstrated a full build file in our project and described many of its details. Our build file uses some shared pieces that all build files in our project use. The shared definitions of our properties give all our build files consistency and maintainability that we could not have achieved through cut-and-paste editing.

The library dependency mappings used in our project give us several benefits, thanks to Ant's property mechanisms. We can easily upgrade a library by simply installing a distribution and changing the version number in a common properties file. We can have one component in our project depend on a different version of a library than the others, if necessary. We can run a single build and test cycle using a new library version to smoke test our project, without forcing an upgrade for everyone until we know it works acceptably well.

Finally, we'd like to congratulate the reader on reaching the end of the first part of this book. You are now equipped with the knowledge and tools necessary to build sophisticated, production-quality build files. While there certainly are more tools and techniques available, they all rely upon the fundamentals covered thus far. In the next section of this book we will apply Ant and the techniques we have covered to a number of common development situations, such as code generation, Enterprise JavaBeans, web development, XML manipulation, web services, and much more.

PART 2

Applying Ant

Once you have a good understanding of Ant's fundamentals, you will want to start applying Ant in enterprise development situations. Typical uses include web application development, XML processing, and Enterprise JavaBeans. In chapters 9 through 18, we show you how to use Ant in such projects, along with other areas such as web services and native code. We also explore how to use Ant in larger projects, addressing migration, continuous integration mechanisms, and the challenge of deploying to production servers.

C H A P T E R 9

Using Ant in your development projects

9.1   Designing an Ant-based
      build process   206
9.2   Migrating to Ant   209
9.3   The ten steps of migration   210
9.4   Master builds: managing
      large projects   212
9.5   Managing child project builds   221

9.6   Creating reusable library
      build files   228
9.7   Looking ahead: large project
      support evolution   230
9.8   Ant project best practices   231
9.9   Summary   233

The first part of this book introduced Ant, showing you how to use Ant to compile, test, run, package, and deploy a Java project.

Now it's time to apply this basic technical knowledge: you need to integrate an Ant-based build process with your software process. This integration needs a bit of care to work properly; if you introduce or implement Ant badly then your build process will be slower and more complex than you need, and may not take advantage of all the facilities that Ant has to offer.

This chapter is going to show you how to use Ant effectively: how to migrate to it, ways to use it with an IDE, what makes a good build file, and what to do when things don't work. We will also cover how to use Ant in a large project that has multiple build files. It is important to know how to do this, as it keeps the project manageable. Finally, we will introduce some of the best practices for Ant build files.

Let's start with the fundamentals: how to design a build file from scratch.

9.1 DESIGNING AN ANT-BASED BUILD PROCESS

As we have already shown, Ant can do much more than just compile Java programs; it can create archive files, test them, deploy them, and even run them. It can act as the means to automate your entire build process. This is only possible if your build process is structured to work with Ant. By build process we mean the mechanics of compiling and delivering the project, not the full software development process, which is a methodology for how the people in the team work. Ant does not dictate what software process you use, but it does have preferences about the build process. It likes a build process that has been thought out in advance and coded into the build file in a way that lets all team members work from the same build file.

9.1.1 Analyzing your project

When you start with a new build file, you have complete control as to what it will do. Where should you begin? Look at what the project has to deliver, and think about how Ant can help you do that.

Determine your deliverables

The type of application you are writing determines what the deliverables are and how you deploy or deliver these outputs. Table 9.1 shows the basic outputs and deployment routes for common Java project types. A complex project may have more than one deliverable, such as a client applet and a web application; you should have separate projects for each of these components.

Table 9.1 Common application types, their deliverables, and deployment routes. The worst-case project combines everything. Ant should be able to create all the deliverables, and address most of the deployment.

Application Type	Deliverables	Deployment
Client application	JAR, Zip, tar; PDF and HTML documentation	Upload to web site; email; Web Start served installation
Applet	JAR, documentation	Upload to web server
Web application	WAR; code+JSP; SQL data	Deploy to web server; reload server
Enterprise application	EAR file containing EJB and WAR files, SQL data	Deploy to application server

Let's use a client application as an example. It will consist of code with a Swing GUI. We will include some HTML documentation, and deploy the program as a Web Start application.

Determine the build stages

Once you have deliverables, you can list the stages needed to make them and dependencies between them. These become your targets. Start with the common targets such as build, test, and deploy, and work backwards to the steps needed to achieve these goals. Each major step in the build should have its own target, for individual testing and use. You should also create targets in a way that minimizes duplication. For example, there should be only one target to make a JAR file of all the code; the tasks to make the WAR and EAR files can simply depend upon this.

Deployment should be in separate targets from the deliverables, as you can have many different deployment routes. It is also nice to be able to reuse deployment targets in multiple projects. We will show you how to reuse build files later in this chapter.

For our example client application, the main targets would be: all, test, dist, deploy, and clean. We will have internal targets compile, archive, doc, and init, with more to come when needed.

Plan your tests

If you plan to have Ant perform unit tests or other validation of the code, now is a good time to pick a mechanism to execute the tests, and write them. We will introduce more testing technologies, such as HttpUnit and Cactus, in chapter 12.

For our hypothetical client application, we have the challenge of testing a Swing GUI. A good split between model and view lets us test the model with normal JUnit tests, leaving only the view as a problem. One of the side exercises in the project will be to browse to junit.org and explore the current options for testing Swing applications. With luck, we should be able to perform the core GUI tests from a <junit> call.

Outline a package hierarchy

You need to have a Java package hierarchy defined so that directories can begin and coding can take place. These are the packages into which you place your Java source by declaring this fact in the with package statements, such as this one for our client application:

```
package com.example.coolapp.view;
```

Ant requires Java source to be stored in a directory tree matching the package hierarchy, here com/example/coolapp/view/. Dependency checking relies on this, and Sun's javac compiler also prefers this layout.

We like having separate packages between the model, the view, and the controller code for any implementation of the Model-View-Controller pattern, as it prevents cross-contamination of the view into the model. For EJB designs we keep the beans in their own tree, split into entity and session beans.

You need to place JUnit tests into the same package as the classes they test if you want to access package-scoped methods. The test classes should all adhere to a standard naming pattern, so that a wildcard such as **/*Test.class can include them in <junit>, and can exclude them from any distribution tasks. In our client application, we would have the layout illustrated in figure 9.1.

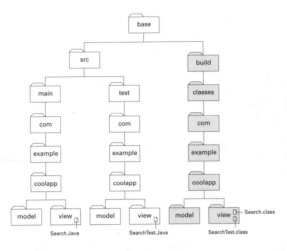

Figure 9.1
How to lay out classes in a large project. You can split the test and the main source into separate trees; a distribution build only compiles the main tree, a test build compiles both. All end up together, giving test classes access to methods scoped at the package access level. Core concepts, here "model" and "view," can be given their own package to emphasize the split between them.

9.1.2 Creating the core build file

With the basic design of the build in place, you can now create the build file for the project, perhaps by taking a standard base build file and customizing it to your project. If no such file exists, start by coding the basic set of targets needed to get yourself and any colleagues building and testing code; other targets can follow as the need arises.

You can create the core build file before there is any code to compile, test, or deploy; all the targets and tasks should just chain together without doing much work. Ant will create the output directories and build a JAR file containing nothing but a manifest.

Having some code, even a stub class and stub test case, provides a better test of the build, as it will use all the tasks which depend upon it, such as `<javac>` and `<junit>`. Ant will make calls to tools such as the compiler and the JUnit library, which will fail if these tools are missing. If they are found, the generated JAR file should then contain the class files in the appropriate place, while a source Zip file should include the stub classes and the build file.

At this point, you have the foundation for your project: check it in, share with others, and start coding.

9.1.3 Evolve the build file

Nobody in the team should be afraid of looking at the build file and adding new targets, be they for deliverables, deployment options, or new intermediate steps in the build process. As they do so, they should try to keep the build file concise yet readable, a few short pages intended to tell readers how to build the project. The practice to beware of is cut-and-paste task reuse; this leads to maintenance problems in build processes as much as it does with source code. Correct use of dependencies is one solution. The other is the `<antcall>` method we covered in chapter 7, section 7.8.1, which lets you reuse targets with a different set of properties defined.

One challenge is deciding what to do when Ant does not directly support your project. Start by looking in the Ant documentation: there are so many tasks, you may find what you want. For our client application, we want to create a Java Web Start installer, so we need to learn how to do that and find out how to do it from Ant. We can't find anything in the documentation, but the External Tools and Tasks page on Ant's web site (http://jakarta.apache.org/ant/external.html) has a pointer to an external project, Vamp, which not only contains the Ant tasks we need, it has the documentation. Extension tasks like these make a complex build possible.

9.2 MIGRATING TO ANT

Migrating an existing project is harder than starting from scratch, as existing projects already have deliverables; JAR and Zip files, test reports, and deployment processes that need to be reimplemented in an Ant-based build. There are also the inevitable time pressure and fear of breaking something. This all makes people reluctant to change an existing process, even if it is hard work to use and extend. In fact, the more ugly and complex the build process is, the more scared people are of "fixing" it. This fear is unfounded: the uglier and more complex the build process is, the more it needs Ant.

We have found that it usually doesn't take that long to move an existing project to Ant: that is, for a build file to compile, run, and archive an application. Extending that build file with tests and deployment does take effort, but that can be an ongoing project.

One particularly troublesome migration was a complex project, comprising eight teams of four to ten engineers, spread across two continents, each with their own sub-project. We used Ant to unify the build, providing an integrated build where none existed before and duplicating everyone's existing projects to run the unified build alongside their original build process. When the ease and benefits of being able to rebuild everyone's code in one go became obvious, the teams eventually began to adopt Ant themselves.[1]

If there were one suggestion we would make about migration, it would be "do it after a deadline." There is almost always some slack time after a milestone to write a build file, or perhaps you can suggest an interim postmortem to see if any aspects of the project could be improved. Most likely, any project would benefit from more tests, automated testing, and automated deployment, so suggest Ant as the means of controlling these tasks.

Next, we are going to look at the basic process for migrating from an IDE or Make to Ant.

---

[1] Some remnants of this effort are the "Ant in Anger" paper (Loughran 2000-2), and the Perl script to start Ant.

9.3 THE TEN STEPS OF MIGRATION

Migrating to Ant is mostly a matter of following a fairly simple and straightforward process. The ten steps of migration are listed in table 9.2.

Table 9.2 Steps to migrate an existing project to Ant

Migration step	Purpose
1. Check in	Check everything in for safety, and tag it with a BEFORE_ANT label.
2. Clean up	Clean out the old .class files to prevent confusion; copy the old JAR files somewhere for safety. There should be no generated files in the project at this point.
3. Determine the deliverables	From examining your existing build tool, make a list of your project outputs and the stages in creating them; build a list of Ant targets and dependencies from this.
4. Define directories	Define your directory structure and the property names used to refer to these different directories.
5. Design the build file	Make an initial design of your build file, or reuse an existing one.
6. Arrange the source	If you need to place the source into new directories, do so now.
7. Implement the build file	Create the build file that you have defined, or customize one you are reusing.
8. Run a verbose build	Run the build, verify that it is working with the -verbose flag.
9. Add some tests	Start writing tests if there were none already.
10. Evolve the build file	Add more targets as you need them.

Migration is slightly trickier than starting with a new project because the existing build process probably works. You need to bring the Ant build up quickly to an equivalent standard, without disrupting anyone else working on the project. You may also need to rearrange the source files and other directories; this makes the migration obvious to the rest of the team, and is the biggest single source of disruption.

If the project is a simple IDE or makefile one, creating a JAR or two, you can consider the migration complete when the same files can be created with Ant. The rest of the Ant development—tests, new deployment targets, and new deliverables—are build file evolution, which are common in all Ant projects.

During the life of the project, you should rarely need to edit the build file to include new source files, documents, or unit tests; they should all be accommodated automatically. If you do need to keep editing the build file for such changes, then something is wrong with your task declarations—usually file path patterns. The only reasons for build file maintenance should be new deliverables, new processing steps, and refactorings to clean up the process, such as moving all hard-coded paths and filenames into properties for easier overriding. Such refactoring is when a working build is most likely to break; as with source, tests help verify that the changes worked. Testing after every little change is the key to a successful build file refactoring.

9.3.1 Migrating from Make-based projects

A Make-based project is usually implemented as a tree of makefiles, one per directory, recursively calling subdirectories to perform the full build. Usually you can replace all makefiles in a stand-alone project by a single build file at the top of the source tree whose build and clean targets invoke the implementations in the subprojects. You can usually derive the targets and deliverables of the Ant file by looking at the targets of the makefile: these name the entry points and list the outputs.

Makefile builds often create the .class files in the same directory as the Java source, which the Ant task should not duplicate, even though it is possible to recreate this effect. Instead, the intermediate and final files should go into separate build and dist directories.

In a large project, with many subprojects, the migration gets harder. Replacing the entire build process in one go is probably too ambitious and dangerous to succeed and, in a multiteam project, not always feasible. Here you can migrate the subprojects one by one. You do not even need to change the master makefile until you are finally ready to replace Make completely. Instead, have the subsidiary makefiles hand off their work to Ant, with a makefile that redirects Make targets to Ant targets:

```
ANT=ant.sh
ANT_COMMANDS=-emacs

all:
        $(ANT) $(ANT_COMMANDS) all

clean:
        $(ANT) $(ANT_COMMANDS) clean
```

All this wrapper file does is pass each target in the makefile down to our nominated Ant wrapper script, setting any options we want to have (here, emacs-style output). The great thing about this tactic is it nominally adheres with a "Make everywhere" build policy: it uses Make everywhere and just hands off parts of the build process to a helper application called Ant. In chapter 17, we shall go the other way, handing off native code generation to make from Ant.

IMPORTANT   The Windows ant.bat file does *not* set the error code when a build fails, because nobody has been able to do this consistently across all supported versions of Windows. Use the Perl version, runant.pl, instead.

9.3.2 Migrating from IDE-based projects

Although Ant provides much more than a traditional IDE does in terms of automating building, testing, and deployment, migrating from an IDE to Ant is difficult for two reasons. First, it is hard to see the complete build process in an IDE at a glance; you need to delve into all the settings dialogs to enumerate the build stages. Secondly, a good IDE integrates coding, compilation, and debugging so well that developers may see little incentive to change their tools. To move to Ant, you need to demonstrate to developers that it is worthwhile, which means showing that Ant can do more than just compile the source.

One of the best ways to migrate to Ant is to find the Ant plug-in for your IDE listed on the Ant web site. You can then stay in the IDE, although unless the plug-in can create a build file from your project's configuration settings, you still have to manually create the build file.

If you want to stay with an IDE that is not Ant aware, invoke Ant from inside it by running the command via some sort of macro. You need to have the IDE parse the Ant error messages so that you can go to a line of source by clicking on the relevant error message: Ant's -emacs option generates output that most development environments can handle.

One danger in working with an IDE ignorant of Ant is that it will have its own means of compiling files. This can cause confusion if the two tools are compiling source files into different places, or with different build options. We can suggest no solutions here, other than to change the key bindings so that the normal "build" keystroke invokes Ant with your preferred target, be it dist or test. The other is to configure Ant and the IDE to compile into different places, but this makes it harder to use the IDE as a debugger.

9.4 MASTER BUILDS: MANAGING LARGE PROJECTS

Large projects create their own problems. There is more to do, they are more visible, so failure and delays are often less acceptable, there are more people on the team, and the integration issues are worse. A small project could have one product, such as a JAR file, and its documentation. A large project could have client-side and server-side components, native library add-ins, and a database somewhere. These all need to be built, tested, and deployed together. If the build process is inadequate, the effort of managing the build can spiral out of control.

Can Ant manage the build for a big project? Yes. It may be great for small to medium projects, but it also scales up to work with large ones. Like any software scaling exercise, scaling up does not come automatically: you need to plan. You also need the other foundational tools of a large project that we will assume you have in place: source control, defect tracking, and perhaps even a change control process.

Our ongoing example project is slowly becoming a large project. It has some core libraries, an Ant task, and a web application, and we are about to write an EJB component. This is a broad mix of deliverables, but we still want to be able to run a single build file to bring it all up to date.

9.4.1 Refactoring build files

The standard solution to size in any software project is to break it into smaller, more manageable child projects, each with their own set of deliverables. For our example application, penciling in some future subprojects gives us a number of child projects, as shown in table 9.3.

Table 9.3 Subprojects within our example project. The EJB project is still on the list of things to do.

Child project	Deliverables
Common	Common libraries
Tools	Utility classes
Ant	Ant task <index>
Index	Ant documentation index
Webapp	Web application
EJB	EJB classes and EAR file

Some of these projects depend upon other projects just as in a build file, targets can depend upon other targets. It would be nice to be able to declare in a master build how these Ant projects were interdependent, so that this tool could then build the projects in the appropriate order. Ant does not integrate subprojects so seamlessly, but it does make it possible to write a master build file that can call the subprojects in the order that the file's authors specify, with significant control over these invoked builds. The key to this is the <ant> task.

9.4.2 Introducing the <ant> task

We covered the <antcall> task in chapter 7. As you may recall, it lets you call a target inside the current build file with a different set of properties. The <ant> task is almost identical except that it also allows you to specify the build file that contains the target. This enables you to divide your build file into subprojects; one for each of the child projects of the actual software project. It also enables you to write library build files. These are build files that contain reusable targets to perform standard actions, such as incrementing a build counter or deploying to a web server.

The basic functionality of the <ant> task is simple: you use it to call any target in any other build file, passing in properties and references if you desire. When you call a target with it, you implicitly invoke any other target in the build file that the invoked target depends upon.

9.4.3 Example: a basic master build file

With all our projects laid out under a single main directory (app), we can create a basic master build file that calls the targets. Listing 9.1 shows a master build file that will build five subprojects. ·

Listing 9.1 A simple master build file to build five subprojects

```
<?xml version="1.0"?>
<project name="Master Build" default="all">
  <target name="all"  description="Build everything">
    <ant dir="ant"    inheritAll="false"/>
    <ant dir="common" inheritAll="false"/>
    <ant dir="tools"  inheritAll="false"/>
```

```
      <ant dir="index"  inheritAll="false"/>
      <ant dir="webapp" inheritAll="false"/>
  </target>
</project>
```

This build file contains one target that lists the order in which to build the sub-projects. We ordered the targets to ensure that all predecessor targets are built before those that depend upon them. We could have placed the dependencies inside the sub-projects themselves, so that calling the webapp project would cause it to build its direct dependents, tools and index, from a predecessors target:

```
<project name="webapp" default="all">
  <target name="all"  depends="predecessors,dist"/>

  <target name="predecessors" />
    <ant dir="../tools" inheritAll="false"/>
    <ant dir="../index" inheritAll="false"/>
  </target>
```

But we rejected this approach for a two reasons:

- *It couples projects too tightly.*
  A subproject does not need to know where the components it needs came from, only that they are available. Sometimes you need to run a project against archived versions of its dependent components; hard coding the steps for generating the predecessor in the build file prevents this. Keeping the dependency rules inside the master build makes it easier to change them, to split subprojects, or change their order.

- *It makes development builds faster.*
  As an example, if you are working on the webapp project, you don't want to run the tools or index build files every time you run your own build file. The other projects have not changed, so there is no need to rebuild them

Examining the master build

With our master build file written, and run with -verbose for detailed output, we can see what the master build is doing. When in verbose mode, the <ant> task names the build files and targets it is invoking, using [default] when it is calling the default entry point for that file:

```
[ant] calling target [default] in build file
        C:\AntBook\app\ant\build.xml
            . . .
[ant] calling target [default] in build file
        C:\AntBook\app\common\build.xml
            . . .
[ant] calling target [default] in build file
        C:\AntBook\app\tools\build.xml
            . . .
```

CHAPTER 9 USING ANT IN YOUR DEVELOPMENT PROJECTS

```
[ant] calling target [default] in build file
        C:\AntBook\app\index\build.xml
    ...
[ant] calling target [default] in build file
        C:\AntBook\app\webapp\build.xml
    ...
BUILD SUCCESSFUL
Total time: 1 minute 7 seconds
```

Just over a minute is a long time for an incremental build. The cause of the delays turns out to be that two build files are creating the index. Such duplication becomes obvious when you create a master build. We can fix this, but there are some other· changes to make first.

Enhancing the build files

We'd like to add some validation to the subproject build files, to verify that the files they need are present. We can do this by adding a `validate` target to each build file which will use a series of `<available>` tests to probe for needed files and classes.

Another enhancement is more fundamental: we want to call different targets from the master build file, such as a global target `clean`. The quick and dirty solution would be to cut-and-paste our `all` target into the `clean` target:

```
<target name="clean"  description="Clean everything">
  <ant dir="ant"    inheritAll="false" target="clean"/>
  <ant dir="common" inheritAll="false" target="clean"/>
  <ant dir="tools"  inheritAll="false" target="clean"/>
  <ant dir="index"  inheritAll="false" target="clean"/>
  <ant dir="webapp" inheritAll="false" target="clean"/>
</target>
```

This works, but what about the next target, `test`, or the one after that, `docs`. Cut-and-paste editing would soon get out of hand—something that you would only notice when you had to add a new subproject, or change the dependency order; every single master build target would need changing.

There must be a better way.

9.4.4   Designing a scalable, flexible master build file

A better way to structure a master build file is to use an intrinsic feature of all single file Ant projects: the ability to divide your build file into targets with explicitly declared dependencies between them. If we define a target in the master build file for each subproject—ant, common, tools, index, and webapp—then we can use the `depends` attribute to state how they depend upon each other, and let Ant control the order in which subprojects are built. We want to be able to call different targets inside the projects without too much cut-and-paste coding. The same set of targets should be able to hand off a `clean` command to subprojects as easily as a `test` command.

The trick will be to use a property to name a common target to invoke on every subproject. Here, the property named `target` lets us control which target to invoke from a set of targets that we implement in every build file. This will let us write a master build file containing targets that call down to the child projects like this:

```
<target name="do-tools" depends="do-ant">
  <ant dir="tools" target="${target}"
    inheritAll="false"/>
</target>

<target name="do-index" depends="do-task">
  <ant dir="index" target="${target}"
    inheritAll="false"/>
</target>

<target name="do-webapp" depends="do-tools,do-index">
  <ant dir="webapp" target="${target}"
    inheritAll="false"/>
</target>
```

With such a build file, calling a target across all the subprojects is a simple as:

```
ant -Dtarget=clean
```

Even better, we can implement the same entry points in the master build file, and use `<antcall>` to set the target property before calling the graph of subprojects.

Defining standard targets for projects

The first step in this process is to define a standard set of target names. We have chosen the set in table 9.4. Most are from the de facto standard set of Ant target names: `all`, `clean`, `dist`, `docs`, and `test`. These should all perform known functions to an experienced Ant user.

Table 9.4   **Our unified set of entry points. We implement these targets across all our child projects.**

Target Name	Function
default	The default entry point
all	Builds and tests everything; creates a distribution, optionally installs
clean	Deletes all generated files and directories
dist	Produces the distributables
docs	Generates all documentation
test	Runs the unit tests
noop	Does nothing but print the name of the project

Two nonstandard targets are `default` and `noop`. The `default` target is going to be the default target for each project, which will usually depend upon `dist` to create a distribution. The `noop` target is a special target we added for two reasons: it lets us test the whole master build more easily and it paves the way for using extra properties to control the individual targets that each subproject executes.

Adding these targets to the subprojects is simply a matter of adding those that we have not already implemented and pointing them at the appropriate internal targets. For the webapp project, for example, we add the following:

```
<target name="default" depends="dist"
  description="default: Make everything" />
<target name="all" depends="dist"
  description="build everything"/>
<target name="test" depends="dist"
  description="run tests" />
<target name="docs" depends="javadocs"
  description="generate documentation" />
<target name="noop" />
```

We now add similar targets for the other projects, resulting in a set of entry points whose meaning is consistent across the projects. It is important that each target brings its project up to date for the sake of the dependents. This means that all the test tasks must also generate the outputs that the dependent projects need. This is why the default, all, and test targets for the webapp project create a distribution, by being dependent upon the dist target. Of course, the noop target consistently does nothing.

After defining the targets, we declare each project's default entry point, as stated in the <project> declaration, to be the target called default. For example:

```
<project name="AntBook - Web App" default="default" basedir=".">
```

We need this default target because once we move to using a property to define a target, we need to know the name of the default target. Passing in an empty string as the target <ant target=""/> does not call the default target; it calls any target named "". Having a target called "" is very silly, as you cannot use it as a dependency. But some projects do use this as their default target, so we cannot change the behavior of <ant>.

After implementing these targets in each of the projects, we manually call each of them once. It is important to know that a build file works on its own before trying to integrate it into a larger project.

Creating a dependency graph

With each subproject implementing the same entry points, we can now create the graph of dependencies between the projects. This tells us the order in which to call the projects from the master build. What we cannot do is have a different dependency graph for different targets in each project: test cannot have a different set of dependencies from docs. We need to combine all predecessor projects of all the entry point targets into a single list. As long as there is no looping created by this process, we are ready for the next step.

Figure 9.2 shows our project's dependency graph.

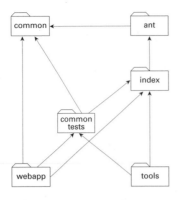

Figure 9.2
The dependency graph of our projects.
To avoid a loop (which must always have
existed), the tests of the common file had
to be pulled out into a separate build file.

This graph is slightly different from the order in listing 9.2. In altering the project common so that we could use the index files created by index for its tests, it became dependent upon that index project. This showed up that we always must have had a circular dependency: the ant project depended upon common, but the test target in common depended upon ant. We hadn't noticed this before because we only clean-built individual projects, not the entire suite. To remove the loop, we moved the tests into the file common-tests and made the test target in common do nothing. The final outputs of the project still depend on passing these tests, which is why webapp and tools depend upon the common-tests project.

We can now rework our single master build target to become a parameterized target that builds the projects, which we show in listing 9.2.

```
<target name="do-all-builds" >
  <ant dir="common" inheritAll="false" target="${target}"/>
  <ant dir="ant"    inheritAll="false" target="${target}"/>
  <ant dir="index"  inheritAll="false" target="${target}"/>
  <ant dir="common"  antfile="common-test.xml"
    inheritAll="false" target="${target}"/>
  <ant dir="tools"  inheritAll="false" target="${target}"/>
  <ant dir="webapp" inheritAll="false" target="${target}"/>
</target>
```

When calling the common-test build file, we have to specify the name of the file as well as the directory in which it exists. When the file you are calling with <ant> is called build.xml, as those of most projects are, then specifying the directory is all you need to do. When you want to call a build file with a different name, then you state the name in the antfile attribute, and the directory in which it is to execute. The name must be relative to the directory in the dir attribute. We will explain later, in our discussion of library build files, why the dir attribute should always be specified when naming a file. For now, take our word that naming the directory containing the build file is a sensible action.

CHAPTER 9   USING ANT IN YOUR DEVELOPMENT PROJECTS

We can then write the well-known entry points to the build file, each invoking the `do-all` target, setting the `target` parameter to the name of the target to execute in every build file. For example, here is the `noop` target.

```
<target name="noop"
    description="do nothing">
  <antcall target="do-all-builds">
    <param name="target" value="noop"/>
  </antcall>
</target>
```

To show it works, we call this target, which will trace out the projects as we execute them:

```
app$ ant noop
Buildfile: build.xml
noop:
do-all:
noop:
    [echo] no-op in AntBook - Common
noop:
    [echo] no-op in AntBook - Custom Ant Tasks
noop:
    [echo] no-op in AntBook - Index
noop:
    [echo] no-op in AntBook - Common - Test
noop:
    [echo] no-op in Antbook - Tools
noop:
    [echo] no-op in AntBook - Web App
BUILD SUCCESSFUL
```

At this point, we can use the master build file to provide a unifying build of our project, adding new entry points for each target name defined in table 9.4. We have lost all the explicit dependency information, but the build file works.

Writing the invocation targets

Even with only a few child projects, our build files are getting complex dependencies between them. This may be a symptom of inadequate decoupling of components, but as a project grows, this trend will only continue; having to order everything ourselves will only get more difficult over time.

We need to hand off ordering build file invocation to Ant itself. It can detect circular dependencies or build the targets in a valid sequence. We just have to create a set of proxy targets, one for each child project, as shown in listing 9.3.

Listing 9.3 Our proxy targets: one per build file, with all direct predecessors stated

```
<target name="do-common">
  <ant dir="common" target="${target}"
    inheritAll="false"/>
</target>
```

```
<target name="do-ant" depends="do-common">
  <ant dir="ant" target="${target}"
    inheritAll="false"/>
</target>

<target name="do-index" depends="do-ant">
  <ant dir="index" target="${target}"
    inheritAll="false"/>
</target>

<target name="do-common-test" depends="do-index,do-common">
  <ant dir="common" antfile="common-test.xml"
    target="${target}"
    inheritAll="false"/>
</target>

<target name="do-tools"
    depends="do-common,do-index,do-common-test">
  <ant dir="tools" target="${target}"
    inheritAll="false"/>
</target>

<target name="do-webapp"
    depends="do-common,do-index,do-common-test">
  <ant dir="webapp" target="${target}"
    inheritAll="false"/>
</target>

<target name="do-all" depends="do-tools,do-common-test,do-webapp"/>
```

The body of each of these targets is one of the individual task declarations of the unified master build target of listing 9.2. We have increased the line count, but also
increased flexibility. We can now define high-level master build targets that depend
upon some, but not all, of the subprojects. And we can easily add new subprojects by
adding new proxy targets and setting up the appropriate dependencies.

Running the master build

Having written the proxy targets, we need to write the entry points for the master
build. We have already introduced the noop target; the others are nearly identical. Of
course, the internal target we invoke (do-all) is new; we make this change to all
the entry points.

```
<target name="all"
  description="build everything">
  <antcall target="do-all">
    <param name="target" value="all"/>
  </antcall>
</target>
```

First, we test the noop target:

```
$ ant noop
Buildfile: build.xml
noop:
```

```
do-common:
noop:
     [echo] no-op in AntBook - Common
do-ant:
noop:
     [echo] no-op in AntBook - Custom Ant Tasks
do-index:
noop:
     [echo] no-op in AntBook - Index
do-common-test:
noop:
     [echo] no-op in AntBook - Common - Test
do-tools:
noop:
     [echo] no-op in Antbook - Tools
do-webapp:
noop:
     [echo] no-op in AntBook - Web App
do-all:
BUILD SUCCESSFUL
```

A quick glance at the project dependency graph shows that we have declared the dependencies correctly, at least to the extent that the targets are executing in a valid order.

The next test is more rigorous: we completely clean build the system:

```
$ ant clean all
... many lines of output omitted ...
BUILD SUCCESSFUL
Total time: 1 minute 36 seconds
```

The success of a clean build, including the execution of all our tests, means that the build is seemingly working. Further tests on the deployed code are needed to verify that the WAR file, when deployed, is complete and correct—a different problem. What we do know is that we can now clean build our entire suite of projects in less than two minutes.

9.5   MANAGING CHILD PROJECT BUILDS

We have just shown how to subdivide a project into a number of stand-alone child projects, each with their own build files, and one master build file to integrate them all.

If there is a problem in this design, it is that we do not want to have to declare the same properties and tasks in all the different child projects. There are ways to do this, which we shall now explore.

9.5.1   How to control properties of child projects

One of the key features of master build files is that they can control their child projects by setting their properties. Because of Ant's property immutability rule, a child project cannot override any property set by a master build file. This lets you write master build files that control complex details of the child project, even child projects that were never

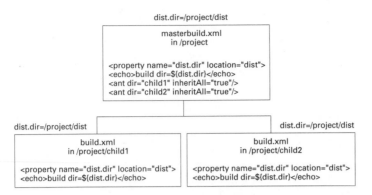

dist.dir=/project/dist

```
masterbuild.xml
in /project

<property name="dist.dir" location="dist">
<echo>build dir=${dist.dir}</echo>
<ant dir="child1" inheritAll="true"/>
<ant dir="child2" inheritAll="true"/>
```

dist.dir=/project/dist

```
build.xml
in /project/child1

<property name="dist.dir" location="dist">
<echo>build dir=${dist.dir}</echo>
```

dist.dir=/project/dist

```
build.xml
in /project/child2

<property name="dist.dir" location="dist">
<echo>build dir=${dist.dir}</echo>
```

Figure 9.3 A master build can set the properties for the child projects, even if those projects try to override them. If the master build had accidentally used `value` instead of `location`, the directory location would have been resolved in the client build files relative to their own directory, which is not what we desire.

written to be called from a master build file. As an example, figure 9.3 shows a master build file that sets the `dist.dir` property for two child projects. The outcome of this operation will be that the two child projects will place all their final distribution files into a single directory, rather than into their own directories.

In all our uses of the <ant> task in section 9.4, we carefully declared the attribute `inheritall` to be false, without actually explaining what the attribute was or why we set it. We actually introduced this attribute in section 7.8.1, in the <antcall> target, when we were explaining property inheritance in that task. The <antcall> task actually uses <ant> to do its work, so the property inheritance model for both is identical.

Although the two tasks share the same implementation code, when creating a master build file you often need to use them slightly differently. An instance of <antcall> calls a target graph inside your own build file with parameters—both properties and references—which you define. The <ant> task can control a complete build file for a project that you may not even have written. This different usage can change how you pass parameters to the called file and target. Take, for example, the problem of setting the release build flag for all our projects, all of which use the technique described in chapter 6 to set the <java> build flags to the release options when `release.build` is set. In a master build, we want to be able to set that flag in one place and have it propagate.

The <ant> task lets you do this, because any of the properties and references that the <ant> task sets for the invoked project is, as usual, immutable. You can control the settings of a child project by predefining any property or path before its own initialization code tries to define it. If the <ant> call defines the `release.build` property, it will enable release builds; if it sets the distribution directory to a single location, then that location becomes the destination directory for all distribution files.

To use this feature, you need to know the rules by which properties are passed down:

- If `inheritAll` is true, all properties set in the master build file are passed to the child projects.
- Any properties defined inside `<ant>` override those set in the master build.
- If `inheritAll` is false, only those properties defined inside the `<ant>` declaration are passed down.
- Properties set on the command line are always passed down, and can never be overridden by any declarations inside the `<ant>` call.

The final rule of the set means that you can configure the master build from the command line and have those changes propagate down to all the child builds:

```
ant -Drelease.build=true -Ddist.dir=/projects/CDimage/dist
```

Designing a project for easy overriding

If the child projects use properties to control all the details of their build options, then their parent projects can tune parameters to ensure that all projects are consistent. Controlling where the projects place their distribution packages is one common control option; others are which tests to run, and which servers to deploy against. For a project to be controllable, it needs to make extensive use of properties.

A good build file should already be using properties to define any string, attribute, or file that is used in multiple places. For easy integration into a larger project, any option that could be overridden should first be defined with a property and then referred to, giving the master build an option to change the value. Of course, this would be far too much effort to do up front: changing build files as needed is the standard approach to making build files overridable. When you do this, use properties of the same name as sibling projects, as it makes configuring the master build file easier. For example, if our `common` project used `make.release.build` as its release build flag, and the `webapp` project used `javac.release.mode` instead, unifying the projects would be much harder than our unified `release.build` property.

One important practice to make overriding work better is to use `<property location>` to define file locations, rather than `<property value>`. In a single build file, using the `value` attribute to define a file location works, because when these properties are resolved to file locations, it will be in the same build file. When you are passing properties around to other build files, using the `location` attribute ensures that relative paths are resolved in the build file declaring the property, not in the build file using the property.

9.5.2 Inheriting properties and references from a master build file

Like the `<antcall>` task, `<ant>` will pass to the target all currently defined properties, unless you tell it not to. In earlier (pre-1.4) versions of Ant, `<ant>` would always pass down *all* current sets of properties. This inheritance rule was simple and straightforward, but it meant that subprojects needed to use unique names for every property to avoid accidental definition by the parent project. If ever you do call a project with <ant> without setting inheritall=false, then this is the behavior you will get. Any definition you have made in the parent file, such as declaring which directory build.dir will refer to, propagates to the child project. Because of Ant's property immutability rules, this will freeze the value of build.dir to that of the parent directory, causing the subproject to place its output in a different location. If this is what you intended, then you have discovered the secret to controlling child projects from a master build file. If it is not, then you have introduced a defect in how your master build works.

To control our compiler options, the master build file can set the appropriate properties and have them propagate down to the child projects:

```
<property name="release.build" value="true"/>
<property name="build.compiler" value="modern"/>

<target name="do-common">
  <ant dir="common" target="${target}"
    inheritAll="true"/>
</target>

<target name="do-ant" depends="do-common">
  <ant dir="ant" target="${target}"
    inheritAll="true"/>
</target>
```

The same technique works for references to paths in a project. A master build file can define classpaths for use in executing and compiling Java programs, and if the inheritRefs attribute is set to true, then these references propagate down the execution chain.

> **WARNING** The default value of the inheritRefs attribute in <ant> is false, whereas the default value for inheritall is true. This is a historical quirk related to backwards compatibility.

9.5.3 Declaring properties and references in <ant>

The <ant> task lets you declare properties that are passed down to a child build, using the <property> and <reference> nested elements. If you have been using <antcall>, this should seem familiar, although in that task the element to set properties is called <param>.

The <property> element of <ant> looks exactly the same as a normal <property> declaration: it can set properties to a value, a location, a file, or a resource. You can even use <property env="env"> to load the environment variables. Loading properties in from a file is powerful, because a single file can then control which properties are set and which are left unset. For example, we could modify our targets to load a common file, the values of which would be set in all the child projects:

```
<target name="do-common">
  <ant dir="common" target="${target}"
       inheritAll="false">
    <property file="masterbuild.properties"/>
  </ant>
</target>
```

Let us assume that the file masterbuild.properties includes the following property declarations:

```
release.build=true
build.compiler=modern
```

These properties would all trickle down to the subprojects, controlling their build options. One of the problems with this approach is that it does not work for relative file references. All properties loaded from a file are treated as simple values, rather than relative file locations, which need to be immediately resolved. This limits the value of this technique.

Setting references requires a declaration of the reference earlier in the build file; a `<reference>` tag must then point to the reference:

```
<reference refid="main.classpath"/>
```

If you want to rename a reference, then you must supply the name of the reference ID by which the path will be known in the destination:

```
<reference refid="main.classpath" torefid="compile.classpath"/>
```

The value of setting such references increases in complex projects, especially with library Ant projects, which we shall cover in section 9.6.

9.5.4 Sharing properties via XML file fragments

Although we have demonstrated the different ways of passing information to child projects, astute readers will have noticed from our master build example that we use of none of these. We use a slightly different technique, which is much more powerful but harder to use.

The problem is that we want to make each child project stand-alone, so that you can call it without having to go via the master build file. Yet we do not want any duplicate definitions of properties or the locations of the library files we use in our projects. Because some of the projects depend on the work of other projects, we also need references to the output files of all our projects–again, with no duplication.

How do we solve this? We use XML file fragments. XML supports the ability to import fragments from other files as entities, inserting these fragments into the local XML file wherever these entities appear. This is roughly equivalent to the `#include` feature in C and C++, which inserts a named text file into the source code. The difference between XML and C or C++ is that the insertion is done in two phases: declaration and then importation.

You first declare the fragment at the beginning of the file, after the `<?xml?>` header and before the XML data itself:

```
<?xml version="1.0"?>
<!DOCTYPE project [
    <!ENTITY properties SYSTEM "file:../properties.xml">
]>
<project name="AntBook - Common" default="default" basedir=".">
```

This does not insert the file yet, merely makes it known to the XML parser using the name `properties`. We will use this name when inserting the file into the text of the build file. Observe that we had to give a URI to the file's location: `file:../properties.xml`. Because the XML parser is importing these files, we cannot use Ant properties here, or Ant's ability to convert between MS-DOS and Unix style paths. Unix-style forward slashes should work across platforms.

Having told the parser about the file, we can now insert it inside the build file simply by preceding the entity name with an ampersand (`&`) and following it with a semicolon (`;`). This is exactly the same syntax we use for inserting unusual characters into the build file, such as angle brackets as `&gt;` and `&lt;`. Here, however, we are inserting significantly more content:

```
<project name="AntBook - Common" default="default" basedir=".">

  &properties;
```

At parse time, before Ant gets to see the file, the XML parser inserts the file's contents into the build file whenever it encounters the entity reference. As with `#include` of C and C++ code, the compiler is reasonably ignorant of the fact that the inclusion took place: Ant sees everything from the included file as if it were in the main XML file. This means that all file references inside the included file have to be either absolute and hence not portable, or relative to the file into which they are being included. Knowing this fact is essential to making inclusion work.

For our properties file, even though it is stored in the base directory of the application, we assume that it is always loaded into a build file one level down, and so can refer up a level with two dots (`..`) to get to the base directory. Listing 9.4 shows some of this build file, to give you a flavor of it. It is primarily a list of file and directory locations.

We have not completely ruled out the option of including this file into a project in a lower level directory. Careful property declaration enables a build file to define the master project base directory, by defining `masterbuild.dir` before including the build file fragment through the entity reference. We would interpret having to do that as a symptom that the project was getting even more complex, and would take steps to simplify the project structure, if possible.

Note that the shared property file lets users override subsequent definitions by defining their values in a properties file to be loaded before any other. Three such files are loaded: a per-application property file in the current directory, a per-user property file in their home directory, and a property file stored in the masterbuild directory.

```
<property environment="env"/>
<property name="user.properties.file"
        location="${user.home}/.build.properties"/>
<property file="build.properties"/>
<property file="${user.properties.file}"/>

<property name="root.dir" location="${basedir}"/>
<property name="masterbuild.dir" location="${root.dir}/.."/>
<property file="${masterbuild.dir}/build.properties"/>
<property name="src.dir" location="${root.dir}/src"/>
<property name="build.dir" location="build"/>
<property name="build.classes.dir"
        location="${build.dir}/classes"/>
<property name="dist.dir" location="dist"/>
<property name="dist.bin.dir" location="${dist.dir}/bin"/>
<property name="doc.dir" location="doc"/>
<property name="javadoc.dir" location="${doc.dir}/javadoc"/>


<property name="lib.dir" location="${root.dir}/../lib"/>
<property name="antbook-ant.jar"
  location="${masterbuild.dir}/ant/dist/antbook-ant.jar"/>

<property name="antbook-common.jar"
  location="${masterbuild.dir}/common/dist/antbook-common.jar"/>
```

Gets the basedir of the current Ant project

Determines the parent directory

Locates a directory under the parent

Locates a file built by one of the projects

Together these enable a developer to customize the build, to store output in new locations, to compile with a different compiler, and to deploy using a different username and password—the kind of thing that becomes ever more important as projects grow and more people work on them.

9.5.5   Sharing targets with XML file fragments

Because XML inclusion pulls arbitrary text into the master build file, you can use it to include any fragment of a build file. Classpath declarations are an obvious option, as are <taskdef> declarations to import new Ant tasks into the build file (which we will cover in chapter 10). You can even include common targets, provided the targets are identical across all projects that use them.

We use the technique of sharing common targets across all build files by referencing a targets.xml entity in all our projects:

```
<?xml version="1.0"?>
<!DOCTYPE project [
    <!ENTITY properties SYSTEM "file:../properties.xml">
    <!ENTITY targets SYSTEM "file:../targets.xml">
]>
```

The file targets.xml initially contains a single target, though more could be added later:

```
<target name="noop">
  <echo>no-op in ${ant.project.name}</echo>
</target>
```

This approach gives you simple maintenance of common targets: change the build file, and all subprojects have their targets updated. These shared targets can still be customized through careful property definitions. You can bypass some targets if the `if` or `unless` conditions on the targets are not met, and other aspects of the target can be altered through predefining different properties and paths. If you find that you are using this approach, and starting to contemplate using `<antcall>` to invoke the shared code, then you should instead opt for a more manageable solution.

9.6   CREATING REUSABLE LIBRARY BUILD FILES

A library build file is our unofficial term for a build file that is entirely self-contained, and provides a small self-contained service in the build. The library file is invoked using `<ant>`, with parameters defined to tell it what to do. The simplest way to view these build files is as a subroutine, with the subroutine parameters supplied as properties and references.

As an example of a library build file, we are going to move our uses of the `<javadoc>` task into a single library build file that the child projects can invoke. This is a good choice because it has so many options; in a library file they can be configured once for all projects.

Writing the library build file

First, we write the component build file and save it in our masterbuild directory. Listing 9.5 shows this file. It takes a number of parameters: four properties and one classpath. Any undefined property has a default value given that is a valid value for this project. Other library build files may want to test for essential properties and `<fail>` if they are missing.

> **Listing 9.5   A self-contained build file to javadoc a directory**

```
<?xml version="1.0"?>
 <project name="javadoc" default="javadoc"
  basedir="." >

  <target name="javadoc" description="make java docs" >
    <property name="javadoc.packages"
      value="org.*,com.*,net.*,edu.*" />
    <property name="javadoc.src.dir"  location="src" />
    <property name="javadoc.dest.dir" location="docs/javadoc" />
    <property name="javadoc.title"  value="ant book" />
    <mkdir dir="${javadoc.dest.dir}"/>
    <javadoc author="true"
             destdir="${javadoc.dest.dir}"
```

```
                  packagenames="${javadoc.packages}"
                  sourcepath="${javadoc.src.dir}"
                  use="true"
                  version="true"
                  windowtitle="${javadoc.title}"
                  private="true"
                  >
         <classpath refid="javadoc.classpath"/>
      </javadoc>
   </target>
</project>
```

This file is a parameterized wrapper around the `<javadoc>` task, adding the creation of the destination directory as a convenience feature. With this file stored in the master build directory, it will not work as is; there is no subdirectory called src containing files to document. Another build file must invoke it with a different base directory from the one in which it lives.

Invoking the component build file

We use `<ant>` to invoke the library build file, here from our child project that creates our Ant task:

```
<target name="javadocs" depends="compile"
    description="make the java docs" >
  <ant antfile="${masterbuild.dir}/javadoc.xml"
      dir="."
      inheritall="false">
      <property name="javadoc.title"  value="index task" />
      <reference refid="compile.classpath"
        torefid="javadoc.classpath"/>
  </ant>
</target>
```

We only set one property, the title, and leave the packages, source, and destination unchanged. So how does the javadoc build file know to run in the current subdirectory? The `dir` attribute tells the `<ant>` task which directory for an invoked build file to treat as its base. By naming the file with `antfile`, then setting `dir` to `"."`, we tell the task to run the build file in the current directory. When it runs, it has no way of determining its original location, other than by inspecting the property `ant.file`. All relative file declarations will now be relative to the directory of the project that invoked the library project. This will cause our invoked target to create the javadoc documentation from the src and build directories of the current child project. When we do so there will be some classpath complaints, however, as we haven't explicitly included the Ant libraries on the supplied classpath:

```
javadocs:
javadoc:
  [javadoc] Generating Javadoc
  [javadoc] Javadoc execution
  [javadoc] Loading source files for package org.example.antbook.ant.lucene...
```

```
[javadoc] Constructing Javadoc information...
[javadoc] javadoc: warning - Import not found:
    org.apache.tools.ant.BuildException - ignoring!
[javadoc] javadoc: warning - Import not found:
    org.apache.tools.ant.DirectoryScanner - ignoring!
[javadoc] javadoc: warning - Import not found:
    org.apache.tools.ant.Project - ignoring!
[javadoc] javadoc: warning - Import not found:
    org.apache.tools.ant.Task - ignoring!
[javadoc] javadoc: warning - Import not found:
    org.apache.tools.ant.types.FileSet - ignoring!
[javadoc] javadoc: warning - Cannot find class
    org.apache.tools.ant.types.FileSet
[javadoc] javadoc: warning - Cannot find class
    org.apache.tools.ant.BuildException
[javadoc] Building tree for all the packages and classes...
[javadoc] Building index for all the packages and classes...
[javadoc] Building index for all classes...
[javadoc] Generating /home/ant/app/ant/doc/javadoc/stylesheet.css...
[javadoc] 7 warnings
BUILD SUCCESSFUL
Total time: 8 seconds
```

Be aware that the <ant> task has some quirky behavior regarding directory definition that only makes sense from a historical perspective. If you always set the dir
attribute, this will not be an issue. The quirks are rules about what the default directory is when the directory is not specified, and it varies upon the value of inheritall. Consult the task documentation if you are curious, then follow our example
and always specify the dir attribute.

Writing library files is a powerful technique in a single large build file, but it is
equally powerful across sequential projects. If one project's build processes are factored
out into reusable library files, then the successor project can reuse the testing, auditing,
reporting, and deployment codes without having to do much cut-and-paste reuse.
You can also share them with other projects, adding functionality to Ant without forcing developers to write new tasks.

9.7   *LOOKING AHEAD: LARGE PROJECT SUPPORT EVOLUTION*

We avoid talking much about the future of Ant in this book, because it is so hard to
predict. One thing is clear: as Ant-based projects get bigger, the tools and techniques
for scaling them will improve. One interesting question is, "Can you build independent subprojects simultaneously?" Indeed you can, using the <parallel> task.
However, there are many thread-safety risks inherent in running multiple Ant builds
simultaneously. A forking version of <ant> could address this.

One proposed enhancement is a version of <ant> that could take a path or fileset,
and call all build files therein. This could be used in a master build file that would
automatically build all Ant projects placed underneath it. Although people have
posted implementations of this (the <antOn> task) to the Ant mailing lists, none has

made it into the official distribution. Writing a master build file as we have done, stating dependencies between subprojects, is more reliable and provides more information to the build tool and to other developers. Yet for some projects, such as the Apache Axis project, this proposed <anton> task is exactly what is needed to run a separate build file for every test case, that being how many of their tests are implemented. Some form of this task will emerge, although perhaps not in the main Ant distribution.

The requirements list for Ant2.0 explicitly includes the ability for a project to state that it depends upon another project, and for a target to depend upon a target in another build file. This should eliminate the need to use low-level XML mechanisms for importing fragments of a build file. Instead, initialization targets will be able to define properties, paths, and tasks that can be used by dependent targets in other files. When a version of Ant supports this facility, it will be easier to integrate large projects, but it will still require care. A single master build file managing the process for its children is still a better tactic than binding together many peer-level projects through explicit interdependencies.

Layering on top of Ant, even using the techniques we have discussed in this chapter to share common build file pieces and control a complex project with a master build file, still can get unwieldy. Fortunately, there are efforts under way to provide layers on top of Ant to hide many of these complexities and to more abstractly and cleanly define your build steps. At the time of writing this book, there are two such efforts in development, both of which are in production use for several projects and maturing rapidly. These two projects are:

Centipede—http://www.krysalis.org/centipede/

Maven—http://jakarta.apache.org/turbine/maven/

Both of these projects have a common goal to be a Java project management tool that does much more than simply build a distributable. Project descriptors are used to define a higher level view of your directory structure, library dependencies, and desired steps such as unit testing, code metrics generation, cross-referenced views of source code, change logs, and many other project artifacts. Maven and Centipede support automatic downloading of library dependencies as part of the build process if they are not already present. We encourage you to keep an eye on these efforts, as they are likely to form the basis of future Java project best practices. Ant is the engine under the covers of both of these tools, and for simple projects these tools can even hide the fact that Ant is there altogether. For more complex build processes, Ant customization and expertise is still needed to accomplish steps that fall outside their capabilities.

9.8 ANT PROJECT BEST PRACTICES

If good source is as readable as a book, a good build file should be as readable as a booklet, including short, concise, and clear instructions on what the project creates and how it goes about creating these deliverables. In this section, we cover two aspects of managing Ant projects that become increasingly important as a project evolves.

Remember, small projects become large projects, so keep these points in mind when you begin setting up a projects build process. Refactoring should also be applied to build files, not just your Java source code.

In appendix D, we cover more general suggestions as to how to lay out a build file to be readable. If you wish to diverge from these, then try to be consistent within all the build files you create. We have derived these best practices from common uses, although there is no single standard for how to name directories and targets or structure a build file. Even in the Apache Jakarta projects, there is little consistency on what to name the directory for distributable packages; both `dist` and `target` are used. We encourage you to strive for greater consistency within your own team and organization.

Having a consistent layout across projects means that people can understand their way around your code, so adding new people to a team is easier. It also makes it easier to cut and paste targets and tasks between projects, which is a common practice when starting up a new project. The best approach is for an organization to have a set of template build files that can be used for different projects, or a collection of targets to bring together to form a build file.

9.8.1 Managing libraries

A particularly tricky situation arises in the management of external library dependencies. These dependencies are typically third-party products, such as many of the fine Jakarta offerings. These dependencies may also be in-house components that are built, packaged, and versioned for use in other projects. Regardless of the source of the libraries, the issues are the same: Where should libraries exist within the software configuration management (SGM) and project directory structure? How can different projects use different library versions? How can an individual developer's build incorporate a different library than the production build of a project?

Whether or not you keep libraries in the SCM is a decision that we cannot make for you. We do, however, recommend that little or no local configuration be required to replicate a build, other than pulling the code from the repository to a clean machine. We even store Ant itself in our SCM so that we know our builds will work in the future even if a future version of Ant breaks them. We can simply run our builds with the version that we've always used.

We discussed in chapter 8 how we deal with third-party libraries by using Ant property mapping indirections. Whether you go to the extreme shown in those examples or use a simpler scheme with few mappings is up to you, but we do recommend that a build be capable of running with a different version of a library easily if desired. At the very least, having mappings like `${lucene.jar}` to refer to the JAR location allows a user to override that value, if desired.

9.8.2 Implementing processes

Because Ant can be used for automated builds, tests, and deployment, use it that way. Invest the time in learning how to use the test frameworks, the deployment mechanisms, and set up an automated smoke test. The time invested will be paid back in the current project and those that follow. We recommend that you:

- Do a clean build at least once a day on every system. This stops cruft accruing in the output directory.
- Set up an automated smoke test for nightly or even hourly builds. We cover how to do that in chapter 16.
- Automate as much of the build, test, and deploy process as you can.
- Make a ghost copy of the disk image and restore it once a week, after setting up any server with the appropriate system software for staging tests. This helps test automated installation processes. You may not like this extra work, but operations will love you for it.

9.9   SUMMARY

Applying Ant to a project requires careful integration with the rest of the software development and build processes. As it is only a build tool, and should not be dictating how to organize your software process, though it has certain preferences for the build process itself.

We have outlined the steps that we recommend for starting a new project using Ant, and for migrating an existing project to Ant. We advise learning Ant with a new project until you are comfortable with the tool because migrating is a more difficult process.

Large projects are a challenge in their own right. The core technique to cope with large projects and their complex build processes is to subdivide the projects and have a master build file in a parent directory that invokes the others using <ant>. We have shown you our approach to doing this, with proxy targets in the master build file to model dependencies in the subprojects. Coupled with a set of well-known build targets inside each build file, this prevents the master build file itself from becoming a maintenance problem.

Another aspect of large projects that we have covered is managing properties in the child projects. There are many ways to address this. Defining the properties in the master build and passing them down is one, reading them in from shared property files is another. A third approach, importing XML fragments as entities, is a powerful one, but to be used carefully.

In a large project, applying best practices to build files themselves matters greatly. These best practices boil down to writing build files to be readable by others and consistent with other projects.

As seen with the Web Start example earlier in this chapter, there are Ant tasks out there to help in practically every situation. We are next going to explore the different types of Ant tasks, including more third-party tasks that can add great value to our build process.

C H A P T E R   1 0

Beyond Ant's core tasks

10.1 Understanding types of tasks   235

10.2 Optional tasks in action   237

10.3 Using software configuration management tasks   245

10.4 Using third-party tasks   247

10.5 Notable third-party tasks   248

10.6 The ant-contrib tasks   253

10.7 Sharing task definitions among projects   258

10.8 Best practices   258

10.9 Summary   259

Ant is only as useful as its tasks. It comes with many necessary and useful tasks; you can accomplish a great deal with an out-of-the-box Ant installation. You are, however, very likely to encounter a need for more than the built-in functionality offered. At the very least, you are likely to be integrating unit testing into your build process.

There are also a growing number of tasks freely available, yet separate from the Ant distribution. The Ant development team is now intentionally keeping many third-party and vendor-specific tasks from being incorporated into the core. This frees Ant's developers from maintenance headaches and pushes task development and maintenance to the tool authors and vendors. This chapter explains the different types of Ant tasks and provides examples of their use. We cover several very special Ant tasks that increase the power of your build file and accomplish powerful results with little effort.

10.1 UNDERSTANDING TYPES OF TASKS

There are four primary types of Ant tasks:

- *Core* or *built-in*—Tasks that work out-of-the-box and are immediately available for use with a properly configured Ant installation. Most of the tasks that were covered in previous chapters are core tasks, such as `<javac>`, `<jar>`, and `<copy>`.

- *Optional*—Tasks that ship natively with Ant (in its optional.jar) but typically require libraries or external programs that do not ship with Ant. A couple of optional tasks—`<junit>` and `<junitreport>`—were covered previously. The `<junit>` task requires the JUnit library and `<junitreport>` requires an XSLT engine—neither of these components ships with Ant.

- *Third-party*—Tasks that were developed by others and which can be dropped into an Ant installation.

- *Custom*—Tasks that you have written and compiled yourself.

These terms can cause some confusion, especially when discussing the difference between core tasks and optional tasks. This chapter deals with optional and third-party tasks only. Custom task development is covered in chapter 20. Core tasks are covered throughout this book in all other chapters. We also provide solutions to the few technical hitches that can occur when using optional and third-party tasks. For a complete summary of all of Ant's tasks, refer to the Ant Task Reference in the appendix, and to the Ant online documentation.

10.1.1 So, what is an "optional" task?

In previous versions of Ant, the term "optional" task referred to those tasks not normally distributed with Ant; they were in an add-on library that users downloaded separately. As of version 1.5, Ant ships with complete sets of core and optional tasks. But there are still distinctions between the two task types. Ant's optional tasks are stored in different libraries and the online documentation divides tasks into core and optional.

With current distributions, the distinction between core and optional tasks may seem odd or unnecessary, but there are some remaining differences. A key one is that optional tasks are generally viewed as less essential than the core tasks to the majority of build files. Although `<junit>` is an optional task, we consider it to be a mandatory feature in all build files. The other difference is that nearly all the optional tasks depend upon external libraries or programs to work. Unlike core tasks, optional tasks are not typically stand-alone.

Thus to use nearly any optional task, you must download and install the extra libraries or programs. These additional downloads have been the source of many support issues. The expectation by many users was that once the optional JAR was downloaded, everything would work. When it didn't, many concluded there was a bug in Ant. As a consequence of the many erroneous bugs reported, the error message received when referencing an "optional" task is now very explicit in version 1.5. It boils down to: don't file a bug report, it isn't a real defect. The message received when an unknown task is encountered lists many possible causes, but probably the most common causes after simple spelling errors are a missing optional.jar or missing libraries for the task.

10.1.2 Ant's major optional tasks

Table 10.1 categorizes the majority of Ant's optional tasks.

Table 10.1 Ant's optional tasks. Most of these tasks require installation of additional components.

Task Category	Description of tasks
Source Code Management[†]	ClearCase, Continuus, Perforce, PVCS, StarTeam, Visual SourceSafe / SourceOffSite
EJB	<ejbjar> and others. Chapter 14 covers the EJB tasks.
Archiving / Distribution	CAB, RPM
Compilers / Grammars / Language	ANTLR, Depend, JavaCC, Javah, JSPC, iContract, NetRexxC, .NET
Utilities	PropertyFile, Native2Ascii, ReplaceRegExp, Translate
Testing	JUnit, JUnitReport
Networking	Telnet, FTP, MimeMail
Miscellaneous	Jlink, Script, Sound, XmlValidate
Metrics / Coverage Analysis	JDepend, JProbe, Metamata

† CVS support is provided as built-in task.

Many of these tasks require that dependencies be in the classpath of Ant's JVM, and this typically means that the dependencies should be in ANT_HOME/lib (JUnit and Log4j for example) or in the system classpath. Any dependencies required for the optional tasks are noted in the documentation.

Beyond what is covered in this chapter, several of Ant's optional tasks are given special attention elsewhere in this book. JUnit integration is covered in chapter 4 ("Testing"). FTP and Telnet are covered in chapter 7 ("Deployment"). XmlValidate is covered more extensively in chapter 13. Emailing file attachments is covered in chapter 7. The Script task is covered in chapter 20. Javah is covered in chapter 18 ("C++ integration"). JSPC is covered in chapter 12. There are many additional optional tasks that we do not cover in detail in this book because they are only useful in specific environments and are not generally applicable to the majority of Java development situations; however, these tasks are covered in Ant's documentation.

Many useful, and probably necessary, tasks are considered optional in the Ant documentation, even though you are unlikely to consider some of them optional! Tasks such as <junit> and <xmlvalidate> are indispensable for build best practices.

10.1.3   Why third-party tasks?

Because it is impractical and even illegal[1] for Ant to ship all Ant tasks that exist, third-party tasks are often a necessary addition to your build file. Having tasks maintained closer to the vendor or application programming interface (API) on which they operate is best for both Ant and for the vendor or project being wrapped in a task. Why? Because the Ant developers are already maintaining a framework for build process automation as well as many core and optional tasks, and are not necessarily domain experts on the vendor or API. The Ant web site contains a resource section with pointers to many third-party tasks.

Third-party tasks offer interesting and useful capabilities such as code-style checking and database object-relational mapping code generation. Although third-party tasks are easily integrated into an Ant build file, they require some build file writer effort that the core and optional tasks do not.

10.2   OPTIONAL TASKS IN ACTION

Even though we cover many of commonly needed optional tasks elsewhere (see section 10.1.2 for pointers), we want to introduce you to several that are commonly used to add powerful capabilities to build processes. We also toss in two fun ones to lighten things up a bit. In this section, you learn to work with these optional tasks:

- <propertyfile>
- <depend>
- <javacc>
- <replaceregexp>
- <sound> and <splash>

Most of these tasks illustrate the optional nature of the tasks and require additional components to be installed in order to function properly. For each task, we discuss the specific requirements it has and how to configure your system to run it.

10.2.1   Manipulating property files

One of the easiest and most common methods of carrying around metadata such as configuration information or localized text is via Java property files. Property files are simply textual key/value pairs: less powerful than XML configuration files, but much easier to read and write. The <propertyfile> task provides several powerful features for creating and manipulating property files, such as incrementing numbers and dates. Java provides easy access to property file data by using the java.util. Properties API, which allows your production code to access property files generated during the build process.

---

[1] Specifically the Apache Software Foundation software license is less stringent than the GNU General Public License (GPL), so GPL licensed tasks can not be included with Ant, nor even tasks bound to GPL or Lesser GPL libraries.

Capturing build information for application use

By using a combination of the `<property>` and `<propertyfile>` tasks we capture the build date, time, machine name, user, and operating system into a properties file, which we later incorporate into our projects distributable. Listing 10.1 illustrates the build file pieces used to build the dynamic properties file.

Listing 10.1 Using `<propertyfile>` to capture build-time information

```
<property environment="env"/>
<property name="env.COMPUTERNAME" value="${env.HOSTNAME}"/>

<propertyfile comment="Build Information"
              file="${build.classes.dir}/build.properties">
    <entry key="build.date"
           type="date"
           pattern="EEEE MMM dd, yyyy"
           value="now"/>
    <entry key="build.time"
           type="date"
           pattern="kk:mm:ss"
           value="now"/>
    <entry key="build.host" value="${env.COMPUTERNAME}"/>
    <entry key="build.user.name" value="${user.name}"/>
    <entry key="build.os.name" value="${os.name}"/>
</propertyfile>
```

The `<propertyfile>` task, somewhat misleadingly, does not actually set any Ant properties. It creates or updates a properties file. To load those properties as Ant properties you need to use `<property file="..." />` afterwards, perhaps using its `prefix` attribute to keep from clashing with already existing properties.

TIP: Here's how to ensure getting the hostname (or computer name) across many platforms:

```
<property environment="env"/>
<property name="env.COMPUTERNAME" value="${env.HOSTNAME}"/>
```

This works in both standard Windows and Linux environments and provides the machine name as `${env.COMPUTERNAME}`. It works because of the immutability of properties. Loading the environment variables on a Linux machine would not pick up an `env.COMPUTERNAME` property, and it will be set on the property assignment. On a Windows machine, `env.COMPUTERNAME` would be set from the environment variables and the following assignment would be ignored. If you'd rather have the property named `env.HOSTNAME`, just switch the order of the two properties on the second line.

Incrementing build number and setting expiration date

Capturing build time information is one thing you can do with `<propertyfile>`, but it can do more. The `<propertyfile>` task can also be used to increment numbers and dates. Ant includes a built-in `<buildnumber>` task to accomplish the same thing, only more concisely. In listing 10.2, we use both tasks to create/update a properties file at build-time, which not only stores the build number, but also an expiration date that our software could use to restrict the life of a demo version, for example.

Listing 10.2 Build file segment showing how to increment build numbers and perform a date operation

```
<property name="metadata.dir" location="metadata"/>

<property name="buildprops.file"
          location="${metadata.dir}/build.properties"/>
<property name="buildnum.file"
          location="${metadata.dir}/build.number"/>

<buildnumber file="${buildnum.file}"/>              ◁────────── Increments and stores
<echo message="Build Number: ${build.number}"/>               into build.number

<delete file="${buildprops.file}"/>
<propertyfile comment="Build Information"
              file="${buildprops.file}">

    <entry key="build.number" value="${build.number}"/>  ◁──── Writes build
                                                                number

    <entry key="expiration.date"
           type="date"
           operation="+"
           value="1"                    Generates a date one
           default="now"                month from today
           unit="month" />
</propertyfile>
```

The `<entry>` element of the `<propertyfile>` task has several attributes that work in conjunction with one another. The `type` attribute allows for `int`, `date`, or the default `string`. The `operation` attribute is either +, -, or the default of =. Date types support a `unit` attribute and a special `default` of now. Refer to the documentation for more coverage of the `<entry>` attributes. Existing property files are not completely overwritten by the `<propertyfile>` task, as `<propertyfile>` is designed to edit them, leaving existing properties untouched unless modified explicitly with an `<entry>` item. Comments, however, get lost in the process.

10.2.2   Adding audio and visual feedback during a build

We cannot help but mention two interesting optional tasks, `<sound>` and `<splash>`. The `<sound>` task is a fun addition to a build file and it could be useful when running an involved build process. The `<sound>` task enables audible alerts when a build completes; even different sounds, depending on build success or failure. The `<splash>` task displays a graphic during the build, providing eye candy but also the ability to personalize or brand a build.

"Ding, your build is done!"

Listing 10.3 demonstrates an example use of the `<sound>` task.

Listing 10.3   Using the `<sound>` task to alert on build success or failure

```
<project name="Sound" default="all">
  <property file="build.properties"/>
  <target name="init">
    <sound>
      <success source="${sound.dir}/success.wav" duration="500"/>
      <fail source="${sound.dir}/fail.wav" loops="2"/>
    </sound>
  </target>

  <target name="fail" depends="init">
    <fail/>
  </target>

  <target name="success" depends="init"/>

  <target name="all" depends="success"/>
</project>
```

A couple of bells and whistles about `<sound>` are the `duration` and `loops` attributes. If `source` is a directory rather than a file, a file is randomly picked from that directory. When the build completes, either the `<success>` or `<fail>` sound is played based on the build status. Any sound file format that the Java Media Framework recognizes will work with `<sound>`, such as WAV and AIFF formats. Java 1.3 or the JMF add-on is a `<sound>` dependency requirement.

A picture is worth a thousand words

The new Ant 1.5 `<splash>` task displays either the Ant logo or an image of your choosing while the build is running. As the build runs, a progress bar across the bottom moves along with every event, such as a tasks starting and finishing (build events are covered in chapter 21 in detail). Figure 10.1 shows an example of using a custom graphic.

Figure 10.1
Custom <splash> display, showing the build progress along the bottom

This task has potential for abuse, though, and it provides nothing functional to the build. It would be wrong to incorporate it into automated build processes, which run unattended. It is cute, though! This build file demonstrates its use:

```
<project name="splash" default="main">

  <target name="init">
    <splash imageurl="http://www.ehatchersolutions.com/logo.gif"
            showduration="5000"/>
    <sleep seconds="1"/>
    <sleep seconds="1"/>
    <sleep seconds="1"/>
    <sleep seconds="1"/>
    <sleep seconds="1"/>
    <sleep seconds="1"/>
  </target>

  <target name="main" depends="init"/>

</project>
```

The `<sleep>` tasks were added to demonstrate the progress bar moving as the build progresses. Note that while the progress bar along the bottom progresses as the build proceeds, it is not an indicator of how much work there is remaining.

10.2.3 Adding dependency checks

The `<javac>` dependency logic to ensure that out-of-date classes are recompiled during incremental builds implements a rudimentary check that only passes .java files to the compiler if the corresponding .class file is older or nonexistent. It does not rebuild classes when the files that they depend upon change, such as a parent class or an imported class. The `<depend>` task looks at the generated class files, extracts the references to other classes from these files, and then deletes the class files if any of their dependencies are newer. This clears out files for `<javac>` to rebuild. One fly in the ointment is that because compile-time constants, such as primitive datatype values and string literals, are inlined at compile time, neither `<javac>` nor `<depend>` can tell when a definition such as `Constants.DEBUG_BUILD` has changed from `true` to `false`.

Projects that do not have a substantial number of .java files can get away with simply doing a clean build and recompiling their entire source to ensure all is in sync. In situations where there is a large number of Java source files and the time to rebuild the entire source tree is prohibitive, the `<depend>` task is a great benefit to ensure incremental builds are as in sync as possible. Adding the dependency check to the build process is fairly simple; we just paste it in to the compile target above the `<javac>` call, as shown here:

```
<target name="compile" depends="init,release-settings">
  <depend srcdir="${src.dir}"
          destdir="${build.dir}/classes"
```

```
            cache="${build.dir}/dependencies"
            closure="true">
    <classpath>
      <pathelement location="${antbook-ant.jar}"/>
      <pathelement location="${antbook-common.jar}"/>
    </classpath>
  </depend>
  <javac destdir="${build.dir}/classes"
         debug="${build.debug}"
         includeAntRuntime="no"
         srcdir="src">
    <classpath refid="compile.classpath"/>
  </javac>
</target>
```

We inserted <depend> inside the compile target as it is only ever needed before the
<javac> call; there was little merit in providing a separate target. We considered writing a reusable target, either by pasting a new target into our shared targets.xml file, or by writing a stand-alone library build file. The former is easier to integrate with compile, just another dependency in the target's list; the latter is more reusable. We refrained from either action until we had integrated it into all the targets, to see how much classpath variation there was, and so determine what parameters to support.

The two mandatory attributes of the <depend> task are srcdir, which points to the Java source, and destdir, which points to the classes. The cache attribute names a directory that is used to cache dependency information between runs. The task looks inside the class files to determine which classes they depend on, and as this information does not change when the source is unchanged, it can be safely cached from run to run to speed up the process. Because it does speed up the process, we highly recommend you always specify a cache directory. The final attribute we are using is closure, which tells the task whether to delete .class files if an indirect dependency has changed. The merits of this one are unclear: it may be safer to set closure=true, but faster to leave it unset.

There is also a nested attribute to specify a classpath. This is not mandatory; <depend> is not compiling the source and it does not need to know where all the packages the source depends upon are stored. Instead, the task uses any supplied classpath as a list of classes that may also have changed, and so dictate a rebuild of the local source. It looks inside JAR files to see the timestamps of the classes therein, deleting local .class files if needed classes in the JAR have changed. For speed, we only list the JAR files that our sibling projects create; a change in an external library such as ant.jar or lucene.jar is not detected. We usually only rebuild those libraries from their CVS repositories once a day, and we know to run a clean build of our own projects afterwards.

You can also include or exclude source files from the dependency checking by using nested <includes> and <excludes> elements. We have never done this, because, like <javac>, the task includes all Java files under the source directory automatically, and we have always wanted to check the dependency of our entire source.

Running the target adds one more line to the compilation target's output; here stating that two files were deleted:

```
compile:
   [depend] Deleted 2 out of date files in 0 seconds
    [javac] Compiling 3 source files to C:\AntBook\app\webapp\build\classes
```

Because this task ensures that source code changes are picked up more reliably, we always use this task in our projects. Sometimes the fact that it cannot detect dependencies upon imported constants (static final data) catches us out, as their changes do not propagate: remember to clean build every time you change a public constant. A regular clean build is always a good idea.

10.2.4 Grammar parsing with JavaCC

The Lucene indexing and search engine that we've incorporated into our example application allows for sophisticated search expressions such as these:

```
(foo OR bar) AND (baz OR boo)
title:ftp AND NOT content:telnet
```

Under the hood, Lucene's API can perform searches by using a Query object, which can be constructed either through the API directly (for example, a nested set of BooleanQuery objects), or more simply using the QueryParser, which takes expressions like those just shown and parses them into a Query object. The parsing of such expressions into Java objects can be done by using a grammar compiler. There are two grammar compilers with built-in Ant support: ANTLR and JavaCC. Because our particular application uses Lucene and because Lucene takes advantage of JavaCC, we feature it here.

JavaCC is a Java grammar compiler that compiles .jj files into .java source code. The Lucene query parser, for example, is written using JavaCC, compiled into .java files during Lucene's build process, and then compiled using the standard <javac> task. If you're writing your own meta-language by using JavaCC, the Ant <javacc> task is the quickest way to integrate the two-step sequence into your build process. The <javacc> task is simply a wrapper around the JavaCC command-line compiler.

Listing 10.4 is a piece of Lucene's own build file that uses the <javacc> task.

Listing 10.4 Lucene's own build, which uses Ant's JavaCC task

```
<target name="compile" depends="init,javacc_check" if="javacc.present">

  <!-- ... -->
  <javacc                                          Outputs to temporary directory
    target="${src.dir}/org/apache/lucene/queryParser/QueryParser.jj"
    javacchome="${javacc.zip.dir}"
    outputdirectory="${build.src}/org/apache/lucene/queryParser"/>

  <javac
    srcdir="${src.dir}:${build.src}"          ◄─── Compiles both
    includes="org/**/*.java"                         source trees
```

```
        destdir="${build.classes}"
        debug="${debug}">
      <classpath refid="classpath"/>
    </javac>
</target>
```

10.2.5   Regular expression replacement

If you're coming from a Unix and a Make-based build, chances are you'll be wondering where sed, awk, and Perl are hiding in Ant. The <replaceregexp> task is not quite a full-fledged version of those handy tools, but it can be just what you need to solve some of those tricky build process issues. Let's demonstrate regular expression replacement with an example: an application uses a file display.properties to define sort.order as a comma-delimited list. The application uses this information to provide default sorting of names displayed.

```
sort.order=lastName,firstName
```

Suppose certain customers want to deviate from this default and swap the order. Rather than provide a separate properties file for each customer, we could use the <replaceregexp> task to maintain a single file and note the exceptions (perhaps in a customer-specific properties file loaded in Ant), as the following code illustrates:

```
<project name="Regexp" default="default">
  <property name="customer" value="normal"/>
  <property file="${customer}.properties"/>

  <target name="init">
    <delete dir="output"/>
    <mkdir dir="output"/>
  </target>

  <target name="default" depends="init" if="customer.different">
    <copy file="display.properties" todir="output"/>
    <replaceregexp file="output/display.properties"
                   match="sort.order=(.*),(.*)"
                   replace="sort.order\2,\1"
                   byline="true" />
  </target>

</project>
```

The <replaceregexp> shown matches a comma-delimited sort.order line and replaces it with the two fields swapped. The <replaceregexp> task modifies files in place. Notice that the source file was copied to a working directory prior to replacement.

Although the main point is to demonstrate a use of <replaceregexp>, the conditional flag was added to provide some insight into how Ant properties can be used to make life easier, even given exceptions to rules. In this example, an `acme.properties` file could be provided with `customer.different=true` and Ant run with `ant -Dcustomer=acme`. Alternatively, `customer.different` could be enabled directly using `ant -Dcustomer.different=yes`.

10.3 USING SOFTWARE CONFIGURATION MANAGEMENT TASKS

SCM is the foundation to any successful software project. We expect that you are using some form of SCM to look after your code, as any software professional should. Ant happily works with most SCM systems, and can coexist with any of them. There are a multitude of optional tasks that enable you to make calls to your SCM system from inside Ant. These tasks let you check in and check out code, sometimes even to add labels. The exact set of services available depends upon the particular SCM tool in use: each tool has a unique set of corresponding Ant tasks.

At the time of writing, Ant supports these SCM tools: CVS, Perforce, ClearCase, SourceSafe, SourceOffsite, StarTeam, Merant PVCS, and Continuus. Each has its own tasks and its own set of operations. Table 10.2 lists the core set of corresponding Ant tasks.

Table 10.2 Ant-supported SCM systems and the core actions supported by Ant's tasks.

SCM System	update	check out	check in	label
CVS	`<cvs command="update">`	`<cvs command="checkout">`	`<cvs command="commit">`	`<cvs command="label">`
ClearCase	`<ccupdate>`	`<cccheckout>`	`<cccheckin>`	N/A
Continuus	N/A	`<ccmcheckout>`	`<ccmcheckin>`	N/A
PVCS	`<pvcs>`	N/A	N/A	N/A
SourceSafe	`<vssget>`	`<vsscheckout>`	`<vsscheckin>`	`<vsslabel>`
SourceOffSite	`<sosget>`	`<soscheckout>`	`<soscheckin>`	`<soslabel>`
StarTeam	N/A	`<stcheckout>`	`<stcheckin>`	`<stlabel>`
Perforce	`<p4sync>`	`<p4edit>`	`<p4submit>`	`<p4label>`

All the tasks need some external support to run. Except for StarTeam, all rely on a native executable on the path, such as `cvs`, `p4`, and `cleartool`. The StarTeam tasks use a Java library supplied by the vendor, which must be dropped into the ANT_HOME\lib directory. All of the SCM tasks, except for the `<cvs>` task, are optional tasks. Ironically, and perhaps understandably because of its popularity, the `<cvs>` task is a built-in task, although it does require the CVS command-line executable to be available. The rest of this section briefly touches on a few of these SCM tasks, noting any issues that we are aware of.

10.3.1 CVS

During the development of this book, we used a CVS server as our repository for source and the book's chapters themselves. Our automated builds that were developed for the CruiseControl section of chapter 16 required that we update our build machine from our SCM. The code to do this uses one `<cvs>` task, as shown here:

```
<property name="root.dir" location="${env.TEMP}"/>
<property name="cvs.username" value="${user.name}"/>
<property name="cvs.host" value="localhost"/>
<property name="cvs.root"
          value=":pserver:${cvs.username}@${cvs.host}:/home/cvs/projects"/>
<property name="cvs.passfile" value="../.cvspass"/>
<property name="cvs.dir" location="${root.dir}"/>
<property name="cvs.package" value="AntBook/app"/>

<cvs cvsRoot="${cvs.root}"
     command="checkout"
     dest="${root.dir}"
     package="${cvs.package}"
     passfile="${cvs.passfile}"
     failonerror="yes" />
```

The important things to note are that we use a temporary directory for our continuous builds (we use the environment's TEMP directory) and that we set `failonerror` to ensure that a <cvs> failure is fatal, which is not the default.

Generating change reports from a CVS repository

Ant 1.5 adds two nice core tasks that work with CVS repositories: <cvschangelog> and <cvstagdiff>. The <cvschangelog> task generates an XML file containing all the changes that have occurred within a specified date range on CVS modules. The <cvstagdiff> task generates an XML file containing the differences between two CVS tags. Pleasantly, Ant ships with the Extensible Stylesheet Language (XSL) files changelog.xsl and tagdiff.xsl, both in ANT_HOME/etc, which turn these XML files into attractive hypertext markup language (HTML) reports. Refer to Ant's documentation for more details on these tasks, but we leave you with an example of how to generate a report from a CVS change log:

```
<cvschangelog destfile="changelog.xml"/>

<xslt in="changelog.xml"
      out="changelog.html"
      style="${ant.home}/etc/changelog.xsl">
  <param name="title" expression="AntBook ChangeLog"/>
  <param name="module" expression="AntBook"/>
</xslt>
```

Chapter 13 covers the <xslt> task in more detail.

10.3.2   ClearCase

Although you can check files out, the current tasks don't follow the strict application of the Rational process, in which you have to name a particular task or defect related to the check out. Nor is there any method by which to label files from Ant, which is a feature desperately needed for completely automated deployment.

We have encountered odd behavior when, after an "ant clean" deleted the build and dist directories in a ClearCase file system, Ant could not build again until the system was rebooted. If you encounter the same problem, try the same solution.

10.4   USING THIRD-PARTY TASKS

Because of the increasing number of useful third-party tasks, it is very likely that you will decide to use one or more of them in your build process. The types of tasks available vary widely from source code style checkers to application server deployment tasks. Regardless of the task you want to use, the process for integrating it into an Ant build file is all the same: simply declare the task(s) with <taskdef>.

This section discusses using the <taskdef> task in more detail.

10.4.1   Defining tasks with <taskdef>

Ant automatically knows which Java class implements each of the core and optional tasks. But to use a new third-party task in a build file, you need to tell Ant about it. This is what the <taskdef> task is used for. The <taskdef> task itself is a core task. To define a task, you specify a name and a fully qualified Java class name. The name is arbitrary, but unique within the build file, and is used as the XML element name to invoke the task later in the build file.

To demonstrate how to declare a third-party task, we'll use XDoclet, a task that we cover in the next chapter. The following code shows how to declare the XDoclet <document> task:

```
<taskdef name="document"
         classname="xdoclet.doc.DocumentDocletTask"
         classpath="${xdoclet.jar}"/>
```

The class xdoclet.doc.DocumentDocletTask exists in the JAR file referenced by the ${xdoclet.jar} property. Our build file now has the capability to use the <document> task in the same manner as any other task is used. Defining multiple tasks can be accomplished simply with multiple <taskdef> tasks, but if multiple related tasks are being used there is an alternative.

Defining multiple tasks, an alternative

Because task declarations are essentially name/value pairs, multiple tasks can be defined in a single properties file and loaded either directly as a properties file, or as a resource from a classpath. For example, to define two of the XDoclet tasks we could use an xdoclet_tasks.properties file as shown here:

```
document=xdoclet.doc.DocumentDocletTask
xdoclet=xdoclet.DocletTask
```

Loading this properties file by using the file variant would define both tasks, <document> and <xdoclet>, in one <taskdef>:

```
<taskdef file="xdoclet_tasks.properties"
         classpath="${xdoclet.jar}"/>
```

If the task definition properties file is in the classpath, then the resource variant may be used:

```
<taskdef resource="taskdef.properties">
  <classpath refid="task.classpath"/>
</taskdef>
```

NOTE Using the resource variant is a nice feature that is demonstrated more fully in the XDoclet chapter. It is the same mechanism that Ant uses. In Ant's ant.jar, there is a properties file named org/apache/tools/ant/taskdefs/defaults.properties with the task/class name pairs listed for all of Ant's built-in and optional tasks.

Unrelated tasks should be declared using individual `<taskdef>`'s because they each have their own dependencies and classpaths. The XDoclet tasks, however, are all in the same library and have the same dependency requirements. We encourage third-party Ant task providers to embed a taskdef.properties file in the root folder of the distributable JAR to enable users to more easily incorporate tasks into a build.

10.5   NOTABLE THIRD-PARTY TASKS

There are several third-party tasks that stand out and deserve coverage. Unfortunately, we do not have the space to do justice to them all. Here are a few of our favorites.

10.5.1   Checkstyle

Do you catch yourself day-dreaming about a warm tropical island beach, gentle breeze blowing, and your source code devoid of hard tabs? We do! Bringing up the topic of coding standards is often followed by heated dead-end "discussions" on where curly brackets should go. This is serious business, and seeing two senior developers duke it out over whether public member variables are allowed is not a pretty sight. Because the authors take coding standards seriously[2] and even more seriously the desire to shift work to the build process and off of the people, our build is integrated with a style-checking task.

Checkstyle is currently a SourceForge-hosted project, delivering a stand-alone command-line tool and an Ant task. It has the capability to check the following, and more:

- Unused and duplicate import statements
- Proper and preferred Javadoc tag usage
- License header in all modules
- Preferred placement of curly brackets
- Existence of tabs
- Line length maximum
- Naming conventions for classes, methods, and variables
- Java Language Specification recommended modifier ordering

---

[2] Hey, we're human, too, so be gentle on us if we inadvertently miss adhering to our own strict standards. If we address issues reported by Checkstyle, however, we'll catch most mistakes.

Checkstyle's default settings claim to adhere to Sun's coding conventions (Sun 2000), and if those defaults aren't sufficient for your needs, its many configuration options will likely get you to your in-house coding standards. Listing 10.5 shows our task for this, which is implemented in a reusable library build file.

Listing 10.5   Checkstyle.xml: checking our coding style standards

```xml
<?xml version="1.0"?>
<!DOCTYPE project [
    <!ENTITY properties SYSTEM "properties.xml">      <----  Our project-wide
]>                                                          property settings
<project name="Checkstyle" default="main">

  <!-- Override typical lib.dir, which is by default relative to
       our subdirectory projects -->
  <property name="lib.dir" location="lib"/>

  <!-- Load in all standard app-wide properties -->
  &properties;
                                                      Default project to check,
  <property name="project" value="ant"/>      <----  but typically overridden

  <property name="checkstyle.src.dir" location="${project}/src"/>
  <property name="output.dir" location="checkstyle/${project}"/>
  <property name="checkstyle-noframes.xsl"
            location="xdocs/stylesheets/checkstyle-noframes.xsl"/>

  <path id="checkstyle.classpath">
    <pathelement location="${checkstyle.jar}"/>
  </path>

  <taskdef resource="checkstyletask.properties"
           classpathref="checkstyle.classpath"/>

  <target name="init">
    <echo message="Checking style of ${project}"/>
    <mkdir dir="${output.dir}"/>
  </target>

  <target name="checkstyle" depends="init">                 Don't be too harsh
    <checkstyle failOnViolation="false"   <--------------   about violations!
                maxLineLen="67"
                cacheFile="${output.dir}/checkstyle.cache">
      <formatter type="plain"/>  <-----
    <formatter type="xml" toFile="${output.dir}/checkstyle.xml"/>
      <fileset dir="${checkstyle.src.dir}" includes="**/*.java"/>
    </checkstyle>
                                                                 Displays
                                                               interactively
    <style basedir="${output.dir}" destdir="${output.dir}"    and logs for
           includes="checkstyle.xml"                            reporting
           style="${checkstyle-noframes.xsl}"/>
  </target>

  <target name="main" depends="checkstyle"/>
</project>
```

Like `<junitreport>` (covered in chapter 4) the `<checkstyle>` task has formatters to allow its output to be written to the console or log file, as well as to XML format for integrated reporting. We demonstrate the transformation for reporting in chapter 13's section on XSL and the `<style>` task (an alias for the `<xslt>` task).

The checkstyle.xml file lives in our project root directory, and because our directory naming conventions are consistent among all subprojects, it is easy to check any project from the command-line from any subdirectory:

```
ant -find checkstyle.xml -Dproject=webapp
```

This command searches towards the root directory until it finds checkstyle.xml and then checks the coding standards of our webapp project.

Installing Checkstyle

Obtain the latest Checkstyle release version from http://checkstyle.sourceforge.net (we used version 2.1). The easiest install is simply to extract the "-all" JAR from the distribution into your ANT_HOME/lib directory. In our case, the JAR name is checkstyle-all-2.1.jar. Rather than putting the JAR into ANT_HOME/lib, we placed the Checkstyle distribution into our global SCM-maintained lib directory and mapped the `checkstyle.jar` property to the JAR location in our project-wide properties.xml.

10.5.2 Torque–object-relational mapping

One of the best kept secrets from the Jakarta Project is Torque, a persistence layer that provides object-relational mapping to relational databases. Previously Torque was a component of the Turbine application server framework, but has been decoupled for general-purpose use. If you don't need the sophisticated features of Enterprise JavaBeans, such as distributed transactions, Torque is likely to provide everything you need in a persistence layer. Torque includes several third-party Ant tasks, which are described in table 10.3.

Table 10.3   Torque's Ant tasks

Task name	Task description
TorqueCreateDatabase	Generates simple scripts for creating databases on various platforms
TorqueDataDTDTask	Generates data DTD from an XML Schema describing a database structure
TorqueDataDumpTask	Dumps data from db into XML
TorqueDataSQLTask	Generates SQL source from an XML data file
TorqueJDBCTransformTask	Generates an XML Schema of an existing database from JDBC metadata
TorqueObjectModelTask	Uses the Velocity template engine to generate schema-based source code
TorqueSQLExecTask	Inserts an SQL file into its designated database
TorqueSQLTask	Generates SQL source from an XML Schema describing a database structure
TorqueSQLTransformTask	Generates an XML Schema from an SQL schema
TorqueDocumentationTask	Generates HTML or XML documentation for XML Schemas

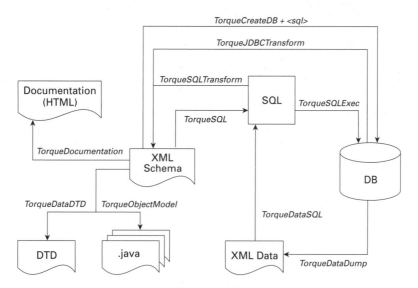

Figure 10.2 Torque's Ant tasks. The schema can be generated from a database, or the database generated from the schema. SQL scripts, data dump to XML, and schema documentation are among Torque's other build-time features.

These tasks are illustrated in figure 10.2, demonstrating the numerous ways in which Torque's tasks can benefit a build process.

Even if your project is not using Torque's persistence layer, its Ant tasks could still be useful. The XML representation of a database schema and flexible ways of using that representation to build a database or generate code from the XML Schema are incredibly powerful build-time behaviors. Torque's code-generation engine relies on Velocity, another of Jakarta's projects, for generating source code from template files. When starting with Torque, the first question is: "What is the one definitive source of my schema?" The idea is to get your schema into Torque's schema XML format. Although using the XML format as the definitive schema source is typical, SQL scripts could be the root schema source, or even an existing database that can be accessed using JDBC. Remember, pragmatic programmers keep a single unambiguous representation of all metadata!

Torque in action

Our project takes advantage of Torque's persistence and uses several of its Ant tasks. Our web applications' persistence only consists of a single table, USER. The table columns represent username, password, and a full name. We modeled this table in Torque's XML Schema format as shown in listing 10.6.

```xml
<?xml version="1.0" encoding="ISO-8859-1" standalone="no" ?>
<!DOCTYPE database SYSTEM "http://jakarta.apache.org/turbine/dtd/data-
base.dtd">

<database name="default" package="org.example.antbook.model" defaultId-
Method="native" baseClass="BaseObject" basePeer="BasePeer">
  <table name="USER" javaName="User">
    <column name="USER_ID" javaName="UserId" primaryKey="true"
           required="true" type="INTEGER" />
    <column name="USERNAME" javaName="Username"
           required="true" type="VARCHAR" size="64"/>
    <column name="PASSWORD" javaName="Password" required="true"
           type="VARCHAR" size="64"/>
    <column name="FULLNAME" javaName="Fullname" required="true"
           type="VARCHAR" size="128"/>
  </table>
</database>
```

This single representation is responsible for generating several other pieces during the stages of our build process:

1 Prior to compilation, we use the TorqueObjectModelTask (`<torque-om>` is our mapping to it) to generate Java code representing our data as "base" and "peer" objects, providing abstraction to hide the persistence mechanism. The code is generated into a gensrc subdirectory of build.

2 Later in the build process SQL files are generated using the `<torque-sql>` task. Again, the output goes to the build directory in an sql subdirectory.

3 A data document type definition (DTD) is generated for use in the next step from a sample data XML file in order to ship our application with built-in data. The `<torque-datadtd>` task takes care of this.

4 The generated DTD and a sample data XML file are used by `<torque-datasql>` to generate Structured Query Language (SQL) commands for populating the database with the data defined in the XML file.

5 Ant's built-in `<sql>` task constructs a new database with the schema SQL generated in step 2.

6 The `<sql>` task is used again, this time to populate the database with sample data.

It is unlikely that most Torque-based projects need all of these steps. We have the added steps for generating an embedded prepopulated sample database. These steps can be optimized with clever use of `<uptodate>` to prevent regeneration of files that will not change until the schema itself changes. We are using the lightweight Hypersonic SQL database, which allows us to run a complete database within our web application (no separate server process is needed). The Torque project is still working on a 3.0 release at the time of writing, so we used a development version. Because some of the details may change, it is best for us not to show the specifics of Torque's Ant task syntax. The Torque distribution provides detailed documentation and examples, and the user community is helpful and responsive.

> **NOTE** A great benefit of having a single source representation of schema metadata surfaced while writing this chapter. The original table was named SEARCH_USER during some experimentation. For example purposes, we wanted it shortened to USER. Simply changing it in one place in antbook-schema.xml was all it took, combined with a clean build, to ensure the old generated code and SQL files were eradicated. Many database-driven projects have serious domino effect nightmares if a table or column changes name or type. Torque and Ant make such issues much less severe and more easily managed.

Installing Torque

Because at the time of writing a new release or Torque was on the horizon, we encourage you to check with the Jakarta web site to get the latest version and installation/usage instructions. There are a number of dependencies that the Torque tasks require, and these currently ship with release versions of Torque.

10.6 THE ANT-CONTRIB TASKS

SourceForge hosts the ant-contrib (note the dash, a seemingly inactive project without it also exists) project. This project contains several Ant tasks that have been rejected for inclusion into the core Ant code base or that are being developed and tested prior to submission to Ant. These tasks are well developed (two of Ant's committers are actually members of this project) and maintained. Here are a few tasks that exist in ant-contrib:

- C++ compiling and linking tasks—we discuss these tasks in more detail in chapter 17.
- <propertycopy>—allows for property expansion to dereference properties dynamically, similar to the trick shown in chapter 3.
- <osfamily>—sets a property to indicate the operating system family, such as mac, windows, and unix. This is much simpler than using Ant's <condition> task to accomplish the same effect.
- The controversial logic tasks: <if>, <switch>, <foreach>, and <try-catch> tasks. Although these tasks may make your build seem more pleasant, resist the temptation to program your build files in a procedural way. Use these with caution and with knowledge of the alternatives.

Installing the ant-contrib tasks

The ant-contrib project is available at http://sourceforge.net/projects/ant-contrib/. At the time of writing, only the CPP tasks were available as a binary download, so be prepared to build the others yourself by pulling the ant-contrib project to your local system by using a CVS client and by using its own provided Ant build file to create a JAR file to use within your own projects. The build incorporates a `<taskdef>` usable properties file into its JAR, allowing all tasks to be defined with a single `<taskdef>`:

```
<property name="ant-contrib.jar"
          location="lib/ant-contrib-0.1.jar"/>

<taskdef resource="net/sf/antcontrib/antcontrib.properties"
          classpath="${ant-contrib.jar}"/>
```

Copying properties

In section 3.10.1 we demonstrate an obscure way to dereference property values by using Ant's built-in capabilities. The ant-contrib `<propertycopy>` task makes property dereferencing much cleaner and easier to understand. We have refactored the example we presented earlier to use `<propertycopy>`:

```
<target name="propertycopy">
  <property name="X" value="Y"/>
  <property name="Y" value="Z"/>
  <propertycopy name="A" from="${X}"/>
  <echo message="A = ${A}"/>
</target>
```

The value of `${X}` is "Y". The `from` attribute of `<propertycopy>` refers to an Ant property name, "Y" in this example. The value of the property Y is "Z", so the output is "A = Z". This is a much nicer alternative than using the `refid` tricks.

Operating system family

Ant relieves us of many platform-specific issues, but there are settings that typically need to vary across platforms. The ant-contrib `<osfamily>` task enables us to set an Ant property with the value `mac`, `windows`, `dos`, or `unix`. By using this value, we can load a platform-specific properties file, for example:

```
<target name="osfamily">
  <osfamily property="os.family" />
  <echo message="O/S family is ${os.family}"/>
  <property file="${os.family}.properties"/>
</target>
```

Executing this target on a Windows 2000 machine would load windows.properties. Loading properties based on operating system family, or by hostname, enables build files to adapt easily to their operating environment.

Using if/then/else logic

A common frustration that folks new to Ant experience is that its declarative nature can seem overly constraining. Performing if/then/else and switching logic using Ant's built-in capabilities is by design difficult. Ant's XML "language" was not meant to be a generalized scripting language. To the rescue come the logic tasks from ant-contrib for those who simply must have explicit logic in a build process. Here is an example of an `<if>`/`<then>`/`<else>` construct straight from the ant-contrib API documentation:

```
<target name="if">
  <if>
    <equals arg1="${foo}" arg2="bar" />

    <then>
      <echo message="The value of property foo is bar" />
    </then>

    <else>
      <echo message="The value of property foo is not bar" />
    </else>
  </if>
</target>
```

A single condition, which could be anything that the `<condition>` task accepts, including the `<and>` or `<or>` construct, is contained within the `<if>` tag. As expected, if the condition is true the tasks within the `<then>` section are executed, otherwise the ones within the `<else>` section execute.

Multiple value switching

Along the same vein as the `<if>` task, ant-contrib includes a `<switch>` task, which enables a single value to control the execution branch:

```
<target name="switch">
  <switch value="${foo}">

    <case value="bar">
      <echo message="The value of property foo is bar" />
    </case>

    <case value="baz">
      <echo message="The value of property foo is baz" />
    </case>

    <default>
      <echo message="The value of property foo is not sensible" />
    </default>

  </switch>
</target>
```

The <case> task container specifies the value that must equal the <switch> value for the containing tasks to be executed. A <default> container is executed if the value does not match any of the <case> values.

Catching task exceptions

A failing Ant task normally immediately stops the build with a BUILD FAILED banner. If, for some reason, you want the build to continue when a task fails, use the <trycatch> ant-contrib task. Mirroring Java's exception handling facilities, <trycatch> has nested <catch> and <finally> containers to allow tasks to execute in those two conditions. This example demonstrates its usage:

```
<target name="trycatch">
  <trycatch property="exception.message"
            reference="exception.ref">

    <try>
      <fail>Oops!</fail>
    </try>

    <catch>
      <echo>Caught</echo>
    </catch>

    <finally>
      <echo>Finally</echo>
    </finally>

  </trycatch>

  <echo>As property: ${exception.message}</echo>
  <property name="exception.value" refid="exception.ref" />
  <echo>From reference: ${exception.value}</echo>
</target>
```

Executing this target produces this output:

```
trycatch:
 [trycatch] Caught exception: Oops!
     [echo] Caught
     [echo] Finally
     [echo] As property: Oops!
     [echo] From reference: C:\AntBook\Sections\Applying\tasks\
                ant-contrib.xml:72: Oops!

BUILD SUCCESSFUL
```

Of note is that the build succeeded despite <fail> executing. Both the <catch> and <finally> execute when a failure is encountered in the <try> block. If no failure had occurred, only the <finally> block would have subsequently executed.

Using explicit iteration

You may find yourself wishing there was a way to perform a set of Ant tasks for every file in a fileset, or iterating over a list of values. With the ant-contrib `<foreach>` task, such iteration is easily accomplished. In our example, we iterate over a set of string values as well as a set of files.

```
<target name="for-each">
  <foreach list="1,2,3" target="loop" param="var"
           delimiter=",">
    <fileset dir="."/>
  </foreach>
</target>

<target name="loop">
  <echo message="var = ${var}"/>
</target>
```

The `<foreach>` task has two lists that it iterates, one specified using the `list` attribute, followed by each file in the optional nested `<fileset>`. Typical usage would not include the use of both `list` and `<fileset>` but using both is acceptable as well. The `target` and `param` attributes are required. The target attribute specifies an Ant target in the same build file that will be invoked for each iteration, with the param-named property being set to the `list` item or file name.

In our example, the `loop` target will be executed repeatedly, with the `var` property being set to 1 for the first iteration, then to 2 and to 3. After the `list` values complete, the filenames in the fileset are provided as `var` values. The output is

```
for-each:

loop:
     [echo] var = 1

loop:
     [echo] var = 2

loop:
     [echo] var = 3

loop:
     [echo] var = C:\AntBook\Sections\Applying\tasks\ant-contrib.xml

loop:
     [echo] var = C:\AntBook\Sections\Applying\tasks\build\build.properties
 .
 .
 .
```

The target is invoked for each iteration by using the underlying mechanism that the `<antcall>` task uses, which means that the dependencies of the target are reevaluated each iteration.

10.7   SHARING TASK DEFINITIONS AMONG PROJECTS

In larger build environments in which many components, products, and build files exist, centralizing common pieces used by builds is important. Using a central properties file is a good technique for defining the name/class pairs for all third-party or custom tasks. Classpath issues make this more difficult because all dependencies of all tasks defined need to be in a single classpath for `<taskdef>`.

Another technique is to use XML entity references, as demonstrated in chapter 9. In our application build system, we created a taskdef.xml file containing:

```
<path id="xdoclet.classpath">
  <pathelement location="${xdoclet.jar}"/>
  <pathelement location="${log4j.jar}"/>
  <!-- javadoc is needed -->
  <pathelement path="${java.class.path}"/>
  <path refid="test.classpath"/>
</path>
<taskdef name="document"
         classname="xdoclet.doc.DocumentDocletTask"
         classpathref="xdoclet.classpath"/>
<taskdef name="xdoclet"
         classname="xdoclet.DocletTask"
         classpath="${xdoclet.jar}"/>

<path id="checkstyle.classpath">
  <pathelement location="${checkstyle.jar}"/>
</path>
<taskdef name="checkstyle"
         classname="com.puppycrawl.tools.checkstyle.CheckStyleTask"
         classpathref="checkstyle.classpath"/>
```

Each build file that will be using these tasks specifies the entity reference at the top of its build.xml:

```
<!DOCTYPE project [
    <!ENTITY taskdef SYSTEM "file:../taskdef.xml">
]>
```

Our projects all live one directory below where the XML file resides, so a relative path is used to point up a directory. Later in our build file, before any targets are defined, the entity reference is used:

```
&taskdef;
```

Using entity references does have its drawback because the path from the build file to the included file must be a fixed, although likely relative, path. If the build file is moved, so must any relative-referenced entities.

10.8   BEST PRACTICES

We routinely use Ant's optional tasks, as well as third-party and custom tasks. We consider `<junit>` and `<junitreport>` mandatory tasks in a build process.

All major projects we work on incorporate the `<propertyfile>` task to capture build-time information.

Do not be put off by tasks that require you to download additional dependencies. Typically, dropping JAR files into ANT_HOME/lib is all that it takes to get up and running with the optional tasks that require an external library, such as `<ftp>`. However, we actually recommend keeping as much out of ANT_HOME/lib as possible. Many tasks can be used by specifying their classpath in `<taskdef>`; unfortunately, however, there are classloader issues that require some libraries to be in the system classpath. Experiment with libraries outside of ANT_HOME/lib, because this allows you to locate them in a more centralized directory structure minimizing installation issues for users of your build files.

Ask your vendors for Ant support to make your build life easier. Vendors recognize the value of working with Ant and many are already providing custom tasks, but make it known to them if deployment or other integration is too difficult to automate with Ant.

Keep external task libraries and their dependencies under source code control. Building your system should be as easy as pulling from the repository, perhaps making a few *documented* configuration changes, and executing an Ant build.

When a need arises for a task that you feel does not exist within Ant's core or optional tasks, check with the Ant web site, which maintains a list of resources for third-party tasks hosted elsewhere. If that fails to identify what you're looking for, inquire on the Ant-user list. Odds are that what you need can already be done in some way. The Ant-user community is the resource we recommend after reading Ant's documentation and consulting Ant's resource links.

10.9 SUMMARY

Inevitably, you will need to add additional tasks to your build process. Ant provides built-in (or core) tasks and also ships with optional tasks that typically require additional components in order to function properly. Vendors or authors of other open-source software projects have developed third-party Ant tasks to provide benefits specific to their products. These tasks are easily integrated into an Ant build by using `<taskdef>`. After reading this chapter, you should be comfortable with setting up and using Ant's optional tasks and integrating third-party tasks into a build file.

There are some very powerful Ant tasks in existence, many of which are not provided with Ant's distribution. Torque and Checkstyle are just a couple of our favorites. The next chapter is dedicated entirely to another very special set of Ant tasks: XDoclet.

Ant's web site provides links to additional third-party tasks. If Ant doesn't provide what you need, check with the Ant web site or with the vendor of the product you are automating around. If all else fails, check with the Ant user community email list before reinventing the wheel by creating a custom task. Writing your own task can be fairly easy, depending on its goal. We will show you how to write your own Ant task in chapter 19.

C H A P T E R   1 1

XDoclet

11.1   Installing XDoclet   261
11.2   To-do list generation   261
11.3   XDoclet architecture   262
11.4   Writing your own XDoclet template   265

11.5   Advanced XDoclet   273
11.6   The direction of XDoclet   275
11.7   XDoclet best practices   276
11.8   Summary   277

XDoclet is definitely in the running for one of the coolest and most powerful third-party Ant tasks currently available. Technically, it is an extended Javadoc Doclet engine that facilitates the use of custom at sign (@) Javadoc tags as metadata to dynamically generate files at build time. The XDoclet developers like to refer to it as "attribute-oriented programming." It was initially named EJBDoclet and designed for generating EJB artifacts such as deployment descriptors and stub code, but evolved into a more generic tool. Its usefulness is quite generic already, but it has many vendor- and product-specific built-in capabilities such as those listed in table 11.1.

Table 11.1   XDoclet vendor-specific capabilities

Vendor	Capability
EJB	Generates deployment descriptors and other artifacts from entity beans. Capabilities for vendor-specific metadata exist for WebLogic, WebSphere, JBoss, Castor, Struts, and others.
Struts	Action mappings and ActionForm bean definitions can be pulled from metadata to generate struts-config.xml.
Web	Provides web.xml generation pulling metadata for filters, listeners, and servlets.
	Provides JSP Tag Library Descriptor (TLD) generation from Taglib classes.
Other	Other vendors provide Apache SOAP, Castor, and JMX.

11.1 INSTALLING XDOCLET

XDoclet is freely available from http://xdoclet.sourceforge.net. Its installation is simply a matter of copying xdoclet.jar into ANT_HOME/lib. It also depends on Log4j (a logging utility that is a member of the Jakarta family); placing either log4j.jar or log4j-core.jar into ANT_HOME/lib is sufficient. We actually prefer to keep as many dependencies out of ANT_HOME/lib as possible. In the case of XDoclet, it is possible; and in our examples in this chapter, you will see `classpathref` used on `<taskdef>` to accomplish it. Please consult XDoclet's documentation for updated installation instructions, because the release following the version we used (1.1.2) will change the dependencies and installation.

11.2 TO-DO LIST GENERATION

Before moving into the gory details of XDoclet's structure as it relates to Ant build files, we want to first show a simple use for it: the generation of hyperlinked HTML to-do lists from source code comments.

It is common practice to add special comments in your code such as `/*TODO: ... */` or `//FIXME`. These notations enable code to be revisited later for cleanup or refactoring—you just search through the text for the comments. One of XDoclet's capabilities is generation of a Javadoc-like frame-based HTML report of all classes that have a particular "@" tag. This can be used to mark up classes for later work, with a tag named `@fixme`, `@todo`, or `@revisit`. The XDoclet tool comes with a task to process a tag and generate documentation of all outstanding uses of the tag. The `@todo` tag is special in that a future version of Javadoc will support this as a standard. Until `<javadoc>` supports it directly, `<xdoclet>` can be used to generate the report. An example of `@todo` usage in our sample application is in this class:

```
/**
 * A DocumentHandler implementation to delegate responsibility to
 * based on a files extension.  Currently only .html and .txt
 * files are handled, other extensions ignored.
 *
 * @author    Erik Hatcher
 * @created   October 28, 2001
 * @todo Implement dynamic document type lookup
 */
public class FileExtensionDocumentHandler
                                implements DocumentHandler {
  // implementation omitted
}
```

When running `<javadoc>` from JDK 1.4 over this source, it complains that you are using a tag that they plan to support in future:

```
Custom tags that could override future standard tags:  @todo. To avoid
potential overrides, use at least one period character (.) in custom tag names.
```

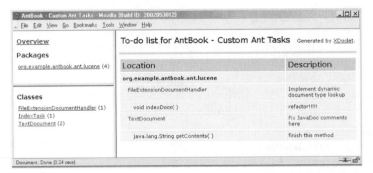

**Figure 11.1
To-do list generated
by XDoclet.**

Ignore this message; as long as you use the `@todo` tag for its intended purpose, to document code needing work, then the warning is irrelevant. Figure 11.1 shows a generated to-do list report.

By using the `<document>` task, generating the to-do list is simple:

```
<taskdef name="document"
        classname="xdoclet.doc.DocumentDocletTask"
        classpathref="xdoclet.classpath"/>
<document sourcepath="${src.dir}"
         destdir="${build.dir}/todo"
         classpathref="xdoclet.classpath">
  <fileset dir="${src.dir}">
    <include name="**/*.java" />
  </fileset>
  <info header="To-do list"
        projectname="Custom Ant Task"
        tag="todo"/>
</document>
```

The tag being reported can be changed, and could easily be some other tag of your choice, with "todo" being a generally useful usage of the `<info>` subtask. Interestingly, if the `projectname` attribute is not specified, it defaults to the Ant `<project>` name value, demonstrating that custom Ant tasks have access to container context information.

A typical process with the `@todo` reports is to generate them nightly for everyone to see. A technical team lead could run the to-do list reports manually to see what has been done and what is left to do. Chapter 16 discusses these periodic and continuous build processes.

11.3   *XDOCLET ARCHITECTURE*

Rather than delving into the implementation details of XDoclet, which date rapidly in the open-source world, we cover how XDoclet works from a build file perspective. XDoclet consists of several Ant tasks, each specific to a particular area, such as EJB or web development needs. Each task allows a set of *subtasks* to be nested within to provide specific generation for the parent tasks *context* and share configuration.

11.3.1 XDoclet's Ant tasks

There are several Ant custom tasks built into the XDoclet distribution. Each of these main tasks allow for specific subtasks nested as XML elements. Table 11.2 describes each of XDoclet's Ant tasks and subtasks.

Table 11.2 XDoclet's tasks and their supported subtasks.

Name	Classname (prefixed by xdoclet.)	Allowed subtasks	Subtask Purpose
DocletTask	`DocletTask`	`<template>`	Custom template subtask.
		`<xmltemplate>`	Enhanced template capabilities enabling validation of XML generation.
DocumentDocletTask	`doc.DocumentDocletTask`	`<info>`	General tag HTML reporting (see to-do list generation in section 11.2).
		`<documenttags>`	XDoclet uses XDoclet to document itself!
EjbDocletTask	`ejb.EjbDocletTask`	Many (See chapter 14 for more details.)	Generation of many EJB artifacts from vendor-specific deployment descriptors to value objects.
JMXDocletTask	`jmx.JMXDocletTask`	`<mbeaninterface>` `<mlet>` `<mx4jdescription>`	
WebDocletTask	`web.WebDocletTask`	`<webxml>` `<jbosswebxml>` `<jrunwebxml>` `<weblogicwebxml>`	
		`<jsptaglib>`	JSP Taglib descriptor (TLD) generation.
		`<strutsconfig>`	Jakarta Struts configuration file generation.
		`<webworkactiondoc>`, `<webworkconfigproperties>`	

Although the amount of information in table 11.2 is a bit overwhelming, it is quite straightforward to incorporate the pieces you need. As an example, let's revisit the to-do list generation. From table 11.2, the `<info>` subtask is served by the Document-DocletTask:

```
<taskdef name="document"
         classname="xdoclet.doc.DocumentDocletTask"
         classpathref="xdoclet.classpath"/>
```

The `<info>` tag is nested under `<document>`. Another useful bit of XDoclet trivia is that all of these tasks extend from DocletTask, which means that all attributes and elements for DocletTask work within them all. For example, the `<template>` sub-task can be nested within any of the other tasks, which can reduce some build file complexity if you need custom template generation as well as, say, web.xml generation (in which case only WebDocletTask needs to be task-defined).

11.3.2 Templating

All artifacts generated from the built-in subtasks are defined in template files (embedded in XDoclet's JAR file). Currently these template files are a mixture of fixed text and XDoclet *template tags* (future versions intend to support pluggable template engines such as Velocity). This syntax mirrors that of JavaServer Pages (JSP) taglibs, being XML-like tags. There are two classifications of the tags, *block tags* and *content tags*. Again, similar to JSP taglibs, content tags generate output directly while the block tags control the processing of their nested content. Block tags facilitate looping and conditional template processing.

A content tag that outputs the fully qualified class name:

```
<XDtClass:fullClassName/>
```

A block tag to loop over all methods implemented in the current class (excluding methods inherited from superclasses):

```
<XDtMethod:forAllMethods  extent="concrete-type">
  . . .
</XDtMethod:forAllMethods>
```

Tag namespaces

Each XDoclet template tag exists within a namespace to allow logical grouping of tag responsibilities. There are quite a few namespaces provided with XDoclet's distribution; here are a few:

- *XDtClass*—Tags for dealing with a Java class
- *XDtMethod*—Tags for dealing with methods within a class
- *XDtMerge*—Tag for pulling in external files to include or process and include the results
- *XDtConfig*—Tags to allow configurable control over template processing

Unlike JSP taglibs, tags can be nested within another tag's attributes, something that takes a bit of getting used to for those of us entrenched in JSP taglib syntax (examples of this are shown in listing 11.2). XDoclet comes with a plethora of tags covering everything from looping over all methods of a class to merging in external files during processing. There are many domain-specific tag features, particularly in the area of Enterprise JavaBeans. Section 11.3 provides examples of custom template files and their usage of a few of the template tags.

11.3.3 How XDoclet works

XDoclet internally contains a custom Javadoc doclet[1] that collects the "model" of all the classes it processes. This model contains all of the information that you typically see in the HTML Javadoc pages such as

- Inheritance hierarchy
- Methods and their return types, parameters, exceptions
- Javadoc comments at the class, method, and field levels
- Javadoc tags including, of course, the extensible tags that contain domain-specific metadata for the associated class, method, or field

The model is then handed to each of the nested subtasks for processing. These subtasks have the responsibility of controlling how those classes are processed. For example, in the `<info>` subtask shown in section 11.1, a handful of HTML files are created for the index, overview of classes, overview of packages, and then an HTML file for each package and each class. The generalized `<template>` subtask (covered in section 11.3) does far less work, by either handing the complete model to a single template or by processing the specified template for each class individually.

11.4 WRITING YOUR OWN XDOCLET TEMPLATE

A major part of our sample application is the development of a custom Ant task to build a Lucene index from an Ant fileset. As explained in section 10.4.1, custom tasks require the use of `<taskdef>` in order to be recognized. The `<taskdef>` task, as previously shown, enables tasks to be defined in a properties file. Our custom indexing task, as well as any other related custom Ant tasks that may be developed in the future, should be easily incorporated into another build process. Our properties file, named taskdef.properties, defines the task names and classes:

```
index=org.example.antbook.ant.lucene.IndexTask
```

Our build process embeds this properties file into the generated JAR. Defining the tasks embedded in our component is accomplished simply:

```
<path id="task.classpath">
  <pathelement location="${antbook-ant.jar}"/>
  <pathelement location="${lucene.jar}"/>
  <pathelement location="${tidy.jar}"/>
</path>

<taskdef resource="taskdef.properties">
  <classpath refid="task.classpath"/>
</taskdef>
```

---

[1] Currently, it keys off Ant's own `<javadoc>` task, a fact that will be obsolete by the time this is published. The related XJavadoc project is replacing this dependency on Sun's javadoc tool and increases XDoclet's performance and capabilities dramatically.

Only ${antbook-ant.jar}, a property with the full path to our tasks JAR file, is needed for the <taskdef>, but Lucene and JTidy are used by the task itself when invoked and so all dependencies used in the task should be included.

The properties file is generated dynamically from a template by using XDoclet. Later, if we implement more Ant tasks in our project, it won't be necessary to have another, often overlooked, manual step to add the task to the properties file. The only missing piece to generate the properties file is the task name. It is added to Index-Task as a class-level Javadoc comment: @ant.task name="index":[2]

```
/**
 *  Ant task to index files with Lucene
 *
 *@author     Erik
 *@created    October 27, 2001
 *@ant.task name="index"
 */
public class IndexTask extends Task {
    // ...
}
```

During our build, another target, taskdef, is added, as shown in listing 11.1.

Listing 11.6 Generation of a properties file based on extended Javadoc metadata

```
<taskdef name="xdoclet"
         classname="xdoclet.DocletTask"
         classpathref="xdoclet.classpath"/>

  <target name="taskdef" depends="init" unless="taskdef.uptodate"  ◁─────
    <echo message="Building taskdef descriptors"/>
    <xdoclet sourcepath="${src.dir}"
             destdir="${build.classes.dir}"                      The unless
             classpathref="xdoclet.classpath">               clause is covered
      <fileset dir="${src.dir}">                                in section 11.7.1
        <include name="**/*.java" />
      </fileset>
      <template templateFile="${taskdef.template}"
                destinationfile="${taskdef.properties}">
        <configParam name="date" value="${DSTAMP} @ ${TSTAMP}"/>
      </template>
    </xdoclet>                          The <template> subtask of XDoclet
  </target>                        powers the generation of our properties
                                    file using the specified templateFile
```

---

[2] Before the release of JDK 1.4, XDoclet used a colon as a separator on custom Javadoc tags. JDK 1.4's javadoc tool command-line tag option uses a colon as a separator character, and thus makes it impossible to use the -tag switch with @tags containing a colon. XDoclet was modified to allow either a colon or a dot.

The final piece to our properties file generation puzzle is the template. For our properties file, this template is used:

```
# Created: <XDtConfig:configParameterValue paramName="date"/>
<XDtClass:forAllClasses>
  <XDtClass:ifHasClassTag tagName="ant.task" paramName="name">
<XDtClass:classTagValue tagName="ant.task"
  paramName="name"/>=<XDtClass:fullClassName/>
</XDtClass:ifHasClassTag>
</XDtClass:forAllClasses>
```

In plain English, this template is iterating over all classes (`<XDtClass:forAllClasses>`), and processing the class if it has our custom `ant.task name="..."` tag. For each class with our tag, it writes out the value of that tag, `index` in our case, an equals sign, and then the full class name of the class being processed. The `<configParam>` child element of `<template>` and the corresponding `<XDtConfig:configParameterValue>` entry in the template file demonstrate XDoclet's ability to be customized from the Ant build itself by using the timestamp properties created by previous `<tstamp/>` (in our init target).

This is a very simple example of XDoclet's capabilities, yet it does provide our project with a tangible benefit—a programmer only needs to be aware of the XDoclet tags that need to be added to a class, method, or field. This metadata is only specified once and is used to dynamically generate other artifacts that require it. *The Pragmatic Programmer* (Hunt 2000) advocates this approach with these tips:

- *DRY—Don't Repeat Yourself*: For example, in the EJB domain it is common to duplicate metadata by manually creating several classes just for a single entity bean. This is unnecessary duplication, which can be avoided with XDoclet.

- *Program Close to the Problem Domain*—Putting information directly with the classes, fields, and methods by using domain-specific terms such as `@ant.task` enables us to be clear about meaning.

- *Write Code that Writes Code*—Why write a properties file that mirrors the same information that is already available in the code? Let the code itself define how related artifacts are generated. In most common cases, if you're using XDoclet, you don't even write code that writes code—you write a few extra Javadoc comments that cause code to be written with the XDoclet engine.

XDoclet does come with a small price: the slight curve involved in learning the template tags. The benefits are enormous, and the learning curve is time well spent.

11.4.1 Code generation

A project that one of the authors worked on had a situation in which there were value objects that represented a selection filter for constraining search results. These value objects were objects conforming to the JavaBean naming conventions and contained simple datatypes such as `String`, `Integer`, `Boolean`, and `Timestamp`. Struts implemented the web presentation tier. Struts forms[3] themselves adhere to the same bean-naming conventions, but are more than just data placeholders because a reset method is needed to initialize the values.[4] In this project, literally hundreds of these data classes existed, each requiring its own custom Struts ActionForm subclassSee figure 11.2.

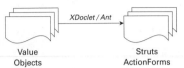

Figure 11.2
Using XDoclet for custom code generation

Value Objects

Struts ActionForms

XDoclet came to the rescue in order to avoid the manual creation of all this code. Having these classes autogenerated also reduced the maintenance headaches involved when we renamed, added, or removed a field. A sample value object looks like:

```
package org.example.antbook.filters;

import java.sql.Timestamp;

public class PersonSearch {

    private boolean active;
    private String lastName;
    private Integer minimumAge;
    private Timestamp startDate;

    // ... getters/setters removed for brevity ...
}
```

Take note of the package name and data types used in PersonSearch. The corresponding Struts ActionForm bean is generated as:

```
package org.example.antbook.view;

import javax.servlet.http.HttpServletRequest;
import org.apache.struts.action.ActionError;
import org.apache.struts.action.ActionErrors;
import org.apache.struts.action.ActionForm;

import org.apache.struts.action.ActionMapping;

public class PersonSearchForm extends ActionForm {

    private java.lang.String lastName;
    private java.lang.Integer minimumAge;
    private String startDate;
    private boolean active;
```

---

[3] A typical Struts form is a JavaBean class that contains setters/getters for all the fields of an HTML form.

[4] This is primarily because an unchecked check box in a web form does not get sent as part of the request.

```
void setLastName (java.lang.String lastName) {
    this.lastName = lastName;
}

java.lang.String getLastName () {
    return lastName;
}

void setMinimumAge (java.lang.Integer minimumAge) {
    this.minimumAge = minimumAge;
}

java.lang.Integer getMinimumAge () {
    return minimumAge;
}

void setStartDate (String startDate) {
    this.startDate = startDate;
}

String getStartDate () {
    return startDate;
}

void setActive (boolean active) {
    this.active = active;
}

boolean isActive () {
    return active;
}

public void reset(ActionMapping mapping, HttpServletRequest request) {
    setLastName("");
    setMinimumAge(null);
    setStartDate("");
    setActive(false);
}
}
```

Again, take note of package name and datatypes comparing PersonSearch to PersonSearchForm. The Timestamp datatype is represented simply as a String on a Struts form (validation occurs elsewhere). Generating the Struts form bean using XDoclet was accomplished with the template in listing 11.2 (XDoclet tags are in boldface).

Listing 11.7   struts_form.template: a mildly sophisticated value object converter

```
package <XDtPackage:packageOf><XDtClass:fullClassName/></XDtPackage:packageOf>;

import javax.servlet.http.HttpServletRequest;
import org.apache.struts.action.ActionError;
import org.apache.struts.action.ActionErrors;
import org.apache.struts.action.ActionForm;
import org.apache.struts.action.ActionMapping;
```

```
public class <XDtClass:className/>Form extends ActionForm {
<XDtMethod:forAllMethods   extent="concrete-type">
  <XDtMethod:ifHasMethod name="<XDtMethod:setterMethod/>"
parameters="<XDtMethod:methodType/>">
    <XDtType:ifIsOfType value="return-type" type="java.sql.Timestamp"
extent="concrete-type">
    private String <XDtMethod:propertyName/>;
    </XDtType:ifIsOfType>
    <XDtType:ifIsNotOfType value="return-type" type="java.sql.Timestamp"
extent="concrete-type">
    private <XDtMethod:methodType/> <XDtMethod:propertyName/>;
    </XDtType:ifIsNotOfType>
  </XDtMethod:ifHasMethod>
</XDtMethod:forAllMethods>

<XDtMethod:forAllMethods   extent="concrete-type">
  <XDtMethod:ifHasMethod name="<XDtMethod:setterMethod/>"
parameters="<XDtMethod:methodType/>">

    <XDtType:ifIsOfType value="return-type" type="java.sql.Timestamp"
extent="concrete-type">
    void <XDtMethod:setterMethod/> (String <XDtMethod:propertyName/>) {
        this.<XDtMethod:propertyName/> = <XDtMethod:propertyName/>;
    }

    String <XDtMethod:getterMethod/> () {
        return <XDtMethod:propertyName/>;
    }

    </XDtType:ifIsOfType>

    <XDtType:ifIsNotOfType value="return-type" type="java.sql.Timestamp"
extent="concrete-type">
    void <XDtMethod:setterMethod/> (<XDtMethod:methodType/>
<XDtMethod:propertyName/>) {
        this.<XDtMethod:propertyName/> = <XDtMethod:propertyName/>;
    }

    <XDtMethod:methodType/> <XDtMethod:getterMethod/> () {
        return <XDtMethod:propertyName/>;
    }

    </XDtType:ifIsNotOfType>
  </XDtMethod:ifHasMethod>
</XDtMethod:forAllMethods>

    public void reset(ActionMapping mapping, HttpServletRequest request) {
<XDtMethod:forAllMethods   extent="concrete-type">
  <XDtMethod:ifHasMethod name="<XDtMethod:getterMethod/>"
parameters="<XDtMethod:methodType/>">
    <XDtType:ifIsOfType value="return-type" type="java.lang.String"
extent="concrete-type">
        <XDtMethod:setterMethod/>("");
    </XDtType:ifIsOfType>
```

If the current method is a setter...

Convert Timestamp to String

Create reset method to initialize all fields

```
        <XDtType:ifIsOfType value="return-type" type="java.lang.Number"
extent="hierarchy">
            <XDtMethod:setterMethod/>(null);
        </XDtType:ifIsOfType>
        <XDtType:ifIsOfType value="return-type" type="java.sql.Timestamp"
extent="concrete-type">
            <XDtMethod:setterMethod/>("");
        </XDtType:ifIsOfType>
        <XDtType:ifIsOfType value="return-type" type="java.lang.Boolean"
extent="concrete-type">
            <XDtMethod:setterMethod/>(Boolean.FALSE);
        </XDtType:ifIsOfType>
        <XDtType:ifIsOfType value="return-type" type="boolean"
extent="concrete-type">
            <XDtMethod:setterMethod/>(false);
        </XDtType:ifIsOfType>
    </XDtMethod:ifHasMethod>
</XDtMethod:forAllMethods>
        }
}
```

While the template shown in listing 11.2 may seem daunting at first glance, the developer coding and maintenance time it saved far outweighed the learning curve of the XDoclet tag capabilities. XDoclet template tags are well documented and many samples exist to help get started. Our build file section to generate and compile is:

```
<target name="codegen" depends="init">
  <document sourcepath="${src.dir}"
            destdir="${gen.dir}"                            Short-cut
            classpathref="xdoclet.classpath">                 trick
    <fileset dir="src">
      <include name="**/filters/*.java" unless="class.name"/>
      <include name="**/${class.name}.java" if="class.name"/>  ◁──
    </fileset>
    <template templateFile="${template.file}"
              destinationfile="{0}Form.java">  ◁────────────
      <packageSubstitution packages="filters" substituteWith="view"/>
    </template>
  </document>
</target>                                                    Per-class
                                                            generation
<target name="compile" depends="codegen">
  <javac srcdir="${src.dir};${gen.dir}"
         destdir="${classes.dir}"
         debug="${javac.debug}"
         classpathref="compile.classpath"/>
</target>
```

The shortcut trick shown was also demonstrated in chapter 4 to enable individual test cases to be run. In this case, an individual class can be processed with our build file by running:

```
ant -Dclass.name=PersonSearch
```

NOTE   Because our `includes` pattern is `"**/${class.name}.java"` it will process all classes with the same name in our directory tree. The convenience of not having to specify the full package directory path outweighs the rare event of processing more than one file. This technique allows us to experiment with the template without having to wait for all of our source code to be processed.

We do not want our Struts form to be in the same package as the value object. The `<packageSubstitution>` subelement causes filters to be replaced with view in our package name. The `destinationfile` attribute of `<template>` allows the specification of per-class processing, substituting the *source* class package directory structure for `{0}`. Appending `"Form.java"` allowed us to rename the class according to our naming conventions.

Active and passive code generation

While there are certainly other solutions to the package problem, such as passing a configuration parameter to the template or creating your own custom subtask (see section 11.5.1), the `<move>` and `<mapper>` trick sufficed here. Depending on your needs, you could use this type of technique for *active* or *passive* code generation. Active code generation is an integral part of a build routine and the resultant code is completely throwaway and can be regenerated as needed. Our example is an active process, as our form bean code will only ever be code generated and not manually edited. Passive generation is a one-time process to create starter code that is designed for manual customization and should be incorporated into a source code repository along with the rest of the codebase. Whenever possible, opt for active code generation because this allows the metadata (in this case, the structure of the value object) to change and to be accounted for automatically. Regenerating customized code, of course, causes the loss of those customizations. However, subclassing actively generated code is a nice trick to achieve customization and dynamic generation.

Within Ant, active code generation is likely to be part of the main dependency graph so that a clean build would execute the code generation prior to compilation. Passive code generation should be implemented in a build file as a stand-alone target (or set of targets perhaps) that could be run when desired but was outside of the main build dependencies.

11.4.2   Per-class versus single-file generation

Our taskdef.properties XDoclet process only creates a single output file. Our Struts code generator produces an output file for each class processed. We accomplish this by specifying a `{0}` in the `<template>` `destinationfile` attribute. The `{0}` is replaced by the full package directory path of each class being processed. For example, specifying `{0}.xml` for `destinationfile` would generate a file *destdir*/org/ example/antbook/SomeClass.xml when processing org.example.antbook. SomeClass, where destdir is the directory specified on the main XDoclet task element. Just to clarify and to avoid possible confusion, the {0} substitution is an XDoclet feature, and not related to Ant's property substitution at all.

11.4.3 Filtering classes processed

There are several ways to filter the classes processed in order to accomplish fine grained needs.

- Limit the `<fileset>` to only the desired Java classes using includes/excludes.
- In per-class mode (that is, using {0} in `destinationfile`), use the `ofType`, `extent`, and `havingClassTag` attributes on the `<template>` subtask.
- In non-per-class mode, use the constraints on `<XDtClass:forAllClasses>`: `abstract`, `type`, and `extent`. Also, the conditions such as `<XDtClass:ifHasTag>`/`<XDtClass:ifDoesntHaveTag>` allow precise control.

The possible values of extent are concrete-type, superclass, and hierarchy. Using `extent="concrete-type"` with a specified type restricts processing to only classes of precisely that type, whereas specifying `extent="hierarchy"` allows processing of all classes that extend, even indirectly, from the specified type.

You may wonder why we did not employ this kind of filtering when building our `taskdef.properties`. Because of Ant's flexible introspective handling of custom tasks, tasks do not necessarily subclass from `org.apache.tools.ant.Task`. The only required piece for a Java class to become an Ant task is a method with the signature `void execute()`. (See chapter 19 for information about writing custom Ant tasks.) A greatly enhanced version of the XDoclet work to process Ant tasks is currently under way to autogenerate Ant's own documentation and metadata from the task source code.[5] This enhanced version accomplishes much greater filtering capabilities using custom built XDoclet subtasks and tag handlers.

Even though template-based generation is powerful all on its own, there are instances where you need more specialized functionality. For example, the `<info>` subtask generates many HTML files all based on the specified tag attribute. XDoclet's API is quite accessible and creating a subtask to accomplish sophisticated multifile generation is a lot easier than having to hand code and deal with the maintenance headaches that would inevitably follow from duplicated metadata being strewn throughout a project's files.

11.5 ADVANCED XDOCLET

For most purposes, the existing XDoclet capabilities are sufficient for your code or metadata generation needs. However, like Ant itself, XDoclet is easily extensible in a couple of ways. First, you can write a custom XDoclet subtask to control generation processes such as creating output file names, locations, and multiple file output.

---

[5] And, in fact, this work was used to build the task reference appendix in this book.

Second, you can create your own XDoclet template tags that can encapsulate more sophisticated logic than would be feasible or pleasant using the built-in template tags. Custom subtasks can more finely control the filtering of classes processed. XDoclet's API is both beyond the scope of this book and subject to change beyond our control. The next two sections give a generalized overview of these features.

11.5.1 Custom subtasks

A custom subtask is the controller of template processing. Using a custom subtask is as simple as specifying the class name in a build file:

```
<document sourcepath="${src.root}"
          destdir="${gen.dir}"
          mergedir="${basedir}/src"
          classpathref="xdoclet.classpath">
  <fileset dir="${src.dir}">
    <include name="**/*.java" unless="class.name"/>
    <include name="**/${class.name}.java" if="class.name"/>
  </fileset>
  <template subTaskClassName="org.apache.tools.ant.xdoclet.AntSubTask"
            templateFile="${task.properties.template}"
            destinationfile="task_defaults.properties"/>
  <template subTaskClassName="org.apache.tools.ant.xdoclet.AntSubTask"
            templateFile="${xdoc.template}"
            destinationfile="{0}.xml"/>
</document>
```

This example was taken from the initial prototypes for generating Ant documentation directly from its own source code, as well as generating the task property mappings file (which Ant uses internally itself to define the built-in and optional tasks). The AntSubTask contains the logic to filter processing to only actual Ant tasks, which is not a trivial check! For example, abstract classes and classes without a void execute() method in their hierarchy are omitted. This type of filtering is not possible using the default <template> subtask.

11.5.2 Creating a custom tag handler

Introspecting Ant's source code to build its own documentation requires a fair bit of sophisticated logic. This logic may have been possible using the standard XDoclet tags, but it would have been extremely difficult to write and understand. Pushing the handling of this logic into a custom XDoclet tag handler makes our properties file template as simple as this:

```
<XDtTagDef:tagDef namespace="Ant"
        handler="org.apache.tools.ant.xdoclet.AntTagsHandler"/>
<XDtAnt:forAllTasks><XDtAnt:taskName/>=<XDtClass:fullClassName/>
</XDtAnt:forAllTasks>
```

The <XDtTagDef:tagDef> makes our custom tags available to the template. The custom <XDtAnt:forAllTasks> block tag iterates over all classes that are themselves Ant tasks. The <XDtAnt:taskName/> content tag provides the Ant task name.

This is a similar, but enhanced, version of what was shown previously with our own custom task properties file generation. An Ant task name, in Ant's source code, does not have to be specified with `@ant.task name="..."` because most of the class names are also the same as the mapped task name, with only the exceptions explicitly specified; this logic is encapsulated in the `<XDtAnt:taskName/>` tag, allowing it to be hidden from the template.

11.6   *THE DIRECTION OF XDOCLET*

XDoclet is now a suite of interrelated projects. The projects consist of XJavadoc, Middlegen, XDoclet GUI, and Reverse XDoclet. These are all in varying stages of development, with XJavadoc currently the focus of the XDoclet development team.

XJavadoc is designed to be a replacement for Sun's javadoc command-line tool to increase performance, allow for tags to be inserted back into the source code through its API, and allow tighter integration with the core XDoclet capabilities. One of the major advantages XJavadoc will have over the current custom doclet, besides performance increases, is that the actual source code of the classes being processed will be available in the model. The possibilities of this are quite staggering! For example, it will be possible to mutate a class, rather than generate a new class. XDoclet GUI uses this technique.

Middlegen is a powerful tool that reads JDBC metadata information and code generates the starter pieces needed for EJB environments. The code generated contains XDoclet tags enabling the generation of many other EJB artifacts. Some vendor-specific support is already provided, and more will certainly be added as this tool matures. We explore the combination of Middlegen and XDoclet in chapter 14.

XDoclet GUI is a stand-alone extensible Javadoc @tag editor, which may lead to IDE integration. It comes aware of current XDoclet tag capability, allowing for easy editing of tags such as `@ejb.bean`. And, finally, the Reverse XDoclet project is still on the drawing board, but its goals are to enable reading a deployment descriptor and automatically inserting the appropriate tags into the source code. Such reverse engineering of existing metadata will enable projects to rapidly switch EJB application server vendors, for example.

11.6.1   XDoclet versus C#

C#, the language recently developed by Microsoft as part of its .NET offering, was designed partly to address the shortcomings of Java. A major advance incorporated into C#, and other .NET languages, is introspectable metadata. At compile time, the metadata annotations on a class, method, or field are compiled into the generated assembly, so that at run time a program can use reflection to examine this metadata. In contrast, the metadata used by XDoclet is only accessible at compile time, when it must be used to generate the configuration files that are read when the compiled code is executed or deployed. The result is that you can use XDoclet to replicate much of the metadata functionality of the .NET languages, but it requires more build-time effort.

11.6.2 Looking into Java's future: JSR 175 and 181

In response to the needs to embed metadata into source code, Sun, through its Java Community Process, has created Java Specification Request (JSR) 175 to define language enhancements to capture metadata at class, interface, method, and field levels and to make it available to tools such as code generators and IDEs. Part of this JSR is to define the delivery mechanisms so that metadata can be accessed at deploy and run time. It is too early to tell how this JSR will affect the future of XDoclet and extensible @tags, but it is proof that XDoclet was ahead of its time and that it is a necessary and powerful mechanism. In addition, JSR 181 defines a set of standard @tags for web services that XDoclet promises to support.

11.7 XDOCLET BEST PRACTICES

Javadoc comments are certainly the right place for a lot of information, but it is not appropriate for everything. For example, XDoclet has the capability to generate the Struts struts-config.xml based on `@struts.action` and `@struts.form` tags. In addition, a `@struts.action-forward` tag defines the local forwards. This could be seen as a major time saver to developers, but also oversteps the boundaries of Model-View-Controller in the Struts paradigm. In other words, a Struts Action should not know or care about the actual path(s) used. The moral of this story is that it is easy to get carried away with metadata. The point of a lot of common metadata, especially in Enterprise JavaBeans, is to actually separate information from the source code, such that the information bound at deployment time rather than build time.

Often metadata needs to be pulled together from multiple places, some residing in @tags and some residing in external files. Chapter 12 demonstrates the use of merge points in an XDoclet template to accomplish the building of the infamous web.xml. This file contains servlet definitions that can be gathered from source code, but also allows for merging in the definition of third-party servlets.

11.7.1 Dependency checking

While we are still waiting for XJavadoc to appear, we must make do with what we have. With XDoclet's current implicit reliance on Ant's `<javadoc>` task (which wraps Sun's javadoc command-line utility), the processing speed leaves a bit to be desired. Churning through Ant's own codebase and generating XML files for each of its tasks and a couple of properties files takes about 90 seconds. This is not the type of thing you would put on your main development build dependency graph. Internally, XDoclet does its own dependency checking, only regenerating files when needed, but it still goes through a lengthy javadoc phase to gather the complete model before deciding whether or not to regenerate files. There are a couple of solutions to this problem:

- Narrow the `<fileset>` processed by XDoclet to the smallest set of files necessary.
- Use `<uptodate>` to implement your own dependency checking and skip the entire process if the generated artifacts are newer than the source code.

The dependency checking capabilities of XDoclet will no doubt improve dramatically as it gains popularity and widespread use.

Using <uptodate>

In the build for our Ant task subproject, we can bypass the XDoclet step by checking all source file timestamps against the generated taskdef.properties file. The `"init"` target contains our timestamp check:

```
<uptodate property="taskdef.uptodate"
          targetfile="${build.classes.dir}/${taskdef.properties}">
  <srcfiles dir="${src.dir}" includes="**/*.java"/>
  <srcfiles dir="${template.dir}" includes="taskdef.template"/>
</uptodate>
```

Our `"taskdef"` target uses conditional target execution by specifying an `unless` clause:

```
<target name="taskdef" depends="init" unless="taskdef.uptodate">
  <!-- ... -->
</target>
```

The effect is that Ant only runs the XDoclet task when any file in the Java source is newer than our properties file. In a large project, we may want to be more selective in the patterns we pass to <uptodate>, so that Ant runs XDoclet only when relevant packages in the project have changed. In the example, we could restrict XDoclet to run only when files in the antbook.ant package were changed:

```
<srcfiles dir="${src.dir}" includes="**/antbook/ant/**.java"/>
```

11.8   SUMMARY

Why has XDoclet earned a complete chapter in a book on Ant? XDoclet is a powerful build-time templating engine that provides access to Java code structure and metadata. At the time of writing, XDoclet was intertwined with Ant and was not a stand-alone utility. Even if it eventually becomes decoupled (and it should; tight code dependencies are bad!) from Ant's API, it will always be available as a set of Ant tasks. The primary use of XDoclet is to generate from a single source of metadata the necessary artifacts that are incorporated into a build distributable. Such uses include the generation of

- Property files
- Deployment descriptors
- Documentation
- Helper or adaptor Java code
- Other XML descriptor files

Being knowledgeable with XDoclet's capabilities is guaranteed to be a positive influence in your build process. Metadata should ideally only reside in a single source location and should be used to generate artifacts if necessary. By eliminating metadata duplication and placing it close to the source, developers can focus on business logic development rather than being bogged down with plumbing maintenance (Peltz 2000).

CHAPTER 12

Developing for the web

12.1 How are web applications
      different? 279
12.2 Working with tag libraries 280
12.3 Compiling JSP pages 288
12.4 Customizing web applications 292

12.5 Generating static content 297
12.6 Testing web applications with
      HttpUnit 299
12.7 Server-side testing with Cactus 310
12.8 Summary 315

Web applications are an essential part of most server-side Java development. Most J2EE systems are likely to have a web application as part of the middle tier, and many other applications bypass the EJB model to become a pure web application. We are going to cover EJB development with Ant in chapter 14. Before then, we will look at the processes associated with building web applications.

Many of the other chapters also cover aspects of web application development. In section 6.7, we introduced the `<war>` task for WAR archive creation, while in section 11.4.1 we showed how the XDoclet task could simplify web sites built with the Struts framework. The Web is integral to so many server-side applications that almost all Ant tasks find a role in building and deploying a single project.

12.1 HOW ARE WEB APPLICATIONS DIFFERENT?

How is a web application different from a stand-alone server application? One difference is that the programs you deploy are not stand-alone; a servlet container hosts them. This container, be it a stand-alone servlet engine or a full J2EE server, needs to know how to execute the web application. This requires a standard packaging mechanism: the WAR file, which contains your code, dependent libraries, and metadata critical for deployment. The metadata can be hand coded, or you can use Ant and its tasks to create it for you.

Another key difference is that the code contained in web applications comes in different forms. As well as the basic servlet, there are JSP pages. Although you can embed Java source straight into these pages within <% %> delimiters, displaying member variables and method results using <%= %> delimiters, doing so is dangerous. It leads you down to a slippery slope of mixing the model and view, and generally increasing future maintenance issues. If you have code in the JSP pages, it stays uncompiled until someone fetches the page: errors only show after deployment. Furthermore, people with no Java skills need to edit the JSP pages; copywriters, graphic artists, and other web site designers all create pages, and they should not be exposed to Java source. Together these problems mean that the risk of scriptlet error is high, but it is not easy to find the problems early on in the build/test/deploy process.

Tag libraries (taglibs) are a solution: Java classes that implement new markup tags, letting you add functionality to web pages without any Java code going into the JSP pages. In use, tags in tag libraries are very similar to Ant tasks, with the additional prefixes to distinguish tags from different libraries:

```
<happy:happy verbose="true" fail="true"/>
```

In implementation, taglibs are portable across different containers, but they have their own deployment descriptors, which are extra development effort. If you do not make any special effort, then most of the validation of JSP pages and the XML metadata

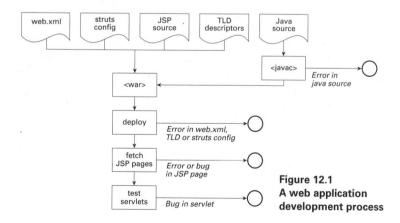

**Figure 12.1
A web application
development process**

you have to write only takes place server side. For example, you have to deploy to a server and then remember to retrieve changed JSP pages to see if the changes generate Java source that compiles. This process may work as you begin a project, but as the number of pages increases, it soon becomes unworkable. Figure 12.1 shows the typical development process of a web application.

In this manual process, there are too many files that developers create by hand—files only validated during and after deployment. We need to automate the tests, run them earlier in the process, and stop writing so many deployment descriptors. Our new development process will look like figure 12.2:

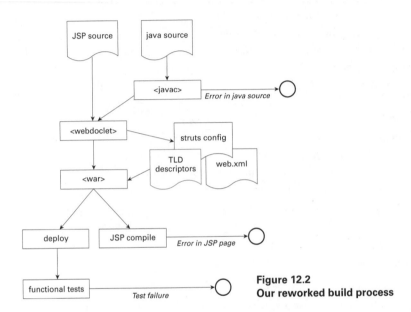

**Figure 12.2
Our reworked build process**

12.2 WORKING WITH TAG LIBRARIES

Tag libraries are the safest way to add code to JSP pages. That does not mean they are the easiest. Historically the creation of the XML taglib descriptor was one of those manual chores that added extra work to the build process. Like most manual stages, it is prone to error, and as it is not particularly complicated, it is an ideal target for automating. The tool for automating such a process is XDoclet. As we demonstrated in chapter 11, XDoclet is capable of examining source files and building XML, text, or source files based on tags used to mark up classes and source.

12.2.1 Creating a tag library

First, we need a tag to mark up; we will write a simple one to test system happiness and return an error code if we think there is anything wrong. We could use this in our build file, fetching the page and failing the build if it returns an error. That means we have to catch the error, which implies that either the page generates an HTTP response of 500 or greater, or we parse the text received and look for an error string, maybe return XML text and have it parsed properly. We choose the simple route: generate an error response. In fact, we choose an even simpler route: throw an exception and let the container generate an error response. This may not be too portable, but we will address that when we encounter problems.

Listing 12.1   A simple tag to test server state against our requirements

```
package org.example.antbook.web.taglibs;

import javax.servlet.ServletContext;
import javax.servlet.jsp.JspException;
import javax.servlet.jsp.tagext.TagSupport;
import java.io.IOException;

/**
 * @jsp.tag name="happy" body-content="empty"      ❶
 */

public class HappyTag extends TagSupport {

    private boolean verbose=false;
    private boolean fail=false;

    /**
     * @jsp.attribute required="false"
     */
    public void setVerbose(boolean verbose) {
        this.verbose=verbose;
    }

    /**
     * @jsp.attribute required="false"
     */
    public void setFail(boolean fail) {
        this.fail=fail;
    }

    public int doStartTag() throws JspException {
        testServletVersion();
        testFailureBehavior();
        return SKIP_BODY;
    }

    public void testServletVersion() throws JspException {      ❷
        ServletContext context = pageContext.getServletContext();
        int major = context.getMajorVersion();
        int minor = context.getMinorVersion();
        if (major < 2 || (major == 2 && minor < 3)) {
            String text= "Servlet version (" + major + "." + minor
                    + ") too old; 2.3+ required";
```

```
            throw new JspException(text);
        }
        log("version =" + major + "." + minor);
    }

    public void testFailureBehavior() throws JspException {        ❸
        if(fail) {
            throw new JspException("Failure requested");
        }
    }

    public void log(String message) throws JspException {
        if (verbose) {
            try {
                pageContext.getOut().println(message);
            }
            catch (IOException e) {
                throw new JspException(e);
            }
        }
    }
}
}
```

Listing 12.1 shows our simple tag to make the test. The routine only contains one
realistic test, that of verifying that the servlet API supported by the container is version 2.3 or later ❷. It also has a second test ❸ that we can manually trigger; this lets
us test the error handling. This test depends upon the state of the `fail` member variable, which can be set via an attribute in the tag. We have also written a log method,
which logs test information if the `verbose` Boolean is set, and which is an attribute
controllable in the tag.

In traditional tag library development, we would need to write the XML taglib
descriptor, listing the class name, its tag name, and tag information, such as the fact
that this tag supported two optional attributes, `fail` and `verbose`. Here we are not
doing traditional taglib development; we are using Ant and XDoclet. Our class-level
Javadoc comment has a new tag, `@jsp.tag`, that names the tag ❶. There is a different Javadoc tag for each of the attributes' setter methods, declaring that the method
maps to an attribute of the tag, and that in each case these attributes are optional.

This is all the information we need in order to generate the tag library, which the
`<webdoclet>` task does for us. Like all the XDoclet tasks, this needs the external
XDoclet library, a manual task declaration, and the classpath configured correctly.
Our communal taskdefs.xml build file fragment addresses this initialization, so we just
add the creation of the tag library descriptor to the process of generating all our web
application descriptors, as shown in listing 12.2.

```
<target name="make-webxml" depends="compile">
  <webdoclet sourcepath="${src.dir}"
             destdir="${build.webinf.dir}"
             mergedir="templates">
    <classpath>
      <path refid="xdoclet.classpath"/>
      <pathelement location="${antbook-common.jar}"/>
    </classpath>
    <fileset dir="${src.dir}">
      <include name="**/*.java" />
    </fileset>
    <deploymentdescriptor servletspec="2.3" validatexml="true">   ❶
      <welcomefile file="index.jsp"/>
    </deploymentdescriptor>
    <jsptaglib validatexml="true" destinationfile="antbook.tld"/>  ❷
  </webdoclet>
</target>
```

This target contains one task declaration, `<webdoclet>`, which performs two services for our web application. First, it creates the web.xml file from files in the templates directory that the `mergedir` attribute is set to, adding any extra declarations we include inside the `<deploymentdescriptor>` element ❶. The latter tells `<webdoclet>` to create a web.xml deployment descriptor for version 2.3 of the servlet specification, and to validate the XML against the appropriate DTD. We add a declaration as a nested element, stating that files called index.jsp are to be served up when browsing to directories. The task scans the javadoc comments looking for @web tags, of which we have only one, declaring a servlet that the application server should run on startup:

```
/**
 *@web:servlet name="init" load-on-startup="1"
 */
public class InitServlet extends HttpServlet {

    // initialization code here
}
```

The `@web:servlet` tag tells `<webdoclet>` to add a new servlet entry to the web.xml file, with the load-on-startup option set. Other tags that you can insert into the source let you declare filter classes (`@web:filter`), and many of the servlet configuration options. We are not listing these; consult the XDoclet documentation for their details. The reason we are not listing them is that we do not believe that the Java source is the appropriate place for the configuration options of a web application. Javadoc tags are appropriate for declaring what components you implement in the source, but not how they should be used.

Returning to listing 12.2, the second function of the task is to generate tag library descriptors. With the single line ❷, the task generates the taglib antbook.tld at the same time it generates the servlet information. Minimizing the number of sweeps over the source is important for speed. By stating that the target depends upon the compile target, we ensure that the source does at least compile before we invest the time in running XDoclet. Adding an <uptodate> check will enable Ant to skip the entire target if the generated files (web.xml and antbook.tld) are newer than the source.

When Ant executes the make-web target, the <webdoclet> task creates the file antbook.tld in the build/web/WEB-INF directory:

```
<?xml version="1.0" encoding="UTF-8"?>
<!DOCTYPE taglib
  PUBLIC "-//Sun Microsystems, Inc.//DTD JSP Tag Library 1.2//EN"
  "http://java.sun.com/dtd/web-jsptaglibrary_1_2.dtd">
<taglib>
  <tlib-version>1.0</tlib-version>
  <jsp-version>1.2</jsp-version>
  <short-name></short-name>
  <tag>
    <name>happy</name>                                                  ❶
    <tag-class>org.example.antbook.web.taglibs.HappyTag</tag-class>
    <body-content>empty</body-content>
    <attribute>                                                         ❷
      <name>fail</name>
      <required>false</required>
    </attribute>
    <attribute>                                                         ❸
      <name>verbose</name>
      <required>false</required>
    </attribute>
  </tag>
</taglib>
```

Looking at this descriptor, the tag we have written is declared ❶, along with its fail ❷ and verbose ❸ attributes—exactly what we wanted. We still need to get a reference to this descriptor into the application's web.xml file, which we can do with <webdoclet>. We mentioned in passing that in listing 12.2 we set the merge-dir="templates" attribute, which tells the <webdoclet> task to merge XML fragments, in separate files in this directory, into our web.xml file. These files are called merge points.

There are many different merge points, clearly documented in XDoclet's distribution. These include setting security roles, mappings for the request filters added in the Servlet 2.3 API, EJB binding information, and even MIME-type bindings. All of these files are optional; the task does not require any of them to generate the web.xml file, but they are the way to customize web applications with <webdoclet>. We create the merge file templates/taglibs.xml and fill it with the declaration of our taglib, binding the URI to its physical location in the file:

```
<taglib>
<taglib-uri>/WEB-INF/antbook.tld</taglib-uri>
<taglib-location>/WEB-INF/antbook.tld</taglib-location>
</taglib>
```

We then modify our `<war>` task to pull in WEB-INF/antbook.tld, and we are ready to test the tag library. First, we create a JSP page, happy.jsp, which contains our test:

```
<%@ page contentType="text/plain" %>
<%@ taglib uri="/WEB-INF/antbook.tld" prefix="happy" %>
<happy:happy/>
We are happy
```

We have to build the web application and then deploy the file, which we do using the Tomcat deployment targets of chapter 7. Browsing to the page http://localhost:8080/antbook/happy.jsp we get the string "We are happy" a few lines down the page. This shows that we can generate a tag that a JSP page will process and that the servlet version test is succeeding: the container is of an acceptable version. A final test is to verify that the tag works correctly when unhappy, so we write the JSP page unhappy.jsp to force a failure:

```
<%@ page contentType="text/plain" %>
<%@ taglib uri="/WEB-INF/antbook.tld" prefix="happy" %>
<happy:happy verbose="true" fail="true"/>
We are unhappy
```

When we fetch this page, we get a servlet 500 error reported, with an error trace including the error string:

```
javax.servlet.jsp.JspException: Failure requested
   at org.example.antbook.web.taglibs.HappyTag.testFailureBehavior(HappyTag.java:78)
   at org.example.antbook.web.taglibs.HappyTag.doStartTag(HappyTag.java:49)
   at org.apache.jsp.unhappy$jsp._jspService(unhappy$jsp.java:69)
   at org.apache.jasper.runtime.HttpJspBase.service(HttpJspBase.java:107)
   at javax.servlet.http.HttpServlet.service(HttpServlet.java:853)
```

Just to make fully sure that the response code is being sent to the receiver, we telnet in and retrieve the URL by hand:

```
GET /antbook/unhappy.jsp HTTP/1.0
```

The response is as we hoped. It is an HTTP error that the `<get>` task can pick up, as the Java networking classes underlying its implementation will throw an exception when they see a response in the 5XX region:

```
HTTP/1.1 500 Internal Server Error
```

The Ant task will be unable to retrieve the body of the response on a Java1.3 system, but a manual visit to the web page will reveal the cause of failure. Overall, our tag works as planned: it is silent when the server state meets its requirements. When the tag detects an unacceptable condition, it raises an error whose text is intelligible to engineers and an error code that is intelligible to Ant. These behaviors may be different on different platforms: some application servers refuse to give a stack trace on failure, for security reasons. Nor is a stack trace directly useful on a production system managed by an operations group; they see "Java error" and call the software team up. As we move the web application closer to production, we may want to consider writing an error-handling JSP page that emails the stack-trace to operations via email, rather than expose a system failure to normal users.

12.2.2 Integrating tag libraries

For many problems, there is no need to write a taglib: reusing an existing library is much easier. As well as Struts, the Apache Jakarta project hosts a complete set of tag libraries in its taglibs project (http://jakarta.apache.org/taglibs/). Jakarta Taglibs is also hosting the reference implementation of the JSP Standard Tag Library (JSTL), which is the official tag library under development with the Java Community Process. Whenever any of these libraries is used, it needs to be included in the WAR file, and in the file templates/taglibs.xml; <webdoclet> will then include its declarations into the web application. To add Struts support, for example, we paste the Struts declarations into this file, below the declaration of our own tag library:

```
<taglib>
  <taglib-uri>/WEB-INF/antbook.tld</taglib-uri>
  <taglib-location>/WEB-INF/antbook.tld</taglib-location>
</taglib>

<taglib>
  <taglib-uri>/WEB-INF/struts-bean.tld</taglib-uri>
  <taglib-location>/WEB-INF/struts-bean.tld</taglib-location>
</taglib>

<taglib>
  <taglib-uri>/WEB-INF/struts-html.tld</taglib-uri>
  <taglib-location>/WEB-INF/struts-html.tld</taglib-location>
</taglib>

<taglib>
  <taglib-uri>/WEB-INF/struts-logic.tld</taglib-uri>
  <taglib-location>/WEB-INF/struts-logic.tld</taglib-location>
</taglib>

<taglib>
  <taglib-uri>/WEB-INF/struts_template.tld</taglib-uri>
  <taglib-location>/WEB-INF/struts-template.tld</taglib-location>
</taglib>
```

With these tag libraries pulled in to WEB-INF/lib as a set of JAR files, our target to build the WAR file is getting more complex, as listing 12.3 demonstrates.

Listing 12.3   The target to create the WAR file

```
<target name="make-war"
      depends="compile,make-webxml,index">
  <war destfile="${warfile}"
    compress="false"
    webxml="${build.webinf.dir}/web.xml">
    <classes dir="${build.classes.dir}"/>
    <webinf dir="${build.dir}" includes="index/**"/>
    <webinf dir="${struts.dir}/lib" includes="*.tld,*.dtd"/>
    <webinf dir="${build.webinf.dir}" includes="*.tld"/>
    <fileset dir="web"/>
    <lib dir="${antbook-common.dist.dir}" includes="antbook-common.jar"/>
    <lib dir="${struts.dist.dir}" includes="*.jar"/>
    <lib dir="${lucene.dist.dir}" includes="${lucene.jarname}"/>
    <lib dir="${log4j.dist.dir}" includes="log4j.jar"/>
  </war>
</target>
```

This target to create the WAR file now includes at least four dependent libraries: our common classes, everything in the Struts distribution, the Lucene search engine, and the Log4j logging package. The equivalent target to create the unexpanded WAR file, for direct deployment to Tomcat, is getting even more complex—enough so to make us reconsider using that tactic at all, even though it worked in chapter 6 as a preamble to deployment. From now on, we may want to use the <war> task to create the WAR file, then <unzip> to expand it before deploying. Although slower, it is easier:

```
<property name="war.expanded.dir"
  location="${build.dir}/war" />

<target name="unwar" depends="make-war">
  <unzip src="${warfile}" dest="${war.expanded.dir}"/>
</target>
```

This target expands the WAR file into a directory in the build tree. The <unzip> task uses dependency checking, so after the first run it is quite fast.

12.2.3   Summary of taglib development with Ant

As we have explained, taglibs are the best way to provide functionality to a JSP page. They are far better than scriptlets. It is a tricky process to get right, but Ant and XDoclet can take most of the manual labor out of the process. The <webdoclet> task supports more @jsp tags than we have covered. We are going to point you at the XDoclet documentation to cover these, as it would take another book to do complete justice to taglibs and XDoclet. We have shown you how to build the source and extract the metadata, then insert the generated tag library descriptor into your WAR file and its deployment descriptor, which are the roles of Ant in the process.

12.3 COMPILING *JSP* PAGES

Even if JSP pages only contain taglibs and HTML source, you still need to verify that the taglibs are used correctly. If the pages contain some Java code, then you definitely need to make sure it is all correct.

Normally the web application server compiles the pages; the validity of the page, the taglib references, or any Java code are unknown until you have deployed. This makes it easy to do some things: add new files to a live system, fix a deployed file, and even decouple page development from the code side of a project. This can be convenient, but is at odds with any rigorous web site development process, in which you write pages under SCM control, test them on staging, and then deploy them to the production site. In this process, run-time compilation introduces delays, as the JSP files need to be translated into Java before being compiled down to bytecodes on every server. What is worse, source code errors in the files do not show up until the pages are deployed on a web server. This puts it at odds with the build-test-deploy sequence we have been using up until now.

Dynamic JSP compilation also forces the Java Development Kit to be installed on the server system, which can increase the security risk. If anyone were to gain write access to directories in a server, then new JSP pages could be written and executed under the identity of the web server. A locked-down Java web server makes this path of attack harder by not supporting dynamic JSP compilation.

We can address this problem by compiling the JSP pages during the build. This finds syntax errors early, and enables deployment to locked-down Java servers. There has been an optional task to do this for Weblogic 4.5.1 for some time, but Ant 1.5 added a new factory-based task for compiling JSP pages, <jspc>. This task can support multiple back-end JSP compilers, and is very similar to the <javac> task in syntax. The task translates from .jsp files to .java files: the actual compilation to bytecodes needs a separate <javac> task. Both tasks are needed to fully test the pages.

One complication in the process of compiling JSP pages is that application servers have the right to implement their own JSP-to-Java translation, so some vendors mandate their translation engine over a common standard. A different translation engine not only creates different code, it can even generate different class names for JSP pages that do not have a legal valid class name (any keyword or something like 123-45.jsp). You should never attempt to run any generated JSP servlet on a different platform from that of the <jspc> compiler: it will not work. However, even if the generated code does not work in the targeted application server, compiling down the JSP pages will find errors in the code faster than any other mechanism.

The current Ant distribution only includes support for the Jasper JSP compiler of Tomcat 4.x, which is the reference implementation of the JSP 1.2 specification, and only generates Java code for the Servlet 2.3 standard. The Java code it generates will not work on previous implementations, as the source will not even compile against the older libraries. We recommend Tomcat 4.1 version, as it fixes bugs found in the Tomcat 4.0 release.

Extra support for different application servers is inevitable. Check with the online documentation to see what the current support is. The latest unreleased version of Ant, the one at the head of the CVS repository, may have even broader support.

12.3.1 Installing the \<jspc> task

The \<jspc> task is in the optional library, and it needs support libraries for the particular JSP compiler you intend to use. For Jasper, three support libraries listed are required; these are listed in table 12.1.

Table 12.1   Libraries needed for compiling JSP pages with Jasper

Library	Location
servlet.jar	Servlet 2.3 API
jasper-compiler.jar	Tomcat 4.0 distributions
jasper-runtime.jar	Tomcat 4.0 distributions

These libraries do not need to live in the Ant library directory, as the task takes a classpath that can point to these files. However, the task also needs an XML parser, so you must either add crimson.jar into the same directory as the rest of the Jasper files, or include a reference to the Ant run-time classpath with the element \<pathelement path="${java.class.path}"/> inside the \<jspc> task's classpath declaration.

12.3.2 Using the \<jspc> task

Listing 12.4 shows our target to compile the JSP pages in our project. Notice how we are running the \<jspc> task against the source in our web application, not the JSP source pages in our web source directory. We will explain why in a moment.

Listing 12.4   How to compile all JSP pages in a web application

```
<property name="build.jspc.java.dir"
  location="${build.dir}/jspc/java"/>

<property name="build.jspc.classes.dir"
  location="${build.dir}/jspc/classes"/>

<path id="jasper.classpath">
  <fileset dir="${jasper.dir}">
    <include name="**/*.jar"/>
  </fileset>
</path>

<target name="compile-jsp" depends="unwar">
  <mkdir dir="${build.jspc.classes.dir}" />
  <mkdir dir="${build.jspc.java.dir}" />
```

```
<jspc    ◄─────────────────────────────────    Creates the Java files
    srcdir="${war.expanded.dir}"
    destdir="${build.jspc.java.dir}"
    >
    <include name="**/*.jsp"/>
    <classpath refid="jasper.classpath"/>
</jspc>
<javac   ◄─────────────────────────────────    Compiles the Java files
    debug="${build.debug}"
    includeAntRuntime="false"
    srcdir="${build.jspc.java.dir}"
    destdir="${build.jspc.classes.dir}"
    >
    <classpath>
      <path
        location="${war.expanded.dir}/WEB-INF/classes"/>
      <fileset dir="${war.expanded.dir}/WEB-INF/lib">
        <include name="**/*.jar"/>
      </fileset>
      <path refid="jasper.classpath"/>
    </classpath>
  </javac>
</target>
```

This `compile-jsp` target compiles the JSP pages into a temporary directory using
`<jspc>`, then runs `<javac>` over the created files. When run, it will state how
many files it compiled down:

```
compile-jsp:
    [mkdir] Created dir: C:\AntBook\app\webapp\build\jspc\classes
    [mkdir] Created dir: C:\AntBook\app\webapp\build\jspc\java
    [jspc] Compiling 9 source files to C:\Ant-
Book\app\webapp\build\jspc\java
    [javac] Compiling 9 source files to C:\Ant-
Book\app\webapp\build\jspc\classes
BUILD SUCCESSFUL
Total time: 29 seconds
```

Having shown the task working, we should explain some of the details. As with
`<javac>`, the task takes a `srcdir` and a `destdir` attribute, both of which are
mandatory. We chose a new directory under `build.dir` to store the generated Java
files. The source directory is more interesting: we have to run the task against our
unzipped WAR file, rather than the original source. This is because the `<jspc>` task
needs to find a directory WEB-INF somewhere above the source files. It needs this
directory to determine the root of the web application, used for references in the JSP
pages, such as:

```
<%@ taglib uri="/WEB-INF/antbook.tld" prefix="happy" %>
<%@ include file="/html/sometext.html %>
```

It also uses the directory tree between this root and the JSP pages to determine where to place the output files; files that the task creates in a matching directory tree under the destination directory. Although we do have a WEB-INF directory under the directory containing our JSP source files, it is incomplete: it does not contain the files we have created using XDoclet. We don't want to risk the source by copying generated files into the source tree, so we have to copy the source files into some appropriately structured folders in the build directory tree. As the make-war and unwar targets do exactly that, we just mark our new target's dependencies appropriately and point <jspc> at the expanded WAR file. If you are not dynamically generating web.xml and TLD metadata, you do not need to do all this.

One advantage of running <jspc> against the expanded WAR file is that we can follow this by running <javac> against the generated Java files, *using the libraries shipping in the WAR file*. This verifies not only that the JSP pages are valid, but also that only those libraries that we are distributing will be available for the JSP pages to use. There is one complication: the generated pages also need to link against the Jasper run time, and perhaps even the J2EE JAR file. These substitute for the libraries provided by the application server. For example, in listing 12.4, we have to include the Jasper run time.

Having written this target, what do we do with it? Currently we think the best use of the JSP compilation target is to validate the code prior to deploying to a web server. We enforce this by modifying our dist target to depend on the JSP pages compiling successfully:

```
<target name="dist" depends="make-war,compile-jsp"
  description="creat a distribution" />
```

With this addition, we know that it is almost impossible to deploy our project's WAR file if the JSP pages are incorrect. We say almost, because there are some flaws with the <jspc> task that could cause problems. First, the dependency checking is not smart enough to track changes files included into the JSP pages, or referenced taglib descriptors. If a TLD is changed, the JSP pages may need a rebuild, but <jspc> will not notice. Regular clean builds are the only solution. There are other issues too, some of which need addressing inside Jasper, and then the fixes pulled back into Ant. Using an up-to-date copy of Jasper is important, as is checking the online Ant documentation; maybe even the bug database (http://nagoya.apache.org/bugzilla/) for any Ant bugs with the word JSPC in the title.

12.3.3   JSP compilation for deployment

Moving beyond compilation for testing, we come to compilation for deployment, and for deployment to more secure servers. For this to be viable using the Jasper compiler with <jspc>, the target system must be running a compatible version of the servlet engine, which currently means Tomcat 4.x. We are not convinced that the combination of <jspc> and the Jasper libraries are mature or stable enough for precompilation yet.

For this reason, we are not including an example of this, leaving it as an exercise for the reader instead. The generated class files need to be included into the class tree of the web application, and the servlet declarations created. You can accomplish the latter by setting the `webinf` attribute of the `<jspc>` task to the name of the file you want. This file needs to go in web.xml, somehow, perhaps by using XDoclet.

Trying to automate this with the approach we use—creating the WAR file, unzipping it, then building the JSP pages—leads to a recursive model. After creating this transient WAR file, you need to create a new one containing the final web.xml and the new classes. You could perhaps do this by building straight into the expanded WAR file, overwriting its web.xml, then `<jar>` this up for deployment.

12.3.4 Other JSP compilation tasks

WebLogic has its own JSP compiler, `<wljspc>`, which predates the `<jspc>` by many months. The documentation states that it has not been widely tested, and so it should be used with caution.

Now that Ant 1.5 provides in `<jspc>` an extensible task for JSP compilation, we would hope that the vendors of web application servers provide plug-in compilers for this task, and if not these vendors, then people in the Ant community. The external tasks page on the Ant web site (http://jakarta.apache.org/ant/external.html) will be a good starting point.

12.4 CUSTOMIZING WEB APPLICATIONS

When you are deploying a web application to more than one physical server, you need to change configuration data. Even worse, if you deploy on more than one type of application server, you may need to change details like which libraries you include in the archive file.

The most common action is probably that of dynamically altering a deployment descriptor based upon current settings and the destination system. Indeed, a common irritation with the WAR file format in a complex project is that you need to configure the web.xml file for different target systems, which means you need to build a different WAR file for each destination.

Ant can address that need, but it requires some help to do so.

12.4.1 Filterset-based customization

One tactic to customize the deployment descriptor file is to use `<copy>` with a filter. Take the problem of conditionally enabling a servlet on different systems, such as the Cactus test servlet, the details of which we will discuss in section 12.7. Cactus uses two servlets to allow in-container unit testing of classes and EJB objects. The servlet definitions need to be in the development web.xml files, but to enable them in production is to create a potential security hole. By using XML comments, our build can turn on the testing servlets by uncommenting pieces of web.xml.

Listing 12.5 shows a section of our original web.xml.

```
<!-- Cactus configuration
Note: Do not place any XML comments in this Cactus configuration section (Ant's
filtered copy is used to activate this configuration when the test web
application is built)
-->
<!-- Begin Cactus Configuration @start.cactus.config@
    <servlet>
        <servlet-name>ServletRedirector</servlet-name>
        <servlet-class>
            org.apache.cactus.server.ServletTestRedirector
        </servlet-class>
    </servlet>

    <servlet>
        <servlet-name>JspRedirector</servlet-name>
        <jsp-file>/cactus/jspRedirector.jsp</jsp-file>
    </servlet>

  @end.cactus.config@ End Cactus Configuration -->
```

The `<copy>` task to enable the Cactus configuration replaces "`@start.cactus.`
`config@`" and "`@end.cactus.config@`" with ending and beginning XML comment notation, respectively:

```
<copy todir="build/WEB-INF"
      file="web/WEB-INF/web.xml"
      overwrite="yes">
  <filterset>
    <filter token="start.cactus.config" value="--&gt;" />
    <filter token="end.cactus.config" value="&lt;!--" />
  </filterset>
</copy>
```

When this filtered copy is applied, it uncomments the servlet declarations:

```
<!-- Begin Cactus Configuration -->
    <servlet>
        <servlet-name>ServletRedirector</servlet-name>
        <servlet-class>
            org.apache.cactus.server.ServletTestRedirector
        </servlet-class>
    </servlet>

    <servlet>
        <servlet-name>JspRedirector</servlet-name>
        <jsp-file>/cactus/jspRedirector.jsp</jsp-file>
    </servlet>
```

```
<!-- End Cactus Configuration -->
```

There is, of course, another section in web.xml to define the servlet mappings; we enable or disable both sections in the single-filtered `<copy>`.

To apply this in a build, we would place it inside a target that set the filter parameters based on a condition flag, such as the following:

```
<target name="copy-build-file">
  <condition property="start.tag" value="--&gt;">
    <isset property="cactus.enabled"/>
  </condition>
  <property name="start.tag" value=""/>
  <condition property="end.tag" value="&lt;!--">
    <isset property="cactus.enabled"/>
  </condition>
  <property name="end.tag" value=""/>

  <copy todir="build/WEB-INF"
        file="web/WEB-INF/web.xml"
        overwrite="yes">
    <filterset>
      <filter token="start.cactus.config"
          value="${start.tag}" />
      <filter token="end.cactus.config"
          value="${end.tag}" />
    </filterset>
  </copy>
</target>
```

When Ant calls this target, it only sets the start and end markers into the end and start XML comments if the `cactus.enabled` property is set.

One weakness of this process is that we have to set the `overwrite` attribute of the `<copy>` task to true, otherwise the commenting/uncommenting only takes place if the destination file is missing. With the `overwrite` flag set, the copy and filter always takes place, but this induced change will propagate along the rest of the build and deploy, taking extra time when the conditional option does not change from build to build.

Another weakness is that in a big project, the number of options to control gets more complex, with conditional inclusion of other components alongside Cactus servlets, and with target-specific configuration data. A simple filtered copy may not be enough.

12.4.2 Customizing deployment descriptors with XDoclet

As we are using XDoclet to create the deployment descriptor, we may as well use it to conditionally include or exclude fragments of our build file. We can do this by setting configuration parameters to the task, then modifying the templates to include fragments if these parameters are set. For our Cactus problem, we define a configuration parameter `enable.cactus` whose value is bound to that of the Ant property of the same name:

```
<target name="make-webxml" depends="init">
  <webdoclet sourcepath="${src.dir}"
             destdir="${build.dir}"
             mergedir="templates" force="true">
    <configParam name="enable.cactus" value="${enable.cactus}"/>
    <classpath>
      <path refid="xdoclet.classpath"/>
      <pathelement location="${antbook-common.jar}"/>
    </classpath>
    <fileset dir="${src.dir}">
      <include name="**/*.java" />
    </fileset>
    <deploymentdescriptor servletspec="2.3" validatexml="true"/>
  </webdoclet>
</target>
```

We can now add conditional content into the template files that this task uses, specifically templates/servlets.xml and templates/servlet-mappings.xml. When the `<webdoclet>` task merges the different template files it interprets its own XML tags in these files as it does so. Most of the tags are only of interest to anyone trying to write a new source processing task on par with `<webdoclet>`. But there are two configuration tags that are of interest, `ifConfigParamEquals` and `ifConfigParam-NotEquals`, which can be used to conditionally include and exclude content based on any conditional parameters we define inside a declaration of `<webdoclet>`. For our problem, we modify the servlets.xml file to make some of the servlet declarations dependent upon this parameter being equal to true:

```
<XDtConfig:ifConfigParamEquals paramName="enable.cactus" value="true">
    <servlet>
        <servlet-name>ServletRedirector</servlet-name>
        <servlet-class>
        org.apache.cactus.server.ServletTestRedirector
      </servlet-class>
    </servlet>

    <servlet>
        <servlet-name>JspRedirector</servlet-name>
        <jsp-file>/test/jspRedirector.jsp</jsp-file>
    </servlet>
</XDtConfig:ifConfigParamEquals>
```

If the Ant property is undefined, the configuration parameter will be set to the string `${enable.cactus}`, which, as it does not match the string `true`, is evaluated to be false by XDoclet; the content contained within the conditional element will not be included. Note that we are literally comparing against the string `true` next, so be careful not to use `on` or `yes` simply because other Ant tasks accept these true values (here is room for a new XDoclet template tag—to evaluate the string as Ant does!). A similar modification to the template file servlet-mappings.xml applies the change to the second half of the servlet deployment files:

```
<XDtConfig:ifConfigParamEquals
    paramName="enable.cactus" value="true">
  <servlet-mapping>
    <servlet-name>ServletRedirector</servlet-name>
    <url-pattern>/ServletRedirector/</url-pattern>
  </servlet-mapping>

  <servlet-mapping>
    <servlet-name>JspRedirector</servlet-name>
    <url-pattern>/JspRedirector/</url-pattern>
  </servlet-mapping>
</XDtConfig:ifConfigParamEquals>
```

When Ant executes the `<webdoclet>` task with the `enable.cactus` property set to `true`, this will set the task's configuration parameter to the same value, and the task will include the two servlet declarations.

To use this technique across multiple servers, we recommend you apply techniques that will be recognized by experienced users of C/C++ conditional inclusion with `#ifdef`. One option is to make the inclusion conditional on a particular machine, based on the value of a target server machine name:

```
<XDtConfig:ifConfigParamEquals
    paramName="server.name" value="ranier">
  <servlet-mapping>
    <servlet-name>ServletRedirector</servlet-name>
    <url-pattern>/ServletRedirector/</url-pattern>
  </servlet-mapping>

  <servlet-mapping>
    <servlet-name>JspRedirector</servlet-name>
    <url-pattern>/JspRedirector/</url-pattern>
  </servlet-mapping>
</XDtConfig:ifConfigParamEquals>
```

This is a valid approach for configuration options that are definitely per-system, such as the URL of a database server, but for many options, such as these Cactus servlets, it is the wrong approach. It gets overly complicated when more than one server needs to have the same servlets included: you need to copy the same XML fragments into separate conditional statements.

Instead, you should tease out each attribute into its own property (`cactus.enabled`, `log4j.enabled`, `jndi.enabled`), then have a configuration for each system that enables or disables these properties as appropriate. A property file for each server would be the ideal place to keep this configuration data; Ant could load the appropriate file for a server before creating the deployment descriptor.

12.4.3 Customizing libraries in the WAR file

Altering the web.xml deployment descriptor lets you target different systems as destinations for your web application, but it is not enough. Different application servers have different built-in libraries; web applications need to avoid creating conflicts with these built-in libraries by omitting duplicate or incompatible versions. The XML parser is the classic problem, but a simpler one is whether to include packages such as the JavaMail API in mail.jar packages, which all J2EE servers include. WAR files built for a pure web server such as Tomcat need to include those libraries. Versions built for a full J2EE server should omit them.

We could generate the different WAR files with different declarations of the WAR task, each including different libraries. Alternatively, we can write a reusable target that takes a path or a reference to fileset, listing all the libraries to include, and invoke it with <antcall>. Even better, we can take advantage of the if/unless attributes on patternsets to allow for conditional inclusion or exclusion of files. We will postpone this work until we get to deployment in chapter 18, and actually have to start worrying about supporting different target systems.

12.5 GENERATING STATIC CONTENT

Static content often goes alongside dynamic content generated by JSP pages and servlets. In a large system, developers often offload this content to front-end servers running something like the Apache web server, reducing the load on the application server systems that need the CPU cycles for the dynamic content.

Ant can help with static content in two ways. First, it can create static content or customize existing content. Second, it can deploy the content.

12.5.1 Generating new content

Ant can generate any content that you can create from Ant tasks, or by running Java or native programs during the build. As a complex example, to create custom artwork, you could somehow generate some SVG, the XML-based image description language, then render it to an image with Batik, the SVG-rendering tool from Apache's XML project. Ant could invoke the renderer and include the generated images into a WAR file.

A simpler example is to include the javadoc-generated API documentation in the web application. We do this by running our usual javadocs target before we create the WAR file, and including its output in the archive. First, we configure the javadocs target to leave out the author tags and any private methods and member variables, as we do not want those details included in the public documentation:

```
<target name="javadocs"  description="make the java docs" >
  <javadoc author="false"
           destdir="${javadoc.dir}"
           packagenames="org.example.antbook.*"
           sourcepath="src"
           use="true"
```

```
            version="true"
            windowtitle="ant book webapp"
            package="true"
            >
      <classpath refid="compile.classpath"/>
    </javadoc>
</target>
```

Next, we modify the make-war target to depend on the generation of the Javadocs. As the target is collecting too many dependencies, we decide to factor out the targets to create documentation into their own subtarget:

```
<target name="make-web-docs"
    depends="index,javadocs"
    />
```

Two targets may not seem worth the effort, but we are planning on adding more in the near future; having all documentation targets callable from one place makes it easier to see what major stages the build really goes through. We next tweak the target to create the WAR file to depend upon this interim target, and then include the generated content in the archive where we want it, which is under a directory called api:

```
<target name="make-war"
    depends="compile,make-webxml,make-web-docs">
    <war destfile="${warfile}"
      compress="false"
      webxml="${build.webinf.dir}/web.xml">
        <classes dir="${build.classes.dir}"/>
        <webinf dir="${build.dir}" includes="index/**"/>
        <webinf dir="${struts.dir}/lib" includes="*.tld,*.dtd"/>
        <webinf dir="${build.webinf.dir}" includes="antbook.tld"/>
        <fileset dir="web"/>
        <zipfileset dir="${javadoc.dir}" prefix="api" />
        <lib dir="${antbook-common.dist.dir}" includes="antbook-common.jar"/>
        <lib dir="${struts.dist.dir}" includes="*.jar"/>
        <lib dir="${lucene.dist.dir}" includes="${lucene.jarname}"/>
        <lib dir="${torque.dist.dir}" includes="*.jar"/>
        <lib dir="${log4j.dist.dir}" includes="log4j.jar"/>
    </war>
</target>
```

The net effect of these changes is that our classes' API is now visible on the web application, under the path antbook/api.

12.5.2   Creating new files

We want to put a build status file up on the web site, too, so we can browse straight to a system and see what version is running there:

```
<target name="make-build-properties" depends="init" >
    <property name="buildprops.filename"
        value="build.properties"/>
    <property name="buildprops.path"
        location="${build.dir}/${buildprops.filename}"/>
```

```
<propertyfile comment="Build Information"
            file="${buildprops.path}">
  <entry key="build.date"
    type="date"
    pattern="EEEE MMM dd, yyyy"
    value="now"/>
  <entry key="build.time"
    type="date"
    pattern="kk:mm:ss"
    value="now"/>
  <entry key="build.timestamp"
    type="date"
    pattern="yyyy-MM-dd'T'HH:mm:ss"
    value="now"/>
  <entry key="build.user.name" value="${user.name}"/>
  <entry key="build.counter"
      operation="+" value="1" default="1" type="int"/>
</propertyfile>
</target>
```

Running this creates a property file such as the following:

```
#Build Information
#Sat Mar 16 11:54:58 PST 2002
build.time=11\:54\:58
build.user.name=slo
build.date=Saturday Mar 16, 2002
build.timestamp=2002-03-16T11\:54\:58
build.counter=31
```

The build counter is a simple, self-incrementing number that gets lost whenever a clean build is done; we should really pull in the SCM-managed build version counter from chapter 10. It is, however, adequate for a manual or automated check that the code being served matches that which we have just built.

12.5.3 Modifying existing files

Ant can also modify existing files before they are deployed, usually by inserting strings into placeholder locations. Using <copy> with a filter is the standard technique; this is useful to replace filter tokens inside static HTML pages.

12.6 TESTING WEB APPLICATIONS WITH HTTPUNIT

How do you test a web application once you have deployed it? The answer is that you can test the skin of a web site with HttpUnit (http://www.httpunit.org/), which is an extension of JUnit. We cannot do this test framework justice in a few paragraphs. For more detail we would direct you to the online documentation or Hightower & Lesieki 2001.

HttpUnit extends JUnit by providing the code to have a conversation with a web server as if your test case were a client web browser. It can start a session with a server, fetch pages, fill in forms, and navigate around the site. Along the way, it can validate web pages, looking at elements in the page such as the title, forms, and text. You can write code to follow links, letting you validate further pages off your starting page. If you really know what you are doing, it will give you the actual DOM of a server response for you to validate, which can be a complex process. Because it is actually testing what the server is generating, it can perform functional testing of the complete system. So the "unit" in the title is a bit of a misnomer, but it does emphasize its intended use within JUnit test cases.

To use HttpUnit, the first step is to download the latest version from the httpunit.org web site and unzip it somewhere. It contains the documentation and the two files you need to run the tests httpunit.jar and jtidy.jar, the latter being the Java version of Dave Raggett's HTML parsing and tidying code.

12.6.1 Writing HttpUnit tests

To test your web pages you can write JUnit test case classes and methods, just as if you were testing local classes. However, the code inside these methods does not create and test local classes. Instead, it uses the HttpUnit classes to talk to a web server, fetching and testing the pages these helper classes retrieve.

The first lines of code import the test libraries into our class, which we name `HttpUnitTest` to be consistent with our existing test case naming policy:

```
package org.example.antbook.test;

import com.meterware.httpunit.*;
import junit.framework.TestCase;

public class HttpUnitTest extends TestCase {
    private String url;

    public HttpUnitTest(String name) {
        super(name);
    }
```

The class just declares itself a normal JUnit `TestCase` class; the HttpUnit classes do not replace any existing aspects of the JUnit framework. Indeed, the classes work perfectly well outside the JUnit framework, which is convenient when you want to interact with web sites from any Java code; the library lets you scrape pages and fill in forms to your heart's content. Our class declares one instance variable, the field `url`, which we will use to point to the base of our application. This field needs to be defined at run time, which we will do by defining a Java system property when we invoke the JUnit tests.

Next, we write the setup method:

```
public void setUp() {
    url=System.getProperty("server.url");
    HttpUnitOptions.setExceptionsThrownOnErrorStatus(true);
    HttpUnitOptions.setMatchesIgnoreCase(true);
    HttpUnitOptions.setParserWarningsEnabled(true);
}
```

This method starts by fetching the URL supplied as a parameter to the test. The remaining lines set static options in the HttpUnit library, telling it to throw an HttpException for any error response codes, to be case insensitive in its matches, and to print out any parser warnings of dubious HTML.

We then add our first test case: a test case to fetch our index page, validate its title, then follow a named link off this page to our happy.jsp test page:

```
public void testIndex() throws Exception {
    assertNotNull("server.url not set",url);
    WebConversation session = new WebConversation();
    WebRequest request = new GetMethodWebRequest(url);
    WebResponse response= session.getResponse(request);
    assertEquals("Ant Book",response.getTitle());
    WebLink linkToHappy=response.getLinkWithID("happy");
    WebRequest nextRequest=linkToHappy.getRequest();
    WebResponse happyStatus=session.getResponse(nextRequest);
    assertEquals("happy",happyStatus.getTitle());
}
```

The first line of the test verifies that our URL property was defined when running the test case, and if not, we print a meaningful error message, rather than fail with a NullPointerException. Next, the test case starts a new conversation with a server—a session with its own state and cookies—and fetches our base URL. We expect back an index file with the title "Ant Book"; if the title is different, then we fail the test. This verifies that the server returns the file index.html when we fetch the application's directory. Our test index page initially looks like the following, although it will be changed soon:

```
<html>
<head>
  <title>Ant Book</title>
</head>
<body>
  <ul>
  <li><a href="login,jsp">login</a></li>
  <li><a href="search.jsp">search</a></li>
  <li><a href="api">api</a></li>
  <li><a href="happy.jsp" id="happy">happy test</a></li>
  <li><a href="unhappy.jsp" id="unhappy">unhappy test</a></li>
  </ul>
</body>
</html>
```

The test then looks inside the body of the response, and finds the link with the ID happy. We could have used getLinkWith("happy test") instead, but this would have been more vulnerable to changes in the skin of the web page. Having found the link to the happy page, we fetch it. There is little need to examine the result, as in the setUp method we told HttpUnit to throw an exception on any error response code sent back by the web server. We check the title anyway, to verify we have fetched the correct file and that the link in the index page was correct.

We also want to verify that our unhappy.jsp page is working correctly, that it returns a 500 error code when fetched. We use a separate test for this:

```
public void testUnhappy() throws Exception {
    assertNotNull("server.url not set",url);
    WebConversation session = new WebConversation();
    WebRequest request = new GetMethodWebRequest(url+"/unhappy.jsp");
    try {
        WebResponse response= session.getResponse(request);
        fail("should have raised an exception");
    } catch(HttpException e) {
        assertEquals("Expected Internal Server Error 500",
            500,
            e.getResponseCode());
    }
}
```

This test fetches the page and fails the test unless the attempt fails with a response code of 500. A successful fetch or an error code of any other value (such as a 404 "not found" response) constitutes a test failure.

Together these tests can verify that our taglib works, that our web application deployed, and that our index page is as we intended it to be. This constitutes a good start at functional testing of the server, although we still have to write tests that verify the login process to protected pages, and to fill in the search form and get sensible responses back. HttpUnit lets you write these tests through its methods to examine tables and to examine and manipulate forms. All these are covered in the library's online documentation; we are going to focus on how to build and execute our tests in Ant.

12.6.2 Compiling the tests

Being Java based, we have to compile the tests before we can run them. We save the tests in a test source subdirectory, which keeps them out of the normal compile and packaging targets. We add a simple <javac> in what is a new target in the web application build file, compile-tests. This is a normal compilation target, a new output directory (build/test/classes), and the following classpath:

```
<path id="functional-test.compile.classpath">
  <pathelement location="${httpunit.jar}"/>
  <pathelement location="${junit.jar}"/>
  <pathelement location="${jtidy.jar}"/>
</path>
```

Calling the compile target now creates the file HttpUnitTest.class in the appropriate directory, so we are ready to run the tests as soon as the web application is deployed.

12.6.3 Preparing to run HttpUnit tests from Ant

Before executing our tests from Ant, we need to find the right place in the build file for them. The application must be deployed first, so they are dependent upon the deployment tasks. Because the main webapp/build.xml file is getting a bit large, we first pull out all the deployment routines we wrote in chapter 7 into a separate deploy.xml build file, which we call from the main build file with <ant>. A deploy target in build.xml hands off the deployment to the subsidiary file:

```
<target name="deploy" depends="dist">
  <ant dir="."
    antfile="deploy.xml"
    target="default"
    inheritall="false"/>
</target>
```

In the deploy.xml file, we create a default entry point that initially deploys to a local Tomcat server:

```
<target name="default"
  depends="deploy-localhost-remotely"
  description="deploy to a local tomcat4 server"
  />
```

We verify that this refactoring works by doing a clean build and deploy, then looking at the local deployment of the properties file we created earlier, which is accessible as http://127.0.0.1:8080/antbook/build.properties. As all looks well, we can proceed. When we start deploying to different application servers, this splitting up of deployment targets from the rest of the build becomes invaluable, but having a reusable deployment library early on is cleaner.

12.6.4 Running the HttpUnit tests

We add the functional tests to the deployment file, to integrate them with the deployment process. To this end, we make the test case a target designed for <antcall> invocation, a call that must pass in the server URL to provide an endpoint for the tests. The functional test target is simply a <junit>/<junitreport> pair, with a classpath set up to include the httpunit.jar and jtidy.jar files. It is dependent upon the compile-tests target, which we also move into the deploy.xml build file along with its classpath declaration. Notice how the <junit> task maps the Ant property server.url into a system property of the JVM:

```
<path id="functional-test.classpath">
  <path refid="functional-test.compile.classpath"/>
  <pathelement location="${build.test.classes.dir}"/>
</path>

<target name="functional-tests"
  depends="compile-tests" >
  <mkdir dir="${test.data.dir}"/>
  <junit printsummary="false"
```

```
                errorProperty="test.failed"
                failureProperty="test.failed"
                fork="true">
        <classpath
          refid="functional-test.classpath"/>
        <sysproperty key="server.url"
          value="${server.url}"/>
        <formatter type="xml"/>
        <formatter type="brief" usefile="false"/>
        <test name="${testcase}" if="testcase"/>
        <batchtest todir="${test.data.dir}" unless="testcase">
          <fileset dir="${src.dir}" includes="**/*Test.java"/>
        </batchtest>
      </junit>
      <junitreport todir="${test.data.dir}">
        <fileset dir="${test.data.dir}">
          <include name="TEST-*.xml"/>
        </fileset>
        <report format="frames" todir="${test.reports.dir}"/>
      </junitreport>
      <fail message="Functional tests failed"
        if="test.failed"/>
    </target>
```

The target resembles all our declarations of the `<junit>` task we have in our build files, because it is a perfectly normal JUnit test as far as Ant is concerned. The fact that it is now testing the deployed code on a local or remote web server is almost invisible to the build process.

12.6.5   Integrating the tests

We have the tests and we have the target to call them. All that remains is to pull this into the build process, which we do by invoking the test target after performing the deployment itself. We can accomplish this by adding this invocation to the deployment target we wrote in section 7.6:

```
<target name="deploy-remote-server"
    depends="build-remote-urls,remove-remote-app,ftp-warfile">
  <property name="target.port" value="8080"/>
  <property name="redist.url"
    value="file://${target.directory}" />
  <!-- install the new -->
  <property name="target.url.params"
    value="path=/${target.appname}&amp;war=${redist.url}" />
  <get
    src="${target.manager.url}/install?${target.url.params}"
    dest="deploy-remote-install.txt"
    username="${target.username}"
    password="${target.password}"
    />
  <loadfile property="deploy.remote.result"
    srcFile="deploy-remote-install.txt"/>
  <echo>${deploy.remote.result}</echo>
```

```
  <property name="server.url"
    value="http://${target.server}:${target.port}/${target.appname}"
    />
  <antcall target="functional-tests">
    <param name="server.url"
      value="http://127.0.0.1:8080/antbook"/>
  </antcall>
</target>
```

The four lines at the end of the target invoke our functional tests against the current server. The property declaration immediately preceding the `<antcall>` derives the `server.url` parameter from the values already passed to the target. We have to be sure that the server port is defined, so we add one line at the top to set that to a default value of 8080—the Tomcat default port—rather than the port 80 of a normal web server.

What happens when we run the new deployment targets, from an ant deploy call in the webapp directory? After building everything and uploading the changed files, Ant now runs our functional tests happily against our local server:

```
functional-tests:
    [junit] Testsuite: org.example.antbook.test.HttpUnitTest
    [junit] Tests run: 2, Failures: 0, Errors: 0, Time elapsed: 3.645 sec
```

Our tests ran, and both passed. This is exactly what we want to hear. Against the test server "eiger" (Running Linux and Tomcat 4.01 on Java1.4), we get a different result:

```
functional-tests:
    [junit] Testsuite: org.example.antbook.test.HttpUnitTest
    [junit] Tests run: 2, Failures: 0, Errors: 1, Time elapsed: 2.35 sec
    [junit]
    [junit] Testcase: testIndex(org.example.antbook.test.HttpUnitTest):
               Caused an ERROR
    [junit] Error on HTTP request: 500 Internal Error
               [http://eiger:8080/antbook/happy.jsp]
    [junit] com.meterware.httpunit.HttpInternalErrorException:
               Error on HTTP request: 500 Internal Error
               http://eiger:8080/antbook/happy.jsp]
    [junit] TEST org.example.antbook.test.HttpUnitTest FAILED
    [junit] at com.meterware.httpunit.WebClient.validateHeaders
               (WebClient.java:350)
    [junit] at com.meterware.httpunit.WebClient.updateClient
(WebClient.java:299)
    [junit] at com.meterware.httpunit.WebClient.getResponse
(WebClient.java:72)
    [junit] at org.example.antbook.test.HttpUnitTest.testIndex
(HttpUnitTest.java:57)
```

This is not what we really wanted to see: something has gone wrong and somebody is going to have to fix it. In this particular instance, something is wrong with Tomcat itself, and we are going to have to look at its configuration.

Tests like this are exactly the kind of result we want from a functional test calling deployment status pages. We want to know immediately if there is any kind of configuration problem preventing our application from running, and the taglibs we have written, combined with the HttpUnit tests, are providing the information we need. Integrating these tests with Ant simply ensures that the tests are run against the servers as we deploy to them. There certainly won't be any success emails being sent out after this build.

12.6.6 Limitations of HttpUnit

Although HttpUnit strives to act like a normal browser, supporting cookies and redirects, it does not interpret any JavaScript that comes with a page, or non-HTML content like applets. If you need to test such things, you must find an alternate solution, or extend HttpUnit. No doubt, the HttpUnit team would gratefully accept such contributions, as they would increase the power of the tool further. As it stands, complex DHTML pages cannot be tested with the tool.

A further limitation is that it is somewhat inelegant to write Java code to test HTML. Higher-level descriptions of pages should be usable for validating HTML, so developers do not need to write code to test web pages written by the web page designers. Still, using Java gives the tests power and flexibility, and enables them to integrate well with Ant. If the final web pages are maintained by someone other than the developer, such as a graphic designer, it is important to write tests that are not bound too closely to the content. Using ID attributes of labels, forms, and tables is a good tactic in this situation.

Despite these limitations, being able to integrate functional tests of a web site with the rest of the Ant-based build and deploy process is a tremendous boost to code quality, and even to developer productivity. If everything works, there is no need to browse to individual web pages to verify it, and if it didn't, you know where to start looking.

12.6.7 Canoo WebTest

Layered on top of HttpUnit and JUnit is an open-source product by Canoo called WebTest. It provides an Ant task interface to writing web site validation tests. In order to verify that our web application is generating the data that it should, we are going to write a few simple WebTest steps. The pages we will walk through are shown in figures 12.3 through 12.5.

Figure 12.3
Login page of our example web application

Figure 12.4
The search page of our web application. Note the powerful Google-like expression that is used for searching Ant's documentation.

Figure 12.5
The results page of our web application

As mentioned in section 12.6.6, writing HttpUnit tests is a low-level exercise and likely involves rework and recompilation when site navigation changes. WebTest provides a higher-level way to describe functional web tests. Listing 12.6 shows our build file to test these three pages.

Listing 12.6 WebTest example build file

```
<!DOCTYPE project [
    <!ENTITY properties SYSTEM "file:../properties.xml">
]>
<project name="canoo" default="main">
  &properties;

  <taskdef name="testSpec"
        classname="com.canoo.webtest.ant.TestSpecificationTask">
```

```
      <classpath>
        <fileset dir="${webtest.dist.dir}"
                  includes="*.jar"/>
      </classpath>
</taskdef>


<property name="output.dir" location="build/canoo"/>
<property name="xsl.file"
            location="xdocs/stylesheets/canoo.xsl"/>


<property name="app.context" value="antbook"/>
<property name="app.port" value="8080"/>
<property name="app.host" value="localhost"/>
<property name="app.username" value="erik"/>
<property name="app.password" value="hatcher"/>


<property name="query" value="(http AND wait) -title:API"/>
<property name="expected" value="WaitFor Task"/>


<target name="init">
  <mkdir dir="${output.dir}"/>
</target>


<target name="clean">
  <delete dir="${output.dir}"/>
</target>


<target name="main">

  <testSpec name="test our site">
    <config host="${app.host}"
            port="${app.port}"
            protocol="http"
            basepath="${app.context}"
            summary="true"
            verbose="false"
            saveresponse="true"
            resultpath="${output.dir}"
            haltonerror="true"
            haltonfailure="true"/>
    <steps>
      <invoke stepid="go to login page" url="login.jsp"/>
      <setinputfield stepid="set user name"
                     name="username"
                     value="${app.username}" />
      <setinputfield stepid="set password"
                     name="password"
                     value="${app.password}" />
      <clickbutton stepid="login" name="submit"/>
      <setinputfield stepid="set query"
                     name="query"
                     value="${query}"/>
      <clickbutton stepid="search" name="submit"/>
      <verifytext stepid="${expected} found" text="${expected}"/>
```

Defines the WebTest task

Defines default query and expected result

<testSpec name="test our site"> ◁—— **Begins testing steps**

```
        </steps>
    </testSpec>

    <xslt basedir="${output.dir}"
          destdir="${output.dir}"
          includes="TestSummary*xml"      Transforms
          extension=".html"               results into
          style="${xsl.file}"             HTML
    />

  </target>
</project>
```

The `<testSpec>` task encapsulates a series of steps, and in our case the steps are:

1 Navigate to the login page.

2 Fill in the username and password fields, then submit the form.

3 Enter a query into the search form and submit it.

4 Verify that the results page includes the expected text.

Ant properties are used to represent our query (`${query}`) and a string expected (`${expected}`) to be on the results page. We could easily rerun a test for a different query and expected result, for example:

```
> ant -f canoo.xml
      -Dquery="+steve +anger" -Dexpected="Ant in Danger"[1]
Buildfile: canoo.xml

main:

BUILD FAILED
Failure: Test "test our site" failed at step "Ant in Danger found"
  with message
"Step "Ant in Danger found" (8/9): Text not found in page.
 Expected <Ant in Danger>"

Total time: 3 seconds
```

It is beyond the scope of this book to cover the Canoo's WebTest task in more detail. The WebTest distribution found at http://webtest.canoo.com contains robust documentation and examples. One of the very handy things that can be done with WebTest, thanks to Ant's XML build file format, is to transform another XML file into a complete WebTest build file or build file fragment. A friend of ours, David Eric Pugh, has done this very thing by automating the construction of functional test cases from a DBForms model into WebTest steps. DBForms[2] is an open-source project to

---

[1] The actual document is called "Ant in Anger."

[2] http://www.dbforms.org

generate Model-View-Controller-style JSP pages from an XML descriptor (which can be generated from database metadata).

The `<xslt>` task, a task we will cover in chapter 13, is used to turn the results written from the `<testSpec>` task into an easily navigable HTML file. One of the great benefits to WebTest is its capturing of the pages as it executes the steps. It saves each page it encounters to a separate HTML file in the `resultpath` directory, allowing you to see exactly what WebTest sees as it is executing. Then, with the `<xslt>` task, Ant creates an index for all these pages for easy analysis.

12.7   SERVER-SIDE TESTING WITH CACTUS

Cactus is the Jakarta project's J2EE container unit testing framework for unit testing server-side code. It deals with the thorny issues of testing server-side code that is dependent upon container-provided services, ranging from J2EE to SQL database access. It deals with this in a way that is simpler to describe than to implement: by running all the unit tests on the server.

For example, we have developed a utility method that returns a specific parameter or attribute from an `HttpServletRequest` object. This is a useful utility for cases where either the URL (or form POST) contains a parameter or it has been injected into the request scope attributes during server-side forwards. There is no single method to retrieve the parameter regardless of which of these two scopes it is in, so we have to write one:

```
package org.example.antbook;

import javax.servlet.http.HttpServletRequest;

public class RequestUtil {
    public static final String getValue
                        (HttpServletRequest request, String key) {
        String value = request.getParameter(key);
        if (value != null) {
            return value;
        }

        value = (String) request.getAttribute(key);
        if (value != null) {
            return value;
        }

        return null;
    }
}
```

Having written a class, we now need to test it. How can we test this class and its `getValue` method with JUnit? There are two popular methods: Mock Objects and Cactus. Mock Objects are emulations of objects such as the servlet API, which you can then use inside normal `<junit>` tests to invoke code inside a mock server. They would be handled with <junit> as covered in chapter 4. We are not going to cover Mock Objects, but rather refer you to http://www.mockobjects.com for further exploration. Mock Objects are powerful in their own way. We are going to take a look at Cactus, because its model for server-side unit tests is unique and tightly integrated with Ant.

Our coverage of Cactus is intentionally brief. It is a fairly complex framework to explain architecturally, and it has been documented beautifully by Vincent Massol at the Cactus web site (http://jakarta.apache.org/cactus/), as well as in our good friends' book, *Java Tools for Extreme Programming* (Hightower & Lesiecki 2001).

12.7.1 Cactus from Ant's perspective

Let's take a look at what makes Cactus tick from an Ant perspective. To run test cases in a J2EE container, you first need a running container, of course. Yet, we do not want the burden of manually having to deploy, start, and stop our application server. Cactus does this for us with its <runservertests> Ant task. This task is part of the Cactus distribution, and looks quite elegant in our build file. Listing 12.7 shows the build file pieces used to run our Cactus unit tests. Our example was adapted easily from the sample provided with the Cactus distribution with very few changes, mostly in a build.properties file to configure the location of libraries needed for compilation and deployment.

Listing 12.7 Part of a build file to run server-side tests with Cactus

```xml
<target name="tests_tomcat_40"
        depends="prepare_tests_tomcat_40"
        if="tomcat.home.40">

  <runservertests testURL="http://localhost:${test.port}/test"
                  startTarget="start_tomcat_40"
                  stopTarget="stop_tomcat_40"
                  testTarget="tests"/>

</target>

<target name="start_tomcat_40">

  <java classname="org.apache.catalina.startup.Bootstrap"
      fork="true">
    <jvmarg value="-Dcatalina.home=${tomcat.home.40}"/>
    <arg value="-config"/>
    <arg value="${out.tomcat40.full.dir}/conf/server.xml"/>
    <arg value="start"/>
    <classpath>
      <pathelement path="${java.class.path}"/>

      <fileset dir="${tomcat.home.40}">
        <include name="bin/bootstrap.jar"/>
        <include name="server/catalina.jar"/>
      </fileset>
    </classpath>
  </java>

</target>

<target name="stop_tomcat_40">

  <java classname="org.apache.catalina.startup.Bootstrap"
      fork="true">
    <jvmarg value="-Dcatalina.home=${tomcat.home.40}"/>
    <arg value="stop"/>
    <classpath>
      <pathelement path="${java.class.path}"/>

      <fileset dir="${tomcat.home.40}">
        <include name="bin/bootstrap.jar"/>
        <include name="server/catalina.jar"/>
      </fileset>
    </classpath>
  </java>

</target>
```

12.7.2 How Cactus works

Again, we'll refer you to the Cactus documentation for more details about how it works, but here is a brief description. You write test cases that extend from the Cactus base test case classes: `ServletTestCase`, `JspTestCase`, or `FilterTestCase`. Your test cases are compiled and deployed on an application server and also remain on the client where Ant is running. The `<runservertests>` task is an interesting beast: it accepts other Ant target names as parameters and uses those in a multi-threaded way. First, the target specified by `startTarget` is executed in its own thread to keep the process from blocking, followed by the `testTarget` and finally the `stopTarget`. The `startTarget` for Tomcat, as shown in listing 12.7, starts Tomcat from our freshly built deployment directory. A configuration file is built dynamically using filtered `<copy>` tasks to customize the environment for our desired settings.

The tests run using the standard `<junit>` techniques shown in chapter 4. There is no distinction within Ant's `<junit>` between a Cactus test case and any other JUnit test case. Figure 12.6 shows what happens under the covers.

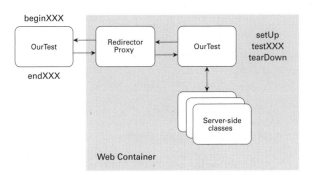

Figure 12.6
Cactus unit tests run server-side, using a proxy servlet to bind them to the Ant-hosted tests.

The client-side (from Ant) test case is executed through the `<junit>` framework. On the client side, methods beginning with `begin` and `end` are invoked before and after executing the actual test method on the server side. The proxy invokes the standard `setUp` and `tearDown` methods on the server side. The `begin`-prefixed method is used for configuring the HTTP request parameters, such as cookies, HTTP headers, and URLs to simulate. The `end`-prefixed method is more complex in that it can have one of two different method signatures. There is a Cactus `WebResponse` and an HttpUnit `WebResponse` class. This lets you use HttpUnit, as described earlier in this chapter, to do sophisticated, test-generated, HTML results content testing. If your test does not require HttpUnit testing, then simply use the Cactus `WebResponse` class in the `endXXX` method signature. The `beginXXX`, `endXXX`, `setUp`, and `tearDown` methods are all optional.

12.7.3 And now our test case

To test our `getValue` method using Cactus, we create two test methods. One tests that a parameter is obtained from the URL parameters. Another tests that, if a parameter exists in both request scope and part of the URL parameters, the URL parameter overrides the one from request scope. Listing 12.8 shows our test case to exercise the `getValue` method. The `ServletTestCase` provides access to the HttpServletRequest object as the member variable `request`.

Listing 12.8 Cactus test case

```
package org.example.antbook;

import org.apache.cactus.ServletTestCase;
import org.apache.cactus.WebRequest;

public class RequestUtilTest extends ServletTestCase
{
    public RequestUtilTest(String theName)
    {
        super(theName);
    }

    public void beginGetValueParam(WebRequest theRequest) {
        theRequest.setURL("localhost:8080", "/antbook",
                          "/test/test.jsp", null, "param=url");
    }

    public void testGetValueParam() {
        request.setAttribute("param", "request");
        assertEquals("url",
                     RequestUtil.getValue(request, "param"));
    }

    public void testGetValueAttribute() {
        request.setAttribute("param", "request");
        assertEquals("request",
                     RequestUtil.getValue(request, "param"));
    }
}
```

Adds `?param=url` to URL

Ensures value is from URL

Ensures request-scope value works when no URL parameter is present

One of the easily misunderstood facets of Cactus is that it does not actually make a connection to the URL provided, as shown in the `beginGetValueParam` of listing 12.8. The connection is made to one of the Cactus redirectors.

12.7.4 Cactus summary

Cactus is the premiere way to test server-side objects through a J2EE web container. It takes care of all the hard work involved in starting and stopping application servers. There are many application servers with Cactus support already provided, but it can be easy to add new vendor support if your vendor is not one of them. All J2EE-compliant application servers should work with Cactus tests. The trick is how to start, stop, and deploy to them automatically from Ant. We tested using Tomcat 4 (a.k.a. Catalina), which of course has excellent Cactus support. Much of Cactus is web related, and it communicates to the server through a web container. Cactus also can be used to test EJB container code, although that is a bit more difficult and beyond the scope for this chapter.

We recommend that you separate Cactus tests and pure client-side tests in your directory and package structure, or do so by naming conventions. This lets you run tests in environments where the container is not accessible or configured, and having the option to run only the client-side tests is nice. Consider also using Cactus tests as part of a continuous integration process, such that your in-container tests are executed with the latest integrated codebase on a periodic basis.

Cactus tests tag libraries, Struts actions, servlets, and any other server-side classes that are accessible. As with pure client-side JUnit tests, there are techniques and base classes that you can use to make testing of server-side APIs easier. For example, there is a `StrutsTestCase` base class available that facilitates testing Struts actions by asserting that you get an `ActionForward` that was expected.

12.8 SUMMARY

This chapter has explored some of the web application specific issues of Java development, and shown how Ant can integrate with other open source tools to automate the development and test process for web applications.

Writing JSP tag libraries is much easier with the XDoclet `<webdoclet>` task, which can extract tag declaration data from the javadoc comments in the code. You can also use this task for the conditional inclusion of content into the web.xml deployment descriptor, which is convenient when you need to distinguish between development and release versions of your application, or configure multiple servers' versions differently.

To compile JSP pages before deployment, you can use the `<jspc>` task. This task converts JSP pages into Java source files, which a normal `<javac>` task can compile. Of the two uses for this task, validation and actual precompilation, we are most comfortable with the former. Feel free, however, to experiment with inclusion of the generated servlets into your application.

We have introduced HttpUnit for functional testing of web sites, and shown how to use it from Ant, validating web applications the moment that deployment has completed. Together, the automated generation of deployment metadata, JSP precompilation, and postdeployment testing can raise your Ant-based builds far beyond what an IDE-based build process can accomplish. It may seem that we have turned a fairly simple build process into a complex one, and certainly for the size of our example application it does seem overkill. However, we now have a build process that can cope with a larger project: as new taglibs and JSP pages are added, all we need to do is add new HttpUnit tests.

Finally, we have presented the Cactus in-container JUnit testing framework. It takes the hard work out of the issues involved with automating the start, stop, and deploy to J2EE application servers. Cactus is a great way to test code that relies on container-managed classes like `HttpServletRequest`. Not only can testing your code with Cactus ensure that it works, Cactus gives you regressions tests for when you need to run on a new application server, or simply a new version of your current server.

For your own projects, we recommend that you gradually adopt these advanced build process techniques as the need arises. The need for functional testing will probably arise first, but compiling JSP pages can make JSP page development a lot faster. Tag libraries are always going to be tricky to write and test: the moment you write a taglib you should adopt the XDoclet-based TLD generation process to save time and effort. Cactus does take time to understand and work with, and you do need to invest the effort in writing the tasks to start and stop your server. However, once you have your Cactus test framework working, it soon becomes an integral part of servlet and EJB testing. No other mechanism lets you run detailed unit tests upon the internal components of your server-side application.

CHAPTER 13

Working with XML

13.1 Preamble: all about XML libraries 318
13.2 Validating XML 319
13.3 Transforming XML with XSLT 323
13.4 Generating an XML build log 327

13.5 Loading XML data into Ant properties 331
13.6 Next steps in XML processing 332
13.7 Summary 332

XML is rapidly becoming a language that most Java projects have to work with in one way or another. It hosts the configuration data for so much of Java, describing everything from web applications to the downloadable files of a client-side program deployed with Java Web Start. Nor can we forget Ant's build file format itself. XML can find many more places in a large project, which means that Ant needs to work with it.

XML can act as a structured file format for programs to use as source of input or configuration data: build files are an example of this use. XML can also be the output format of an application; this output can be fed into another program that uses the same format. XML can work as a marshalling format for data in a remote procedure call; XML-RPC, SOAP and SOAP + Attachments are all examples of this. One powerful use of XML is as a presentation-independent representation of documents; from a single XML document, you can generate HTML, PDF, and bitmap representations of the text. All these examples are not merely theoretical uses of XML; they are some of the things you may wish to do with XML during a build process.

Ant provides the basic set of tasks to enable many of these actions in a build. First, it can validate the XML, verifying that it is well formed and matches a DTD or other schema. Second, it can transform XML, by using XSLT transformations or simple text file filtering. The third way that Ant can work with XML is that a custom task can

317

take XML input and act on this and other files in the build process to perform some operation. The <xdoclet> task, introduced in chapter 11, is an example of this use, taking documents and a configuration in XML syntax to generate new output, usually XML files themselves.

To keep the build process fast and reliable, we need to automate all these XML operations. We are particularly fond of using Ant to validate deployment XML files used by the program, because it is always better to find out something is broken as early on as you can.

13.1 PREAMBLE: ALL ABOUT XML LIBRARIES

If you have not experienced "XML parser hell" then you are either very lucky or have not worked much with XML. For those readers who are blissfully unaware of the problem, here is a short recap. It may seem messy but the problem is related to the rate of change of the specifications; Windows programmers will have experienced similar MSXML version grief if they have worked in XML.

Java supports multiple XML parsers, lightweight ones such as Crimson, full-powered ones such as Xerces, and others provided by various vendors; these libraries all implement the SAX event-based parser in the org.w3c.sax packages, and the World Wide Web Consortium (W3C) XML Document Object Model (DOM) of an XML file with the org.w3c.dom packages. To resolve the potential conflict of all these multiple libraries all implementing the same classes, the JAXP API provides a factory API through which caller programs ask for a DOM or SAX parser, stating the required attributes of the parser, validating and namespace-aware being the key pair. All parsers that the JAXP factory can find must be in the current or accessible parent classloader, and not in a child classloader. Many problems with applications stem from the JAXP libraries (often in a library such as jaxp.jar or xml-apis.jar) being in a different classloader from the implementation of the APIs which the program needs. Certainly, many Ant installation support issues have this as their root cause. Other problems arise when the parsers supplied by the factory are inadequate for the needs of the program; Crimson may be small and nimble, but Xerces is much more complete. Xerces is a 1.7MB file, rather than the 200KB of Crimson, which is why it has been distributed less.

Alongside the XML parser API is the API transforming XML, TRaX. Xalan is the Apache XSLT engine that implements the TRaX API. Xalan is the standard XSLT engine used by Ant tasks; other implementations of TRaX may work, but they are not so widely used.

To complicate the matter further, Java 1.4 includes its own built-in implementation of the JAXP APIs. To an extent, this is good: you know what to expect when your program finds it is running on Java 1.4. It just complicates the whole process of locating XML parsers and XSLT engines; complications that programs like Ant have to address.

What this all boils down to is that a normal Ant 1.5 installation of Ant comes with the Xerces XML parser, which can be used for parsing and validating XML. If you want to perform any XSLT transforms in Ant, you also need version 2 of Xalan;[1] you can download it from http://xml.apache.org/. Prior to Ant 1.5, Ant shipped with Crimson and JAXP libraries. The xalan.jar library must go into ANT_HOME/lib. Although some tasks, such as <xslt>, have classpath support that lets you point to the location of the XSLT engine, the mysteries of classloaders mean that this may or may not work; certainly the results will differ from system to system. Placing the libraries in the Ant's lib directory is the safest action.

13.2   VALIDATING XML

Raise your hand if you've ever deployed a Struts application only to later realize that struts-config.xml had parse errors. (Both authors' hands go up.) Okay, not everyone develops Struts applications, but certainly most of us use XML files that are hand edited. Configuration files for the application server, such as web.xml and ejb-jar.xml, all need to be verified if you are not creating them with XDoclet (and even then XDoclet can provide built-in validation of deployment descriptors it creates). If you are using XML for the storage of structured configuration data inside your application, there are often other XML files in the JAR. Prevalidating these configuration files can avoid a problem that only surfaces when some machine needs to read in a particular XML file. See figure 13.1.

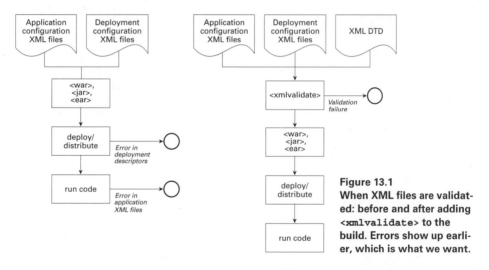

Figure 13.1
When XML files are validated: before and after adding <xmlvalidate> to the build. Errors show up earlier, which is what we want.

One of Ant's optional tasks can save time and headaches by validating XML at build time rather than at deploy time. The <xmlvalidate> task is straightforward: give it the name of an XML file and it will validate it, or give it a <fileset> and it will

---

[1]   At the time of writing it was being debated whether to include Xalan with the Ant 1.5 distribution. It is likely that it will be included in the final release, so check before installing it yourself.

validate many files in one pass. To validate our Struts configuration, we write a target to run it against our struts-config.xml file:

```
<target name="validate-struts-config">
  <xmlvalidate warn="false" file="web/WEB-INF/struts-config.xml"/>
</target>
```

Our Struts config file begins with a declaration of the DTD, so as well as being able to verify that the file is well formed, the task can validate it against the DTD:

```
<?xml version="1.0" encoding="ISO-8859-1" ?>
<!DOCTYPE struts-config PUBLIC
 "-//Apache Software Foundation//DTD Struts Configuration 1.0//EN"
 "http://jakarta.apache.org/struts/dtds/struts-config_1_0.dtd">

<struts-config>
 ...etc.
```

When we run the task, it validates the file, but we get a warning message:

```
[xmlvalidate] Could not resolve
 ( publicId:
  -//Apache Software Foundation//DTD Struts Configuration 1.0//EN,
  systemId:http://jakarta.apache.org/struts/dtds/struts-config_1_0.dtd)
   to a local entity
[xmlvalidate] 1 file(s) have been successfully validated.
```

This warning indicates that the task had to fetch the DTD from the remote web server. Despite the warnings, it actually validated the XML file against the DTD and guarantees that we are deploying a well-formed and valid XML document. Our target is working, but only when the system running the build can reach the remote server; run the build offline or behind a firewall and it fails with an error message:

```
[xmlvalidate] C:/AntBook/app/webapp/web/WEB-INF/struts-config.xml:5:
  External entity not found:
     "http://jakarta.apache.org/struts/dtds/struts-config_1_0.dtd".
BUILD FAILED
C:\AntBook\app\webapp\build.xml:198: Could not validate document C:\Ant-
Book\app\webapp\web\WEB-INF\struts-config.xml
```

Obviously, this is not what we want. We shall have to fix that shortly. Note that if we set the attribute lenient="true" of <xmlvalidate>, the task verifies that a file is well formed, but not that it matches the DTD. This allows you to check the basic structure of an XML file, even if you do not have the DTD on hand.

13.2.1 When a file isn't validated

What happens if a file isn't valid? As a test, we pulled out a handwritten web.xml file from a shipping production service, one that avoided DTD resolution problems by pasting the Servlet 2.2 DTD into the file itself. Although this application loaded happily on Tomcat 3.x and a production application server, our validate task was not so forgiving:

```
validate-xml:
[xmlvalidate] /projects/svg/WEB-INF/web.xml:216:
    Element "web-app" does not allow "servlet" here.
[xmlvalidate] /projects/svg/WEB-INF/web.xml:219:
    Element "servlet" does not allow "description" here.
[xmlvalidate] /projects/svg/WEB-INF/web.xml:224:
    Element "web-app" does not allow "servlet-mapping" here.
[xmlvalidate] /projects/svg/WEB-INF/web.xml:229:
    Element "web-app" does not allow "servlet" here.
[xmlvalidate] /projects/svg/WEB-INF/web.xml:232:
    Element "servlet" does not allow "description" here.
[xmlvalidate] /projects/svg/WEB-INF/web.xml:237:
    Element "web-app" does not allow "servlet-mapping" here.
[xmlvalidate] /projects/svg/WEB-INF/web.xml:242:
     Element "web-app" does not allow "servlet" here.
[xmlvalidate] /projects/svg/WEB-INF/web.xml:245:
    Element "servlet" does not allow "description" here.
[xmlvalidate] /projects/svg/WEB-INF/web.xml:250:
    Element "web-app" does not allow "servlet-mapping" here.
[xmlvalidate] /projects/svg/WEB-INF/web.xml:255:
    Element "web-app" does not allow "servlet" here.
[xmlvalidate] /projects/svg/WEB-INF/web.xml:258:
    Element "servlet" does not allow "description" here.
[xmlvalidate] /projects/svg/WEB-INF/web.xml:263:
    Element "web-app" does not allow "servlet-mapping" here.
BUILD FAILED
/projects/svg/build.xml:608:
    /projects/svg/WEB-INF/web.xml is not a valid XML document.
```

That is a lot of errors for a file that we thought was okay—it worked, after all. We could just ignore these errors, but there is a risk that other application servers will be less forgiving, so we should fix them. Having a test makes it easy to identify and fix the problems, which all turn out to be due to the incorrect ordering of declarations in the web.xml file. After reordering them, the application now works on a Tomcat 4.*x* server, which rigorously validates web application descriptors and rejects such invalid files.

This shows that XML validation not only lets you find XML errors earlier in the development cycle, it also lets you find them when the run-time system, be it an application server or your own code, does not validate XML documents rigorously. This is a mirror of the "compile-and-test" philosophy for Java sources, applying it to XML files as well as code.

13.2.2   Resolving XML DTDs

Standard XML files, such as struts-config.xml and web.xml, use standard DTDs that point to HTTP-accessible resources. Because they also supply a `publicId` for the DTD, we can resolve them against a local file. We do this by declaring the mapping in the `<dtd>` nested element of the task. This element has two attributes, the `publicID` of the DTD and the location of the local copy. Adding one of these to our `<xmlvalidate>` means that it can validate files offline:

```
<target name="validate-struts-config">
  <xmlvalidate warn="false" file="web/WEB-INF/struts-config.xml">
    <dtd publicId=
      "-//Apache Software Foundation//DTD Struts Configuration 1.0//EN"
      location=
      "${struts.dir}/lib/struts-config_1_0.dtd"/>
  </xmlvalidate>
</target>
```

Running this version results in a near-silent validation of the files:

```
validate-struts-config-standalone:
[xmlvalidate] 1 file(s) have been successfully validated.
BUILD SUCCESSFUL
Total time: 4 seconds
```

If you want to bulk validate a set of XML files, files that may be based on different DTD files, all you have to do is list all the possible DTD IDs and locations inside the <xmlvalidate> target. As an example, if we wanted to verify a web.xml file alongside the Struts configuration file, we could do both in the same task:

```
<target name="validate-xml-files">
 <xmlvalidate warn="false">
  <fileset dir="web/WEB-INF" includes="struts-config.xml,web.xml"/>
  <dtd publicId=
    "-//Apache Software Foundation//DTD Struts Configuration 1.0//EN"
    location="${struts.dir}/lib/struts-config_1_0.dtd"/>
  <dtd publicId=
    "-//Sun Microsystems, Inc.//DTD Web Application 2.3//EN"
    location="${j2ee.dir}/lib/web-app_2_3.dtd"/>
 </xmlvalidate>
</target>
```

The `location` attribute of the nested `<dtd>` elements can be a file, resource, or URL. As both j2ee.jar and servlet.jar contains the web-app_2_2.dtd file as a resource, we could have declared a reference to it by naming the resource as the location:

```
<dtd publicId=
  "-//Sun Microsystems, Inc.//DTD Web Application 2.3//EN"
  location="javax.servlet.resources.web-app_2_3.dtd"/>
```

The `<xmlvalidate>` task provides classpath specification support so that j2ee.jar could be referenced by using `classpath="${j2ee.jar}"`, with the usual mapping of the `j2ee.jar` property to the location of the actual JAR file.

Validating XML should be part of the whole testing regimen. It is one more sanity check that you can easily add to a build, ensuring that one less thing can go wrong at run time.

13.2.3   Supporting alternative XML validation mechanisms

There are competing successors to XML DTDs that provide more powerful ways to describe valid XML documents. These all use XML representations for easier manipulation of the DTD-equivalent schema itself, and offer a richer specification language. The most well-known is XML Schema, but there is a lighter-weight alternative called RELAX NG. Ant can validate XML files against this schema language using the third-party `<jing>` task, a task listed on the Ant web site.

We are not aware of any tasks that exist specifically to validate XML Schema-based XML files. This would seem a useful feature for any web service work, so one may be forthcoming in the Ant 1.6 timeframe. We may even have to write it ourselves.

13.3 TRANSFORMING XML WITH XSLT

XML is a great way to keep data separate from formatting. It is the ideal format for documentation because it lets you transform it into display or print formats, such as HTML and PDF. This can be done at run time, perhaps with a framework such as Cocoon or XML-FO, in a very sophisticated use of XML in an application. A simpler use is to convert the XML into the output format at build time, which is what we are about to do.

With our application, we store the user documentation in XML format but want it generated as JSP pages in the web application. JSP pages are desired rather than static HTML files because we want to take advantage of some dynamic elements such as using Struts templates to generate headers and footers.

Ant's built-in `<xslt>` task performs XSL transformations. Transforming an entire fileset of XML files with a single XSL stylesheet is easy. See figure 13.2.

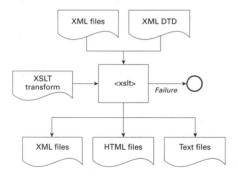

Figure 13.2
The <xslt> task transforms XML into other file formats or into new XML files.

Our actual source documents all have a simple structure, similar to the structure of xdocs/about.xml:

```
<?xml version="1.0" encoding="UTF-8" ?>
<doc>
  <section title="About">
  This is the web application to provide an online
  searchable version of the Ant documentation
  </section>
</doc>
```

To turn this into a JSP file we have an XSLT file, xdocs/stylesheets/docs.xsl, which looks quite complex because we have to escape out all the angle brackets around the JSP tags we plan to insert:

```
<xsl:stylesheet
    xmlns:xsl="http://www.w3.org/1999/XSL/Transform"
    xmlns:template="struts template"
    version="1.0">
<xsl:output method="text"/>
<xsl:template match="/">
&lt;%@ taglib uri="/WEB-INF/struts-html.tld"
    prefix="html" %&gt;
&lt;%@ taglib uri="/WEB-INF/struts-template.tld"
    prefix="template" %&gt;
&lt;template:insert template='/WEB-INF/templates/wrapper.jsp'&gt;
    &lt;template:put name='title'
        direct='true'
        content='<xsl:value-of select="/doc/section/@title"/>'/&gt;
    &lt;template:put name='content'&gt;
      <xsl:value-of select="/doc/section"/>
    &lt;/template:put&gt;
&lt;/template:insert&gt;
</xsl:template>
</xsl:stylesheet>
```

All this template does is add the taglib prefixes we want at the top of the document, and then places the section text inside one of the Struts tags and the title of the section into another tag. Because we only allow one section per document, we should add a DTD and validate our files before transforming them. If we didn't have the JSP-specific <@ tags we could avoid having to escape the angle brackets; generating XML format JSP pages might be cleaner.

To apply the stylesheet to all XML files in our xdocs directory, we use the `<xslt>` task in a new target, webdocs:

```
<target name="webdocs" depends="init">
  <xslt basedir="xdocs" destdir="${build.dir}/webdocs"
        includes="*.xml"
        extension=".jsp"
        style="xdocs/stylesheets/doc.xsl"/>
</target>
```

The following code creates a JSP file for every XML file in the directory. The about.xml file shown earlier is transformed into this JSP:

```
<%@ taglib uri="/WEB-INF/struts-html.tld"
    prefix="html" %>
<%@ taglib uri="/WEB-INF/struts-template.tld"
    prefix="template" %>
<template:insert template='/WEB-INF/templates/wrapper.jsp'>
    <template:put name='title'
        direct='true'
        content='About'/>
```

```
<template:put name='content'>

  This is the web application to provide an online
searchable version of the Ant documentation

    </template:put>
</template:insert>
```

By default, the `<xslt>` task generates files with the .html extension, which we override by setting the `extension` attribute to .jsp. The task is an implicit fileset task, with `basedir` mapped to the standard fileset `dir` attribute; consequently, by setting `includes="*.xml"`, we select all XML files in the xdocs directory. These files are transformed with doc.xsl, producing the JSP files in the directory `${build.dir}/webdocs`. The task is dependency aware about both the source files and the stylesheet, so the task recreates the about.jsp file whenever about.xml or doc.xsl is newer than the existing copy of the file.

We now need to pull these JSP pages into the WAR file. We do this by adding a new `<zipfileset>` to the WAR file, by inserting the following line into our existing `<war>` task, the task in listing 12.3:

```
<zipfileset dir="${build.dir}/webdocs" prefix="help"/>
```

This extra declaration includes the files, but what about our JSP verification process introduced in chapter 12? It turns out that because we run `<jspc>` against the unzipped copy of the WAR file, our generated JSP pages are automatically validated by compiling them with Jasper. Together the tasks ensure that we can create valid JSP pages from source data stored in XML files.

There are numerous other reasons to transform XML during build time. One useful action is the postprocessing of the output of tasks and Java programs executed in the build. This can be simply the generation of reports about tests or it could be the extraction of content from a database and presentation in XML format. The `<xslt>` task is the foundation for the postprocessing needed between data generation and the presentation or deployment of the results.

13.3.1 Using the XMLCatalog datatype

Both the `<xslt>` and `<xmlvalidate>` tasks support local copies of DTD's in Ant 1.5 with the `<xmlcatalog>` nested element. This lets you transform XML documents whose SYSTEM URIs and entity references aren't resolvable. To demonstrate this, we add a DTD for our documentation page:

```
<?xml version="1.0" encoding="UTF-8" ?>
<!DOCTYPE doc PUBLIC
  "-//Antbook//DTD xdoc 1.0//EN"
  "nap:chemical+brothers"
  >
<doc>
  <section title="About">
  This is the web application to provide an on
```

```
line searchable version of the Ant documentation
   </section>
</doc>
```

Because the `nap:` URI will not resolve in the absence of Napster and an appropriate plug-in for the JRE, the URI is effectively unresolvable; our current `<xslt>` transform fails:

```
[xslt] : Fatal Error! java.net.MalformedURLException: unknown protocol:
   nap Cause: java.net.MalformedURLException: unknown protocol: nap
[xslt] Failed to process C:\AntBook\app\webapp\xdocs\about.xml
```

```
BUILD FAILED
```

Just like `<xmlvalidate>`, the `<xslt>` task needs to find the DTDs of the files it transforms, and fails if it cannot resolve any. First, we have to write the DTD itself, which we create in xdocs/stylesheets/doc.dtd:

```
<!ELEMENT doc (section) >
<!ELEMENT section (#PCDATA)>
<!ATTLIST section title CDATA #IMPLIED>
```

Next, we add the DTD to the `<xslt>` task, adding an `<xmlvalidate>` as a precursor. We are probably being overcautious, as `<xslt>` will reject invalid XML itself.

```
<target name="webdocs" depends="init">
  <xmlvalidate warn="false">
    <fileset dir="xdocs" includes="**/*.xml"/>
    <dtd publicID="-//Antbook//DTD xdoc 1.0//EN"
      location="xdocs/stylesheets/doc.dtd"/>
  </xmlvalidate>
  <xslt basedir="xdocs" destdir="${build.dir}/webdocs"
        includes="*.xml"
        extension=".jsp"
        style="xdocs/stylesheets/doc.xsl">
    <xmlcatalog>
      <dtd publicID="-//Antbook//DTD xdoc 1.0//EN"
        location="xdocs/stylesheets/doc.dtd"/>
    </xmlcatalog>
  </xslt>
</target>
```

The `<xmlcatalog>` datatype that `<xslt>` uses could be more powerful if someone were to add support for loadable XML catalog files. You would then be able to refer to a single catalog file that could be shared across multiple build files, and with other development tools, such as a DTD aware IDE. Note that `<xmlvalidate>` also supports nested `<xmlcatalog>` elements, so we share a common catalog definition among both tasks.

What you can do today is refer to XML catalogs by ID inside a file, even declaring them outside any individual target, just as you can for a path or a patternset:

```
<xmlcatalog id="xdocs.catalog">
 <dtd publicID="-//Antbook//DTD xdoc 1.0//EN"
   location="xdocs/stylesheets/doc.dtd"/>
</xmlcatalog>

<target name="webdocs" depends="init">
  <xmlvalidate warn="false">
    <fileset dir="xdocs" includes="**/*.xml"/>
    <xmlcatalog refid="xdocs.catalog"/>
  </xmlvalidate>
  <xslt basedir="xdocs" destdir="${build.dir}/webdocs"
        includes="*.xml"
        extension=".jsp"
        style="xdocs/stylesheets/doc.xsl">
    <xmlcatalog refid="xdocs.catalog"/>
  </xstl>
</target>
```

13.3.2   Generating PDF files from XML source

We stated in this chapter's introduction that you could generate binary files such as PDF documents from an XML source. You can use XSL:FO to accomplish this. We do not cover this activity, except to point you toward Ted Neward's excellent paper on how to do this within Ant, X-Power (Neward 2001).

13.3.3   Styler–a third-party transformation task

Although Ant's built-in <xslt> task is sufficient for most purposes, it lacks some features of a LGPL-licensed project called Styler, which lets you build a pipeline of XML transformations and work with alternate input sources, such as HTML or any other format for which you can write a reader.

You can find Styler at http://www.langdale.com.au/styler/. We won't cover the <styler> task here, but will point out that its ability to chain together SAX event handlers lets you use Ant to build an XML processing chain, which could find more uses than merely build-time processing. If you need this kind of pipeline, you are into some serious XML hacking, or need to do some HTML scraping as part of your build process.

As an aside, there is a working group under way at the W3C on a pipeline processing model for XML, and one of the submissions has actually based its pipeline workflow language on Ant!

13.4   GENERATING AN XML BUILD LOG

At the beginning of this chapter, we mentioned that applications could generate XML output for other applications. One such application is Ant itself: you can make it generate an XML format log instead of the normal text log. You can then transform this log into readable HTML, or feed into some other application for postprocessing. To create the XML version of the build log, you list the name of the XML logger class after the -listener option (see figure 13.3):

```
ant -listener org.apache.tools.ant.XmlLogger
```

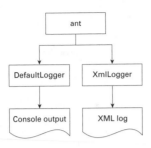

Figure 13.3
Ant splits the output of the build when the XML logger listens in.

This saves the log into a file called log.xml. Because it will overwrite any existing file, make sure that you do not have a file called log.xml in the build directory. In addition, the file isn't saved until the build completes: if for any reason the build exits unexpectedly, perhaps when an unforked application calls System.exit, there is no log file left behind.

When we run the web application build file with logging, we get a 350KB file. Why is it so big? Let's look at the first few lines:

```
<?xml version="1.0" encoding="UTF-8" ?>
<?xml-stylesheet type="text/xsl" href="log.xsl"?>
<build time="54 seconds">
 <message priority="debug"><![CDATA[
  Detected Java version: 1.3 in: c:\java\JDK\jre]]>
 </message>
 <message priority="debug"><![CDATA[
  Detected OS: Windows 2000]]>
 </message>
 <message priority="debug"><![CDATA[ +User task: propertyfile
   org.apache.tools.ant.taskdefs.optional.PropertyFile]]>
</message>
```

The log contains all messages output, rather than those messages displayed at the output level specified on the command line with -debug, -verbose, and -quiet, or the default of information-level messages only. We explain why this happens in chapter 20.

13.4.1 Stylesheets

At the top of the generated log file, is a reference to a log file, log.xsl. This file is in ANT_HOME/etc; it transforms the log files into readable HTML. You need to copy this into your destination directory, or tell the listener to use a different stylesheet by setting the Ant property ant.XmlLogger.stylesheet.uri. You can use this property to bind directly to the log.xsl file in the Ant directory by pointing the property at it:

```
<property name="ant.XmlLogger.stylesheet.uri"
    location="${ant.home}/etc/log.xsl" />
```

You can just as easily bind to a stylesheet on a web server:

```
<property name="ant.XmlLogger.stylesheet.uri"
    location="http://localhost/styles/log.xsl" />
```

This approach stops your having to copy XSL files around, but it does need a continually available server.

13.4.2 Output files

Similarly, to choose a different output file you can set the `XmlLogger.file` property either on the command line or inside the file, such as this one in deploy.xml:

```
<property name="XmlLogger.file"
    location="deploy-log.xml" />
```

When doing this, take care not to overwrite the build file or other valuable XML source file by accident. Saving the files in a separate directory is safer.

One option here is to configure Ant to copy the log file to a web server; so that users get a full log of what happened; some web browsers will handle the XSLT transform themselves:

```
<property name="log.dir"
    location="${env.CATALINA_HOME}/webapps/ROOT/log"/>
<property name="XmlLogger.file"
    location="${log.dir}/deploy-log.xml" />
```

Figure 13.4 shows what the generated HTML page looks like in a web browser that can transform the XML itself. When the build fails, as it does in this figure, the summary message appears with a red background, for an at-a-glance status message.

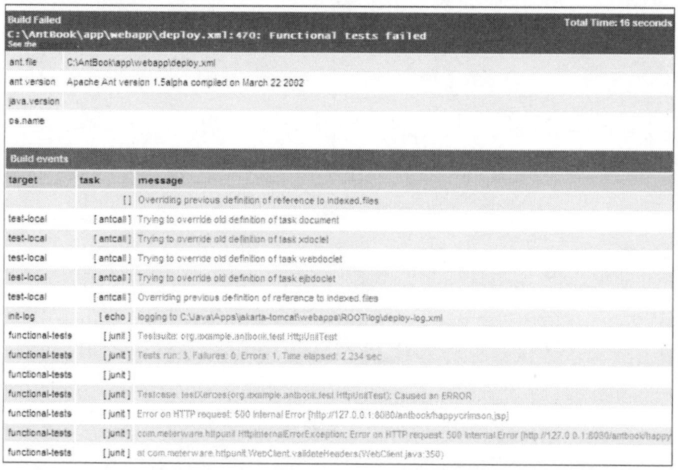

Figure 13.4   The XML log of a failed build, saved to a local web server, and then viewed from the browser, which is transforming the XML itself.

13.4.3 Postprocessing the build log

If you create an XML log for a master build file, it will include all the trace information of all the nested files. This soon becomes a lot of data; the XmlLogger class can also be used as a build logger and will adhere to the verbosity level set, such as -quiet.

You could apply the log.xsl style sheet to the output to generate the HTML report for direct viewing or placement on a web server. Ant can do this, but only from a build separate from the one whose log we are trying to process; the log is not created until the first build finishes.

Here is a helper build file that can create a log file from an input file; we keep this in the directory app/tasklibs, but want to call it from the parent directory and have relative files right. We do that by setting the basedir attribute of the project to point to the parent:

```
<?xml version="1.0"?>
  <project name="tohtml" default="default"
    basedir=".." >

  <target name="default"
    description="create html from an xml log" >
    <fail unless="in.filename">
      Property ${in.filename} is not defined
    </fail>
    <fail unless="out.filename">
      Property ${out.filename} is not defined
    </fail>
    <property name="in.path" location="${in.filename}"/>
    <property name="out.path" location="${out.filename}"/>
    <xslt out="${out.path}"
          in="${in.path}"
          style="${ant.home}/etc/log.xsl">
    </xslt>
  </target>
</project>
```

We invoke this from its parent directory, pointing it at files relative to this directory:

```
C:\AntBook\app>ant -f tasklib\create-html-log.xml
    -Din.filename=log\deploy-log.xml -Dout.filename=log\deploy.html
```

Because the project set its base directory to be .., all files are resolved relative to the parent directory, rather than the one in which the build file itself lives. This is a convenience if you want to keep helper build files in a subdirectory, controlling directory clutter. The output log indicates that the build file did locate the files we wanted:

```
Buildfile: tasklib\create-html-log.xml

default:
    [style] Processing C:\AntBook\app\log\deploy-log.xml to
            C:\AntBook\app\log\deploy.html
    [style] Loading stylesheet C:\Java\Apps\jakarta-ant\etc\log.xsl

BUILD SUCCESSFUL
```

Converting the full XML log into a more succinct HTML file (here from 160KB to 7KB), lets people download the log over slow network connections or via email. The <mail> task could easily mail the results to a mailing list. There is an easier way to send a success or failure message, the MailLogger, which we will cover in chapter 20. That approach, however, does not generate HTML files of the build log.

13.5 LOADING XML DATA INTO ANT PROPERTIES

We covered the <xmlproperty> task in chapter 3, but it deserves mention here as well. If you have XML data files that contain values needed in your build process, the <xmlproperty> task may be able to help. It has some notable issues, however: it does not perform local DTD resolution and it only provides access to the first element or attribute value if there are duplicate names. An example data file:

```
<?xml version="1.0" encoding="UTF-8" ?>
<data>
  <element attribute1="attribute1">element1</element>
  <element attribute2="attribute2">element2</element>
</data>
```

We load this data file in Ant:

```
<xmlproperty file="data.xml"
             keepRoot="false"
             collapseAttributes="true"
/>
<echo>
  Values
  ------
  element = ${element}
  element.attribute1 = ${element.attribute1}
  element.attribute2 = ${element.attribute2}
</echo>
```

This results in the following output:

```
[echo]          Values
[echo]          ------
[echo]          element = element1
[echo]          element.attribute1 = attribute1
[echo]          element.attribute2 = attribute2
```

Despite the shortcomings, such as the second <element> value becoming inaccessible and the confusing way in which attribute1 and attribute2 are both accessible, this task can be handy when you have well-known simple XML data and need access to a piece of it during the build process.

13.6 NEXT STEPS IN XML PROCESSING

A feature likely to be available in the very near future is JAXB support: the new process for creating Java classes from an XML description, classes that at run time you can bind to an XML document; all the parsing of the document and mapping of XML data to class data will be handled for you. This will make handling of XML documents whose structure you know at compile time much easier. Obviously, an Ant task to create the classes is the way to integrate this with an Ant-based build process. We would expect such a task to appear shortly after Sun finally releases JAXB. There is also an open source project, Castor, (at exolab.org), that, among other things, creates Java classes from an XSD schema. We use Castor in our projects, simply with a `<java>` call; it's good, but needs an Ant task with dependency checking to be great.

13.7 SUMMARY

Ant uses XML to describe the build, so it is a highly XML-centric build tool. It can also process XML during the build. Validating XML is the obvious first step; the `<xmlvalidate>` task enables you to ensure that your XML is well formed and matches the DTD or XSD description of the file.

The `<xslt>` task enables you to transform XML during the build. This lets you store content in XML form and then dynamically generate HTML, WML, or JSP pages from it. The `<xslt>` task is a very powerful tool, but you first have to put in the effort to learn XSL.

Ant itself can generate an XML version of its build log; this can be transformed using XSL to produce a readable HTML file. Ant could then perform some follow-on action, such as copying the file to a local web server, or emailing it to the development team.

C H A P T E R   1 4

Enterprise JavaBeans

14.1 EJB overview   333
14.2 A simple EJB build   335
14.3 Using Ant's EJB tasks   336
14.4 Using <ejbjar>   337
14.5 Using XDoclet for EJB
       development   340

14.6 Middlegen   345
14.7 Deploying to J2EE
       application servers   348
14.8 A complete EJB example   349
14.9 Best practices in EJB projects   354
14.10 Summary   354

Building Enterprise JavaBeans applications is a complex Java development process. The sheer volume of Java code needed for each entity bean forces the need for code organization and management. Ant plays a crucial role in the building of EJB-based projects by tackling the tough issues, allowing developers to concern themselves with development rather than with building and deployment.

14.1   EJB OVERVIEW

Enterprise JavaBeans play a prominent role in the Java 2 Enterprise Edition (J2EE) suite of specifications. The EJB specifications provide component-based distributed computing. The goal of J2EE is to allow component developers to focus on developing business models and processes that leverage container-provided services such as distributed transactions, declarative security, and persistence. The separation of roles, development, assembly, deployment, and administration, is often touted as a primary benefit of EJB.

It is hard work to create a good bean model in EJB development, and handing off the database binding of beans to the container can be a performance bottleneck; implementing persistence yourself is extra work. Some of the premium enterprise IDEs make EJB development easier, but it has still been mostly a manual task. In the past, the effort and the cost of full J2EE servers have been barriers to adoption too, but now you can get high-quality application servers such as JBoss[1] and HP Application Server for free.

Ant and XDoclet do make EJB development significantly easier, leaving only architectural issues to the developers.

14.1.1 The many types of Enterprise JavaBeans

In the EJB 2.0 specifications, there are three types of EJBs: entity beans, session beans, and message-driven beans. An entity bean typically represents business model data and can either take advantage of container-managed persistence (CMP) or provide its own persistence implementation (bean-managed persistence, BMP). Session beans typically represent business processes such as workflow and control, and facilitate complex entity bean transactions. Session beans come in two flavors: stateful and stateless. Stateful session beans may represent, for example, a single-user's shopping cart. A stateless session bean is useful for providing services that can be accomplished without storing state between method invocations. Finally, message-driven beans (MDBs) are new to the EJB 2.0 specification and exist to process asynchronous messages received from a Java Message Service (JMS).

The EJB 2.0 specification also has other interesting features such as container-managed relationships (CMR) and local interfaces. Prior to the EJB 2.0 specification, all EJB clients, regardless of location, were required to use remote interfaces. Now you can use high-performance local interfaces, which avoid the overhead of remote method invocation (RMI).

14.1.2 EJB JAR

The primary artifact of EJB development is the EJB JAR file. An EJB JAR file can consist of one or more Enterprise JavaBeans and all of the .class files associated with each EJB. Within the META-INF directory of an EJB JAR file is a deployment descriptor named ejb-jar.xml, as well as any vendor-specific metadata. Figure 14.1 illustrates the typical components in an EJB application.

The developer creates the actual entity or session bean. The EJBHome interface and the EJBObject remote interface for the EJB are also historically developer-created modules, although XDoclet or other code generators do away with these tedious steps.

In the simplest possible EJB JAR, the contents are

- A single EJB
- A home interface
- A remote interface
- An XML deployment descriptor

---

[1] JBoss (jboss.org) isn't J2EE certified because it doesn't have access to the tests; HP Application Server (http://www.hpmiddleware.com) is J2EE certified, but you don't get the source. Both seem good value for money.

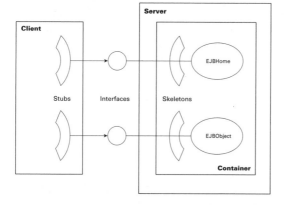

Figure 14.1
Typical EJB scenario with home and remote interfaces accessed from the client through RMI

With the simplest possible EJB JAR file containing four pieces, the build process of a large EJB project can get quite complex. Luckily, there are Ant-based tools to make the job a bit easier.

14.1.3 Vendor-specific situations

The cause of many headaches when using EJB is the vendor-specific nature of EJB deployment. Most application servers have their own specific additional deployment descriptors. Often vendor-specific processes, such as the generation of support classes, need to occur. For example, IBM WebSphere requires several metadata files: Schema.dbxmi, Map.mapxmi, ibm-ejb-jar-bnd.xmi, and ibm-ejb-jar-ext.xmi. Such vendor-specific files are often generated from vendor supplied tools, or can be built using XDoclet or other code-generation techniques.

14.2 A SIMPLE EJB BUILD

The most rudimentary way to build an EJB JAR file is to create all the necessary Java code and a deployment descriptor yourself, compile the code, and then use the `<jar>` task to bundle it all. If your project has only one or a small number of fixed EJB JAR files, this is the best solution. It is simple, but it does not scale. Listing 14.1 provides an example.

Listing 14.1   Building an EJB JAR using <jar>

```
<target name="compile" depends="init">
  <javac destdir="${build.classes.dir}"
         debug="${build.debug}"
         srcdir="${src.dir}">
    <classpath refid="compile.classpath"/>
    <include name="**/*.java"/>
  </javac>
</target>
```

```
<target name="jar" depends="compile">
  <jar destfile="${dist.dir}/${ejbjar.name}"
       basedir="${build.classes.dir}">
    <metainf dir="metadata" includes="ejb-jar.xml"/>
  </jar>
</target>
```

The code in listing 14.1 compiles all the Java source code and builds an EJB JAR file with the metadata/ejb-jar.xml file built into the META-INF directory. The main difference in the code shown here and the `<jar>` usage shown in section 6.3.2 is the inclusion of the deployment descriptor in the META-INF directory.

14.3 USING ANT'S EJB TASKS

Ant includes a handful of EJB-related tasks, most of which are vendor specific. The vendor-specific tasks are now showing their age, though, and may not be applicable to the latest versions of the application servers. Check the Ant documentation for the specific version information.

WebLogic

WebLogic is the most well represented J2EE application server in terms of EJB tasks. The tasks include:

- `<wlrun>` and `<wlstop>` to start and stop the WebLogic server. You can use `<wlrun>` inside the `<parallel>` task in order to allow other tasks to execute against the running server.
- `<ddcreator>` to create ejb-jar.xml deployment descriptors from text-based descriptor files.
- `<ejbc>` to compile WebLogic-specific support classes including the RMI stubs and skeletons. This task is for an older version of WebLogic; it is more likely that the nested `<weblogic>` element of `<ejbjar>` would be used instead.
- `<serverdeploy>`, new in Ant 1.5, using a nested `<weblogic>` subelement, to hot-deploy an EAR, WAR, or JAR to WebLogic servers.

iPlanet Application Server

There is an `<iplanet-ejbc>` task to build the EJB stubs and skeletons for the iPlanet Application Server. The `<ejbjar>` task has a nested `<iplanet>` element that you should probably use instead.

Borland Application Server

Specific to the Borland Application Server, but needed in a more general sense, is the `<blgenclient>` task. It creates the client EJB JAR from the server EJB JAR file.

14.4   USING <EJBJAR>

In projects where the use of EJB is more sophisticated than what the simple <jar> capabilities can handle, use <ejbjar>. The <ejbjar> task provides two services. It can introspect ejb-jar.xml-compliant files and build EJB JAR files with the classes specified and their dependencies. It also provides vendor-specific deployment build tools as nested elements inside the task.

The <ejbjar> task scans a directory structure for deployment descriptors and uses the matched descriptors to build an EJB JAR for each deployment descriptor that it processes. This allows it to generate any number of EJB JAR files in one sweep as opposed to having to do them individually with their own <jar> tasks. Another great advantage of <ejbjar> is that it pulls in dependencies for the classes named in the deployment descriptors it processes. In particular, it automatically locates superclasses and incorporates them into the resultant JAR. There are many bells and whistles to the <ejbjar> task, but we only touch upon a few of them in the examples provided. The documentation provided with the Ant distribution is the best source for detailed information on the many attributes and options.

> **NOTE**   Ant 1.5's <ejbjar> task supports EJB 2.0, including local interfaces and message-driven beans. Ant 1.4.1 does not support these and ignores them when processing ejb-jar.xml files.

Packaging a bean with <ejbjar>

Our application takes advantage of EJB by providing stateless session bean access to our searching functionality. Very simply, our session bean code is:

```
package org.example.antbook.session;

import org.example.antbook.common.Document;
import org.example.antbook.common.SearchException;
import org.example.antbook.common.SearchUtil;

import javax.ejb.SessionBean;
import javax.ejb.SessionContext;

public class SearchSessionBean implements SessionBean {
    public void setSessionContext(SessionContext context) {
    }

    public void ejbCreate() {
    }

    public void ejbRemove() {
    }

    public void ejbActivate() {
    }

    public void ejbPassivate() {
    }
```

```
    public Document[] search(String query) throws SearchException {
        return SearchUtil.findDocuments(query);
    }

    public void init(String indexDir) throws SearchException {
        SearchUtil.init(indexDir);
    }
}
```

Using our common library search functionality, our session bean merely acts as a wrapper to this functionality, which can also be used directly from our stand-alone command-line search tool and our web interface. The search and init[2] methods are direct pass-through methods to our SearchUtil capability. Our deployment descriptor, shown in listing 14.2, is typical and contains references to the home, remote, and entity beans.

Listing 14.2   The EJB deployment descriptor for the enterprise application

```
<ejb-jar>

<description>
AntBook EJB
</description>
<enterprise-beans>
    <session>
        <description>
          Search Bean
        </description>
        <ejb-name>SearchSessionBean</ejb-name>
        <home>org.example.antbook.session.SearchSessionHome</home>
        <remote>org.example.antbook.session.SearchSessionRemote</remote>
        <ejb-class>org.example.antbook.session.SearchSessionBean</ejb-
class>
        <session-type>Stateless</session-type>
        <transaction-type>Container</transaction-type>
    </session>
</enterprise-beans>

<assembly-descriptor>
    <container-transaction>
        <method>
            <ejb-name>SearchSessionBean</ejb-name>
            <method-name>*</method-name>
        </method>
        <trans-attribute>Supports</trans-attribute>
    </container-transaction>
</assembly-descriptor>
</ejb-jar>
```

---

[2] The init method would be better handled as JNDI lookup, but does have the advantage of allowing the client to control the index being searched.

Building the EJB JAR file by using `<ejbjar>`:

```
<ejbjar srcdir="${build.classes.dir}"
        descriptordir="metadata"
        destdir="${dist.dir}"
        basejarname="${ejbjar.name}"
        genericjarsuffix="">
  <include name="ejb-jar.xml"/>
</ejbjar>
```

The `basejarname` and `genericjarsuffix` attributes, as well as several other attributes unused in this example, provide control over the names of the generated EJB JAR files. Because this example is only generating a single EJB JAR file (note that it only includes a single ejb-jar.xml file), we want to control the name of the JAR precisely. Again, you should refer to Ant's documentation for more details on JAR file naming as it involves complexity beyond what we cover.

The `srcdir` attribute, somewhat confusingly, refers to the directory containing the classes referred to by the deployment descriptor files, not to the actual source code. The `descriptordir` is the base directory to use when scanning for deployment descriptors. Deployment descriptors do not have to be named ejb-jar.xml; some developers name them to match the generated EJB JAR file. The task renames deployment descriptor to ejb-jar.xml when embedded in the JAR file regardless of its original name. The `destdir` attribute specifies where the generated JAR files should be written. Depending on the options selected, the JAR files could be written into a directory hierarchy mirroring the hierarchy of the deployment descriptors processed, which gives you flexibility.

14.4.1   Vendor-specific `<ejbjar>` processing

Nested within the `<ejbjar>` task are vendor tags to tackle vendor-specific needs. Table 14.1 shows the vendors and capabilities currently supported.

Table 14.1   The vendor-specific subtasks for `<ejbjar>`. Some vendors also supply their own version of Ant with other extensions to the task.

Vendor	Tag	Capabilities
Borland Application Server	`<borland>`	Generates and compiles the stubs and skeletons, builds the server JAR, and, optionally, the corresponding client JAR file.
iPlanet Application Server	`<iplanet>`	Builds the specific skeletons and stubs needed and incorporates any iPlanet-specific deployment descriptors.
JBoss	`<jboss>`	JBoss does not require any pregeneration or compilation of stubs and skeletons, but there are JBoss-specific deployment descriptors that are incorporated: jboss.xml and jaws.xml.
Java Open Application Server (JOnAS)	`<jonas>`	Generates the JOnAS stubs and skeletons and incorporates its vendor-specific deployment descriptors.

continued on next page

Table 14.1 The vendor-specific subtasks for <ejbjar>. Some vendors also supply their own version of Ant with other extensions to the task. (continued)

Vendor	Tag	Capabilities
WebLogic	`<weblogic>`	Invokes the WebLogic `ejbc` tool to build the WebLogic EJB JAR. There are some issues with this process, so refer to the Ant documentation for details.
WebSphere	`<websphere>`	Incorporates the WebSphere specific deployment descriptors and can optionally invoke the WebSphere `ejbdeploy` tool. This is probably the trickiest vendor `<ejbjar>` plug-in to work with. Depending on the options used, it can require that the IBM JDK be used, and configuration of the classpath to locate all of the necessary WebSphere classes is involved.

Although new vendors or users can easily create the necessary customizations to add to the list of supported deployment tools, Ant's current architecture does not provide the capability to dynamically add subelements to <ejbjar>. Adding new ones requires a change to the actual task code of <ejbjar>.

One consequence is that where some vendors provide their own extension elements, they do so by providing their own modified version of the Ant jar files, which can cause no end of confusion. This restriction is unfortunate and needs to be addressed in a future version of Ant.

14.5 *USING XDOCLET FOR EJB DEVELOPMENT*

If you've ever felt the pain of dealing with the enormous amount of support code for an EJB project you will likely find XDoclet's EJB support invaluable. In chapter 11, we explored XDoclet's @todo and templating capabilities, but it really shines with EJB.

The goal of XDoclet's EJB support is to enable developers to write Enterprise Java-Beans without ever having to write a deployment descriptor or remote interface. Instead, you just code the bean implementation, mark it up with a few custom Javadoc tags, and have all the support structures generated for you.

Returning to our stateless session search bean, figure 14.2 demonstrates the use of two simple @tags to generate of all the needed EJB support components. The class-level @ejb.bean type="Stateless" marks the class as a stateless session bean, rather than as stateful. Both methods that we want to expose to our remote clients get flagged with an @ejb.interface-method tag.

Using an optional view-type attribute on the @ejb.interface allows the method to be exposed as a remote or local (EJB 2.0) interface, or both, giving great control over such details.

This example only demonstrates a session bean, but XDoclet also generates entity bean-specific code such as primary key classes and data access objects. The utility methods generated consist of helper getHome methods to return the home interface from the InitialContext. This Ant code generated all the files shown in figure 14.2:

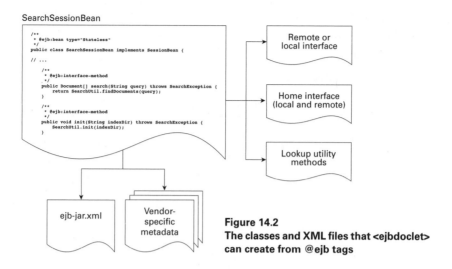

Figure 14.2
The classes and XML files that <ejbdoclet> can create from @ejb tags

```
<ejbdoclet
    sourcepath="src"
    destdir="${build.dir}"
    classpathref="xdoclet.classpath"
    excludedtags="@version,@author"
    ejbspec="1.1">

    <fileset dir="src">
      <include name="**/*Bean.java" />
    </fileset>

    <remoteinterface/>
    <homeinterface/>
    <utilobject/>
    <deploymentdescriptor destdir="${build.dir}/ejb/META-INF"/>
    <jboss/>
</ejbdoclet>
```

The ejbspec attribute tells XDoclet to do the right things code and deployment descriptor generation-wise for the desired EJB specification (1.1 or 2.0). While migrating from one container version to another is not likely to be headache-free, XDoclet performs a lot of the work for you.

14.5.1   XDoclet subtasks

Because of the variability in deployment descriptors between various EJB containers as well as the sheer volume of architectural options with EJB in general, XDoclet has many configuration possibilities. The <ejbdoclet> usage shown in section 14.5 illustrates the build-file writer's control over what artifacts are generated. In that example, the generation includes remote interfaces, home interfaces, utility objects, standard EJB deployment descriptor, and vendor-specific JBoss deployment descriptors.

Nested within the `<ejbdoclet>` Ant task are *subtasks*, the XDoclet term for nested elements in its Ant tasks. Table 14.2 shows the available subtasks for the `<ejbdoclet>` task. We cover vendor-specific subtasks in section 14.5.3.

Table 14.2 `<ejbdoclet>` subtasks

Subtask	Artifacts Generated
`<dao>`	Abstract data access object interfaces
`<dataobject>`	EJB data objects
`<deploymentdescriptor>`	EJB standard-compliant deployment descriptor, ejb-jar.xml
`<entitybmp>`	Entity bean BMP classes derived from the abstract entity bean classes
`<entitycmp>`	Entity bean CMP classes derived from the abstract entity bean classes
`<entitypk>`	Primary key classes
`<homeinterface>`	Home interfaces
`<localhomeinterface>`	Local (EJB 2.0) home interfaces
`<localinterface>`	Local (EJB 2.0) interfaces
`<remoteinterface>`	Remote interfaces
`<session>`	Session bean classes derived from the abstract session bean classes
`<utilobject>`	Utility objects for local/home interface lookups
`<valueobject>`	Value object classes

The `<template>` (discussed in chapter 11) and `<xmlTemplate>` subtasks are also valid subtasks for `<ejbdoclet>`, which allows custom XDoclet templating to occur in the same sweep of the source code that EJB generation uses. Each subtask has its own share of attributes, and there are standard attributes that all subtasks share. Each subtask can override the `destdir`, `mergedir`, and `templatefile` for added control over output location and merge files, and to override the XDoclet template used. There are many other options to the subtasks; consult the excellent XDoclet documentation for the details.

14.5.2 XDoclet's @tags

The power of XDoclet comes from the metadata stored in the @tags. Another major piece of information that is gathered from source code analyzed by XDoclet is the class structure, specifically the inheritance hierarchy, interfaces implemented, and the method names and signatures. XDoclet uses many EJB-specific @tags to define metadata and to control the generation process. From XDoclet's documentation, here is a typical example of a class-level entity bean Javadoc block:

```
/**
 * This is an account bean. It is an example of how to use the
 * EJBDoclet tags.
 *
 * @see Customer Accounts are owned by customers, and a customer can
 * have many accounts.
```

```
 *
 * @ejb.bean    name="bank/Account"
 *              type="CMP"
 *              jndi-name="ejb/bank/Account"
 *              primkey-field="id"
 * @ejb.finder  signature="Collection findAll()"
 *              unchecked="true"
 * @ejb.interface remote-class="test.interfaces.Account"
 */
```

14.5.3 Supporting different application servers with XDoclet

Even by using XDoclet's automation, we cannot escape vendor-specific issues. Fortunately, XDoclet handles this cleanly with vendor-specific @tags that can be interspersed with the general XDoclet EJB tags. The result is a single bean class with all of the needed tags to generate all the desired artifacts, perhaps with quite a lot of tags if a project targets multiple application servers. Despite the possible mess of @tags, the benefits are enormous: multivendor support with automatic code generation of all the ugliness freeing you to work on business logic rather than fighting with the gory details. See table 14.3.

Table 14.3 XDoclet's vendor-specific subtasks for EJB development

Vendor	Subtask	Description
Apache SOAP	`<apachesoap>`	Generates Apache SOAP deployment descriptors from EJB classes and non-EJB classes. Methods to expose are tagged with @soap:method.
Bluestone (now HP Application Server)	`<bluestone>`	Produces HPAS-specific deployment descriptors.
Castor	`<castormapping>`	Creates a Castor mapping.xml file.
JBoss	`<jboss>`	Produces jaws.xml and jboss.xml.
JRun	`<jrun>`	Creates JRun-specific deployment descriptor.
MVCSoft	`<mvcsoft>`	Generates MVCSoft configuration file.
Orion	`<orion>`	Creates Orion-specific deployment descriptor.
Pramati	`<pramati>`	Generates Pramati-specific deployment descriptor.
Struts (from Apache Jakarta)	`<strutsform>`	Creates Struts form-bean source code from entity beans.
WebLogic	`<weblogic>`	Produces WebLogic-specific deployment descriptors.
WebSphere	`<websphere>`	Generates WebSphere-specific deployment descriptors such as Schema.dbxmi.

14.5.4 Ant property substitution

An interesting and powerful feature of XDoclet is its Ant property substitution feature. XDoclet uses the same syntax that Ant uses for property expansion: ${ }. If an Ant property exists for the name between the brackets, XDoclet replaces it with the value of the Ant property.

To illustrate, we use the `<strutsform>` subtask. Tagging entity bean classes with an `@struts:form` tag causes Struts `ActionForm` classes to be generated. One of the optional parameters to `@struts:form` is an `extends` attribute specifying the base class to extend for the generated Java code, defaulting to the Struts `org.apache.struts.action.ActionForm` class. Our entity bean class consists of two XDoclet tags at the class level:

```
package org.example.antbook.ejb;

import javax.ejb.CreateException;
import javax.ejb.EJBException;
import javax.ejb.EntityBean;
import javax.ejb.EntityContext;
import javax.ejb.FinderException;

/**
 *   Sample entity bean
 *
 *@ejb.bean type="BMP"
 *@struts:form extends="${struts.base.class}"
 */
public class SomeEntityBean implements EntityBean {
    // . . .
}
```

We could have specified our base class directly or have had the default Struts base class used by not specifying the `extends` attribute at all. By providing a bit of insulation between our application and the Struts API, we allow ourselves the flexibility to inject new functionality (perhaps form validation features). By using `${struts.base.class}`, our build can dynamically change the base class that gets used on the generated code. Our `<ejbdoclet>` task now looks like this:

```
<property name="struts.base.class"
          value="org.apache.struts.action.ActionForm"/>
<ejbdoclet
        sourcepath="${java.src.dir};src"
        destdir="${java.src.dir}"
        excludedtags="@version,@author"
        ejbspec="2.0"
        classpathref="xdoclet.classpath">

  <packageSubstitution packages="ejb" substituteWith="interfaces"/>

  <fileset dir="${java.src.dir}">
    <include name="**/*Bean.java" />
  </fileset>

  <fileset dir="src" includes="**/*Bean.java"/>

  <!-- Several XDoclet subtasks omitted here -->
```

```
  <strutsform>
    <packageSubstitution packages="ejb" substituteWith="struts"/>
  </strutsform>

</ejbdoclet>
```

By default, the standard Struts base class is used; however, if a different base class is desired, the property `struts.base.class` can be overridden. This override could occur at many levels, depending on your needs, but typically it would be from a properties file (see Ant properties in chapter 3). You could even define a new base class from the command-line:

```
ant -Dstruts.base.class=org.example.antbook.struts.BaseForm
```

Overriding a base class at build time is perhaps an extreme example of XDoclet's Ant property substitution, and use of a factory-like design pattern could certainly accomplish similar capabilities. The possibilities that open up with this feature are astounding—code-generation with build-time control over switches and parameters.

Note the use of `<packageSubstitution>` nested in `<ejbdoclet>` and within `<strutsform>`. By default, generated code gets placed in the same package as the original source code being processed. Code can be relocated to more meaningful packages, and their corresponding directories, by using `<packageSubstitution>`. For example, our sample entity bean is in package `org.example.antbook.ejb`. All code, except from `<strutsform>`, is generated into `org.example.antbook.interfaces`. The `<strutsform>`-generated code overrides the global package substitution and its code generates into package `org.example.antbook.struts`.

14.6 MIDDLEGEN

Having `<ejbdoclet>` generate all the EJB support code and descriptors is great, but the common practice of going from a database to the EJB models takes time. By using XDoclet, we can save an enormous amount of effort by simply creating a single Java file for each bean with the appropriate tags. Perhaps you already have an existing database that you want to reverse engineer into entity beans. This is precisely the purpose of a great tool called Middlegen, created by Aslak Hellesøy, who is also a member of the XDoclet development team. See figure 14.3.

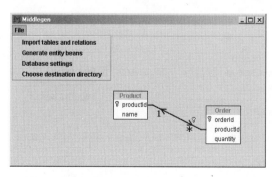

Figure 14.3
Middlegen user interface,
displaying a table relationship

To create entity beans from a database, we simply point Middlegen at our (SQL Server) database.

```
<taskdef
        name="middlegen"
        classname="middlegen.MiddlegenTask"
        classpath="${middlegen.jar}"
/>

<middlegen
        gui="${gui}"
        destination="${java.src.dir}"
        driver="${db.driver}"
        databaseurl="${db.url}"
        username="${db.username}"
        password="${db.password}"
        schema="${db.schema}"
        catalog="${db.catalog}"
        package="org.example.antbook.ejb"
        interfacepackage="org.example.antbook.interfaces"
/>
```

The <middlegen> task works in two modes, based on the gui switch: classes may be generated automatically or interactively (the latter through the user interface shown in figure 14.3). Our database schema simply has two tables, Product and Order, which are linked with a one-to-many relationship. The Middlegen task creates a single-entity bean class for each table processed. The code contains the necessary @tags to be further processed by XDoclet's <ejbdoclet> task. Listing 14.3 shows a sample class generated for our Product table.

Listing 14.3   Example entity bean generated from Middlegen

```
package org.example.antbook.ejb;

/**
 * @author <a href="http://boss.bekk.no/boss/middlegen/">Middlegen</a>
 *
 * @ejb.bean                              Standard XDoclet container
 *    type="CMP"                          managed persistence tags
 *    cmp-version="2.x"
 *    name="Product"
 *    local-jndi-name="org.example.antbook.interfaces.ProductLocal"
 *    view-type="local"
 *
 * @weblogic:table-name Product
 * @weblogic:data-source-name middlegen.database    Automatic
 * @weblogic:persistence                            vendor-specific
 *                                                   support added
 * @jboss:table-name Product
 */
public abstract class ProductBean implements javax.ejb.EntityBean {
```

```
/**
 * Context set by container
 */
private javax.ejb.EntityContext _entityContext;

/**
 * Returns the productId
 *
 * @return the productId
 *
 * @ejb.persistent-field
 * @ejb.pk-field
 *
 * @weblogic:dbms-column ProductID
 *
 * @jboss:column-name ProductID
 */
public abstract java.lang.Long getProductId();

// ... some code removed for brevity ...

/**
 * Returns a collection of local Orders
 *
 * @return a collection of local Orders
 *
 * @ejb.relation
 *     name="product-order"
 *     role-name="product-has-order"
 *
 * @weblogic:column-map
 *     foreign-key-column="ProductID"
 *     key-column="ProductID"
 * @jboss:relation
 *     fk-constraint="true"
 *     fk-column="ProductID"
 *     related-pk-field="ProductID"
 */
public abstract java.util.Collection getOrders();

// ... some code removed for brevity ...

}
```

Relationship with Order table

The next step is to have XDoclet process these generated files and build all of the other necessary pieces, including vendor-specific deployment descriptors. In section 14.8, a complete build incorporating Middlegen, XDoclet, compilation, and building the EJB JAR and EAR files is shown.

Middlegen in practice

Middlegen is still in its infancy and has a few notable issues that may preclude out-of-the-box use:

- It is geared to EJB 2.0, so it does not generate EJB 1.*x*-compliant code.
- At the time of writing, only WebLogic and JBoss vendor-specific tags are being generated, although this will change quickly.
- We ran into issues with JDBC drivers and were unable to use Hypersonic SQL and Microsoft Access.[3] Middlegen was unable to determine the table relationships with those databases. Some JDBC metadata calls that Middlegen uses are unsupported by at least a few drivers. We finally got our example relationships working against Microsoft SQL Server 2000.

Even if Middlegen does not work out of the box for a particular database or EJB container vendor, the time invested in tweaking Middlegen's freely available source code or XDoclet entity bean template is likely to be well spent. The combination of Middlegen and XDoclet is a great benefit to EJB developers. There are many database EJB reverse-engineering tools available, but the open-source and easily tweakable nature of these two products make them very attractive. The community support available is unlikely to be matched by any commercial product vendors. It's quite common for developers to write their own code generators, but it might just be time to roll up your sleeves and contribute to efforts such as Middlegen instead!

To use Middlegen effectively, we recommend that you explore its capabilities gradually, starting with a few tables in a simple database. If you send it up against a 30-table database with lots of relations between the entries, you will be intimidated by the amount of code that it generates. The generated code should be left alone, if at all possible; if you do change it, copy it away to safety first. You do not want an automated tool stomping on your source.

14.7 DEPLOYING TO J2EE APPLICATION SERVERS

Before the release of version 1.5, Ant has had no specific support for EJB deployment. Although with a friendly JBoss server running locally, development deployment can be as simple as using `<copy>` to move an EJB JAR, WAR, or EAR to its `deploy` directory. Production deployment is an entirely different situation, however; we cover it in more detail in chapter 18. Ant 1.5 ships with a `<serverdeploy>` task designed similarly to the `<ejbjar>` task in that it is a container for vendor-specific subelements. At the time of writing, only two vendors have `<serverdeploy>` support: WebLogic and JOnAS. Deploying to a WebLogic server can be accomplished by using the nested `<weblogic>` element:

---

[3] We wanted a lightweight and easily distributable working example, thus our preference for using Hypersonic SQL for our database examples.

```
<serverdeploy action="deploy"
          serverUrl="t3://myserver:7001"
          classpath="${classpath}"
          username="${user.name}"
          password="${user.password}"
          source="${lib.dir}/ejb_myApp.ear">
  <weblogic application="myapp"
          component="ejb_foobar:myserver,productionserver"
  />
</serverdeploy>
```

We predict that other vendors will be supported in the near future.

14.8   *A COMPLETE EJB EXAMPLE*

While we have typically refrained from long, boring code listings in this book, it is important to show a complete example of how all the pieces fit together to build an EJB JAR by using most of the techniques and tasks discussed in this chapter.

Listing 14.4 demonstrates using Ant to build a database from SQL, reverse engineering it into entity beans by using Middlegen, generating many EJB artifacts from the Middlegen-generated entity beans and manually built source code, compiling it all, and then bundling it all into an EJB JAR. Figure 14.4 shows this graphically.

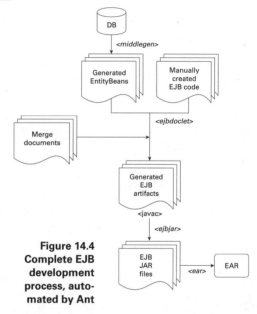

Figure 14.4 Complete EJB development process, automated by Ant

Listing 14.4   EJB JAR generation all the way from database metadata

```
<?xml version="1.0" encoding="UTF-8" ?>
<!DOCTYPE project [
    <!ENTITY properties SYSTEM "file:../../../app/properties.xml">
]>
<project name="EJB Examples" default="main" basedir=".">

  &properties;

  <property name="name" value="ejbexample"/>
  <property name="build.dir" location="build"/>
  <property name="src.dir" location="src"/>
  <property name="gen.src.dir"
          location="${build.dir}/src/java"/>
  <property name="java.classes.dir"
```

```
                location="${build.dir}/classes"/>
    <property name="ejb.dd.dir"
                location="${java.classes.dir}/META-INF"/>
    <property name="standard-ejb.dir"
                location="${build.dir}/standard-ejb"/>
    <property name="ejb.jar.file"
                location="${standard-ejb.dir}/${name}-ejb.jar"/>

    <property name="sql.dir" location="sql"/>
    <property name="sql.create.file"
                location="${sql.dir}/create.sql"/>

    <property name="application.xml"
                location="metadata/application.xml"/>

    <property name="db.dir" location="${build.dir}/db"/>
    <property name="db.name" value="example"/>
    <property name="db.url" value="jdbc:hsqldb:${db.dir}/${db.name}"/>
    <property name="db.driver" value="org.hsqldb.jdbcDriver"/>
    <property name="db.username" value="sa"/>
    <property name="db.password" value=""/>

    <path id="compile.classpath">
      <pathelement location="${j2ee.jar}"/>
      <pathelement location="${struts.jar}"/>
    </path>

    <path id="xdoclet.classpath">
      <pathelement location="${log4j.jar}"/>
      <pathelement location="${xdoclet.jar}"/>
      <pathelement location="${j2ee.jar}"/>

      <!-- javadoc is needed -->
      <pathelement path="${java.class.path}"/>
    </path>

    <!-- ======================================================= -->
    <!-- Default starting point                                  -->
    <!-- ======================================================= -->
    <target name="main" depends="ear"/>


    <!-- ======================================================= -->
    <!-- Clean everything                                        -->
    <!-- ======================================================= -->
    <target name="clean" description="Clean all generated stuff">
      <delete dir="${build.dir}"/>
      <delete dir="${db.dir}"/>
    </target>

    <!-- ======================================================= -->
    <!-- Create sample DB                                        -->
    <!-- ======================================================= -->
    <target name="build-db"
            description="Build sample database">
```

```
    <mkdir dir="${db.dir}"/>
    <sql driver="${db.driver}"
         url="${db.url}"
         userid="${db.username}"          Creates the
         password="${db.password}"        database from
         print="true"                     SQL CREATE
         autocommit="true"                TABLE script
         src="${sql.create.file}"
         onerror="continue">
      <classpath>
        <pathelement location="${hsqldb.jar}"/>
      </classpath>
    </sql>
</target>


<!-- ======================================================= -->
<!-- Run Middlegen                                           -->
<!-- ======================================================= -->
<target name="middlegen" depends="build-db"
        description="Run Middlegen">
  <mkdir dir="${gen.src.dir}"/>

  <taskdef name="middlegen"
           classname="middlegen.MiddlegenTask"
           classpath="${middlegen.jar};${xdoclet.jar};${hsqldb.jar}"
  />

  <middlegen gui="${gui}"
             destination="${gen.src.dir}"        Middlegen produces
             driver="${db.driver}"               XDoclet-configured
             databaseurl="${db.url}"             entity bean classes
             username="${db.username}"              for each table
             password="${db.password}"
             package="org.example.antbook.ejb"
             interfacepackage="org.example.antbook.interfaces"
  />
</target>


<!-- ======================================================= -->
<!-- Run XDoclet                                             -->
<!-- ======================================================= -->
<target name="xdoclet" depends="middlegen"
        description="Generate artifacts from EJBs">
  <mkdir dir="${ejb.dd.dir}"/>

  <taskdef name="ejbdoclet"
           classname="xdoclet.ejb.EjbDocletTask"
           classpath="${xdoclet.jar}"
  />

  <property name="struts.base.class"
            value="org.apache.struts.action.ActionForm"/>
```

```
<ejbdoclet sourcepath="${gen.src.dir};${src.dir}"
           destdir="${gen.src.dir}"
           excludedtags="@version,@author"
           ejbspec="2.0"
           classpathref="xdoclet.classpath">

    <packageSubstitution packages="ejb"
                         substituteWith="interfaces"/>

    <fileset dir="${gen.src.dir}">
      <include name="**/*Bean.java" />
    </fileset>

    <fileset dir="${src.dir}" includes="**/*Bean.java"/>

    <dataobject/>
    <valueobject/>
    <localinterface/>
    <utilobject/>
    <localhomeinterface/>
    <entitypk/>
    <entitycmp/>
    <homeinterface/>
    <remoteinterface/>
    <entitypk/>
    <strutsform>
      <packageSubstitution packages="ejb" substituteWith="struts"/>
    </strutsform>
    <deploymentdescriptor destdir="${ejb.dd.dir}"
                          validatexml="true"
    />

    <jboss version="2.4"
           xmlencoding="UTF-8"
           destdir="${ejb.dd.dir}"
    />
  </ejbdoclet>
</target>
```

XDoclet generates EJB artifacts from Middlegen and our own code

```
<!-- ========================================================= -->
<!-- Compile everything                                        -->
<!-- ========================================================= -->
<target name="compile" depends="xdoclet"
        description="Compile source code">
  <javac destdir="${java.classes.dir}"
         classpathref="compile.classpath">
    <src path="${gen.src.dir};${src.dir}"/>
  </javac>
</target>
```

Compiles both generated and maintained code

```
<!-- ========================================================= -->
<!-- Build EJB JARs                                            -->
<!-- ========================================================= -->
<target name="ejb-jar" depends="compile"
        description="Make EJB JAR files">
  <mkdir dir="${standard-ejb.dir}"/>
```

```
        <ejbjar srcdir="${java.classes.dir}"
                descriptordir="${ejb.dd.dir}"
                destdir="${standard-ejb.dir}"
                naming="ejb-name"
                genericjarsuffix="-ejb.jar">
          <include name="ejb-jar.xml"/>
          <dtd publicId="-//Sun Microsystems, Inc.//
DTD Enterprise JavaBeans 1.1//EN
location="${j2ee.dir}/${j2ee.subdir}/ejb-jar_1_1.dtd"/>
        </ejbjar>
      </target>

    <!-- ========================================================= -->
    <!-- Build EAR                                                 -->
    <!-- ========================================================= -->
    <target name="ear" depends="ejb-jar"
            description="Build EAR file">
      <mkdir dir="${dist.dir}"/>
      <ear destfile="${dist.dir}/${name}.ear"
           appxml="${application.xml}">
        <fileset dir="${standard-ejb.dir}"/>
      </ear>
    </target>

</project>
```

Builds EJB JAR file based on XDoclet-generated deployment descriptor

Packages EJB JAR file into EAR

There are some things to note about listing 14.4:

- Keep the generated code separate from the code you write. We do this with temporary directories built by Middlegen and XDoclet and referenced in `<ejbdoclet>` and `<javac>`.

- Typically, Middlegen would not be an integral part of a build process because of its time-consuming nature on large schemas and because a build process should not generally require a database server to run. The Middlegen target could be made conditional on a flag, or taken out of the main dependency graph. Perhaps even the entity beans generated by Middlegen would be moved to the source code repository and only updated when the schema changes.

- Ant properties are used for everything that could conceivably need to be overridden, including the location for the EAR's `application.xml` file using `${application.xml}`.

- Until XDoclet's dependency checking and speed improves, the `xdoclet` target should be made conditional on an `<uptodate>` set flag to ensure it is only run when needed.

14.9   BEST PRACTICES IN *EJB* PROJECTS

When you start creating entity beans, you end up with many little bean classes. If these classes are autogenerated with Middlegen, then you have directories full of beans; follow it through with individual EJB JAR, and you have many JARs to deal with. Tame this chaos by following these conventions:

- Keep interfaces/datatypes separate for easy reuse in client apps
- Use `<ejbjar>` to build unified JAR files

14.10   SUMMARY

Enterprise JavaBeans are a complex, yet powerful, addition to the J2EE suite. Ant has what it takes to tackle the additional build chores associated with EJB projects. In the simplest cases with hand-made (or generated using non-Ant-based tools) EJB code, simple compilation and packaging into a JAR file is all that is needed. Larger projects, which are more the norm for EJB use, need more capabilities. Ant, along with some additional open-source tools, provides the features demanded in large-scale EJB projects.

Ant's provided `<ejbjar>` task builds a dynamic number of EJB JARs, in addition to providing vendor-specific build capabilities for many application servers. It uses standard EJB deployment descriptors. These deployment descriptors can be built any number of ways from vendor supplied tools to handcrafting them in a text editor, but XDoclet is our recommended automation tool for EJB code and deployment descriptor generation.

Middlegen provides an XDoclet entity bean-generation process based on database metadata. Reverse engineering a schema into entity beans in an Ant-automated way, and employing the other EJB techniques in this chapter, can mean the difference between a smooth-flowing project and one riddled with domino-effect manual maintenance problems. If you are using EJB, do yourself and your project a big favor: investigate these tools and evaluate them for use in your environment.

CHAPTER 15

Working with web services

15.1 What are web services and
     what is SOAP? 356
15.2 Creating a SOAP client
     application with Ant 357
15.3 Creating a SOAP service with
     Axis and Ant 363
15.4 Adding web services to an
     existing web application 367
15.5 Writing a client for our
     SOAP service 371

15.6 What is interoperability, and
     why is it a problem? 376
15.7 Building a C# client 376
15.8 The rigorous way to build a
     web service 381
15.9 Reviewing web service
     development 382
15.10 Calling Ant via SOAP 383
15.11 Summary 384

Web services are an emerging target of software development. Put simply, a web service is a web or enterprise application that provides a way for other programs to call it by using XML as the means of exchanging data. If you can build and deploy a web application, you can build and deploy a web service.

If it's all so easy, why do we have a whole chapter on web services? Because they add new problems to the process: integration and interoperability. Client applications need to be able to call your web service, including applications that are written in different languages or that use different web service toolkits. We need to extend our existing development process to integrate client-side and interoperability tests.

In this chapter, we extend the web application we wrote in chapter 12, adding a SOAP interface to it. We use the Apache Axis library to provide our SOAP interface, rather than the Sun version, because it comes from a sister project to Ant and because we like it. After adding SOAP to our application, we build tests for it, first with a Java client, and then with a C# client running on the .NET platform. As we said, integration and interoperability are the new challenges of a web service development process.

We do not delve deeply into the details of SOAP and web services; we encourage you to read books on the subject (for example, Wesley 2002, and Graham 2001), as well as the SOAP specifications hosted in the web services working group at the W3C (http://www.w3.org/2002/ws/). We do explain the basic concepts behind web services, however, and show how you can use Ant to build, test, and call a web service.

15.1 WHAT ARE WEB SERVICES AND WHAT IS *SOAP*?

Web services use XML as the language of communication to provide computing functionality as a service over the Internet. Web services extend the web, so every service exposes itself as one or more URLs, URLs that provide functionality in response to POST or GET requests. The exact details of the communication are still evolving; SOAP (Simple Object Access Protocol) and REST (Representational State Transfer) are the current competing ideologies. REST is a conceptual model of how to expose objects, properties, and methods as URLs (Fielding 2000); to implement a REST service you export URLs for all the objects and attributes you wish callers to have access to; callers send and receive data to and from the URLs in the format they prefer. SOAP has more of a Remote Procedure Call (RPC) flavor. A single URL acts as an *endpoint*; a SOAP endpoint can receive different requests/method calls in the posted request, and return different XML responses for the different methods.

Central to SOAP is WSDL, the Web Services Description Language. This is roughly the SOAP equivalent of an Interface Definition Language (IDL). SOAP 1.1 clients use it to examine a remote API, and that services use to define which API they export, as shown in figure 15.1. Unlike the old RPC world, where writing an IDL file was mandatory, in the new SOAP universe, you can write your classes and let the run time generate the WSDL from it. Many web service practitioners consider this to be a bad thing, as it makes interoperability with other SOAP implementations, and maintenance in general, that much harder. It is, therefore, a shame that WSDL is even harder to work with than classic IDL.

Figure 15.1
SOAP-based web services offer service metadata in their WSDL file and method invocation with XML requests and responses.

SOAP 1.2, still under development, looks to be moving away from an RPC model, in which the caller blocks till the response is received, to a more asynchronous model in which SOAP messages are routed to a destination. Some of the low-level APIs used to support XML messaging in Java can work with this model, specifically the JAXM API for XML messaging.

15.1.1 The SOAP API

The Java API for XML-based RPC (JAX-RPC) is a higher level SOAP API. Both the Apache and Sun toolkits implement JAX-RPC. This API comprises the `javax.xml.soap` and `javax.xml.rpc` packages; the different libraries provide their own implementations of these APIs. Apache Axis has its own API under `org.apache.axis`. Although these APIs are powerful, they are also complex. Although we will use these APIs and their implementation, we will avoid learning the APIs ourselves by handing off the grunge work to Axis and associated tools.

15.1.2 Adding web services to Java

SOAP support in Java is still evolving; initially Sun neglected it—with Java everywhere, there was no need for web services. However, Sun has pulled enough of a U-turn to embrace SOAP, with full support promised in J2EE 1.4. They also provide the Java web services Developer Pack as a download from http://java.sun.com/webservices/. This large download includes many well-known Apache components: Tomcat, Xerces, Xalan, and even Ant. Other vendors provide their own toolkits for supporting web services in Java.

We stick with the Apache Axis library, from the sibling project of Jakarta, because it is nice to be able to step into the code to debug everything. We also know that if there is anything we don't like about the implementation we can get it fixed, even if that means doing it ourselves. You can download Apache Axis from its home page, http://xml.apache.org/axis/; we have used the beta-1, beta-2, and later CVS versions. Like all open source projects, it is continually evolving, so some details may have changed since we wrote this.

Both the Sun and Apache implementations have a moderately complex deployment process: the Sun server library only works with a specially modified version of Tomcat, whereas the Apache implementation prefers that you add your services to their example web application, rather than write your own. We will be patching our existing web service to support Axis, which involves some effort and some more testing.

15.2 CREATING A SOAP CLIENT APPLICATION WITH ANT

Before we build our own service, we will pick an existing web service and build a client for it. This lets us explore the client-side experience and build process, before we go deeper into web service development. All that we learn here will apply to our own integration tests.

The Apache Axis library contains two programs for use at build time: WSDL2Java and Java2WSDL. These programs create Java classes from a WSDL description and vice versa. There are also two tasks—`<java2wsdl>` and `<wsdl2java>`—which are Ant wrappers around the programs. Unfortunately, in the beta-2 release, these tasks are not part of the binary distribution; they live in the test package, and you must build them yourself. Because these tasks are not part of the official distribution, and because they are undocumented, we are not going to cover them. Instead, we will call the documented programs with the <java> task. Figure 15.2 shows the overall workflow of our Ant build file.

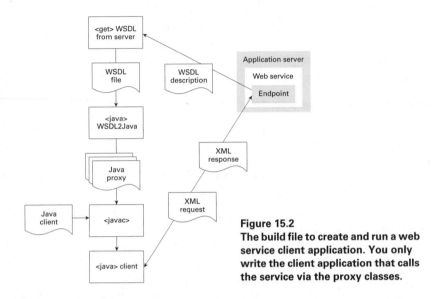

Figure 15.2
The build file to create and run a web service client application. You only write the client application that calls the service via the proxy classes.

15.2.1 Preparing our build file

The first step in our build process is to name the endpoint, the URL of the service that we will call. We will use one of the services offered by xmethods (http://xmethods.net), a service that provides a stock quote. First, we set a property to point to the WSDL file of the service:

```
<property name="endpoint"
 value=
 "http://services.xmethods.net/soap/urn:xmethods-delayed-quotes.wsdl"
 />
```

We then define the directory locations to store the cached file, and to store any generated Java. As usual, we do not want to place generated source into our source tree, because of the risk of accidental overwriting. We also need an init target to set up the build.

```
  <property name="axis.dir"
    location="${lib.dir}/xml-axis" />
  <property name="xercesxalan.dir"
    location="${lib.dir}/xercesxalan" />

  <property name="build.dir" location="build"/>
  <property name="fetched.dir" location="${build.dir}/fetched"/>
  <property name="generated.dir" location="${build.dir}/generated"/>
```

```
<target name="init">
 <mkdir dir="${fetched.dir}"/>
 <mkdir dir="${generated.dir}"/>
 <mkdir dir="${cached.dir}"/>
 <mkdir dir="${build.classes.dir}"/>
 <condition property="offline">
  <not>
  <http url="${endpoint}"/>
  </not>
 </condition>
</target>
```

Our `init` target probes for the endpoint being reachable, and sets a property if we are offline. When offline, we will not be able to run the service, but we still want to be able to compile the code against a cached copy of the WSDL file.

Retrieving the WSDL from the remote server

The remote server describes the SOAP API from a WSDL file, which it serves along-side the SOAP endpoint. We fetch this WSDL file by using the `<get>` task:

```
<target name="fetch-wsdl" depends="init" unless="offline">
  <get src="${endpoint}" dest="${fetched.dir}/api.wsdl"/>
</target>
```

To run this target behind a firewall, you may need to set the Java proxy properties to get to the remote endpoint; the `<setproxy>` task lets you do this inside your build file:

```
<setproxy proxyhost="web-proxy" proxyport="8080" />.
```

15.2.2 Creating the proxy classes

After retrieving the file, we can create Java proxy stubs from the WSDL-described API. These classes allow us to talk to a SOAP service from our own code, without having to refer to `javax.xml.soap` or `org.apache.axis` in our code. It also adds compile time-type safety into our use of the SOAP service—the generated classes talk to the SOAP API, so we don't have to. To create the stubs, we first set up the Axis classpath, then write a target to create the Java classes from the WSDL we have just fetched.

```
<path id="axis.classpath">
  <fileset dir="${axis.dist.dir}">
    <include name="**/*.jar"/>
  </fileset>
  <fileset dir="${xercesxalan.dist.dir}">
    <include name="*.jar"/>
  </fileset>
</path>

<target name="import-wsdl" depends="fetch-wsdl">
  <java
    classname="org.apache.axis.wsdl.WSDL2Java"
```

```
            fork="true"
            failonerror="true"
            classpathref="axis.classpath"
            >
            <arg file="${fetched.dir}/api.wsdl"/>
            <arg value="--output"/>
            <arg file="${generated.dir}"/>
            <arg value="--verbose"/>
            <arg value="--package"/>
            <arg value="soapapi"/>
        </java>
    </target>
```

This target runs the org.apache.axis.wsdl.WSDL2Java program to convert the WSDL interface description into Java source. We do this with <java>, taking care to set up the classpath to include all the files in the Axis lib directory. We also had to add an XML parser to the classpath, so we include Xerces in the path. The alternative approach is to add the Ant classpath to the <java> call, but we prefer to keep things self-contained. We also run the class in a new JVM, so that if the program returns an error by calling System.exit(), we get an exit code instead of the sudden death of Ant.

The parameters to the task tell WSDL2Java to create classes from the downloaded WSDL file, into the package soapapi, into the directory build/generated. The result of the build, with many long lines wrapped to make them readable is:

```
import-wsdl:
    [java] Parsing XML file:
        build/fetched/api.wsdl
    [java] Generating portType interface:
        build/generated/soapapi/StockQuoteService.java
    [java] Generating client-side stub:
        build/generated/soapapi/StockQuoteServiceSoapBindingStub.java
    [java] Generating service class:
        build/generated/soapapi/StockQuoteServiceService.java
    [java] Generating service class:
        build/generated/soapapi/StockQuoteServiceServiceLocator.java
    [java] Generating fault class:
        build/generated/soapapi/Exception.java

BUILD SUCCESSFUL
```

The program generated Java proxy classes for the endpoint. Let's look at them to see how we can use them.

What WSDL2Java creates

The target creates five Java classes that implement the client-side proxy to this service, and one interface listing the methods offered by the remote service:

```
/**
 * StockQuoteService.java
 *
```

```
 * This file was auto-generated from WSDL
 * by the Apache Axis Wsdl2java emitter.
 */

package soapapi;

public interface StockQuoteService extends java.rmi.Remote {
    public float getQuote(java.lang.String symbol) throws
                    java.rmi.RemoteException, soapapi.Exception;
}
```

The program also creates a proxy class that implements this interface and redirects it to a remote endpoint, and a locator class that finds the endpoint at run time and binds to it.

15.2.3 Using the SOAP proxy classes

To use these generated classes, simply create a Java file that imports and invokes them:

```
import soapapi.*;

public class SoapClient {

    public static void main(String args[]) throws java.lang.Exception {
        StockQuoteServiceServiceLocator locator;
        locator=new StockQuoteServiceServiceLocator();
        StockQuoteService service;
        service= locator.getStockQuoteService();
        for(int i=0;i<args.length;i++) {
            float quotation=service.getQuote(args[i]);
            System.out.println(args[i]+"="+quotation);
        }
    }
}
```

This service first creates a locator instance to locate the endpoint. In this example, it always returns the same endpoint, but it is conceivable that a locator could use a Universal Description, Discovery, and Integration (UDDI) registry or other directory service to locate a service implementation dynamically.

After creating the locator we bind to the service by asking the locator for a binding; it returns an implementation of the remote interface—the stub class that WSDL2Java created. With this binding, we can make remote calls, here asking for the stock price of every argument supplied to the main method, that being the classic simple web service.

15.2.4 Compiling the SOAP client

Before we can run that method, we have to compile the source:

```
<target name="compile" depends="import-wsdl">
  <javac
   srcdir="src;${generated.dir}"
   destdir="${build.classes.dir}"
```

```
    classpathref="axis.classpath"
    debuglevel="lines,vars,source"
    debug="true"
    includeAntRuntime="false"
    />
</target>
```

We supply a path to the source directory to include both our source and the generated files. One irritation of the current SOAP import process is that the Java files are
always regenerated, which means they always need recompilation. This makes the
build longer than it need be. Unless WSDL2Java adds dependency checking, you
should use something similar to <uptodate> to bypass the import-wsdl target
when it is not needed. There is an extra complication here; you need to use a <files-
match> test inside a <condition> to verify that the file you just fetched with
<get> hasn't changed. We omit all this because it is so complex.

15.2.5   Running the SOAP service

With compilation complete, there is one more target to write:

```
<target name="run" depends="compile" unless="offline">
  <java
    classname="SoapClient"
    fork="true"
    failonerror="true"
    >
    <arg value="SUNW"/>
    <arg value="MSFT"/>
    <classpath>
      <path refid="axis.classpath"/>
      <pathelement location="${build.classes.dir}"/>
    </classpath>
  </java>
</target>
```

This target runs the stock quote client, fetching the stock price of Sun and Microsoft,
producing a result that we cannot interpret as good news for either of them, at least
during May 2002:

```
run:
    [java] SUNW=6.67
    [java] MSFT=52.12
```

If we were ambitious, we could save the output of the run to a properties file, and then
load the output as Ant properties and somehow act on them.[1]

---

[1] Having applications output their results in the properties file format makes it very easy to integrate
     their results into Ant or, indeed, into any other Java application. We have used this trick for Win32/
     Java communications. XML is more powerful, but harder to work with.

15.2.6   Reviewing SOAP client creation

As we have shown, Ant can create a build file that goes from a remote WSDL description to Java code and then it can compile and run this code to make remote SOAP RPC calls.

More SOAP services could provide extra functionality for the build, such as returning information from a remote database, information that could populate a file used in the build or one of the build's redistributables.

Alternative implementations to the Apache Axis SOAP libraries have different processes for creating stub code from WSDL services. We have not looked at the process for using alternate implementations in any detail, but they should be amenable to a similar build process. If multiple Java SOAP implementations do become popular, we may eventually see Ant adding a task to import WSDL that supports different implementations, just as `<javac>` supports many Java compilers.

15.3   *CREATING A **SOAP** SERVICE WITH **AXIS** AND **ANT***

Apache Axis enables you to develop SOAP services in three ways: the simple way, the rigorous way, and the hard way. The simple method is to save your Java files with the .jws extension and then save them under the Axis web application; when you fetch these files in a web browser Axis compiles them and exports them as web services. The rigorous method is to write the WSDL for services, create the bindings and web service deployment descriptors, copy these to the Axis servlet, and register these deployment descriptors with the servlet.

The hard way is to retrofit an existing application with SOAP support and then use either of the previous two approaches. It is a lot easier to develop under Axis than it is to add SOAP to an existing web application.

Installing Axis on a web server

Axis is a web application. It is redistributed in the expanded form, rather than as a WAR file. To install it, you copy everything under webapp/axis to the directory webapp/axis in Tomcat. Because many versions of Tomcat 4 do not allow libraries in WEB-APP/lib to implement `java.*` or `javax.*` packages, you also need to copy jaxrpc.jar and saa.jar to CATALINA_HOME/common/lib. Make sure you have the right lib directory—CATALINA_HOME/server/lib and CATALINA_ HOME/lib are the wrong places. If you are trying to install Axis on other application servers and you are using Java1.4, then you may need to configure the server so that the system property `java.endorsed.dirs` includes the directory containing the jaxrpc.jar file.

If these URLs load, you know that you have a successful installation, assuming that your copy of Tomcat is running on port 8080:

```
http://localhost:8080/axis/servlet/AxisServlet
http://localhost:8080/axis/StockQuoteService.jws?wsdl
```

The first of these verifies that all the libraries are in place and all is well; the second forces the Axis servlet to compile the sample web service and run it. The service is, of course, a version of the infamous stock option service. If either URL is unreachable, you may not be running Tomcat on that port; alter the URL to point to your server. If you receive the 500 error code (internal server error), it is probably because the libraries are not in the right place. Failing that, check the installation guide in the Axis documents and FAQ at the Axis web site for more advice.

15.3.1 The simple way to build a web service

Now that Axis is in place and working, let us write our simple web service, which will export the indexed search as a web service, enabling calling applications to send a search term and then get the result back as a list of URLs. We will also tack in a management call to tell us the last search string submitted.

The easiest way to write a web service in Axis is to implement the service API as a Java class, save it with the extension .jws, and copy it into the Axis web application anywhere outside the WEB-INF directory. We could do that, but it is too reminiscent of the JSP problem: if the server compiles the code, bugs only show up after deployment. Given that .jws files are really .java files, why can't we compile them in advance, just to make sure they work? We can, and that's what we are going to do.

There are two ways to do this. We could work with the .jws files and then copy them to files with a .java extension to test compile them. However, if we do that and we find a bug, clicking on the error string in the IDE will bring up the copied file, not the .jws original. Java IDEs don't know that .jws files are really Java source, so we would lose out on the method completion, refactoring, and reformatting that we expect from a modern IDE. Clearly, the second approach—save as .java files and copy to .jws during deployment—is the only sensible one. Of course, we have to differentiate the service files from normal Java files, which we do by keeping them out of the src directory tree, placing them into a directory called soap instead. In our build process, we have to give these files a .jws extension before copying them to a web server or into a WAR file. Figure 15.3 shows the build process.

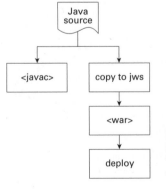

Figure 15.3
Our simple web service build process. The <javac> step is only there to validate files before deployment.

This is what our simple service looks like, with a stub implementation of our search call:

```
public class SearchService {

    private static String lastSearch="";
    private static final String[] emptyArray=new String[0];

    public String[] search(String keywords) {
        setLastSearch(keywords);
        return emptyArray;
    }

    public String getLastSearchTerm() {
        return lastSearch;
    }

    private void setLastSearch(String keywords) {
        lastSearch=keywords;
    }
}
```

The methods in bold are our service methods: one for end users, the search method that always returns the same empty string array, and the other a management call to see what is going on. A real system should split the management API into a separate endpoint, so that access could be restricted, but we aren't going to worry about that here.

To compile this code in Java, we have a short build file; it is so short, we include it in its entirety as listing 15.1

Listing 15.1 A build file to add a web service to an existing Axis installation

```
<?xml version="1.0"?>
 <project name="soapserver" default="default"
  basedir="." >

  <property name="endpoint"
    value="http://localhost:8080/axis/SearchService.jws"/>

  <property environment="env"/>
  <property name="build.dir" location="build"/>
  <property name="build.classes.dir" location="build/classes"/>

  <target name="default" depends="test"
    description="create a web service" >
  </target>

  <target name="init">
   <mkdir dir="${build.classes.dir}"/>
   <fail unless="env.CATALINA_HOME">Tomcat not found</fail>
  </target>

  <target name="clean">
   <delete dir="${build.dir}"/>
  </target>
```

```
<target name="compile" depends="init">                              ❶
  <javac
    srcdir="soap"
    destdir="${build.classes.dir}"
    debuglevel="lines,vars,source"
    debug="true"
    includeAntRuntime="false"
    >
  </javac>
</target>

<target name="deploy" depends="compile">
  <copy                                                             ❷
    todir="${env.CATALINA_HOME}/webapps/axis/">
    <fileset dir="soap" includes="**/*.java"/>
    <mapper type="glob" from="*.java" to="*.jws"/>
  </copy>
</target>

<target name="test" depends="deploy">
  <waitfor timeoutproperty="deployment.failed"                      ❸
    maxwait="30"
    maxwaitunit="second">
    <http url="${endpoint}?wsdl" />
  </waitfor>
  <fail if="deployment.failed"
    message="application not found at ${verify.url}" />
  <echo>service is live on ${endpoint}</echo>
</target>
</project>
```

The first few targets are the traditional init, clean, and compile targets; the only
difference is the source directory for the compiler is now "soap" ❶. We do not
need to add any of the Axis libraries to the classpath, because we do not reference
them. All we need to do is declare public methods in our class and they become
methods in a SOAP web service. We do have to be careful about our choice of
datatypes if we want real interoperability; by restricting ourselves to integers, strings,
and arrays of simple datatypes, we are confident that other SOAP implementations
can call us.

The actual deployment task is a simple copy ❷ of all the Java files under the web
directory into the CATALINA_HOME/webapps/axis/ directory tree. If we were
deploying remotely, we would use FTP instead. That's it. No configuration files; no
need to restart the server. If only all deployments were so simple.

Simple deployment or not, we need to verify that the deployment worked. Our
test target tries to retrieve the WSDL description of the service for 30 seconds ❸;
if it is successful, it reports that the service is live and the build succeeds.

15.4   ADDING WEB SERVICES TO AN EXISTING WEB APPLICATION

Now that we have shown the basics of web services and how to configure Tomcat to work with Axis, it is time to retrofit a SOAP endpoint to our existing web application. To do this we have add the appropriate libraries to the WEB-INF/lib directory, and then configure Axis to work. We need to make some changes to the web.xml configuration file to achieve that, but there we can use XDoclet.

15.4.1   Configuring the web application

Recall that in section 12.3.2, we configured the template files used by <webdoclet> to include servlets conditionally. We now need to add the Axis configuration details to the same template files. The first step is to extract the settings from the Axis/WEB-INF/web.xml file, so we open it in an editor and find the <servlet> and <servlet-mapping> tags. The servlet settings we insert into the servlets.xml file that <webdoclet> uses to build our web application's web.xml file is as follows:

```
<servlet>
  <servlet-name>AxisServlet</servlet-name>
  <display-name>Apache-Axis Servlet</display-name>
  <servlet-class>
    org.apache.axis.transport.http.AxisServlet
  </servlet-class>
</servlet>

<servlet>
  <servlet-name>AdminServlet</servlet-name>
  <display-name>Axis Admin Servlet</display-name>
  <servlet-class>
      org.apache.axis.transport.http.AdminServlet
  </servlet-class>
  <load-on-startup>100</load-on-startup>
</servlet>
```

The servlet mappings file sets up the bindings of these servlets to URL patterns beneath the server, one for the Axis admin servlet, the others providing the SOAP endpoints for the service clients. We find the values further down the Axis web.xml file and paste them into our templates/servlet-mappings.xml file:

```
<servlet-mapping>
  <servlet-name>AxisServlet</servlet-name>
  <url-pattern>*.jws</url-pattern>
</servlet-mapping>

<servlet-mapping>
  <servlet-name>AxisServlet</servlet-name>
  <url-pattern>/servlet/AxisServlet</url-pattern>
</servlet-mapping>

<servlet-mapping>
  <servlet-name>AxisServlet</servlet-name>
```

```
  <url-pattern>/services/*</url-pattern>
</servlet-mapping>

<servlet-mapping>
  <servlet-name>AdminServlet</servlet-name>
  <url-pattern>/servlet/AdminServlet</url-pattern>
</servlet-mapping>
```

The configuration data you need to paste may well vary from the beta-2 release, the latest version at the time of writing, and the final version, so follow the process we have described to get the most up-to-date settings.

15.4.2 Adding the libraries

The servlet configuration is not enough—we need to add the Axis libraries. We do this by bringing all the JAR files from the xml-axis/lib directory into our WAR file. Rather than do this naively, we first filter out any files that we don't need, such as log4j-core.jar and crimson.jar. We move these into a subdirectory called not_to_server. This lets us use the pattern lib/**/*.jar to pull in all the Axis jar files needed client side, while lib/*.jar works as the server-side pattern.

15.4.3 Including SOAP services in the build

Everything is ready; it is time to extend our web application with the SOAP entry point. We do this with three property declarations and one new target:

```
<property name="soap.src.dir"
  location="soap"/>

<property name="soap.classes.dir"
  location="${build.dir}/soap/classes"/>

<property name="soap.jws.dir"
  location="${build.dir}/soap/jws"/>

<target name="make-soap-api"
  depends="init">
  <mkdir dir="${soap.classes.dir}"/>
  <javac
    srcdir="${soap.src.dir}"
    destdir="${soap.classes.dir}"
    includeAntRuntime="false"
    >
    <classpath>
      <path refid="compile.classpath"/>
      <pathelement location="${build.classes.dir}"/>
    </classpath>
  </javac>
  <copy todir="${soap.jws.dir}">
    <fileset dir="${soap.src.dir}"
      includes="**/*.java"/>
    <mapper type="glob" from="*.java" to="*.jws"/>
```

```
    </copy>
  </target>
```

This target compiles the service source using the full classpath of the project, including any Java files we have compiled. If that succeeds, it copies the Java files into a staging directory, renaming the files in the process. We then need to add two lines to our existing `<war>` task declaration, in the target `make-war`, and declare that this target depends upon our new `make-soap-api` target. The result is that the Axis libraries and our SOAP endpoint are now in our web application.

15.4.4 Testing the server for needed classes

We need to make sure the changes we have made to build process works, which means writing tests. Ant already runs the HttpUnit tests we wrote in chapter 12 immediately after deployment. We now need to add a test to fetch our endpoint's WSDL description to verify that Axis is working.

Because Axis configuration and deployment is more complex—needing someone to deploy the jax-rpc.jar outside the WAR file—this test is inadequate. If something goes wrong with the configuration, then the test will fail, but it won't provide clues as to a solution. It may provide an error trace starting with a `ClassNotFoundException`, but those errors mean nothing to the operations people who often install and configure production web servers. To avoid them calling in the engineering staff (us!) to diagnose the problem, we have to write tests with simpler diagnostics.

Our solution is to extend our JSP `<happy>` tag with a `classMustExist` attribute, which if set, triggers an attempt to instantiate the class with `Class.forName()` and throws a JSP exception if that attempt failed for any reason. Then we add a new attribute, `errorText`, which, if set, overrides the text of the `JspException` thrown when a test fails and provides more useful error messages. We had to do a bit of refactoring to do this cleanly. The result of these changes is that we can write a test file, happyaxis.jsp, containing tests for classes found in the different Axis libraries:

```
<%@ taglib uri="/WEB-INF/antbook.tld" prefix="happy" %>
<html><head><title>happy</title></head>
<body>
<happy:happy
  classMustExist="javax.xml.soap.SOAPMessage"
  errorText="saaj needs to be installed correctly"/>
<happy:happy
  classMustExist="javax.xml.rpc.Service"
  errorText="jax-rpc needs to be installed correctly"/>
<happy:happy
  classMustExist="org.apache.axis.transport.http.AxisServlet"
  errorText="axis.jar not found"/>
<p>Axis libraries are present</p>
</body>
</html>
```

This is a server-side mirror of the technique of using `<available>` and `<fail>` in a build file to validate build-time requirements; now we can test for classes existing on the server. This is a useful technique for any project with a complex deployment process.

15.4.5 Implementing the SOAP endpoint

With Axis integrated into our web application, and the deployment tests written, all that remains is to generate client side JUnit tests, write the real client application, and to bind the SOAP endpoint to our search code. We are going to tackle these in reverse order, implementing the API first. Writing the basic code to implement the searching from the SOAP endpoint turns out to be easy, although we are only returning the local path to the documents, not a network accessible URL.

```
public String[] search(String keywords) {
    try {
        setLastSearch(keywords);
        String[] results;
        Document[] docs = SearchUtil.findDocuments(keywords);
        results=new String[docs.length];
        for (int i=0; i < docs.length; i++) {
            results[i]=docs[i].getField("path");
        }
        return results;
    }
    catch (SearchException e) {
        return emptyAarray;
    }
}
```

Some more work needs to done to return the documents—perhaps a new method that returns the files as MIME attachments or a JSP page that serves it up in response to a GET. We could also turn any local exceptions into AxisFault exceptions; Axis will send these back over the network to the caller. We can evolve these features over time.

15.4.6 Deploying our web service

How do we deploy this web service? We already do this, because all we are doing is adding new libraries, files, and configuration data to our existing web application. The command `ant deploy` in our webapp directory is all we need to update our application.

After deploying, there are two web pages that we can fetch to test. First is our happy page:

```
http://localhost:8080/antbook/happyaxis.jsp
```

This should return the message "Axis libraries are present." We have added this page to our list of pages to fetch using HttpUnit, so our deployment target triggers an automatic probe of this page. The next page we fetch is the Axis-generated WSDL file for the service:

```
http://localhost:8080/antbook/SearchService.jws?wsdl
```

If the result of this fetch is an XML file, then everything is working. Axis has compiled the file and generated a WSDL description from its methods. Again, we modify our HttpUnit test to fetch this file during deployment, so that we automatically verify that Axis is working and that our SOAP endpoint is present whenever we deploy.

15.5   WRITING A CLIENT FOR OUR *SOAP* SERVICE

As usual, we want some unit tests, too, but this time we don't need to write them—we are going to make WSDL2Java do the work. The Axis utility will even generate JUnit test cases, one for each method, simply by setting the --testcase option. We do all this in a build file that is separate from the server and in a separate directory. We need nothing of the server other than its endpoint and the WSDL we can get from it. We will make Ant create the proxy classes and basic JUnit tests for us, and then we will write and execute the real tests and Java client. Figure 15.4 shows the process we will be implementing.

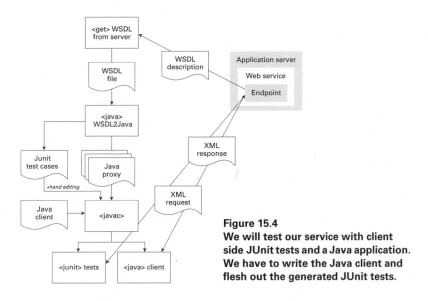

Figure 15.4
We will test our service with client side JUnit tests and a Java application. We have to write the Java client and flesh out the generated JUnit tests.

15.5.1   Importing the WSDL

To import the WSDL from our service, we just reuse our <get> target from 15.2.1. This time we bypass all the connectivity tests, because we are binding to a local server:

```
<property name="endpoint"
  value="http://localhost:8080/antbook/SearchService.jws?wsdl" />


<target name="fetch-wsdl" depends="init">
  <get src="${endpoint}" dest="${local.wsdl}"/>
</target>
```

```
<target name="import-wsdl" depends="fetch-wsdl">
  <java
    classname="org.apache.axis.wsdl.WSDL2Java"
    fork="true"
    failonerror="true"
    classpathref="axis.classpath"
    >
    <arg file="${local.wsdl}"/>
    <arg value="--output"/>
    <arg file="${generated.dir}"/>
    <arg value="--verbose"/>
    <arg value="--package"/>
    <arg value="soapapi"/>
    <arg value="--testCase"/>
  </java>
</target>
```

When we run the `import-wsdl` target, the WSDLToJava program creates the following files in the directory named in `${generated.dir}/soapapi`:

```
SearchService.java
SearchServiceService.java
SearchServiceServiceLocator.java
SearchServiceServiceTestCase.java
SearchServiceSoapBindingStub.java
```

These classes comprise the locator and proxy for the web service, as we saw in section 15.2, and a new class containing an automatically generated JUnit test case. We can use this generated test case as the framework for our test.

15.5.2 Implementing the tests

The generated JUnit test cases only test a call to the endpoint's methods with some parameters. For example, the test generated for the `search` method sends an empty string as the search term and does nothing with the return value:

```
package soapapi;

public class SearchServiceServiceTestCase extends junit.framework.TestCase
{

    public SearchServiceServiceTestCase(String name) {
        super(name);
    }

    public void test1SearchServiceSearch() {
        soapapi.SearchService binding;
        try {
            binding = new soapapi.SearchServiceServiceLocator().
                getSearchService();
        }
        catch (javax.xml.rpc.ServiceException jre) {
            throw new junit.framework.
            AssertionFailedError("JAX-RPC ServiceException caught: " + jre);
        }
```

```
    assertTrue("binding is null", binding != null);

    try {
        java.lang.String[] value = null;
        value = binding.search(new java.lang.String());
    }
    catch (java.rmi.RemoteException re) {
        throw new junit.framework.
            AssertionFailedError("Remote Exception caught: " + re);
    }
}
```

Notice that this is a ready-to-compile JUnit test case; it subclasses `junit.frame-work.TestCase` and provides a valid constructor. Even without writing another line of code, we can test basic operation of our SOAP endpoint, and we can edit the test cases to test the service properly. There are three things that we must do to create real test cases. First, we must copy the generated file into our source tree, where it will not be overwritten, and move it outside the `soapapi` package, so that if we compile our source, and the generated directories, then no source file overwrites the other .class file. Next, we edit the test methods to send valid data to the SOAP service, and check for valid data coming back. For the test case above, we send a real search term and require a nonempty array back:

```
try {
    java.lang.String[] value = null;
    value = binding.search("test");
    assertTrue("should have got an array back",
        value!=null && value.length>0);
}
catch (java.rmi.RemoteException re) {
    throw new junit.framework.
        AssertionFailedError("Remote Exception caught: " + re);
}
```

For the test of the `getLastSearchTerm` method, we search on a string and then verify that the service returns this string if we immediately call `getLastSearchTerm`. Doing so introduces a small race condition on a laden system, but we ignore it:

```
public void test2SearchServiceGetLastSearchTerm() {
    soapapi.SearchService binding;
    try {
        binding = new soapapi.SearchServiceServiceLocator()
            .getSearchService();
    }
    catch (javax.xml.rpc.ServiceException jre) {
        throw new junit.framework.
            AssertionFailedError("JAX-RPC ServiceException caught: "
            + jre);
    }
    assertTrue("binding is null", binding != null);
```

```
try {
    java.lang.String value = null;
    String searchTerm="test2";
    binding.search(searchTerm);
    value = binding.getLastSearchTerm();
    assertEquals(searchTerm,value);
}
catch (java.rmi.RemoteException re) {
    throw new junit.framework.
        AssertionFailedError("Remote Exception caught: " + re);
}
}
```

To run the tests we have to compile the tests and proxy classes, now with a classpath containing Axis, Xerces, and JUnit, then use `<junit>`, to call the tests. We configure the task to search for `**/*TestCase.java`, rather than the usual `**/*Test.java`, and do this over the source and generated directories:

```
<target name="test" depends="compile"
        description="Execute unit tests">
  <junit printsummary="yes"
         errorProperty="test.failed"
         failureProperty="test.failed"
         fork="true">
    <classpath>
      <path refid="axis.classpath"/>
      <pathelement location="${build.classes.dir}"/>
    </classpath>
    <batchtest>
      <fileset dir="${client.src.dir}"
               includes="**/*TestCase.java"/>
    </batchtest>
  </junit>
</target>
```

The first time we ran these tests it failed in `test2SearchServiceGetLast SearchTerm`—we weren't getting back the last term we searched for. It turned out that Axis was creating a new object instance for each request, but we had expected a servlet style reentrant invocation. Until we made the `lastSearchTerm` field in our `SearchService` class static, it was being reset every invocation, causing the test to fail. This is, of course, exactly what functional tests are for: to validate your assumptions.[2]

---

[2] The web service deployment descriptor can enable sessions, but it also has to be set up on the client side. With JWS drop-in services, you do not get the option to specify this.

15.5.3 Writing the Java client

After the tests pass, we can write the real Java client:

```
import soapapi.*;

public class SearchClient {

    public static void main(String args[]) throws Exception {

        SearchServiceServiceLocator locator;
        locator=new SearchServiceServiceLocator();          ❶
        soapapi.SearchService service=locator.getSearchService();

        String lastTerm=service.getLastSearchTerm();         ❷
        System.out.println("last search = "+lastTerm);

        String[] results=service.search(args[0]);            ❸
        for(int i=0;i<results.length;i++) {
            System.out.println(results[i]);
        }
    }
}
```

This client has three stages.

❶ It finds and binds to the service.

❷ It retrieves and displays the previous search term, for curiosity .

❸ It sends the first argument of our application to the web service as a search term, and prints the results.

We have to run the program, of course, so let's write a target to invoke it with <java>:

```
<target name="run" depends="test">
  <java
    classname="SearchClient"
    fork="true"
    failonerror="true"
    >
    <arg value="deployment"/>
    <classpath>
      <path refid="axis.classpath"/>
      <pathelement location="${build.classes.dir}"/>
    </classpath>
  </java>
</target>
```

What happens when we run this? Well, we run the search and get a list of Ant documents that contain the word "deployment":

```
[java] last search = deployment
[java] /home/ant/docs/manual/OptionalTasks/ejb.html
[java] /home/ant/docs/manual/OptionalTasks/serverdeploy.html
             ...
[java] /home/ant/docs/manual/Integration/VAJAntTool.html
```

This means we have completed our example web service, from integration with our application all the way to our client, including both configuration checks to probe for Axis, and client-side functional tests to verify that the service does what we expect. We are now very close to being able to declare the service ready for production. One missing item is the extra server-side functionality to retrieve the indexed files; we will leave this until version 2.0. What we do have to do for version 1.0 is verify that our service is interoperable.

15.6 WHAT IS INTEROPERABILITY, AND WHY IS IT A PROBLEM?

Interoperability, or interop, as it is often called, is an ongoing issue with SOAP. The developers of SOAP toolkits, the SOAPBuilders, all work on interoperability tests to verify that foundational datatypes such as strings, integers, Booleans, arrays, and base64 encoded binary data can all be exchanged between clients and servers.

This is all very well, but it is not enough; complex types are not yet standardized. Consider the HashTable class: Java implements java.util.HashTable and .NET has its own implementation in System.Collections.HashTable. You can return one of these from a service you implement in your language of choice:

```
public HashTable getEmptyHashTable() {
    return new HashTable();
}
```

A client written to use the same toolkit as the service will be able to invoke this SOAP method and get a hashtable back. A client written in another toolkit, or in a different language, will not be able to handle this. If we were writing our server API by coding a WSDL file first and then by writing entry points that implemented this WSDL, we would probably notice that there is no easy way to describe a hashtable; consequently, we would define a clean name-value pair schema to represent it. Because we are developing web services the lazy way, by writing the methods and letting the run time do the WSDL generation, we do suffer from the hashtable problem. There is no warning at build time that the datatypes we are using in our service are not usable by other SOAP libraries, which means that we may only find out that we have an interop problem some time after we have deployed our service. We need to rectify this.

15.7 BUILDING A C# CLIENT

To detect interoperability problems early, we need to create a client with a different SOAP toolkit and then verify that it can call our service.

Although we could use the Sun web services toolkit, we chose, instead, to make life seemingly more complex by creating a C# client. It is a little known fact that there is a task in Ant to compile C# programs, the <csc> task, and that Ant 1.5 added the <wsdltodotnet> task to go alongside <csc>, purely to make C#-based interoperability testing inside Ant possible and easy. Because these tasks call down to programs in the .NET framework SDK, they only work on a Windows PC with the SDK installed. You do not need the commercial Visual Studio.Net, just the downloadable SDK. The jEdit editor has a C# mode for editing, and we will build with Ant. The Ant .NET tasks have not been tested with either the Rotor public source version of .NET for FreeBSD or with the Ximian team's Mono implementation.

Building a .NET client for our service is nearly identical to building a Java version: we run a program to generate the stub classes, add an entry point class, build them, and then run the program with our chosen arguments. See figure 15.5.

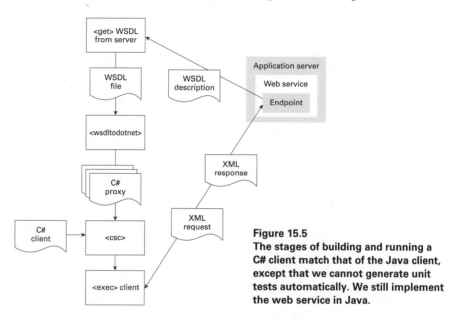

Figure 15.5
The stages of building and running a C# client match that of the Java client, except that we cannot generate unit tests automatically. We still implement the web service in Java.

15.7.1   Probing for the classes

Because we are only supporting the Windows implementation of .NET, we can only build the .NET client on Windows, and then only those versions with the .NET SDK installed and on the PATH. How do we restrict this? With a few moderately complex conditions:

```
<target name="probe_for_dotnet_apps" >
 <condition property="wsdl.found">
    <or>
     <available file="wsdl"     filepath="${env.PATH}" />
     <available file="wsdl.exe" filepath="${env.PATH}" />
     <available file="wsdl.exe" filepath="${env.Path}" />
    </or>
  </condition>
 <echo> wsdl.found=${wsdl.found}</echo>
 <condition property="csc.found">
    <or>
```

```
    <available file="csc"     filepath="${env.PATH}" />
    <available file="csc.exe" filepath="${env.PATH}" />
    <available file="csc.exe" filepath="${env.Path}" />
  </or>
 </condition>
<echo> csc.found=${csc.found}</echo>
<condition property="dotnetapps.found">
   <and>
    <isset property="csc.found"/>
    <isset property="wsdl.found"/>
   </and>
  </condition>
 <echo> dotnetapps.found=${dotnetapps.found}</echo>
</target>
```

These conditions ultimately set the `dotnetapps.found` property if we can find the programs wsdl and csc on the PATH; we don't tie ourselves to Windows explicitly, so if new platforms add the programs, we will try and use them.

15.7.2   Importing the WSDL in C#

The first step in creating the client is to generate C# source from the WSDL. We use the `<wsdltodotnet>` task to do this, feeding it the file we downloaded in section 15.5.2 in the `fetch-wsdl` target:

```
<property name="out.csc" location="${generated.net.dir}/soapapi.cs"/>

<target name="import-dotnet" depends="probe_for_dotnet_apps,fetch-wsdl"
  if="dotnetapps.found">
  <wsdltodotnet destFile="${out.csc}"
    srcFile="${local.wsdl}"
    />
</target>
```

This target creates a single file that contains the web service proxy class. Here is a fragment of the file:

```
[System.Web.Services.WebServiceBindingAttribute(
    Name="SearchServiceSoapBinding",
    Namespace="http://localhost:8080/antbook/SearchService.jws")]

public class SearchServiceService :
    System.Web.Services.Protocols.SoapHttpClientProtocol {

...

    /// <remarks/>
    [System.Web.Services.Protocols.SoapRpcMethodAttribute("",
      RequestNamespace="http://localhost:8080/antbook/SearchService.jws",
      ResponseNamespace="http://localhost:8080/antbook/SearchService.jws")]

    [return: System.Xml.Serialization.SoapElementAttribute("return")]

    public string getLastSearchTerm() {
```

```
        object[] results = this.Invoke("getLastSearchTerm", new object[0]);
        return ((string)(results[0]));
    }
    ...
}
```

We don't need to understand the details of this code, any more than we need to understand the proxy code that Axis generates. Note, however, that all the declarations in front of class and methods are *attributes*; these are like XDoclet tags except that you are really declaring constructors for objects that get serialized into the binary files. At run time, you can introspect the code to see what attributes are associated with the program, the class, the methods, or member variables. In our code, the web service support code in the .NET framework uses our declarations to bind properly to our service at run time.

15.7.3   Writing the C# client class

We can now write our C# client:

```
using System;

public class DotNetSearchClient {

    public static void Main(String[] args)  {

    SearchServiceService service=new SearchServiceService();

    String lastTerm=service.getLastSearchTerm();
    Console.WriteLine("last search = "+lastTerm);

    String[] results=service.search(args[0]);
    for(int i=0;i<results.Length;i++) {
        Console.WriteLine(results[i]);
        }
    }
}
```

By comparing this to the Java client in section 15.5.3, you will see that there is almost no difference between the Java and the C# client; indeed, we used cut-and-paste to create the C# client.

15.7.4   Building the C# client

Let's compile this code by using the <csc> task:

```
<property name="out.app" location="${build.net.dir}/netclient.exe"/>

<target name="build-dotnet" depends="import-dotnet"
    if="dotnetapps.found">
    <copy toDir="${generated.net.dir}">
        <fileset dir="${src.net.dir}" includes="**/*.cs" />
    </copy>
```

❶

```
<csc
  srcDir="${generated.net.dir}"
  destFile="${out.app}"
  targetType="exe"
  >
  </csc>
</target>
```

The <csc> task will compile all C# files in and below the srcDir directory, just as the <javac> task compiles Java source. Unlike <javac>, the output is not a directory tree full of object files. The task creates the executable, library, or DLL straight from the source files. The task does check dependencies, and rebuilds the target file if any of the input files have changed.

One little irritant of the task is that you can only specify one source directory. This prevents us from building our handwritten source together with the generated source. To fix this, we have to copy our handwritten source to the generated directory ❶, before running the build. A consequence of this is that when we click on any error line in an Ant hosting IDE, the IDE brings up the duplicate file, the one being compiled, not the master copy. We have to be very careful which file we are editing. We may enhance this task to support multiple source directories; as usual, check the documentation.

15.7.5 Running the C# client

With the code compiled, it is time to run it, this time with <exec>:

```
<target name="dotnet" depends="build-dotnet" if="dotnetapps.found">
  <exec
    executable="${out.app}"
    failonerror="true"
    >
    <arg value="deployment"/>
  </exec>
</target>
```

What is the result of this? Well, we get nearly the same results as before—because we are running against a local server on a Windows system, the file paths we get back are all Windows based:

```
[exec] last search = deployment
[exec] C:\jakarta-ant\docs\manual\OptionalTasks\ejb.html
[exec] C:\jakarta-ant\docs\manual\OptionalTasks\serverdeploy.html
   . . .
[exec] C:\jakarta-ant\docs\manual\Integration\VAJAntTool.html
```

This is exactly what we wanted—to call our Java web service from a C# client. Now that we have this dual-language client import-and-build process working, we can keep using it as we extend the classes.

15.7.6   Review of the C# client build process

As you can see, it is not that much more complicated to build a C# program in Ant than it is to build a Java application: the fact that Ant is the ubiquitous Java build tool does not mean that it can only build Java programs, that is merely what it is best at. In chapter 17, we will go one step farther and build native C++ code.

The reason we are compiling C# code here is not because we have a big C# project, but because we need to verify that our Java-based web service is interoperable with the other SOAP implementations. The process for doing so is the same for all target languages: import the WSDL, write an entry point or other test case, and run them. Were we writing our web service in another language such as C# or Perl, we would be able to use our build file to create an Axis/Java client to test the service, complete with generated JUnit test cases.

Often the act of running the WSDL importers is a good initial test of interoperability, extending the entry point even better. It's a pity that the Microsoft toolkit doesn't generate NUnit tests for us to use alongside the JUnit tests; we have to do these by hand. If we did start developing a complex .NET client, we might find ourselves taking a closer look at NAnt, a .NET version of Ant, found at SourceForge (http://nant.sourceforge.net), and maybe <exec>, the NAnt build from our Ant task. Alternatively, we might write an <nunit> task for Ant.

Finally, we need to state that the hashtable problem is a fundamental problem with web services: it is too easy to write a web service whose methods can only be called by clients that use the same language and toolkit implementation as the service. This belies the whole notion of using XML-based web services as a way to communicate across languages. Something needs to be done to address this.

15.8   THE RIGOROUS WAY TO BUILD A WEB SERVICE

The most rigorous approach to building a web service is to create a WSDL specification of the interface, and perhaps an XSD description of all the datatypes. SOAP has its own syntax for declaring simple datatypes, but because XSD is more standardized, we encourage you to follow the XSD path.

The other aspect of rigorous service development is to implement the service in a Java file, and not as a JWS page, which lets you bypass the copy-based renaming of Java source to JWS pages. The Java files just live in the same source tree as the rest of the web application, and are validated by the build-time <javac> compile of the main source tree.

We don't go into detail on this more rigorous server-side development process. We could probably write a whole new book on how to build, test, and deploy web services with Ant, and get into much more detail into how SOAP and Axis work. What we can do is provide some directions for you to follow, if you want to explore this problem. One of the best starting points is actually the test server classes you can find in the Axis CVS tree; these are the most up-to-date examples of service generation.

To turn a Java class into a SOAP endpoint, you need to provide a Web Service Deployment Descriptor (WSDD) that tells the Axis run time what the attributes of the service are. In the descriptor, you must name the service and the class that implements it, and which class methods are to be accessible via SOAP. You can also register handlers for SOAP headers. These are the SOAP equivalent of headers in an HTTP request: little fragments of information that the SOAP endpoint or other server-side code can use to implement features such as security and sessions. You could use HTTP headers instead, but the SOAP header model integrates better with an XML-based communication system, and works when you use alternative transports such as email.[3] If you want to do complex SOAP handling, a deployment descriptor file is mandatory; this means that you must use Java and not JWS files to implement your service.

After deploying your application, you have to register your WSDD files with the Axis administration servlet. Unless you change this server to be accessible remotely, you need to run code server side to register each deployment descriptor, and you need to make a list of all the WSDD files to register. You can call the administration program from a build file via <java>, so registering local builds is easy.

Based on our past examples of generating XML descriptor files from Java source, readers no doubt expect a new XDoclet task at that point. Unfortunately, we can't provide one because XDoclet does not support Axis at the time of writing. We expect this to be fixed eventually; the XDoclet team has promised us that they will be writing tags for the Sun toolkit, so a matching Axis set makes sense.

When you are being fully rigorous, you write the XSD and then the WSDL files before you implement your service class. Writing these files can be problematic; the CapeClear editor (http://www.capeclear.com/) is the best there is for this purpose. After writing the WSDL file, call WSDL2Java with the -server attribute, and the program generates the server-side stubs for your service You can take these generated classes and implement your web service behind them.

15.9   REVIEWING WEB SERVICE DEVELOPMENT

We have just set up an advanced build process to add SOAP support to our application. Adding the Axis libraries and configuration settings to our existing web application was relatively simple, but it forced us to add new deployment tests for missing classes, implemented through our existing <happy> JSP page. With the libraries and configuration all working, we can create web services simply by saving Java source files with a .jws extension in the main web application directory.

Writing the service is half the problem; testing it, the remainder. The Axis client-side utilities come into play here, creating Java proxy classes from our services' WSDL description. The WSDL2Java class can even generate basic JUnit test cases, which can act as a foundation for hand-coded unit tests.

---

[3]   There is still one good reason for using cookies: hardware load balancers can direct requests to specific servers based on cookie values.

Web services are an area of heated development. Axis will evolve, Sun is coming out with its own web service package, and, inevitably, Ant will acquire wrapper tasks to simplify the stages of the build using Apache, Sun, and other toolkits.

Ultimately, web services are distributed applications scaled up. If you are writing one, you are writing an application to work across the Internet, interoperating with systems written in other languages, communicating over a protocol (HTTP) that is chosen because it can get through firewalls, not because it is the best protocol for such things (it isn't). This is a major undertaking. Ant alone is not adequate. What Ant gives you is the means to build, deploy, and test your code, including automated generation of client-side stub classes and test cases. It is not a silver bullet. It is, however, along with JUnit, an essential tool for this kind of project.

15.10 CALLING ANT VIA SOAP

If calling SOAP services from a build file lets your program use remote services from the build file, what is a good service to use? How about Ant itself?

Rant, Remote Ant, is a project under way at SourceForge (http://sourceforge.net/projects/remoteant/). This project contains a web application that gives you remote Ant access via a SOAP interface. You can submit a request from a remote system, naming a build file and a target in the file to execute. The servlet executes the build, returning success or failure information.

This is a nice model for implementing a distributed build process, in which different machines in a cluster take on different parts of a big build. It could also be useful for a build process in which a single central machine was the reference build system; developers could use Rant to trigger a new build on this system from their own machine. If the build process is sufficiently complex, especially if it integrates with native compilers or a local database, a centralized build does start to make sense, even if a replicable build environment were preferable. To trigger a remote build you simply invoke it via an Ant task:

```
<taskdef name="rant"       ⟵——————————————————————  Declares the task
  classname="com.einnovation.rant.RantTaskDef">
  <classpath>
    <fileset dir="lib">
      <include name="*.jar"/>
    </fileset>
  </classpath>
</taskdef>

<property name="endpoint"
  value="http://127.0.0.1:8080/rant/servlet/rpcrouter" />
<property name="target.file" location="../soap/soap.xml" />

<target name="default" >
  <rant buildFile="${target.file}"
     soapURL="${endpoint}"          │ Calls the
     target="default"/>             │ remote build
</target>
```

That SOAP is the marshaling layer is irrelevant, except that it lets you trigger remote Ant builds from any language that has a compatible SOAP library: Perl, Python, maybe even the Microsoft.NET framework.

You should not place the Rant service up on a generally accessible web server. Allowing any caller to invoke any Ant file in the system is a significant security issue. Even worse, if the server supported anonymous FTP, a malicious person could upload the build file before referring to it.

Neither of the authors uses this tool in any serious manner, but we like the idea. If we did use it, we would change the API so that you could only select from a limited number of build files, which would significantly lessen the security implications. The other major issue that needs fixing in the current release, version 0.1, is that the service does not return the output of the remote build. All you get now is a success message or the failure exception; it needs to return the log as XML for postprocessing. There is also the issue that Rant uses the original Apache SOAP product, not Axis; Axis has better interoperability.

To use Rant, you need to install its web application on your server. After the application server expands the application, you may need to update rant/WEB-INF/lib with later Ant versions, and any libraries you need for optional tasks. This is because it contains its own version of Ant in the web application's lib directory.

Because the Rant tool is still in its infancy, we would expect it to address issues such as these in future versions. It could become an essential and useful part of every complex build process, replacing those deployment processes in which the client build file uses the <telnet> task to connect to a remote server and run Ant remotely.

15.11 SUMMARY

We explored some aspects of integrating with SOAP-based web services. We demonstrated how to fetch a WSDL description of a web service, and how to use Axis to generate local proxy classes that you can integrate with your own source to create a working web service client. As web services become more common and the SOAP implementations more stable, an increasing number of people will use Ant to build web service servers or clients. What we covered here is a foundation.

The easy way to add a web service to your existing web application is to give a Java file the .jws extension and place it in the web application alongside HTML or JSP pages. Axis, if you have installed and configured it correctly, will compile the file and export it as a SOAP endpoint.

After exposing the endpoint, comes the other half of the problem: the client side. We covered how to build Java and C# clients in Ant, both of which follow a similar process. You fetch the WSDL description of the service, generate proxy classes, and then compile and run these classes against hand-coded client applications. Because interoperability is such an issue with SOAP, you need to continually import and build client applications in as many languages and frameworks as you can manage.

If you only build clients in the same language and SOAP toolkit as that of the server, you may not discover that your service suffers from the hashtable problem until the service goes live, which is never a good time to find out that you have a fundamental design problem.

If you are working in the web services area, you should read some of our other work, which will give you more insight into how to design, develop, and deploy these systems (Loughran 2002-1, Loughran 2002-2). Working with web services can be fun, but there are many challenges to address. Ant can certainly make the process more tractable.

C H A P T E R   1 6

Continuous integration

16.1 Scheduling Ant builds with
     the operating system   387
16.2 CruiseControl   388
16.3 Anthill   397

16.4 Gump   401
16.5 Comparison of continuous
     integration tools   405
16.6 Summary   406

Now that your interactive builds are working for you locally, it's time to automate! In single-developer environments, such automation may be overkill, but more than likely, you are part of a team (whose members may be across the hall or around the world). To keep control (and your sanity!) of larger-scale development efforts, an integration build and routine deployment is needed.

Ant gets us most of the way there for continuous integration. Builds can be easily scheduled and automated with Ant by using operating system job-scheduling capabilities, but it's still not enough. Here are some features that our builds accomplish by using the techniques and tools in this chapter:

- Automated routine builds
- Build logs captured
- Application deployment to test server
- In-container test suite run
- Direct reporting of failures to the developer(s) causing them
- Build numbering
- Web-based reporting

After you have created a complete set of tests, wouldn't it be good to run them every night against a fresh build of the source? And if you can do that, wouldn't it be even nicer to run the task two or three times a day? How about whenever somebody checks in some new source?

We also want our builds and tests to report failures; not to just broadcast build failures, but to notify the actual developer that broke the build. We also want logging of build results, tagging of build numbers, and a web-based history of what has and what hasn't worked.

16.1   SCHEDULING ANT BUILDS WITH THE OPERATING SYSTEM

The most basic way to automate Ant builds is to use your operating system's features to schedule builds on a periodic basis. On Windows NT-based systems, including Windows XP, the Task Scheduler service can be used to schedule a routine job. The AT command queues a job that the service executes at the specified intervals. On Unix-flavored systems, the queuing of a `cron` job is comparable to scheduling a job. We'll only demonstrate Windows and Unix automation, but you can do the same thing on other platforms by writing a small shell script to fetch your source and run your Ant build files.

16.1.1   The Windows way

Our Windows `build.bat` command file is quite short:

```
set OLDCP=%CLASSPATH%
set CLASSPATH=
cd \AntBook\app
cvs update -P -R -d
call %ANT_HOME%\bin\ant.bat clean all
set CLASSPATH=%OLDCP%
```

This batch file simply updates the local SCM sandbox and executes our build. It's best to craft your build files so that no system-specified classpath is needed; that is why we temporarily unset CLASSPATH in our batch file. We do rely on CVS being in the execution PATH, and the user having logged in once with `cvs login`, so that the password is retained for later commands. To schedule the file using AT, we issue the following command-line:

```
C:\>at 01:00 /every:M,T,W,Th,F,S,Su "c:\jobs\build.bat"
Added a new job with job ID = 1

C:\>at
Status ID   Day                       Time            Command Line
-------------------------------------------------------------------------
        1   Each M T W Th F S Su      1:00 AM         c:\jobs\build.bat
```

Executing `at` with no parameters displays the jobs scheduled. This example schedules our builds to run at 1 a.m. every day of the week.

16.1.2 The Unix version

First, we create a shell script such as this one:

```
cd ~/Projects/Antbook/app
cvs update -P -R -d
ant clean all
```

Then we modify our crontab file (using `crontab -e`) to schedule the build:

```
# run at 00:30 every day 30 0 * * * $HOME/Projects/AntBook/app/rebuild.sh
```

Our build will now run every night, with email delivered whether or not it works. This is good, but it is not frequent enough and we don't want to be bothered when the build worked. To get this to work, we set ANT_HOME in the system profile file /etc/profile, and added ANT_HOME/bin to the path; assigning ANT_HOME in the shell script and hard coding the path would avoid this.

16.1.3 Making use of scripting

Taking advantage of your operating system's scheduling capabilities is a quick way to automate builds, but does require writing a shell, batch, or Perl wrapper script. Unless you've built SCM project code fetching into your build file or wrapper script, simply automating a build does not accomplish a lot. There are several ways to improve these types of scheduled builds to be more robust:

Put your SCM system's update commands in your wrapper script, or within a separate target of your build file that uses Ant's SCM tasks (see section 10.3).

- Add a `MailLogger` to the Ant invocation so that failed and/or successful builds send email alerts (see chapter 20 for details on MailLogger).
- Have build logs and JUnit test results from `<junitreport>` published to an intranet-accessible directory. This can be accomplished with property overrides from the command line used to invoke Ant (see section 3.12.6) during automated builds and use of the `-logger` command-line switch. We showed how to do this in section 13.6, including how to save the files to a web server.

Great benefits come with a simple wrapper scripts and SCM integration. If you are in need of quick automation, this is the way to go. Perhaps even this level of automation will suffice for your needs, but read further to evaluate other tools available that add many more features to continuous integration builds.

16.2 CRUISECONTROL

CruiseControl is an automated build support tool from Martin Fowler and colleagues at ThoughtWorks. It continually rebuilds and retests your system after changes are detected in your codebase. It is an open source project hosted under SourceForge at http://cruisecontrol.sourceforge.net/. Although it is a powerful tool, it can be tricky to get working as of the 1.2.1a release available at the time of writing.

16.2.1 How it works

CruiseControl consists of two pieces: a stand-alone Java application that runs the builds and a web application that reports build status. Figure 16.1 shows the Cruise-Control architecture. The command-line Java application drives the builds. It sits in an infinite loop, cycling over a project's build. When it wakes up for a new cycle, it runs one of two special targets in your build file. Mostly, it runs a *master build* target, which does an incremental update from the SCM. Periodically, after a specified number of incremental build attempts, it runs a *clean build* target.

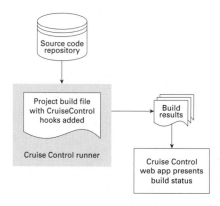

Figure 16.1
CruiseControl architecture. The web reporting interface is separate from the main build process, and your own build file controls the repository fetches.

16.2.2 It's all about the cruise—getting the build runner working

The CruiseControl distribution includes enough information to get it running, but it requires some trial and error to get it started the first time. We describe the steps we used to get it running on our project, but be sure to check the documentation, especially if you are using a newer version.

Standard steps to get CruiseControl into the build

- Download and install the CruiseControl distribution (we used version 1.2.1a).
- Based on your scheme for managing third-party tasks, place the cruisecontrol.jar appropriately—or simply leave it in the install directory.
- Add these new targets to your project build file: `modificationset`, `masterbuild`, and `cleanbuild`. These targets can be copied from one of the example build files that are provided with the CruiseControl installation. There are samples for several different SCM systems—pick the appropriate one for your environment.

With our project, we created a CruiseControl-specific build file called cruisecontrol.xml. This file contains the CruiseControl needed targets, and a `build` target to `<ant>` to our main build. This is a nice way to keep your main build file separate and distinct from how the continuous integration process works on your project. Listing 16.1, which we'll get to in a moment, shows our cruisecontrol.xml.

The flow is straightforward. The CruiseControl runner application sits in a loop for a specified number of seconds, and when it's time the process kicks off the appropriate build target, either `cleanbuild` or `masterbuild`. Running a clean build every so often ensures that no previously generated build artifacts are interfering with the build results. The numbers in figure 16.2 represent the ordering of multiple dependencies on the `cleanbuild` and `masterbuild` targets.

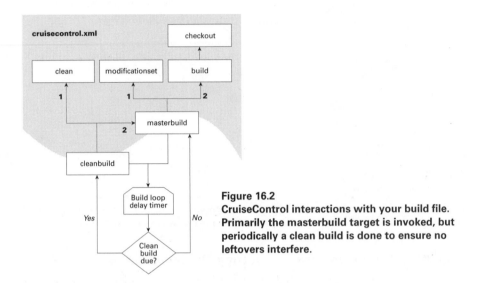

Figure 16.2
CruiseControl interactions with your build file. Primarily the masterbuild target is invoked, but periodically a clean build is done to ensure no leftovers interfere.

ModificationSet

The heart of CruiseControl's capabilities is the *modification set*. The `modification-set` target in our build file executes the CruiseControl-provided Ant task `<modifi-cationset>`. Nested within `<modificationset>` are nested elements providing your specific repository information. The `<modificationset>` task queries the repository for modifications since the last build, using the `log` command internally, for example, for a CVS repository. CruiseControl provides a `lastBuildAttemptTime` property that you must provide to `<modificationset>`. If no changes are found in the repository since that last build attempt, the `<modificationset>` task fails, which, in turn, causes the build to fail. This failure is a normal and routine condition only noticeable when watching the runner application console output.

The `<modificationset>` task collects information in an XML file. If changes are detected since the last build attempt, the build continues. After a build has completed, successfully or otherwise, the XML-generated build log file, modification set results, and any other XML files specified in the CruiseControl configuration that are generated by your build, are collected into a single log XML file.

Our build file

Listing 16.1 comprises our complete CruiseControl build file. Let's take a closer look at the details.

```xml
<project name="AntBook - CruiseControl" default="masterbuild" basedir=".">

  <property file="cruisecontrol.properties"
          prefix="cruisecontrol"/>                          Gets access
  <property name="test.data.dir"                            to our CC
          location="${cruisecontrol.logDir}/testresults"/>  configuration

  <property environment="env"/>
  <!-- On Windows env.TEMP will already be set,
       so set it for Linux-->
  <property name="env.TEMP" location="/tmp"/>


  <!-- The next few lines of loading property files is copied from
       build.xml - perhaps entity reference include is warranted -->
  <property name="user.properties.file"
          location="${user.home}/.build.properties"/>

  <!-- Load the application specific settings -->
  <property file="build.properties"/>

  <!-- Load user specific settings -->
  <property file="${user.properties.file}"/>

  <property name="root.dir" location="${env.TEMP}"/>        Defines our
                                                            repository
                                                            settings
  <!-- CVS Info -->
  <property name="cvs.username" value="${user.name}"/>
  <property name="cvs.host" value="localhost"/>
  <property name="cvs.root"
        value=":pserver:${cvs.username}@${cvs.host}:/home/cvs/projects"/>
  <property name="cvs.passfile" value="../.cvspass"/>
  <property name="cvs.dir" location="${root.dir}"/>
  <property name="cvs.package" value="AntBook/app"/>

  <target name="init">
    <mkdir dir="${root.dir}"/>
    <echoproperties/>
  </target>

  <target name="clean">
    <echo>Cleaning build directory</echo>
    <delete dir="${root.dir}/AntBook/app"/>
  </target>

  <target name="modificationset"
          depends="init"
          description="Check modifications since last build">
    <taskdef name="modificationset"
          classname="net.sourceforge.cruisecontrol.ModificationSet"
```

```
                        classpath="lib/cruisecontrol/cruisecontrol.jar"
    />

    <!-- set the CruiseControl timestamp when it is not defined -->
    <tstamp>
      <format property="lastBuildAttemptTime"
              pattern="yyyy-MM-dd HH:mm:ss"
              offset="-24" unit="hour"
      />
    </tstamp>
```

Allows use outside CC's runner

```
    <echo>
      Checking for modifications since ${lastBuildAttemptTime}
    </echo>

    <modificationset lastbuild="${lastBuildAttemptTime}"
                     quietperiod="60"
                     dateformat="yyyy-MMM-dd HH:mm:ss">
      <cvselement cvsroot="${cvs.root}"
                  localworkingcopy="${root.dir}/${cvs.package}"
      />
    </modificationset>
  </target>
```

Checks for repository changes

```
  <target name="checkout" depends="init">
    <cvs cvsRoot="${cvs.root}"
         dest="${root.dir}"
         package="${cvs.package}"
         passfile="${cvs.passfile}"
         failOnError="yes"
    />
  </target>
```

Gets latest from repository

```
  <target name="build" depends="checkout">
    <ant dir="${root.dir}/${cvs.package}"
         inheritAll="false">
      <!-- accumulate test results into a global location -->
      <property name="test.data.dir" location="${test.data.dir}"/>

      <!-- force any properties we set here to propogate down -->
      <property name="inheritAll" value="true"/>
    </ant>
  </target>
```

Executes our build

```
  <target name="masterbuild"   <─────────────────────
          depends="modificationset,build"
          description="CruiseControl master build"
  />
```

CruiseControl hook

```
  <target name="cleanbuild"   <─────────────────────
          depends="clean,masterbuild"
          description="CruiseControl clean build"
  />

</project>
```

CruiseControl hook

After you have configured the build file, either with the CruiseControl targets added to your project build file or through a separate build file as we did, you need to configure the properties CruiseControl uses while running. The distribution provides a well-documented starter `cruisecontrol.properties`, and very little needs to be changed. We copied this file into our project's main directory. Some of the properties we tweaked are:

```
antfile = cruisecontrol.xml
auxlogfiles = modificationset.file, test.data.dir
mailhost = <our mail server>
```

There are several other properties to control the master and clean build target names, the cycle interval between clean builds, time interval between build cycles, the URL to the build servlet, email mapping file, several other email notification options, and a custom build-label incrementer.

The `auxlogfiles` property deserves some mention. It is a comma-separated list of Ant property names that represent either files or directories. The `modification-set.file` is the default value, and we added `test.data.dir`. As covered in chapter 4, our `<junit>` and `<junitreport>` tasks save files to this directory. When a build completes, the build log, modification set data, and XML files specified by auxlogfiles (or if the property is a directory, XML files in that directory) are put into a single XML file. The log files are then accessible to the reporting web application.

TIP   By ensuring that Ant property names are used for build output, it becomes very easy to interface with external systems such as CruiseControl—the properties are simply overridden when run with CruiseControl to allow output to be collected where CruiseControl desires.

Starting the CruiseControl runner

The CruiseControl distribution provides .bat and .sh startup scripts. Working on a Windows machine, we used cruiseControl.bat as a basis, renaming it cc.bat. We copied this file into our application directory and modified it to match our environment. CruiseControl 1.2.1a is built on Ant 1.4, but we are using Ant 1.5 so it required adjustments to the classpath used. We recommend that you try the standard Cruise-Control scripts, but expect that there will be issues that require fine tuning. Starting CruiseControl for the first time requires some one-time initialization parameters. Running cc.bat without these parameters generates the details to help decipher what to do next:

```
[masterbuild] ***** Starting automated build process *****

Reading build information from : c:\AntBook\app\buildcycleinfo
Cannot read build information.
Usage:

Starts a continuous integration loop
```

```
java MasterBuild [options]
where options are:
    -lastbuild timestamp   where timestamp is in yyyyMMddHHmmss format.
       note HH is the 24 hour clock.
    -label label           where label is in x.y format, y being an integer.
     x can be any string.
    -properties file        where file is the masterbuild properties file,
     and is available in the classpath
```

Our first run started with this command:

```
cc.bat -lastbuild 20020101010101 -label 1.1.1
```

Running CruiseControl subsequently picks up from where it left off and the parameters are not needed. The -properties parameter defaults to cruisecontrol.properties if not specified. Typical output generated from the build runner application is:

```
[masterbuild] ***** Starting automated build process *****

Reading build information from : c:\AntBook\app\buildcycleinfo
[masterbuild] ***** Starting Build Cycle
[masterbuild] ***** Label: 1.1.1
[masterbuild] ***** Last Good Build: 20020101010101
[masterbuild]

[masterbuild] Opening build file: cruisecontrol.xml
[masterbuild] Using clean target: cleanbuild

clean:
     [echo] Cleaning build directory

init:
[echoproperties] #Ant properties
 .
 .
 .

modificationset:
     [echo]
       Checking for modifications since 20020404110915

[CVSElement] Executing: cvs -d :pserver:erik@localhost:/home/cvs/projects
  -q log -N "-d>2002-04-04 16:09:15 GMT" C:/temp/AntBook/app

BUILD FAILED
C:\AntBook\app\cruisecontrol.xml:68: No Build Necessary

Total time: 14 seconds
[masterbuild]

[masterbuild] ***** Ending Build Cycle, sleeping 30.0 seconds until next
               build.

[masterbuild] ***** Label: 1.1.1
[masterbuild] ***** Last Good Build: 20020101010101
[masterbuild]
```

16.2.3   Build log reporting

The reporting piece of CruiseControl is a web application. It presents a slick interface to navigate the build logs. A WAR file is provided with the CruiseControl distribution.

Configuring the web application

The WAR file provided deploys easily in a web container such as Tomcat. Here are the steps we followed:

- Install the WAR file into the web application deployment directory. Start the web application, which should expand the WAR file into actual physical files.
- Edit `WEB-INF/web.xml` to point to where you keep the CruiseControl logs. Restart the web server to ensure these changes are in effect.
- Test the installation by pointing to `/buildservlet/cruise.jsp` on the web server.

Unless you have run an initial build with CruiseControl already, the first thing you should see is an error about missing files—unless the CruiseControl maintainers have made the JSP page more helpful in its reporting:

```
java.lang.NullPointerException
        at java.io.File.(File.java:180)
        at org.apache.jsp.cruise$jsp$InitData
           .getLastBuildLogFilename(cruise$jsp.java:49)
```

After you have generated some build results, the CruiseControl web interface should be similar to figure 16.3.

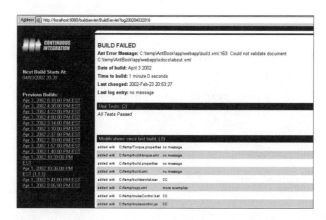

**Figure 16.3
CruiseControl web interface presents attractive build summary reports.**

The CruiseControl interface is generated by a combination of JSP and XML/XSLT. The left side of figure 16.3 is generated within `cruise.jsp`, while the details of a specific build are transformed by using XSLT from the consolidated XML file generated for each build. The stylesheet used can be customized to suit your needs.

16.2.4 Email notifications and build labeling

When a build fails, CruiseControl can send emails directly to the user(s) who last committed files to the repository. Because there is not necessarily a direct mapping between repository user names and email addresses, mapping capability is provided. Email address aliasing capabilities exist to enable you to specify that build failure notifications are sent to, for example, "developers."

After a successful build, the build label is incremented. The default incrementer simply adds one to the last number of the last label. A custom build-label incrementer may be used and is configured in cruisecontrol.properties; this allows CruiseControl to work with your preferred build-labeling scheme rather than forcing you to use its default scheme. Consult the CruiseControl documentation for details of incrementing a build-label incrementer.

16.2.5 CruiseControl summary

CruiseControl is, at this time, the Cadillac of Java continuous integration tools. It provides a nice addition to a project's toolset. Its configuration is tricky and, even though fairly well documented, difficult to get running. Once you've got it configured and running, the results are well worth the effort. We certainly expect that future releases will be much more user friendly and far less difficult to install and run.

Using CruiseControl can force you into better Ant habits by ensuring that you are defining properties for output files, thus allowing overridability.

Another issue is to decide what really defines a clean build. In our case, we cleared the entire project directory structure and refetched everything from our SCM, but it is just as reasonable to simply remove build artifacts leaving repository maintained files in place.

16.2.6 Tips and tricks

- CruiseControl recommends that you use Jikes instead of `javac` because it is faster and leaks less memory.
- Likewise, if you do use the javac compiler or another big Java program, set `fork="true"`.
- Get a mobile phone with SMS messaging and set up an email alias, and then you can get paged when things go wrong—and when they start working again.

16.2.7 Pros and cons to CruiseControl

During our integration efforts with CruiseControl we noted several pros and cons to it. Here are the things we felt were problems and some suggestions for improvement:

- Requires web.xml webapp configuration. This would be problematic for web containers that do not expand WAR files into physical files. You will have to replace the web.xml inside the WAR file manually in such situations. The configuration really should be done via a web interface.

- Requires a somewhat involved modification to your build file and requires an understanding of Ant's optional SCM tasks for your particular repository. Perhaps in the future, the CruiseControl engine itself could deal with the SCM and not require build file modifications. In all fairness, CruiseControl ships with examples for many repositories that can be cut and pasted into your project.

- The auxlogfiles feature does not recursively process XML files. This would have been useful in our situation, where we are running a build of many subprojects from a single master build. Although we could handle this situation by having a separate Ant output property for each subproject, or by making sure all file names generated are unique, it would require some effort to handle these ourselves.

- Version labeling is not integrated with the SCM. The labels assigned to successful builds by CruiseControl is merely an identifier on the log files. We could implement such labeling as part of our build process ourselves, because Cruise-Control provides the label as an Ant property label.

- Multiple projects would require multiple runners configured, and you would likely want separate web applications for each.

Things we really liked about CruiseControl include:

- Once it is set up and starts running it's very reliable.

- Reporting is well done, attractive, and easily customizable. The ability to incorporate any XML file into the results provides great extensibility.

- Version label incrementing can be customized.

- Direct emailing to the developer(s) that broke the build.

- Highly configurable email settings, even with group aliases.

The best thing about CruiseControl is that once it is working, it works very well. It provides an automated build and test system that harangues developers when they break something, while management gets a web view that keeps them happy. Because it can run tests from a build file, the more JUnit, HttpUnit, Cactus, or other Ant-hosted tests you write, the more testing you can do on a system. And, of course, the more testing you do, the better your product becomes.

16.3 ANTHILL

Anthill is a freely available continuous integration tool created by Urbancode (http://www.urbancode.com). Anthill integrates with your SCM system (currently only a CVS adapter is provided) and runs scheduled automated builds through an installed web application. Not only are build results made available through the web interface, but project build artifacts can also be made available. These artifacts typically include Javadoc API documentation, and source and binary distributions. The Anthill distribution also includes Java2HTML,[1] which produces hyperlinked and color-coded views of the latest versions of your project source code. Anthill's purpose is more than just for ensuring that integration builds work, it is also designed to be a build artifact publishing service.

16.3.1 Getting Anthill working

Installing and running Anthill is straightforward and well documented. Here are the steps we followed to get it installed, configured, and running against our project.

Installing Anthill

Anthill consists primarily of a single web application; its binary distribution contains a WAR file that easily deploys in your favorite J2EE-compatible web container. Here are the steps we used to install Anthill:

1 Download the latest Anthill binary release build from http://www.urban-code.com.

2 Extract the downloaded archive into an installation directory (c:\tools\anthill in our case).

3 Create a publish directory under the installation directory. (This will likely not be necessary in future versions, but is a bug we encountered.)

4 Copy anthill.war from the installed dist directory into our web application server deployment directory.

5 Start the web application server.

6 Navigate to root of the Anthill web application with a web browser: http://localhost:8080/anthill/ (trailing slash was mandatory in the version we used, but this should be fixed in future versions).

7 Create an anthill.version file in your project's root directory. This is simply a text file that initially contains the version number you'd like your project to start with. A value of 1.1.1 is a reasonable start. This file needs to be committed to your source code repository.

Getting Anthill to work with Ant 1.5

Anthill comes with Ant 1.3 and Ant 1.4, but our builds require features found only in Ant 1.5. We copied our Ant 1.5 installation into an ant1.5 directory under our installation's lib directory, and in the Anthill Properties settings of the web administration, we set anthill.ant.home to lib/ant1.5. It was that easy!

After the web application is up, the configuration screen displays, as shown in figure 16.4.

This is a one-time configuration that persists its value in a .anthill.properties file in the user.home directory (the user the webapp is running as, that is). To verify that Ant-

---

[1] Available separately at http://www.java2html.com/

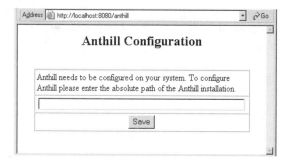

Figure 16.4
Anthill is configurable from a web form.

hill is working correctly, we installed their example application in our CVS repository and configured it appropriately by using the web-based project configuration.

16.3.2 How Anthill works

Anthill maintains project and scheduling configuration information in its own installation directory. The web application performs configuration administration, build running, and an interface to generated results. Anthill takes care of the SCM repository communication itself before running a build. If new files are present, a build runs. Figure 16.5 illustrates Anthill's architecture.

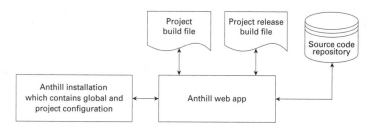

Figure 16.5   **Anthill architecture. The Anthill application controls repository access, and the main build file does not need to be modified.**

Not only does Anthill operate on your project's main build file, it also requires an additional build file that is invoked after the build is successful. This second build file is for publishing build artifacts. Comments within Anthill's web administration indicate that this additional build file will not be needed in the future and that publishing of build artifacts will be delegated to the main build file instead.

Each Anthill-configured project is associated with a schedule. You define a schedule simply as an interval (in minutes). Specifying an interval of zero keeps the builds from running automatically—a stoppedSchedule comes configured by default. You can also run builds manually through the web interface by clicking the Build hyperlink on the main page.

After a successful build, the version stored in the version file (anthill.version in our case) is incremented and the repository is tagged with this value. Anthill provides the capability to lock this file in the repository to ensure that there are no race conditions on it, but in our environment, locking did not function properly, so we disabled it (which, fortunately, was a setting in the Anthill configuration). See figure 16.6.

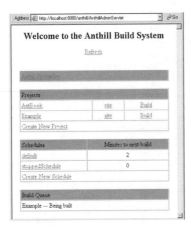

Figure 16.6
Anthill's main screen allows easy manually forced builds and project configuration.

16.3.3   Anthill summary

Anthill is very nicely done, and despite its relatively recent appearance, it works very well and requires little effort to install and configure. There is room for improvement, however. We offer our cons:

- The secondary publish build file seems unnecessary and confusing. We would prefer that Anthill have project-level configuration to specify Ant properties referencing files and directories of build artifacts to be published.
- Much improvement is needed to the build status presentation. We would like to see a summary page for each project with its build outcome, results of unit tests, and links to other build artifacts such as documentation and distributions.

Here is what we liked about Anthill:

- Very straightforward installation and configuration
- Multiple project support
- The scheduler handles multiple projects within a single instance of the Anthill web application.
- Unobtrusive to our build file.
- Anthill takes care of SCM fetching outside of our build file, which made configuration much simpler but also currently limits Anthill to CVS repositories. Having the secondary publish build file violates this unobtrusiveness a bit, so we hope that a better solution is on the horizon.
- Customizable version-labeling scheme.

- Automatic repository tagging of version.
- Capability to manually start a build regardless of its schedule.

16.4 GUMP

Builds are like a box of chocolates. Gump has repeatedly proven that "you never know what you're going to get" when running continuous integration builds of the world's most popular open-source projects many times per day. At the time of writing, Gump still lives in a very small corner of Jakarta's CVS repository. There are no binary distributions of it, and it is used primarily to build Jakarta projects and other key open-source dependencies. Its usefulness is not limited to open-source projects, and you customize it to work as a local continuous integration build tool.

Gump not only provides the Java open-source world with continuous integration feedback, it also produces interproject cross-reference information, up-to-date published Javadocs, and JAR files of the projects it builds. Gump's most recent success was building all the projects against JDK 1.4 before its final release to alert project development teams of incompatibilities.

16.4.1 Installing and running Gump

Gump's installation is perfect for those of us who love to roll up our sleeves and dig under the covers of the tools we use. It's not going to be as pleasant for those who want a simple installation and to be up and running quickly. The documentation available at the Gump web site is much more thorough than we provide, and it is continually improving. We recommend consulting the most current online documentation for installation instructions, but we will now provide an overview of the steps we followed to give you a preview. Here are the installation steps we used to set up our own Gump process for the AntBook project:

1 Use a CVS client to login and checkout the jakarta-alexandria module to the machine that will be running the Gump process. From the command-line, this is:

```
cvs -d :pserver:anoncvs@cvs.apache.org:/home/cvspublic login
password: anoncvs

cvs -d :pserver:anoncvs@cvs.apache.org:/home/cvspublic
        checkout jakarta-alexandria
```

2 Learn the details of Gump's configuration by reading the documentation at http://jakarta.apache.org/gump. The configuration files live in the jakarta-alexandria/proposal/gump directory and below.

3 Configure a workspace XML file in the main Gump directory. It should be named *hostname*.xml, where *hostname* is the name of the machine. The workspace file is the one place where platform-specific and absolute path information is configured.

4 From this point forward, configuration is dependent upon your workspace settings. We cover more details of our configuration in the next section.

5 Once configuration is complete, the fun begins.

Our workspace configuration is as follows:

```xml
<?xml version="1.0" ?>
<workspace basedir="c:\temp\gump" pkgdir="C:\tools\gump" version="0.3">

  <property name="build.sysclasspath" value="first"/>

  <profile href="profile/erik.xml"/>

  <project name="ant" home="c:\AntBook\jakarta-ant-1.5">
    <jar name="lib/ant.jar"/>
    <jar name="lib/optional.jar"/>
    <jar name="lib/junit.jar"/>
    <jar name="lib/log4j.jar"/>
  </project>

</workspace>
```

This workspace definition tells the builds to set the special `build.sysclasspath`[2] property so that system classpath comes before all paths used internal to a build. The profile definition defines projects we want to build, and the `<project>` element defines where our Ant installation resides. We could have gone even further and had our project depend on the build of Ant itself, but we opted to simply point Gump to an already built version of Ant.

Our profile, `erik.xml`, defines what projects we want to build and which repositories are available:

```xml
<profile name="erik">
  <module href="project/antbook.xml"/>
  <module href="project/xdoclet.xml"/>

  <repository href="repository/eiger.xml"/>
  <repository href="repository/sourceforge.xml"/>
</profile>
```

We build our project and the XDoclet project. If we wanted to, we could even pull down Ant itself, then perhaps Tomcat and Apache Axis. Sure, the build would get slower, but we would know the moment any of these tools broke our code, and we could then either fix our code or raise the issue with whoever changed the code we depend upon.

This shows one of the interesting ways that using open source tools can change your perspective. Instead of being a consumer of finished products, your project can

---

[2] We do not cover build.sysclasspath in this book. It is rarely needed for Ant users. Ant's documentation provides details on its purpose and possible values.

stand on the shoulders of the daily builds of all the tools you depend upon. That may seem a bit bleeding edge, and sometimes it is, but another way to look at it is as continuous integration raised up a notch. You are no longer integrating your code against older versions of libraries; you are building on a daily basis against the latest code developed. This may seem unduly hazardous, but open-source developers tend to put all bug fixes at the head of the CVS tree, and prefer bug reports from the nightly build, too. Bug reports with old versions are less welcome, because someone has to determine whether the problem has already gone away.

Generating the scripts

From a command prompt at the main Gump directory, execute either gen.bat or gen.sh, depending on the platform you're using. This script uses the workspace configuration file and any other needed configuration files to build scripts specific to your platform and settings. These scripts are built to the `basedir` specified in the workspace definition.

Updating and building

The generation process creates an update.bat/.sh file and a build.bat/.sh file. First execute the update script, which updates the local copy of the project from the repository. Next, execute the build script to build all projects in their dependency order.

Automating these steps is simply a matter of wrapping them in a recurring job. See section 16.1 for additional details on scheduling a job on your platform.

16.4.2 How Gump works

Gump does a fantastic job at modeling complex build processes. It separates the concepts of project, module, repository, profile, and workspace into individual XML configuration files, allowing them to be reused easily. Table 16.1 defines these concepts further.

Table 16.1 Gump's configuration files

Gump terminology	Definition
project	Represents a buildable project or an installable package such as a fixed external library. The project definition names the JARs that it exports, which are available to dependent projects.
module	A collection of projects stored in a single repository.
repository	Defines the CVS information needed to access repositories such as SourceForge, Jakarta, or your own CVS server.
profile	Defines a collection of projects and repositories.
workspace	Global controlling configuration. Defines which projects are built, directly or via profile definitions. Platform-specific and path information is kept here.

Figure 16.7 illustrates Gump output for a typical run, this particular one using JDK 1.4. It demonstrates that not only does Gump show build failures, it also shows whether a project cannot be built because a prerequisite failed, which is noted by a different status. Build failures can trigger email nags, but you need to install Perl to use this feature.

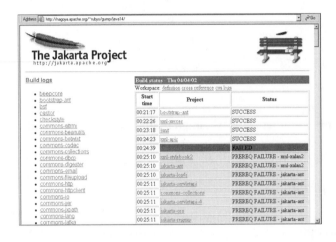

**Figure 16.7
How the failure of one open-source project to build breaks everything else. Here Xalan is broken, which stops Ant from building, so nothing else will be built either.**

16.4.3   Summary of Gump

We are intentionally being short on details with Gump because we feel the online documentation of Gump is superb. In addition, the details are in continual flux and whatever we can say here will probably be out of date shortly. Gump has stood the test of time by being a workhorse of the open-source Java world. Gump does have some negatives, however:

- Currently, Gump supports only CVS.

- Configuration, execution, and automation are not for the faint of heart. In addition, a solid understanding of Gump's architecture and configurations are needed to really get rolling with it.

- The non-Java aspects of Gump are likely to scare off many developers. There are shell scripts that automate the generation of other shell scripts. Perl is used for failure email notification, but not it is not a required component to run Gump.

Negatives aside, Gump has capabilities that are not present in other continuous integration tools and likely gets much more of a workout than any other similar tool. Its outstanding features are:

- Interproject dependencies. A typical project has dependencies on other libraries. Having those other libraries built from the latest (HEAD in CVS terminology) codebase prior to your projects build can provide early warning of API changes or assurances that all is well.

- Very well done output and user interface. All projects are hyperlinked to their dependencies' builds. The CVS update log is one click away. Project cross-references are extremely helpful in visualizing a complex set of interconnected projects.

16.5 COMPARISON OF CONTINUOUS INTEGRATION TOOLS

The main deciding feature in choosing a continuous integration tool is likely to be SCM support. If you are not using CVS then you have two options: script your SCM integration into a shell script that you automate with your operating system's scheduling capabilities or use CruiseControl. Both Anthill and Gump could be adapted to other SCM systems if desired, but would require you to put forth a low-level effort to implement it yourself unless it has been implemented since we reviewed them. See table 16.2.

Table 16.2   Feature comparison of continuous integration tools

Feature	CruiseControl	Anthill	Gump
Setup/configuration difficulty	Moderately difficult.	Easy.	Difficult
Requires modifications to project build files	Yes.	No.	No.
Multiple project dependencies	No.	No.	Yes.
SCM Support	CVS, VSS, ClearCase, MKS, Perforce, PVCS, StarTeam, and file system.	CVS only.	CVS only.
Controls SCM itself	No (you have to code this into your build file manually).	Yes.	Yes.
Process to support multiple project builds	Set up another instance of the runner application and configure each project's build file with the CruiseControl hooks.	Add another project definition through the web interface.	Add another project to your profile or workspace configuration and regenerate/rerun the scripts.
Version labeling	Default and custom labeling are available. SCM is not tagged.	Default and custom labeling are available. SCM is tagged automatically after successful builds.	Builds are timestamped; no other labeling support is provided. SCM is not tagged.

16.6 SUMMARY

Continuous integration is a necessary step in taming the complexities we continue to introduce into our software development lives. Projects are more complex, time scales are shorter, teams are becoming distributed, making communication more difficult, and many other forces are acting against our ability to maintain tight control over our process. We covered four ways to implement a continuous integration process into your development environment that can really help keep a handle on growing complexities.

If you are using a CVS repository, you have all these options to explore, but with any other repository your options are either to implement your own custom automated build process or to use CruiseControl. We would be doing a disservice to each of these fine tools to recommend one over the others, as they each have pros and cons. Nevertheless, here is a quick set of good points of each:

- *Custom shell scripting build automation*—Quick and easy, and of course highly customizable!
- *CruiseControl*—Excellent reporting and default support for reporting unit test results.
- *Anthill*—Easy installation and full control through the web application.
- *Gump*—The only game in town if you need interproject dependencies and cross-reference reporting.

Installation and configuration of all of these continuous integration tools require a bit of effort, but in the end, it is effort well spent. Regardless of the tool you use, having automated builds with failure email notification is a wonderful thing. We can make one unequivocal recommendation: use continuous integration in your projects!

CHAPTER 17

Developing native code

17.1 The challenge of native code 407
17.2 Using existing build tools 408
17.3 Introducing the <cc> task 410
17.4 Building a JNI library in Ant 412

17.5 Going cross-platform 422
17.6 Looking at <cc> in more detail 425
17.7 Distributing native libraries 429
17.8 Summary 430

We want to take a quick detour into how to include native code generation into an Ant project. Readers who never have to do this can skip this chapter entirely, returning only when something alters their plans. This chapter will show you how to use Ant to build native code applications and libraries as and when the need arises.

17.1 THE CHALLENGE OF NATIVE CODE

In a Java software project of any significant complexity, you eventually encounter native code. It may be a native library to access some OS feature not directly supported by Java, which you must bridge to using the Java Native Interface (JNI). It may be a CORBA component bridging to existing code. It may even be a COM object. Alternatively, you may have to write a stand-alone native executable. The build process needs to cover these parts of the project, which means you need to compile native code from Ant.

We don't want to add native code into our ongoing application for the sake of it, so we have chosen an example problem that we can use in the application, but whose use is not mandatory. We want to bridge to some native code that extracts and returns the Pentium CPU clock timer: this will give us performance data on our Java code down to individual CPU clock cycles. This code will only work on x86 processors, but it is operating-system independent. This makes it somewhat of a special case: we can explore native code build techniques without having any platform-specific OS calls to worry about.

This lets us explore how to build native code in Ant, and integrate it into a Java project, without going into the deep details of using JNI to bridge Java and native code. For that, we will refer you to Sun's documentation (Sun 2002, Liang 1999).

17.2   USING EXISTING BUILD TOOLS

Ant may be the best build tool for Java programs to date, but it is weak for C or C++ development. Makefiles and IDEs have long been the standard tools used to compile and link native code. Yet these tools retain the fundamental reasons for Ant's existence: they are not portable and can be hard to use. The tools are also invariably weak in other areas where Ant is strong: deployment and integration with the Java compiler and JUnit based testing. The historical solution for building native code has been to suffer the portability and maintenance hit and delegate the native code portion of the build to an IDE or makefile.

17.2.1   Delegating to an IDE

Before we cover how we want you to build your native code with Ant, let's look at what the core compilation target would be if we handed it off to an IDE. This would let us delegate all the complex stages of the build process to the native tool chain, which makes it easier to work with very large native projects, such as COM or CORBA integration exercises.

For example, if we wanted to use Microsoft Visual Studio 6 for the build, we could use <exec> to hand off the C++ stages to a local copy of the IDE, relying on msdev.exe being on the executable path:

```
<target name="msdev" depends="headers">
    <exec
        executable="msdev.exe"
        failonerror="true" >
        <arg file="CpuInfo.dsw" />
        <arg value="/MAKE"/>
        <arg value="&quot;CpuInfo - Release&quot;"/>
    </exec>
</target>
```

This works, but threatens the whole stability and portability of the build file. A new version of the IDE may force you to rework the entire target. Indeed, to support Microsoft Visual Studio.Net, the <exec> command needs a major rewrite:

```
<target name="devenv" depends="headers">
    <exec
        executable="devenv.exe"
        failonerror="true" >
        <arg file="CpuInfo.sln" />
```

```
        <arg value="/build"/>
        <arg value="Release"/>
    </exec>
</target>
```

With this new version of the IDE, you need devenv.exe on the executable path. As this is not the default, you need to manually configure the systems, or, alternatively, specify the path to the IDE in a property stored in a per-user properties file, and alter the `executable` attribute of <exec> appropriately.

Handing off to the IDE means you have to chase version issues to keep your build files current. Equally problematic is ensuring this build works on other systems, even with the same OS. IDE-based builds are usually barely portable; they invariably contain too many hardcoded paths and dependencies to work across systems. The only way to stay in control is to lock down the systems so they all look alike, be they an NFS-based workstation cluster or PCs with a standard disk image. In a large project, or over time, this eventually breaks, leaving you with a build that does not work.

17.2.2   Using Make

If we don't believe the IDE is the approach you should take, is Make any better?

Despite everything that we do not like about Make, it can at least give you a build process you can share among colleagues. You can also integrate it with any of the automated continuous integration processes we covered in chapter 16. To run Make, call it using <exec>:

```
<target name="make" depends="headers">
    <exec
        executable="make"
        failonerror="true" >
        <arg value="-f"/>
        <arg file="CpuInfo" />
        <arg value="release"/>
    </exec>
</target>
```

As with all <exec> based invocations of programs, we have to make sure that we set the `failonerror` attribute to true. Its default value is false, which stops Ant from picking up any failure in the makefile to compile our source.

We do not actually want to use Make, if we can at all avoid it. Its dependency specification process is tricky, and it really requires a broad suite of GNU or Unix commands to work properly. For cross-platform portability, having the GNU tool chain is not enough, you may need to use autoconf to configure your makefile for the platform. Overall then, adding Make support makes your build significantly more complex. Ant was created precisely because Make did not work well for cross-platform development.

Here is a little secret: you can compile and link C and C++ source using Ant tasks especially written for the purpose.

17.3 INTRODUCING THE <CC> TASK

Ant does not have C and C++ compilation and linking tasks in the Ant 1.5 distribution, but it may well have them in future versions. The task being groomed for inclusion currently lives in the Ant-Contrib project on SourceForge (http://sf.net/projects/ant-contrib/). This project hosts some Ant tasks that aren't yet (or may never be) part of the official Ant distribution, some of which we introduced in chapter 10. In particular, the team's logic tasks, <foreach> and <switch>, are too procedural to go into the Ant codebase, yet they are the reference implementation to which Ant users are directed if they really need them.

The native code development task offered by the SourceForge project is <cc>. With it, you can write a single build file that compiles the C++ code for multiple platforms, and link it down to an appropriate executable for the platform. The task is powerful, and much more than a simple wrapper around a compiler. Indeed, some of the features that the associated data types offer, such as an inheritance model, are interesting examples of how the whole of Ant could evolve in the future. Even the dependency checking tasks, which parses source files to find the header files they depend upon, are more advanced than the dependency checking in <java>.

17.3.1 Installing the tasks

First, check your online documentation to see if the task is bundled with your copy of Ant, as we ultimately expect it to be. If not, download the cpp-tasks archive from the project's home on SourceForge. We are using version 1.0a, so it may have changed somewhat since the time of writing.

The task comes in the cpp-tasks.jar file; you must add this to your project's lib directory then declare the <cc> task in your project, along with its four supporting data types:

```
<path id="cc.classpath">
  <pathelement location="lib/cpptasks.jar"/>
</path>

<taskdef resource="cpptasks.tasks"
  classpathref="cc.classpath"
  loaderRef="cctasks"/>
<typedef resource="cpptasks.types"
  classpathref="cc.classpath"
  loaderRef="cctasks"/>
```

If the tasks become part of Ant, these declarations will not be needed in your build files, but until that time declaring the tasks is important. The <typedef> definition lets you define the task's datatypes outside of a <cc>, which can be useful in a complex build. For everything to work, the datatypes and the tasks must all be loaded in the same classloader; otherwise, the <cc> task cannot resolve references to the datatypes. We have to tell Ant to use the same classloader, which we do with the two loader-Ref="cctasks" attributes, one each for the <typedef> and the <taskdef> declarations. All tasks and types declared with the same string in the loaderRef attribute share the same classpath.

17.3.2 Adding a compiler

These tasks also need a compiler to perform the actual work. All the compilers listed in table 17.1 are supported, and no doubt some more will be in later releases. If the compiler you need is missing, you can write your own adapter class in Java and plug it in to the framework

Table 17.1 Supported compilers. Notice that resource, IDL, and Fortran compilers are in there alongside the C/C++ ones. The gcc compiler is the default on all platforms.

Compiler	Description
aCC	HP aCC compiler and linker
bcc	Borland C++ (Windows only; free from borland.com)
brc	Borland resource compiler for Windows
CC	Sun Forte C++ compiler
df	Compaq Fortran compiler
gcc	GNU C++ compiler and linker
icl	Intel 32- bit compiler for Windows
icc	Intel 32- bit compiler for Linux
ecl	Intel 64- bit compiler for Windows
ecc	Intel 64- bit compiler for Linux
midl	Microsoft IDL compiler
msvc	Microsoft C++ compiler
msrc	Microsoft RC resource compiler
os390	Compiler and linker for IBM mainframes
xlC	IBM Visual Age compiler for AIX

Whichever compiler you use, it has to be installed and working from the command line. That means that the compiler command is on the path, and any other settings (such as INCLUDE and LIB environment variables) are correctly configured.

17.3.3 A quick introduction to the <cc> task

The core feature of this task is that it acts as a wrapper for all the stages of building native C and C++ programs on multiple platforms. In particular it accomplishes the following:

- Compiles C and C++ source in files with any of the suffixes .c, .cc, .cxx, .cpp, or .c++.
- Creates intermediate object files, executables, shared libraries, and static libraries.
- Can build files simply by specifying a fileset such as src/**/*.cpp.
- Parses files to determine dependencies.
- Supports multiple platforms and tool chains.

The task tries hard to bring the <javac> experience to the C and C++ world. It comes close to this with its automatic inclusion of all the source files in a directory tree, and its dependency checking. This avoids your having to replicate the makefile practice of listing naming dependencies, yet still gives you fast compilation.

The other feature of the task is cross-platform support. It does as well as it can here, given how radically different the build process is for different platforms and different tools. They have tried hard to stop things from getting too ugly, but it is still complicated. One of the hardest parts of this portability problem is that you do need to code and test your build on all platforms you intend to support. Furthermore, if you are using any but the most basic compiler options, you need to work out the specific options for every compiler and linker you intend to support.

This makes the <cc> task more complicated to use than most other Ant tasks. However, it is attempting to describe the entire native code build process for multiple platforms and tools in a single nested task:

```
<cc debug="false"
    link="executable"
    outfile="dist/application"
    objdir="build/objects"
    multithreaded="true"
    exceptions="true" >
    <compiler name="msvc" if="use-msvc"/>
    <compiler name="gcc" if="use-gcc"/>
    <fileset dir="src/cpp" includes="*.cpp"/>
    <linker name="msvc" if="use-msvc"/>
    <linker name="gcc" if="use-gcc"/>
    <syslibset libs="kernel32,user32"/>
</cc>
```

This single task declaration will build an application with the GNU and Microsoft tool suites, enabling multithreading and exceptions in the code, and producing a release build (debug="false"). That is quite an impressive achievement for 15 lines of XML.

We will return to the details if this task after exploring how we can use it in our JNI project.

17.4   BUILDING A JNI LIBRARY IN ANT

Java calls out to native libraries through JNI. This is a complex and powerful mechanism, so complex that whole books are needed to cover the subject adequately, and there are projects in the SourceForge Java foundry devoted to making it easier (specifically, JNI++). We do not want to get into these details, merely explore how to build and test JNI code inside Ant.

17.4.1 Steps to building a JNI library

The JNI core concept is that Java methods declared with the prefix `native` are bound to native libraries, libraries that are then dynamically loaded by the Java run-time. On Windows the native libraries are Dynamic Link Libraries (DLL), while on Unix shared libraries (.so) provide the same functionality. Other platforms have their own equivalents.

To write a new JNI library, take the following steps:

1 Write a Java class with `native` methods.

2 Compile the Java source into bytecodes.

3 Create a C++ header from the compiled classes with the javah tool.

4 Incorporate this header in a C++ project that creates a dynamic or shared library as its output.

5 Write the C++ code to perform the actual functionality needed.

6 Compile the code, pulling in the JNI header files from the JDK.

7 Link to library files in the JDK as needed to resolve external references.

Figure 17.1 is a graphic representation of the build process that we will implement in Ant.

Executing the native code requires a few more steps. The native library must be in the path of the Java run time. If the library is not in the path, the run time throws the error `java.lang.UnsatisfiedLinkError`, which should be familiar to most JNI developers. Indeed, getting the native library somewhere appropriate is often one of the foundational problems of any JNI project. Products like Java Web Start are taking steps at addressing this, but there is still much room for improvement.

When developing JNI libraries in a team, another minor problem is importing the JNI header files and libraries. These are all in the JDK, so unless all team members install their JDK in the same place, you cannot place hard-coded references to these files. You must use the JAVA_HOME environment variable as the base location of these files, and take into account OS-specific directory names.

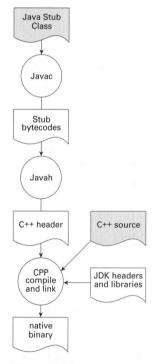

Figure 17.1
The core JNI build process combines Java and C++ build processes.

17.4.2 Writing the Java stub

Writing the Java code to export the native method calls is the easiest step:

```
package org.example.antbook.cpu;

public class CpuInfo {

    native long getCpuClock();

    static {
        System.loadLibrary("CpuInfo");
    }
}
```

This `CpuInfo` class currently exports one method, `getCpuClock`, containing a static initializer that loads the shared library by name.

Compiling this class is no different from a normal build.

```
<target name="compile" depends="init" >
  <javac srcdir="src" includes="**/*.java"
    destdir="${classes.dir}"/>
</target>
```

After running this task, we have a stub Java .class file, from which we can create the header file

Creating the C++ header

The C++ header file is from the class, through the task <javah>, which is a wrapper around the javah tool from the JDK. Although an optional task, it needs no external libraries other than those in the JDK:

```
<target name="headers" depends="compile">
  <javah destdir="${generated.dir}"
    force="yes"
    classpath="${classes.dir}">
      <class name="org.example.antbook.cpu.CpuInfo"/>
  </javah>
</target>
```

The task takes a classpath containing the stub class to work from, the name of the class, and an output directory, generating a header file in that directory named org_ tasklibs_CpuInfo.h. The javah program derives the name from the package and class declarations. The <javah> task does no dependency checking on the Java source, so it does not know when to generate a file. The force="true" attribute tells the task to always create header files, even if the destination exists. This is inefficient: the task always creates the header file, so the C++ compiler will always rebuild the library, even if nothing has changed. Unless and until the <javah> task gets dependency checking, you need to keep it off the main build or use an <uptodate> call to make the header generation target conditional on the destination file being out of date. Here we take the pain of recompilation, because our project is so small.

17.4.3 Writing the C++ class

The next step of the JNI development process is to write the C++ code. The Win32 version of this library is short and terse, relying on the inline assembler of Visual C++ to compile the code; the compiler understands the Pentium instruction `rdtsc` to read the timestamp counter, which is the core of our function. We implement this function in the file org_example_antbook_cpu_CpuInfo.cpp:

```
#include "org_example_antbook_cpu_CpuInfo.h"
JNIEXPORT jlong JNICALL
    Java_org_example_antbook_cpu_CpuInfo_getCpuClock
      (JNIEnv *,
      jobject) {
    __int64 timestamp;
    __int64 *pTimestamp=&timestamp;
    _asm rdtsc;
    _asm mov ecx,pTimestamp;
    _asm mov [ecx],eax;
    _asm mov [ecx+4],edx;
    return timestamp;
}
```

The `rdtsc` instruction stores the CPU clock tick count into two of the processor's 32-bit registers; we move each half of the result into a separate half of a variable that becomes the `jlong` result. This is the native mapping of Java's `long` integer. On Windows this maps to the nonstandard `__int64` datatype; we use this type explicitly to make clear what we are working with. We are planning to completely rewrite the function when we move to Linux, so there is no need to be portable at this stage.

To create the function prototype, we copied the declaration of the function from the header file, adding a reference to that file at the start of our C++ file source. This header file pulls in the JDK's header file jni.h, which declares all the Java datatypes and methods. This means that your C++ source files do not need to include any of the JDK files themselves, only those header files providing access to other libraries, such as the OS API itself.

Dealing with header files

The compiler needs access to all the included header files, the linker to any associated libraries. If you want to use an IDE to compile the source, you need to point the IDE at your JDK, which is very brittle and unlikely to work on different systems. Better to copy the files over into your source tree, either by hand or by using an Ant task:

```
<target name="includes">
  <copy todir="${build.dir}/imported/jni">
    <fileset dir="${env.JAVA_HOME}/include" includes="**/*.h" />
  </copy>
</target>
```

We do not need to do this with `<cc>`; instead we will point the task at the files in JDK using its `<include>` element. We will eventually have to deal with the fact that there is always a platform-specific subdirectory under JAVA_HOME/include that we need to pull in, such as include/win32 and include/linux.

17.4.4 Compiling the C++ source

Everything is ready for us to declare the `<cc>` task to build the C++ file. We do this in a target that depends upon the headers

```
<target name="cc-windows" depends="headers" >
  <cc debug="${build.debug}"
      link="shared"
      outfile="${dist.filename.nosuffix}"
      objdir="${obj.dir}"
      multithreaded="true"
      exceptions="true" >
      <compiler name="msvc" />
      <fileset dir="src/cpp/windows"/>
      <includepath location="${generated.dir}" />
      <sysincludepath location="${env.JAVA_HOME}/include" />
      <sysincludepath location="${env.JAVA_HOME}/include/win32" />
      <linker name="msvc" >
        <syslibset libs="kernel32,user32"/>
      </linker>
  </cc>
</target>
```

This is a complicated task declaration, so let's look at it in pieces. The task declaration covers the two tasks required by a C or C++ program: compilation and linking. Each of these has its own elements inside the task to control the specifics of that stage.

The opening tag

The opening tag of the task provides details about what we want to generate. All the attributes in the `<cc>` tag itself are cross-platform. For example, setting the debug attribute tells the compiler to generate debug information, and the linker to include it at link time. Every class written to support a specific compiler or linker will generate the appropriate options for that tool, but users of the task do not need to worry about such details, merely select the options:

```
<cc debug="${build.debug}"
    link="shared"
    outfile="CpuInfo"
    objdir="${obj.dir}"
    multithreaded="true"
    exceptions="true" >
```

The link attribute tells the task how to link the object files, to create library files or executables. Table 17.2 lists the possibilities. One interesting feature of the task is that you do not need to specify the full name of the library or executable file you want to generate, merely the basename; the task itself will determine the final name. For our shared library, we say `outfile="CpuInfo"`; it will become CpuInfo.dll on

Windows and CpuInfo.so on Unix. There are similar rules for the other output options; when generating library files it even adds a prefix to the start of the file name to indicate it is a library.

Table 17.2 The different types of output the \<cc\> task can generate

Link type	Meaning
Shared	Shared library, .so or .dll
Application	Executable; has .exe ending on Windows
Static	Static library, .a or .lib extension; Unix adds *lib* prefix
None	No linking

One mild inconvenience of the task as it stands is that there is no way to determine the name of the file that the task generates; you have to reinstate the rules yourself in a series of <condition> tests. If the task lets you name a property that would be set to the final file name, life would be easier.

The objdir parameter tells the task where intermediate object files should go; the final two options, multithread and exceptions, specify more options for the compiler and linker.

Configuring the compiler

Inside the task declaration, the first five nested elements are instructions to the compiler:

```
<compiler name="msvc" />
<fileset dir="src/cpp/windows" includes="**/*.cpp"/>
<includepath location="${generated.dir}" />
<sysincludepath location="${env.JAVA_HOME}/include" />
<sysincludepath location="${env.JAVA_HOME}/include/win32" />
```

First comes the selection of the compiler itself; the default is always GNU gcc. We will cover compiler declaration and configuration more in section 17.5. The next element is a fileset declaration pulling in our source files. We have created Windows and Unix subdirectories under the source, to keep everything separate. In a complex project, you may have common source as well as platform- and compiler-specific files, making fileset inclusion more complex. Conditional patternsets are the key to managing this.

The compiler also needs to know the location of include files in external directories. We use the <includepath> and <sysincludepath> elements to describe this. We list the javah-generated header file in an <includepath> element, and the Java JNI header files in two <sysincludepath> elements. We don't need to refer to Visual Studio's own header files, provided the INCLUDE environment variable is configured correctly.

Header files listed in the `<sysincludepath>` directory are not included in the dependency checks; they are assumed to never change. We do want dependency checking on the generated header file, which is why we point to that directory using `<includepath>`.

Configuring a linker

After compilation comes linking, which we specify with the linker element:

```
<linker name="msvc" >
  <syslibset libs="kernel32,user32"/>
</linker>
```

We do not specify the path to the library files here; the LINK tool must extract this from the LIB environment variable. We do have to specify which libraries we want to include, above and beyond the C or C++ run time. You can declare a library set inside the `<cc>` task, or inside the linker declaration itself. Once you add multiple conditional linkers to a `<cc>` task, declaring libraries inside the different linker declarations soon becomes the preferred option.

There are many linker options, such as setting a base address for the library, or enabling incremental linking, but we do not need any of those. The task documentation has complete details; we will look at some of the options when we customize a linker in section 17.6.4.

Running the compiler

With everything declared, we are ready to run the compiler. Let's see the output:

```
compile:
     [javac] Compiling 1 source file to
       C:\AntBook\Sections\Applying\cpp\build\classes
headers:
     [javah] ClassArgument.name=
              org.example.antbook.cpu.CpuInfo
cc-windows:
        [cc] 1 total files to be compiled.
        [cc] org_example_antbook_cpu_CpuInfo.cpp
        [cc] Creating library CpuInfo.lib and object CpuInfo.exp
```

The `compile` target compiles the Java source down to the .class file that the headers target uses to generate a native header file. This provides the foundation for the cc-Windows target, which then creates the DLL file. Clearly, its output messages could do with some improvement; a check at the output directory reveals that CpuInfo.dll has been created, even though this was not stated in the log. The logging messages will apparently be improved; all we see today are those of the compiler.

We now have our native library; let's try using it.

17.4.5   Deploying and testing the library

We are now at the testing and local deployment stage. We can test using JUnit, as usual, with a bit of planning.

Designing the test

The first test should be that the library loads and the method returns. A second test can verify that the clock count increases each call. With some knowledge of expected round-trip times it would be possible to verify that the round-trip time is in a sensible range; this could be added for a regression test in the future, but is vulnerable to changes in Java run time behavior. A third test can call the target repeatedly to determine the overhead of the call itself after the JIT has optimized everything. This number can be subtracted from any real performance measurements to give accurate measurements.

```
package org.example.antbook.cpu;
import junit.framework.*;

public class CpuInfoTest extends TestCase {

    private CpuInfo clock;

    public CpuInfoTest(String name) {
        super(name);
    }

    public void setUp() {
        clock=new CpuInfo();
    }

    public void testClockCallReturns() {
        long time1=clock.getCpuClock();
    }

    public void testClockCodeWorks() {
        long time1=clock.getCpuClock();
        long time2=clock.getCpuClock();
        long diff=time2-time1;
        System.out.println("Invocation time="+diff+" cycles");
        assertTrue(diff>0);
    }

    public void testJitOptimization() {
        int iterations=10000;
        long diff=spin(iterations);
        diff=spin(iterations);
        assertTrue(diff>0);
        int average=(int)(((float)diff)/iterations);
        System.out.println("Total time=" + diff+" cycles");
        System.out.println("Invocation time="+average+" cycles");
    }
```

```
    public long spin(int iterations) {
        long time1=clock.getCpuClock();
        long time2=0;
        for(int i=0;i<iterations;i++) {
            time2=clock.getCpuClock();
        }
        long diff=time2-time1;
        return diff;
    }

}
```

To calculate the average round-trip time after any JIT hotspot optimizations have taken place, we have to preheat everything, stressing the loop enough to trigger the optimizations. We do this by implementing the iterative loop in its own method, spin, and calling this twice, only logging the iteration time of the second loop.

Deploying the library

Before the test stands a chance of succeeding, the native library needs to be deployed to somewhere Java will pick it up. A reliable location appears to be the bin subdirectory of the JDK, at least on our test systems. We make no guarantee that the same directory will work on other systems; it may depend upon JRE settings.

```
<property name ="deploy.dir"
    location="${env.JAVA_HOME}/bin" />

<target name="deploy" depends="cc-windows">
  <copy
    file="${dist.dir}/${libname}"
    todir="${deploy.dir}" />
  <echo message="deployed to ${deploy.dir}" />
</target>
```

Running this target copies the file if it has changed, which it currently does every time we run the build, because <javah> regenerates the header files every run, and <cc> parses the source to determine header file dependencies.

```
deploy:
    [copy] Copying 1 file to C:\java\JDK\bin
    [echo] deployed to C:\java\JDK\bin
```

This deployment target will not work if the destination DLL exists and is in use, which happens if any running JVM has loaded it. The copy will fail, breaking the build.

The test target

We can invoke the test with <junit>, as we have done many times before. Here we configure <junit> to continue after any failure, using a conditional <fail> to stop the build if any test was unsuccessful. This lets us run every test, even if the predecessors fail.

```
<target name="test" depends="deploy">
  <junit printsummary="withOutAndErr"
    failureproperty="tests.failed"
    fork="yes">
    <classpath>
      <pathelement location="${classes.dir}" />
      <pathelement path="${dist.dir}" />
      <pathelement path="${java.class.path}" />
    </classpath>
    <formatter type="plain" usefile="false"/>
    <test name="org.example.antbook.cpu.CpuInfoTest" />
  </junit>
  <fail if="tests.failed">Tests failed</fail>
</target>
```

If the test succeeds then the tail of the output of the executing ant test will be a trace similar to the following, showing the round-trip time from Java to a native library.

```
test:
    [junit] Testsuite: org.example.antbook.cpu.CpuInfoTest
    [junit] Tests run: 3, Failures: 0, Errors: 0,
            Time elapsed: 0.371 sec
    [junit] ------------- Standard Output ---------------
    [junit] Invocation time=761 cycles
    [junit] Total time=1514496 cycles
    [junit] Invocation time=151 cycles
    [junit] ------------- --------------- ---------------
    [junit]
    [junit] Testcase: testClockCallReturns took 0.221 sec
    [junit] Testcase: testClockCodeWorks took 0 sec
    [junit] Testcase: testJitOptimization took 0.02 sec
BUILD SUCCESSFUL
```

What does this tell us? Well, it shows that the library is loading (testClockCall-Returns), and that repeated calls increment the counter (testClockCode-Works), so the assembler code is working. We can also see that the first test took 0.221 seconds, which must be the time to load the Java classes and the DLL; this is the overhead of loading a library. The second test takes 761 cycles, on a par with the 600-cycle, round-trip time for a Windows NT Ring Zero API call from a Win32 application.

The round-trip time after optimization drops to 151 cycles, which is a more acceptable number.[1] We can now consider using this library to time the execution of routines in our application.

---

[1] Test specifics: Java1.4 on Windows XP on a PII/333 laptop, in battery mode, in midflight between Los Angeles and Portland, Oregon. Your results may vary.

Improving library lookup

The least elegant part of this build and test process is the need to place native libraries onto the path of the run time. Java 1.2 added a new property, `java.library.path`, to specify the search path for native libraries. Let's try setting this property in our JUnit test and see if it works. Here is the new target:

```
<target name="test" depends="cc-windows">
  <junit printsummary="withOutAndErr"
    failureproperty="tests.failed"
    fork="yes">
    <sysproperty key="java.library.path"
      value="${dist.dir}"/>
    <classpath>
      <pathelement location="${classes.dir}" />
      <pathelement path="${dist.dir}" />
      <pathelement path="${java.class.path}" />
    </classpath>
    <formatter type="plain" usefile="false"/>
    <test name="org.example.antbook.cpu.CpuInfoTest" />
  </junit>
  <fail if="tests.failed">Tests failed</fail>
</target>
```

Notice how we have removed the `deploy` target from our dependency list; we no longer need it, nor do we need to remove a library from our JRE as part of the clean target. We should find supporting other operating systems easier too, as we no longer need to worry about the OS-specific name of the shared library that `<cc>` is going to generate.

What happens when we clean up the previous build and run this target? It all works as planned, provided the `fork` attribute is set to true. Set it to false and the run time does not pick up the property setting, so the library is not loaded: all the tests fail. Remember when using `<java>` to run Java programs with native libraries, always fork the JVM.

17.5   GOING CROSS-PLATFORM

Now that we know Ant can build and test a native library, we have to ask: how does it support a Unix build as well as a Windows library? We want to rebuild our code for Linux/x86, using the GNU tools: gcc and ar, to build our library. We have waited until we have the build process working on one platform before addressing a second.

All the Java code is going to work cross-platform, so all the build and test stages related to the Java source should work without changes. That leaves two areas: the C++ source and the targets to compile it.

17.5.1   Migrating the C++ source

Although the same machine code to measure the clock will work independently of the operating system, describing that machine code in a C++ source file depends upon the compiler. To get started, we first comment out all the assembler and create a stub implementation that returns zero every call. Once we have the build and test process working, we will port the assembly code.

17.5.2 Extending the build file

The <cc> task lets you state the compilation settings for multiple compilers, with different conditional <compiler> and <linker> elements. Theoretically, we could extend our existing <cc> task declaration to support Linux by adding the appropriate tool declarations, and then make the choice of Windows and Linux tools conditional on if-windows and if-linux properties. We choose not to take this path for two reasons. First, we would have to extend this conditional inclusion even to source and <sysincludepath> references, which would make for a very complex target. Second, we don't want to break a target that works on one platform. Instead, we will copy the contents of the existing cc-windows target to a new one, cc-linux, which we will configure to support the GNU tools on Linux.

The core customization is simply to select the GNU compiler and linker, then pull the Linux version of the JNI headers into our compile. We also make the target conditional upon the OS being Linux, by setting a property when Ant processes the build file on Linux on an x86 family CPU, and then retrofitting a Windows-specific test to the original target:

```
<condition property="is-linux">
    <os name="linux" arch="x86" />
</condition>
<condition property="is-windows">
  <os family="windows"/>
</condition>

<target name="cc-linux" depends="headers" if="is-linux">
  <cc debug="${build.debug}"
      link="shared"
      outfile="${dist.filename.nosuffix}"
      objdir="${obj.dir}"
      multithreaded="true"
      exceptions="true" >
    <compiler name="gcc"/>
    <fileset dir="src/cpp/linux" includes="**/*.cpp" />
    <includepath location="${generated.dir}" />
    <sysincludepath location="${env.JAVA_HOME}/include" />
    <sysincludepath location="${env.JAVA_HOME}/include/linux"/>
    <linker name="gcc" />
  </cc>
</target>
```

We have to add a high-level target, cc, which depends on both of the conditional compilation targets; only one of which will ever run on a single platform's build.

```
<target name="cc" depends="cc-windows,cc-linux"/>
```

We then alter the existing dependent targets of cc-windows, such as test, to depend upon the cc target, so that they will run the appropriate compiler target for their platform.

17.5.3 Testing the migration

As we have not yet migrated the assembly language, we don't expect all the tests to work, but the first test, that a call to the method returns, should already work. Let's run the build and see:

```
cc-linux:
        [cc] Starting dependency analysis for 1 files.
        [cc] Parsing build/generated/org_example_antbook_cpu_CpuInfo.h
        [cc] 0 files are up to date.
        [cc] 1 files to be recompiled from dependency analysis.
        [cc] 1 total files to be compiled.test:
     [junit] Running org.example.antbook.cpu.CpuInfoTest
     [junit] Tests run: 3, Failures: 2, Errors: 0, Time elapsed: 0.129 sec
     [junit] Testcase: testClockCallReturns took 0.023 sec
     [junit] Testcase: testClockCodeWorks took 0.017 sec
     [junit] FAILED
```

This fragment of the build file shows first that the cc-linux target was called to build the files, and then that our first test did pass, but the second two failed. We now have a build process that can create JNI headers from Java files, compile C++ classes to implement the methods on two different platforms, and then test them. Actually implementing the native code on the second platform is the one remaining task.

17.5.4 Porting the code

The final bit of work is to port the timer code, or, to be precise, find the appropriate code fragment with Google, then customize it:

```
JNIEXPORT jlong JNICALL
    Java_org_example_antbook_cpu_CpuInfo_getCpuClock
      (JNIEnv *,
      jobject) {
    long long int timestamp;
    asm volatile (".byte 0x0f, 0x31" : "=A" (timestamp));
    return timestamp;
}
```

Now, we can run the build and see what the results are:

```
test:
     [junit] Running org.example.antbook.cpu.CpuInfoTest
     [junit] Tests run: 3, Failures: 0, Errors: 0, Time elapsed: 0.091 sec
     [junit] Testsuite: org.example.antbook.cpu.CpuInfoTest
     [junit] Tests run: 3, Failures: 0, Errors: 0, Time elapsed: 0.091 sec
     [junit] ------------ Standard Output --------------
     [junit] Invocation time=594 cycles
     [junit] Total time=1469967 cycles
     [junit] Invocation time=146 cycles
```

```
[junit] ------------- ---------------- ---------------
[junit]
[junit] Testcase: testClockCallReturns took 0.023 sec
[junit] Testcase: testClockCodeWorks took 0.003 sec
[junit] Testcase: testJitOptimization took 0.023 sec
BUILD SUCCESSFUL
```

These are the timings on a system identical to the Windows box, still with Java 1.4, but this time running Redhat 7.1 Linux. Notice that the optimized round-trip time takes nearly exactly the same time as the Windows system.

We believe that the Linux version of the C++ code should work on any x86 platform that supports gcc, from Windows to Solaris Intel Edition. If we had set out to work only with gcc, it would have been easier for us to migrate the code as there would be one version of the C++ source, and only one <cc> task needed. We would have had to make the <sysincludespath> references to includes/windows, includes/linux, and includes/solaris conditional, but that is all we would need to do to rebuild our JNI library on each platform we support.

This makes using gcc across the board a very attractive option for JNI development with Ant, even for developers with a copy of the Microsoft tools and debugger, the latter being the main compelling reason to stick with the Microsoft product.

17.6   *LOOKING AT <CC> IN MORE DETAIL*

We promised earlier that we would return to the <cc> task after showing it in use. It is time to look at some of the features we did not use. Before we do so, we want to repeat an important caveat: none of this is stable; all of it may change. Indeed, one reason we kept our example so simple was to increase its stability. That said, there are some interesting features in the <cc> task, and while some of the required and optional attributes may change, the core features will be present in some form or other.

17.6.1   Defining preprocessor macros

Once you have native code building, a possible immediate requirement is to define preprocessor macros. You can use the <defineset> datatype to do this. The simplest way to do this is to declare your definitions inside the compiler task:

```
<target name="cc-linux" depends="headers" if="is-linux">
  <cc debug="${build.debug}"
      link="shared"
      outfile="${dist.filename.nosuffix}"
      objdir="${obj.dir}"
      multithreaded="true"
      exceptions="true" >
      <compiler name="gcc"/>
      <fileset dir="src/cpp/linux" includes="**/*.cpp"/>
      <defineset defines="DEBUG"/>
      <includepath location="${generated.dir}" />
      <sysincludepath location="${env.JAVA_HOME}/include" />
      <sysincludepath location="${env.JAVA_HOME}/include/linux"/>
```

```
      <linker name="gcc" />
   </cc>
</target>
```

We do not want to do this, because we want to share the definitions among different tasks. Instead, we create a `<defineset>` in our `init` target:

```
<condition property="build.debug.istrue">
  <istrue value="${build.debug}" />
</condition>
<defineset id="build.defines">
  <define name="DEBUG" if="build.debug.istrue" />
  <define name="RELEASE" unless="build.debug.istrue" />
</defineset>
```

This datatype has an ID, so we can refer to it later. Its two definitions are conditional on the `build.debug` property; if the property is true then DEBUG is defined; if it is not true then RELEASE is defined. Because the condition in the `<define>` tag is based on whether or not a property is defined, and because when we do a release build we set `build.debug` to false, we need to create a new property that is only defined when `build.debug` is true. Hence we place the `<condition>` test immediately before we declare our definesets. We can now refer to these preprocessor definitions in both our compiler targets, simply by referring to them in the task:

```
<target name="cc-linux" depends="headers" if="is-linux">
  <cc debug="${build.debug}"
      link="shared"
      outfile="${dist.filename.nosuffix}"
      objdir="${obj.dir}"
      multithreaded="true"
      exceptions="true" >
      <compiler name="gcc"/>
      <fileset dir="src/cpp/linux"/>
      <defineset refid="build.defines"/>
      <includepath location="${generated.dir}" />
      <sysincludepath location="${env.JAVA_HOME}/include" />
      <sysincludepath location="${env.JAVA_HOME}/include/linux"/>
      <linker name="gcc" />
  </cc>
</target>
```

17.6.2   Linking to libraries with <libset>

To link against libraries other than the compiler's default set, you need to name them using the `<libset>` datatype, which you can declare inside the `<cc>` task, or inside the linker element.

```
<cc
    outfile="build/app"
    multithreaded="true"
    exceptions="true" >
    <compiler name="gcc"/>
    <fileset dir="src"/>
```

```
    <linker name="gcc" />
    <libset libs="cclib/tools,cclib/services">
</cc>
```

You do not need to give the libraries the platform-specific extension; it uses the appropriate one, such as .a and .so for Unix, and .lib for Windows libraries. Different implementations may have different ways of accessing system libraries: the Microsoft linker relies on the LIB environment variable; the gcc linker searches for well-known library locations such as /usr/lib.

If you want to share libraries between targets, you can do it by declaring them as a datatype with an ID.

```
<libset id="common.libset" libs="cclib/tools,cclib/services" />
```

To use the libraries in a compilation, you just refer to the `<libset>` by ID:

```
<cc
    outfile="build/app"
    multithreaded="true"
    exceptions="true"
    >
    <compiler name="gcc"/>
    <fileset dir="src"/>
    <linker name="gcc" />
    <libset refid="common.libset">
</cc>
```

As well as declaring libraries in a `<libset>` to keep a large native application's build under control, you might find it useful to keep common `<libset>` declarations in an XML file fragment, which we introduced in section 9.5.4. You could group different libraries into different sets—corba, com, mozilla, for examples—and then reuse them in projects as needed.

17.6.3   Configuring compilers and linkers

There is one final area of customization in a native language project, and that is changing the settings on compilers and linkers. The `<compiler>` and `<linker>` elements of the `<cc>` target not only let you do this, they are stand-alone datatypes, enabling you to declare the common linker and compiler for your entire project, and using it where appropriate. The value of this grows with the size and complexity of your project.

Configuring compilers

Inside the compiler element, whether it is inside a `<cc>` task or a stand-alone datatype declaration, you can nest the `<defineset>` element that we introduced in section 17.5.1. Here, for example, is a declaration for a compiler configuration derived from msvc, with extra options for items such as warnings and code generation for the Pentium Pro and a conditional definition of a preprocessor macro in debug builds.

```
<compiler id="studio" name="msvc">
  <compilerarg value="/G6"/>
  <compilerarg value="/W3"/>
  <compilerarg value="/Ze"/>
  <compilerarg value="/Zc:forScope"
    if="msvc.version.is.devenv"/>
  <defineset>
    <define name="_CRTDBG_MAP_ALLOC"
      if="build.debug.istrue"/>
  </defineset>
</compiler>
```

To use this declaration, we just reference it inside the <cc> task:

```
<compiler refid="studio" />
```

You can also extend an existing configuration, which is an interesting idea:

```
<compiler id="studio2" extends="studio">
  <compilerarg value="/Gm"/>
  <compilerarg value="/ZI"/>
</compiler>
```

This extended definition retains all the previous customization and adds more arguments. A likely use would be to define separate debug and release compilers, each with a different set of optimization and compilation flags.

When you use a configured compiler inside a <cc> task, all the compiler settings you add in the task also apply. This means that you can configure your core compiler settings, then in different <cc> tasks, add different options to this base configuration.

One fact worth knowing is that the <cc> task caches the arguments that went into building the output files, the compiler arguments for each object file, and the linker arguments for the linked file. When you change the compiler or linker arguments, the task notices and rebuilds the affected files. There is therefore no need to run the clean target whenever you change your settings, though we still think it is a good idea.

17.6.4   Customizing linkers

Linkers, and indeed any of the <cc> task's processors, can be configured similarly to compilers. Nested arguments and tags can change behavior, and you can give linkers an ID for later reference. In addition, you can extend a linker definition from a previous one. As an example, let's configure a linker that restricts our Windows DLL to a minimum version of Windows, and sets the base address of the library:

```
<linker id="nt4linker" name="msvc"
    base="201333515">
  <linkerarg value="/version:4.0" />
  <syslibset libs="kernel32,user32"/>
</linker>
```

Again, you can reference a linker inside the <cc> task:

```
<linker refid="nt4linker" />
```

As with customizable compilers, if you want to configure linkers you must be doing some complex native code. One of the example build files that comes with the task is designed to build the C++ version of Xerces, showing that you can build a very complex C++ project in a single build file.

17.7 DISTRIBUTING NATIVE LIBRARIES

Remember how we had to set the `java.library.path` property to the directory containing our JNI library before running the JVM?

If you are distributing code you need to do the same in any `<java>` calls that run JNI programs, or any shell scripts that start the programs. When trying to integrate native libraries with a web application, you need either to modify the application server's own startup properties or get the library into the execution path. An Ant-based install script could copy the library into place, just as our `deploy` target did. However you do it, you should shut down the application server first, to ensure that Ant can overwrite any existing version of library, and that the application server will reload the new library.

For client-side code, applets cannot download native libraries for security reasons. Java Web Start does let end users download and run native libraries, and is smart enough to download the appropriate libraries for the client platform.

Java Web Start

A good way to redistribute native libraries with Java applications is to use Java Web Start. This is because it will download whatever native libraries a signed Web Start application declares that it needs.

There is no built-in support for Java Web Start in Ant, but this is corrected by the Venus Application Publisher Vamp product family (http://www.vamphq.com). Along with their publisher toolset comes a couple of Ant tasks for Web Start code delivery. One of these tasks, `<vampwar>`, builds a WAR file containing a web application comprised of the application you wish to distribute and the servlet you need to enable Web Start clients to download your application using the JNLP wire protocol. The task will even sign the downloadable JAR files if you provide it with the right information.

This means that the task can take your code and other resources, and generate a ready-to-go web application to deliver to end users. You just need to get that web application to the server, which is the classic deployment problem for Ant to solve.

You are still going to have to learn about Java Web Start and JNLP from the SDK documentation, and invest time getting your JNLP descriptors right, but the mundane steps of altering your web application to support JNLP and then setting up all the build process steps to package up your application are handled for you by the Vamp tasks.

17.8   SUMMARY

Writing native code to integrate with Java is a complex process, especially once you go cross-platform. You could drop down to an IDE or Make, but these bring with them all their inherent problems inherent in these tools, problems that Ant fixed for pure Java code some time ago. If you resort to external build tools for the native code sections, you make your build more complex and less portable than it needs to be.

The <cc> task, available as a download from http://sf.net/projects/ant-contrib, is the key to compiling native code in Ant. In one single declaration, you can compile and link a directory tree full of C or C++ source, creating your application library. It may seem complex, with the <compiler> and <linker> elements to configure the stages of the build, and the <libset>, <defineset>, and <includespath> elements to provide input to the stages. Consider, however, what you get in return. You get to replace one or more makefiles with one or two targets in your build file. You stop having to worry about header file dependencies, and you get to integrate your C++ code with your Java build, test, and deploy process.

The <cc> task is being used to build libraries or programs as part of a larger Java project, and for large, stand-alone native applications. As the task matures, more people may use Ant as a build tool for pure C++ programs because it makes sense. You can write portable build files that use the <cc> task with all of Ant's packaging and deployment facilities; build files that are easy to maintain. Who knows, the era of the makefile may be drawing to a close.

You don't need to wait for that to happen to use the <cc> task. We have shown how to use it for JNI code generation, with an admittedly simple native library. Yet our build file will scale with new code; all you need to do to add new native classes is write the Java stub, the C++ implementation, and the JUnit tests, and then add the stub class to the <javah> class list. Ant build files work with C++ scale just as well as they do for Java projects.

C H A P T E R   1 8

Production deployment

18.1 The challenge of different
     application servers   432
18.2 Working with operations   437
18.3 Addressing the deployment
     challenge with Ant   440
18.4 Introducing Ant's deployment
     power tools   442

18.5 Building a production
     deployment process   446
18.6 Deploying to specific
     application servers   456
18.7 Verifying deployment   459
18.8 Best practices   462
18.9 Summary   463

We introduced Ant's deployment tasks in chapter 7. We have covered web applications, EJB applications, web services, and even native libraries, and it is time to look again at the deployment problem. This time we will address the challenge of deploying an enterprise or web application to a production application server rather than a local development box.

What differentiates a production system deployment from a development one? Here are some of the attributes of a production system that you may encounter:

- An operations team manages the system, rather than the developers themselves.
- Different application servers may host the application.
- The servers may be remote and deployment harder because of security systems in place.
- The deployment process needs to be more robust, with a rollback mechanism.
- The content deployed is more complex: static content as well as a web/EJB application.
- You may need to deploy to a cluster of multiple servers, with a rolling update to try to keep the system live throughout the process.

Ant can address most of the technical problems one way or another. The hardest is probably that of a live update of a server cluster. That needs coordination with load balancing routers or with server-specific tools to automate the process, though even here Ant can assist. That leaves the fact that someone else manages the system.

We are going to look at production-side deployment, first by examining what problems supporting different application servers adds to the build process, then by introducing some of the advanced deployment tasks that Ant offers. We will then design and demonstrate a build process for deploying to multiple servers of different types. After looking at some server-specific deployment techniques, we will finish with a test to validate the deployment process itself.

18.1 THE CHALLENGE OF DIFFERENT APPLICATION SERVERS

If you can avoid having to target different application servers, do so, because they all have their differences, both major and minor. If you cannot avoid it, it is best to find out early and start preparing. Here are some of the problems you may encounter.

18.1.1 Fundamentally different underlying behaviors

The application servers may support the same API, but have slightly different implicit behaviors. This is a consequence of the different implementations of the servlet and J2EE specifications.

As an example, on Tomcat 3.2, `HttpRequest.getCookies` returns an array of cookies of zero length when there are no cookies; Tomcat 4.0 returns a null pointer instead. This means that although this code works on Tomcat 3.2, on Tomcat 4.0 it throws a `NullPointerException`:

```
public Cookie getAuthCookie(HttpServletRequest request) {
    Cookie authCookie = null;
    Cookie[] cookies = request.getCookies();
    for (int i = 0; i < cookies.length; i++) {
        if (cookies[i].getName().equals("auth")) {
            return cookies[i];
        }
    }
    return null;
}
```

The problem is that some implementations of the servlet API return an empty array when there are no cookies, others return `null`. The specification says `null` is correct, but the erroneous behavior of the two systems on which we developed lulled us into writing incorrect code, shown here in bold. The fix is quite simple; we add a check for a `null`:

```
public Cookie getAuthCookie(HttpServletRequest request) {
    Cookie authCookie = null;
    Cookie[] cookies = request.getCookies();
    int limit = (cookies!=null) ? cookies.length : 0;
```

```
        for (int i = 0; i < limit; i++) {
            if (cookies[i].getName().equals("auth")) {
                return cookies[i];
            }
        }
        return null;
    }
```

This kind of defect can live anywhere in your system; anywhere it holds an assumption about the behavior of the underlying implementation. This can be hard to track down. We found and fixed this particular bug by redeploying a version of the program with full debug information included; once we found that the errant line contained the `cookies.length` test, we could infer what the problem was.

The only way to find these problems is through extensive tests; HttpUnit and Cactus are your friends. The role of Ant is executing these functional tests on every target system and presenting the reports cleanly.

18.1.2   Different Java run-time behavior

Is the target system running the same JVM version as the staging systems? With the same version of the JVM: client or server? What threading mechanism is it using? How is its memory and garbage collector configured?

Any difference in the underlying JRE is going to affect your code somehow, be it performance, synchronization, or memory usage. You should, of course, be using the same JVM in development as production. Operations staff, as do developers, sometimes take the initiative to upgrade or downgrade JVM for reasons of their own, which makes synchronizing JVM versions and configurations harder to control than one might think.

We could add a new test that validates properties to our `<happy>` JSP tag, which would let us name a property and its required value. Then, we could write JSPs to assert what our system properties must be:

```
<happy:happy property="java.version" value="1.3.1_02"/>
<happy:happy property="java.vm.name" value="Java HotSpot(TM) Server VM"/>
```

The problem here is that a change between Java version 1.3.1_02 and version 1.4 might happen some time after deployment, and it may be an improvement. Either you update the JSP to support the new version and not the old one, or you enhance the tests to support a list of valid numbers, maybe substring matches. Maintenance like this after deployment is unwelcome; if you design forward-looking rules, you may find that they don't actually work six months after the go-live date when someone updates the system. It is much better to leave such versioning details to people rather than hardcoded tests.

What we can do is write a JSP to list all properties, though of course a security manager may intercept that; an alternate approach would be a JSP that takes a property name as an argument and returns the value as a response. You can then query settings in a browser to diagnose problems, or use HttpUnit tests to fetch the values, parse them, and verify that the server is what you expected.

We make do with a JSP to list the properties, neglecting security manager issues until we encounter them. We should password protect this file and all other administrative pages, of course.

```
<%@ page language="java"  %>
<%@ page session="false"  %>
<%@ page import="java.util.Enumeration" %>
<%@ page import="java.util.Properties" %>
<html><body><table>
<%
    Properties props=System.getProperties();
    for (Enumeration e = props.propertyNames(); e.hasMoreElements();) {
      String key=(String)e.nextElement();
      String value=props.getProperty(key);
      %>
      <tr><td><%=key%></td><td><%=value%></td></tr>
     <%
    }
%>
</table></body></html>
```

This page is purely for human diagnostics; we do not run any automated tests against it. We also want to tack in some version tests.

Asserting which libraries must be included in the system

Since section 15.4.4, our <happy> JSP tag has offered a way of asserting that a named class must exist. This lets you dictate the minimum version of Java supported, such as with a statement that Java 1.4 or later is required:

```
<happy:happy classMustExist="java.lang.CharSequence"
  errorText="We need Java 1.4 or later"/>
```

This technique is an effective way of setting an absolute barrier against old versions of Java. This assertion technique is useful when you have many external libraries that you depend upon; a single JSP can probe for all of them, providing a single file you can retrieve to verify that the libraries are all present and available. You could fetch this file by hand; we point you at <get>, HttpUnit, and Canoo WebTest as the automated choices.

18.1.3   Coping with different API implementations

A server may give you its own implementations of the JAXP APIs, or other elements of the J2EE library, or other standard packages such as the Java management API, JMX. If you redistribute your own versions things may break; if you rely on the supplied version you need to retest everything. As an example, many complex applications depend upon Xerces being present; if your application server supplies something different, things might break.

Usually experimentation and experience help you determine what works and what doesn't. We went back to our HappyTag.java tag for configuration and added a test for the XML parser, one that extracts the parser name and verifies that it found the string we passed as parser name. See listing 18.1.

Listing 18.1   Additions to HappyTag.java to verify parsers

```java
private String parserName = null;

/**
 *@jsp:attribute      required="false"
 */
public void setParserName(String parserName) {
    this.parserName = parserName;
}

public void testParserName() throws JspException {
    if(parserName!=null) {
        String parser=getParserName();
        if(parser.indexOf(parserName) == -1) {
          throw new JspException("Parser "+parserName
                +" was not found; we are using "
                +parser);
        }
    }
}

public String getParserName() throws JspException {
    try {
        SAXParserFactory saxParserFactory =
            SAXParserFactory.newInstance();
        SAXParser saxParser = saxParserFactory.newSAXParser();
        String saxParserName = saxParser.getClass().getName();
        return saxParserName;
    } catch (Exception e) {
        throw new JspException(e);
    }
}
```

With the addition of a call to testParserName() in our class's doStartTag() method, we can then have a test in a file such as

```
<happy:happy parserName="crimson"/>
```

When this page is loaded, either everything is happy, or we see an error such as

```
javax.servlet.jsp.JspException: Parser crimson was not found;
   we are using org.apache.xerces.jaxp.SAXParserImpl
```

Throwing an error in this situation is a bit extreme as almost everything that works with Crimson should work with Xerces. However, the opposite is not true: there are many things that work with Xerces, but not Crimson. We can enforce our need for Xerces by stating this in the happiness test:

```
<happy:happy parserName="xerces"/>
```

There is no point running this test every 15 minutes on a live server, but when you bring up a new system or run regression tests after an update, you should run through all these tests; the HttpUnit tests should fetch the happy.jsp health page after every deployment.

These tests are somewhat brittle against improvements in the underlying system; we don't know that a SAX implementation bound via JNI to the Expat XML parser won't work; we just haven't tested it yet. However, we take the view that the choice of implementations of XML parsers, web service APIs, and the like is so important we need to make sure that the run time provides the versions we want.

18.1.4 Vendor-specific libraries

Sometimes you need access to vendor-supplied libraries. For a cross-platform application, you need to call vendor-specific classes using reflection, or simply by having wrapper classes that provide access; your application must then load the appropriate wrapper class at run time. Ant provides no help in this process, unless you want selective inclusion of source files at compile time. What you can do with Ant is explicitly differentiate between those libraries you depend upon at build time, and those you include in the WAR file.

18.1.5 Deployment descriptors

The deployment descriptors for each platform often need tuning. We showed how to generate custom web.xml files in section 12.4. The mechanics of customizing deployment descriptors are relatively straightforward with XDoclet, though determining what needs tuning is hard.

Targeting different application servers with EJBs is complicated, because you need to generate the server-specific deployment descriptors. Here you can use the different `<ejbdoclet>` subtasks, and the different `<ejbjar>` nested tasks to create the specific EJB JAR files for your target system.

18.1.6 Server-specific deployment processes

The actual deployment mechanism for each platform can vary wildly. Ant can address this, and you can always deploy by hand until you are ready to write the Ant support. Although this can be labor intensive, it is actually one of the least dangerous differences between servers, and much less worrisome than subtle run-time variations.

18.1.7 Server-specific management

The operational aspects of the server—security, performance, load balancing options, and the management interface—are usually significantly different. There is little Ant can do in this area. When the Java Community Process working group on server management has finished, we may have a standard API for managing and working with application servers. Ant could then add some tasks to issue calls to the servers, calls that work against multiple platforms. Do not hold your breath for these tasks; we will all have to muddle along for some time.

18.2 WORKING WITH OPERATIONS

In a production environment, people other than the developers look after the system. This is good. They understand about security and system management, and *they* can answer the pager at three in the morning. We developers have to build a system that meets their needs; one that is secure, manageable, and doesn't usually generate support calls late at night. We also have to look after our own interests: we do not want the first action of operations to be "wake up the developers."

How do you design, build, and deploy a system to work with operations? The key is to treat operations problems as just another part of the big software development process, with use cases, tests, and defect tracking; all under SCM.

18.2.1 Operations use cases

The tasks that operations need to perform on the system— back up and restore the database, track down why one user cannot log in, identify the IP address of a heavy user—are all use cases that your server needs to support, one way or another. Work with operations to find out what they want to do, and support it, either directly in the application, or in accompanying software and documentation.

18.2.2 Operations tests

Where there are use cases, there are tests. Once you know what operations wants to do, you can write semiautomated tests, and then run them. Regression tests on configuration are a particular area of interest: imagine if a configuration failure causes the clock on a network drive to be eight hours out, confusing the housekeeping routine into deleting files the moment the server creates them. It's easy enough to fix the problem on a single system, but why not write a test routine that you run server-side first? A routine to verify that the remote system's clock is within an acceptable range.

We have actually been writing such tests as we go along, especially in chapters 12 and 13. All of our server-side happiness tests, implemented in our JSP <happy> tag and JSPs and tested through HttpUnit, are in fact regression tests for configuration issues we have encountered.

With Ant we can build, deploy, and run these regression tests every time we build and deploy our service. This does not mean that the tests are easy to write; a web service we were working on had some tests that took whole days to write and validate. Yet just as the benefit of unit tests grows over time, the value of having tests to validate the server configuration and operations' use cases grows over the operational lifespan of the service. As a successful service should run for much longer than its development time takes, these tests do pay for themselves.

18.2.3   Operations defect tracking

If you have use cases and regression tests, you need to round everything off with defect tracking. A web server running Scarab (from tigris.org) or bugzilla (http://www.mozilla.org/projects/bugzilla/) should suffice.

For the defect tracking database to be useful, all the symptoms of the problems must be noted, such as "throughput a quarter of that expected," along with the cause, "accidental use of CAT-3 LAN cable," and the fix, "replaced with new CAT-5 cable." This is all obvious stuff. What is essential is that you do not wait until the system is in staging before you start creating this database: the defect tracking should begin the moment you first start bringing up the first version of the application on your local server. The developers, through building and deploying a service many times a day, gain more early experience in the issues than anyone else does. This knowledge needs to be stored in the defect tracking system unless they want to carry the pager every weekend.

18.2.4   Integrating operations with the build process

The obvious implication of the previous ideas is that the operations team needs to be involved early. You cannot build a system and then just hand it off for delivery. There is no room for the waterfall model in modern software development processes, and we must prevent the final stage of the project, deployment, from taking on the look and feel of the waterfall. We all know the waterfall doesn't work. It isn't flexible or responsive, which is why modern processes abhor it. Yet, as figure 18.1 shows, it is still there.

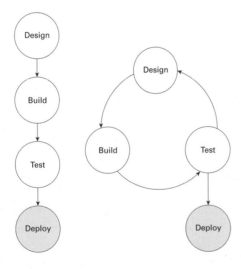

Figure 18.1
The waterfall process, on the left, we all know is broken. But look how an iterative development cycle can revert to a waterfall at the final stage.

What can we do? We can bring operations in from the beginning. Have them support your local developer servers, rather than just the staging and deployment systems. Then whenever you make a new build, you can deploy it through their processes.

Anyone who has worked with operations organizations will immediately know that the notion of fully automated deployment from the developer's own systems will not fly. Some operations teams believe that deployment consists of developers giving them a "gold disk" of the server software on CD, which operations manually install and test on staging servers before the final deployment. Some teams won't give developers access to the system for security reasons, even though they don't audit code line by line, or JAR files class by class. Clearly, our proposal for a tightly integrated process will not immediately mesh with such groups, but we don't see that the classic waterfall deployment process is adequate, especially for web services. The problem with web services, in particular, is that you need access to the production server with a debugger to solve integration problems. The waterfall model of handing off, staging, and finally deploying to the live site does not address such integration problems, and isn't responsive or flexible enough.

Integrating deployment

What do we propose? As we said: involve operations from the outset. They manage your development servers and get used to dealing with all the problems of the system. They can also get used to dealing with system updates taking place on an hourly basis by letting Ant and automated build tools take a central role in the deployment process. See figure 18.2.

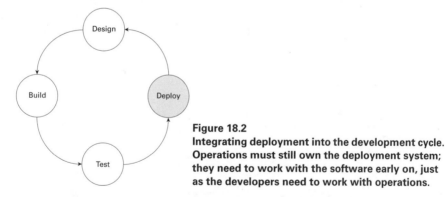

Figure 18.2
Integrating deployment into the development cycle. Operations must still own the deployment system; they need to work with the software early on, just as the developers need to work with operations.

Moving operations-managed deployment into the core development cycle won't be easy. Developers will have to work with operations earlier than normal; operations will have to deploy raw code and help support development tasks such as debugging, rebuilding clean systems, and just having more boxes to manage. These reasons are exactly why you need to do it: these are the problems that the teams need to solve together, automating all of the build, test, and deploy processes, then working together to address the manageability and scalability of the system. Try it; it might just work.

18.3 ADDRESSING THE DEPLOYMENT CHALLENGE WITH ANT

Ant cannot directly address source level or operations issues, but it can produce different WAR and EAR files for each targeted platform, and then deploy to them. It can also execute functional tests after deployment to validate that the system does behave as expected. It can also be the core of any continuous integration process, automating the build and deployment of the software.

18.3.1 Have a single source tree

The first tactic is to have a unified source tree, compiling all your code for all possible target systems in one single <javac> statement. With a unified source tree, you can build all the core server files together, and then create a single JAR of these classes. Ant can incorporate this JAR file into different WAR or EAR files, one for each target platform or system. These custom archive files can contain custom libraries and deployment descriptors.

18.3.2 Have a unified target for creating the archive files

As well as a single source tree, we want to have single targets to create the web.xml and WAR/EAR files. Ideally, we would like to have a single archive file we could reuse, but that is unrealistic because of the differences in library files and web.xml configurations that different target systems will need.

To enable single targets with different configurations, we use property files and set all the different options for a build, as shown in figure 18.3.

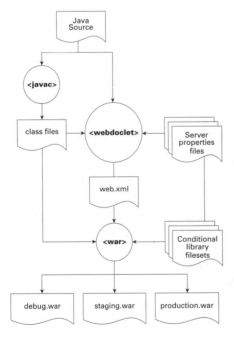

Figure 18.3
Creating custom WAR files from a single source file, using server-specific properties to controlling the <webdoclet> and <war> tasks

With a properties file for each target loaded in at the beginning of the run, we can create different WAR files for each target. Each of these has its own name, to avoid confusion.

The alternate tactic is to have separate build file targets for each target platform, with their own custom invocations of <webdoclet>, <war>, <ejbjar>, and other tasks. This gives you the most flexibility, and if you are only targeting two different systems, the cut-and-paste coding is manageable. However, you have two targets to maintain, and because you are no longer using the same build targets for deployment as production, you may not notice that you are failing to keep the targets in sync until you go live. Single targets with property-file based customization are more robust.

18.3.3   Run Ant server-side to deploy

How are we going to use Ant to deploy to different systems, even through firewalls and with an operations team in charge of the process? We are going to run it server-side. First, we need to list the actions we have to perform, by hand and with Ant, to prepare for this.

1   Create subdirectories under dist/ for each destination system.

2   Build the WAR files into the subdirectories.

3   Implement a separate deployment build file for each server type. These build files are designed to deploy to a local server, using environment variables and a properties file to customize the deployment to the specific platform.

4   Copy deployment build files and shell scripts into the dist subdirectories.

If we do all this, we will have separate localhost deployment packages for each target platform. We can run these locally, to deploy to our development system, run them on the staging systems, or run them on the deployment servers and update them in situ.

The Ant files run on the server can get quite complex; one project of ours had a deployment build file that not only deployed the WAR file, it also copied the existing one out of the way into a history directory, giving it the current date and time. This created a log of when updates had taken place, and permitted a rapid rollback if the update broke something. Other uses of Ant during server-side installation include <sql> tasks to manipulate the database and <chmod> tasks to set file permissions. You can effectively move the final stage of your build process to the destination system.

The remote servers do, of course, need Ant installed. If you are making your own builds of Ant, you need to keep the servers up to date with your build and all dependent libraries. You may want to set up a deployment process to keep Ant up to date across the servers, unless you are sticking with a standard version of Ant.

18.3.4 Automate the upload and deployment process

Now that we have per-system deployment packages, they can be uploaded via FTP or SSH, emailed to the destination,[1] burned onto CD-ROM and handed off to operations, or pushed up via WebDAV. It doesn't matter how they get there, only that the right target gets to the right server, and that you run the install script under an account with the appropriate permissions.

For our continuous integration process to work, this upload and deploy has to be fully automated, both from your desktop and from your automated build service, be it CruiseControl or Cron.

18.4   INTRODUCING ANT'S DEPLOYMENT POWER TOOLS

Production deployment problems are so complex and different that you will usually need to build your deployment targets using a string of tasks. We are about to run through the tasks you may need. These are the Ant equivalent to power tools: in the hands of an Ant professional, they can solve problems in a snap.

18.4.1   The <copy> task

It seems somewhat ironic that one of Ant's core deployment tasks is also one we have been using for a long time: <copy>. If you are deploying to a network server whose file system you can access, you can just copy the files with a simple <copy> command. It is obvious that this works against local NFS or CIFS shares, but on some development platforms you can use copy to deploy to a WebDAV server. On Windows XP, for example, you can just mount the remote server

```
net use z: https://remoteserver.example.org/ password
```

Linux has similar capabilities with the davfs file system under development on Source-Forge (http://dav.sourceforge.net/), and MacOS X supports DAV out of the box. WebDAV is nice as it runs through firewalls, talks straight to web servers, and, with digest authentication, always keeps your password safe. With HTTPS deployment, your documents are also kept private. One day Ant will support WebDAV out of the box, probably using the Jakarta Slide code, and then we can wave goodbye to <ftp>.

When deploying with <copy>, consider setting overwrite="true". This forces Ant to copy the files you are installing over any that exist already, even if they are newer at their destination. If this flag is unset you cannot use Ant to roll back distributions, and some deployment actions (CD-based installation) can fail in obscure circumstances. Setting this flag does, of course, force Ant to overwrite any files that were updated on the server. If you are implementing persistence by saving data to files under your web application, you are already playing a dangerous game; <copy>

---

[1]   Email isn't as daft as you think; we once had Ant email to a free email account on myrealbox.com, then pull the file down using the service's web-based UI, the latter through the Windows terminal services remote access system. Ugly and insecure, but it worked in a pinch.

just triggers the crisis. Here you should control the copy with `overwrite=`
`"${force}"`, for case-by-case control of overwriting.

18.4.2 The \<serverdeploy\> task

A recent addition to the Ant armory of deployment tasks is `<serverdeploy>`. This task is a container for different server-specific deployment elements. The ultimate aim of this task is to grow to be the one-stop-shop for deployment; it is designed so that different providers can write deployment elements for use inside the task.

In Ant 1.5, the task only deploys to two severs, WebLogic and JOnAS(from http://www.objectweb.org/jonas/).

18.4.3 Remote control with \<telnet\>

The `<telnet>` task lets you connect to a remote host and issue a sequence of commands. With an insecure login and no channel encryption, production servers rarely accept inbound calls on telnet from anywhere but the local system. Most development servers, on the other hand, are malleable to `<telnet>` control. Table 18.1 lists the task's attributes. Just like the `<ftp>` task, you need optional.jar and netcomponents.jar in Ant's lib directory.

Table 18.1 Most attributes of `<telnet>`. You should set the first three unless you want to connect using a different port and hence protocol, in which case you should omit the `userid` and `password`. The `timeout` attribute is a safety net that you should always use.

Attribute	Meaning
server	Remote hostname or address
userid	Username for login
password	Login password
port	Port to connect to, if not port 23
timeout	Timeout for commands
initialCR	Flag to trigger sending a carriage return before waiting for the login prompt

You must supply the server name; for a normal login, you should supply `userid` and `password`. If you don't supply these then you must implement the entire login process inside the task declaration. The `timeout` attribute has a default timeout of zero, which is interpreted as no timeout. We recommend always supplying a timeout, even one of a few minutes, to ensure that server-side problems do not lock up the build indefinitely. A timeout occurring will, of course, break the build.

With this task, it is easy to connect to a server:

```
<telnet server="${deploy.server}"
  userid="guest" password="secret"
  timeout="30" >
```

> **NOTE** If you cannot connect to a Windows NT server, you need to disable NTLM telnet authentication on the server; without this `<telnet>` can not authenticate the user.

Once the connection is open, you need to make use of it, which you do by using nested <read> and <write> elements. Each <read> statement declares a string that the task waits to receive before it continues. Usually the read command waits for the prompt of the remote shell, be it >, #, or some different and perhaps longer string. The longer the string, the less likely it is that executed commands will accidentally print it. The following are examples of valid reads, all examples of different prompts that we have encountered. The final prompt is an escaped angle bracket (/>), common to many servers:

```
<read string="%"/>
<read timeout="30">/home/root%</read>
<read string="$"/>
<read string="&gt;"/>
```

The <write> element is the mirror image of <read>: its text goes down the wire to be interpreted by the shell or program at the far end. By default, the command string is echoed to the Ant log; there is an echo attribute you can set to false to prevent this. The following example <write> statements are representative of commands you may want to send to a server:

```
<write string="rm /home/web/webapps/oldapp.war" />
<write string="rm -f ${server.webappdir}/${projectname}.war" />
<write >cd %JAVA_HOME%</write>
<write >cd $JAVA_HOME</write>

<write >ps -ef | grep java &gt; javapps.txt </write>
<write echo="false">${admin.password}</write>
```

In these examples, we use Ant properties and environment variables on the remote system. Environment variables can be used to great advantage during deployment, as the remote site itself can be preconfigured with information about where to deploy things. Apart from property expansion, Ant performs no transformations to the command string: file paths must be in the appropriate format for the target server. There is a nice task called <pathconvert> that can turn a path into a property in the appropriate form for both Unix and Windows; you may find this convenient in preparing data for this task.

To use the <telnet> task, as we stated before, <read> and <write> statements need to be interlaced, with commands being issued after responses are received. Listing 18.2 shows this.

Listing 18.2 Shutting down a remote server with telnet

```
<target name="shutdown-remote-server">
  <property name="deploy.server" value="eiger" />
  <property name="deploy.server.prompt"
        value="bash-2.04$$" />

  <telnet server="${deploy.server}"
      userid="tomcat" password="********"
```

```
        timeout="30" >
    <read string="${deploy.server.prompt}"/>
    <write string="cd $CATALINA_HOME/bin" />
    <read string="${deploy.server.prompt}"/>
    <write>./shutdown.sh</write>
    <read string="${deploy.server.prompt}"/>
  </telnet>
</target>
```

After connecting to the server, we wait for the login prompt then change to the server's bin directory, where we call the shutdown script. With properties defined for the server and the prompt, this telnet target is nearly ready for factoring out into its own library build file. We could then use <ant> to call it from multiple build files, or against multiple servers.

Notice how we close the telnet session with a <read> of the command prompt, to keep the connection open until the final command has completed. This is vital. Without this <read>, the server at the far end may not completely execute the final command sent.

When we run this target against our remote server, the output will, if all is successful, look something like the following:

```
shutdown-remote-server:
    [telnet]
Red Hat Linux release 7.1 (Seawolf)
Kernel 2.4.2-2 on an i686
login:
    [telnet] tomcat
    [telnet]   Password:
    [telnet]
bash-2.04$
    [telnet] cd $CATALINA_HOME/bin
    [telnet]   cd $CATALINA_HOME/bin
bash-2.04$
    [telnet] ./shutdown.sh
    [telnet]   ./shutdown.sh
Using CLASSPATH:
 /opt/Java/Apps/jakarta-tomcat-4.0.1/bin/bootstrap.jar:
 /usr/java/j2sdk1.4.0/lib/tools.jar
Using CATALINA_BASE: /opt/Java/Apps/jakarta-tomcat-4.0.1
Using CATALINA_HOME: /opt/Java/Apps/jakarta-tomcat-4.0.1
Using JAVA_HOME:     /usr/java/j2sdk1.4.0
bash-2.04$

BUILD SUCCESSFUL
Total time: 8 seconds
```

One of the inconveniences of this approach is that you have to spell out in detail each command, often in a platform- and shell-specific manner, and list the responses you expect. The other is that you cannot deal well with any failure of a command in the chain. It is best to write a shell script or batch file to run on the remote machine, FTP it over, then run it.

NOTE   Before Ant 1.5, the `<telnet>` task did not expand properties in nested text inside `<read>` and `<write>`, but did in their `string` attributes. If you want to write a build file that uses properties inside `<telnet>` consistently, use attributes instead of nested text:

```
<read string="$$"/>
<write string="nohup ${command}&amp;"/>
```

This was one of those tough "should we fix this behavior and maybe break things" problems; the change only stayed in because we made some other fixes to system behavior to keep more things working (i.e., Ant stopped silently removing single dollar signs from strings). The consensus was that stopping this odd behavior was so important that the risk to some build files could be tolerated, but it was not at all clear-cut.

We are going to use the `<telnet>` task to execute the deployment build files we have uploaded to the remote servers. This gives Ant absolute control of the build without us having to write and test complex `<telnet>` sequences.

18.5   *BUILDING A PRODUCTION DEPLOYMENT PROCESS*

Enough talking, let's sit down and write the build file, using the tools we have introduced in section 18.4 and the process we described in section 18.3.

18.5.1   The plan

Here is our simple plan to support remote deployment to multiple servers:

1 Move deployment out to a new build file, remotedeploy.xml.

2 Use a configuration file for each application server type to indicate at build time which libraries are needed.

3 Use a configuration file for each target system to provide information about the system: server type, upload account, password and directory, and whether the system is a debug or release server.

4 Have a separate install-time build file for each application server type; a build file that is run on the target system.

5 Have a system-specific configuration file containing install-time configuration data—the ultimate deployment directory—and an application server username and password if needed.

6 Have the main build file create a WAR file for a particular server, upload it to the destination, then use `<telnet>` to run the appropriate installation file.

One of the interesting tricks here is that we will dynamically determine the hostname in the build file. On the remote server, this lets us pick the appropriate properties file for the machine. On the local build server, we can do the same thing to pick up the name of our build time configuration file. This lets us keep all the deployment details for individual developers under CVS, if the security is adequate.

18.5.2 The directory structure

First, we create a new directory tree under webapp to house all the configuration files. We need one configuration file per server type and two per target server, one at build time and one to be uploaded and used during the installation process. The uploaded configuration files should not contain system usernames and passwords, for security reasons, though they may need app server account details. See figure 18.4.

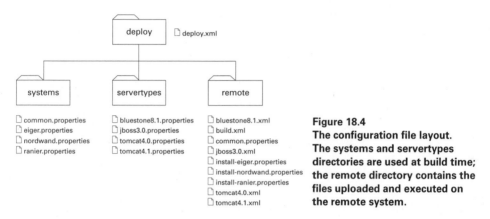

Figure 18.4
The configuration file layout. The systems and servertypes directories are used at build time; the remote directory contains the files uploaded and executed on the remote system.

18.5.3 The configuration files

If this looks complicated, don't panic. You need one configuration file and one installation build file per server type, and two configuration files per target system. If you are using the same application server everywhere, then you don't need many server-type specific files, just those per-system configuration files and a pair of common configuration files to minimize duplication. We are going to start by targeting Tomcat 4.0 on different systems, addressing other server types when the need arises.

18.5.4 The build files

The complete build files are too large to place in their entirety in this chapter. We shall just cover the core pieces of the process, and state the gist of what we have omitted.

18.5.5 The remote build.xml build file

A centerpiece of this process is a build file that developers or operations will run on the remote server. This file determines the identity of the target system, loads the appropriate configuration file, determines the type of application server in use, and calls the appropriate build file for that server.

Identifying the local host

We identify the local host by looking at the standard environment variables:

```
<property environment="env"/>
<property name="env.HOSTNAME" value="${env.COMPUTERNAME}"/>
<property name="hostname" value="${env.HOSTNAME}"/>
```

This extracts the hostname from both the Windows NT and the Unix environment variables. Apparently, it does not work on Mac OS X; non-Unix platforms are an unknown. We have a `<hostname>` task in the pipeline that will work across all platforms, but it came in too late for Ant 1.5.

Loading in the system-specific details

With the hostname, we can load in hostname-specific properties

```
<property name="config.file"
  location="install-${hostname}.properties"/>
<property file="${config.file}" />
<property file="common.properties" />
```

These steps read in the configuration file type for the local system, such as this one:

```
target.servertype=tomcat4.0
target.username=admin
target.password=password
target.port=8080
```

Ant then loads the common properties file, containing the definitions you do not want to duplicate:

```
target.appname=antbook
target.warfile=${target.appname}.war
```

Handing off to the specific build files

With the name of our application server, Ant can choose the appropriate build file for the install:

```
<property name="build.file"
  location="${target.servertype}.xml"/>
```

Running this is a matter of an `<ant>` call:

```
<target name="install" depends="init">
  <ant antfile="${build.file}"
    inheritall="false"/>
</target>
```

The full build file contains validation tests in the `init` target, for a more robust build. In particular, the target verifies that all the configuration files were present, and that `target.servertype` is defined.

18.5.6 Writing the build file for installing to a server

For our Tomcat 4.0 deployment, we have taken the code from section 7.7, somewhat simplified as we know we are always deploying to the local host. We do want to be rigorous in deployment, however, copying the files in under the CATALINA_HOME/webapps directory, so that when the server restarts our application restarts with it.

Reusing the same tricks of section 18.5.5 to load application-specific content, we set up some properties to point to the destination directories and files:

```
<property name="target.deploy.directory"
  location="${env.CATALINA_HOME}/webapps"/>
<property name="webapp.expanded.dir"
 location="${target.deploy.directory}/${target.appname}" />
<property name="webapp.copied.file"
 location="${target.deploy.directory}/${target.appname}.war" />
```

We copy the unexpanded WAR file for server restart, and then expand it for the installation onto the running server.

Unloading the current installation

We will omit the unload target, which issues a `<get>` against

```
http://localhost:8080/manager/remove?path=/${target.appname}
```

We have demonstrated this in section 7.7. Obviously, we can override the port; most production servers run at port 80.

One option to consider here is to actually shut down the application server entirely. This guarantees that any spawned threads are destroyed, and all memory is released. If you do this then you do not need to register the application with Tomcat after deployment, you need to restart Tomcat which is a harder task.

Cleaning up the installation

For production, we always clean out the previous set of files; after unloading the application from Tomcat, we wait a few seconds then delete the WAR file in its expanded and unexpanded state.

```
<target name="clean" depends="unload"
    description="clean up: unload app and delete all files">
  <sleep seconds="${target.sleep.seconds}" />
  <delete file="${webapp.copied.file}" />
  <delete dir="${webapp.expanded.dir}" />
</target>
```

Some servers do not always unload all libraries, especially for JAR files containing `javax` packages. We could set the `failonerror` flag to `false` to keep going, but we may encounter problems at unzip time. If this is a common issue, you will need to shut down the web server every deployment.

Copying the files

After cleanup, we copy in the new files:

```
<target name="install-files" depends="clean">
  <copy file="${target.warfile}"
    tofile="${webapp.copied.file}"/>
  <unzip src="${webapp.copied.file}"
    dest="${webapp.expanded.dir}"/>
</target>
```

This leaves us ready to run the application through a server restart or via a management URL call. The paranoid will restart the server, but we will go for the hot-update.

Loading the application

Again, a manager URL call will start the program; a `<get>` against

```
http://localhost:8080/manager/install?path=/${target.appname}
                                  &war=file://${webapp.expanded.dir}
```

That's it. It takes a few seconds longer than usual, with the delete, the copy, and the expansion, but it still only takes 15-20 seconds, all in.

18.5.7 Uploading to the remote server

We need to get our local installation and configuration files to the remote server. FTP is the path we shall choose, for now. We do all this in our top-level deploy.xml file, a file that resides in the webapp directory and presides over deployment.

Configuring the upload

First Ant must determine which files are needed at the far end. We don't want to send any more files than are needed, to prevent confusion and maintain security. If we build different WAR files for different targets, it is critical that nobody installs them on the wrong machine; stripping out the other build and configuration files helps achieve this.

Although we repeat the same hostname trick of section 18.5.5, we expect the system to usually be called with a remote hostname defined, such as from the command line:

```
ant -Dhostname=eiger
```

The build file loads in the property files for the hostname and makes a list of which files are needed.

```
<property name="config.file"
  location="${systems.dir}/${hostname}.properties"/>
<property file="${config.file}" />
<property file="${systems.dir}/common.properties" />
<property name="servertype.file"
```

```
             location="${servertypes.dir}/${target.servertype}.properties"/>
<property file="${servertype.file}" />
<property name="redeploy.dir" location="dist/redeploy" />
<property name="remote.config.file"
  location="${remote.dir}/install-${hostname}.properties"/>
<property name="remote.build.file"
  location="${remote.dir}/${target.servertype}.xml"/>
```

The configuration files at build time contain more information than those we upload. In particular, they can contain passwords to the server:

```
target.server=eiger
login.userid=tomcat4
login.password=topsecret
ftp.remotedir=/home/tomcat4/install
telnet.cd.directory=${ftp.remotedir}
target.servertype=tomcat4.0
target.server.debug=false
target.isUnix=true
```

We derive some other values from these properties; the aim is to allow target systems to define them in their configuration files if necessary, such as with different FTP and telnet login accounts, or with different servers and ports for SSH-tunneled connections:

```
<property name="ftp.server" value="${target.server}"/>
<property name="ftp.port" value="21"/>
<property name="telnet.server" value="${target.server}"/>
<property name="telnet.port" value="23"/>
<property name="ftp.userid" value="${login.userid}"/>
<property name="ftp.password" value="${login.password}"/>
<property name="telnet.userid" value="${login.userid}"/>
<property name="telnet.password" value="${login.password}"/>
```

The build files also read in the application server-specific configuration files. These state what features are in the server:

```
server.isj2ee=false
server.jsp.version=2.3
server.j2ee.version=0
server.xerces.needed=false
```

These settings can be used to control WAR file generation, either in conditional <patternset> includes of JAR files, or in the <webdoclet> task. We don't need to do this, yet, but the option is important. Obviously, these configuration files are reusable across many projects.

Building a directory of upload files

Based on the configuration details, Ant knows which files to upload, so it copies them to a new redeployment directory, combining the configuration files with the WAR file itself.

```
<target name="build-deployment-package" depends="init">
  <copy todir="${redeploy.dir}" file="${warfile}"/>
  <copy todir="${redeploy.dir}" file="${remote.config.file}"/>
  <copy todir="${redeploy.dir}" file="${remote.build.file}"/>
  <copy todir="${redeploy.dir}" file="${remote.dir}/build.xml"/>
  <copy todir="${redeploy.dir}"
    file="${remote.dir}/common.properties"/>
</target>
```

A local deployment can run straight from this directory; this is the simplest way to test the process. Indeed, a quick test for ${hostname} equaling ${env.HOST-NAME} lets the build file deploy this way on a local system:

```
<target name="install-local"
  depends="build-deployment-package"
  if="is.localhost">
  <ant dir="${redeploy.dir}" inheritall="false"/>
</target>
```

Uploading the files

We will rely on the trusty `<ftp>` task for deployment, called three times in a row.

```
<target name="upload" depends="build-deployment-package"
    unless="is.localhost" >

  <echo>connecting to ${target.server}
    as ${ftp.userid} into ${ftp.remotedir}
  </echo>

  <ftp server="${ftp.server}" port="${ftp.port}"
    action="mkdir"                                      ❶
    remotedir="${ftp.remotedir}"
    userid="${ftp.userid}"
    password="${ftp.password}"
    verbose="true" passive="true"
    ignoreNoncriticalErrors="true"
    />

  <ftp server="${ftp.server}" port="${ftp.port}"
    remotedir="${ftp.remotedir}"
    userid="${ftp.userid}" password="${ftp.password}"
    depends="true" verbose="true" passive="true"
    binary="true"
    ignoreNoncriticalErrors="true"
    >
    <fileset dir="${redeploy.dir}">                     ❷
      <include name="**/*.war"/>
    </fileset>
  </ftp>

  <ftp server="${ftp.server}" port="${ftp.port}"
    remotedir="${ftp.remotedir}"
    userid="${ftp.userid}" password="${ftp.password}"
```

```
      depends="true" verbose="true" passive="true"
      binary="false"
      ignoreNoncriticalErrors="true"
      >
      <fileset dir="${redeploy.dir}">
        <include name="**/*.xml"/>                    ❸
        <include name="**/*.properties"/>
      </fileset>
    </ftp>
  </target>
```

The first `<ftp>` call ❶ creates the destination directory. The second uploads the WAR file ❷. The third one is special ❸; it uploads the XML and properties files in text mode, so that `<telnet>` can convert the line endings to those appropriate for the destination. This is not critical for the files we are currently uploading. If we added text or shell scripts, it would matter a lot.

Preparing to run the remote build

With the files on the remote server, it is time to run the build remotely. This is where `<telnet>` makes an appearance.

Before calling `<telnet>` we need to address the different-servers-different-prompts problem, by defining the initial prompt for the different target platforms we support, and the different commands needed to reset the prompt to something under our control. If we leave them as is, with a $ or a > as the prompt, Ant may mistake program output as the prompt.

```
<target name="unix-prompts" if="target.isUnix">
  <property name="telnet.prompt.command"
    value="export PS1=${telnet.prompt}"/>
  <property name="telnet.initial.prompt" value="$"/>
</target>

<target name="windows-prompts" unless="target.isUnix">
  <property name="telnet.prompt.command"
    value="PROMPT ${telnet.prompt}"/>
  <property name="telnet.initial.prompt" value="&gt;"/>
</target>
```

If we were to support many more platforms, we would factor these settings out into platform-specific settings files, each loaded in dynamically based on a `target.platform` property.

Now, let us deploy.

Calling Ant remotely

```
<target name="install-remote"
    depends="upload,unix-prompts,windows-prompts"
    unless="is.localhost">
```

```
    <telnet server="${telnet.server}"  port="${telnet.port}"
        userid="${telnet.userid}" password="${telnet.password}"
        timeout="${telnet.timeout}" >
      <read string="${telnet.initial.prompt}"/>
```

```
      <write>${telnet.prompt.command}</write>     ⟵——  Set the prompt to a more
      <read string="${telnet.prompt}"/>                 complex one, such as [done]
```

```
      <write>cd ${telnet.cd.directory}</write>    ⟵——  Change to the directory where
      <read string="${telnet.prompt}"/>                 the files were uploaded
```

```
      <write>ant</write>                          ⟵——  Call Ant
      <read string="${telnet.prompt}"/>
    </telnet>
  </target>
```

This target connects to a remote server, using a supplied username and password. We
have a timeout, which must be at least as long as the maximum possible time to run
the build file remotely; we choose 300 seconds for safety. Then we issue three commands down the wire

For this to work, Ant must already be installed, and on the path of the account running the build. If the build fails, the local build file does not notice; it is only at test
time that trouble is detected. This is why the Rant tool introduced in section 15.10
looks so promising; if it can add security and better reporting, then it will be a great
way to run a remote build, not least because SOAP goes through firewalls.

18.5.8   The remote deployment in action

When you actually run the build, the most surprising thing is how ordinary it is. Getting passwords right on remote systems configured with Java, Tomcat, and Ant are
chores, but the build itself flies along nicely. We show a fragment of the full build in
listing 18.3, omitting the preceding FTP upload, and the functional tests that follow.

Listing 18.3   Ant running Ant remotely, via <telnet>

```
install-remote:
    [telnet] Red Hat Linux release 7.1 (Seawolf)
    [telnet] Kernel 2.4.2-2 on an i686
    [telnet] login:
    [telnet] tomcat4
    [telnet]  Password:
    [telnet]
    [telnet] [tomcat4@eiger tomcat4]$
    [telnet] export PS1=[done]
    [telnet]  [done]
    [telnet] cd /home/tomcat4/install
    [telnet] [done]
    [telnet] ant
    [telnet] Buildfile: build.xml
    [telnet] init:
    [telnet] install:
```

```
[telnet] init:
[telnet] unload:
[telnet]      [get] Getting:
                 http://127.0.0.1:8080/manager/remove?path=/antbook
[telnet]     [echo] OK - Removed application at context path /antbook
[telnet] clean:
[telnet]   [delete] Deleting: /home/tomcat4/tomcat4.0/webapps/antbook.war
[telnet]   [delete] Deleting directory
                     /home/tomcat4/tomcat4.0/webapps/antbook
[telnet] install-files:
[telnet]     [copy] Copying 1 file to /home/tomcat4/tomcat4.0/webapps
[telnet]    [unzip] Expanding:
                 /home/tomcat4/tomcat4.0/webapps/antbook.war into
                 /home/tomcat4/tomcat4.0/webapps/antbook
[telnet] deploy:
[telnet]      [get] Getting:
                 http://127.0.0.1:8080/manager/install?path=/antbook
                     &war=file:///home/tomcat4/tomcat4.0/webapps/antbook
[telnet]     [echo] OK - Installed application at context path /antbook
[telnet] default:
[telnet] BUILD SUCCESSFUL
[telnet] Total time: 35 seconds
[telnet] [done]
```

The log shows that Ant has successfully logged in to the remote server, and then run the remote Ant build that it just uploaded. This build file does exactly what it does on a local system: install Ant to the local Tomcat server.

If the remote build failed, the local build continues, oblivious to the fact. We could modify the `<telnet>` task so that it waits for the BUILD SUCCESSFUL string, timing out after a few minutes if it receives a BUILD FAILED message. Instead, we just rely on the functional tests, and a new test we will write in section 18.8.

18.5.9   Reviewing the deployment process

This process seems a bit complex, given that we have demonstrated nothing more than deployment to the same two systems we were deploying to in chapter 7. However, look at what we have gained: scalability, flexibility, and some more security.

- *Scalability*—To add a new server: add two configuration files, one local and one remote; you don't need to touch the build file itself. Developers can easily add their systems to the project without storing passwords in the SCM system, and one single trusted and secured server can keep the details on production systems safe.

- *Flexibility*—We can now support many different server types. Each one needs its own installation build file, with a default target to install the web application based on the configuration file for the local host, but all the details are left to it. These files can be reused across projects, or they can be customized to perform extra tasks, such as configuring the application server itself.

- *Security*—Perfect security is a distant ideal; if you have a password in a computer, you have a security risk. Our deployment process is amenable to working on secured systems where server controls keep the Tomcat management application inaccessible to all but local callers. It will also work through SSH tunnels, using the `passive="true"` option on `<ftp>` and the option to customize ports and servers for `<ftp>` and `<telnet>`.

We have also gained the ability to work with those operations groups that want to control the process. They can keep the configuration files for their servers on their system, and run the code. We can even deploy via email or CD: just `<mail>` the deployment files to operations with a please install message, or `<copy>` the files to a CD-ROM that you can physically hand to them. No matter how the files get to the server, running `ant` at the command prompt will get the application installed.

This is a powerful build process. We have not delved into generating custom WAR files in this task, but the steps are obvious: use the properties in the per-target and per-server configuration files to control `<webdoclet>` and `<war>`. You do need to run a clean build on the system when switching targets. Rather than remembering to do this every time, save the target server's name to a properties file in the dist directory. Next build, load, and compare this to the current target. When the server names are different, your build file should trigger a cleanup.

Now that we have put our deployment process in place, we will take a brief look at the deployment processes of some different application servers.

18.6 DEPLOYING TO SPECIFIC APPLICATION SERVERS

There are so many different application servers, each with its own deployment steps, that we could probably dedicate multiple chapters to the subject. Instead we are going to look at some of the servers that have special `<ant>` tasks, and then discuss how to work with the others.

18.6.1 Tomcat 4.0 and 4.1

Tomcat 4.0 and 4.1 share the same deployment process; Ant issues HTTP GET requests to the management servlet. Tomcat 4.1 makes this process slightly easier, but if you have a process that deploys to Tomcat 4.0, it should still work with the later version.

Deploying to Tomcat 4.0

We have already shown how to deploy to Tomcat 4.0. The management servlet is a security risk: anyone can pick up the base-64 coded authentication string and control the web server.

This is a big issue; the `<get>` task does not support digest authentication so you cannot safely deploy to a production system with it. Anyone could listen to the deployment requests and then issue their own.

You must secure the servlet with an IP address valve, which restricts access to a given IP address. For maximum security, configure the valve to permit management requests from the local server, with this fragment in server.xml:

```
<Context path="/manager" docBase="manager"
  debug="0" privileged="true">
  <Valve
    className="org.apache.catalina.valves.RemoteAddrValve"
    allow="127.0.0.1" />
</Context>
```

The deployment process introduced in section 18.5 works perfectly well with systems so configured.

Deploying to Tomcat 4.1

At the time of writing, Tomcat 4.1 is still only in an Alpha release phase. It contains some features that make it very appealing as a development target: a JMX management API, a reworked management applet designed for integration with build tools, and its own Ant task to install and remove applications:

```
<install url="http://${target.server}:${target.port}/manager"
    username="${target.username}"
    password="${target.password}"
        path="${target.appname}"
         war="file://${webapp.path}"/>
```

Alongside the <install> task, there are others such as the <reload> and <remove> tasks to reload and remove web applications, and a <list> task to list all loaded applications. The tasks hand off the requests to the reworked version of the manager applet. They seem pretty much a drop-in replacement for the Tomcat 4.0 deployment targets we have been using, although they need a failonerror flag so that we can tell <remove> to not break the build if the application is missing. If we wanted to use it now, we would have to use an <http> test in a <condition> task to probe for the application running before unloading it.

Under the hood, these tasks are simply issuing HTTP GET requests against the same URLs we constructed in chapter 7; they might also work against Tomcat 4.0. As with our <get> requests, the password goes over the wire in base64 encoding, so it is not at all secure.

We like the idea of these tasks, but have not yet sat down to see how well they work over time. The manual claims that the tasks only work against the local host, but that is really a server-side configuration issue, and the current alpha releases of Tomcat 4.1 still permit remote management. For secure production deployment, you must configure the server for local management only, as with Tomcat 4.0. To find out more about these tasks, consult the Tomcat documentation (Tomcat 2002).

18.6.2   BEA WebLogic

There is a `<weblogic>` element inside `<serverdeploy>`. This requires the weblogic.jar file on the classpath; you can use the `classpath` attribute to do this.

```
<serverdeploy
    action="deploy"
    source="${webapp.path}">
  <weblogic
    application="${target.appname}"
    component="webapp:${target.server}"
    server="t3://${target.server}:7001"
    username="${target.username}"
    password="${target.password}"
    classpath="${env.WEBLOGIC_HOME}/lib/weblogic.jar"
    />
</serverdeploy>
```

WebLogic 7.0 comes with its own copy of Ant. We recommend that you rename its version of ant.bat and ant.sh, so that you do not accidentally use that version. It is very confusing when there is more than one version of the Ant shell script/batch file on your path, as you may accidentally use an older version of Ant, and may not be adding optional libraries to the appropriate directory.

18.6.3   HP Bluestone application server

This application server ships with its own deployment task; something we should expect from all application servers in the future.

The `<hpas-deploy>` task uploads a WAR or EAR file to a running instance of the HP-AS application server, authorizing the request using the account and password supplied as attributes. We think it uses a custom wire protocol talking to the JMX server.

```
<taskdef name="hpas-deploy"
    classname="com.hp.mwlabs.tools.pacman.ant.HPASDeploy" />
</target>

<target name="deploy" depends="init"
    description="Deploy to HP-AS server">

  <hpas-deploy
    host="${target.server}"
    uri="${target.appname}"
    port="2000"
    username="${target.username}"
    password="${target.password}"
    jarfile="${webapp.path}">
  </hpas-deploy>
</target>
```

You can also specify a set of files to upload as a `<fileset>` inside the task; when you do this you can no longer specify the deployment path; the tool uses the name of each file in the fileset instead. Single file deployment is clearly more flexible.

The development team's choice to provide an Ant task for deployment, rather than a GUI tool, is a welcome sign of how Ant has become the standard build tool for projects, and it demonstrates how developers of commercial products can serve their users by supporting Ant explicitly. Of course, it would be nice to have source access, so we could write a nested element that lets us specify a deployment URI for each element uploaded. It would also be nice to see vendors plugging into the `<serverdeploy>` task.

There is currently one major flaw with this task—it does not work from a normal Ant execution environment, only the vendor's RadPak Ant GUI tool. We don't know why this is the case, but it stops you deploying via this task from any automated build and deploy process.

18.6.4 Other servers

There are many more application servers, each with its own deployment process, but without explicit Ant support. We leave deploying to these servers as an exercise to the reader. The process for creating a build file to deploy to each server is usually the same: look at its documentation and sample deployment scripts, then replicate the steps in Ant. URL-based manager applications succumb to `<get>` requests; helper programs can be called with `<java>` and `<exec>`, and any server that supports hot deployment is amenable to `<copy>` calls.

The batch files are often the most informative source of information, as they show the classpaths and parameters needed to call their Java-based programs. You can replace each such script file with a single `<java>` call in your application.

All in all, we estimate that it can take a day or two to get a working build file to deploy to a new server type, but once written it can be reused again and again. Perhaps the Apache Ant project should put together a repository of deployment targets for the usual suspects of application servers.

18.7 VERIFYING DEPLOYMENT

"Trust, but verify."

The Russian proverb that Reagan quoted when dealing with the Warsaw Pact in treaties on Strategic Armaments also applies to the deployment problem. Even though the individual components of a production deployment process are there to help you, together they can be an implacable obstacle.

We already have the HttpUnit tests to verify that the system works; we wrote those in section 12.6. These make sure that our application is working. There is just one remaining question: how can you be sure that deployment worked?

We may not be able to tell from the functional tests whether the version of the WAR file we just built was the one we just built, or whether an older version is still running. This is rare, but we have encountered it when getting deployment working, and again when a system was misconfigured.

What are we to do? The answer is actually very simple. For every build, we will create a timestamp file that gets included in the web application. Ant can then compare the local timestamp with the copy served up by the just deployed application, and fail the build if they are different.

18.7.1 Creating the timestamp file

First, we give the file a name and a place.

```
<property name="timestamp.filename"
  value="timestamp.txt"/>

<property name="timestamp.path"
  location="${build.dir}/${timestamp.filename}"/>
```

The file will be served from the web site by the same name, such as

```
http://127.0.0.1:8080/antbook/timestamp.txt
```

If after deployment the remote and local files have different contents, then deployment has failed. We need to put a timestamp in the file, of course, which we do by getting the current date and time into a property, then saving this to a file with <echo>.

```
<target name="make-timestamp" depends="init" >
  <tstamp>
    <format property="buildtime"
      pattern="yyyy-MM-dd'T'HH:mm:ss" />
  </tstamp>
  <echo file="${timestamp.path}"
    message="build.timestamp=${buildtime}" />
</target>
```

We could use <propertyfile> for similar effect, but we prefer the terse one-line timestamp for easier-to-read error messages.

18.7.2 Adding the timestamp file to the application

To include this file in the application, we add another fileset to the <war> task and a new dependency to the target:

```
<target name="make-war"
  depends="compile,make-webxml,make-web-docs,make-timestamp,make-soap-api">
  <war destfile="${warfile}"
    compress="false"
    update="true"
    webxml="${build.webinf.dir}/web.xml">
    <classes dir="${build.classes.dir}"/>
    <webinf dir="${build.dir}" includes="index/**"/>
    <webinf dir="${struts.dir}/lib" includes="*.tld,*.dtd"/>
    <webinf dir="${build.webinf.dir}" includes="antbook.tld"/>
    <fileset dir="${build.dir}" includes="${timestamp.filename}"/>
    <fileset dir="web"/>
    ...
  </war>
</target>
```

We could check that this file is there by hand, but we want Ant to do the work. This is what the target in listing 18.4 is for, a target that Ant executes after the `<telnet>`-based remote deployment has returned.

Listing 18.4   A target to fetch the timestamp and verify that it matches
                           our local copy

```
<target name="verify-uptodate"
    depends="install" >
  <property name="verify.url"
    value="${test.url}/${timestamp.filename}" />
  <property name="verify.local.path"
    location="${dist.dir}/deployed-on-${target.server}.txt"
    />
  <waitfor timeoutproperty="deployment.failed"             ❶
    maxwait="30"
    maxwaitunit="second">
    <http url="${verify.url}" />
  </waitfor>

  <fail if="deployment.failed">
    timestamp page not found at ${verify.url}"
  </fail>

  <get src="${verify.url}"                                 ❷
    dest="${verify.local.path}" />

  <condition property="verify.uptodate.successful">         ❸
    <filesmatch
      file1="${timestamp.path}"
      file2="${verify.local.path}"
      />
  </condition>

  <loadfile property="verify.expected"
    srcFile="${timestamp.path}" />
  <loadfile property="verify.found"
    srcFile="${verify.local.path}" />

  <fail unless="verify.uptodate.successful">
    file match failed;
      expected [${verify.expected}]
      found    [${verify.found}]
</target>
```

This target has three phases. After creating the URL to the remote timestamp, it uses `<waitfor>` ❶ to spin until the file is present. This is to give the server time to reload the application.

If the file is present, then a `<get>` task retrieves it and saves it to a local file ❷. This is followed by a `<condition>` test to compare the two files, our original timestamp, and this newly downloaded version ❸. If they are not equal, then the target fails the build, with a helpful error message stating the difference between what we expected and what we got.

18.7.3   Testing the timestamp

In a normal successful build, the output of the target is something to be ignored:

```
verify-uptodate:
     [get] Getting: http://eiger:8080/antbook/timestamp.txt
```

It is only when something has gone wrong that the target contains any message of importance:

```
verify-uptodate:
     [get] Getting: http://eiger:8080/antbook/timestamp.txt

BUILD FAILED
C:\AntBook\app\webapp\newdeploy.xml:273:
     file match failed;
        expected [build.timestamp=2002-04-26T00:42:42]
        found    [build.timestamp=2002-05-26T00:42:42]
```

That is all there is to it. Some new properties, two new targets, and some other minor changes to the build file have self-validated your deployment process: Ant verifies that the deployment went through, then the HttpUnit, Cactus, or Canoo tests verify that the program actually works. Together, they ensure that the production service is ready to go live.

18.8   BEST PRACTICES

When it comes to production deployment, the two core practices are *be rigorous* and *work with operations*. By rigorous we mean: design build files that do not take shortcuts or make too many assumptions about systems such as where applications are installed. In addition, include many tests.

Since chapter 12 in this book, we have been intermittently writing functional tests for the program and happiness tests for the system configuration. The happiness test, our taglib to probe for needed classes and other important configuration data, is one of our secret weapons for successful production deployment. If your functional tests fail, it could be the fault of your program or the system. If the configuration tests fail, it is the fault of the system. The more easily trouble can be located, the more easily it can be fixed. In addition, configuration problems don't merit waking the development team up at 3 a.m.—in theory, anyway. In practice, it is going to happen. The purpose of the tests then becomes to give you 15 minutes more sleep before they call you.

The other key purpose for tests is to verify that the program works on different application servers. We have explored some of the problems here, but there is no core way to address them other than to use the same application server everywhere. Sun is developing validation tools to help here, but there are so many other subtleties of deploying to and operating a different application server that it probably is not enough.

Ant helps by providing the unified deployment and testing system. Even so, keeping the number of application servers to an absolute minimum—one—is very helpful.

The other area of focus is working with operations. From its perspective, the ideal server is one that works so well, they forget where it is located or how to log in to it. It just works. It is far beyond the scope of this book to address the techniques needed to achieve such a goal. We have introduced our thoughts on a process that may move toward that goal: that of treating operations needs as use cases, and the problems it encounters as defects to be logged, tracked, tested, and fixed.

18.9 SUMMARY

We have explored the challenges of deploying to production servers, the subtle differences you may encounter, and the complications of working with operations-managed systems.

We have shown how to create a deployment process driven by per-system and per-application server configuration files that can deploy to different systems and application servers. This deployment process uses an install-time build file for each application server type; this file deploys the application onto the local system. The main build file has to decide which install and configuration files to upload, and then uses <ftp> or a similar tool to get them onto the machine. For automated deployment, Ant can make a <telnet> call and run the remote task from the local system. You can also install the software by running Ant on the server by hand, which permits alternative upload processes such as email and CD-ROM delivery.

Ant's task suite for deployment is still growing, and we are optimistic for the future, but today deployment is usually a matter of putting together a sequence of <copy>, <get>, and <java> calls.

We finished the chapter with a look at how to verify that deployment worked. When you are writing your deployment build files, we strongly encourage you to use this technique from the outset, as it is easy to do, and the price of having a broken deployment process is high.

This chapter marks the end of our exploration of how to apply Ant to advanced development projects. Our next section goes one level deeper, looking at how to extend and customize Ant through writing new tasks, or changing existing ones. This is not hard to do, and gives you the power to address problems in Ant that would otherwise seem impossible.

PART 3

Extending Ant

If you are pushing the limits of Ant's built-in capabilities, chapters 19 and 20 are for you. We first cover writing custom Ant tasks and the essentials of Ant's API. Then, we explore scripting inside Ant build files and, finally, creating your own build listeners, loggers, filter readers, mappers, and selectors. This section enables you to extend Ant to meet the specific needs of your projects.

C H A P T E R   1 9

Writing Ant tasks

19.1 What exactly is an Ant task? 468
19.2 Ant API primer 470
19.3 How tasks get data 474
19.4 Creating a basic Ant Task subclass 483
19.5 Operating on a fileset 485
19.6 Error handling 486
19.7 Testing Ant tasks 487
19.8 Executing external programs 487
19.9 Executing a Java program within a task 490
19.10 Supporting arbitrarily named elements and attributes 493
19.11 Building a task library 495
19.12 Supporting multiple versions of Ant 497
19.13 Summary 497

You know that you are a serious Ant user when you start wanting to extend it through code. Although it seems an expert use of the tool, there is no need to feel intimidated. The word expert can bring into peoples' minds visions of experts-only ski runs: steep and narrow descents where any failure results in life-threatening injuries. Ant is not like that. Extending it is an advanced use of the tool, but it is simple and painless.

There comes a time in everyone's complex project where it suddenly becomes clear that Ant does not do everything you need to control the entire build. It may be that something minor is missing, such as being able to sleep for thirty seconds during installation or testing. It may be that something major is missing, like having no way to deploy EJB packages to the target application server. It may even be that a common Ant task does not work quite right. This happens to everyone and there is always a solution. Ant was designed to be extendible through Java classes, and it only takes a small amount of Java coding to write a new Ant task. If the problem lies in the actual Ant source itself, then the fact that an entire Ant source tree is a download away comes into play. If Ant does not work right, then it can be fixed.

Adding a new Java class requires Java development experience, and the tools to compile the source and make a JAR file from the generated bytecodes. This is exactly the same development skill that anyone using Ant for Java development has, and as for the tools needed—Ant and the Java SDK are all that is required.

People overcoming their projects' build problems wrote all the Ant tasks that come with Ant today. The time and effort those developers invested have benefited not only themselves, but all other Ant users. The same benefits apply to new tasks written, and extensions to existing classes. If the libraries are reused in one project or organization, the cost of development is soon covered; if they are shared with the rest of the Ant community, then not only do others benefit from the development, but also they can share the maintenance effort among themselves.

19.1   WHAT EXACTLY IS AN ANT TASK?

The definition of what makes a Java class into an Ant task is quite simple: it must have an execute() method. Yes, it really is that simple! Ant's core engine has a relatively sophisticated introspection mechanism to allow a lot of freedom in how tasks plug into it.

19.1.1   The world's simplest Ant task

Here is an example of one of the simplest Ant tasks imaginable:

```
package org.example.antbook.tasks;

public class SimpleTask {

    public void execute() {
        System.out.println(">>>> SimpleTask <<<<");
    }

}
```

Notice that our class extends from no base class (except java.lang.Object implicitly, of course) and only has a single method: execute. The execute method must be public and take no arguments, and the class must be capable of instantiation (i.e., the class cannot be abstract) with a no-argument constructor. Those are effectively the only rules that you must follow to turn a Java class into an Ant task. The execute method may have a return value, but it is ignored and a warning is generated when the task is defined. The execute method may throw exceptions, and doing so will cause the build to fail appropriately.

NOTE   Writing to System.out or System.err during task execution is allowed, but Ant captures the output and logs it to the appropriate logging level. The MSG_INFO level is used for System.out, and MSG_ERR is used for System.err. See section 19.2.1 for more information on logging. Running Ant with the -quiet option will not show System.out output, which may surprise you at first. We recommend, however, that you extend org.apache.tools.ant.Task and use the logging methods provided.

19.1.2 Compiling and using a task in the same build

The build file shown in listing 19.1 outputs

```
simpletask:
[simpletask] >>>> SimpleTask <<<<
```

The trick is using `<taskdef>` before executing our task, but after compiling it. When integrating third-party tasks into a build file, you can specify the `<taskdef>` outside a target so that tasks are defined globally to that build file. The `<taskdef>` task, of course, requires that the class file(s) of the tasks being declared exists within its visible classpath. In order to use a task that is being compiled as part of the same build process, the `<taskdef>` has to occur after the compilation. We accomplish this by simply defining the task in the same target where we use it.

> **Listing 19.1   The build file to compile and execute a task all in the same build**

```
<?xml version="1.0" ?>
<project name="tasks" default="main">

  <property name="build.dir" location="build"/>

  <target name="init">
    <mkdir dir="${build.dir}"/>
  </target>

  <target name="compile" depends="init">
    <javac srcdir="src" destdir="${build.dir}"/>      <--- Compiles it
  </target>

  <target name="simpletask" depends="compile">
    <taskdef name="simpletask"
            classname="org.example.antbook.tasks.SimpleTask"
            classpath="${build.dir}"                       Defines it
    />

    <simpletask/>      <--- Uses it
  </target>

  <target name="clean">
    <delete dir="${build.dir}"/>
  </target>

  <target name="main" depends="simpletask"/>

</project>
```

19.1.3 Task lifecycle

How Ant maps from XML task declarations to Java classes is a miracle of informal data binding. We will soon show you how attributes and elements are mapped to Java methods, but before that comes the task lifecycle. There are different stages in the processing of a build file, and the objects that implement tasks are used throughout the stages.

Here is the lifecycle of Ant tasks. The build begins with Ant loading and parsing the build file.

1 As Ant parses the build file, it creates an instance of the appropriate subclass of Task for every declaration of a task in the file, using its empty constructor.

2 Ant then informs the task about its containing project, target, and some other minor details, such as which line of the build file contains it.

3 Ant calls the init() method of the Task class. Most tasks do not override this.

4 Ant proceeds to execute the targets in the order it determines is appropriate, conceivably not executing all of them, depending upon whether conditional targets have their conditions met.

5 The tasks inside a target are executed one by one, For each task, Ant configures it with the attribute and element values in the build file, then calls its execute() method

This does not quite explain how a class that does not extend org.apache.tools. ant.Task works. The answer is that there is a TaskAdapter in Ant's API that does extend from Task, and contains an instance of the Object, and invokes its execute method. The TaskAdapter is used internally to Ant for tasks that do not extend from Task.

19.2   ANT API PRIMER

Before delving into task development any further, it helps to have an understanding of some of Ant's API. You do not need to understand all of the classes and structures that make up the Ant codebase, but several key classes that are used in the majority of Ant tasks are worth noting. This is an intentionally brief and focused view of Ant's API. In practice, these are the classes and methods that you will work with most frequently. Ant ships with complete Javadoc references and is well documented. With Ant's source code being open, it is easy to learn Ant task development tricks by looking at the source code for tasks that are most like the functionality you need. Each subsection that follows represents a single Ant class, with the important methods of the class noted.

19.2.1   Task

The org.apache.tools.ant.Task abstract class is the typical base class for Ant tasks. It is the main unit of work during an Ant build. Classes that extend from Task should at a minimum implement the execute method. The Task class provides access to the Project object using the project-protected member variable. Use the log methods to output to the Ant process—this is much preferable over System.out.println. The init and execute methods are designed to be overridden. The log methods are designed to be called.

- `public void init() throws BuildException`
  The `init` method is called when a task is encountered during the parsing phase of the build file. This is rarely overridden in practice, since any preliminary configuration could be done in the `execute` method instead.

- `public void execute() throws BuildException`
  Here is where it all happens! The execute method is the heart of a task. If something goes awry, simply throw an `org.apache.tools.ant.BuildException`.

- `log(String msg, int msgLevel)` and `log(String msg)`
  The log methods are helpers to call the `Project` log methods. There are five logging levels, listed in descending priority:

  - MSG_ERR
  - MSG_WARN
  - MSG_INFO
  - MSG_VERBOSE
  - MSG_DEBUG

    A `BuildLogger`, discussed in chapter 20, is capable of filtering the output based on the logging level selected. The command-line switches -debug (all levels), -verbose (MSG_VERBOSE and up), and -quiet (MSG_WARN and up) affect the output generated by the default logger. Note that MSG_ERR and MSG_WARN are always output, even in -quiet mode. The overloaded `log` method without the `msgLevel` parameter logs at the MSG_INFO level.

- `public Project getProject()`
  This method allows a task access to project-wide information so it can do things like set new properties or access the values of existing ones. See the `Project` class description for more details.

19.2.2 Project

- `String getProperty(String name)`
  The `getProperty` method returns the value of an Ant property, or null if it is not defined. Because Ant automatically expands properties in attributes before handing the value to the task, this method is rarely needed in tasks.

- `void setNewProperty(String name, String value)`
  Call this method to assign a value to a property. Keep in mind that Ant properties are immutable and this method ensures that the immutability rules are obeyed, so the property will not be changed if it already exists.

- `void setProperty(String name, String value)`
  This is the predecessor to `setNewProperty` from Ant 1.4 and before. It lets the caller override properties, though a warning is printed whenever you do this. If you are writing a task to work with older versions of Ant, you must use this method to set properties.

- `String replaceProperties(String value)`
  Properties are automatically expanded in XML attributes before your task receives the data, but this method is useful when receiving element text that is not automatically expanded.
- `java.io.File getBaseDir()`
  This method returns the project's base directory. This is useful for resolving relative paths, although in practice it is rarely needed because of Ant's automatic file and path expansion feature.
- `String getName()`
  The `getName` method returns the project's name, as specified in the `name` attribute of the `<project>` element.
- `java.io.File resolveFile(String filename)`
  This method returns a File object with an absolute path to the file name specified. If the file name is relative, it is resolved relative to the project's base directory.

19.2.3   Path

- `String toString()`
  `Path` overrides the default `Object.toString` method to provide the full path as a completely resolved and platform-specific path.
- `static String[] translatePath(Project project, String path)`
  This utility method provides an array of path elements from a single path containing elements separated by colon (`:`) or semicolon (`;`) separators.
- `int size()`
  Returns the number of path elements within the `Path` instance.
- `String[] list()`
  Returns an array of path elements from the `Path` instance.

19.2.4   FileSet

- `DirectoryScanner getDirectoryScanner(Project project)`
  To process files from a fileset object, first call this method to get a `Directory-Scanner` object. The `DirectoryScanner` API is then used to iterate over the files. See section 19.5 for an example.
- `java.io.File getDir(Project project)`
  Returns the base directory specified for this `FileSet` instance.

19.2.5   DirectoryScanner

- `String[] getIncludedFiles()`
  This method returns all file names that are included, taking into account the includes/excludes patterns. The file names returned are relative to the root directory specified. See section 19.5 for an example.

19.2.6   EnumeratedAttribute

By requiring that an attribute be one of a list of possible values, Ant makes it easy to take care of simple validation issues. For example, the <echo> task has an optional `level` attribute that can only be set to the values `error`, `warning`, `info`, `verbose`, or `debug`. This constraint is accomplished using an `EnumeratedAttribute` subclass. A subclass must implement the `getValues` method, and the `getValue` method is used to retrieve the value set from the build file.

- `abstract String[] getValues()`
  Implemented by subclasses, returns the set of allowed values.

- `String getValue()`
  Returns the value set, which is guaranteed to be one of the values returned by `getValues`.

- `int getIndex()`
  If the position of the value within the list returned by `getValues` is needed, this method supplies it.

19.2.7   FileUtils

- `static FileUtils newFileUtils()`
  Most of `FileUtils` methods are instance methods, as a placeholder for possible future cross-platform customization. Use this method to return a `FileUtils` instance.

- `copyFile` (many overloaded signatures)
  Using these methods to copy files takes care of several minor details, including optionally filtering token substitution and creating parent directories.

- `java.io.File createTempFile(String prefix, String suffix, File parentDir)`
  This is a handy method to return a currently nonexistent temporary file name. Contrary to the method name, it does not actually create a file, only ensures that the name it generates is not an existing file.

- `java.io.File normalize(String path)`
  This utility method cleans up an absolute file or directory path, ensuring that it is a valid absolute path on the current platform. It will make the drive letter uppercase, if there is one, remove redundant slashes, and resolve `.` and `..` references.

- `java.io.File resolveFile(java.io.File file, String filename)`
  Resolves and normalizes a file path relative to another `file` if the `filename` is not already an absolute path.

- `void setFileLastModified(File file, long time)`
  This is a reflection-based wrapper around `File.setLastModified`, a wrapper that handles Java 1.1 by silently doing nothing. Use this method to alter the timestamp of a file.

19.3 How tasks get data

As you've seen throughout this book, tasks are specified in a build file as XML elements that contain attributes, subelements, and even body text. Ant provides a very elegant and easy way for tasks to obtain this information in rich, domain-specific ways. For example, the `<javac>` task accepts a `debug` attribute to turn on or off the debug flag during compilation. The values `on`, `yes`, or `true` all turn the debug flag on, yet the `<javac>` task internally does not have to deal with string comparisons. It simply gets a `boolean` value: `true` or `false`. While the intricacies involved in describing how this works may at first seem complex, please bear with us, as understanding how this works can mean the difference between letting Ant do the hard work for you or reinventing the wheel and coding something unnecessarily.

During build file execution, Ant creates instances of the tasks used and hands it the attribute and subelement information. Using Java introspection, Ant looks for specially named methods and invokes them with the data from the build file. During this data population stage, an Ant task is not treated specially. Each element in a build file corresponds to an object, some of which are tasks, others are datatypes, and there are also objects that correspond to targets as well as the project. Figure 19.1 illustrates an Ant build file section and its corresponding task. We detail this task later in section 19.8.

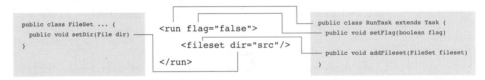

Figure 19.1 Illustration of Ant's introspection mechanisms mapping task attributes, subelements, and their attributes to corresponding methods. Ant will automatically instantiate instances of objects corresponding to nested elements when the `add`-prefixed methods are used.

19.3.1 Setting attributes

An XML attribute simply consists of a name and a textual value. Simple, right? Well, not so fast—there is much more to it than passing the string value to your task instance. In the simplest case, you have a task using an attribute:

```
<sometask value="some value"/>
```

And the task has a `setValue` method:

```
private String value;
public void setValue (String value) {
    this.value = value;
}
```

This is similar to JavaBeans-style naming conventions, where a property corresponds to a setter method with the prefix `set`.

NOTE Before Ant calls a setter method for an attribute, property references are expanded. Tasks receive only the expanded values for attributes. We discuss this further in section 19.4.1.

A `String` parameter is the most straightforward attribute type since its value corresponds directly, including property value substitution, to the text for the attribute in the build file. A `String` type is only the first of many types that can be used, though.

Ant's introspection mechanism does its best to determine the proper setter methods to call, but in the case where a setter method name is overloaded, a non-String setter takes precedence over a String parameter setter. If there are multiple non-String setters for a single attribute name, the one that is located first is JVM dependent. We, of course, recommend that you do not overload setter methods.

True/False settings

Many times a task simply needs to have a true/false, on/off, or yes/no type of toggle. By having your setter parameter take a `boolean` (or `java.lang.Boolean`), your task will get `true` (or `Boolean.TRUE`) if the value is `yes`, `on`, or `true`, and `false` (or `Boolean.FALSE`) otherwise.

```
private boolean toggle = false;

public void setToggle(boolean toggle) {
    this.toggle = toggle;
}
```

The task use in the build file is

```
<setter toggle="on"/>
```

Because of implicit attribute expansion, our task doesn't know the difference when the build file writer specifies

```
<property name="toggle.state" value="on"/>
<setter toggle="${toggle.state}"/>
```

The `setToggle` method is invoked with `true` in both cases—provided, of course, that the `toggle.state` property has not been set earlier to a value that evaluates to `false`.

Accepting numbers

Attribute introspection provides facilities for all the Java primitives and wrapper types. Most of the primitives and corresponding wrapper classes are for numeric data. The numeric types are

- `byte` / `java.lang.Byte`
- `short` / `java.lang.Short`
- `int` / `java.lang.Integer`
- `long` / `java.lang.Long`

- `float / java.lang.Float`
- `double / java.lang.Double`

Setter methods accepting any of these types can be declared, and, if the value of the attribute can be converted to the desired type, all will be well. If an error occurs converting the text to the appropriate numeric type, a `NumberFormatException` will be thrown, halting the build.

A single character

While a single character is not likely to be a commonly used attribute type, Ant allows you to have a setter that takes a `char` or `java.lang.Character` type. The character provided to your setter is the first character of the attribute value, ignoring any additional characters.

File or directory attribute

It is extremely common for a task to need a file or directory passed to it as an attribute. Ant provides built-in support for file or directory attributes by implementing a setter with a `java.io.File` parameter. The benefit of using a `File` parameter as opposed to a `String` parameter is that the path is resolved to an absolute path when a relative path is specified in the build file. If the path specified in the build file is not already an absolute path, it is resolved relative to the project's base directory.

Here is an example of using the `File` attribute type. Our task desires a destination directory, which is specified as a relative path:

```
<mytask destdir="output"/>
```

Our task implements a `setDestDir` method:

```
private File destDir;
public void setDestDir(File destDir) {
    this.destDir = destDir;
}
```

(Notice that case does not matter.)

Our `execute` method verifies that we are dealing with an existing directory:

```
if (!destDir.isDirectory()) {
    throw new BuildException(destDir + " is not a valid directory");
}
```

Path

Tasks that need to operate on paths, such as a classpath, may use a setter with an `org.apache.tools.ant.types.Path` parameter. The benefit to allowing Ant to give you a `Path` object, rather than simply a delimited `String`, is in Ant's cross-platform capabilities. The build file can specify a path using semicolons or colons to separate path elements and back or forward slashes to separate directories, and conversion to the current platform's delimiters is automatic. Relative paths, from the project's base directory, may also be specified within the attribute value. Ant deals with the unpleasant issues of path and directory separators, giving your task a rich data structure that encapsulates it all. To support a `path` attribute in your task, implement a `setPath` method:

```
private Path path;
public void setPath(Path path) {
    this.path = path;
    log("path = " + path);
}
```

And in the build file, perhaps a path is set in this manner:

```
<property environment="env"/>
<setter path="${env.TEMP}:build/output"/>
```

Note that the path is specified in a Unix style with a colon path separator and a forward slash as a directory separator. But running this on a Windows platform yields this result:

```
[setter] path = C:\temp;C:\AntBook\Sections\Extending\tasks\build\output
```

Ant has automatically adjusted the path to suit our current platform regardless of the path style used in the build file. Also, notice that the relative path `build/output` has been set to the absolute path for us automatically.

Enumerated attribute

Ant does a lot to ease writing tasks, and the `EnumeratedAttribute` class is a prime example. If you only allow the value of an attribute to be from a fixed set of possible values, using Ant's `EnumeratedAttribute` type can save some validation coding time. Listing 19.2 shows a task with a `version` attribute that only allows the values 2.2 or 2.3.

Listing 19.2   Using EnumeratedAttribute to restrict an attribute value

```
package org.example.antbook.tasks;

import org.apache.tools.ant.Task;
import org.apache.tools.ant.types.EnumeratedAttribute;

public class EnumTask extends Task {

    private String version = "2.3";        ⟵── Sets default value

    public void setVersion(ServletVersion ver) {
        version = ver.getValue();          ⟵──────────── Retrieves value from our
    }                                                     EnumeratedAttribute
                                                          subclass
    public void execute() {
        log("Servlet version = " + version);
    }
```

```
public static class ServletVersion
            extends EnumeratedAttribute {
    public String[] getValues() {
        return new String[] {"2.2", "2.3"};
    }
}
```

**Defines the allowable
values in an inner class**

```
}
```

EnumeratedAttribute is an abstract class with getValues being an abstract
method that you must implement. The standard practice is to use a nested class
unless there are other tasks that need to share the same enumerated values, in which
case you can create a stand-alone class to be reused by other classes. Use getValue
to retrieve the String value set by the build file, which Ant guarantees to be one of
the allowed values. You can also retrieve the int index of the specified value using
getIndex.

Class

If your task has dynamic swappable implementations as part of its functionality using
Class.forName, using a java.lang.Class setter ensures that the class exists or
the build fails. This variant is only marginally useful because it will only search for
classes within Ant's operating classpath, whereas tasks typically should be flexible
enough to allow the build file to specify its own classpath. This reduces your build's
dependency on its operating environment. We cover how to write tasks that operate
on user-defined classpaths in section 19.9.1. We recommend that you use a String
type for attributes that specify a classname, and use Class.forName to retrieve
classes from the task's classpath specified with <taskdef>, or use AntClass-
Loader.loadClass to get classes from a different classpath.

User-defined types

Last, but not least, for attribute setter types is the capability for you to define your
own type. Any class type that has a public String constructor is allowed, and this is
actually the same mechanism the numeric datatypes use, since all the wrapper classes
have constructors that take a single String parameter.

This flexibility is a pleasant addition to writing tasks, allowing you to deal with
richer objects in your task than simple strings. Inspired by a request by one of the
developers of the <cc> task who asked that Ant support hexadecimal numbers
natively, we decided to add our own support for it by defining a Hex type[1] shown in
listing 19.3.

---

[1] A variant of this was added to Ant's codebase as org.apache.tools.ant.types.FlexInteger.
It allows octal, hexadecimal, or decimal numbers to be used in Ant attributes.

Listing 19.3   Defining our own type to use as an Ant attribute type

```
package org.example.antbook.tasks;

public class Hex {
    private Integer value;

    public Hex(String hex) {
        value = Integer.decode(hex);
    }

    public int intValue() {
        return value.intValue();
    }

    public String toString() {
        return "0x" + Integer.toHexString(value.intValue());
    }
}
```

The important thing to note about the Hex class is that it has a String-argument constructor. When Ant populates an object from its attributes and encounters a setter with an argument type that it does not recognize natively, it attempts to instantiate that object with a String constructor using the value of the attribute. The setter within our task is simply:

```
private Hex hex;
public void setHex(Hex hex) {
    this.hex = hex;
}
```

Our task's execute method demonstrates that we have an instance of the Hex class by logging the hexadecimal value and the integer value.

```
public void execute() {
    if (hex != null) {
        log(hex + " = " + hex.intValue());
    }
}
```

Our build file specifies a hexadecimal number:

```
<setter hex="0x1A"/>
```

The output from the task is

```
[setter] 0x1a = 26
```

Our Hex class is perhaps a bit misnamed, as it actually will accept any legitimately specified decimal, octal, or hexadecimal formatted value and decode it properly. It does, however, effectively demonstrate that it is easy to support attributes using whatever types are most appropriate for your custom task.

Datatype references

Reusable datatypes is one of Ant's greatest strengths. Datatypes used as nested elements implicitly support reuse without any additional coding efforts, but if your task needs to accept an `id` of a previously defined datatype as attribute, use the `org.apache.tools.ant.types.Reference` type. This is really a special case of the `String`-arg constructor capabilities. To accept a path datatype as a reference for a `classpathref` attribute, implement `setClasspathRef`:

```
public void setClasspathRef(Reference r) {
    createClasspath().setRefid(r);
}
```

This example is shown in more detail in listing 19.6.

19.3.2 Supporting nested elements

Throughout this book, you have seen the use of many of Ant's tasks that use nested elements to provide rich and hierarchically structured data to the enclosing task. For example, a typical `<javac>` looks like this with a nested `<classpath>` element:

```
<javac destdir="${build.classes.dir}"
       debug="${build.debug}"
       srcdir="${src.dir}">
  <classpath refid="compile.classpath"/>
</javac>
```

While the actual code to support nested elements is quite straightforward, there is a sophisticated mechanism within Ant to facilitate it. Like attributes, Ant looks for specially named methods in your task to invoke when it encounters nested elements. There are three distinct subelement scenarios that Ant handles using specially named methods. These scenarios and methods are listed in table 19.1.

Table 19.1 Methods used for subelement handling

Scenario	Method
Ant can construct the object using a no-arg constructor, and prepopulation is not needed.	public void add*ElementName*(*ObjectType* obj)
Ant can construct the object using a no-arg constructor, but prepopulation is needed.	public void addConfigured*ElementName*(*ObjectType* obj)
Your task needs to construct the object.	public *ObjectType* create*ElementName*()

For example, a task to support nested file sets would typically have an `addFileset` method:

```
package org.example.antbook.tasks;

import java.util.Vector;

import org.apache.tools.ant.Task;
import org.apache.tools.ant.types.FileSet;
```

```
public class NestedTask extends Task {

    private Vector filesets = new Vector();

    public void addFileset(FileSet fileset) {
        filesets.add(fileset);
    }

    public void execute() {
        log("# filesets = " + filesets.size());
    }

}
```

The addition of this single method allows our task to support the full range of possibilities of the FileSet datatype (see chapter 3). We could use our task in this manner:

```
<taskdef name="nested"
         classname="org.example.antbook.tasks.NestedTask"
         classpath="${build.dir}"
/>

<fileset dir="src" excludes="**/*.java" id="non.java.files"/>

<nested>
  <fileset dir="images">
    <include name="**/*.gif"/>
  </fileset>
  <fileset refid="non.java.files"/>
</nested>
```

Deciding which method to implement for nested elements

We strongly recommend that you use the add*XXX* or addConfigured*XXX* methods for nested task elements. The primary reason for preferring this method over create*XXX* is to allow polymorphism of types. For example, a custom extension to FileSet could be used by refid on tasks that use the add-prefixed methods accepting a FileSet.

The addConfigured-prefixed method is useful if your task needs a fully populated object immediately, rather than waiting for the execute method, but in practice it is rarely needed. Use the create-prefixed method in situations where your task needs to construct the object itself, perhaps because it does not have a no-argument constructor, or because additional steps are needed beyond what the add-prefixed methods provide.

19.3.3   Supporting datatypes

As far as a task implementation goes, there is no difference between tasks that support nested datatypes and nested custom classes. Ant's introspection mechanism handles them both identically, with the added benefit that datatypes support reusability using id/refid attributes. Nested datatypes implicitly support references using refid, so your task code does not need to explicitly add this support. We do not cover writing custom datatypes in this book, as it's not commonly done even when writing custom tasks. Refer to Ant's source code for examples on writing custom datatypes.

Note that if you are trying to import references to a custom datatype, your task and datatype must be loaded by the same classloader. This happens automatically if you place the JAR files into Ant's lib directory. If you are specifying a classloader in the `<taskdef>` and `<datatype>` declarations, then you must set the `loaderref` attribute to the same classloader reference in all your declarations.

19.3.4 Allowing free-form body text

For some tasks, the constraints of XML attribute and element structure is too rigid. It could be prohibitive to require users of your task to work around the character-escaping issues required within attribute values. For example, to use the `<echo>` task to display "6 < 9" using the message attribute requires entity reference use.

This is illegal XML:

```
<echo message="6 < 9"/>
```

It produces the following output:

```
>ant echo-example
Buildfile: build.xml

BUILD FAILED
build.xml:81: Use "&lt;" for "<" in attribute values.
```

Modifying the build file to use entity references, `<echo>` now works as expected, but is not as easily read by humans:

```
<echo message="6 &lt; 9"/>
```

Indeed this would be a major headache if we had to entity-reference encode, for example, a block of SQL commands. Fortunately, this is easily overcome by allowing tasks access to the element text. Adding an `addText` method to your task instructs Ant to allow elements to contain textual body either directly or inside a CDATA section (see appendix B for more details on CDATA and XML syntax). The `<echo>` task supports body text, and our example is better specified using CDATA instead:

```
<echo><![CDATA[
  6 < 9
]]></echo>
```

In this case CDATA is needed because the < character is still illegal in element body text unless inside a CDATA section. It is important to note that Ant properties are not expanded automatically before calling `addText`. We demonstrate the use of `addText` in section 19.4.2 as well as how to have properties expanded if desired.

19.4 CREATING A BASIC ANT TASK SUBCLASS

Our tasks from now on will extend from `org.apache.tools.ant.Task`. The primary reason for subclassing from `Task` is to gain access to Ant's internal APIs. The `Task` class provides the following:

- Access to the containing target
- Access to the current project
- Logging facilities

A class that does not extend from `Task` can still gain access to the project instance and logging facilities through that instance by implementing a `setProject` method:

```
public void setProject (org.apache.tools.ant.Project project)
```

This makes extending from `Task` unnecessary for all practical purposes. The best reason not to do so would be to avoid a dependency on Ant from your class, as well as to keep your own inheritance hierarchy. But if you are going to have a `setProject` method, you've already created an Ant dependency. As for the argument of keeping your own inheritance hierarchy, we recommend encapsulating your other Java classes inside a `Task` subclass; this acts as a wrapper and allows you to change the inner workings of your encapsulated code and keep the task and build file interface unchanged.

19.4.1 Adding an attribute to a task

In keeping with our recommendations, here is a basic Ant task that extends from `Task`. It also demonstrates an optional attribute:

```java
package org.example.antbook.tasks;

import org.apache.tools.ant.Task;

public class MessageTask extends Task {

    private String message = "";

    public void setMessage(String message) {
        this.message = message;
    }

    public void execute() {
        log(message);
    }

}
```

Use it in a build file like this:

```xml
<target name="messagetask" depends="compile">
  <taskdef name="message"
           classname="org.example.antbook.tasks.MessageTask"
```

```
                classpath="${build.dir}"
    />

    <property name="the.message" value="blue scooter"/>
    <message message="${the.message}"/>
</target>
```

With the following results:

```
messagetask:
  [message] blue scooter
```

This task is a bare-bones task similar to <echo> and does nothing but log (at the MSG_INFO level) the value assigned to the message attribute. It is an example of using Ant's attribute introspection and population, and demonstrates the use of logging through the Task.log method. An important fact to note is that Ant handles property expansion in XML attributes automatically for you, as you can see, since our task got the value of the.message property rather than the text "${the.message}".

19.4.2   Handling element text

Element text is handed to its containing object, typically the task itself, or possibly a nested element, using the addText method. Of note is that the text is provided as is, and no property references are expanded. Here is a simple example of a variant of the original MessageTask to take the message text as the element data rather than from an attribute:

```
package org.example.antbook.tasks;

import org.apache.tools.ant.Task;

public class MessageTask2 extends Task {

    private String message = "";

    public void addText(String message) {        Special method to
        this.message = message;                  accept element text
    }

    public void execute() {
        log(message);
    }

}
```

Our build file fragment using this task is:

```
    <property name="another.message" value="light up ahead"/>
    <message2>${another.message}</message2>
```

It generates this output:

```
[message2] ${another.message}
```

Having the unaltered body text provided to the task is beneficial for data that may contain such strings that appear like property references, but if you need those references resolved, it's a simple matter of adding a call to a `Project` method. Our execute method now becomes:

```
public void execute() {
    log(getProject().replaceProperties(message));
}
```

The results now have the property references resolved:

```
[message2] light up ahead
```

19.5   OPERATING ON A FILESET

Ant's datatypes make writing tasks that deal with many of the typical Java build domain objects such as paths and filesets much simpler. If you are writing a task to process files in a single directory tree and would like your task to act as an implicit fileset, the base class `org.apache.tools.ant.taskdefs.MatchingTask` can save a lot of work. Listing 19.4 shows a task to process a set of files.

Listing 19.4   A task to act upon an implicit fileset

```
package org.example.antbook.tasks;

import java.io.File;
import org.apache.tools.ant.BuildException;
import org.apache.tools.ant.DirectoryScanner;
import org.apache.tools.ant.Task;
import org.apache.tools.ant.Project;
import org.apache.tools.ant.taskdefs.MatchingTask;

public class FileProcTask extends MatchingTask {

    private File dir;

    public void setDir (File dir) {
        this.dir = dir;
    }

    public void execute() throws BuildException {
        if (dir == null) {
            throw new BuildException("dir must be specified");
        }

        log("dir = " + dir, Project.MSG_DEBUG);

        DirectoryScanner ds = getDirectoryScanner(dir);
        String[] files = ds.getIncludedFiles();

        for (int i = 0; i < files.length; i++) {
            log("file: " + files[i]);
```

```
        }
        dir = null;
    }
}
```

Using `MatchingTask` provides some nice freebies that mirror the `<fileset>` datatype:

- includes/excludes attributes
- defaultexcludes attribute
- `<include>`/`<exclude>` / `<includesfile>` / `<excludesfile>` elements
- `<patternset>` element

The one piece that you must provide in your own code is the directory to use with the implicit fileset. In our example we implemented a `setDir` method and required that a `dir` attribute be specified by throwing a `BuildException` in execute if it was not specified. The `MatchingTask` base class provides a `getDirectoryScanner(File baseDir)` method to get a `DirectoryScanner` instance, taking into account all the specified inclusion and exclusion rules.

Although many Ant tasks are derived from `MatchingTask`, the current trend is away from this task; explicit filesets have proven to be more flexible. If you are writing your own task, the ease of using MatchingTask as a base class still makes it appealing. Tasks that extend from `MatchingTask` should only deal with a single implicit fileset. Tasks that need to support multiple nested filesets should extend from `Task` instead.

19.6   ERROR HANDLING

It is up to you, as a task developer, to decide how to handle abnormal conditions that may occur during the configuration or execution of your task. Ant will catch exceptions that are thrown from the task methods it invokes and make the build fail at that point. Throw Ant's `org.apache.tools.ant.BuildException`, which is a `RuntimeException` subclass, when you wish a build to fail for any reason.

You may want the failure of a build to be user-specified, in which case a simple pattern to follow is adding a `failonerror` attribute similar to many of Ant's core tasks like `<java>`. Here is a simple `Task` class allowing the build file to control if a build failure occurs or not:

```
package org.example.antbook.tasks;

import org.apache.tools.ant.Task;
import org.apache.tools.ant.BuildException;

public class ConditionalFailTask extends Task {
    private boolean failOnError = true;
```

```
public void setFailOnError(boolean failOnError) {
    this.failOnError = failOnError;
}

public void execute() throws BuildException {
    if (failOnError) {
        throw new BuildException("oops!");
    }
    log("success");
}
}
```

We recommend that failure on error be set by default, forcing a build file writer to explicitly turn off build failure if desired. This is consistent with the design of most built-in Ant tasks, although unfortunately, there are some exceptions.

19.7   TESTING ANT TASKS

The Ant codebase contains not only the source code to Ant's core and optional tasks, but also a growing number of JUnit test cases that help to verify that coding changes do not break expected functionality. Presently the Ant binary distribution does not ship with the base test case class or the testing infrastructure, but it is freely available through Ant's CVS repository.

Since our recommended design of Ant tasks is to wrap existing functionality inside an Ant task façade, it is easier and more straightforward to write unit tests against the underlying API being wrapped. However, you may desire to unit test sufficiently sophisticated Ant tasks. The best source of this information is to access Ant's CVS repository and use the org.apache.tools.ant.BuildFileTest base class. Ant's own build file has the <junit> task to execute the test cases. Test cases can be written to assert that certain messages are logged, properties have expected values, or that a BuildException is thrown when expected.

19.8   EXECUTING EXTERNAL PROGRAMS

A common reason to write an Ant task is to wrap native programs and allow their functionality to support more sophisticated capabilities such as iterating over filesets and doing dependency checking. Before resorting to writing a custom task to wrap an executable program that you would need to invoke during the build process, investigate the built-in <apply> task to see if it can accomplish your needs.

After you determine that a custom task is really needed because <apply> or <exec> is not sufficient, it is time to dig into Ant's API a bit deeper. It is not easy to successfully support launching another program from Ant in a cross-platform manner, and a lot of hard work has gone into Ant's facilities to handle these issues. Listing 19.5 demonstrates a task to execute myprog once for each file specified by nested <fileset> elements.

Listing 19.5   Executing a native program from within a task

```
package org.example.antbook.tasks;

import java.io.File;
import java.io.IOException;
import java.util.Enumeration;
import java.util.Vector;

import org.apache.tools.ant.BuildException;
import org.apache.tools.ant.DirectoryScanner;
import org.apache.tools.ant.Project;
import org.apache.tools.ant.Task;
import org.apache.tools.ant.taskdefs.Execute;
import org.apache.tools.ant.taskdefs.LogStreamHandler;
import org.apache.tools.ant.types.Commandline;
import org.apache.tools.ant.types.FileSet;

public class RunTask extends Task {

    private Vector filesets = new Vector();
    private boolean flag = true;


    public void addFileset(FileSet fileset) {
        filesets.add(fileset);
    }

    public void setFlag(boolean flag) {
        this.flag = flag;
    }

    public void execute() {

        int fileCount = 0;
        int successCount = 0;
        Enumeration enum = filesets.elements();
        while (enum.hasMoreElements()) {
            FileSet fileset = (FileSet) enum.nextElement();

            DirectoryScanner ds =
                        fileset.getDirectoryScanner(getProject());
            String[] files = ds.getIncludedFiles();

            for (int i = 0; i < files.length; i++) {
                fileCount++;
                File f = new File(fileset.getDir(getProject()), files[i]);
                if (process(f)) {
                    successCount++;
                }
            }
        }
    }
```

Allows nested filesets

Supports boolean flag attribute

Gets list of file names from a fileset

Gets absolute file name

```
        log(successCount + " out of " +
            fileCount + " files processed successfully");
    }

    protected boolean process(File file) {
        Commandline cmdline = new Commandline();
        cmdline.setExecutable("myprog");
        if (flag) {
            cmdline.createArgument().setValue("-flag");
        }
        cmdline.createArgument().setValue(file.toString());

        LogStreamHandler streamHandler =
                new LogStreamHandler(this, Project.MSG_INFO,
                                        Project.MSG_WARN);
        Execute runner = new Execute(streamHandler, null);
        runner.setAntRun(project);
        runner.setCommandline(cmdline.getCommandline());

        int retVal = 0;
        try {
            retVal = runner.execute();   <─── Executes it
        }
        catch (IOException e) {
            log(e.getMessage(), Project.MSG_DEBUG);
            return false;
        }

        return true;
    }

}
```

Constructs the command-line

Configures the Execute object

The RunTask class is utilizing several classes provided by Ant. Let's explain what is going on in a bit more detail. RunTask collects an arbitrary number of filesets using the addFileset method. The execute method iterates over each fileset, and for each fileset it uses a DirectoryScanner to get the list of included files. The values in the String[] returned by getIncludedFiles are not full paths—each value is the relative path from the fileset's root directory. We construct a File object using the fileset's root directory as the parent, which gets us the absolute file name.

Within our process method, we use Ant's Commandline object to construct the full command line to our custom executable "myprog", with a conditional switch enabled or disabled using the flag attribute. Ant's Execute class takes care of many ugly process-invoking issues, ensuring that various JDKs and platforms are supported, which each have their own idiosyncrasies in how external processes are invoked. Launcher scripts are utilized when appropriate, which are included in the ANT_HOME/bin directory: antRun.bat, antRun, and antRun.pl.

19.8.1 Dealing with process output

The `LogStreamHandler` that is provided to our `Execute` instance is used to direct standard output and error to the desired Ant logging levels. Had our task required capturing the output of the executed process, we could have used a `Pump-StreamHandler` and provided our own output streams. We do not provide an example of capturing output internal to a task. Please consult Ant's source code for tasks that do.

19.8.2 Summary of native execution

Ant makes launching native executables and scripts from a build file much easier with its many APIs already designed to do the hard work. Make sure that `<apply>` and `<exec>` are insufficient for your needs before writing a custom Ant task to wrap native execution. Had we not needed the conditional flag attribute in our contrived `RunTask` example, we could have used `<apply>`.

19.9 EXECUTING A JAVA PROGRAM WITHIN A TASK

Executing a Java program could be done in the same manner as a native program, which would occur in a new JVM and incur startup overhead. Alternatively, a Java program can be invoked within Ant's own JVM, greatly increasing performance. The `<java>` task uses both methods, depending on the value of the `fork` attribute. The primary reason for wrapping Java execution is because you do not control the source code to the program you are wrapping. If you control the source code, you would be better off writing a task to wrap the API directly rather than running `main` (or an executable JAR).

If the `<java>` task is insufficient for your needs and you want to build a wrapper task to execute a Java program, there are two good methods for doing so. The first method is to create a `Task` extension and encapsulate the `<java>` task, controlling it directly. The second is to create an extension of the `<java>` task, enabling you to inherit all of its built-in capabilities to allow the build file writer to control the classpath, forking, environment, and other parameters.

Both methods allow you to quickly get the functionality to execute Java programs, but we recommend encapsulation, allowing you to expose as much or as little of the `<java>` capability that you want. Either way, you will work with `org.apache.tools.ant.taskdefs.Java`, the class to which the `<java>` task maps.

19.9.1 Example task to execute a forked Java program

As an example, we are going to pretend that we do not have the source code to our search engine command-line tool program. (See listing 5.1 for the source code similar to this program.) We are given a tool that takes a command line:

```
java org.example.antbook.tasks.Searcher index query
```

Here *index* is the directory path to a Lucene index, and *query* is our search query.

We want a task wrapper to this functionality instead of using the `<java>` task. Invoking it with `<java>` is accomplish in this manner:

```
<java classname="org.example.antbook.tasks.Searcher"
      fork="true"
      classpathref="task.classpath">
  <arg file="${index.dir}"/>
  <arg value="${query}"/>
</java>
```

There is actually a good reason to wrap `Searcher` in a custom task instead of using `<java>`. If the correct number of command-line arguments is not provided, the program performs a `System.exit(-1)`. Therefore, if a user inadvertently omits the parameters, Ant will actually die immediately without even a BUILD FAILED message if the process is not forked. While setting `fork="true"` keeps Ant alive and well even when the parameters are not correct, it is risky because it requires a build file writer to know all of this. Wouldn't it be better if the build file looked like the following?

```
<searcher classpathref="task.classpath"
          index="${index.dir}"
          query="${query}"
/>
```

We think so! The risk is removed because internal to the `<searcher>` task, the forking mode is always enabled. In addition, there are benefits to allowing better readability and coupling between the actual program being run and the Ant task. Specifically, the attributes `index` and `query` can be specified in any order to indicate explicitly what they mean, and the user doesn't have to remember the class name.

The secret to accomplishing this easily is in reusing Ant's `<java>` capabilities. Listing 19.6 shows how to do this.

Listing 19.6 Executing a Java program from within an Ant task

```
package org.example.antbook.tasks;

import java.io.File;

import org.apache.tools.ant.BuildException;
import org.apache.tools.ant.Task;
import org.apache.tools.ant.taskdefs.Java;
import org.apache.tools.ant.types.Path;
import org.apache.tools.ant.types.Reference;

public class SearcherTask extends Task {

    private Path classpath;
    private File indexDir;
    private String query;

    public void setClasspath(Path classpath) {        Supports
        this.classpath = classpath;                    classpath
    }                                                  attribute
```

```java
public void setClasspathRef(Reference ref) {
    createClasspath().setRefid(ref);
}

public Path createClasspath() {
    if (classpath == null) {
        classpath = new Path(this.getProject());
    }
    return classpath.createPath();
}

public void setIndex(File indexDir) {
    this.indexDir = indexDir;
}

public void setQuery(String query) {
    this.query = query;
}

public void execute() throws BuildException {
    Java javaTask = (Java) getProject().createTask("java");
    javaTask.setTaskName(getTaskName());

    javaTask.setClassname("org.example.antbook.tasks.Searcher");

    javaTask.setClasspath(classpath);

    javaTask.createArg().setFile(indexDir);
    javaTask.createArg().setValue(query);

    javaTask.setFork(true);
    if (javaTask.executeJava() != 0) {
        throw new BuildException("error");
    }
}
}
```

Supports classpathref attribute

Supports nested classpath elements

Reuses the <java> task internally ◁

We call `setTaskName` with our current task name, from `getTaskName()`, so the output is prefixed with our custom task name instead of `[java]`. In this case, output from `Searcher` will be prefixed by `[searcher]`.

The `SearcherTask` shown in listing 19.6 demonstrates several key techniques useful for wrapping a Java program within a task façade. Most importantly it provides flexibility in how the classpath is specified, allowing either a `classpath` or `classpathref` attribute, or nested `<classpath>` elements. Each of these required work in our task code, but the effort was minimal thanks to Ant's API. The main trick employed in `SearcherTask` is the use of the `<java>` task internally. While this does have a hackish feel to it, it's the easiest way to deal with the complexities of forking, classpath, command-line parameters, and JVM parameters. From the knowledge you've gained in this chapter about how Ant populates tasks with data, you are equipped with the know-how to see how this is working. We simply call the setters and other special methods, such as the `create`/`add`-prefixed methods, just as Ant would do if we used `<java>` literally in a build file.

19.10 SUPPORTING ARBITRARILY NAMED ELEMENTS AND ATTRIBUTES

Before Ant 1.5, tasks could not dynamically add new attributes or elements at run time. As an example of this, you cannot add new <condition> tests, or other elements, inside <ejbjar> without changing Ant's source. Any task that needed to be dynamically extensible had to do so in an ugly manner. For example, a task that needed to support user-defined parameters would typically be specified like this in a build file:

```
<paramtask>
  <param name="username" value="erik"/>
  <param name="hostname" value="localhost"/>
</paramtask>
```

It would be written in Java code in this manner:

```java
package org.example.antbook.tasks;

import org.apache.tools.ant.Task;

import java.util.Vector;
import java.util.Iterator;

public class ParamTask extends Task {
    private Vector params = new Vector();

    public Param createParam() {
        Param p = new Param();
        params.add(p);
        return p;
    }

    public void execute() {
        Iterator iter = params.iterator();
        while (iter.hasNext()) {
            Param p = (Param) iter.next();
            log(p.getName() + " = " + p.getValue());
        }
    }

    public static class Param {
        private String name;
        private String value;

        public String getName() {
            return name;
        }

        public void setName(String name) {
            this.name = name;
        }
```

```
        public String getValue() {
            return value;
        }

        public void setValue(String value) {
            this.value = value;
        }
    }
}
```

It is nicer to have user-defined parameters specified as attributes to our task, rather than the clunkier <param> subelements.

```
<dynatask username="erik" hostname="localhost"/>
```

Ant 1.5 added a dynamic configuration mechanism to let you do just that. The changes haven't trickled into Ant's own tasks, yet, but you can use it in your own code. With the DynamicConfigurator interface, your task can support new attributes and elements. See listing 19.7.

Listing 19.7 DynamicConfigurator allows tasks to dynamically support new attributes and elements

```
package org.example.antbook.tasks;

import org.apache.tools.ant.BuildException;
import org.apache.tools.ant.DynamicConfigurator;
import org.apache.tools.ant.Task;

import java.util.Enumeration;
import java.util.Properties;

public class DynaTask extends Task implements DynamicConfigurator {
    private Properties params = new Properties();

    public void setDynamicAttribute(String name, String value)       Accepts
            throws BuildException {                                   dynamic
        params.setProperty(name, value);                             attribute
    }

    public Object createDynamicElement(String name)       Rejects dynamic
            throws BuildException {                              elements
        throw new
          BuildException("Element " + name + " is not supported");
    }

    public void execute() {
        Enumeration enum = params.keys();
        while (enum.hasMoreElements()) {
            String name = (String) enum.nextElement();
            log(name + " = " + params.get(name));
        }
    }
}
```

The `DynaTask` shown in listing 19.7 implements the two methods from the `DynamicConfigurator` interface, `setDynamicAttribute` and `createDynamic-Element`. In this example, we only support dynamic attributes by throwing a `BuildException` from `createDynamicElement`. Ant's introspection mechanism has special handling for classes which implement the `DynamicConfigurator` interface and hands attribute names and values to `setDynamicAttribute` and element names to `createDynamicElement`.

The example `DynaTask` does not support arbitrarily named elements, but it easily could use a factory-style design pattern, using the element name to look up and instantiate a class instance to return. Ant populates the object returned from `create-DynamicElement` in the same manner as all other Ant elements, even supporting nested `DynamicConfigurator` objects.

The `DynamicConfigurator` capability was added to Ant just before the Ant 1.5 feature cutoff so, unfortunately, there are no tasks within Ant 1.5 that use this capability. In the future, container tasks such as `<ejbjar>` and `<serverdeploy>` will likely take advantage of this dynamic capability to allow more flexible and configurable vender extensibility without requiring the modification of core Ant tasks. XDoclet is taking advantage of `DynamicConfigurator` in this manner, so that it dynamically consults descriptors for implementation details on the supported subtasks.

19.11 BUILDING A TASK LIBRARY

Building a library of reusable tasks makes using your tasks much easier for build file writers. To consolidate tasks into a library is as simple as building a JAR of them. We recommend that you also include a properties file in your library, which allows quick mapping of build file task names to the actual implementation Java class names. We demonstrated this technique in chapter 11 using XDoclet to build the properties file dynamically from `@ant.task` tags in the Javadoc comments of each tag. The result is a JAR containing a properties file. Several tasks presented in this chapter are mapped using this properties file:

```
simpletask=org.example.antbook.tasks.SimpleTask
message=org.example.antbook.tasks.MessageTask
message2=org.example.antbook.tasks.MessageTask2
enum=org.example.antbook.tasks.EnumTask
fileproc=org.example.antbook.tasks.FileProcTask
nested=org.example.antbook.tasks.NestedTask
run=org.example.antbook.tasks.RunTask
```

For this example, we did not use XDoclet, although we prefer to use it in order to save double-maintenance when new tasks get added. Our jar target is simply:

```
<target name="jar" depends="compile">
  <copy file="${meta.dir}/taskdef.properties"
        todir="${build.dir}"/>
```

```
    <jar destfile="${dist.dir}/tasks.jar"
         basedir="${build.dir}"/>
</target>
```

A build file can utilize our task library easily without having to know the class names of each task. Listing 19.8 shows an example of using the library of tasks just built.

Listing 19.8   Using a task library in a build file

```
<?xml version="1.0" ?>
<project name="library" default="main">

  <property name="tasks.jar" location="dist/tasks.jar"/>
  <taskdef resource="taskdef.properties" classpath="${tasks.jar}"/>   <─┐
                                                                         │
  <target name="usetasks">                              Defines all tasks
    <simpletask/>                                      contained within
                                                        the task library
    <property name="the.message" value="blue scooter"/>
    <message message="${the.message}"/>

    <property name="another.message" value="light up ahead"/>
    <message2>${another.message}</message2>

    <enum version="2.3"/>

    <fileproc dir="${basedir}">
      <include name="**/*.java"/>
    </fileproc>

    <nested>
      <fileset dir="images">
        <include name="**/*.gif"/>
      </fileset>
      <fileset refid="non.java.files"/>
    </nested>

    <run flag="off">
      <fileset dir="." excludes="**/*.class"/>
    </run>
  </target>

  <target name="main" depends="usetasks"/>
</project>
```

Note that only one <taskdef> is used, but all the tasks within taskdef.properties are defined and several are used in the usetasks target.

19.12 Supporting Multiple Versions of Ant

Tasks written for previous versions of Ant should work fine in future versions of Ant 1.x (and possibly Ant 2.0), but the converse is not necessarily true. Ant's API evolves, and newer features, of course, are not supported in earlier versions. Ant developers work very hard to keep newer versions as backwards-compatible as possible, such that build files and tasks written for previous versions will still work when upgrading to a newer version of Ant.

In order to write tasks that will work with, say, Ant 1.4.1 and Ant 1.5, you must avoid all newer API capabilities such as `Project.setNewProperty` and `DynamicConfigurator`. The best way to ensure compatibility is to compile your tasks with the oldest version of Ant you wish to support, and of course, test your tasks on each version to ensure all is well.

19.13 Summary

The key to writing a task in Ant as efficiently as possible is to understand the infrastructure that Ant provides to tasks. Datatypes can be used easily in tasks with very little code or effort, and nested datatypes implicitly support references without your task being aware of it. We have not provided an in-depth API reference to Ant. Ant ships with a complete Javadoc set and Ant's own source code is readily available. We encourage you to consult these indispensable references when you begin writing your own tasks. Simply coding by example, cutting and pasting relevant pieces from Ant's own tasks that are similar to what you need to accomplish, is the quickest method to writing sophisticated tasks. With the information in this chapter, which you cannot easily glean from reading source code, you now have an understanding of how Ant provides data to tasks. Java introspection and method naming conventions are the secret. A lot of complex details are buried under the hood of these mechanisms, allowing you to write tasks at a much higher, domain-specific level.

C H A P T E R   2 0

Extending Ant further

20.1 Scripting within Ant   499
20.2 Listeners and loggers   502
20.3 Developing a custom mapper   514
20.4 Creating custom selectors   515
20.5 Implementing a custom filter   517
20.6 Summary   520

Ant's extensibility does not end with custom Java tasks. Ant allows for extensibility and customization in several more ways:

- Scripting ad-hoc tasks using many popular scripting languages with the <script> task
- Monitoring or logging of the build process with custom build listeners and loggers
- Custom <mapper> implementations
- Powerful fileset filtering with specialized selectors
- Filters to transform text streams

Regardless of whether or not you use these features, it is useful to know that these exist in case you encounter them in a build you inherit or come across a situation that could benefit from them.

20.1 SCRIPTING WITHIN ANT

The `<script>` task supports multiple script language commands to invoke tasks and manipulate other Ant objects. The script can be written in JavaScript (Mozilla's Rhino implementation, to be precise), or a number of other languages. It is therefore a simple way to extend Ant from inside a build file, without having to distribute extra libraries or even add another source file to the project.

The basis of the `<script>` task is the Bean Scripting Framework from IBM: their bsf.jar needs to be downloaded and dropped into ANT_HOME/lib. The URL for this file is listed in the library dependencies section of the Ant documentation. The framework is a foundational package to bridge arbitrary scripting languages to Java applications; you also need to provide the implementation of the scripting language you wish to use. The Mozilla Rhino version of JavaScript is a popular choice, but Python is another possibility, as are others. Again, the URLs to these libraries are listed in the Ant documentation.

The example problem chosen to demonstrate the value of the script task is that of assigning a random number to a property. This number can then be used as a parameter to another task, as shown in listing 20.1.

> **Listing 20.1 Using `<script>` to generate a random number and assign it to an Ant property**

```
<project name="script_example" default="test-random">
  <description>
    Use a script task to generate a random number, then
    print it
  </description>

  <target name="random">
    <script language="javascript"><![CDATA[
      //NB: an unqualified Math is the JavaScript object
      var r=java.lang.Math.random();
      var num = Math.round(r*10);
      project.setNewProperty("random", num);
      self.log("Generated random number " + num, project.MSG_DEBUG);
    ]]>
    </script>
  </target>

  <target name="test-random" depends="random">
    <echo>Random number is ${random}</echo>
  </target>

</project>
```

Running the `test-random` target should print out the value of the `${random}`, which will be between zero and ten, inclusive.

```
random:

test-random:
     [echo] Random number is 2

BUILD SUCCESSFUL
```

20.1.1 Implicit objects provided to <script>

The <script> task provides two fixed-name implicit objects to the script context: project and self. The project object is a reference to the actual org.apache. tools.ant.Project instance, which is handy for setting and accessing properties through the Project object API (see chapter 19 for more details). The self object is a reference to the org.apache.tools.ant.taskdefs.optional.Script instance, which is a subclass of org.apache.tools.ant.Task. The self reference is useful for logging messages, using either of the log methods that Task provides. In listing 20.1, we used both project and self, calling project.setNewProperty to assign a property and self.log to generate a message at the debugging level.

Project references

Along with self and project, the <script> task provides Ant properties, targets, and references to the scripting context. Properties and targets are provided by their name, and references by their id or name. References include datatypes, tasks, and the project itself. It can be a bit confusing to work with these references, and there is one important caveat to note: the implicit objects whose names do not represent a valid Java identifier are ignored and not placed into the scripting context. Here is an example demonstrating the various implicit objects that are accessible to the scripting context:

```xml
<?xml version="1.0" ?>
<project name="script_context" default="main">

  <property name="legalName" value="accessible"/>
  <property name="illegal name" value="inaccessible?"/>

  <target name="main">
    <script language="javascript"><![CDATA[
      self.log("legalName = " + legalName);
      self.log("illegal name = " + project.getProperty("illegal name"));
      self.log("test = " + test);
      self.log("echo_task = " + echo_task);
      self.log("script_context = " + script_context);
      self.log("project = " + project);

      echo_task.setMessage("invoked via <script>");
      echo_task.execute();
    ]]>
    </script>
  </target>
```

CHAPTER 20   EXTENDING ANT FURTHER

```
  <target name="test">
    <echo id="echo_task"/>
  </target>

</project>
```

The output is:

```
main:
    [script] legalName = accessible
    [script] illegal name = inaccessible?
    [script] test = test
    [script] echo_task = org.apache.tools.ant.taskdefs.Echo@7a8a02
    [script] script_context = org.apache.tools.ant.Project@7ebe1
    [script] project = org.apache.tools.ant.Project@7ebe1
       [echo] invoked via <script>
```

The `legalName` property is directly accessible, but because `illegal name` contains a space, it is only accessible through `project.getProperty`. The `test` reference displays "test" because the `Target` object has a `toString` method that returns the target name. The `script_context` reference is provided because of the `name` attribute on `<project>`, but it is preferable to access the project reference through `project` (which you can see is equivalent). An interesting facet to the `<script>` task is the ability to script the actual invocation of other targets, as shown by the invocation of the `echo_task` task. You can use `<script>` to configure a task before it runs—but remember that any attributes set in the task have priority, because they are set just before the task executes.

20.1.2   Scripting summary

The scripting framework is very powerful. Any Java class can be used by giving its full package name, and objects in the build file can be referred to by using the names or `id` values assigned to them. Usually, it is rare to see any task declaration in an Ant file given an `id`, but to access tasks within `<script>` code, an `id` is needed.

We could cover the `<script>` task in more detail, providing many examples of its use. However, we prefer to encourage readers to write full Java tasks instead, as covered in chapter 19. For all the power the `<script>` task offers, it does not keep a build file simple, and it limits the reuse opportunities of the code. Too much use of the task often indicates that someone is trying to turn a build file into a make file, or that it is time to refactor the script into an Ant task.

The counter argument is that `<script>` code gives you power without writing and distributing Java libraries, and is faster to write. If a project does use script tasks, then the best way to stay in control is to pull the scripts out into individual files and then use the `<script file="random.js">` option to refer to the file directly. This lets you keep the scripts separate from the build; and they may be reused more easily. The other issue is that the scripting framework is uninformative when things do not work. For example, casting with `(int)` to convert the floating point random number to an integer caused the error `undefined: identifier is a reserved word (<ANT>; line 3)` when executing the script. JavaScript, or ECMAScript to give its official name, is not Java, yet it is close enough to mislead.

Besides the Ant documentation, a useful online resource for the `<script>` task lives at http://www.sitepen.com/ant/javascript.html.

20.2   LISTENERS AND LOGGERS

Ant provides capability to monitor its progress during execution. There are two tightly related concepts used for this monitoring: listeners and loggers. In order to develop custom listeners and loggers, it is worthwhile to understand the underlying architecture used by Ant. Let's first take a look at the UML for the `BuildListener` and `BuildLogger` interfaces, shown in figure 20.1.

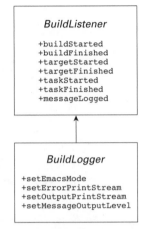

Figure 20.1   UML diagram of Ant's BuildListener and BuildLogger interfaces

Attached `BuildListeners` are notified of seven events during the build lifecycle. The events are: build started/finished, target started/finished, task started/finished, and logging of messages. Any number of build listeners can be attached to a `Project`, and Ant internally attaches some of its own to notify itself of events, particularly the build finished event, for cleanup purposes. Each of the events is handed a `BuildEvent` object. This `BuildEvent` encapsulates either a String message, a reference to the `Project`, a `Target`, or a `Task` depending on the event being triggered. Table 20.1 lists the available `BuildEvent` information for each `BuildListener` method. It also provides access to an exception if one was thrown. For messages logged, a priority is also provided, which could be used to filter output.

To use a listener, you must specify it on the command line using the `-listener` command-line switch. To use the listener, we will write in section 20.2.1, for example, the command line is

```
ant -listener org.apache.tools.ant.listener.CommonsLoggingListener
```

Table 20.1   BuildEvent contents

BuildListener method	BuildEvent contents
buildStarted and buildFinished	Project via getProject() and exception via getException()
targetStarted and targetFinished	Target via getTarget() and exception via getException(). Project object also accessible.
taskStarted and taskFinished	Task via getTask() and exception via getException(). Project and target objects also accessible.
messageLogged	Message via getMessage() and priority of message via getPriority(). Depending on where the message is logged in the build process, getTask, getTarget, or getProject will also available for use.

The `BuildLogger` interface builds upon its parent `BuildListener` by adding access to the output and error print streams. Two other additional methods that the `BuildLogger` interface extends beyond `BuildListener` allow for setting emacs mode and the message output level. The `DefaultLogger` uses the emacs mode to provide output formatted for IDE integration, as the emacs representation of error locations in files is something most IDEs can parse. The message output level is used by `DefaultLogger` to filter the output based on the logging level.

An Ant project can only have one associated `BuildLogger`. Because the logger has access to the error and output print streams, only one attached logger makes sense. The command line allows specification of a `BuildLogger` via the `-logger` switch. Using `-emacs` enables emacs mode. The `-quiet`, `-verbose`, and `-debug` switches specify the logging level. The default output level used is informational, which is between the quiet and verbose options with respect to the output generated. The `BuildLogger` is attached internally as a listener to the project, so that it receives the events exactly like any attached listeners.

NOTE   There is some console output from Ant that occurs prior to the involvement of the logger or listeners that cannot be captured by using them. If an error occurs outside the scope of the project (e.g., a missing build.xml), this output will only be available in the console or log file.

20.2.1   Writing a custom listener

The example listener we demonstrate here was written by Erik during the development of this book, contributed to the Ant codebase, and is already available in the Ant distribution. This custom listener is a wrapper for the Jakarta Commons Logging API, which itself is a façade over several popular logging APIs, including Log4j, LogKit, and Java 1.4's logging facility. The documentation, source, and binaries of this library are available at http://jakarta.apache.org/commons/logging.html. Listing 20.2 shows our implementation of a `BuildListener` that hands off build events to this logging façade.

> **Listing 20.2 CommonsLoggingListener, allowing custom logging through a number of logging APIs**

```
package org.apache.tools.ant.listener;

import org.apache.commons.logging.Log;
import org.apache.commons.logging.LogConfigurationException;
import org.apache.commons.logging.LogFactory;
import org.apache.tools.ant.BuildEvent;
import org.apache.tools.ant.BuildListener;
import org.apache.tools.ant.Project;
import org.apache.tools.ant.Target;
import org.apache.tools.ant.Task;

/**
 * Jakarta Commons Logging listener.
```

```
 * Note: do not use the SimpleLog as your logger implementation as it
 * causes an infinite loop since it writes to System.err, which Ant traps
 * and reroutes to the logger/listener layer.
 *
 * @author Erik Hatcher
 * @since Ant 1.5
 */
public class CommonsLoggingListener implements BuildListener {

    private boolean initialized = false;

    private LogFactory logFactory;

    public CommonsLoggingListener() {
        try {
            logFactory = LogFactory.getFactory();
        } catch (LogConfigurationException e) {
            e.printStackTrace(System.err);
            return;
        }

        initialized = true;
    }

    public void buildStarted(BuildEvent event) {
        if (initialized) {
            Log log = logFactory.getInstance(Project.class);
            log.info("Build started.");
        }
    }

    public void buildFinished(BuildEvent event) {
        if (initialized) {
            Log log = logFactory.getInstance(Project.class);
            if (event.getException() == null) {
                log.info("Build finished.");
            } else {
                log.error("Build finished with error.", event.getExcep-
tion());
            }
        }
    }

    public void targetStarted(BuildEvent event) {
        if (initialized) {
            Log log = logFactory.getInstance(Target.class);
            log.info("Target \"" + event.getTarget().getName() +
                    "\" started.");
        }
    }

    public void targetFinished(BuildEvent event) {
        if (initialized) {
            String targetName = event.getTarget().getName();
```

```
            Log log = logFactory.getInstance(Target.class);
            if (event.getException() == null) {
                log.info("Target \"" + targetName + "\" finished.");
            } else {
                log.error("Target \"" + targetName
                        + "\" finished with error.", event.getException());
            }
        }
    }

    public void taskStarted(BuildEvent event) {
        if (initialized) {
            Task task = event.getTask();
            Log log = logFactory.getInstance(task.getClass().getName());
            log.info("Task \"" + task.getTaskName() + "\" started.");
        }
    }

    public void taskFinished(BuildEvent event) {
        if (initialized) {
            Task task = event.getTask();
            Log log = logFactory.getInstance(task.getClass().getName());
            if (event.getException() == null) {
                log.info("Task \"" + task.getTaskName() + "\" finished.");
            } else {
                log.error("Task \"" + task.getTaskName()
                        + "\" finished with error.", event.getException());
            }
        }
    }

    public void messageLogged(BuildEvent event) {
        if (initialized) {
            Object categoryObject = event.getTask();
            if (categoryObject == null) {
                categoryObject = event.getTarget();
                if (categoryObject == null) {
                    categoryObject = event.getProject();
                }
            }

            Log log = logFactory.getInstance(
                        categoryObject.getClass().getName());
            switch (event.getPriority()) {
                case Project.MSG_ERR:
                    log.error(event.getMessage());
                    break;
                case Project.MSG_WARN:
                    log.warn(event.getMessage());
                    break;
                case Project.MSG_INFO:
                    log.info(event.getMessage());
                    break;
                case Project.MSG_VERBOSE:
```

```
                        log.debug(event.getMessage());
                        break;
                    case Project.MSG_DEBUG:
                        log.debug(event.getMessage());
                        break;
                    default:
                        log.error(event.getMessage());
                        break;
                }
            }
        }
    }
```

It is beyond the scope of this book to cover the Jakarta Commons Logging API, although its use is quite simple. Every event has to be logged in a *category;* here we use the class name. As noted in the class comments, you must not use a logging implementation that writes to `System.out` or `System.err` because of the infinite loop possibility. Ant traps `System.out` and `System.err` calls and forwards them on to attached listeners through the `messageLogged` method.

20.2.2   Using Log4j logging capabilities

Ant includes both a `Log4jListener` and a `CommonsLoggingListener`. The `Log4jListener` was developed before the Commons Logging API existed, both of which can output to Log4j. The `CommonsLoggingListener` is recommended in environments that need to be flexible in which logging API is used, although an additional dependency is required beyond the Log4j dependency: commons-logging.jar. We demonstrate Log4j capabilities using the `CommonsLoggingListener`, although this would work just as well using the `Log4jListener`.

When an event is logged from an application, it is logged to a specific *category*. Categories are hierarchical, based on a dotted textual representation. Ant's `Commons-LoggingListener` class uses as the category name the fully qualified class name of the context provided by the `BuildEvent`. Each event is logged to a *priority* level of DEBUG, WARN, INFO, ERROR, or FATAL (note: FATAL is not used by the `CommonsLoggingListener`, but the other priority levels are). Log4j initializes itself from a `log4j.properties` file (or using `ANT_OPTS=-Dlog4j.configuration=<filename>`). The Log4j configuration properties file could reside wherever most appropriate, but by default, it is picked up from the current directory. `CommonsLoggingListener` fires every event, including debugging information, through Log4j[1] which in turn allows configuration control over what events are logged, where they are logged, and what format is used.

---

[1] Consult the Jakarta Commons Logging API for configuration details. Log4j is the default logging implementation if Log4j is found in the classpath.

The `CommonsLoggingListener` is useful in a continuous integration process. In an environment where builds are running every time code is checked into the source code repository, it is important to be able to filter the log information so that you are alerted only when something goes wrong rather than being inundated by routine successful build notifications. It is also important to keep detailed logs for reference when tracking down a problem. However, it's not important to keep too much historical information, as it's not useful for very long. Integrating Ant with Log4j gives us these powerful capabilities with minimal configuration. Here is the `log4j.properties` file that accomplishes these goals:

```
log4j.rootCategory=INFO,file
log4j.category.org.apache.tools.ant.Project=INFO,file,mail
```
Configures categories

```
log4j.appender.file=org.apache.log4j.RollingFileAppender
log4j.appender.file.layout=org.apache.log4j.TTCCLayout
log4j.appender.file.file=build.log
log4j.appender.file.maxBackupIndex=3
log4j.appender.file.maxFileSize=100KB
```
Configures file appender

```
log4j.appender.mail=org.apache.log4j.net.SMTPAppender
log4j.appender.mail.layout=org.apache.log4j.HTMLLayout
log4j.appender.mail.Threshold=ERROR
log4j.appender.mail.SMTPHost=localhost
log4j.appender.mail.bufferSize=1
log4j.appender.mail.to=erik@example.org
log4j.appender.mail.from=erik@example.org
log4j.appender.mail.subject=Build Failure!
```
Configures mail appender

Let's look at an example of using the `CommonsLoggingListener` with the configuration in the example, and both commons-logging.jar and log4j.jar in Ant's lib directory. Here is a trivial build.xml file that causes a build failure:

```
<project default="fail">
  <target name="fail">
    <fail message="Example build failure"/>
  </target>
</project>
```

The command line is:

```
ant -listener org.apache.tools.ant.listener.CommonsLoggingListener
```

The console outputs this:

```
Buildfile: build.xml

fail:

BUILD FAILED
C:\AntBook\Sections\Extending\listeners\build.xml:3: Example build failure

Total time: 1 second
```

Also, during the execution, build.log is created or appended to, with output like this:

```
[main] INFO org.apache.tools.ant.Project - Build started.
[main] INFO org.apache.tools.ant.Project - Build started.
[main] INFO org.apache.tools.ant.Target - Target "fail" started.
[main] INFO org.apache.tools.ant.taskdefs.Exit - Task "fail" started.
[main] ERROR org.apache.tools.ant.taskdefs.Exit - Task "fail" finished with error.
C:\AntBook\Sections\Extending\listeners\build.xml:3: Example build failure
        at org.apache.tools.ant.taskdefs.Exit.execute(Exit.java:90)
        at org.apache.tools.ant.Task.perform(Task.java:317)
        at org.apache.tools.ant.Target.execute(Target.java:309)
        at org.apache.tools.ant.Target.performTasks(Target.java:334)
        at org.apache.tools.ant.Project.executeTarget(Project.java:1216)
        at org.apache.tools.ant.Project.executeTargets(Project.java:1160)
        at org.apache.tools.ant.Main.runBuild(Main.java:605)
        at org.apache.tools.ant.Main.start(Main.java:195)
        at org.apache.tools.ant.Main.main(Main.java:234)
[main] ERROR org.apache.tools.ant.Target - Target "fail" finished with error.
C:\AntBook\Sections\Extending\listeners\build.xml:3: Example build failure
        at org.apache.tools.ant.taskdefs.Exit.execute(Exit.java:90)
        at org.apache.tools.ant.Task.perform(Task.java:317)
        at org.apache.tools.ant.Target.execute(Target.java:309)
        at org.apache.tools.ant.Target.performTasks(Target.java:334)
        at org.apache.tools.ant.Project.executeTarget(Project.java:1216)
        at org.apache.tools.ant.Project.executeTargets(Project.java:1160)
        at org.apache.tools.ant.Main.runBuild(Main.java:605)
        at org.apache.tools.ant.Main.start(Main.java:195)
        at org.apache.tools.ant.Main.main(Main.java:234)
[main] ERROR org.apache.tools.ant.Project - Build finished with error.
C:\AntBook\Sections\Extending\listeners\build.xml:3: Example build failure
        at org.apache.tools.ant.taskdefs.Exit.execute(Exit.java:90)
        at org.apache.tools.ant.Task.perform(Task.java:317)
        at org.apache.tools.ant.Target.execute(Target.java:309)
        at org.apache.tools.ant.Target.performTasks(Target.java:334)
        at org.apache.tools.ant.Project.executeTarget(Project.java:1216)
        at org.apache.tools.ant.Project.executeTargets(Project.java:1160)
        at org.apache.tools.ant.Main.runBuild(Main.java:605)
        at org.apache.tools.ant.Main.start(Main.java:195)
        at org.apache.tools.ant.Main.main(Main.java:234)
[main] ERROR org.apache.tools.ant.Project - Build finished with error.
C:\AntBook\Sections\Extending\listeners\build.xml:3: Example build failure
        at org.apache.tools.ant.taskdefs.Exit.execute(Exit.java:90)
        at org.apache.tools.ant.Task.perform(Task.java:317)
        at org.apache.tools.ant.Target.execute(Target.java:309)
        at org.apache.tools.ant.Target.performTasks(Target.java:334)
        at org.apache.tools.ant.Project.executeTarget(Project.java:1216)
        at org.apache.tools.ant.Project.executeTargets(Project.java:1160)
        at org.apache.tools.ant.Main.runBuild(Main.java:605)
        at org.apache.tools.ant.Main.start(Main.java:195)
        at org.apache.tools.ant.Main.main(Main.java:234)
```

The output above was generated by the TTCCAppender,[2] which displays the name of the thread ([main]), the event priority (INFO, ERROR, etc.), and the event message,

---

[2] TTCC is short for time, thread, category, and context.

including the stack trace of any exceptions logged. The failure exception is generated three times because it is logged as a `Task` failure, a `Target` failure, and finally a `Project` failure. This could be filtered further with additional configuration in log4j.properties. When build.log reaches the specified limit of 100KB in size, backup files are generated (`backup.log.1`, `backup.log.2`, and so on) with a maximum number of three backup files.

Because we only want a single email sent for each build failure, the configuration has a special entry for the `org.apache.tools.ant.Project` category. This entry overrides any parent category configuration, so it is necessary to specify both the file and mail appenders, as we still want informational project messages logged to the `build.log` file. We then set the mail appender, log threshold to ERROR, to ignore any events with lower priority. During the run of the example build, a single HTML-formatted email detailing the error is sent, as shown in figure 20.2.

Figure 20.2
Log4j SMTP appender email using the HTMLLayout

The Log4j package provides extremely flexible logging capabilities by configuring itself from a properties file at run time. Output can be turned off, filtered by priority, formatted, and logged to any number of appenders, including automatically rotating log files, a TCP/IP socket, JDBC, or even SMTP. Given the flexibility and extensibility of Log4j, most event-based logging needs can be accomplished using either `Log4jListener` or `CommonsLoggingListener`. JDK 1.4's logging API can be invoked by configuring the `CommonsLoggingListener` appropriately as well; consult the Jakarta Commons Logging documentation for details.

20.2.3 Writing a custom logger

A custom `BuildLogger` is simply a `BuildListener` with four additional required methods, as shown in figure 20.1. During the development of this chapter, we took the opportunity to provide a frequently requested capability: sending an email of the complete build log.

One of the most commonly desired features of a build process is having the build results sent via email. Using Log4j's `SMTPAppender` will not quite work because it is designed to email every event logged individually (or buffer a specified number of events to email less frequently, but buffering did not seem to flush when a build finished). This section will demonstrate the development of the `MailLogger` class. Ant's built-in DefaultLogger allows subclasses to receive the output generated by overriding the log method. By subclassing DefaultLogger, the MailLogger will be capable of generating console output, and buffering that same output for the body of an email. Listing 20.3 showcases our MailLogger code, which is now part of the Ant distribution.

Listing 20.3 MailLogger—an example of creating a custom BuildLogger by subclassing from Ant's DefaultLogger

```
package org.apache.tools.ant.listener;      ←—— Confusing package
                                                 name, we know!
import org.apache.tools.ant.BuildEvent;
import org.apache.tools.ant.DefaultLogger;
import org.apache.tools.ant.Project;
import org.apache.tools.ant.util.StringUtils;
import org.apache.tools.mail.MailMessage;

import java.io.FileInputStream;
import java.io.IOException;
import java.io.InputStream;
import java.io.PrintStream;
import java.util.Enumeration;
import java.util.Hashtable;
import java.util.Properties;
import java.util.StringTokenizer;

// Code comments omitted for brevity
public class MailLogger extends DefaultLogger {
    private StringBuffer buffer = new StringBuffer();

    public void buildFinished(BuildEvent event) {      Overrides buildFinished,
        super.buildFinished(event);                    calls parent first

        Project project = event.getProject();
        Hashtable properties = project.getProperties();    Allows for con-
                                                           figuration via
        Properties fileProperties = new Properties();      properties file
        String filename = (String)
                properties.get("MailLogger.properties.file");
        if (filename != null) {
            InputStream is = null;
            try {
                is = new FileInputStream(filename);
                fileProperties.load(is);
            } catch (IOException ioe) {
                // ignore because properties file is not required
            } finally {
                if (is != null) {
                    try {
                        is.close();
                    } catch (IOException e) {
                    }
                }
            }
        }
```

```
            }

        for (Enumeration e = fileProperties.keys();       Substitutes
                e.hasMoreElements();) {                  Ant properties
            String key = (String) e.nextElement();
            String value = fileProperties.getProperty(key);
            properties.put(key, project.replaceProperties(value));    <──┐
        }

        boolean success = (event.getException() == null);
        String prefix = success ? "success" : "failure";

        try {
            boolean notify = Project.toBoolean(getValue(properties,
                    prefix + ".notify", "on"));

            if (!notify) {                                   Should we
                return;                                    send email?
            }

            String mailhost = getValue(properties, "mailhost",
                                       "localhost");
            String from = getValue(properties, "from", null);

            String toList = getValue(properties, prefix + ".to",
                                     null);
            String subject = getValue(properties,
                        prefix + ".subject",
                        (success) ? "Build Success" : "Build Failure");

            sendMail(mailhost, from, toList, subject,
                     buffer.toString());
        } catch (Exception e) {
            System.out.println("MailLogger failed to send e-mail!");
            e.printStackTrace(System.err);
        }
    }                                                   Overrides
                                                  DefaultLogger.log,
                                                  capture messages
    protected void log(String message) {
        buffer.append(message).append(StringUtils.LINE_SEP);
    }


    private String getValue(Hashtable properties, String name,
                            String defaultValue) throws Exception {
        String propertyName = "MailLogger." + name;
        String value = (String) properties.get(propertyName);

        if (value == null) {
            value = defaultValue;
        }

        if (value == null) {
```

```
            throw new Exception("Missing required parameter: " +
                    propertyName);
        }

        return value;
    }


    private void sendMail (String mailhost, String from,
                        String toList, String subject,
                        String message) throws IOException {
        MailMessage mailMessage = new MailMessage(mailhost);   ◁─┐
                                                                  │  Uses Ant's
        mailMessage.from(from);                                   │  built-in mailer

        StringTokenizer t = new StringTokenizer(toList, ", ", false);
        while (t.hasMoreTokens()) {
            mailMessage.to(t.nextToken());
        }

        mailMessage.setSubject(subject);

        PrintStream ps = mailMessage.getPrintStream();
        ps.println(message);

        mailMessage.sendAndClose();
    }
}
```

It is important to note that the buildFinished method initially delegates to
DefaultLogger's implementation of buildFinished. This is necessary so that
the final output is generated to the console or log file before sending the email. There
are several configurable parameters that are needed to create a robust email logger:
from email address, to email address(es), and subject. Beyond those parameters, we
will allow the ability to enable/disable failure and success messages separately, have
different email address lists for failure and success emails, as well as have different
subjects based on the success or failure of a build.

Parameters are configurable through a properties file and through Ant properties,
with Ant properties taking precedence and overriding those specified in the properties
file. This order of precedence allows common settings to be used across multiple
projects, but also allows settings to be controlled on a per-project or per-user basis. We
can use the special project property MailLogger.properties.file (Ant calls
this one of its magic properties) to define the location of the configuration file, then
load it and overlay the project properties. The success status of a build is based on
whether the BuildEvent contains an exception or not.

20.2.4 Using the MailLogger

To use the `MailLogger`, which, again, is already part of Ant since version 1.5, we must provide the necessary configuration parameters. We recommend using an external properties file. This allows multiple projects to share the settings, which can be overridden on a per-project basis simply by overriding the properties using `<property>` or any other property setting technique. Our maillogger.properties file contains:

```
MailLogger.from = erik@example.org
MailLogger.failure.to = erik@example.org
MailLogger.mailhost = localhost
MailLogger.success.to = erik@example.org
MailLogger.success.subject = ${ant.project.name} - Build success
MailLogger.failure.subject = FAILURE - ${ant.project.name}
MailLogger.success.notify = off
```

Notice how we use Ant properties within this configuration file. We use the built-in `${ant.project.name}` property to insert the project name into the subject of the emails sent, allowing us to easily identify which project is being reported at a quick glance. Our example build file to demonstrate the `MailLogger` is:

```
<project name="MailLogger example" default="test">

  <target name="test">
    <echo message="hello out there"/>
  </target>

  <target name="fail"><fail/></target>
</project>
```

From the command line, we specify the configuration file and invoke the fail target:

```
> ant -f buildmail.xml
    -logger org.apache.tools.ant.listener.MailLogger
    -DMailLogger.properties.file=maillogger.properties
    fail
Buildfile: buildmail.xml

fail:

BUILD FAILED
C:\AntBook\Sections\Extending\listeners\buildmail.xml:7: No message

Total time: 1 second
```

Because we have `MailLogger.success.notify` set to `off`, we only receive build failure emails. Setting ANT_ARGS with the appropriate `-logger` and `-DMail-Logger.properties.file` settings allows us to invoke Ant simply as ant -f buildmail.xml fail. See appendix A for details on using ANT_ARGS.

20.3 DEVELOPING A CUSTOM MAPPER

Several Ant tasks support the <mapper> datatype, allowing file names to be mapped to one or more corresponding files. Section 3.10 discusses the built-in mappers in detail. In almost all cases, the provided mappers are sufficient, but you may find a need to write a custom one. In fact, we found such a need during the writing of this book, and we will use it as an example. We wanted to speed up our builds that incorporated unit tests, but the <junit> task simply reruns all tests each time it is encountered. By using <uptodate> to compare timestamps on the unit test results with the actual Java source files, we are able to bypass testing if they have already been run. The problem encountered was that the Java source files are in a directory structure based on package names, while the unit test results are written to a flat directory structure with the dotted package name used in the XML file name. Section 4.8 provides more details on this short-circuiting technique. We developed the package mapper to solve this problem (which is now part of Ant, as of version 1.5), shown in listing 20.4.

Listing 20.4   The package mapper implementation

```
public class PackageNameMapper extends GlobPatternMapper {
    /**
     * Returns the part of the given string that matches the * in the
     * &quot;from&quot; pattern replacing file separators with dots
     *
     *@param name   Source filename
     *@return       Replaced variable part
     */
    protected String extractVariablePart(String name) {
        String var = name.substring(prefixLength,
                name.length() - postfixLength);
        return var.replace(File.separatorChar, '.');
    }
}
```

A custom mapper must implement the org.apache.tools.ant.util.FileName-Mapper interface, which glob mapper class does. We subclass the GlobPattern-Mapper to inherit the asterisk (*) pattern-matching capability. By overriding its extractVariablePart method, all that was needed was to replace file separators with dots.

The FileNameMapper interface's primary method has this signature:

```
String[] mapFileName(String sourceFileName)
```

In our case, the GlobPatternMapper implements this, but you may wish to implement FileNameMapper directly, providing an array of files that translate from the source file name. To use a custom mapper in a build file, simply specify a class-name and optionally a classpath, classpathref, or a nested <classpath> element to the <mapper>:

```
<uptodate property="is.uptodate">
  <srcfiles dir="${some.dir}"/>
  <mapper classname="org.example.antbook.MyCustomMapper"
          classpathref="mapper.classpath"
          from="*Test.java" to="${test.data.dir}/TEST-*Test.xml"/>
</uptodate>
```

Because our example mapper is now part of the Ant distribution, you can simply refer to it by name:

```
<uptodate property="is.uptodate">
  <srcfiles dir="${some.dir}"/>
  <mapper type="package"
          from="*Test.java" to="${test.data.dir}/TEST-*Test.xml"/>
</uptodate>
```

20.4   CREATING CUSTOM SELECTORS

One of Ant's strengths is its ability to represent domain-specific needs at a high level, such as that provided by filesets, which represent a collection of files rooted from a base directory. Patternsets provide the ability to include or exclude files based on file name patterns, and the built-in selectors provide even more selection capability, such as selecting only files that contain a certain string or were modified after a certain date. Section 3.6 covers the built-in selectors in more detail. Our goal here is to write a custom selector that implements something new: selecting files that are read-only.

Our `ReadOnlySelector` code is quite short and sweet, as shown in listing 20.5.

Listing 20.5   ReadOnlySelector includes only files that are not writable

```
package org.example.antbook;

import org.apache.tools.ant.BuildException;
import org.apache.tools.ant.types.selectors.BaseExtendSelector;

import java.io.File;

public class ReadOnlySelector extends BaseExtendSelector {
    public boolean isSelected(File basedir, String filename, File file)
            throws BuildException {
        return (!file.canWrite());
    }
}
```

Because Ant's documentation already provides extensive coverage of writing custom selectors, we will not cover it in detail here. The main things to do are extending `BaseExtendSelector` and implementing the `isSelected` method. Custom selectors can also take parameters using nested <param> tags. For example, we could have written our selector to be a generic file attribute selector and allow a nested `<param name="attribute" value="readonly"/>` (or `value="writable"`). Again, the Ant documentation covers this in detail, so we refer you there.

20.4.1   Using a custom selector in a build

The build file in listing 20.6 compiles and tests our custom selector.

> **Listing 20.6   Using a custom selector, and demonstrating cross-platform testing of file attribute settings**

```
<project name="selectors" default="main">

  <property name="build.dir" location="build"/>
  <property name="temp.dir" location="${build.dir}/temp"/>
  <property name="src.dir" location="src"/>
  <property name="data.dir" location="data"/>

  <target name="init">
    <mkdir dir="${build.dir}"/>

    <condition property="is.windows">          Sets a flag for
      <os family="windows"/>                   Windows platforms
    </condition>
  </target>

  <target name="clean">
    <delete dir="${build.dir}"/>
  </target>

  <target name="compile" depends="init">
    <javac srcdir="${src.dir}" destdir="${build.dir}"/>
  </target>

  <target name="setup-test-init">
    <delete dir="${temp.dir}"/>
    <mkdir dir="${temp.dir}"/>

    <delete dir="${data.dir}"/>
    <mkdir dir="${data.dir}"/>

    <echo file="${data.dir}/writable.dat">writable</echo>         Creates two
    <echo file="${data.dir}/nonwritable.dat">nonwritable</echo>   test files
  </target>

  <target name="setup-test-windows" if="is.windows">
    <exec executable="cmd.exe">
      <arg line="/c attrib +R"/>
      <arg file="${data.dir}/nonwritable.dat"/>
    </exec>                                              Sets the attributes
    <exec executable="cmd.exe">                          on Windows
      <arg line="/c attrib -R"/>                         platforms
      <arg file="${data.dir}/writable.dat"/>
    </exec>
  </target>

  <target name="setup-test"
          depends="setup-test-init,setup-test-windows">
    <chmod file="${data.dir}/nonwritable.dat" perm="u-r"/>    Sets the attributes
    <chmod file="${data.dir}/writable.dat" perm="u+r"/>       on non-Windows
  </target>                                                   platforms
```

```
<target name="test" depends="compile,setup-test">

  <selector id="selector">
    <custom classname="org.example.antbook.ReadOnlySelector"       Defines
           classpath="${build.dir}"/>                              reusable
  </selector>                                                       selector

  <copy todir="${temp.dir}">
    <fileset dir="${data.dir}">
     <selector refid="selector"/>   <────  Uses custom defined selector
    </fileset>                             to copy read-only file
  </copy>

  <available file="${temp.dir}/writable.dat"
             property="test.failed"/>
  <fail if="test.failed">
    Failed!  Writable file copied!
  </fail>
  <echo>Test passed</echo>
</target>

<target name="main" depends="test"/>

</project>
```

This build file is overly elaborate to demonstrate how we were able to test our custom read-only file selector. It creates two files and sets one as writable, and one as nonwritable using `attrib` on Windows platforms through <exec>. The <chmod> task is executed on all platforms, but does nothing on Windows platforms because the `chmod` tool is not natively supported. We then construct a fileset which encompasses both files, but uses our custom selector to only pick read-only files. An <available> check, followed by a conditional <fail> ensures that we have not copied the writable file.

Using the <not> selector container, the logic could be reversed to copy only writable files instead. This eliminates the need for us to write two selectors or parameterize this selector to be more generic.

20.5 IMPLEMENTING A CUSTOM FILTER

In section 3.9, we covered the FilterChain and its nested FilterReaders, which can be used in a few of Ant's tasks. You are not limited to just the built-in FilterReaders, and can write your own if you have a need that is not fulfilled by the handful of built-in ones. The problem we will solve with an example FilterReader is the use of a properties file to customize an XML file for deployment. First, our templated XML data file:

```
<root>
  <description>${description}</description>
</root>
```

We are going to use an <expandproperties> FilterReader in a <copy> to replace ${description}. We are going to read the description property from a properties file, which might contain characters that are illegal in an XML file. Our server.properties file contains:

```
description=<some description>
```

If literally "<some description>" was substituted into ${description} in the XML file, the resultant file would be invalid. Angle brackets are special characters in XML files, and must be escaped in most cases (see appendix B for more on special characters in XML). The <loadproperties> task is similar to <property>, except that it allows for a nested <filterchain>. There is no built-in FilterReader to do the proper escaping, so we will write one, and use it in this manner:

```
<loadproperties srcfile="${data.dir}/server.properties">
  <filterchain>
    <filterreader classname="org.example.antbook.EscapeFilter"
                  classpath="${build.dir}"
    />
  </filterchain>
</loadproperties>

<echo>description=${description}</echo>

<copy tofile="${build.dir}/server.xml"
      file="${data.dir}/template.xml"
      overwrite="true">
  <filterchain>
    <expandproperties/>
  </filterchain>
</copy>

<xmlvalidate file="${build.dir}/server.xml" lenient="true"/>
```

This build file piece is in a target that depends on the compilation target, so that EscapeFilter can be used in the same build file in which it is compiled. The output produced is:

```
     [echo] description=&lt;some description&gt;
     [copy] Copying 1 file to C:\AntBook\Sections\Extending\filters\build
[xmlvalidate] 1 file(s) have been successfully validated.
```

The description property loaded is different than the value from the properties file. The angle brackets have been replaced with their corresponding XML entity references. Had we omitted the <filterchain> within <loadproperties>, the XML validation would have failed.

20.5.1 Coding a custom filter reader

Listing 20.7 shows our relatively straightforward EscapeFilter implementation.

Listing 20.7 EscapeFilter—a custom filter reader implementation

```
package org.example.antbook;

import org.apache.tools.ant.filters.BaseFilterReader;
import org.apache.tools.ant.filters.ChainableReader;

import java.io.Reader;
import java.io.IOException;

public class EscapeFilter extends BaseFilterReader
    implements ChainableReader {

    private String queuedData = null;

    public EscapeFilter(final Reader in) {
        super(in);
    }

    public Reader chain(Reader rdr) {
        EscapeFilter newFilter = new EscapeFilter(rdr);      Allows
        newFilter.setProject(getProject());                  ourselves
        return newFilter;                                    to chain
    }

    public int read() throws IOException {
        if (queuedData != null && queuedData.length() == 0) {
            queuedData = null;
        }

        int ch = -1;
        if (queuedData != null) {
            ch = queuedData.charAt(0);                        Pulls one
            queuedData = queuedData.substring(1);            character at
            if (queuedData.length() == 0) {                  a time from
                queuedData = null;                           the queue
            }
        } else {
            ch = in.read();
            if (ch == -1) {
                return ch;                                   End of data
            }
            queuedData = getEscapeString(ch);
            if (queuedData != null) {
                return read();        ←——————————————— Starts reading from the queue
            }
        }
        return ch;
    }

    private String getEscapeString(int ch) {
        String output = null;
```

```
        switch (ch) {
            case '<' : output = "&lt;"; break;
            case '>' : output = "&gt;"; break;
            case '"' : output = "&quot"; break;
            case '\'' : output = "&apos;"; break;
        }

        if (output != null) {
            return output;
        }

        if (ch < 32 || ch > 127) {
            return "&#x" + Integer.toHexString(ch) + ";";
        }

        return null;
    }

}
```

FilterReaders use the standard `java.io.Reader`, which is implicitly available as the in member variable from the parent class `BaseFilterReader`. If we had wanted our class to be configurable through the build file, we would have had to extend from `BaseParamFilterReader` instead. The `chain` method comes from the `ChainableReader` interface, and allows our FilterReader to be linked to a successive FilterReader, passing the modified stream through to it.

The `read` method can be a bit complicated, and care must be taken to return -1 when `in.read()` returns it, otherwise an infinite loop can occur as we experienced in our first iteration of `EscapeFilter`. The `read` method is initially called from the Ant framework, but we also call it internally when escaped strings are queued. Each call of `read` returns only a single character (as an `int`), so buffering is necessary when text is added, as is the case in `EscapeFilter`.

We found that writing a FilterReader was a bit trickier than other Ant customizations, but was well worth the effort. Had we not had custom filter reader capability in this situation, we probably would have opted to change our business process by mandating that data be already encoded for XML inclusion within the properties file. However, we may want to use that same data outside of XML for other purposes and the situation would have gotten more complex. Luckily, filter readers saved the day by allowing us to have the data cleanly in the properties file, and escape the characters when needed.

20.6   SUMMARY

This chapter has covered several odds and ends with respect to Ant extensibility. While these techniques are not normally needed in the majority of builds, they are each quite powerful and handy when the situations arise for their use.

Scripting using any of the Bean Scripting Framework supported languages allows ad-hoc task writing within an Ant build file, without the need to write, compile, and package custom Java tasks. It is not nearly as powerful or robust as using custom Java tasks, and there are several reasons why using <script> is not preferred. Writing script tasks can be a useful prototyping method before converting to Java tasks, or can automate controlling other tasks and targets in bizarre and fun ways.

Build listeners and loggers are the key to IDE and external integration with Ant, and custom-writing them is easy. Ant comes with several listeners and loggers already, which are detailed in Ant's documentation. Familiarize yourself with these before embarking on custom development. Pay particular attention to the Log4j and Jakarta Commons Logging listeners, which are highly configurable and will meet most custom listening needs already.

Developing custom mappers and selectors provides extensibility in how Ant processes sets of files. Mappers are used to translate one file name to other file names, and a custom one can provide just the trick you need at times. Selectors nest within filesets, allowing sophisticated filtering of files within a directory tree. Writing a custom selector can add enormous capabilities to file selection, such as the read-only file selector we developed here.

FilterReaders allow for powerful data transformations, and chaining FilterReaders together accomplishes something similar to piping commands from one to another in Unix shell scripting. Developing a custom FilterReader is one of Ant's more complex customizations, but still within reach of skilled Java programmers. Our simple EscapeFilter enabled our build process to deal with issues straightforwardly rather than forcing us to change our business process or spend valuable time designing and implementing a more complex solution.

The most important point we can leave you with is: familiarize yourself with all of Ant's out-of-the-box capabilities before beginning customizations. Very likely, you will find that Ant can already handle your needs. Consult the provided Ant documentation, our book, and online resources such as the ant-user email list, where you will find a helpful and often quick-responding crew of Ant users around the world—including ourselves.

APPENDIX A

Installation

A.1 Before you begin   523
A.2 The steps to install Ant   524
A.3 Setting up Ant on Windows   524

A.4 Setting up Ant on Unix   525
A.5 Installation configuration   527
A.6 Installation troubleshooting   527

If there is one area where Ant could be improved, it is installation. It is still a fairly manual installation process, and a few things can go wrong. Here is a summary of how to install Ant, and also a troubleshooting guide in case something goes awry.

A.1 BEFORE YOU BEGIN

Before installing Ant, it is worthwhile verifying that a full Java Development Kit or J2SE Software Development Kit, normally abbreviated to JDK for historical reasons, is installed on the target system. Type `javac` at a command prompt; if a usage message does not appear, then either a JDK needs to be installed or the path is not set up correctly. Sun distributes its versions of this for Windows, Linux, and Solaris products under http://java.sun.com/j2se/—you need the appropriate Java 2 Standard Edition Software Development Kit for your system. Other vendors such as IBM, Apple, HP, and Novell provide versions for their systems from their own web sites.

> **IMPORTANT** Installing the Java SDK on a path without spaces in it, such as c:\java\ jdk, instead of a path such as c:\Program Files\Java is highly recommended, as sometimes spaces confuse Ant and other programs.

After installing the SDK, Ant requires the environment variable `JAVA_HOME` be set to the directory into which the SDK was installed. It is also usual to append

JAVA_HOME\bin to the PATH environment variable, so that you can run the SDK's programs from the command line. Some Ant tasks depend upon this, since they rely on these very same programs.

The standard test for the Java SDK being installed is that typing `javac` from a command line should bring up a usage message, not an error about the command being unknown.

A.2 THE STEPS TO INSTALL ANT

The core stages of the Ant installation process are the same regardless of the platform:

1 Download Ant.

2 Unzip or expand it into your chosen destination.

3 Add it to the path for command line invocation.

4 Set up some environment variables to point to the JDK and usually Ant.

5 Add any optional libraries to Ant that you desire or need. This can be done later.

The exact details vary from platform to platform, and as Ant works to varying degrees on everything from Linux mainframes to Netware servers, it is not possible to cover all the possible platforms you may want to install Ant onto; instead we will cover only the most common Windows and Unix platforms.

Ant distributions come as source or binary distributions. Binary distributions should work out of the box, whereas source editions need to be built using the Ant bootstrap scripts. It is probably safest to hold off getting the source editions until and unless you want to get into extending Ant in Java, at which time grabbing the latest build from the CVS server is the best way to get an up-to-date copy.

When downloading a binary version, get either the latest release build, or a beta release of the version about to be released. Nightly builds are incomplete and built primarily as a test, rather than for public distribution.

A.3 SETTING UP ANT ON WINDOWS

Download the zipped Ant binary file from the Apache web server to your local disk. Then unzip it to where you want the files to live, making sure that the unzip tool preserves directory structure. There is always an unzip tool built into the JDK: type `jar xvf jakarta-ant-X.X-bin.zip` to unzip the file. Let's assume you unzipped it to c:\java\apps\ant. This new directory you have created and installed Ant into is called ant home.

You should add the bin subdirectory of ant home to the path, so it can be called from the command line. You should also set the ANT_HOME environment variable to point to the ant home directory. The batch file that starts Ant can usually just assume that ANT_HOME is one directory up from where the batch file lives, but sometimes it is nice to know for sure.

Windows 9x

To install successfully on Windows 9x, you must use a path with short (8.3) file names rather than long ones. This is a quirk of batch file execution, which the Ant team cannot fix.

The environment variable declarations, PATH and ANT_HOME, need to be placed into autoexec.bat; they will not be picked up until the system is rebooted. Do not include the final backslash in the directory name.

```
SET PATH=%PATH%;c:\java\apps\ant
SET ANT_HOME=c:\java\apps\ant
```

After rebooting, test the environment by typing ant -version at the command line. The printed version number must match that of the version you have just downloaded; anything else means there is still a problem.

Windows NT/2000/XP

The environment variable declarations need to be placed somewhere in the registry, which is normally done in the system section of the control panel applet, in the Advanced tab pane, under Environment Variables.... This dialog is somewhat cramped and noticeably less usable than a text file, but such is progress. After closing the dialog box, any new console windows or applications started should pick up the altered settings. If that does not happen, verify the settings (type SET at the command prompt), or try logging out and in again.

To test the settings, type ant -version at a newly opened console. The printed version number must match that of the version you have just downloaded; anything else means there is still a problem.

A.4   SETTING UP ANT ON UNIX

The first step is to download and install a recent JDK, making note of the location where you installed it, which should be assigned to the JAVA_HOME environment variable. This is usually a subdirectory of /usr/java or /opt/java. You should add the bin subdirectory of the JDK to the PATH environment variable, if it is not done for you.

The second step is to download a recent Ant build from the Jakarta web site. This is intermittently available in RPM format for Linux systems and other Unix systems that handle that format. Alternatively, pull down the tarred and gzipped file. Because tar knows about file permissions, it is the best way to install onto Unix if the RPM format is not suitable. The tar files will not untar properly using the official version that comes with Solaris and MacOS, as they do not handle long file names properly. Use the GNU version of the tar tool instead. Zip files can always be unzipped with the JDK even if unzip does nothing: use jar xvf file.zip, but afterwards you may need to set the execute bit on files in the bin directory. You may even encounter problems with line endings in some of the scripts being in MS-DOS format with extra carriage returns rather than the line-feed-only format of Unix.

As with Windows, try not to install Ant in a directory with spaces in it. The scripts *should* all cope with it, but if they don't, it will be up to you to fix them.

Here is the log of a Linux install into the subdirectory of a user: installation for the entire team would need to be done as root and with an editing of system profile files. This is important if you are planning to have an automated build process later on; whatever account the automated build runs under it needs to have a copy of Ant.

```
[Apps]$ pwd
/home/slo/Java/Apps
[Apps]$ ls
jakarta-ant-1.5-bin.tar.gz
[Apps]$ ls
jakarta-ant-1.5-bin.tar.gz
[Apps]$ tar xzf jakarta-ant-1.5-bin.tar.gz
[Apps]$ ls
jakarta-ant-1.5  jakarta-ant-1.5-bin.tar
[Apps]$ cd jakarta-ant-1.5/bin
[bin]$ ./ant -version
Apache Ant version 1.5Beta3 compiled on June 22 2002
[bin]$
```

The third step is to add the environment variable(s) needed to get it to work.

To set the Bash environment, add this to the profile file that is usually .profile or .bash_profile. System administrators setting these up for an entire system should modify /etc/profile instead, which can be convenient unless different users plan to use different Ant versions. The settings for the profile file should look something like:

```
export JAVA_HOME= (wherever the JDK is installed)
export ANT_HOME= (wherever Ant is installed)
export PATH=$PATH:$ANT_HOME/bin:$JAVA_HOME/bin
```

The environment settings for tcsh have a different syntax but the same behavior, and go into the equivalent file: .cshrc or .tcshrc.

```
setenv JAVA_HOME= (wherever the JDK is installed)
setenv ANT_HOME= (wherever Ant is installed)
setenv PATH=$PATH\:$ANT_HOME/bin\:$JAVA_HOME/bin
```

There is a place where Ant options (such as ANT_OPTS) can be set in Unix, the .antrc file in the user's home directory, which is read in by the Ant shell script. Other mechanisms for starting Ant under Unix, such as the Perl on Python scripts, do not read this file.

After logging off and on again, test the environment by typing ant -version in a shell: a version message that matches the version you have just downloaded indicates that all is well.

A.5 INSTALLATION CONFIGURATION

There are two useful environment variables that the Ant wrapper scripts use when invoking Ant: ANT_OPTS and ANT_ARGS. Neither of these is typically set by users, but each can provide value for certain situations.

A.5.1 ANT_OPTS

The ANT_OPTS environment variable provides options to the JVM executing Ant, such as system properties and memory configuration. During the development of this book, the index we built was over 20MB in size and crashed the Ant JVM. We solved this by setting ANT_OPTS to increase the Java initial heap size. On Windows this is

```
SET ANT_OPTS=-Xmx500M
```

A.5.2 ANT_ARGS

In a similar fashion to ANT_OPTS, the ANT_ARGS environment variable is passed to Ant's main process as command-line arguments, in addition to the arguments that you specify on the command line. This could be useful, for example, if you always want to use Ant's NoBannerLogger to remove the output from empty targets.

```
SET ANT_ARGS=-logger org.apache.tools.ant.NoBannerLogger
```

A.6 INSTALLATION TROUBLESHOOTING

Getting started with Ant is difficult: you do not know exactly what to expect, and there are a few complex steps to go through. The error messages do not make sense, and if you file a bug report on the issue tracking web site, a WORKSFORME response is reasonably likely. This is where you discover that a consequence of free, open source software is that nobody staffs the support lines but you and people like you.

Because Ant does work fine on most systems, any installation that does not work is almost always due to some configuration issue with the local machine. Something is missing, something is misconfigured, or some other piece of software is interfering with Ant.

Just before this book went to press, a -diagnostics command-line switch was added to display diagnostic information about an Ant installation, such as Ant's ant.jar and optional.jar version numbers, whether all tasks defined are actually present in the JAR files, system properties, and ANT_HOME/lib JAR information. This output may help to determine the caues of any installation or configuration problems.

Problem: Java not installed/configured

If Java is missing, then Ant does not work.

Test: Run java from the command line; if this is not a known command then either Java is not installed or the path is wrong.

Fix: Install the JDK; set up JAVA_HOME to point to the install location.

Problem: JDK not installed/configured

Ant needs to find the JDK so that it can use classes in tools.jar, such as the Java compiler. Without this, some Ant tasks will fail with class not found exceptions. The environment variable JAVA_HOME is used to find the JDK—if it is not set, Ant will warn you on startup with an error message:

```
Warning: JAVA_HOME environment variable is not set.
```

This may just be a warning, but it is a warning that some tasks will not work properly. More insidiously, if JAVA_HOME is wrong, Ant will not notice until some tasks fail, usually `<javac>` and `<javadoc>`.

Test 1: Run `javac` from the command line; if this is not a known command then either Java is not installed or the path is wrong.

Test 2: Use `set` or `setenv` to verify that the environment variable JAVA_HOME exists. Verify that the file tools.jar can be found in the subdirectory JAVA_HOME /lib.

Fix: Install the JDK; set up JAVA_HOME to point to the install location.

Problem: Ant not on the path

Ant is started by a platform-dependent batch file or shell script, or by a portable script in a language such as Perl or Python. If the path does not include Ant's bin directory, these scripts are not found and so Ant cannot start.

Test: Run `ant -version` from the command line: a version number and build time should appear. If the command interpreter complains that `ant` is unknown, then the path is wrong. If the error is that the Java command is unknown, then the problem is actually with the Java installation, covered earlier.

Fix: Modify the environment path variable to include the Ant scripts, log out, reboot or otherwise reload the environment to have the change applied.

Problem: Another version of Ant is on the path

Because there are few restrictions on Ant redistribution, and because it is so popular, other Java products sometimes include a version of Ant. Tomcat has done this in the past. Having a separate version of Ant on the path is problematic for a number of reasons. First, it may be an older version of Ant. Second, the installation may be incomplete; dependent libraries or even dependent batch files, such as lcp.bat, which ant.bat uses, may be missing.

Test: One trick is to have a build file that contains a target with the string `<echo message="${ant.home}"/>` to see the Ant home directory. Another is to search for all copies of `ant.bat`, `ant.jar` or just plain `ant` in the file system, which can highlight potential problems.

Fix: Remove or rename other copies, or reorder your path to place the version you want first.

Problem: Ant fails with an error about a missing task or library

This can mean that a library containing needed task definitions is missing. Unless your build file uses nonstandard extension libraries, the most common reason for missing many task definitions is that the `optional.jar` file has not been loaded and added to the ANT_HOME/lib directory.

Test: Look in the ANT_HOME/lib directory for the optional JAR file.

Fix: Download this file from the jakarta.apache.org web site, and drop it into the directory.

Problem: Ant still fails with an error about a missing task or library

The error message can also mean that a task depends on one or more external JAR files that it cannot find.

Test: Determine which task failed by looking at the error text, then use the Ant manual to see what dependencies the task has. Next, check to see if the JAR file is on the system, either in the CLASSPATH environment variable or in the ANT_HOME/lib directory.

Fix: Download any needed JARs; place them in the ANT_HOME/lib directory.

Problem: The ANT_HOME directory points to the wrong place

You should not actually need to set the ANT_HOME environment variable: most Ant launcher scripts will just assume that it is one directory up from where they are, then perhaps call other batch files, such as ANT_HOME/bin/lcp.bat, to set up the classpath. If ANT_HOME is set, but set to the wrong location, much confusion can arise. A warning about lcp.bat being missing is one obvious sign when calling ant.bat; another is failure to find ant.jar, with a Java error about the class `org.apache.tools.ant.Main` not being found.

Test: Look at the value of ANT_HOME and verify it is correct.

Fix: Either set the variable to the correct location, or omit it.

Problem: Incompatible Java libraries on the classpath

If you set up the CLASSPATH environment variable with a list of commonly needed JAR files, there is a risk that versions of common libraries, xmlParserAPIs.jar and xerces.jar in particular, clash with the versions Ant needs. If this is a problem (it is very rare), then XML parsing is the most likely part of the Ant build to fail.

Test: Look at the value of CLASSPATH and verify it is empty or does not contain any XML parsers.

Fix: Either clear the environment variable completely or pull out the XML parser libraries.

Problem: Java extension libraries conflicting with Ant

Java 1.2 and later supports extension libraries—JAR files placed into JAVA_HOME\jre\lib\ext are loaded by the run time—using a different classloader than normal. This can cause problems if any code in the extension libraries (such as `jaxp.jar`) tries to locate classes loaded under a different classloader.

Test: Look in JRE/lib/ext directory for any JAR files that have crept in as extension libraries, and are confusing Ant.

Fix: Move the XML parser libraries to a different directory.

Problem: Sealing violation when running Ant

This exception happens when a library has been marked as sealed but another library implements classes in one of the packages of the sealed library. This exception means there is an XML parser conflict, perhaps from an older version on the classpath or extension library, perhaps from some other library that contains a sealed copy of the JAXP API. The underlying cause will be one of the two problems above: extension library conflicts or classpath incompatibilities.

Fix: The message should identify which libraries have sealing problems. Use this to identify the conflict, and fix it, usually by removing one of the libraries. You can unseal a JAR file by editing its manifest, but this only fixes a symptom of the conflict, not the underlying problem.

Problem: Calling Ant generates a Java usage message

If the Java invocation string that the Ant launcher scripts is somehow corrupt, then the `java` program will not be able to parse it, so it will print a message beginning `Usage: java [-options] class [args...]`.

This is usually caused by one of the environment variables, JAVA_HOME, ANT_HOME, ANT_OPTS, or CLASSPATH being invalid.

Test: Examine the environment variables to see if there are any obvious errors.

Fix: Fix any obvious errors. Otherwise, unset each variable in turn until Ant works; this will identify the erroneous variable.

Problem: Illegal Java options in the ANT_OPTS variable

The environment variable ANT_OPTS provides a means to pass options into Ant, such as a permanent definition of some properties, or the memory parameters for Java. The variable must contain only options the local JVM recognizes. Any invalid parameter will generate an error message such as the following (where ANT_OPTS was set to –3):

```
Unrecognized option: -3
Could not create the Java virtual machine.
```

If the variable contains a string that is mistaken for the name of the Java class to run as the main class, then a different error appears:

```
Exception in thread "main" java.lang.NoClassDefFoundError: error-string
```

   Test: Examine ANT_OPTS and verify that the variable is unset or contains valid JVM options.

   Fix: Correct or clear the variable.

If the cause still cannot be found, a useful next step is to edit the Ant invocation scripts to provide more debugging information. In the case of the Windows batch file, commenting out the first line (@echo off) gives a detailed trace of the file. The Perl script has a debug flag that can be set to get some debug information from the Ant invocation route.

XML primer as it applies to Ant

Because Ant uses XML as the means of describing what to build, creating Ant build files by hand forces you to understand a bit about XML. XML can get very complex, once you get into the details of parsing, XML namespaces, schemas, Java support issues, and indeed the whole politics of XML implementations. Very little of that is relevant to Ant, so here is a brief description of basic XML, which is sufficient for writing build files.

XML provides a way of representing structured data that is intelligible to both humans and programs. It is not the easiest of representations for either party, but it lets humans create structured files that machines can understand. Since it looks like HTML, it is not too hard to read or write once you have learned it.

An XML document should begin with an XML prolog, which indicates the version and optionally the character set of the XML file—here the string `<?xml version="1.0"?>`. XML (and therefore Ant) supports different character sets, including Unicode documents in the UTF-8 encoding, which can be useful in international applications.

Applications can validate XML documents against another document describing what is valid inside it: a Document Type Description (DTD) or an XML Schema. There is no DTD for Ant, because it can add support for new XML elements during the execution of a build. It is, however, possible to generate or download a somewhat inaccurate DTD to describe Ant build files for use in XML editors.

After the prolog comes the XML content. This must consist of a single XML root element, which can contain zero or more elements nested inside. Each XML element is delimited with the angle bracket characters (< >) and must be the name of the element. A closing tag of the same element name must close it. An example element inside an Ant build file to print a string could be a reference to the echo task, which outputs a message:

```
<echo></echo>
```

This would only actually print an empty string, because it contains no child elements or other description of a message to print. XML tags support attributes, which are named string assignments in the opening tag of an element. For example, the echo task supports the message attribute, printing the result:

```
<echo message="hello world"></echo>
```

Ant often uses attributes to control stages in a build process, and it makes extensive use of nested elements. At its simplest, these are text nodes, such as in the <echo> task, which accept child text elements as an alternate means of stating which message to display:

```
<echo>hello world</echo>
```

Note that <echo> allows a message to be specified as an attribute or as an embedded text element.

Sometimes, the child elements are complex XML declarations of their own:

```
<target name="compile">
  <javac srcdir="." destdir="." />
</target>
```

In this example, one XML element <target> contains another element, <javac>; each element has one or more attributes. The child element, <javac>, has no body, so needs to be closed with a </javac> tag. We have cheated by ending the opening tag with the text />. This tells the XML parser that the tag element is closed with no child elements at all. It is a common shortcut used in Ant files, as it reduces the amount of typing. It is a bit deceptive at first as the closing / may not catch the eye, but the XML parser certainly catches its presence or absence and reminds you if it has been omitted.

XML cannot contain binary data directly; it has to be encoded using techniques like base-64 encoding. This is never an issue in Ant build files. A more common problem is that certain characters, specifically > and < cannot be used except when marking the beginning or ending of tags. Instead they need to be *escaped* using the strings > and < respectively. This should be familiar to anyone who has written a lot of low-level HTML content. When assigning values to attributes, you may need to escape single or double quotation marks; there are escape sequences for these two characters, although this tends to be less of an issue in Ant files. Any Unicode character can also be described in XML by providing its numeric value in a very similar manner: and   both refer to the ASCII space character, decimal value 32, hexadecimal value 0x20 This trick can be sporadically useful in dealing with minor internationalization issues. When needed, a line such as

```
<echo message="&apos;&lt;$&gt;&amp;&quot;" />
```

would be translated to an output such as:

```
[echo] '<$>&"
```

Escaping characters is most common in XML attributes, such as setting the passwords to remote FTP or HTTP servers. Table B.1 lists the most common symbols that you must escape in an Ant file.

Table B.1 How to escape common characters so that the XML parser or Ant can use them

Symbol	Ant XML representation
<	<
>	>
"	"
'	'

newline; \n	

A Unicode character, such as ß (hex value 00df)	ß

Because escaping characters can become very messy and inconvenient, XML provides a mechanism for allowing unescaped text within a CDATA section. In Ant's build files, CDATA sections typically appear around script blocks or SQL commands. CDATA sections begin with <![CDATA[and end with]]>. The ending sequence of a CDATA section is the only set of characters that requires escaping internally. A CDATA example is:

```
<echo><![CDATA[
    <b>hello</b> world
    ]]>
</echo>
```

Unless stated otherwise, XML parsers assume that the character set of input files is not that of the locale of the local system, but instead Unicode in the UTF-8 encoding. The ASCII characters, which are zero to 127, are represented as-is in UTF-8 files, so this subtle file format detail will not show up. However, the moment you add any high bit characters, such as £ or ü, the parser breaks. To avoid having the Ant parse stage failing with an error about illegal characters the moment you add a string like münchen to the file, you must set the encoding of the XML file in the declaration, and use the same encoding in your text editor. For example, to use the ISO Latin-1 encoding, you set the first line of the build file to

```
<?xml version='1.0' encoding="iso-8859-1" ?>
```

APPENDIX B   XML PRIMER AS IT APPLIES TO ANT

This will tell the parser that the encoding is ISO Latin-1 and that the ISO Latin-1 characters from 128 to 255 are valid. Alternatively, save the build files in UTF8 encoding, if your text editor permits that.

XML permits comments inside the delimiters < ! -- and -->. This is very important in an Ant build file, because documentation of the stages in the build process is so critical. A good build file contains well laid out XML declarations as well as comments that describe what is happening. It is also useful for commenting out sections during development, although here the fact that XML does not permit comments inside the angle brackets of an element tag makes it hard to comment out some parts of a build, as shown in the following code fragment:

```
<target name="compile">
   <!-- compile some code -->        <----- This is a legal comment
   <javac srcdir="."
   <!--
    optimize="true"                  This is illegal, as it
   -->                               is inside an XML tag
     />
</target>
```

The normal workaround in this situation is to cut and paste the comment block outside the element tag, which is inelegant and makes it harder to re-enable the attribute later, as you need to remember where it came from. Better still, by using Ant's *property* concept, you can control task attributes without having to resort to commenting them in and out.

A good XML editor reduces the chances for errors and simplifies navigation around the file, although by restructuring the layout of the file, the final aesthetics and readability of the text may be reduced. A good application for creating Ant files without the need to view or edit XML directly can improve productivity, which is why some of the latest generation of Ant-based build tools are valuable. However, XML is the underlying language, and being able to manually edit a build file will remain useful. Even if you somehow manage never to edit the file by hand, tracking down errors or comparing versions of build files in some file difference (or comparison) tool will often use the raw XML text. Also, raw XML makes a great format for people to share parts of a build process, by cutting and pasting steps between your own projects, picking up useful examples from other people's build files, or just making sense of the examples in this book. Even as Ant becomes easier to use, XML will probably remain the power-user representation of an Ant build process.

IDE integration

C.1 Using Ant in an IDE   536
C.2 Some Ant-aware IDEs   537
C.3 Making the most of a combined
     IDE/Ant build process   543

Many developers like their IDEs but need Ant for the full build. These developers should consider using an Ant-aware IDE.

C.1   USING ANT IN AN IDE

Historically, Java IDEs have always been weak in one way or another. Usually the text editors have been inadequate, the debuggers weak, and the package and deployment support limited. They have also been somewhat sluggish and memory hungry if written purely in Java, or restricted to a single platform (usually Windows). Fortunately, the performance of today's entry-level computers is now more than enough for these tools, and the cost of memory is so low that memory is rarely an issue, leaving only debugging, text editing, and build support as problems.

Using Ant from inside IDEs addresses the build process and benefits both the tools and the users. The tools avoid having to implement Ant's functionality; they can merely invoke it and process the results. Users benefit by having the best of both worlds: a graphical editing and debugging tool integrated with a cross-platform and a readily automated build process. The declarative nature of Ant is actually intended to simplify this process; it is possible for development environments to parse the data and present it in ways that make the build file easier to view, edit, and use. Most Ant-aware editors present the build file as a list of targets or tree of targets and tasks, a view that you can use for editing or executing the build file.

Putting an IDE in control of the build file can make it easier to manipulate, but it does tend to make the actual XML harder to read. IDEs may remove any indentations inserted to make the file readable, and can reorder the attributes inside an XML element start tag. As a case in point, all Ant developers declare targets with the name coming before the dependencies or the description:

```
<target name="all"
  description="does everything"
  depends="init, build, package, email" />
```

The tools that edit build files for you have a tendency to reorder the attributes, usually into alphabetical order:

```
<target depends="init, build, package, email"
description="does everything" name="all" />
```

Working with the file after such a tool has edited it is much, much harder. Maybe we need an `<xmltidy>` task to tidy up XML files based on a specification; this could make build files readable again, among other things.

Another issue with Ant integration is the version. There is always a lag between an Ant version being released and support for it in other tools arriving: the more complex the container product the longer the lag. The best tools for developers who keep up-to-date with Ant builds are those that remain loosely coupled to Ant, executing any version preinstalled on the local system. If you are learning Ant, however, a tool that makes build files easy to view, edit, and use is good, especially if it hides XML details.

C.2 SOME ANT-AWARE IDES

In this section we have listed the IDEs with Ant integration with which we are sufficiently familiar to determine the strengths and weaknesses of the Ant integration. We do not cover which editor is best at other tasks, such as editing and debugging, although these are clearly important. Be aware that these tools are continually evolving. The Jakarta-Ant web site is the most up-to-date list of Ant integration resources, and should be the first place to look for more information.

There is no one IDE with Ant integration that we can point to and say this is the tool you need. Maybe everyone should just stick to their favorite editor and debugger and get the appropriate Ant plug-in for it. After doing so, find out where the lib directory of the IDE is, and add all dependent JAR files the tasks you use need, such as NetComponents.jar for the `<ftp>` task. Updating Ant itself is not so easy: sometimes it has been modified to work with the IDE; other times more than ant.jar itself needs to be adjusted, as the parser used to display the file contains its own model of what tasks, elements, and attributes are valid.

jEdit

jEdit editor, from http://jedit.org/, is currently one of our favorite Java and Ant text editors. Its AntFarm plug-in lists all the targets on a build file that you have added to it; selecting a target runs it. Status and error messages appear in the console window; clicking on an error will highlight the file containing an error in Java source or the build file itself.

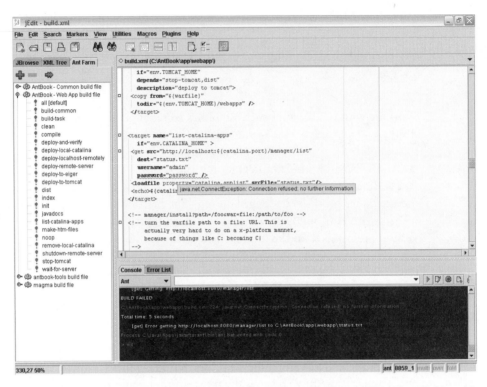

Figure C.1 jEdit executing a build file with AntFarm; the build file is in the main window with some of the targets collapsed for easier navigation; the targets of the file are listed in the pane to the left. We have encountered an error on this run; the line on the build file where this happened is underlined and a ToolTip has popped up the message.

To generate Ant files the tool comes with an excellent XML editor mode that auto-completes many tags and lets you expand and collapse targets for easier navigation. Figure C.1 shows the results of a build, with the build file displayed in Ant mode, which adds highlighting of many of the Ant keywords to the XML view. The jEdit editor does not attempt to rearrange the XML at all, letting you write a build file in a readable form. You do however have to write most of that build file yourself; apart from a few dialogs, which fill out the basic options for tasks such as <javac>.

The final nice feature of jEdit for Ant-based development is that although it ships with a built-in version of Ant, you can select any other installation of Ant on the command line through a dialog box, which is ideal when you are extending or editing Ant itself. Unfortunately, not all changes to Ant are handled so well; some changes to well-known tasks, such as new <condition> tests, need a new version of the AntFarm plug-in, which can be inconvenient. Changes to attributes and the addition of new tasks do not cause this problem. Because of Ant version issues, we actually use some jEdit macros to run Ant targets via the command console, saving files before executing the build. With different macros calling different targets, for example, *build*, *test*, and *deploy*, and keystroke bindings for each target, we can do fast Ant-based development within the IDE without the AntFarm plug-in.

The tool is a great text editor, and compared to the other Java tools it is positively svelte, showing that you can do fast GUI applications in Java if you try hard enough. It is therefore well worth installing and experimenting with, even if you choose to stick to other IDEs.

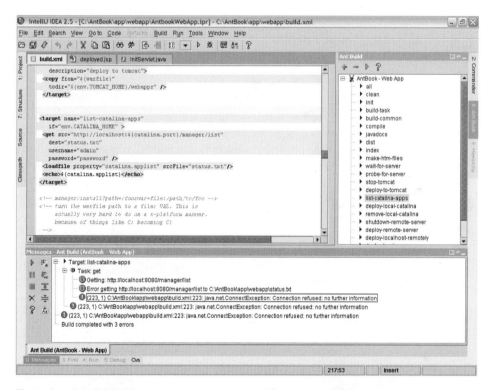

Figure C.2 IntelliJ IDEA, running the same build file and displaying errors. The pane of Ant targets is on the right; these targets are also listed under the build menu for easy access by mouse or keyboard shortcut.

IntelliJ IDEA

This commercial IDE is a very powerful Java source editor that also can debug programs, run JUnit tests, and generally get your code working. From a text-editing standpoint, its method completion, pop-up Javadocs, and refactoring can be great for productivity.

It supports Ant right out of the box; figure C.2 shows it having run into an error executing a target. Our build file required the Ant nightly build; to get IDEA to execute it, we just dropped new versions of ant.jar, optional.jar, into its lib directory. One of our other build files failed because the property ant.home was not being defined; that is one of those gotchas in IDE-hosted build files that can hurt you. We fixed it in an ugly way with a line in our build file:

```
<property name="ant.home" value="${env.ANT_HOME}" />
```

We still could not run our deployment tasks due to library dependencies. This exemplifies the problem with tight IDE integration: you end up having to debug the integration more than your build process itself, and sometimes you are constrained by the IDE as to which tasks you can run.[1] You can download and purchase the IDE from http://intellij.com.

Sun NetBeans/Forte

The NetBeans project is Sun's open source Java development platform; the Forte product is a commercial derivative. NetBeans' Ant support is pretty good; their developers regularly file Ant bug reports and patches, and this shows in the quality of the integration. Not only can you navigate and execute Ant targets from the build file pane, you can insert new tasks, bring up the Ant documentation, and fill in task and target options using property windows. They also keep reasonably up-to-date with Ant versions, a benefit of their frequent release cycle. See figure C.3.

Because this IDE lets you create targets through menus and dialog boxes, it is a great way to learn Ant and to integrate Ant with IDE-based development.

Do not attempt to update Ant on NetBeans by dragging, dropping, and renaming files, as it only stops things from working. You can download release and development versions of NetBeans from http://www.netbeans.org.

---

[1] On a more positive note, someone has recently (January 2002) posted an Ant task which creates an IDEA project as part of the build; this lets someone roll out changes to a project to all team members, reducing the maintenance overhead of IDE-based development.

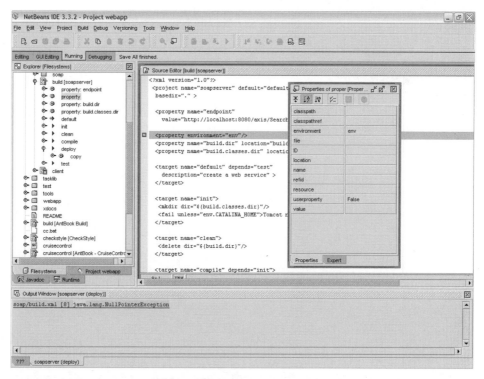

Figure C.3   NetBeans not running a task because of Ant1.4.1 and Java1.4 incompatiblities, but highlighting the error line quite nicely. The pane on the left shows the build file and provides navigation and task creation; the property dialogs let you fill in the values.

IBM Eclipse

The IBM-backed Eclipse project, at http://eclipse.org/, is an alternative to NetBeans; it is a general-purpose development framework targeting Java and C++ development, the latter primarily on Linux. See figure C.4.

Eclipse's Ant integration is through a view called Ant Console. Getting Ant up and running in Eclipse required a visit to the Eclipse FAQ page to find out that tools.jar needed to be added to the Ant classpath. The Ant Console shows each output level as a custom chosen color, and the verbosity level is configurable through the Preferences. Right-clicking on a build.xml file displays the Run Ant... menu item. Choosing this displays a dialog allowing you to pick which targets to run and to provide any additional arguments such as property overrides. You may consult the Eclipse web site for information on upgrading its Ant version, however, it's also possible to get information through the Ant page in Preferences. We look forward to promised improvement in Eclipse's Ant integration in Eclipse 2.0, as it's a nice development environment; but we were unsatisfied with its current Ant features, such as no way to double-click from a compile error directly to the corresponding line of source code.

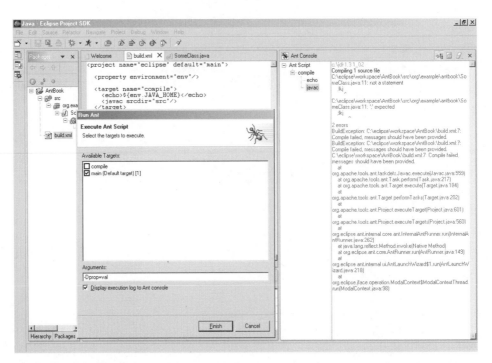

Figure C.4   Eclipse running a simple example project including a compile error. Unfortunately the Ant Console does not directly link to source code and is a passive, display-only view of the build results.

Other tools

We have not listed other tools here because the options are continually changing, and many are not so different from the others. The Ant web site provides up-to-date pointers to IDEs that support Ant, including emacs. Borland/Inprise supports Ant and JUnit in its premium JBuilder Enterprise Edition; for everyone else there is a JBuilder add-on listed on the Ant web site.

What is notable is the emergence of pure Ant execution tools, which provide GUIs for editing and executing a build file. There is an Ant child project, Antidote, which started doing this; work on this may have restarted after a long sabbatical. The HP RadPak is a deployment tool designed to create and deploy WAR and EAR applications to the J2EE server. Among other things it lets you edit XML files and construct build files through dialogs, and it comes with an officially supported task to deploy to the servers. It currently lags a bit regarding Ant versions, there is no way to update it, and it ruins your build file's readability, but otherwise it is slick. Although we prefer to run from the IDE or the command line, the tool can be useful in the hands of non-developers: operations and management.

C.3 MAKING THE MOST OF A COMBINED *IDE*/ANT BUILD PROCESS

The best way to use Ant from an IDE consists of recognizing and using the best features of each product. IDEs are great at debugging and editing text; Ant is good at building, testing, and deploying. Where IDEs are weak is in multideveloper support: each developer has to configure his IDE projects to work on his own system, and changes in the build do not propagate well. So why try and unify the IDE environments? Ant can be all the commonality of the build process developers need. Here are our recommended tactics to combine IDEs and Ant in a team project:

- Let developers choose their favorite IDEs. The boost to productivity and morale here can outweigh most compatibility issues.

- Have everyone install a common IDE, such as jEdit, NetBeans, or even emacs. This ensures everyone on the team has a common working environment on the occasions they need to work on each other's machines. If pair-programming techniques are being used this is invaluable, although key binding standardization soon becomes an issue.

- Integrate tests into the build process, so they are run every build and deploy cycle. Tests and deployment are key reasons for developers to use Ant over the IDE's own compiler.

- Use a team build file to build the code. Any customizations should be in per-user properties, not private build files.

- Have standard target names across projects (a general Ant best practice).

- Have developers set up keystroke shortcuts to run the standardized targets: test, deploy, clean.

Some developers may miss the total integration of a pure IDE build; adding unit tests and deployment to the Ant build, surpassing what the IDE build could do, could help bring them on board. Offering them not only the choice of which IDE to use, but also the funding to buy a commercial product, could also help with motivation.

The elements of Ant style

D.1 General principles 544
D.2 Environment conventions 545
D.3 Formatting conventions 546
D.4 Naming conventions 548
D.5 Documentation conventions 552
D.6 Programming conventions 553

D.1 GENERAL PRINCIPLES

1. Let Ant be Ant

Don't try to make Ant into Make. (Submitted by Rich Steele, eTrack Solutions, Inc.)
Ant is not a scripting language. It is a *mostly* declarative description of steps. The declarative nature of Ant can be a source of confusion for new users, especially if a scripting language is expected.

2. Design for componentization.

A small project becomes a large project over time; splitting up a single build into child projects with their own builds will eventually happen. You can make this process easier by designing the build file properly from the beginning, being sure to:

- Use `<property location>` to assign locations to properties, rather than values. Not only does this stand out, it ensures that the properties are bound to an absolute location, even when they are passed to a different project.
- Always define output directories using Ant properties. This lets master build files define a single output tree for all child projects.

3. *Design for maintenance.*

Will your build file be readable when you get back to it six months after the project is finished? Will it execute on a clean machine? Follow these points:

- Document the build process. XML may be a file format that is both human readable and machine readable, but it is not the most easily read format for either party. A text file covering the build and deploy process will be appreciated by your successors. Of critical importance is the list of which programs and libraries are needed for the build; without it, running the build will be a trial-and-error process.

- Use comments liberally.

- Avoid dependencies on programs and JAR files outside the source tree: keep everything you can under source code control for later re-creation of development environments. That includes Ant itself, especially if you have changed it in any way.

- Keep deployment usernames and passwords out of build files. Passwords should change over time, and security is always an issue. Keep them in property files out of source code control. If a password is required for a build process, the user can be alerted to it being missing by using `<fail message="Provide user.password" unless="user.password"/>`

- Never neglect false positive test case failures. Even if you know that `testWorstCase` always fails, four months later someone else might have the maintenance task and waste ages trying to find out why the build is reporting errors. At best, fix them; otherwise exclude them from the test suite.

D.2 ENVIRONMENT CONVENTIONS

The items in this section assume that you are launching Ant through the wrapper scripts, such as the provided ant.bat, ant.sh, runant.pl, or runant.py.

4. *Run without a CLASSPATH.*

There is no need to manually set your system CLASSPATH environment variable. When running through the Ant wrapper scripts, the libraries in ANT_HOME/lib are automatically placed into the system CLASSPATH before invoking Ant.

5. *Place commonly used Ant library dependencies in Ant's lib directory.*

In some cases it is required that libraries be in the system classpath. JUnit's library is one of them, when using the `<junit>` task.

6. *Use **ANT_OPTS** to control Ant's virtual machine settings.*

Some tasks may require more memory, which you can set in the ANT_OPTS environment variable, using the appropriate mechanism for your platform:

```
set ANT_OPTS=-Xmx500M
export ANT_OPTS=-Xmx500M
```

7. Use **ANT_ARGS** *to set fixed command-line switches.*

You may always want to use the —emacs and the `NoBannerLogger`:

```
set ANT_ARGS=-emacs -logger org.apache.tools.ant.NoBannerLogger
export ANT_ARGS=-emacs -logger org.apache.tools.ant.NoBannerLogger
```

Other settings that may be useful in ANT_ARGS are:

```
-Dbuild.compiler=jikes
-listener org.apache.tools.ant.tools.listener.Log4jListener
-propertyfile my.properties.
```

D.3   FORMATTING CONVENTIONS

Readability and maintainability are the prevailing rationales for most of these items.

NOTE   Some IDE and XML editors have an annoying habit of reformatting build.xml automatically—use these with caution if you care about the aesthetics of your build file.

If your build file will be manually edited and readability is desired, craft it your way; and if a tool attempts to spoil it, complain to the vendor and avoid using it.

8. *Provide the* **<?xml…?>** *directive.*

Include the encoding if there are characters outside the ASCII range:

```
<?xml version="1.0" encoding="iso-8859-1"?>
```

9. *Use consistent indentation.*

Keep <project> at the very left edge, along with the <?xml ... ?> tag. Two or four spaces is typical, no hard tabs. Keep closing elements aligned with opening elements, as in <target> here:

```
<?xml version="1.0">
<project>
..<target name="init">
....<mkdir dir="${build.dir}"/>
..</target>
</project>
```

10. *One-line elements are acceptable.*

This typically only applies to elements that combine their start and finish tags into one.

```
<echo message="hello"/>
```

One line also works for short begin and end pairs.

```
<echo>build.dir = ${build.dir}</echo>
```

11. *Break up long lines.*

Follow conventions similar to Java coding. Lines typically should not be longer than 80 characters, although other considerations may lower this limit. Break lines when they become longer than the limit, or when readability would be increased by breaking them. These guidelines assist in breaking long lines.

Place the first attribute of an XML element on the same line as the start element tag, and place subsequent attributes on new lines indented to the same level as the first attribute.

```
<javac destdir="${build.classes.dir}"
       debug="${build.debug}"
       includeAntRuntime="yes"
       srcdir="${src.dir}"
/>
```

If an attribute value still pushes past the established line length limit, consider splitting the value into multiple properties and concatenating their values.

Close self-contained elements on a new line, as shown here, with the /> characters aligned vertically with the opening <. This helps you visually notice the entire block as a unit.

12. White space is your friend.

Include blank lines between logical groupings. Examples include between logical sets of property definitions, targets, and groupings of tasks within a target.

13. Define tasks, datatypes, and properties before targets.

Some tasks are allowed outside targets: <taskdef>, <typedef>, and <property>. All datatype declarations are also allowed outside of targets. When possible, place task, datatype, and property definitions before the first target as child elements of <project>.

```
<?xml version="1.0" ?>
<project name="library" default="main">

  <property name="tasks.jar" location="dist/tasks.jar"/>
  <taskdef resource="taskdef.properties" classpath="${tasks.jar}"/>

  <path id="the.path" includes="${tasks.jar}"/>

  <target name="usetasks">
    <sometask refid="the.path"/>
  </target>

</project>
```

Some exceptions apply, such as compiling and using a custom task in the same build —this requires the <taskdef> to be inside a target dependent upon compilation.

14. Order attributes logically and consistently.

Define targets with name first so that it is easy to spot visually.

```
<target name="deploy" depends="package" if="deploy.server">
  <!-- ... -->
</target>
```

For commonly used tasks, such as <javac>, establish a preferred ordering of attributes and be consistent across projects:

```
<javac srcdir="${src.dir}"
       destdir="${build.classes.dir}"
       classpathref="compile.classpath"
       debug="${build.debug}"
       includeAntRuntime="yes"
/>
```

Use XML entity references to include common fragments.

```
<?xml version="1.0"?>
<!DOCTYPE project [
    <!ENTITY properties SYSTEM "file:../properties.xml">
]>
<project name="Sub-project" default="main">

  &properties;

</project>
```

D.4   NAMING CONVENTIONS

D.4.1   General

15.   Use a common naming scheme among targets, datatypes, and properties.
Combine meaningful names, such as install, docs, and webapp, with meaningful types, such as docs.patternset, webapp.name, and webapp.classpath.

D.4.2   Targets

16.   Use consistent target names.
Standard target names keep a build file understandable over time and by new developers. In a project with separate subprojects, each with its own build file, it is important to keep the names consistent between projects, not just for the benefit of programmers but for any master build mechanism.

Well-known Ant targets provide a "walk up and use" experience. Table D.1 details several commonly used targets and their purposes.

Table D.1   These targets are common to many builds. Always avoid changing the behavior of a well-known target name. You do not need to implement all of these in a single project.

Target Name	Function
all	Build and test everything; create a distribution, optionally install.
clean	Delete all generated files and directories.
deploy	Deploy the code, usually to a remote server.
dist	Produce the distributables.
distclean	Clean up the distribution files only.
docs	Generate all documentation.
init	Initialize the build: create directories, call <tstamp> and other common actions.

continued on next page

Table D.1 These targets are common to many builds. Always avoid changing the behavior of a well-known target name. You do not need to implement all of these in a single project. *(continued)*

Target Name	Function
install	Perform a local installation.
javadocs	Generate the Javadoc pages.
printerdocs	Generate printable documents.
test	Run the unit tests.
uninstall	Remove a local installation.

Never override a well-known target name with a different behavior, as the build file will then behave unexpectedly to new users. For example, the docs task should not install the system as a side effect, as that is not what is expected.

17. Separate words in target names with a hyphen.

For example, use install-lite instead of installLite, install_lite, or install lite.

18. Use consistent default target names across projects.

A standard default project target name allows for easy invocation from the command line.

```
<project name="elements" default="default">

  <target name="clean">
    <!-- ... -->
  </target>

  <target name="default" depends="..."/>

</project>
```

The targets main and default make good standard default target names, although this is an area of personal preference. Whatever you choose, be consistent across all projects. To invoke a default clean build, run ant clean default.

D.4.3   Properties

19. Use standard suffixes for directory and library properties.

Use .dir for directory paths and .jar for JAR file references.

*20. Prefix compilation properties with **build**.*

The reason is somewhat historical, as build.compiler is Ant's magic property to control which compiler is used. In keeping with this special property, build.debug should be used to control the debug flag of <javac>. Likewise, other <javac> parameters that you wish to control dynamically should use the build. prefix.

21. State the role of the property first, then the type of property.

For example, a property representing whether or no tests need to be run is represented as `tests.uptodate`.

22. Separate words with a dot (.) character in property names.

23. Use lowercase property names.

Environment variables are an exception.

24. Load environment variables with env. prefix.

```
<property env="env"/>
```

The case of the properties loaded will be dependent upon the environment variables, but they are typically uppercase: `env.COMPUTERNAME`, for example, is the computer name on a Windows platform.

25. Use properties to name and locate JAR libraries.

Using indirection keeps a build file decoupled from the location and version of third-party libraries.

`build.xml`:

```
<property name="lib.dir" location="../somewhere/libs"/>
<property file="${lib.dir}/lib.properties"/>


...
<classpath id="compile.classpath"
           path="${oro.jar}:${xalan.jar}"
/>
```

`lib.properties`:

```
xalan.jar=${lib.dir}/java/jakarta-xalan2/xalan.jar
oro.jar=${lib.dir}/java/jakarta-oro/jakarta-oro-2.0.6.jar
```

(Submitted by Stephane Bailliez, stephane.bailliez@haht.com.)

There are several ways to accomplish this indirection to varying degrees of flexibility and complexity. The important point is that a build file should not be hardcoded with library version information.

D.4.4   Datatypes

26. Use property name formatting conventions for datatype IDs.

In other words, lowercase datatype IDs and separate words with the dot (.) character.

27. Standardize datatype suffixes.

Paths that represent classpaths end with `.classpath`, like `compile.classpath`. End patternset ISDs with `.patternset` (or simply `.pattern`, but be consistent). Filesets end with `.files`.

D.4.5 Directory structure

28. Standardize directory structures.

A consistent organization of all projects' directory structures makes it easier for build file reuse, either by cut-and-paste editing, or within library build files. It also makes it easier for experienced Ant users to work with your project.

A good directory structure is an important aspect of managing any software development project. In relation to Ant, a well thought out directory structure can accomplish something simply and elegantly, rather than struggling with tangled logic and unnecessarily complex fileset definitions. Table D.2 lists directory names commonly found in Ant projects.

Table D.2 Common directory names. The build and dist directories should contain nothing in them that Ant cannot build, so clean can clean up just by deleting them.

Directory	Contents
build	Temporary staging area for classes and more
dist	Distribution directory
docs	Documentation files stored in their presentation formats
etc	Sample files
lib	Project dependencies, typically third-party .jar files
src	Root directory of Java source code, package directory structure below
src/xdocs	Documentation in XML format, to be transformed into presentation format during the build process
src/META-INF	Metadata for the JAR file
web	Root directory of web content (.html, .jpg, .JSP)
web/WEB-INF	Web deployment information, such as web.xml

The actual naming and placement of directories are somewhat controversial, as many different projects have their own historical preference. All good layouts, however, tend to have these features:

- Source files are cleanly split from generated files; Java class files are never generated into the same directory as the source. This makes it much easier to clean a project of all generated content, and reduces the risk of any accidental destruction of source files.

- Java files are laid out in package hierarchy, with subdirectories such as com and org, which contain vendor and project names beneath them. This is critical for Ant's Java file dependency checking, and it also helps you to manage very large projects.

- Library files used are kept with the project. This avoids implicit dependencies on files from elsewhere that have been stuck onto the classpath somehow.

- Distribution files are separate from intermediate files. This lets you clean up the intermediate files while keeping the redistributable output.

29. Define a project `<description>`.

This is visible in the build file, but is also displayed when the –projecthelp switch is used.

```
<project name="elements" default="default">
  <description>The Elements of Ant Style project</description>

  <target name="default"
          description="Public target"
  />

</project>
```

Running ant –projecthelp shows the description:

```
Buildfile: build.xml
The Elements of Ant Style project
Main targets:

 default  Public target

Default target: default
```

30. Use comments liberally.

Be succinct and do not repeat what is already obvious from the build file elements. There is no need to say `<!-- compile the code -->` followed by `<javac>`.

Here is an example of a block comment to separate sections visibly.

```
<!-- ======================================================= -->
<!-- Datatype declarations                                   -->
<!-- ======================================================= -->
<path id="compile.classpath">
  <pathelement location="${lucene.jar}"/>
  <pathelement location="${jtidy.jar}"/>
</path>
```

31. Define a usage target.

If mostly new users use your build file, having the default target display some usage information will help them get started.

```
<project name="MyProject" default="usage" basedir="..">
 <target name="usage">
   <echo message="  Execute 'ant -projecthelp' for build file help."/>
   <echo message="  Execute 'ant -help' for Ant help."/>
 </target>
```

(Submitted by Bobby Woolf, woolf@acm.org.)

You may, alternatively, want your default target to perform the primary build of the project but still have a usage target that can be invoked if needed.

32. Use alias target names to provide intuitive entry points.

For example, you may want to have a usage target but users would also type ant help and expect assistance. An alias is simply an empty target that depends on a nonempty target.

```
<target name="help" depends="usage"/>
```

33. Include an **all** target that builds it all.

This may not be your default target though. This target should at least create all artifacts including documentation and distributable, but probably would not be responsible for installation.

34. Give primary targets a description.

Targets with a description appear as Main targets in the –projecthelp output. The description should be succinct and provide information beyond what the actual target name implies.

```
<target name="gen-ejb"
        description="Generate EJB code from @tags"
        depends="init">
  <!-- ... -->
</target>
```

Higher level build process documentation or diagrams can be generated from a build file using XSL transformations or other techniques. (Submitted by Greg Cosmo Haun, GHaun@cenquest.com.) This is a rationale for keeping descriptions short. Use XML comments for more detailed information if necessary.

D.6   PROGRAMMING CONVENTIONS

D.6.1   General

35. Copy resources from source path to classpath.

Metadata resources are often kept alongside source code, or in parallel directory trees, to allow for customer customization or test data, for example. These files are typically property files or XML files, such as resource bundles used for localization.

Tests may assume these files are available on the classpath. Copying these resource files to the directory where source files are compiled allows them to be picked up automatically during packaging and testing.

```
<copy todir="${test.classes.dir}">
  <fileset dir="${test.src.dir}" includes="**/*.properties"/>
</copy>
```

D.6.2   Targets

36. Clean up after yourself.

Make sure that all artifacts generated during a build are removed with a `clean` target. You may also want a `cleandist` target such that the `clean` target only removes the temporary build files but leaves the final distributable, and `cleandist` removes everything including the generated distributable.

D.6.3   Properties

37. Use properties to name anything that could need overriding by the user or a parent project.

Every output directory deserves a unique property name, suffixed by `.dir`. Other items that make good candidates for properties are: configuration files, template files used for code generation, distributable file names, application names, user names, and passwords.

38. Use `location` for directory and file references.

This results in the full absolute path being resolved and used for the property value, rather than just the string (likely relative path) value.

```
<property name="build.dir" location="build "/>
```

39. Handle creation and deletion of property-referenced directories individually.

Do not assume that hierarchically named properties refer to hierarchically structured directories.

```
<project name="DirectoryExample" default="init">
  <property name="build.dir" location="build"/>
  <property name="build.classes.dir" location="${build.dir}/classes"/>

  <target name="init">
    <mkdir dir="${build.dir}"/>
    <mkdir dir="${build.classes.dir}"/>
  </target>

  <target name="clean">
    <delete dir="${build.dir}"/>
    <delete dir="${build.classes.dir}"/>
  </target>
</project>
```

The `<mkdir>` task will make multiple levels of directories if they do not exist, so if only `<mkdir dir="${build.classes.dir}"/>` was used in the `init` target, both the build and build/classes directories would be created. However, because properties are designed to be overridden you cannot assume that `build.classes.dir` is physically under `build.dir`. A master build file may have forced the project to build into a different set of directories.

40. *Understand and utilize property rules.*

Properties are immutable. This fact alone can be the source of frustration for those seeking to implement variables, or the source of great flexibility when used properly. A property sticks with its first value set, and all future attempts to change it are ignored.

Load properties in the desired order of precedence. The needs of the project, development team, and organization dictate the specific order required. Loading user-specific properties is a convention all projects should follow. The following code is an example of typical property ordering:

```
<!-- Load environment variables -->
<property environment="env"/>

<property name="user.properties.file"
          location="${user.home}/.build.properties"
/>

<!-- Load the project specific settings -->
<property file="build.properties"/>

<!-- Load user specific settings -->
<property file="${user.properties.file}"/>
```

This fragment loads all environment variables as Ant properties first. The user-specific properties file is mapped to an Ant property so that its location can itself be overridden, but it is not loaded until after the project-specific properties are loaded. This allows a project to have more control over its settings than a user's preference, if it is needed.

41. *Base hierarchically named directory properties from the parent directory property.*
Don't do this:

```
<property name="build.dir" location="build"/>
<property name="build.classes" location="build/classes"/>
```

Do this instead:

```
<property name="build.dir" location="build"/>
<property name="build.classes" location="${build.dir}/classes"/>
```

The difference becomes apparent when a user or master build wants to override build.dir. In the first example, only build.dir is relocated to the overridden directory, but build.classes will remain under the base directory. In the second example, overriding build.dir has the desired effect of moving all child directories too.

42. *Achieve conditional logic with* `<property>`*.*
New users to Ant often overlook this technique when searching for ways to achieve conditional logic.

Defaulting the `build.number` property to zero if it is not set in a properties file takes advantage of property immutability.

```
<property file="build.properties"/>
<property name="build.number" value="0"/>
```

If `build.number` is loaded from build.properties, the second `<property>` task is essentially ignored.

Setting properties differently depending on the server only requires a single build file line.

```
<property file="${server.name}.properties"/>
```

The `server.name` property could be set at the command line, set from the environment (with some indirection from `<property name="server.name" value="${env.COMPUTERNAME}"/>`), or from a previously loaded properties file.

43. Use **prefix** to uniquely identify similar property names.

Because of property immutability and name clash possibilities, the `<property>` task allows prefixing all loaded properties.

To load two server configuration files with unique prefixes, use `prefix`.

```
<property file="server1.properties" prefix="server1"/>
<property file="server2.properties" prefix="server2"/>
```

Both files may have a `server.name` property, but they will be accessible as `server1.server.name` and `server2.server.name` Ant properties.

D.6.4   Datatypes

44. Define reusable paths.

This eases build file maintenance. Adding a new dependency to the compile classpath, in this example, automatically includes it in the test classpath.

```
<path id="compile.classpath">
  <pathelement location="${lucene.jar}"/>
  <pathelement location="${jtidy.jar}"/>
</path>

<path id="test.classpath">
  <path refid="compile.classpath"/>
  <pathelement location="${junit.jar}"/>
  <pathelement location="${build.classes.dir}"/>
  <pathelement location="${test.classes.dir}"/>
</path>
```

D.6.5 Classpath

This section deals with classpath issues within your build file.

45. Use explicit classpaths wherever possible.

Although some libraries must be in ANT_HOME/lib, keep the ones that are not needed there in a separate location, and refer to them with Ant properties to allow for overriding. Avoid, if possible, using filesets to pull `*.jar` into a path declaration, as this makes the build file break if conflicting JAR files are added later.

```
<path id="task.classpath">
  <pathelement location="${build.dir}"/>
  <pathelement location="${antbook-common.jar}"/>
  <pathelement location="${lucene.jar}"/>
</path>

<java classname="org.example.antbook.tasks.Searcher"
     fork="true"
     classpathref="task.classpath">
  <arg file="${index.dir}"/>
  <arg value="${query}"/>
</java>
```

46. Turn off `includeAntRuntime` on `<javac>`.

By default, `includeAntRuntime` is `true`. There is no need for it to be in the classpath unless you are building custom Ant tasks. Even then, it is not necessary because you can include `${ant.home}/lib/ant.jar` in the classpath manually.

47. Use the `refid <property>` variant for string representation of a path.

This can be useful for debugging purposes, or especially handy when invoking Java programs with `<apply>`.

This example invokes JavaNCSS on a set of source files, producing an XML output file.

```
<path id="ncss.classpath">
  <fileset dir="${ncss.lib.dir}" includes="**/*.jar" />
</path>

<target name="ncss" depends="compile">
  <property name="cp" refid="ncss.classpath" />
  <apply executable="java"
         parallel="true"
         dir="${src.dir}"
         output="${build.dir}/${ant.project.name}-ncss.xml">
    <arg line="-cp %classpath%;${cp}" />
    <arg value="javancss.Main" />
    <arg line="-package -xml" />
    <fileset dir="${src.dir}" includes="**/*.java" />
  </apply>
```

(Submitted by Paul Holser, Paul_Holser@Landsafe.Com.)

D.6.6　Testing

48. *Write tests first!*
While not directly related to Ant, we find this step important enough to say whenever we can. Corollary: if you can't do them first, at least do them second.

49. *Standardize test case names.*
Name test cases `*Test.java`. In the `<junit>` task use `<fileset dir= "${test.dir}" includes="**/*Test.class"/>`. The only files named `*Test. java` are test cases that can be run with JUnit. Name helper classes something else.

    Another useful convention is to name base, typically abstract, test cases `*TestCase`.

50. *Provide visual and XML test results.*
Use `<formatter type="brief" usefile="false"/>` and `<formatter type= "xml"/>`. The brief formatter, without using a file, allows for immediate visual inspection of a build indicating what caused the failure. The XML formatter allows for reporting using `<junitreport>`.

51. *Incorporate the single test case trick.*
The nested `<test>` and `<batchtest>` elements of `<junit>` allow for if/unless conditions. This facilitates a single test case to be run when desired, or all tests by default.

```
<junit printsummary="no"
       errorProperty="test.failed"
       failureProperty="test.failed"
       fork="${junit.fork}">
  <classpath refid="test.classpath"/>

  <test name="${testcase}" if="testcase"/>
  <batchtest todir="${test.data.dir}" unless="testcase">
    <fileset dir="${test.classes.dir}"
             includes="**/*Test.class"
    />
  </batchtest>
</junit>
```

During development, a single test case can be isolated and run from the command line:

```
ant -Dtestcase=org.example.antbook.TroublesomeTest
```

52. *Fail builds when tests fail.*
By default, the `<junit>` task does not halt a build when failures occur. If no reporting is desired, enable `haltonfailure` and `haltonerror`. However, reporting of test cases is often desired. To accomplish reporting of test failures and failing the build together, borrow this example:

```
<junit printsummary="no"
       errorProperty="test.failed"
       failureProperty="test.failed"
       fork="${junit.fork}">
  <!-- ... -->
</junit>

<junitreport todir="${test.data.dir}">
  <fileset dir="${test.data.dir}">
    <include name="TEST-*.xml"/>
  </fileset>
  <report format="frames" todir="${test.reports.dir}"/>
</junitreport>

<fail if="test.failed">
  Unit tests failed. Check log or reports for details
</fail>
```

When tests fail, the property test.failed is set, yet processing continues. The conditional <fail> stops the build after Ant has generated the reports.

53. *Code test cases that need data to adapt.*

Place test data files alongside test cases, copy the files to the test classpath during the build, and access them using Class.getResource. Read test configuration information from system properties, and set them from Ant. Both of these techniques are illustrated in this example.

```
<copy todir="${test.classes.dir}">
  <fileset dir="${test.src.dir}" excludes="**/*.java"/>
</copy>
<junit printsummary="no"
       errorProperty="test.failed"
       failureProperty="test.failed"
       fork="${junit.fork}">
  <classpath refid="test.classpath"/>
  <sysproperty key="docs.dir" value="${test.classes.dir}"/>
  <!-- ... -->
</junit>
```

System.getProperty is used to retrieve the value of docs.dir. Our tests can be controlled easily and values adjusted through Ant properties.

D.6.7   Cross-platform issues

54. *Launch even native scripts in a cross-platform manner.*

Disabling the vmlauncher setting of <exec> executes through Ant's launcher scripts in ANT_HOME/bin.

```
<exec executable="script" vmlauncher="false" />
```

This will launch script on Unix and script.bat on Windows OSs.

This assumes the Unix script version does not have a suffix and the Windows version has a supported suffix as defined in the PATHEXT environment variable. This works because setting the vmlauncher attribute to false causes the command to be executed through cmd.exe on Windows NT/2000/XP, antRun.bat on Windows 9x, and antRun on Unix. Otherwise, with JVMs 1.3 and above, the command is executed directly, bypassing any shell or command interpreter. (Submitted by Bill Burton, billb@progress.com.)

D.6.8 Debugging

55. Log important information at the appropriate level.
The <echo> task has an optional level attribute. Use it to provide information at verbose and debug levels.

```
<echo level="verbose">Seen with -verbose</echo>
<echo level="debug">Seen with -debug</echo>
```

Adding diagnostic output at the debug level can help troubleshoot errant property values, yet the output will not be seen during normal builds. Run ant -debug to see such output.

56. Add a debug target.
Adding a debug target with no dependencies with an <echoproperties> can shed light on possible misconfiguration.

```
<target name="debug">
  <echoproperties/>
</target>
```

Because properties can be defined inside targets, simply running ant debug will not necessarily display them all. Running two targets from a single command line execution will, since properties retain their values across target invocations. For example, if the init target sets properties, running ant init debug will display the properties set by init.

57. Increase Ant's verbosity level.
By default, messages displayed to the console during Ant builds are only a fraction of the messages generated by the Ant engine and tasks. To see all logged output, use the -debug switch:

```
ant -debug
```

The -debug switch generates an enormous amount of output. A good compromise is the -verbose switch, which outputs more than the default informational level of output, but less than the debugging output.

APPENDIX E

Ant task reference

Ant's distribution ships with extensive documentation in HTML format, including details for every task. Why then, do we include a task reference in this book? We felt readers would benefit from a quick reference they could consult while reading the book, or flip through while away from their computers, or as a quick reference to the valid attributes and elements of a task.

We didn't want to rewrite the documentation, as it would have taken a lot of effort for little real benefit. At the same time, we didn't want to include the current documentation as it is too detailed for a quick reference, yet not guaranteed to be accurate. Because Ant's current task documentation is decoupled from the source of the tasks, it is out of sync with the tasks in some places.

To address these needs, we created an automated process to analyze Ant's source code and extract task details directly. This process used XDoclet's custom capabilities, allowing generation of an XML file for each task. These XML files contain information such as task description and all supported attribute and element names, types, and descriptions.[1] We expect the future releases of Ant to adopt this process, improving the online documentation accordingly.

---

[1] The XDoclet work included a custom subtask, tag handler, and template. The process was simple from that point forward. The XML files were merged using `<concat>` and transformed into HTML using `<xslt>`. The code for this autogeneration exists within Ant's source code repository.

Here then is a quick guide to all the tasks, automatically generated from the source itself. It lists all tasks in Ant 1.5 and their nested elements and attributes. We have omitted any examples, or any details, on the nested elements. For these we refer you to the online documentation, and, of course, the many chapters in our book.

E.1   REFERENCE CONVENTIONS

Tasks are listed in the following format:

<task-name>   Brief description of task.

attribute	Attribute description. [Attribute type]
<subelement>	Subelement description. [Element type]

Attributes are listed first, alphabetically, followed by subelements, which are also listed alphabetically. Subelements have angle brackets (< >) around them.

All attributes have a type provided. Element types are only provided for common datatypes. Consult Ant's documentation for specific information on elements when a type is not noted. Boolean attributes are considered true when their values equal on, yes, or true. Any other value is considered false. Path attributes accept platform-independent paths, using either colon (:) or semi-colon (;) as separators and either forward (/) or back slashes (\) as directory separators.

Several tasks are based on a parent *MatchingTask*. MatchingTasks support a number of additional attributes and subelements, and are denoted by an asterisk (*).

E.2   COMMON TASK ATTRIBUTES

All tasks support three common attributes.

id	A unique task instance identifier, which can, for example, be used to refer to the task from <script>. [String]
taskname	An alias for the task; useful for logging purposes, as this name is provided instead. [String]
description	A field useful for commenting purposes, although it is not used or displayed by Ant. [String]

E.2.1   * MatchingTask

Tasks denoted with the asterisk (*) also support the follow attributes and subelements. These tasks operate on an implicit fileset, and typically have an attribute representing the base directory of the fileset.

`casesensitive`	Case sensitivity of the file system. [Boolean]
`defaultexcludes`	If false, turns off the default exclusions. [Boolean]
`excludes`	Comma- or space-separated list of patterns of files that must be excluded. [String]
`excludesfile`	The name of a file; each line of this file is taken to be an exclude pattern. [File]
`followsymlinks`	Indicates whether symbolic links should be followed. [Boolean]
`includes`	Comma- or space-separated list of patterns of files to include. [String]
`includesfile`	The name of a file; each line of this file is taken to be an include pattern. [File]
`<and>`	Selects files that are selected by all of the selectors it contains. [Selector]
`<contains>`	Limits the files selected to only those that contain a specific string. [Selector]
`<custom>`	Adds a custom selector. [Selector]
`<date>`	Selects files based on last modification timestamp. [Selector]
`<depend>`	Selects files whose last modified date is later than another file. [Selector]
`<depth>`	Selects files based on how many directory levels deep they are in relation to the base directory. [Selector]
`<exclude>`	Adds a single pattern to the excludes list.
`<excludesfile>`	Adds patterns contained in a file to the excludes list.
`<filename>`	Functions similarly to the `<include>` and `<exclude>` elements. [Selector]
`<include>`	Adds a single pattern to the includes list.
`<includesfile>`	Adds patterns contained in a file to the includes list.
`<majority>`	Selects files provided that a majority of the contained selectors also select it. [Selector]
`<none>`	Selects files that are not selected by any of the selectors it contains. [Selector]
`<not>`	Reverses the meaning of the single selector it contains. [Selector]
`<or>`	Selects files that are selected by any one of the elements it contains. [Selector]
`<patternset>`	Adds a patternset. [Patternset]
`<present>`	Selects files that have an equivalent file in another directory tree. [Selector]
`<selector>`	Adds selector through a reference. [Selector]
`<size>`	Limits files selected by size. [Selector]

E.3   ANT'S TASKS

\<ant\>   Builds a subproject.

`antfile`	The build file to use. [String]
`dir`	The directory to use as a base directory for the new Ant project. [File]
`inheritall`	If true, pass all properties to the new Ant project; default true. [Boolean]
`inheritrefs`	If true, pass all references to the new Ant project; default false. [Boolean]
`output`	File name to write the output to. [String]
`target`	The target of the new Ant project to execute. [String]
`<property>`	Property to pass to the new project. [See `<property>`]
`<reference>`	Reference element identifying a data type to carry over to the new project.

\<antcall\>   Calls another target in the same project.

`inheritall`	If true, pass all properties to the new Ant project; default true. [Boolean]
`inheritrefs`	If true, pass all references to the new Ant project; default false. [Boolean]
`target`	Target to execute, required. [String]
`<param>`	Property to pass to the invoked target. [See `<property>`]
`<reference>`	Reference element identifying a data type to carry over to the invoked target.

\<antlr\>   Invokes the ANTLR Translator generator on a grammar file.

`debug`	Enables ParseView debugging. [Boolean]
`diagnostic`	Flag to emit diagnostic text. [Boolean]
`dir`	The working directory of the process. [File]
`glib`	Sets an optional super grammar file. [String]
`html`	If true, emits HTML. [Boolean]
`outputdirectory`	The directory to write the generated files to. [File]
`target`	The grammar file to process. [File]
`trace`	If true, enables all tracing. [Boolean]
`tracelexer`	If true, enables lexer tracing. [Boolean]
`traceparser`	If true, enables parser tracing. [Boolean]
`tracetreewalker`	Flag to allow the user to enable tree-walker tracing. [Boolean]
`<classpath>`	Adds a classpath to be set because a directory might be given for ANTLR debug. [Path]
`<jvmarg>`	Adds a new JVM argument.

\<antstructure\> Creates a partial DTD for Ant from the currently known tasks.

output	The output file. [File]

\<apply\> Executes a given command, supplying a set of files as arguments.

append	Sets whether output should be appended or an existing file overwritten. [Boolean]
dest	The directory where target files are to be placed. [File]
dir	The working directory of the process. [File]
executable	The command to execute. [String]
failifexecutionfails	Stop the build if program cannot be started. [Boolean]
failonerror	Fail if the command exits with a non-zero return code. [Boolean]
newenvironment	Do not propagate old environment when new environment variables are specified. [Boolean]
os	List of operating systems on which the command may be executed. [String]
output	File the output of the process is redirected to. [File]
outputproperty	Property name whose value should be set to the output of the process. [String]
parallel	If true, run the command only once, appending all files as arguments. [Boolean]
relative	Sets whether the file names should be passed on the command line as absolute or relative pathnames. [Boolean]
resultproperty	The name of a property in which the return code of the command should be stored. [String]
skipemptyfilesets	If no source files have been found or are newer than their corresponding target files, do not run the command. [Boolean]
type	Type of file to operate on. [file, dir, both]
vmlauncher	If true, launch new process with VM, otherwise use the OS's shell. [Boolean]
\<arg\>	Adds a command-line argument.
\<env\>	Adds an environment variable to the launched process.
\<fileset\>	Source files to operate upon. [Fileset]
\<mapper\>	Adds mapping of source files to target files. [Mapper]
\<srcfile\>	Marker that indicates where the name of the source file should be put on the command line.
\<targetfile\>	Marker that indicates where the name of the target file should be put on the command line.

\<available\> Sets the given property if the requested resource is available at run time.

classname	Classname of a class which must be available to set the given property. [String]
classpath	Classpath to be used when searching for classes and resources. [Path]
classpathref	Classpath by reference. [Reference]

file	File which must be present in the file system to set the given property. [File]
filepath	Path to use when looking for a file. [Path]
ignoresystemclasses	Sets whether the search for classes should ignore the run-time classes and just use the given classpath. [Boolean]
property	Name of the property that will be set if the particular resource is available. [String]
resource	Name of a Java resource which is required to set the property. [String]
type	Sets what type of file is required. [file, dir]
value	Value given to the property if the desired resource is available. [String]
<classpath>	Classpath to be used when searching for classes and resources. [Path]
<filepath>	Path to search for file resources. [Path]

<basename> Sets a property to the base name of a specified file, optionally minus a suffix.

file	File or directory to get base name from. [File]
property	Property to set base name to. [String]
suffix	Optional suffix to remove from base name. [String]

<blgenclient> Generates a Borland Application Server 4.5 client JAR using as input the EJB JAR file.

classpath	Path to use for classpath. [Path]
classpathref	Reference to existing path, to use as a classpath. [Reference]
clientjar	Client JAR file name. [File]
debug	If true, turn on the debug mode for each of the Borland tools launched. [Boolean]
ejbjar	EJB JAR file. [File]
mode	Command launching mode: java or fork. [String]
version	No description. [Integer]
<classpath>	Adds path to the classpath. [Path]

<buildnumber> Reads, increments, and writes a build number in a file.

file	The file in which the build number is stored. [File]

<bunzip2> Expands a file that has been compressed with the BZIP2 algorithm.

dest	The destination file or directory; optional. [File]
src	The file to expand; required. [File]

<bzip2> Compresses a file with the BZIP2 algorithm.

src	The file to compress; required. [File]
zipfile	The required destination file. [File]

<cab> * Creates a CAB archive.

basedir	Base directory to look in for files to CAB. [File]
cabfile	The name/location of where to create the .cab file. [File]
compress	If true, compress the files; otherwise only store them. [Boolean]
options	Sets additional cabarc options that are not supported directly. [String]
verbose	If true, display cabarc output. [Boolean]
<fileset>	Adds a set of files to archive. [Fileset]

<cccheckin> Checks in files with ClearCase.

cleartooldir	Directory where the cleartool executable is located. [String]
comment	Comment string. [String]
commentfile	Specifies a file containing a comment. [String]
identical	If true, allows the file to be checked in even if it is identical to the original. [Boolean]
keepcopy	If true, keeps a copy of the file with a .keep extension. [Boolean]
nowarn	If true, suppresses warning messages. [Boolean]
preservetime	If true, preserves the modification time. [Boolean]
viewpath	Path to the item in a ClearCase view to operate on. [String]

<cccheckout> Checks out files in ClearCase.

branch	Specifies a branch to check out the file to. [String]
cleartooldir	Directory where the cleartool executable is located. [String]
comment	Comment string. [String]
commentfile	Specifies a file containing a comment. [String]
nodata	If true, checks out the file but does not create an editable file containing its data. [Boolean]
nowarn	If true, suppresses warning messages. [Boolean]
out	Creates a writable file under a different file name. [String]
reserved	If true, checks out the file as reserved. [Boolean]
version	If true, allows checkout of a version other than the latest. [Boolean]
viewpath	Path to the item in a ClearCase view to operate on. [String]

<ccmcheckin>	Performs a Continuus checkin command.	
	`ccmdir`	Directory where the `ccm` executable is located. [String]
	`comment`	Specifies a comment. [String]
	`file`	Path to the file that the command will operate on. [File]
	`task`	Specifies the task number used to check in the file (may use default). [String]

<ccmcheckintask>	Performs a Continuus checkin default task command.	
	`ccmdir`	Directory where the `ccm` executable is located. [String]
	`comment`	Specifies a comment. [String]
	`file`	Path to the file that the command will operate on. [File]
	`task`	Specifies the task number used to check in the file (may use default). [String]

<ccmcheckout>	Performs a Continuus checkout command.	
	`ccmdir`	Directory where the `ccm` executable is located. [String]
	`comment`	Specifies a comment. [String]
	`file`	Path to the file that the command will operate on. [File]
	`task`	Specifies the task number used to check out the file (may use default). [String]

<ccmcreatetask>	Creates new Continuus <ccm> task and sets it as the default.	
	`ccmdir`	Directory where the `ccm` executable is located. [String]
	`comment`	Specifies a comment. [String]
	`platform`	Specifies the target platform. [String]
	`release`	Specifies the `ccm` release. [String]
	`resolver`	Specifies the resolver. [String]
	`subsystem`	Specifies the subsystem. [String]
	`task`	Specifies the task number used (may use default). [String]

<ccmreconfigure>	Reconfigures a Continuus project, optionally recursively.	
	`ccmdir`	Directory where the `ccm` executable is located. [String]
	`ccmproject`	`ccm` project on which the operation is applied. [String]
	`recurse`	If true, recurse on subproject (default false). [Boolean]
	`verbose`	If true, do a verbose reconfigure operation (default false). [Boolean]

<ccuncheckout>	Performs a ClearCase Uncheckout command.	
	`cleartooldir`	Directory where the `cleartool` executable is located. [String]
	`keepcopy`	If true, keep a copy of the file with a .keep extension. [Boolean]
	`viewpath`	Path to the item in a ClearCase view to operate on. [String]

<ccupdate> Performs a ClearCase Update command.

cleartooldir	Directory where the `cleartool` executable is located. [String]
currenttime	If true, modification time should be written as the current time. [Boolean]
graphical	If true, displays a graphical dialog during the update. [Boolean]
log	Log file where `cleartool` records the status of the command. [String]
overwrite	If true, overwrites hijacked files. [Boolean]
preservetime	If true, modification time should be preserved from the VOB time. [Boolean]
rename	If true, hijacked files are renamed with a .keep extension. [Boolean]
viewpath	Path to the item in a ClearCase view to operate on. [String]

<checksum> * Creates or verifies file checksums.

algorithm	Specifies the algorithm to be used to compute the checksum. [String]
file	File for which the checksum is to be calculated. [File]
fileext	File extension that is be to used to create or identify destination file. [String]
forceoverwrite	Indicates whether to overwrite existing file, irrespective of whether it is newer than the source file. [Boolean]
property	Property to hold the generated checksum. [String]
provider	MessageDigest algorithm provider to be used to calculate the checksum. [String]
readbuffersize	The size of the read buffer to use. [Integer]
verifyproperty	Verify property. [String]
<fileset>	Files to generate checksums for. [Fileset]

<chmod> Chmod equivalent for Unix-like environments. Some of the attributes are an artifact of the task's implementation as a subclass of <exec>.

append	Indicates whether output should be appended to or overwrite an existing file. [Boolean]
defaultexcludes	Sets whether default exclusions should be used. [Boolean]
dest	The directory where target files are to be placed. [File]
dir	The directory that holds the files whose permissions must be changed. [File]
excludes	Set of exclude patterns. [String]
executable	The command to execute. [String]
failifexecutionfails	Stops the build if program cannot be started. [Boolean]
failonerror	Fail if the command exits with a nonzero return code. [Boolean]
file	The file or single directory for which the permissions must be changed. [File]
includes	Set of include patterns. [String]

newenvironment	Do not propagate old environment when new environment variables are specified. [Boolean]
os	List of operating systems on which the command may be executed. [String]
output	File the output of the process is redirected to. [File]
outputproperty	Property name whose value should be set to the output of the process. [String]
parallel	If true, runs the command only once, appending all files as arguments. [Boolean]
perm	The new permissions. [String]
relative	Indicates whether the file names should be passed on the command line as absolute or relative pathnames. [Boolean]
resultproperty	The name of a property in which the return code of the command should be stored. [String]
skipemptyfilesets	If no source files have been found or are newer than their corresponding target files, do not run the command. [Boolean]
type	Type of file to operate on [file, dir, both].
vmlauncher	If true, launches new process with VM, otherwise uses the OS's shell. [Boolean]
<arg>	Adds a command-line argument.
<env>	Adds an environment variable to the launched process.
<exclude>	Adds a name entry on the exclude list.
<fileset>	Source files to operate upon. [Fileset]
<include>	Adds a name entry on the include list.
<mapper>	Adds mapping of source files to target files. [Mapper]
<patternset>	Adds a set of patterns. [Patternset]
<srcfile>	Indicates where the name of the source file should be put on the command line.
<targetfile>	Indicates where the name of the target file should be put on the command line.

<concat> Concatenates a series of files into a single file. This task supports nested text, which is appended to the end if specified.

append	Behavior when the destination file exists. [Boolean]
destfile	Destination file, or uses the console if not specified. [File]
encoding	Encoding for the input files, used when displaying the data via the console. [String]
<filelist>	List of files to concatenate. [Filelist]
<fileset>	Set of files to concatenate. [Fileset]

<condition> Task to conditionally set a property.

property	The name of the property to set. [String]
value	The value for the property to set, if condition evaluates to true. [String]

`<and>`		True if all nested conditions evaluate to true.
`<available>`		Identical to the `<available>` task.
`<checksum>`		Identical to the `<checksum>` task.
`<contains>`		Tests whether one string contains another.
`<equals>`		Tests whether two strings are equal.
`<filesmatch>`		Tests that two files match, byte for byte.
`<http>`		Checks for a valid response from a web server of a specified URL.
`<isfalse>`		Tests whether a string value is not `<istrue>`.
`<isset>`		Tests whether a property has been set.
`<istrue>`		Tests whether a string evaluates to `true`, on, or yes.
`<not>`		Negates results of single nested condition.
`<or>`		True if one nested condition is `true`.
`<os>`		Tests whether the current operating system is of a given type.
`<socket>`		Checks for the existence of a TCP/IP listener at the specified host and port.
`<uptodate>`		Identical to the `<uptodate>` task.

\<copy\> Copies a file or directory to a new file or directory.

encoding	Character encoding. [String]
failonerror	If false, notes errors to the output but keeps going. [Boolean]
file	Single source file to copy. [File]
filtering	If true, enables filtering. [Boolean]
flatten	When copying directory trees, the files can be flattened into a single directory. [Boolean]
includeemptydirs	Used to copy empty directories. [Boolean]
overwrite	Overwrites any existing destination file(s). [Boolean]
preservelastmodified	Gives the copied files the same last modified time as the original files. [Boolean]
todir	Destination directory. [File]
tofile	Destination file. [File]
verbose	Used to force listing of all names of copied files. [Boolean]
`<fileset>`	Adds a set of files to copy. [Fileset]
`<filterchain>`	Adds a FilterChain. [FilterChain]
`<filterset>`	Adds a filterset. [Filterset]
`<mapper>`	Defines the mapper to map source to destination files. [Mapper]

\<csc\> * Compiles C# source into executables or modules.

additionalmodules	Semicolon-separated list of modules to refer to. [String]
debug	Debug flag on or off. [Boolean]
definitions	Semicolon-separated list of defined constants. [String]
destdir	Destination directory of files to be compiled. [File]

`destfile`	Name of exe/library to create. [File]
`docfile`	File for generated XML documentation. [File]
`extraoptions`	Any extra options that are not explicitly supported by this task. [String]
`failonerror`	If true, fails on compilation errors. [Boolean]
`filealign`	File alignment. [Integer]
`fullpaths`	If true, prints the full path of files on errors. [Boolean]
`includedefault-` `references`	If true, automatically includes the common .NET assemblies, and tells the compiler to link in mscore.dll. [Boolean]
`incremental`	Incremental compilation flag on or off. [Boolean]
`mainclass`	Name of main class for executables. [String]
`noconfig`	Do not read in the compiler settings files csc.rsp. [Boolean]
`optimize`	If true, enables optimization flag. [Boolean]
`outputfile`	Output file. [File]
`referencefiles`	Path of references to include. [Path]
`references`	Semicolon-separated list of DLLs to refer to. [String]
`srcdir`	Source directory of the files to be compiled. [File]
`targettype`	Type of target. [String]
`unsafe`	If true, enables the `unsafe` keyword. [Boolean]
`utf8output`	If true, requires all compiler output to be in UTF8 format. [Boolean]
`warnlevel`	Level of warning currently between 1 and 4 with 4 being the strictest. [Integer]
`win32icon`	File name of icon to include. [File]
`win32res`	File name of a Win32 resource (.RES) file to include. [File]

`<cvs>` Performs operations on a CVS repository.

`append`	Indicates whether to append output when redirecting to a file. [Boolean]
`command`	The CVS command to execute. [String]
`compression`	If true, this is the same as `compressionlevel="3"`. [Boolean]
`compressionlevel`	If set to a value 1–9 it adds `-zN` to the `cvs` command line, else it disables compression. [Integer]
`cvsroot`	The `CVSROOT` variable. [String]
`cvsrsh`	The `CVS_RSH` variable. [String]
`date`	Use the most recent revision, no later than the given date. [String]
`dest`	The directory where the checked-out files should be placed. [File]
`error`	The file to direct standard error from the command. [File]
`failonerror`	Stop the build process if the command exits with a return code other than 0. [Boolean]
`noexec`	If true, report only and do not change any files. [Boolean]
`output`	The file to direct standard output from the command. [File]
`package`	The package/module to operate upon. [String]

passfile	Password file to read passwords from. [File]	
port	Port used by CVS to communicate with the server. [Integer]	
quiet	If true, suppress informational messages. [Boolean]	
tag	The tag of the package/module to operate upon. [String]	
\<commandline>	Adds direct command line to execute.	

\<cvschangelog> Examines the output of CVS log data and groups related changes together.

daysinpast	Number of days worth of log entries to process. [Integer]
destfile	Output file for the log. [File]
dir	Base directory for CVS. [File]
end	Date at which the changelog should stop. [Date]
start	Date at which the changelog should start. [Date]
usersfile	Lookup list of user names & addresses. [File]
\<fileset>	Adds a set of files about which cvs logs will be generated. [Fileset]
\<user>	Adds a user to list changelog knows about.

\<cvspass> Adds a new entry to a CVS password file.

cvsroot	The CVS repository to add an entry for. [String]
passfile	Password file to add the entry to. [File]
password	Password to be added to the password file. [String]

\<cvstagdiff> Examines the output of cvs diff between two tags.

compression	If true, this is the same as compressionlevel="3". [Boolean]
compressionlevel	If set to a value 1–9, it adds -zN to the cvs command line, else it disables compression. [Integer]
cvsroot	The CVSROOT variable. [String]
cvsrsh	The CVS_RSH variable. [String]
destfile	Output file for the diff. [File]
enddate	End date. [String]
endtag	End tag. [String]
failonerror	Stop the build process if the command exits with a return code other than 0. [Boolean]
package	The package/module to analyze. [String]
passfile	Password file to read passwords from. [File]
port	Port used by CVS to communicate with the server. [Integer]
quiet	If true, suppress informational messages. [Boolean]
startdate	Start date. [String]
starttag	Start tag. [String]

<ddcreator> * Builds a serialized deployment descriptor given a text file description of the descriptor in the format supported by WebLogic.

`classpath`	Classpath to be used for this compilation. [String]
`descriptors`	Directory from where the text descriptions of the deployment descriptors are to be read. [String]
`dest`	Directory into which the serialized deployment descriptors are written. [String]

<delete> * Deletes a file or directory, or set of files defined by a fileset.

`defaultexcludes`	Sets whether default exclusions should be used. [Boolean]
`dir`	Directory from which files are to be deleted. [File]
`excludes`	Set of exclude patterns. [String]
`excludesfile`	Name of the file containing the excludes patterns. [File]
`failonerror`	If false, notes errors but continues. [Boolean]
`file`	Name of a single file to be removed. [File]
`includeemptydirs`	If true, deletes empty directories. [Boolean]
`includes`	Set of include patterns. [String]
`includesfile`	Name of the file containing the include patterns. [File]
`quiet`	If true, and the file does not exist, does not display a diagnostic message or modify the exit status to reflect an error. [Boolean]
`verbose`	If true, lists all names of deleted files. [Boolean]
`<exclude>`	Adds a name entry on the exclude list.
`<excludesfile>`	Adds a name entry on the exclude files list.
`<fileset>`	Adds a set of files to be deleted. [Fileset]
`<include>`	Adds a name entry on the include list.
`<includesfile>`	Adds a name entry on the include files list.
`<patternset>`	Adds a set of patterns. [Patternset]

<depend> * Generates a dependency file for a given set of classes.

`cache`	Dependency cache file. [File]
`classpath`	Classpath to be used for this dependency check. [Path]
`classpathref`	Adds a reference to a classpath defined elsewhere. [Reference]
`closure`	If true, transitive dependencies are followed until the closure of the dependency set if reached. [Boolean]
`destdir`	Destination directory where the compiled Java files exist. [Path]
`dump`	If true, the dependency information will be written to the debug level log. [Boolean]
`srcdir`	Directories path to find the Java source files. [Path]
`<classpath>`	Adds a classpath to be used for this dependency check. [Path]

<dependset> * Examines and removes out-of-date target files.

<srcfilelist>	Adds a list of source files. [Filelist]
<srcfileset>	Adds a set of source files. [Fileset]
<targetfilelist>	Adds a list of target files. [Filelist]
<targetfileset>	Adds a set of target files. [Fileset]

<dirname> Determines the directory name of the specified file.

file	Path to take the dirname of. [File]
property	The name of the property to set. [String]

<ear> * Creates an EAR archive.

appxml	File to incorporate as application.xml. [File]
basedir	Directory from which to archive files; optional. [File]
compress	Indicates whether to compress the files or only store them; optional, default=true;. [Boolean]
destfile	The file to create; required. [File]
duplicate	Sets behavior for when a duplicate file is about to be added. [add, preserve, fail]
encoding	Encoding to use for file names, defaults to the platform's default encoding. [String]
filesonly	If true, emulates Sun's JAR utility by not adding parent directories; optional, defaults to false. [Boolean]
index	Indicates whether to create an index list for classes. [Boolean]
manifest	The manifest file to use. [File]
update	If true, updates an existing file, otherwise overwrites any existing one; optional, defaults to false. [Boolean]
whenempty	Behavior of the task when no files match. [fail, skip, create]
<archives>	Adds zipfileset. [ZipFileset]
<fileset>	Adds a set of files. [Fileset]
<manifest>	Allows the manifest for the archive file to be provided inline in the build file rather than in an external file.
<metainf>	Adds a zipfileset to include in the META-INF directory. [ZipFileset]
<zipfileset>	Adds a set of files that can be read from an archive and given a prefix/fullpath. [ZipFileset]
<zipgroupfileset>	Adds a group of Zip files. [Fileset]

<echo> Writes a message to the Ant logging facilities. A message may be supplied as nested text to this task.

append	If true, append to existing file. [Boolean]
file	File to write to. [File]
level	Logging level. [error, warning, info, verbose, debug]
message	Message to write. [String]

<echoproperties> Displays all the current properties in the build.

destfile	File to store the property output. [File]
failonerror	If true, the task will fail if an error occurs while writing the properties file, otherwise errors are just logged. [Boolean]
prefix	If the prefix is set, then only properties that start with this prefix string will be recorded. [String]

<ejbc> * Builds EJB support classes using WebLogic's ejbc tool from a directory containing a set of deployment descriptors.

classpath	Classpath to be used for this compilation. [String]
descriptors	Directory from where the serialized deployment descriptors are to be read. [String]
dest	Directory into which the support classes, RMI stubs, etc. are to be written. [String]
keepgenerated	If true, ejbc will keep the intermediate Java files used to build the class files. [String]
manifest	Name of the generated manifest file. [String]
src	Directory containing the source code for the home interface, remote interface, and public key class definitions. [String]

<ejbjar> * Provides automated EJB JAR file creation.

basejarname	Base name of the EJB JAR that is to be created if it is not to be determined from the name of the deployment descriptor files. [String]
basenameterminator	The string that terminates the base name. [String]
classpath	Classpath to use when resolving classes for inclusion in the JAR. [Path]
dependency	Analyzer to use when adding in dependencies to the JAR. [String]
descriptordir	Descriptor directory. [File]
destdir	Destination directory. [File]
flatdestdir	Controls whether the destination JARs are written out in the destination directory with the same hierarchical structure from which the deployment descriptors have been read. [Boolean]
genericjarsuffix	Suffix for the generated JAR file. [String]
manifest	Manifest file to use in the JAR. [File]
naming	Naming scheme used to determine the name of the generated JARs from the deployment descriptor. [ejb-name, directory, descriptor, basejarname]
srcdir	Source directory, which is the directory that contains the classes that will be added to the EJB JAR. [File]
<borland>	Adds a deployment tool for Borland server.
<classpath>	Adds to the classpath used to locate the super·classes and interfaces of the classes that will make up the EJB JAR. [Path]
<dtd>	Creates a DTD location record.
<iplanet>	Adds a deployment tool for iPlanet Application Server.

`<jboss>`	Adds a deployment tool for JBoss server.
`<jonas>`	Adds a deployment tool for JOnAS server.
`<support>`	Adds a fileset for support elements. [Fileset]
`<weblogic>`	Adds a deployment tool for WebLogic server.
`<weblogictoplink>`	Adds a deployment tool for WebLogic when using the Toplink Object-Relational mapping.
`<websphere>`	Adds a deployment tool for Websphere 4.0 server.

<exec> Executes a given command if the OS platform is appropriate.

`append`	Sets whether output should be appended to or overwrite an existing file. [Boolean]
`dir`	The working directory of the process. [File]
`executable`	The command to execute. [String]
`failifexecution-fails`	Stop the build if program cannot be found or started; default true. [Boolean]
`failonerror`	Fail if the command exits with a nonzero return code. [Boolean]
`newenvironment`	Do not propagate old environment when new environment variables are specified. [Boolean]
`os`	List of operating systems on which the command may be executed. [String]
`output`	File the output of the process is redirected to. [File]
`outputproperty`	Property name whose value should be set to the output of the process. [String]
`resultproperty`	The name of a property in which the return code of the command should be stored. [String]
`vmlauncher`	If true, launch new process with VM, otherwise use the OS's shell. [Boolean]
`<arg>`	Adds a command-line argument.
`<env>`	Adds an environment variable to the launched process.

<fail> Exits the active build, giving an additional message if available. The message may be specified as nested text, or with the `message` attribute.

`if`	Only fail if a property of the given name exists in the current project. [String]
`message`	A message giving further information on why the build exited. [String]
`unless`	Only fail if a property of the given name does not exist in the current project. [String]

<filter> Sets a token filter that is used by the file copy tasks to do token substitution.

`filtersfile`	The file from which the filters must be read. [File]
`token`	The token string without @ delimiters. [String]
`value`	The string that should replace the token during filtered copies. [String]

<fixcrlf> * Converts text source files to local OS formatting conventions, as well as repair text files damaged by misconfigured or misguided editors or file transfer programs.

destdir	Destination where the fixed files should be placed. [File]
encoding	Specifies the encoding Ant expects the files to be in. Defaults to the platform's default encoding. [String]
eof	Specifies how DOS EOF (control-z) characters are to be handled. [add, asis, remove]
eol	Specifies how EndOfLine characters are to be handled. [asis, cr, lf, crlf]
javafiles	Sets to true if modifying Java source files. [Boolean]
srcdir	Source dir to find the source text files. [File]
tab	Specifies how tab characters are to be handled. [add, asis, remove]
tablength	Specifies tab length in characters. [Integer]

<ftp> Uploads or downloads files using FTP.

action	FTP action to be taken. [send, put, recv, get, del, delete, list, mkdir, chmod]
binary	If true, uses binary mode, otherwise text mode; default is true. [Boolean]
chmod	File permission mode (Unix only) for files sent to the server. [String]
depends	Sets to true to transmit only files that are new or changed from their remote counterparts. [Boolean]
ignorenon-criticalerrors	If true, skip errors on directory creation. [Boolean]
listing	The output file for the list action. [File]
newer	A synonym for depends. [Boolean]
passive	Specifies whether to use passive mode. [Boolean]
password	Login password for the given user ID. [String]
port	FTP port used by the remote server. [Integer]
remotedir	Remote directory where files will be placed. [String]
separator	Remote file separator character. [String]
server	FTP server to send files to. [String]
skipfailed-transfers	If true, enables unsuccessful file put, deletes, and gets operations to be skipped with a warning and transfers the remainder of the files. [Boolean]
umask	Default mask for file creation on a Unix server. [String]
userid	Login user ID to use on the specified server. [String]
verbose	Set to true to receive notification about each file as it is transferred. [Boolean]
<fileset>	A set of files to upload or download. [Fileset]

<genkey>   Generates a key in a keystore.

alias	The alias to add under. [String]
dname	The distinguished name for entity. [String]
keyalg	The method to use when generating name-value pair. [String]
keypass	Password for private key (if different than storepass). [String]
keysize	Indicates the size of key generated. [String]
keystore	Keystore location. [String]
sigalg	The algorithm to use in signing. [String]
storepass	Password for Keystore integrity. [String]
storetype	Keystore type. [String]
validity	Indicates how many days certificate is valid. [String]
verbose	If true, enables verbose output when signing. [Boolean]
<dname>	Distinguished name list.

<get>   Gets a particular file from a URL source, usually a web server.

dest	Where to copy the source file. [File]
ignoreerrors	If true, log errors but do not treat as fatal. [Boolean]
password	Password for basic authentication. [String]
src	URL to get. [URL]
username	Username for basic authentication. [String]
usetimestamp	If true, conditionally download a file based on the timestamp of the local copy. [Boolean]
verbose	If true, show verbose progress information. [Boolean]

<gunzip>   Expands a file that has been compressed with the GZIP algorithm.

dest	The destination file or directory; optional. [File]
src	The file to expand; required. [File]

<gzip>   Compresses a file with the GZIP algorithm.

src	The file to compress; required. [File]
zipfile	The required destination file. [File]

<icontract> *   Instruments Java classes with iContract DBC preprocessor.

builddir	Build directory for instrumented classes. [File]
classdir	Class directory (uninstrumented classes). [File]
classpath	Classpath to be used for invocation of iContract. [Path]
classpathref	Adds a reference to a classpath defined elsewhere. [Reference]
controlfile	Control file to pass to iContract. [File]
failthrowable	Throwable (Exception) to be thrown on assertion violation. [String]
instrumentdir	Instrumentation directory. [File]
invariant	Turns on/off invariant instrumentation. [Boolean]

post	Turns on/off postcondition instrumentation. [Boolean]
pre	Turns on/off precondition instrumentation. [Boolean]
quiet	Tells iContract to be quiet. [Boolean]
repbuilddir	Build directory for instrumented classes. [File]
repositorydir	Build directory for repository classes. [File]
srcdir	Source directory. [File]
targets	Name of the file where targets will be written. [File]
updateicontrol	If true, updates iControl properties file. [Boolean]
verbosity	Verbosity level of iContract. [String]
<classpath>	Classpath. [Path]

<ilasm> * Assembles .NET Intermediate Language files.

debug	Debug flag on or off. [Boolean]
extraoptions	Any extra options that are not explicitly supported by this task. [String]
failonerror	If true, fails if ilasm tool fails. [Boolean]
keyfile	The name of a file containing a private key. [File]
listing	If true, produces a listing; default is false. [Boolean]
outputfile	Output file. [File]
resourcefile	Name of resource file to include. [File]
srcdir	Source directory containing the files to be compiled. [File]
targettype	Type of target, either exe or library. [String]
verbose	If true, enables verbose ilasm output. [Boolean]

<input> Reads an input line from the console. The message can also be specified using nested text.

addproperty	Defines the name of a property to be created from input. [String]
message	Message that gets displayed to the user during the build run. [String]
validargs	Defines valid input parameters as comma-separated strings. [String]

<iplanet-ejbc> Compiles EJB stubs and skeletons for the iPlanet Application Server.

classpath	Classpath to be used when compiling the EJB stubs and skeletons. [Path]
debug	If true, debugging output will be generated when ejbc is executed. [Boolean]
dest	Destination directory where the EJB source classes must exist and where the stubs and skeletons will be written. [File]
ejbdescriptor	Location of the standard XML EJB descriptor. [File]
iasdescriptor	Location of the iAS-specific XML EJB descriptor. [File]
iashome	May be used to specify the "home" directory for this iAS installation. [File]
keepgenerated	If true, the Java source files generated by ejbc will be saved. [Boolean]
<classpath>	Adds to the classpath used when compiling the EJB stubs and skeletons. [Path]

<jar> * Creates a JAR archive.

basedir	Directory from which to archive files; optional. [File]
compress	Sets whether to compress the files or only store them; optional, default is true. [Boolean]
destfile	The file to create; required. [File]
duplicate	Sets behavior for when a duplicate file is about to be added. [add, preserve, fail]
encoding	Encoding to use for file names, defaults to the platform's default encoding. [String]
filesonly	If true, emulates Sun's JAR utility by not adding parent directories; optional, defaults to false. [Boolean]
index	Sets whether to create an index list for classes. [Boolean]
manifest	The manifest file to use. [File]
update	If true, updates an existing file, otherwise overwrites any existing one; optional, defaults to false. [Boolean]
whenempty	Sets behavior of the task when no files match. [fail, skip, create]
<fileset>	Adds a set of files. [Fileset]
<manifest>	Allows the manifest for the archive file to be provided inline in the build file rather than in an external file.
<metainf>	Adds a zipfileset to include in the META-INF directory. [ZipFileset]
<zipfileset>	Adds a set of files that can be read from an archive and be given a prefix/full path. [ZipFileset]
<zipgroup-fileset>	Adds a group of Zip files. [Fileset]

<jarlib-available> Checks whether an extension is present in a fileset or an extension set.

file	The JAR library to check. [File]
property	The name of property to set if extensions are available. [String]
<extension>	Extension to look for.
<extensionset>	Adds a set of extensions to search in.

<jarlib-display> Displays the Optional Package and Package Specification information contained within the specified JARs.

file	The JAR library to display information for. [File]
<fileset>	Adds a set of files about which library data will be displayed. [Fileset]

<jarlib-manifest> Generates a manifest that declares all the dependencies.

destfile	The location where generated manifest is placed. [File]
<attribute>	Adds an attribute that is to be put in main section of manifest.
<depends>	Adds a set of extensions that this library requires.
<extension>	Adds an extension that this library implements.
<options>	Adds a set of extensions that this library optionally requires.

<jarlib-resolve> Tries to locate a JAR to satisfy an extension and place the location of the JAR into a property.

checkextension	If true, libraries returned by nested resolvers should be checked to see if they supply an extension. [Boolean]
failonerror	If true, failure to locate library should fail build. [Boolean]
property	The name of the property in which the location of library is stored. [String]
<ant>	Adds Ant resolver to run an Ant build file to generate a library.
<extension>	Specifies extension to look for.
<location>	Adds location resolver to look for a library in a location relative to project directory.
<url>	Adds a URL resolver to download a library from a URL to a local file.

<java> Launcher for Java applications.

append	If true, append output to existing file. [Boolean]
classname	Java class to execute. [String]
classpath	Classpath to be used when running the Java class. [Path]
classpathref	Classpath to use, by reference. [Reference]
dir	The working directory of the process. [File]
failonerror	If true, then fail if the command exits with a return code other than 0. [Boolean]
fork	If true, execute in a new VM. [Boolean]
jar	The location of the JAR file to execute. [File]
jvm	Command used to start the VM (only if not forking). [String]
jvmargs	Command-line arguments for the JVM. [String]
jvmversion	JVM version. [String]
maxmemory	Corresponds to -mx or -Xmx, depending on VM version. [String]
newenvironment	If true, use a completely new environment. [Boolean]
output	File the output of the process is redirected to. [File]
timeout	Timeout in milliseconds after which the process will be killed. [Long]
<arg>	Adds a command-line argument.
<classpath>	Adds a path to the classpath. [Path]
<env>	Adds an environment variable.
<jvmarg>	Adds a JVM argument.
<sysproperty>	Adds a system property.

<javac> * Compiles Java source files.

bootclasspath	Bootclasspath that will be used to compile the classes against. [Path]
bootclasspathref	Adds a reference to a classpath defined elsewhere. [Reference]
classpath	Classpath to be used for this compilation. [Path]
classpathref	Adds a reference to a classpath defined elsewhere. [Reference]
compiler	Chooses the implementation for this particular task. [String]
debug	Indicates whether source should be compiled with debug information; defaults to off. [Boolean]
debuglevel	Keyword list to be appended to the -g command-line switch. [String]
depend	Enables dependencytracking for compilers that support this (jikes and classic). [Boolean]
deprecation	Indicates whether source should be compiled with deprecation information; defaults to off. [Boolean]
destdir	Destination directory into which the Java source files should be compiled. [File]
encoding	Java source file encoding name. [String]
executable	The name of the javac executable. [String]
extdirs	Extension directories that will be used during the compilation. [Path]
failonerror	Indicates whether the build will continue even if there are compilation errors; defaults to true. [Boolean]
fork	If true, forks the javac compiler. [Boolean]
includeantruntime	If true, includes Ant's own classpath in the classpath. [Boolean]
includejavaruntime	If true, includes the Java run-time libraries in the classpath. [Boolean]
listfiles	If true, lists the source files being handed off to the compiler. [Boolean]
memoryinitialsize	The initial size of the memory for the underlying VM if javac is run externally; ignored otherwise. [String]
memorymaximumsize	The maximum size of the memory for the underlying VM if javac is run externally; ignored otherwise. [String]
nowarn	If true, enables the -nowarn option. [Boolean]
optimize	If true, compiles with optimization enabled. [Boolean]
source	Value of the -source command-line switch; will be ignored by all implementations except modern and jikes. [String]
sourcepath	Source path to be used for this compilation. [Path]
sourcepathref	Adds a reference to a source path defined elsewhere. [Reference]
srcdir	Source directories to find the source Java files. [Path]
target	Target VM that the classes will be compiled for. [String]
verbose	If true, asks the compiler for verbose output. [Boolean]

`<bootclasspath>`	Adds a path to the bootclass path. [Path]
`<classpath>`	Adds a path to the classpath. [Path]
`<compilerarg>`	Adds an implementation-specific command-line argument.
`<extdirs>`	Adds a path to extdirs. [Path]
`<sourcepath>`	Adds a path to source path. [Path]
`<src>`	Adds a path for source compilation. [Path]

\<javacc\> Invokes the JavaCC compiler on a grammar file.

`buildparser`	BUILD_PARSER grammar option. [Boolean]
`buildtokenmanager`	BUILD_TOKEN_MANAGER grammar option. [Boolean]
`cachetokens`	CACHE_TOKENS grammar option. [Boolean]
`choiceambiguitycheck`	CHOICE_AMBIGUITY_CHECK grammar option. [Integer]
`commontokenaction`	COMMON_TOKEN_ACTION grammar option. [Boolean]
`debuglookahead`	DEBUG_LOOKAHEAD grammar option. [Boolean]
`debugparser`	DEBUG_PARSER grammar option. [Boolean]
`debugtokenmanager`	DEBUG_TOKEN_MANAGER grammar option. [Boolean]
`errorreporting`	ERROR_REPORTING grammar option. [Boolean]
`forcelacheck`	FORCE_LA_CHECK grammar option. [Boolean]
`ignorecase`	IGNORE_CASE grammar option. [Boolean]
`javacchome`	The directory containing the JavaCC distribution. [File]
`javaunicodeescape`	JAVA_UNICODE_ESCAPE grammar option. [Boolean]
`lookahead`	LOOKAHEAD grammar option. [Integer]
`optimizetokenmanager`	OPTIMIZE_TOKEN_MANAGER grammar option. [Boolean]
`otherambiguitycheck`	OTHER_AMBIGUITY_CHECK grammar option. [Integer]
`outputdirectory`	The directory to write the generated files to. [File]
`sanitycheck`	SANITY_CHECK grammar option. [Boolean]
`static`	STATIC grammar option. [Boolean]
`target`	The grammar file to process. [File]
`unicodeinput`	UNICODE_INPUT grammar option. [Boolean]
`usercharstream`	USER_CHAR_STREAM grammar option. [Boolean]
`usertokenmanager`	USER_TOKEN_MANAGER grammar option. [Boolean]

\<javadoc\> Generates Javadoc documentation for a collection of source code.

`access`	Scope to be processed. [protected, public, package, private]
`additionalparam`	Sets an additional parameter on the command line. [String]
`author`	Includes the author tag in the generated documentation. [Boolean]
`bootclasspath`	Boot classpath to use. [Path]
`bootclasspathref`	Adds a reference to a classpath defined elsewhere. [Reference]
`bottom`	Text to be placed at the bottom of each output file. [String]

charset	Charset for cross-platform viewing of generated documentation. [String]
classpath	Classpath to be used for this javadoc run. [Path]
classpathref	Adds a reference to a classpath defined elsewhere. [Reference]
defaultexcludes	Sets whether default exclusions should be used. [Boolean]
destdir	Specifies directory where the Javadoc output will be generated. [File]
docencoding	Specifies output file encoding name. [String]
doclet	Specifies class that starts the doclet used in generating the documentation. [String]
docletpath	Specifies classpath used to find the doclet class. [Path]
docletpathref	Specifies classpath used to find the doclet class by reference. [Reference]
doctitle	Specifies title of the generated overview page. [String]
encoding	Specifies encoding name of the source files. [String]
excludepackagenames	Specifies list of packages to be excluded. [String]
extdirs	Specifies location of the extensions directories. [Path]
failonerror	Specifies the build process to fail if javadoc fails (as indicated by a nonzero return code). [Boolean]
footer	Places footer text at the bottom of each output file. [String]
group	Groups specified packages together in overview page. [String]
header	Places header text at the top of each output file. [String]
helpfile	Specifies the HTML help file to use. [File]
link	Creates links to javadoc output at the given URL. [String]
linkoffline	Links to docs at url using package list at url2— separates the URLs by using a space character. [String]
locale	Locale to use in documentation generation. [String]
maxmemory	Maximum memory to be used by the javadoc process. [String]
nodeprecated	If true, do not include @deprecated information. [Boolean]
nodeprecatedlist	If true, do not generate deprecated list. [Boolean]
nohelp	If true, do not generate help link. [Boolean]
noindex	If true, do not generate index. [Boolean]
nonavbar	If true, do not generate navigation bar. [Boolean]
notree	If true, do not generate class hierarchy. [Boolean]
old	Indicates whether Javadoc should produce old style (JDK 1.1) documentation. [Boolean]
overview	Specifies the file containing the overview to be included in the generated documentation. [File]
package	Indicates whether only package, protected, and public classes and members are to be included in the scope processed. [Boolean]
packagelist	The name of a file containing the packages to process. [String]
packagenames	Package names to be processed. [String]

`private`	Indicates whether all classes and members are to be included in the scope processed. [Boolean]
`protected`	Indicates whether only protected and public classes and members are to be included in the scope processed. [Boolean]
`public`	Indicates whether only public classes and members are to be included in the scope processed. [Boolean]
`serialwarn`	If true, generates warning about `@serial` tag. [Boolean]
`source`	Enables the `-source` switch; will be ignored if javadoc is not the 1.4 version or a different doclet than the standard doclet is used. [String]
`sourcefiles`	List of source files to process. [String]
`sourcepath`	Specifies where to find source file. [Path]
`sourcepathref`	Adds a reference to a classpath defined elsewhere. [Reference]
`splitindex`	Generates a split index. [Boolean]
`stylesheetfile`	Specifies the CSS stylesheet file to use. [File]
`use`	Generates the use page for each package. [Boolean]
`useexternalfile`	Works around command-line length limit by using an external file for the sourcefiles. [Boolean]
`verbose`	Runs javadoc in verbose mode. [Boolean]
`version`	Includes the version tag in the generated documentation. [Boolean]
`windowtitle`	Title to be placed in the HTML `<title>` tag of the generated documentation. [String]
`<bootclasspath>`	Creates a path to be configured with the boot classpath. [Path]
`<bottom>`	Text to be placed at the bottom of each output file.
`<classpath>`	Creates a path to be configured with the classpath to use. [Path]
`<doclet>`	Creates a doclet to be used in the documentation generation.
`<doctitle>`	Adds a document title to use for the overview page.
`<excludepackage>`	Adds a package to be excluded from the javadoc run.
`<fileset>`	Adds a fileset. [Fileset]
`<footer>`	Footer text to be placed at the bottom of each output file.
`<group>`	Separates packages on the overview page into whatever groups you specify, one group per table.
`<header>`	Header text to be placed at the top of each output file.
`<link>`	Creates link to javadoc output at the given URL.
`<package>`	Adds a single package to be processed.
`<packageset>`	Adds a packageset. [Dirset]
`<source>`	Adds a single source file.
`<sourcepath>`	Creates a path to be configured with the locations of the source files. [Path]
`<tag>`	Creates and adds a `-tag` argument.
`<taglet>`	Adds a taglet.

\<javah\> Generates JNI header files using javah.

bootclasspath	Location of bootstrap class files. [Path]
bootclasspathref	Adds a reference to a classpath defined elsewhere. [Reference]
class	The fully qualified name of the class (or classes, separated by commas). [String]
classpath	The classpath to use. [Path]
classpathref	Adds a reference to a classpath defined elsewhere. [Reference]
destdir	Destination directory into which the Java source files should be compiled. [File]
force	If true, output files should always be written (JDK1.2 only). [Boolean]
old	If true, specifies that old JDK1.0-style header files should be generated. [Boolean]
outputfile	Concatenates the resulting header or source files for all the classes listed into this file. [File]
stubs	If true, generates C declarations from the Java object file (used with old). [Boolean]
verbose	If true, causes javah to print a message concerning the status of the generated files. [Boolean]
\<bootclasspath\>	Adds path to bootstrap class files. [Path]
\<class\>	Adds class to process.
\<classpath\>	Path to use for classpath. [Path]

\<jdepend\> Runs JDepend tests.

classpath	Classpath to be used for this compilation. [Path]
classpathref	Adds a reference to a classpath defined elsewhere. [Reference]
dir	The directory to invoke the VM in. [File]
fork	If true, forks into a new JVM. [Boolean]
format	The format to write the output in. [xml, text]
haltonerror	Sets whether to halt on failure. [Boolean]
jvm	The command used to invoke a forked Java Virtual Machine. [String]
outputfile	The output file name. [File]
\<classpath\>	Adds a path to the classpath. [Path]
\<sourcespath\>	Adds a path to source code to analyze. [Path]

\<jjtree\> Runs the JJTree preprocessor for the JavaCC compiler compiler.

buildnodefiles	BUILD_NODE_FILES grammar option. [Boolean]
javacchome	The directory containing the JavaCC distribution. [File]
multi	MULTI grammar option. [Boolean]
nodedefaultvoid	NODE_DEFAULT_VOID grammar option. [Boolean]
nodefactory	NODE_FACTORY grammar option. [Boolean]
nodepackage	NODE_PACKAGE grammar option. [String]

nodeprefix	NODE_PREFIX grammar option. [String]
nodescopehook	NODE_SCOPE_HOOK grammar option. [Boolean]
nodeusesparser	NODE_USES_PARSER grammar option. [Boolean]
outputdirectory	The directory to write the generated file to. [File]
static	STATIC grammar option. [Boolean]
target	The jjtree grammar file to process. [File]
visitor	VISITOR grammar option. [Boolean]
visitorexception	VISITOR_EXCEPTION grammar option. [String]

<jpcoverage> Runs Sitraka JProbe Coverage analyzer.

applet	If true, runs an applet. [Boolean]
classname	Classname to run as stand-alone or runner for filesets. [String]
exitprompt	Toggles display of the console prompt: always, error, never. [String]
finalsnapshot	Type of snapshot to send at program termination: none, coverage, all. [String]
home	The directory where JProbe is installed. [File]
javaexe	Path to the java executable. [File]
recordfromstart	If you want to start analyzing as soon as the program begins, use all. If not, select none. [coverage, none, all]
seedname	Seed name for snapshot file. [String]
snapshotdir	The path to the directory where snapshot files are stored. [File]
tracknatives	If true, tracks native methods. [Boolean]
vm	Indicates which virtual machine to run. [java2, jdk118, jdk117]
warnlevel	Sets warning level (0-3, where 0 is the least amount of warnings). [Integer]
workingdir	The physical path to the working directory for the VM. [File]
<arg>	Adds a command argument.
<classpath>	Classpath to run the files. [Path]
<fileset>	The classnames to execute. [Fileset]
<filters>	Defines class/method filters based on pattern matching.
<jvmarg>	Adds a JVM argument.
<socket>	Defines a host and port to connect to if you want to do remote viewing.
<triggers>	Defines events to use for interacting with the collection of data performed during coverage.

<jpcovmerge> Runs the snapshot merge utility for JProbe Coverage.

home	The directory where JProbe is installed. [File]
tofile	Output snapshot file. [File]
verbose	If true, perform the merge in verbose mode giving details about the snapshot processing. [Boolean]
<fileset>	Adds a fileset containing the snapshots to include. [Fileset]

<jpcovreport> Runs the JProbe Coverage 3.0 snapshot merge utility.

format	Format of the report. [html, text, xml]
home	The directory where JProbe is installed. [File]
includesource	If true, include text of the source code lines. [Boolean]
percent	A numeric value for the threshold for printing methods. [Integer]
snapshot	The name of the snapshot file that is the source to the report. [File]
tofile	The name of the generated output file. [File]
type	The type of report to be generated. [executive, summary, detailed, verydetailed]
<reference>	Adds a set of classes whose coverage information will be checked against.
<sourcepath>	Adds a path to source files. [Path]

<jspc> * Runs a JSP compiler.

classpath	Classpath to be used for this compilation. [Path]
classpathref	Adds a reference to a classpath defined elsewhere. [Reference]
compiler	Class name of a JSP compiler adapter. [String]
destdir	Destination directory into which the JSP source files should be compiled. [File]
failonerror	Specifies the build to halt if compilation fails (default is true). [Boolean]
ieplugin	Java Plug-in CLASSID for Internet Explorer. [String]
mapped	If true, generates separate write() calls for each HTML line in the JSP. [Boolean]
package	Name of the package the compiled JSP files should be in. [String]
srcdir	Path for source JSP files. [Path]
uribase	The URI context of relative URI references in the JSP pages. [File]
uriroot	The root directory that URI files should be resolved against. [File]
verbose	Verbose level of the compiler. [Integer]
webinc	Output file name for the fraction of web.xml that lists servlets. [File]
webxml	File name for web.xml. [File]
<classpath>	Adds a path to the classpath. [Path]
<webapp>	Adds a single webapp.

<junit> Runs JUnit tests.

dir	The directory to invoke the VM in. [File]
errorproperty	Property to set to true if there is a error in a test. [String]
failureproperty	Property to set to true if there is a failure in a test. [String]
filtertrace	If true, smartly filter the stack frames of JUnit errors and failures before reporting them. [Boolean]
fork	If true, JVM should be forked for each test. [Boolean]
haltonerror	If true, stop the build process when there is an error in a test. [Boolean]

haltonfailure	If true, stop the build process if a test fails (errors are considered failures as well). [Boolean]
includeant-runtime	If true, include ant.jar, optional.jar, and junit.jar in the forked VM. [Boolean]
jvm	The command used to invoke the Java Virtual Machine, default is java. [String]
maxmemory	Maximum memory to be used by all forked JVMs. [String]
newenvironment	If true, use a new environment when forked. [Boolean]
printsummary	If true, print one-line statistics for each test, or withOutAndErr to also show standard output and error. [true, yes, false, no, on, off, withOutAndErr]
showoutput	If true, send any output generated by tests to Ant's logging system as well as to the formatters. [Boolean]
timeout	Timeout value (in milliseconds). [Integer]
<batchtest>	Adds a set of tests based on pattern matching.
<classpath>	Adds path to classpath used for tests. [Path]
<env>	Adds an environment variable; used when forking.
<formatter>	Add a new formatter to all tests of this task.
<jvmarg>	Adds a JVM argument; ignored if not forking.
<sysproperty>	Adds a system property that tests can access.
<test>	Adds a new single testcase.

<junitreport>

Aggregates all <junit> XML formatter test suite data under a specific directory and transforms the results via XSLT.

todir	Destination directory where the results should be written. [File]
tofile	Name of the aggregated results file. [String]
<fileset>	Adds a new fileset containing the XML results to aggregate. [Fileset]
<report>	Generates a report based on the document created by the merge.

<loadfile>

Loads a whole text file into a single property.

encoding	Encoding to use for input, defaults to the platform's default encoding. [String]
failonerror	If true, fail on load error. [Boolean]
property	Property name to save to. [String]
srcfile	File to load. [File]
<filterchain>	Adds the FilterChain element. [FilterChain]

<loadproperties>

Loads a file's contents as Ant properties.

srcfile	File to load. [File]
<filterchain>	Adds a FilterChain. [FilterChain]

\<mail\> A task to send SMTP email.

bcclist	Adds bcc address elements. [String]
cclist	Adds cc address elements. [String]
encoding	Allows the build writer to choose the preferred encoding method. [auto, mime, uu, plain]
failonerror	Indicates whether BuildExceptions should be passed back to the core. [Boolean]
files	Adds a list of files to be attached. [String]
from	Shorthand to set the from address element. [String]
includefilenames	Sets Includefilenames attribute. [Boolean]
mailhost	Host. [String]
mailport	Mail server port. [Integer]
message	Shorthand method to set the message. [String]
messagefile	Shorthand method to set the message from a file. [File]
messagemimetype	Shorthand method to set type of the text message, text/plain by default, but text/html or text/xml is quite feasible. [String]
subject	Subject line of the email. [String]
tolist	Adds to address elements. [String]
\<bcc\>	Adds bcc address element.
\<cc\>	Adds cc address element.
\<fileset\>	Adds a set of files (nested fileset attribute). [Fileset]
\<from\>	Adds a from address element.
\<message\>	Adds a message element.
\<to\>	Adds a to address element.

\<manifest\> Creates a manifest file for inclusion in a JAR.

file	The name of the manifest file to create/update. [File]
mode	Update policy; default is replace. [update, replace]
\<attribute\>	Adds an attribute to the manifest's main section.
\<section\>	Adds a section to the manifest.

\<maudit\> Invokes the Metamata Audit/Webgain Quality Analyzer on a set of Java files.

fix	Automatically fixes certain errors (those marked as fixable in the manual); optional, default false. [Boolean]
list	Creates listing file for each audited file; optional, default false. [Boolean]
maxmemory	Maximum memory for the JVM; optional. [String]
metamatahome	The home directory containing the Metamata distribution; required. [File]
tofile	The XML file to which the Audit result should be written to; required. [File]
unused	Finds declarations unused in search paths; optional, default false. [Boolean]
\<classpath\>	Classpath (also source path unless one explicitly set). [Path]

`<fileset>`	The Java files or directory to audit. [Fileset]
`<jvmarg>`	Additional optional parameters to pass to the JVM.
`<rulespath>`	Classpath for additional audit rules; these must be placed before metamata.jar. [Path]
`<searchpath>`	Search path to use for unused global declarations; required when `unused` is set. [Path]
`<sourcepath>`	Source path. [Path]

<mimemail> See <mail>.

<mkdir> Creates a given directory.

`dir`	The directory to create; required. [File]

<mmetrics> Computes the metrics of a set of Java files and writes the results to an XML file.

`granularity`	Granularity of the audit. [`compilation-units`, `files`, `methods`, `types`, `packages`]
`maxmemory`	Maximum memory for the JVM; optional. [String]
`metamatahome`	The home directory containing the Metamata distribution; required. [File]
`tofile`	Output XML file. [File]
`<classpath>`	Classpath (also source path unless one explicitly set). [Path]
`<fileset>`	The Java files or directory to audit. [Fileset]
`<jvmarg>`	Additional optional parameters to pass to the JVM.
`<path>`	New path (directory) to measure metrics from. [Path]
`<sourcepath>`	Source path. [Path]

<move> Moves a file or directory to a new file or directory.

`encoding`	Character encoding. [String]
`failonerror`	If false, notes errors to the output but keeps going. [Boolean]
`file`	Single source file to copy. [File]
`filtering`	If true, enables filtering. [Boolean]
`flatten`	When copying directory trees, the files can be flattened into a single directory. [Boolean]
`includeemptydirs`	Used to copy empty directories. [Boolean]
`overwrite`	Overwrites any existing destination files. [Boolean]
`preservelast-modified`	Gives the copied files the same last modified time as the original files. [Boolean]
`todir`	Destination directory. [File]
`tofile`	Destination file. [File]
`verbose`	Used to force listing of all names of copied files. [Boolean]
`<fileset>`	Adds a set of files to copy. [Fileset]
`<filterchain>`	Adds a FilterChain. [FilterChain]
`<filterset>`	Adds a filterset. [Filterset]
`<mapper>`	Defines the mapper to map source to destination files. [Mapper]

<mparse> Invokes the Metamata MParse compiler compiler on a grammar file.

cleanup	Remove the intermediate Sun JavaCC file; optional, default false. [Boolean]
debugparser	Set parser debug mode; optional, default false. [Boolean]
debugscanner	Set scanner debug mode; optional, default false. [Boolean]
maxmemory	Maximum memory for the JVM; optional. [String]
metamatahome	The home directory containing the Metamata distribution; required. [File]
target	The .jj file to process; required. [File]
verbose	Set verbose mode; optional, default false. [Boolean]
<classpath>	Creates a classpath entry. [Path]
<jvmarg>	Additional optional parameters to pass to the JVM.
<sourcepath>	Creates a source path entry. [Path]

<native2ascii> * Converts files from native encodings to ASCII.

dest	Destination directory to place converted files into. [File]
encoding	Encoding to translate to/from. [String]
ext	Extension which converted files should have. [String]
reverse	Flag the conversion to run in the reverse sense, that is ASCII-to-native encoding. [Boolean]
src	Source directory in which to find files to convert. [File]
<mapper>	Defines the FileNameMapper to use (nested mapper element). [Mapper]

<netrexxc> * Compiles NetRexx source files.

binary	Sets whether literals are treated as binary, rather than NetRexx types. [Boolean]
classpath	Classpath used for NetRexx compilation. [String]
comments	Sets whether comments are passed through to the generated Java source. [Boolean]
compact	Sets whether error messages come out in compact or verbose format. [Boolean]
compile	Sets whether the NetRexx compiler should compile the generated Java code. [Boolean]
console	Sets whether messages should be displayed. [Boolean]
crossref	Sets whether variable cross-references are generated. [Boolean]
decimal	Sets whether decimal arithmetic should be used for the NetRexx code. [Boolean]
destdir	Destination directory into which the NetRexx source files should be copied and then compiled. [File]
diag	Sets whether diagnostic information about the compile is generated. [Boolean]
explicit	Sets whether variables must be declared explicitly before use. [Boolean]

`format`	Sets whether the generated Java code is formatted nicely or left to match NetRexx line numbers for call stack debugging. [Boolean]
`java`	Sets whether the generated Java code is produced. [Boolean]
`keep`	Sets whether the generated Java source file should be kept after compilation. [Boolean]
`logo`	Sets whether the compiler text logo is displayed when compiling. [Boolean]
`replace`	Sets whether the generated .Java file should be replaced when compiling. [Boolean]
`savelog`	Sets whether the compiler messages will be written to NetRexxC.log as well as to the console. [Boolean]
`sourcedir`	Tells the NetRexx compiler to store the class files in the same directory as the source files. [Boolean]
`srcdir`	Source dir to find the source Java files. [File]
`strictargs`	Tells the NetRexx compiler that method calls always need parentheses, even if no arguments are needed. [Boolean]
`strictassign`	Tells the NetRexx compile that assignments must match exactly on type. [Boolean]
`strictcase`	Specifies whether the NetRexx compiler should be case sensitive. [Boolean]
`strictimport`	Sets whether classes need to be imported explicitly using an `import` statement. [Boolean]
`strictprops`	Sets whether local properties need to be qualified explicitly using `this`. [Boolean]
`strictsignal`	Sets whether the compiler should force catching of exceptions by explicitly named types. [Boolean]
`suppress-` `deprecation`	Sets whether we should filter out any deprecation-messages of the compiler output. [Boolean]
`suppressexcep-` `tionnotsignalled`	Sets whether the task should suppress the `FooException` is in SIGNALS list but is not signalled within the method, which is sometimes rather useless. [Boolean]
`suppressmethod-` `argumentnotused`	Sets whether the task should suppress the "Method argument is not used" in strictargs-Mode, which cannot be suppressed by the compiler itself. [Boolean]
`suppressprivate-` `propertynotused`	Sets whether the task should suppress the "Private property is defined but not used" in strictargs-Mode, which can be quite annoying while developing. [Boolean]
`suppressvariable-` `notused`	Sets whether the task should suppress the "Variable is set but not used" in strictargs-Mode. [Boolean]
`symbols`	Sets whether debug symbols should be generated into the class file. [Boolean]
`time`	Asks the NetRexx compiler to print compilation times to the console. [Boolean]
`trace`	Turns on or off tracing, and directs the resultant output. [trace, trace1, trace2, notrace]
`utf8`	Tells the NetRexx compiler that the source is in UTF8. [Boolean]
`verbose`	Sets whether lots of warnings and error messages should be generated. [verbose, verbose0, verbose1, verbose2, verbose3, verbose4, verbose5, noverbose]

`<p4add>` Adds specified files to a Perforce server.

`changelist`	If specified, the open files are associated with the specified pending changelist number; otherwise the open files are associated with the default changelist. [Integer]
`client`	Specifies the p4 client spec to use; optional, defaults to the current user. [String]
`cmdopts`	Sets extra command options; only used on some of the Perforce tasks. [String]
`commandlength`	Positive integer specifying the maximum length of the command line when calling Perforce to add the files. [Integer]
`failonerror`	Sets whether to stop the build or keep going if an error is returned from the p4 command; default is true. [Boolean]
`port`	Specifies the p4d server and port to connect to; optional, default `perforce:1666`. [String]
`user`	Specifies the p4 username; optional, defaults to the current user. [String]
`view`	Specifies the client, branch, or label view to operate upon; optional default `//....` [String]
`<fileset>`	Files to add. [Fileset]

`<p4change>` Requests a new changelist from the Perforce server.

`client`	The p4 client spec to use; optional, defaults to the current user. [String]
`cmdopts`	Set extra command options; only used on some of the Perforce tasks. [String]
`description`	Description for ChangeList;optional. [String]
`failonerror`	Sets whether to stop the build (true, default) or keep going if an error is returned from the p4 command. [Boolean]
`port`	The p4d server and port to connect to; optional, default `perforce:1666`. [String]
`user`	The p4 username; optional, defaults to the current user. [String]
`view`	The client, branch, or label view to operate upon; optional default `//....` [String]

`<p4counter>` Obtains or sets the value of a Perforce counter.

`client`	The p4 client spec to use; optional, defaults to the current user. [String]
`cmdopts`	Set extra command options; only used on some of the Perforce tasks. [String]
`failonerror`	Sets whether to stop the build (true, default) or keep going if an error is returned from the p4 command. [Boolean]
`name`	The name of the counter; required. [String]
`port`	The p4d server and port to connect to; optional, default `perforce:1666`. [String]
`property`	A property to be set with the value of the counter. [String]
`user`	The p4 username; optional, defaults to the current user. [String]

value	The new value for the counter; optional. [Integer]
view	The client, branch, or label view to operate upon; optional default //.... [String]

<p4delete> Checkout Perforce-managed files for deletion.

change	An existing changelist number for the deletion; optional but strongly recommended. [String]
client	The p4 client spec to use; optional, defaults to the current user. [String]
cmdopts	Set extra command options. [String]
failonerror	Sets whether to stop the build (true, default) or keep going if an error is returned from the p4 command. [Boolean]
port	The p4d server and port to connect to; optional, default perforce:1666. [String]
user	The p4 username; optional, defaults to the current user. [String]
view	The client, branch or label view to operate upon; optional default //.... [String]

<p4edit> Open Perforce-managed files for editing.

change	An existing changelist number to assign files to; optional but strongly recommended. [String]
client	The p4 client spec to use; optional, defaults to the current user. [String]
cmdopts	Set extra command options; only used on some of the Perforce tasks. [String]
failonerror	Sets whether to stop the build (true, default) or keep going if an error is returned from the p4 command. [Boolean]
port	The p4d server and port to connect to; optional, default perforce:1666. [String]
user	The p4 username; optional, defaults to the current user. [String]
view	The client, branch, or label view to operate upon; optional default //.... [String]

<p4have> Lists Perforce-managed files currently on the client.

client	The p4 client spec to use; optional, defaults to the current user. [String]
cmdopts	Set extra command options; only used on some of the Perforce tasks. [String]
failonerror	Sets whether to stop the build (true, default) or keep going if an error is returned from the p4 command. [Boolean]
port	The p4d server and port to connect to; optional, default perforce:1666. [String]
user	The p4 username; optional, defaults to the current user. [String]
view	The client, branch, or label view to operate upon; optional, default //.... [String]

`<p4label>` Creates a new Perforce label and sets contents to reflect current client file revisions.

client	The p4 client spec to use; optional, defaults to the current user. [String]
cmdopts	Set extra command options; only used on some of the Perforce tasks. [String]
desc	Label description; optional. [String]
failonerror	Sets whether to stop the build (true, default) or keep going if an error is returned from the p4 command. [Boolean]
lock	When set to locked, Perforce will lock the label once created; optional. [String]
name	The name of the label; optional, default AntLabel. [String]
port	The p4d server and port to connect to; optional, default perforce:1666. [String]
user	The p4 username; optional, defaults to the current user. [String]
view	The client, branch, or label view to operate upon; optional, default //.... [String]

`<p4reopen>` Reopens Perforce-managed files.

client	The p4 client spec to use; optional, defaults to the current user. [String]
cmdopts	Set extra command options; only used on some of the Perforce tasks. [String]
failonerror	Sets whether to stop the build (true, default) or keep going if an error is returned from the p4 command. [Boolean]
port	The p4d server and port to connect to; optional, default perforce:1666. [String]
tochange	The changelist to move files to; required. [String]
user	The p4 username; optional, defaults to the current user. [String]
view	The client, branch, or label view to operate upon; optional default //.... [String]

`<p4revert>` Reverts Perforce open files or files in a changelist

change	The changelist to revert; optional. [String]
client	The p4 client spec to use; optional, defaults to the current user. [String]
cmdopts	Set extra command options; only used on some of the Perforce tasks. [String]
failonerror	Sets whether to stop the build (true, default) or keep going if an error is returned from the p4 command. [Boolean]
port	The p4d server and port to connect to; optional, default perforce:1666. [String]
revertonly-unchanged	Flag to revert only unchanged files (p4 revert -a); optional, default false. [Boolean]
user	The p4 username; optional, defaults to the current user. [String]
view	The client, branch, or label view to operate upon; optional default //.... [String]

\<p4submit\> Submits a numbered changelist to Perforce.

`change`	The changelist number to submit; required. [String]
`client`	The p4 client spec to use; optional, defaults to the current user. [String]
`cmdopts`	Set extra command options; only used on some of the Perforce tasks. [String]
`failonerror`	Sets whether to stop the build (true, default) or keep going if an error is returned from the p4 command. [Boolean]
`port`	The p4d server and port to connect to; optional, default `perforce:1666`. [String]
`user`	The p4 username; optional, defaults to the current user. [String]
`view`	The client, branch, or label view to operate upon; optional default `//....` [String]

\<p4sync\> Synchronizes client space to a Perforce depot view.

`client`	The p4 client spec to use; optional, defaults to the current user. [String]
`cmdopts`	Set extra command options; only used on some of the Perforce tasks. [String]
`failonerror`	Sets whether to stop the build (true, default) or keep going if an error is returned from the p4 command. [Boolean]
`force`	Force a refresh of files, if this attribute is set; false by default. [String]
`label`	Label to sync client to; optional. [String]
`port`	The p4d server and port to connect to; optional, default `perforce:1666`. [String]
`user`	The p4 username; optional, defaults to the current user. [String]
`view`	The client, branch, or label view to operate upon; optional default `//....` [String]

\<parallel\> Executes the contained tasks in separate threads, continuing once all are completed. Any Ant task can be nested inside this task.

\<patch\> Patches a file by applying a diff file to it; requires `patch` to be on the execution path.

`backups`	Flag to create backups; optional, default=false. [Boolean]
`dir`	The directory to run the patch command in, defaults to the project's base directory. [File]
`ignorewhitespace`	Flag to ignore white space differences; default=false. [Boolean]
`originalfile`	The file to patch; optional if it can be inferred from the diff file. [File]
`patchfile`	The file containing the diff output; required. [File]
`quiet`	Work silently unless an error occurs; optional, default=false. [Boolean]
`reverse`	Assume patch was created with old and new files swapped; optional, default=false. [Boolean]
`strip`	Strip the smallest prefix containing this many leading slashes from file names. [Integer]

\<pathconvert\>	Converts path and classpath information to a specific target OS format.	
	dirsep	Default directory separator string; defaults to current JVM. [String]
	pathsep	Default path separator string; defaults to current JVM. [String]
	property	The property into which the converted path will be placed. [String]
	refid	Adds a reference to a Path, FileSet, DirSet, or FileList defined elsewhere. [Reference]
	setonempty	If false, don't set the new property if the result is the empty string; default true. [Boolean]
	targetos	Sets target platform; required unless pathsep or dirsep are specified. [windows, unix, netware, os/2]
	\<map\>	Creates a nested MAP element.
	\<path\>	Creates a nested PATH element. [Path]

\<property\>	Sets a property by name, or set of properties (from file or resource) in the project.	
	classpath	The classpath to use when looking up a resource. [Path]
	environment	The prefix to use when retrieving environment variables. [String]
	file	The file name of a property file to load. [File]
	location	Property to the absolute file name of the given file. [File]
	name	Name of the property to set. [String]
	prefix	Prefix to apply to properties loaded using file or resource. [String]
	refid	Reference to an Ant datatype declared elsewhere. [Reference]
	resource	The resource name of a property file to load. [String]
	value	Value of the property. [String]
	\<classpath\>	The classpath to use when looking up a resource. [Path]

\<propertyfile\>	Modifies settings in a property file.	
	comment	Optional header comment for the file. [String]
	file	Location of the property file to be edited; required. [File]
	\<entry\>	Specifies a property and how to modify it.

\<pvcs\>	Extracts the latest edition of the source code from a PVCS repository.	
	filenameformat	The format of the folder names; optional. [String]
	force	Specifies the value of the force argument; optional. [String]
	ignorereturncode	If set to true the return value from executing the PVCS commands are ignored; optional, default false. [Boolean]
	label	Only files marked with this label are extracted; optional. [String]
	linestart	What a valid return value from PVCS looks like when it describes a file. [String]
	promotiongroup	Specifies the name of the promotiongroup argument. [String]

pvcsbin	Specifies the location of the PVCS bin directory; optional if on the PATH. [String]	
pvcsproject	The project within the PVCS repository to extract files from; optional, default "/". [String]	
repository	The network name of the PVCS repository; required. [String]	
updateonly	If true, files are fetched only if newer than existing local files; optional, default false. [Boolean]	
workspace	Workspace to use; optional. [String]	
<pvcsproject>	Specifies a project within the PVCS repository to extract files from.	

<record> Adds a listener to the current build process that records the output to a file.

action	Action for the associated recorder entry. [start, stop]
append	Sets whether the logger should append to a previous file. [Boolean]
emacsmode	No description. [Boolean]
loglevel	Level to which this recorder entry should log to. [error, warn, info, verbose, debug]
name	Name of the file to log to, and the name of the recorder entry. [String]

<replace> * Replaces all occurrences of one or more string tokens with given values in the indicated files.

dir	The base directory to use when replacing a token in multiple files; required if file is not defined. [File]
encoding	File encoding to use on the files read and written by the task; optional, defaults to default JVM encoding. [String]
file	Source file; required unless dir is set. [File]
propertyfile	The name of a property file from which properties specified using nested <replacefilter> elements are drawn; Required only if property attribute of <replacefilter> is used. [File]
replacefilterfile	Name of a property file containing filters; optional. [File]
summary	Indicates whether a summary of the replace operation should be produced, detailing how many token occurrences and files were processed; optional, default is false. [Boolean]
token	String token to replace; required unless a nested replace-token element or the replacefilterfile attribute is used. [String]
value	String value to use as token replacement; optional, default is the empty string " ". [String]
<replacefilter>	Adds a replacement filter.
<replacetoken>	The token to filter as the text of a nested element.
<replacevalue>	The string to replace the token as the text of a nested element.

<replaceregexp> Performs regular expression string replacements in a text file.

byline	Process the file(s) one line at a time, executing the replacement on one line at a time. [String]
file	File for which the regular expression should be replaced; required unless a nested fileset is supplied. [File]
flags	The flags to use when matching the regular expression. [String]
match	The regular expression pattern to match in the files; required if no nested `<regexp>` is used. [String]
replace	The substitution pattern to place in the files in place of the regular expression. [String]
`<fileset>`	Lists files to apply the replacement to. [Fileset]
`<regexp>`	A regular expression.
`<substitution>`	A substitution pattern.

<rmic> * Runs the rmic compiler against classes.

base	Location to store the compiled files; required. [File]
classname	The class to run rmic against; optional. [String]
classpath	Classpath to be used for this compilation. [Path]
classpathref	Adds a path to the classpath by reference. [Reference]
compiler	Compiler implementation to use; optional, defaults to the value of the `build.rmic` property, or failing that, default compiler for the current VM. [String]
debug	Generates debug info (passes –g to rmic); optional, defaults to false. [Boolean]
extdirs	Extension directories that will be used during the compilation; optional. [Path]
filtering	Indicates whether token filtering should take place; optional, default=false. [Boolean]
idl	Indicates that IDL output should be generated. [Boolean]
idlopts	Passes additional arguments for `idl` compile. [String]
iiop	Indicates that IIOP-compatible stubs should be generated; optional, defaults to false if not set. [Boolean]
iiopopts	Sets additional arguments for IIOP. [String]
includeantruntime	Sets whether to include the Ant run-time libraries; optional defaults to true. [Boolean]
includejavaruntime	Task's classpath. [Boolean]
sourcebase	Optional directory to save generated source files to. [File]
stubversion	Specifies the JDK version for the generated stub code. [String]
verify	Flag to enable verification, so that the classes found by the directory match are checked to see if they implement `java.rmi.Remote`. [Boolean]
`<classpath>`	Adds a path to the classpath. [Path]
`<compilerarg>`	Adds an implementation-specific command-line argument.
`<extdirs>`	Adds path to the extension directories path. [Path]

`<rpm>`	Invokes the rpm tool to build a Linux installation file.

`cleanbuilddir`	Flag (optional, default=false) to remove the generated files in the BUILD directory. [Boolean]
`command`	What command to issue to the rpm tool; optional. [String]
`error`	Optional file to save `stderr` to. [File]
`output`	Optional file to save `stdout` to. [File]
`removesource`	Flag (optional, default=false) to remove the sources after the build. [Boolean]
`removespec`	Flag (optional, default=false) to remove the spec file from SPECS. [Boolean]
`specfile`	The name of the spec File to use; required. [String]
`topdir`	The directory which will have the expected subdirectories, SPECS, SOURCES, BUILD, SRPMS ; optional. [File]

`<script>`	Executes a script. The script can be nested as text, or an external file referenced using `src`.

`language`	Defines the language (required). [String]
`src`	Load the script from an external file; optional. [String]

`<sequential>`	Container task to execute all nested tasks sequentially. This is useful when nested within `<parallel>`.

`<serverdeploy>`	Controls hot deployment tools for J2EE servers.

`action`	The action to be performed, usually `deploy`; required. [String]
`source`	The file name of the component to be deployed; optional depending upon the tool and the action. [File]
`<generic>`	Creates a generic deployment tool.
`<jonas>`	Creates a JOnAS deployment tool, for deployment to JOnAS servers.
`<weblogic>`	Creates a WebLogic deployment tool, for deployment to WebLogic servers.

`<setproxy>`	Sets Java's web proxy properties, so that tasks and code run in the same JVM can have through-the-firewall access to remote web sites, and remote ftp sites.

`nonproxyhosts`	A list of hosts to bypass the proxy on. [String]
`proxyhost`	The HTTP/ftp proxy host. [String]
`proxyport`	The HTTP/ftp proxy port number; default is 80. [Integer]
`socksproxyhost`	The name of a Socks server. [String]
`socksproxyport`	ProxyPort for socks connections. [Integer]

\<signjar\> Signs JAR or Zip files with the javasign command-line tool.

alias	The alias to sign under; required. [String]
internalsf	Flag to include the .SF file inside the signature; optional; default false. [Boolean]
jar	The JAR file to sign; required. [File]
keypass	Password for private key (if different than storepass); optional. [String]
keystore	Keystore location; required. [File]
lazy	Flag to control whether the presence of a signature file means a JAR is signed; optional, default false. [Boolean]
sectionsonly	Flag to compute hash of entire manifest; optional, default false. [Boolean]
sigfile	Name of .SF/.DSA file; optional. [File]
signedjar	Name of signed JAR file; optional. [File]
storepass	Password for Keystore integrity; required. [String]
storetype	Keystore type; optional. [String]
verbose	Enable verbose output when signing ; optional: default false. [Boolean]
\<fileset\>	Adds a set of files to sign. [Fileset]

\<sleep\> Sleep, or pause, for a period of time.

failonerror	Flag controlling whether to break the build on an error. [Boolean]
hours	Hours to add to the sleep time. [Integer]
milliseconds	Milliseconds to add to the sleep time. [Integer]
minutes	Minutes to add to the sleep time. [Integer]
seconds	Seconds to add to the sleep time. [Integer]

\<soscheckin\> Commits and unlocks files in Visual SourceSafe via a SourceOffSite server.

comment	Comment to apply to all files being labeled; optional, only valid in SOSLabel. [String]
file	File name to act upon; optional. [String]
label	Labeled version to operate on in SourceSafe. [String]
localpath	Override the working directory and get to the specified path; optional. [Path]
nocache	Flag to disable the cache when set; optional, needed if SOSHOME is set as an environment variable. [Boolean]
nocompress	Flag that disables compression when set; optional. [Boolean]
password	SourceSafe password; optional. [String]
projectpath	SourceSafe project path without the $ prefix; required. [String]
recursive	Flag to recursively apply the action (not valid on all SOS tasks); optional, default false. [Boolean]
soscmd	Directory where soscmd is located; optional, soscmd must be on the path if omitted. [String]
soshome	The path to the SourceOffSite home directory. [String]

sosserverpath	Address and port of SourceOffSite Server. [String]
username	SourceSafe username; required. [String]
verbose	Enable verbose output; optional, default false. [Boolean]
version	A version number to get—only works with the SOSGet on a file; optional. [String]
vssserverpath	Path to the location of the ss.ini file; required. [String]

<soscheckout> Retrieves and locks files in Visual SourceSafe via a SourceOffSite server.

comment	Comment to apply to all files being labelled; optional, only valid in SOSLabel. [String]
file	File name to act upon; optional. [String]
label	Labeled version to operate on in SourceSafe. [String]
localpath	Override the working directory and get to the specified path; optional. [Path]
nocache	Flag to disable the cache when set; optional needed if SOSHOME is set as an environment variable. [Boolean]
nocompress	Flag that disables compression when set; optional. [Boolean]
password	SourceSafe password; optional. [String]
projectpath	SourceSafe project path without the $ prefix; required. [String]
recursive	Flag to recursively apply the action (not valid on all SOS tasks); optional, default false. [Boolean]
soscmd	Directory where soscmd is located; optional, soscmd must be on the path if omitted. [String]
soshome	The path to the SourceOffSite home directory. [String]
sosserverpath	Address and port of SourceOffSite Server, e.g. [String]
username	SourceSafe username; required. [String]
verbose	Enable verbose output; optional, default false. [Boolean]
version	A version number to get—only works with the SOSGet on a file; optional. [String]
vssserverpath	Path to the location of the ss.ini file; required. [String]

<sosget> Retrieves a read-only copy of the specified project or file from Visual SourceSafe via a SourceOffSite server.

comment	Comment to apply to all files being labelled; optional, only valid in SOSLabel. [String]
file	File name to act upon; optional. [String]
label	Labeled version to operate on in SourceSafe. [String]
localpath	Override the working directory and get to the specified path; optional. [Path]
nocache	Flag to disable the cache when set; optional, needed if SOSHOME is set as an environment variable. [Boolean]
nocompress	Flag that disables compression when set; optional. [Boolean]
password	SourceSafe password; optional. [String]
projectpath	SourceSafe project path without the $ prefix; required. [String]

recursive	Flag to recursively apply the action (not valid on all SOS tasks); optional, default false. [Boolean]
soscmd	Directory where soscmd is located; optional, soscmd must be on the path if omitted. [String]
soshome	The path to the SourceOffSite home directory. [String]
sosserverpath	Address and port of SourceOffSite Server, e.g. [String]
username	SourceSafe username; required. [String]
verbose	Enable verbose output; optional, default false. [Boolean]
version	A version number to get—only works with the SOSGet on a file; optional. [String]
vssserverpath	Path to the location of the ss.ini file; required. [String]

<soslabel> Labels Visual SourceSafe files via a SourceOffSite server.

comment	Comment to apply to all files being labelled; optional, only valid in SOSLabel. [String]
file	File name to act upon; optional. [String]
label	Labeled version to operate on in SourceSafe. [String]
localpath	Override the working directory and get to the specified path; optional. [Path]
nocache	Flag to disable the cache when set; optional, needed if SOSHOME is set as an environment variable. [Boolean]
nocompress	Flag that disables compression when set; optional, default. [Boolean]
password	SourceSafe password; optional. [String]
projectpath	SourceSafe project path without the $ prefix; required. [String]
recursive	Flag to recursively apply the action (not valid on all SOS tasks); optional, default false. [Boolean]
soscmd	Directory where soscmd is located; optional, soscmd must be on the path if omitted. [String]
soshome	The path to the SourceOffSite home directory. [String]
sosserverpath	Address and port of SourceOffSite Server, e.g. [String]
username	SourceSafe username; required. [String]
verbose	Enable verbose output; optional, default false. [Boolean]
version	A version number to get—only works with the SOSGet on a file; optional. [String]
vssserverpath	Path to the location of the ss.ini file; required. [String]

<sound> Plays a sound file at the end of the build, according to whether the build failed or succeeded.

<fail>	Adds a sound when the build fails.
<success>	Adds a sound when the build succeeds.

\<splash> Creates a splash screen.

`imageurl`	A URL pointing to an image to display; optional, default antlogo.gif from the classpath. [String]
`password`	Proxy password; required if `user` is set. [String]
`port`	Proxy port; optional, default 80. [String]
`proxy`	Name of proxy; optional. [String]
`showduration`	How long to show the splash screen in milliseconds, optional; default 5000 ms. [Integer]
`user`	Proxy user; optional, default=none. [String]

\<sql> Executes a series of SQL statements on a database using JDBC. SQL commands, may optionally be nested as text data.

`append`	Sets whether output should be appended to or overwrite an existing file. [Boolean]
`autocommit`	Auto commit flag for database connection; optional, default false. [Boolean]
`caching`	Caching loaders/driver. [Boolean]
`classpath`	Classpath for loading the driver. [Path]
`classpathref`	Classpath for loading the driver using the classpath reference. [Reference]
`delimiter`	Delimiter that separates SQL statements; optional, default ";". [String]
`delimitertype`	Delimiter type: `normal` or `row` (default `normal`). [normal, row]
`driver`	Class name of the JDBC driver; required. [String]
`encoding`	File encoding to use on the SQL files read in. [String]
`onerror`	Action to perform when statement fails; default is `abort`. [continue, stop, abort]
`output`	Output file; optional, defaults to the Ant log. [File]
`password`	Password; required. [String]
`print`	Print result sets from the statements; optional, default false. [Boolean]
`rdbms`	Execute task only if the lowercase product name of the DB matches this. [String]
`showheaders`	Print headers for result sets from the statements; optional, default true. [Boolean]
`src`	Name of the SQL file to be run. [File]
`url`	Database connection URL; required. [String]
`userid`	User name for the connection; required. [String]
`version`	Version string, execute task only if rdbms version matches; optional. [String]
`<classpath>`	Adds a path to the classpath for loading the driver. [Path]
`<fileset>`	Adds a set of files (nested fileset attribute). [Fileset]
`<transaction>`	Adds an SQL transaction to execute.

<stcheckin> Checks files into a StarTeam project.

adduncontrolled	If true, any files or folders NOT in StarTeam will be added to the repository. [Boolean]
comment	Optional `checkin` comment to be saved with the file. [String]
createfolders	Value of `createFolders`. [Boolean]
excludes	Declare files to exclude. [String]
forced	Flag to force actions regardless of the status that StarTeam is maintaining for the file; optional, default false. [Boolean]
includes	Declare files to include. [String]
password	Password to be used for login; required. [String]
projectname	Name of the StarTeam project to be acted on; required if `url` is not set. [String]
recursive	Flag to set to include files in subfolders in the operation; optional, default true. [Boolean]
rootlocalfolder	Local folder that will be the root of the tree to which files are checked out; optional. [String]
rootstarteam-folder	Root of the subtree in the StarTeam repository from which to work; optional. [String]
servername	Name of StarTeamServer; required if `url` is not set. [String]
serverport	Port number of the StarTeam connection; required if `url` is not set. [String]
unlocked	Set to do an unlocked checkout; optional, default is false; If true, file will be unlocked so that other users may change it. [Boolean]
url	Server name, server port, project name and project folder in one shot; optional, but the server connection must be specified somehow. [String]
username	Name of the StarTeam user, needed for the connection. [String]
viewname	Name of the StarTeam view to be acted on; required if `url` is not set. [String]

<stcheckout> Checks out files from a StarTeam project.

create-workingdirs	Flag (defaults to true) to create all directories that are in the Starteam repository even if they are empty. [Boolean]
delete-uncontrolled	Should all local files not in StarTeam be deleted? Optional, defaults to `true`. [Boolean]
excludes	Declare files to exclude. [String]
forced	Flag to force actions regardless of the status that StarTeam is maintaining for the file; optional, default false. [Boolean]
includes	Declare files to include. [String]
label	Label StarTeam is to use for checkout; defaults to the most recent file. [String]
locked	Set to do a locked checkout; optional default is false. [Boolean]
password	Password to be used for login; required. [String]
projectname	Name of the StarTeam project to be acted on; required if `url` is not set. [String]
recursive	Flag to set to include files in subfolders in the operation; optional, default true. [Boolean]

rootlocalfolder	Local folder that will be the root of the tree to which files are checked out; optional. [String]
rootstarteam-folder	Root of the subtree in the StarTeam repository from which to work; optional. [String]
servername	Name of StarTeamServer; required if url is not set. [String]
serverport	Port number of the StarTeam connection; required if url is not set. [String]
unlocked	Set to do an unlocked checkout. [Boolean]
url	Server name, server port, project name, and project folder in one shot; optional, but the server connection must be specified somehow. [String]
username	Name of the StarTeam user, needed for the connection. [String]
viewname	Name of the StarTeam view to be acted on; required if url is not set. [String]

<stlabel> Creates a view label in StarTeam at the specified view.

description	Optional description of the label to be stored in the StarTeam project. [String]
label	The name to be given to the label; required. [String]
lastbuild	The timestamp of the build that will be stored with the label; required. [String]
password	Password to be used for login; required. [String]
projectname	Name of the StarTeam project to be acted on; required if url is not set. [String]
servername	Name of StarTeamServer; required if url is not set. [String]
serverport	Port number of the StarTeam connection; required if url is not set. [String]
url	Server name, server port, project name and project folder in one shot; optional, but the server connection must be specified somehow. [String]
username	Name of the StarTeam user, needed for the connection. [String]
viewname	Name of the StarTeam view to be acted on; required if url is not set. [String]

<stlist> Produces a listing of the contents of the StarTeam repository at the specified view and StarTeamFolder.

excludes	Declare files to exclude. [String]
forced	Flag to force actions regardless of the status that StarTeam is maintaining for the file; optional, default false. [Boolean]
includes	Declare files to include. [String]
label	List files, dates, and statuses as of this label; optional. [String]
password	Password to be used for login; required. [String]
projectname	Name of the StarTeam project to be acted on; required if url is not set. [String]
recursive	Flag to set to include files in subfolders in the operation; optional, default true. [Boolean]

rootlocalfolder	Local folder that will be the root of the tree to which files are checked out; optional. [String]
rootstarteam-folder	Root of the subtree in the StarTeam repository from which to work; optional. [String]
servername	Name of StarTeamServer; required if `url` is not set. [String]
serverport	Port number of the StarTeam connection; required if `url` is not set. [String]
url	Server name, server port, project name, and project folder in one shot; optional, but the server connection must be specified somehow. [String]
username	Name of the StarTeam user, needed for the connection. [String]
viewname	Name of the StarTeam view to be acted on; required if `url` is not set. [String]

<style> See <xslt>.

<stylebook> Executes the Apache Stylebook documentation generator.

append	If true, append output to existing file. [Boolean]
book	The book xml file that the documentation generation starts from; required. [File]
classname	Java class to execute. [String]
classpath	Classpath to be used when running the Java class. [Path]
classpathref	Classpath to use, by reference. [Reference]
dir	The working directory of the process. [File]
failonerror	If true, then fail if the command exits with a returncode other than 0. [Boolean]
fork	If true, execute in a new VM. [Boolean]
jar	The location of the JAR file to execute. [File]
jvm	Command used to start the VM (only if not forking). [String]
jvmargs	Command-line arguments for the JVM. [String]
jvmversion	JVM version. [String]
loaderconfig	A loader configuration to send to stylebook; optional. [String]
maxmemory	Corresponds to −mx or −Xmx depending on VM version. [String]
newenvironment	If true, use a completely new environment. [Boolean]
output	File the output of the process is redirected to. [File]
skindirectory	The directory that contains the stylebook skin; required. [File]
targetdirectory	The destination directory where the documentation is generated; required. [File]
timeout	Timeout in milliseconds after which the process will be killed. [Long]
<arg>	Adds a command-line argument.
<classpath>	Adds a path to the classpath. [Path]
<env>	Adds an environment variable.
<jvmarg>	Adds a JVM argument.
<sysproperty>	Adds a system property.

\<tar\> *   Creates a tar archive.

basedir	This is the base directory to look in for things to tar. [File]
compression	Set compression method. [none, gzip, bzip2]
destfile	Set is the name/location of where to create the tar file. [File]
longfile	Set how to handle long files, those with a path>100 chars. [warn, fail, truncate, gnu, omit]
\<tarfileset\>	Adds a new fileset with the option to specify permissions.

\<taskdef\>   Adds a task definition to the current project, such that this new task can be used in the current project.

classname	The full class name of the object being defined. [String]
classpath	Classpath to be used when searching for component being defined. [Path]
classpathref	Reference to a classpath to use when loading the files. [Reference]
file	Name of the property file to load Ant name/classname pairs from. [File]
loaderref	Use the reference to locate the loader. [Reference]
name	Name of the property resource to load Ant name/classname pairs from. [String]
resource	Name of the property resource to load Ant name/classname pairs from. [String]
\<classpath\>	Creates the classpath to be used when searching for component being defined. [Path]

\<telnet\>   Task to automate a telnet session or other TCP connection to a server.

initialcr	Send a carriage return after connecting; optional, defaults to false. [Boolean]
password	The login password to use; required if userid is set. [String]
port	TCP port to connect to; default is 23. [Integer]
server	Hostname or address of the remote server. [String]
timeout	Default timeout in seconds to wait for a response, zero means forever (the default). [Integer]
userid	The login ID to use on the server; required if password is set. [String]
\<read\>	A string to wait for from the server.
\<write\>	Adds text to send to the server.

\<tempfile\>   This task sets a property to the name of a temporary file.

destdir	Destination directory. [File]
prefix	Optional prefix string. [String]
property	The property you wish to assign the temporary file to. [String]
suffix	Suffix string for the temp file (optional). [String]

<touch> Touches a file and/or fileset(s); corresponds to the Unix touch command.

datetime	The new modification time of the file in the format MM/DD/YYYY HH:MM AM or PM; optional, default=now. [String]
file	Single source file to touch. [File]
millis	The new modification time of the file in milliseconds since midnight Jan 1, 1970. [Long]
<fileset>	Adds a set of files to touch. [Fileset]

<translate> * Translates text embedded in files using Resource Bundle files.

bundle	Sets family name of resource bundle; required. [String]
bundlecountry	Sets locale-specific country of resource bundle; optional. [String]
bundleencoding	Sets Resource Bundle file encoding scheme; optional. [String]
bundlelanguage	Sets locale-specific language of resource bundle; optional. [String]
bundlevariant	Sets locale-specific variant of resource bundle; optional. [String]
destencoding	Sets destination file encoding scheme; optional. [String]
endtoken	Sets ending token to identify keys; required. [String]
forceoverwrite	Sets whether to overwrite existing file irrespective of whether it is newer than the source file as well as the resource bundle file. [Boolean]
srcencoding	Sets source file encoding scheme; optional, defaults to encoding of local system. [String]
starttoken	Sets starting token to identify keys; required. [String]
todir	Sets destination directory; required. [File]
<fileset>	Adds a set of files to translate as a nested fileset element. [Fileset]

<tstamp> Sets properties to the current time, or offsets from the current time.

prefix	Prefix for the properties. [String]
<format>	Creates a custom format with the current prefix.

<typedef> Adds a data type definition to the current project.

classname	The full class name of the object being defined. [String]
classpath	Classpath to be used when searching for component being defined. [Path]
classpathref	Reference to a classpath to use when loading the files. [Reference]
file	Name of the property file to load Ant name/classname pairs from. [File]
loaderref	Use the reference to locate the loader. [Reference]
name	Name of the property file to load Ant name/classname pairs from. [String]
resource	Name of the property resource to load Ant name/classname pairs from. [String]
<classpath>	Creates the classpath to be used when searching for component being defined. [Path]

<unjar>   See <unzip>.

<untar>   Untars a file.

compression	Set decompression algorithm to use; default=none. [none, gzip, bzip2]
dest	Destination directory. [File]
overwrite	If true, overwrite files in dest, even if they are newer than the corresponding entries in the archive. [Boolean]
src	Path to tar file. [File]
<fileset>	Adds a fileset. [Fileset]
<patternset>	Adds a patternset. [Patternset]

<unwar>   See <unzip>.

<unzip>   Unzip a file.

dest	Destination directory. [File]
overwrite	Should the task overwrite files in dest, even if they are newer than the corresponding entries in the archive? [Boolean]
src	Path to Zip file. [File]
<fileset>	Adds a fileset. [Fileset]
<patternset>	Adds a patternset. [Patternset]

<uptodate>   Sets the given property if the specified target has a timestamp greater than all of the source files.

property	The property to set if the target file is more up-to-date than (each of) the source file(s). [String]
srcfile	The file that must be older than the target file if the property is to be set. [File]
targetfile	The file which must be more up-to-date than (each of) the source file(s) if the property is to be set. [File]
value	The value to set the named property to if the target file is more up-to-date than (each of) the source files. [String]
<mapper>	Defines source to target mapping. [Mapper]
<srcfiles>	Adds fileset to the source files. [Fileset]

<vajexport>   Exports packages from the Visual Age for Java workspace.

defaultexcludes	Sets whether default exclusions should be used; default true. [Boolean]
destdir	Destination directory into which the selected items should be exported; required. [File]
excludes	Set of exclude patterns. [String]
exportclasses	Optional flag to export the class files; default false. [Boolean]
exportdebuginfo	Optional flag to export the debug info; default false. [Boolean]
exportresources	Optional flag to export the resource file; default true. [Boolean]

exportsources	Optional flag to export the Java files; default true. [Boolean]	
includes	Set of include patterns. [String]	
overwrite	If true, files will be overwritten during export. [Boolean]	
remote	Name and port of a remote tool server. [String]	
<exclude>	Adds a name entry on the exclude list.	
<include>	Adds a name entry on the include list.	

<vajimport> Imports source, class files, and resources to the Visual Age for Java workspace.

defaultexcludes	Sets whether default exclusions should be used. [Boolean]
importclasses	Flag to import .class files; optional, default false. [Boolean]
importresources	Imports resource files (anything that doesn't end in .class or .java); optional, default true. [Boolean]
importsources	Imports .java files; optional, default true. [Boolean]
project	The VisualAge for Java Project name to import into. [String]
remote	Name and port of a remote tool server [String]
<fileset>	Adds a set of files (nested `fileset` attribute). [Fileset]

<vajload> Loads specific project versions into the Visual Age for Java workspace.

remote	Name and port of a remote tool server, optional. [String]
<vajproject>	Adds a project description entry on the project list.

<vssadd> Adds files to a Microsoft Visual SourceSafe repository.

autoresponse	What to respond with (sets the -I option). [String]
comment	Comment to apply; optional. [String]
localpath	Local path. [Path]
login	The login to use when accessing VSS, formatted as username, password; optional. [String]
recursive	Sets behavior to recursive or nonrecursive. [Boolean]
serverpath	Directory where srssafe.ini resides; optional. [String]
ssdir ·	Directory where ss.exe resides; optional. [String]
vsspath	SourceSafe path that specifies the project/file(s) you wish to perform the action on; required. [String]
writable	Leave added files writable? Default: false. [Boolean]

<vsscheckin> Checks in files to a Microsoft Visual SourceSafe repository.

autoresponse	What to respond with (sets the -I option). [String]
comment	Comment to apply; optional. [String]
localpath	Local path. [Path]
login	The login to use when accessing VSS, formatted as username, password; optional. [String]
recursive	Flag to tell the task to recurse down the tree; optional, default false. [Boolean]

serverpath	Directory where srssafe.ini resides; optional. [String]	
ssdir	Directory where ss.exe resides; optional. [String]	
vsspath	SourceSafe path that specifies the project/file(s) you wish to perform the action on; required. [String]	
writable	Leave checked in files writable? Default: false. [Boolean]	

<vsscheckout> Checks out files from a Microsoft Visual SourceSafe repository.

autoresponse	What to respond with (sets the -I option). [String]
date	Date to get. [String]
label	Label to get. [String]
localpath	Local path. [Path]
login	The login to use when accessing VSS, formatted as username,password; optional. [String]
recursive	Flag to tell the task to recurse down the tree; optional, default false. [Boolean]
serverpath	Directory where srssafe.ini resides; optional. [String]
ssdir	Directory where ss.exe resides; optional. [String]
version	Version to get; optional. [String]
vsspath	SourceSafe path which specifies the project/files you wish to perform the action on; required. [String]

<vsscp> Performs CP (Change Project) commands on a Microsoft Visual Source-Safe repository.

autoresponse	What to respond with (sets the -I option). [String]
login	The login to use when accessing VSS, formatted as username,password; optional. [String]
serverpath	Directory where srssafe.ini resides; optional. [String]
ssdir	Directory where ss.exe resides; optional. [String]
vsspath	SourceSafe path that specifies the project/files you wish to perform the action on; required. [String]

<vsscreate> Creates a new project in a Microsoft Visual SourceSafe repository.

autoresponse	What to respond with (sets the -I option). [String]
comment	Comment to apply in SourceSafe. [String]
failonerror	Sets whether task should fail if there is an error creating the project; optional, default true. [Boolean]
login	The login to use when accessing VSS, formatted as username,password; optional. [String]
quiet	Sets/clears quiet mode; optional, default false. [Boolean]
serverpath	Directory where srssafe.ini resides; optional. [String]
ssdir	Directory where ss.exe resides; optional. [String]
vsspath	SourceSafe path that specifies the project/files you wish to perform the action on; required. [String]

<vssget> Gets files from a Microsoft Visual SourceSafe repository.

`autoresponse`	What to respond with (sets the `-I` option). [String]
`date`	Date to get; optional. [String]
`label`	Label to get; optional. [String]
`localpath`	Overrides the working directory to get to the specified path; optional. [Path]
`login`	The login to use when accessing VSS, formatted as `username,password`; optional. [String]
`quiet`	Flag to suppress output when true; false by default. [Boolean]
`recursive`	Flag to tell the task to recurse down the tree; optional, default false. [Boolean]
`serverpath`	Directory where srssafe.ini resides; optional. [String]
`ssdir`	Directory where ss.exe resides; optional. [String]
`version`	Version number to get; optional. [String]
`vsspath`	SourceSafe path that specifies the project/files you wish to perform the action on; required. [String]
`writable`	Makes fetched files writable; optional, default false. [Boolean]

<vsshistory> Gets a change history from a Microsoft Visual SourceSafe repository.

`dateformat`	Format of dates in `fromdate` and `todate`; optional. [String]
`fromdate`	Start date for the comparison of two versions; optional. [String]
`fromlabel`	Start label; optional. [String]
`login`	The login to use when accessing VSS, formatted as `username,password`; optional. [String]
`numdays`	Number of days for comparison; optional. [Integer]
`output`	Output file name for the history; optional. [File]
`recursive`	Flag to tell the task to recurse down the tree; optional, default false. [Boolean]
`serverpath`	Directory where srssafe.ini resides; optional. [String]
`ssdir`	Directory where ss.exe resides; optional. [String]
`style`	Specify the output style; optional. [`brief`, `codediff`, `nofile`, `default`]
`todate`	End date for the comparison of two versions; optional. [String]
`tolabel`	End label; optional. [String]
`user`	Name the user whose changes we would like to see; optional. [String]
`vsspath`	SourceSafe path that specifies the project/files you wish to perform the action on; required. [String]

<vsslabel> Labels files in a Microsoft Visual SourceSafe repository.

`autoresponse`	What to respond with (sets the `-I` option). [String]
`comment`	The comment to use for this label; optional. [String]
`label`	Label to apply; required. [String]
`login`	The login to use when accessing VSS, formatted as `username,password`; optional. [String]

serverpath	Directory where srssafe.ini resides; optional. [String]
ssdir	Directory where ss.exe resides; optional. [String]
version	Name of an existing file or project version to label; optional. [String]
vsspath	SourceSafe path that specifies the project/files you wish to perform the action on; required. [String]

<waitfor> Waits for a nested condition to become valid.

checkevery	Time between each check. [Long]
checkeveryunit	Check every time unit. [millisecond, second, minute, hour, day, week]
maxwait	Maximum length of time to wait. [Long]
maxwaitunit	Max wait time unit. [millisecond, second, minute, hour, day, week]
timeoutproperty	Name of the property to set after a timeout. [String]
<and>	True if all nested conditions evaluate to true.
<available>	Identical to the <available> task.
<checksum>	Identical to the <checksum> task.
<contains>	Tests whether one string contains another.
<equals>	Tests whether two strings are equal.
<filesmatch>	Tests that two files match, byte for byte.
<http>	Checks for a valid response from a web server of a specified URL.
<isfalse>	Tests whether a string value is not <istrue>.
<isset>	Tests whether a property has been set.
<istrue>	Tests whether a string evaluates to "true", "on", or "yes".
<not>	Negates results of single nested condition.
<or>	True if one nested condition is true.
<os>	Tests whether the current operating system is of a given type.
<socket>	Checks for the existence of a TCP/IP listener at the specified host and port.
<uptodate>	Identical to the <uptodate> task.

<war> [*] An extension of <jar> to create a WAR archive.

basedir	Directory from which to archive files; optional. [File]
compress	Sets whether to compress the files or only store them; optional, default=true;. [Boolean]
destfile	The file to create; required. [File]
duplicate	Sets behavior for when a duplicate file is about to be added. [add, preserve, fail]
encoding	Encoding to use for file names, defaults to the platform's default encoding. [String]
filesonly	If true, emulates Sun's JAR utility by not adding parent directories; optional, defaults to false. [Boolean]
index	Sets whether to create an index list for classes. [Boolean]

manifest	The manifest file to use. [File]
update	If true, updates an existing file, otherwise overwrites any existing one; optional, defaults to false. [Boolean]
webxml	Deployment descriptor to use (WEB-INF/web.xml); required unless update is true. [File]
whenempty	Sets behavior of the task when no files match. [fail, skip, create]
<classes>	Adds files under WEB-INF/classes. [ZipFileset]
<fileset>	Adds a set of files. [Fileset]
<lib>	Adds files under WEB-INF/lib/. [ZipFileset]
<manifest>	Allows the manifest for the archive file to be provided inline in the build file rather than in an external file.
<metainf>	Adds a zipfileset to include in the META-INF directory. [ZipFileset]
<webinf>	Files to add under WEB-INF. [ZipFileset]
<zipfileset>	Adds a set of files that can be read from an archive and be given a prefix/fullpath. [ZipFileset]
<zipgroup-fileset>	Adds a group of Zip files. [Fileset]

<wljspc> * Precompiles JSPs using WebLogic's JSP compiler (weblogic.jspc).

classpath	Classpath to be used for this compilation. [Path]
dest	Directory containing the source JSPs. [File]
package	Package under which the compiled classes go. [String]
src	Directory containing the source JSPs. [File]
<classpath>	Adds a path to the classpath. [Path]

<wlrun> Starts a WebLogic server.

args	Additional argument string passed to the WebLogic instance; optional. [String]
beahome	The location of the BEA Home; implicitly selects WebLogic 6.0; optional. [File]
classpath	The classpath to be used with the Java Virtual Machine that runs the WebLogic Server; required. [Path]
domain	Domain to run in; required for WL6.0. [String]
home	The location where WebLogic lives. [File]
jvmargs	Additional arguments to pass to the WebLogic JVM. [String]
name	The name of the WebLogic server within the WebLogic home that is to be run. [String]
password	Management password of the server; optional and only applicable to WL6.0. [String]
pkpassword	Private key password so the server can decrypt the SSL private key file; optional and only applicable to WL6.0. [String]
policy	The name of the security policy file within the WebLogic home directory that is to be used. [String]
properties	The name of the server's properties file within the WebLogic home directory used to control the WebLogic instance; required for WL4.5.1. [String]

username	Management username to run the server; optional and only applicable to WL6.0. [String]
weblogicmain-class	Name of the main class for WebLogic; optional. [String]
wlclasspath	WebLogic classpath used by the WebLogic server; optional, and only applicable to WL4.5.1. The WebLogic classpath is used by WebLogic to support dynamic class loading. [Path]
<classpath>	Adds the classpath for the user classes. [Path]
<wlclasspath>	Gets the classpath to the WebLogic classpaths. [Path]

<wlstop> Shuts down a WebLogic server.

beahome	The location of the BEA Home; implicitly selects WebLogic 6.0 shutdown; optional. [File]
classpath	The classpath to be used with the Java Virtual Machine that runs the WebLogic Shutdown command;. [Path]
delay	Delay (in seconds) before shutting down the server; optional. [String]
password	The password for the account specified in the user parameter; required. [String]
url	URL to which the WebLogic server is listening for T3 connections; required. [String]
user	The username of the account that will be used to shut down the server; required. [String]
<classpath>	The classpath to be used with the Java Virtual Machine that runs the WebLogic Shutdown command. [Path]

<wsdltodotnet> Converts a WSDL file or URL resource into a .NET language.

destfile	Name of the file to generate. [File]
extraoptions	Any extra WSDL.EXE options that aren't explicitly supported by the Ant wrapper task; optional. [String]
failonerror	Should failure halt the build? Optional, default=true. [Boolean]
language	Language; default is CS, generating C# source. [CS, JS, or VB]
namespace	Namespace to place the source in. [String]
server	Flag to enable server-side code generation; optional, default=false. [Boolean]
srcfile	The local WSDL file to parse; either url or srcfile is required. [File]
url	URL to fetch. [String]

<xmlproperty> Loads property values from a valid XML file, generating the property names from the file's element and attribute names.

collapseat-tributes	Flag to treat attributes as nested elements; optional, default false. [Boolean]
file	The XML file to parse; required. [File]
keeproot	Flag to include the XML root tag as a first value in the property name; optional, default is true. [Boolean]
prefix	The prefix to prepend to each property. [String]
validate	Flag to validate the XML file; optional, default false. [Boolean]

<xmlvalidate> Checks whether XML files are valid (or only well formed).

classname	Specify the class name of the SAX parser to be used. [String]
classpath	Specify the classpath to be searched to load the parser (optional). [Path]
classpathref	Where to find the parser class; optional. [Reference]
failonerror	Specify how parser errors are to be handled; optional, default is true. [Boolean]
file	Specify the file to be checked; optional. [File]
lenient	Specify whether the parser should be validating. [Boolean]
warn	Specify how parser error are to be handled. [Boolean]
<classpath>	No description. [Path]
<dtd>	Creates a DTD location record; optional.
<fileset>	Specifies a set of files to be checked. [Fileset]
<xmlcatalog>	Adds an XMLCatalog as a nested element; optional. [XMLCatalog]

<xslt> * Processes a set of XML documents via XSLT.

basedir	Base directory; optional, default is the project's basedir. [File]
classpath	Optional classpath to the XSL processor. [Path]
classpathref	Reference to an optional classpath to the XSL processor. [Reference]
destdir	Destination directory into which the XSL result files should be copied to; required, unless in and out are specified. [File]
extension	Desired file extension to be used for the target; optional, default is html. [String]
force	Sets whether to check dependencies, or always generate; optional, default is false. [Boolean]
in	Specifies a single XML document to be styled. [File]
out	Specifies the output name for the styled result from the in attribute; required if in is set. [File]
processor	Name of the XSL processor to use; optional, default is trax. [String]
scanincluded-directories	Sets whether to style all files in the included directories as well; optional, default is true. [Boolean]
style	Name of the stylesheet to use—given either relative to the project's basedir or as an absolute path; required. [String]
<classpath>	Optional classpath to the XSL processor. [Path]
<outputproperty>	Specifies how you wish the result tree to be output.
<param>	Creates an instance of an XSL parameter.
<xmlcatalog>	Adds the catalog to our internal catalog. [XMLCatalog]

<zip> * Creates a Zip file.

basedir	Directory from which to archive files; optional. [File]
compress	Sets whether to compress the files or only store them; optional, default=true;. [Boolean]
destfile	The file to create; required. [File]
duplicate	Sets behavior for when a duplicate file is about to be added. [add, preserve, fail]
encoding	Encoding to use for file names, defaults to the platform's default encoding. [String]
filesonly	If true, emulates Sun's JAR utility by not adding parent directories; optional, defaults to false. [Boolean]
update	If true, updates an existing file, otherwise overwrites any existing one; optional, defaults to false. [Boolean]
whenempty	Sets behavior of the task when no files match. [fail, skip, create]
<fileset>	Adds a set of files. [Fileset]
<zipfileset>	Adds a set of files that can be read from an archive and be given a prefix/fullpath. [ZipFileset]
<zipgroup-fileset>	Adds a group of Zip files. [Fileset]

resources

All URLs listed here were valid at the time of publishing. No doubt some of these change over time. Some of the least stable URLs have been listed by providing the URL of their home server, from where a search may find the document.

WORKS CITED

In print

Beck, Kent. *Extreme Programming Explained: Embrace Change*. Addison-Wesley Longman, 1999.

Bloch, Joshua. *Effective Java Programming Language Guide*. Addison-Wesley, 2001.
  A thorough treatise on Java programming idioms.

Fowler, Martin, et al. *Refactoring: Improving the Design of Existing Code*. Addison-Wesley, 1999.

Gamma, Erich et al. *Design Patterns*. Addison-Wesley, 1995. The Gang of Four book.

Graham, Steve, ed., et al. *BuildingWeb Services with Java: Making Sense of XML, SOAP, WSDL, and UDDI*. Sams, 2001.

Hightower, Richard, and Nicholas Lesiecki. *Java Tools for Extreme Programming: Mastering Open Source Tools, including Ant, JUnit, and Cactus*. John Wiley & Sons, 2001.
  An excellent introduction to the tools used by Java developers. Erik contributed a case study on HttpUnit.

Hunt, Andrew, and David Thomas. *The Pragmatic Programmer: From Journeyman to Master*. Addison-Wesley, 2000.
  A must-read for all developers.

Jeffries, Ron, et al. *Extreme Programming Installed*. Addison-Wesley, 2000.

Krutchen, Philippe. *The Rational Unified Process: An Introduction, 2nd ed*. Addison-Wesley, 1999.

Roman, Ed, et al. *Mastering Enterprise JavaBeans*, 2nd ed. John Wiley & Sons, 2002.

Wesley, Ajamu A. *Programming Web Services with Java*. Manning Publications, 2002.

Vermeulen, Al, ed., et al. *The Elements of Java Style*. Cambridge University Press, 2000.

Online

Almaer, Dion. *Using XDoclet: Developing EJBs with Just the Bean Class*. 2002.
http://www.onjava.com/pub/a/onjava/2002/01/30/xdoclet.html

Ambler, Scott. *The Enterprise Unified Process.* Integrating deployment with the iterative development stage. 2001.
http://www.ronin-intl.com/publications/unifiedProcess.htm

AntFAQ. *Frequently Asked Questions about Ants.* 2000.
http://www.antcolony.org/FAQ2.htm

Bray, Tim. *The Annotated XML Specification.* 1998.
If you have to read the XML specification, this is the version to read.
http://www.xml.com/axml/testaxml.htm

Dorigo. 2000
http://iridia.ulb.ac.be/~mdorigo/ACO/RealAnts.html.

Fielding, Roy Thomas. *Architectural Styles and the Design of Network-based Software Architectures.*
Ph.D. Dissertation, University of California, 2000.
http://www.ics.uci.edu/~fielding/pubs/dissertation/top.htm

Fowler, Martin and Matthew Foemmel. *Continuous Integration.* 2000.
http://www.martinfowler.com/articles/continuousIntegration.html

Free Software Foundation. *GNU Make Manual.*
http://www.gnu.org/manual/make/index.html

Hatcher, Erik. *Automating the build and test process.* 2001.
http://www.ibm.com/developerworks/java/library/j-junitmail/

Koeritz, Chris. *Clam.* 2001.
http://www.gruntose.com/build/clam/manual/clam_root.html

Liang, Sheng. *The Java Native Interface Programmer's Guide and Specification.* 1999.
http://java.sun.com/docs/books/jni/

Loughran, Steve. *Ant in Anger: Using Ant in a Production Environment.* Apache. 2000.
http://jakarta.apache.org/ant/ant_in_anger.html

Loughran, Steve. *When Web Services Go Bad,.* Web Services Developer's Conference. 2002 (1).
http://www.iseran.com/Steve/papers.html

Loughran, Steve. *Making Web Services that Work.* To be published as an HP Laboratories Technical Report. 2002 (2).
http://www.iseran.com/Steve/papers.html

Neward, Ted. *Understanding Class.forName ().* 2000.
This explains why extension libraries confuse programs.
http://www.develop.com/

Neward, Ted. (2001) *X-Power: Use XML to Write Papers.*
http://www.javageeks.com/Papers/PapersXSLFO/

Sun. *Code Conventions for the Java Programming Language.* 2000.
    http://java.sun.com/docs/codeconv/

Sun. *Java Native Interface.* 2002.
    http://java.sun.com/j2se/1.4/docs/guide/jni/

Sun. *Endorsed Standards Override Mechanism.* 2002.
    http://java.sun.com/j2se/1.4/docs/guide/standards/

Sitepen. *Using JavaScript with Ant.* 2002.
    http://www.sitepen.com/ant/javascript.html

Tomcat. *Tomcat Manager How-To.* 2002.
    http://jakarta.apache.org/tomcat/tomcat-4.1-doc/manager-howto.html

ADDITIONAL RESOURCES

In print

Brand, Stewart. *How Buildings Learn: What Happens After They're Built.* Viking Penguin, 1994.
    In an indirect way, this is the best guide ever to designing applications that last.

Eckel, Bruce. *Thinking in Java.* Prentice Hall PTR, 2000.
    Online copy: http://www.mindview.net/Books.

McConnell, Steve C. *Rapid Development: Taming Wild Software Schedules.* Microsoft Press, 1996.
    The most readable of all the modern software development books.

Shirazi, Jack. *Java Performance Tuning.* O'Reilly & Associates, 2000.
    How to make your Java applications go farther, and equally important, insight into how the various JVMs work.

Tremper, Bruce *Staying Alive in Avalanche Terrain.* Mountaineers Books, 2001.
    Software projects, Alpine mountaineering: it's all about risk management.

Online

(ECMA-262) *ECMAScript Reference*, Standard ECMA-262. The JavaScript specification.
    http://www.ecma.ch/; search for it by name on that site.

Peltz, Chris. *10 Best Practices for J2EE Development.* 2000.
    http://www.hpmiddleware.com/newsletters/webservicesnews/features/

Raymond, Erik. *The Jargon File.* 1981.
    The definitive repository of hacker and developer terminology. If you don't read this, you will never be able to talk about cargo cult programming or waving a dead chicken over the source code, among other things.
    http://www.tuxedo.org/~esr/jargon/

More online resources

Ant-contrib	http://sourceforge.net/projects/ant-contrib/
AntHill	http://urbancode.com/
Apache Ant	http://jakarta.apache.org/ant/
Apache Axis	http://xml.apache.org/axis/
Apache Cactus	http://jakarta.apache.org/cactus/
Apache Tomcat Web Server	http://jakarta.apache.org/tomcat/
Canoo WebTest	http://webtest.canoo.com/
Checkstyle	http://checkstyle.sourceforge.net/
Cruise Control	http://cruisecontrol.sourceforge.net/
DBForms	http://www.dbforms.org/
Dbunit Database Testing Framework	http://dbunit.sourceforge.net/
Gump	http://jakarta.apache.org/gump/
Jakarta Tomcat	http://jakarta.apache.org/tomcat/
JBoss Application Server	http://jboss.org/
JOnAS Application Server	http://www.objectweb.org/jonas/
JUnit	http://junit.org/
Rant	http://sourceforge.net/projects/remoteant/
XDoclet	http://xdoclet.sourceforge.net/

index

Symbols

${...}
  definition 51
@tags 342
  for EJB development with
    XDoclet 340
  in XDoclet 276

A

addConfiguredXXX 480
addText() 482
addXXX 480
Amber 13
Ant
  API 470–473
  beyond Java development 21
  command line 36–39
  command-line options 41
  committer 14
  concepts 5–7
  history 14
  how it works underneath 474
  installation configuration 527
  installing 523
  migrating to 209–212
  procedures using 182
  running remotely via Telnet 453
  using for deployment 441
  what is 3–5
  why use 10–14
<ant> task 213–221, 564
  controlling properties 221
  used with CruiseControl 392
Ant Console
  in Eclipse 541
Ant task
  attribute setting 474

backward compatibility 497
character setter 476
developing 467–497
enumerated attribute 477
error handling 486
executing Java main() 490
File setter 476
nested elements 480
numeric attributes 475
Path setter 476
simple example 468
String constructor
  extensibility 478
supporting arbitrary attributes and
  elements 493
supporting datatype
  references 480
supporting text and CDATA 482
testing custom 487
using custom in same build 469
what is 468
wrapping command-line
  tool 487–490
ANT_ARGS 527
ANT_HOME 524
ANT_OPTS 527
  to set Log4j configuration 506
<antcall> task 182–186, 564
AntClassLoader 478
ant-contrib project 253–257
  <cc> task, See <cc> task
  Sourceforge project
    <propertycopy> 81
Anthill 397–401
  installation 398
Antidote 542
<antlr> task 564

<antstructure> task 565
Apache SOAP 343
<apply> task 130, 565
  and custom task development 487
<arg> element
  passing file paths 40
attrib
  executing with <exec> 516
attribute-oriented programming 260
attributes
  setting in custom task 474
automating
  with operating system 387
<available> task 70–72, 565
  checking for class existence 70
  checking for file existence 71
  checking for resource
    availability 72
  probing for executables 377
  testing custom selector 517
  within <condition> 72
Axis
  creating proxy classes with
    WSDL2Java 360
  creating simple web service 364
  installing Axis on a web server 363
  the many ways to implement a web
    service 363
  registering Web Service
    Deployment Descriptors 382
  tools for converting between Java
    and WSDL 357
  using the WSDL2Java generated
    proxy classes 361
  Web Service Deployment
    Descriptor 382
  See also web services 355

B

BaseExtendSelector 515
BaseFilterReader 519
<basename> task 566
BaseParamFilterReader 520
Bash
    configuring Ant installation 526
BEA
    WebLogic, *See* WebLogic
Bean Scripting Framework
    See BSF
<blgenclient> task 336, 566
Bluestone
    See HP-AS
Boolean
    attribute setters 475
Boolean attributes 50
Borland Application Server 336
    and <ejbjar> 339
BSF 499–502
Bugzilla 438
build
    failure 27
    logging in XML 327
    notification, using <sound> 240
build file 5–6
    best practices 231–233
    design for componentization 544
    design for maintenance 545
    example 7
    examples 189
    includes 189
    libraries 228
    philosophy 200
    simple example 24
    specifying which to run 42
build log
    HTML view 329
Build numbering
    See <buildnumber> task
build process 3
    JUnit integration 95
    and operations 438
    what is 4
build tools
    Amber 13
    Cons 13
    Jam 13
    Make 11
BuildEvent
    list 502
BuildException 487
-buildfile 41
buildFinished event 502

building EAR
    See <ear>
BuildListener interface 502
BuildLogger
    for log() method calls 471
BuildLogger interface 502
<buildnumber> task 239, 566
buildStarted event 502
built-in task
    definition 235
<bunzip2> task 566
<bzip> task 567

C

C#
    compiling, *See* <csc> task
    metadata 275
    running a C# program with
        <exec> 380
C/C++
    compilation using 410
<cab> task 567
Cactus 310–315
    how it works 313
    test case example 314
Canoo WebTest
    See WebTest
Castor 332, 343
Catalina
    See Tomcat
<cc> task 410–412
    installing 410
    supported compilers 411
<cccheckin> task 245, 567
<ccheckout> task 245, 567–568
<ccmcheckout> task 245
<ccmreconfigure> task 568
<ccuncheckout> task 568
<ccupdate> task 245, 569
CDATA 534
    withing custom Ant tasks 482
Centipede 231
ChainableReader 519
Checkstyle 248–250
    installing 250
<checkstyle> task 249
Checksum
    using <condition> 73
<checksum> task 569
<chmod> task 145, 569
    testing custom selector 516
class
    forName() 478
    loading in custom task 478

ClassFileset 66
<classpath>
    within <javac> 51
ClearCase 246
    tasks 245
code generation
    active vs. passive 272
    with XDoclet 267
<ccmcheckin> task 245
command line 488
    logging options 41
        See –logger and -logfile
    monitoring build process
        See -listener
    running multiple targets 36, 38
    selecting build file options
        See -buildfile
    setting properties
        See -D and -propertyfile
    setting properties from 74
CommonsLoggingListener 503
<concat>
    Filelist 65
<concat> task 570
<condition> 72–73
<condition> task 570
    determining OS family 516
    probing for web service
        availability 358
    using <filesmatch> for deployment
        verification 461
conditional build failure 78
conditional logic
    using <condition>, *See* <condition>
    using ant-contrib tasks 255
Cons build system 13
console input 172
Continuous integration
    tools comparison 405
continuous integration 386–406
Continuus
    tasks 245
<copy>
    FilterChain 59
    overwrite attribute 58
<copy> task 136–137, 571
    <filterset> example 293
    deployment 442–443
    filtering 299
    overwrite attribute 294
    overwrite attribute for
        deployment 443
    preservelastmodified attribute 137
    replacing tokens 299
    timestamp checking 137

copying files 136–137
Core task
  definition 235
createDynamicElement() 494
createTempFile() 473
createXXX 480
cross-platform
  detection using 254
  directory and path separators 52
CruiseControl 388–397
  architecture 389
  logging 395
  ModificationSet
    See <modificationset> task
  notifications 396
  using 245
<csc> task 571
  compiling C# code 379
Custom task
  ant.jar in classpath 51
  definition 235
CVS
  change log 246
  tasks 245
<cvs> task 572
<cvschangelog> task 246, 573
<cvspass> task 573
<cvstagdiff> task 246, 573

D

-D 41
database
  manipulation with Torque 250
  O/R mapping with Torque 250
datatype
  best practices 82–83
  ClassFileset 66
  element naming conventions 57
  Filelist 65
  overview 48
  references 79
  Selectors 56
  supporting in custom tasks 481
Datestamp
  generating 58
DBForms 309
<ddcreator> task 336, 574
-debug 41
default excludes 53
DefaultLogger 503
defect tracking 438
<delete> task 135–136, 574
  warning 136
deleting files. See <delete>
<depend> task 241–243, 574

dependencies
  graph 7
dependency checking
  beyond <javac>
    See <depend> task
  using 72
<dependset> task 575
  Filelist 65
deployment 163–187
  best practices 462–463
  configuration files 447
  descriptors 436
  HTTP URL based 459
  integration 439
  issues 432–437
  to local Tomcat 174
  planning 446
  precompiled JSP 291
  production 431–463
  remote upload 450
  solving problems 171
  supporting different
    servers 456–459
  task requirements 164
  tasks 164
  testing 187, 437
  vendor-specific libraries 436
  verification with timestamps 460
  via email 173
directory structure 31
DirectoryScanner 488
<dirname> task 575
Dirset 65
<dirset> 65
documentation
  generation 139–145
DTD resolution 321
DynamicConfigurator 493–495

E

<ear> task 575
  <zipfileset> 65
  build file example 353
EAR files
  deployment issues 440
<echo> task 575
  as example of CDATA 482
<echoproperties> task 576
Eclipse 541
EJB 333–354
  Ant tasks 336
  deployment 348–349
  deployment descriptor
    example 338
  JAR 334–335

JAR building with 335
  overview 333
  See also Enterprise JavaBeans
EJB development
  Ant best practices 354
  build example 349
  deployment descriptor
    generation 340
  reverse-engineering database 345
  supporting multiple vendors/
    versions 343
  using XDoclet 340–345
<ejbc> task 576
<ejbdoclet> task 341
<ejbjar> task 337–340, 576
  <borland> element 339
  <iplanet> element 336, 339
  <jboss> element 339
  <jonas> element 339
  <weblogic> element 336, 339
  <websphere> element 339
  basejarname attribute 339
  build file example 353
  compared to <jar> task 337
  deployment issues 441
  descriptordir attribute 339
  genericjarsuffix attribute 339
  lack of DynamicConfigurator
    support 495
  srcdir attribute 339
  vendor-specific handling 339
-emacs 41–42
emacs 542
  mode 503
email
  sending attachments 170
  sending, See <mail> task
Enterprise JavaBeans See EJB
entity reference 189
EnumeratedAttribute 477
  API 473
environment variables
  accessing as properties 69
error handling
  in custom tasks 486
errors
  common mistakes 27
<exec> task 124, 130, 577
  best practices 132
  executing attrib on Windows 516
  executing shell commands 127
  to launch Make 409
  for native code compilation 408
  probing for program existence 129
  setting environment variables 126

<exec> task *(continued)*
  timeout attribute 127
  error handling 126
execute() 468
  definition 471
executing programs
  best practices 132
  limitations 132
  native programs 124
  processing output 131
extending Ant
  writing custom tasks
    See Ant tasks, developing
Extensible Markup Language *See*
  XML 331
external programs
  executing within Ant 111, 133
eXtreme Programming 16
  and unit testing 86

F

–f 41
<fail> task 577
  if/unless 78
Filelist 65
files
  moving, copying,
    deleting 135–139
  setting permissions 145
FileSet 488
  API 472
  in custom task 481
  supporting in custom task 485
<fileset>
  defaultexcludes attribute 53
fileset 52–54
  default excludes 53
  resolution 54
  selectors 56
  See also <fileset>
FileUtils
  API 473
<filter> 59
<filter> task 577
<filterchain> 60
FilterChain 59, 517
filtering
  See <filterset>
  token substitution 138
FilterReaders 59
  writing custom 517–520
<filterset>
  used to customize web.xml 293
filterset 58

-find 41
-find switch
  example 250
<fixcrlf> task 143, 578
Flatten mapper 62
fleset
  examples 53
<foreach> task 257
Forte 540
FTP
  deployment 442
  distribution 171
  probing server availability 166
  Windows FTP server 166
<ftp> task 166, 578
  deployment 452
  uploading 171

G

<genkey> task 152, 579
<get> task 170, 579
  deployment verification 461
  retrieving WSDL from a SOAP
    server 359
  used for Tomcat deployment 456
getBaseDir() 472
getIncludedFiles() 472
getName() 472
getProperty() 471
Glob mappers 63
GlobPatternMapper 514
Gump 401–405
<gunzip> task 579
<gzip> task 579

H

-help 41
Hexadecimal numbers
  as Ant task attributes 478
HP Application Server
  See HP-AS
HP-AS 333
  deployment 458
<hpas-deploy> task 458
HttpUnit 299–310
  running from Ant 303
  and WebTest 306

I

<icontract> task 579
IDE 10, 19
  debugging integration 42
  integration with Ant 536–543
  migrating to Ant 211

IDEA 540
Identity mapper 61
<if> task 255
<ilasm> task 580
includeAntRuntime 51
init() 470–471
<input> task 172, 580
-inputhandler 41
<install> task
  for Tomcat 4.1 deployment 457
installing Ant 523–531
Integrated Development
  Environment
  See IDE
IntelliJ IDEA 540
interactive input 172
Internet
  retrieving files from 170
introspection
  for task population 469, 474
<iplanet-ejbc> task 336
iPlanet Application Server 336
  and <ejbjar> 339
<iplanet-ejbc> task 580

J

Jakarta
  Commons Logging API 503
  Slide 442
  Gump, *See* Gump
Jam 13
<jar> task 148–154, 581
  in EJB development 335
  <zipfileset> 65
JAR building
  See <jar>
JAR files
  adding metadata 152
  signing 152
  testing 149
<jarlib-available> task 581
<jarlib-display> task 581
<jarlib-manifest> task 582
<jarlib-resolve> task 582
Jasper 288
Java
  class constants access in Ant 60
  dependency checking
    See <depend> task
  executing
    See <java>
  executing from within Ant 112,
    124
    See <java> task

Java (continued)
  executing main() 113
  executing programs inside Ant 39
  installing SDK 523
  metadata specifications 276
  package names 32
<java> task 113, 124, 582
  <arg> element 115
  arguments 40
  classpath 114–115
  classpathref attribute 115
  command-line arguments 115
  controlling environment
    variables 118
  executable JARs 120
  executing third-party
    programs 121
  failonerror attribute 119
  forking the JVM 117
  JVM parameters 118
  probing for class existence 123
  running a SOAP client 362
  setting system properties 116
  timeout attribute 124
  used for deployment 459
  used in custom task
    development 490
Java 1.4
  logging using
    CommonsLogging–Listener
    503
Java Native Interface
  building with Ant 412–430
Java programs
  wrapped in custom Ant task 490
<javac>
  always recompiles 33
  attributes 49
  deployment issues 440
  srcdir 51
<javac> task 583
javac
  comparison to <javac> 49
  command-line switches 49
  See <javac>
JavaCC 243
<javacc> task 243, 584
Javadoc 261
  including in distributable 297
  See <javadoc> task
<javadoc> task 142, 584
  including API docs in WAR 297
  using <javadoc> task 142–143
  and JDK 1.4 261
<javah> task 587

JavaScript
  within Ant
    See <script> task
JAXB 332
JBoss 333, 343
  and <ejbjar> 339
  support in Middlegen 348
JBuilder 542
<jdepend> task 587
jEdit 538
Jikes 49
  with CruiseControl 396
<jjtree> task 587
JMS, Java Messaging Service
  and Message-Driven Beans 334
JOnAS
  and <ejbjar> 339
  and <serverdeploy> 348, 443
<jpcoverage> task 588
<jpcovmerge> task 588
<jpcovreport> task 589
JRun 343
JSP
  building dynamically from
    XML 324
  compilation 288–292
  compilation with Jasper 288
JSP tag libraries
  See Tag libraries
<jspc> task 288, 589
  example 289
  installing dependencies 289
  and WEB-INF 290
JUnit
  accessing external resources 93
  Ant best practices 109
  applying 92–94
  architecture 87–91
  asserts 88
  capturing results in XML 98
  compiling test cases 96
  extensions 91
  installation 91
  lifecycle 90
  reporting 100–105
    See also <junitreport> task
  running multiple tests 99
  setting system properties 303
  test case 88
  test runners 88
  testing databases 105
  testing J2EE in-container code
    See Cactus
  TestSuite 90
  UML diagram 87

  and WebTest 306
  what is it 85
  See also <junit> task
<junit>
  capturing results 97
  custom results formatter 100
  directory structure 94
  failures 97
  passing configuration information
    into 104
  result formatters 98
  short-circuiting 105
  viewing System.out/.err 99
  XML formatter 98
  and properties 96
<junit> task 94–97, 589
  <batchtest> 99
  <formatter> 97
  conditional test cases 103
  errorProperty attribute 102
  forking JVM 104
  haltonfailure attribute 97
  initializing environment 103
  issues 108
  printsummary attribute 98
JUnitPerf 91
<junitreport> task 100–105, 590
  customizing output 102
  HTML results 101
  running after test failures 102
  system requirements 101
JVM
  deployment version 433

L

library dependencies
  directory structure 196
  handling 196–200
  installing new version 198
  property mappings 197
  user overrides 199
line endings
  adjusting for platforms 143
-listener 41
  using
    CommonsLoggingListener 502,
    507
listeners 502–513
  writing custom 503
<loadfile> task 590
  deployment verification 461
  FilterChain 59
<loadproperties>
  FilterChain 59

<loadproperties> task 590
log() methods 471
Log4j
   and Commons Logging API 503
   listener configuration 507
   logging build events 506–509
Log4jListener 506
-logfile 41
-logger 41
   with MailLogger 513
loggers 502–513
   writing custom 509–513
logging levels 471
LogKit
   and Commons Logging API 503
LogStreamHandler 488
Lucene 18
   using 243

M

MacOS X
   and WebDAV 442
   localhost issue 448
magic properties
   in MailLogger 512
<mail> task 169–170, 591
   attributes 169
mail
   sending build failure
      notification 509
   sending complete build log 509
MailLogger 388, 510
Make 11
   comparison to Ant 12
   computed variable name 81
   executing from Ant 409
   file dependency counterpart in Ant
      See <apply>
   migrating to Ant 211
   related tools 13
makefile
   See Make
<manifest> task 591
manifests
   creating for 150
mappers 61–64
   flatten 62
   glob 63
   identity 61
   merge 62
   package 64
   regexp 63
   writing custom 514–515
   See <mapper>

MatchingTask 563
<maudit> task 591
Maven 231
Merge mapper 62
messageLogged event 502
Metadata 275
META-INF
   in EJB development 336
Microsoft
   Visual SourceSafe
      See SourceSafe
Microsoft .NET 21
Microsoft Windows
   See Windows
Middlegen 19, 345–348
   build file example 351
   build integration 353
migration to Ant
   steps 210
<mimemail> task 592
<mkdir> task 33, 592
<mmetrics> task 592
Mock Objects 91, 310
<modificationset> task
   example 392
<move> task 137, 592
   FilterChain 59
moving files 137
Mozilla Rhino 499
<mparse> task 593
MSG_DEBUG 471
MSG_ERR 471
MSG_INFO 471
MSG_VERBOSE 471
MSG_WARN 471
MVCSoft 343

N

NAnt
   building .NET applications 381
Native programs
   wrapped in custom Ant task 487
<native2ascii> task 593
.NET
   See also Microsoft .NET
   building web service client 376
   building with NAnt 381
   metadata 275
   testing with NUnit 381
NetBeans 540
<netrexxc> task 593
Neward, Ted 21, 327
NoBannerLogger 527
NUnit
   testing .NET code 381

O

optional tasks 235–237
Orion 343
<osfamily> task 254

P

<p4add> task 595
<p4change> task 595
<p4counter> task 595
<p4delete> task 596
<p4edit> task 245, 596
<p4have> task 596
<p4label> task 245, 597
<p4reopen> task 597
<p4revert> task 597
<p4submit> task 245, 598
<p4sync> task 245, 598
Package mapper 64
PackageNameMapper 514
packaging 134–162
   adding data files 141
   install scripts 143
   process diagram 135
   testing 161
<parallel> task 336, 598
<patch> task 598
path 51–52
   API 472
   cross-platform handling 52
   datatype definition 51
   string representation 80
   See also <path>
<pathconvert> task 599
   Filelist 65
<pathelement> 51
<patternset>
   conditional deployment 451
   if/unless 78
patternset 54–56
   conditional 297
   conditional patterns 78
   nesting using references 81
pausing the build
   See <sleep>
PDF
   generation from XML 327
Perforce
   tasks 245
Platform-specific
   setting property
      See <condition>
Pramati 343
production deployment
   See deployment

<project> 25
  <description> element 45
project 6
  API 471
  directory structure 31
  example 7
  sharing common properties 225
project management 205–233
  designing a build process 206–209
  directory structure 551
  generating to-do lists from
    source code 192
  implementing processes 232
  library management 232
  managing subprojects 221–228
  master builds 212
-projecthelp 41, 44
properties 66–79
  <ant> task 221
  best practices 82–83
  built-in 66
  copying 253
  creating property files
    See <propertyfile> task
  dereferencing 80, 253
  <equals> task 72
  expansion in attribute setters 475
  expansion in attributes 483
  expansion in <telnet> 446
  immutability exceptions 69
  immutability of 69
  inheriting 223
  <isfalse> 72
  <isset> 72
  <istrue> 72
  loading environment variables 69
  loading from properties file 68
  loading from XML file 76
  magic
    See magic properties
  manually expanding in
    element text 485
  override design 223
  overriding 68, 74
  overriding with <ant> 224
  overview 48
  prefixing names using
    <property> 68
  relative paths 68
  setting
    See <property>
  setting to file paths 69
  setting value 67
  sharing across projects 225

  sharing across sub-projects 194
  substituting with XDoclet 343
  undefined value 71
<property> 67–70, 599
  environment variant 69
  file variant 68
  location variant 69
  value variant 67
<propertycopy> task 81, 254
-propertyfile 41
<propertyfile> task 237–239, 599
  <entry> element 239
  example in web development 298
propertyfile 9
PVCS
  task 245
<pvcs> task 245, 599
Python
  scripting within Ant
    See <script> task

Q

-quiet 41

R

RadPak
  See HP-AS
Rant
  remotely invoking Ant 383
<rant> task
  for executing Ant as a web
    service 383
Rational Unified Process 17
ReadOnlySelector 515
<record> task 600
Refactoring 86
References 79–82
  inheriting 223
refid attribute 79
Regexp mapper 63
regular expressions
  mapper 63
  replacing
    See <replaceregexp> task
<replace> task 600
replaceProperties() 472
<replaceregexp> task 244–245, 601
replacing tokens
  See <copy> task, filtering
resolveFile() 472–473
Rhino
  for scripting 499
<rmic> task 601

RPM
  installing Ant 525
<rpm> task 602
Ruby, Sam 15
<runservertests> task 311

S

Scarab 438
scheduling
  See automating
SCM
  ClearCase 245
  Continuus 245
  CVS, See <cvs> task
  Perforce 245
  PVCS 245
  scheduling 388
  SourceOffSite 245
  SourceSafe 245
  StarTeam 245
  tasks 245
<script> task 499–502, 602
  generating random number 499
  implicit objects 500
scripting within Ant
  See <script> task
SDK
  installing 523
selectors 56
  read-only files 515
  writing custom 515–517
self
  in 500
<sequential> task 602
server
  management 436
  shutdown with <telnet> 444
<serverdeploy> task 348, 443, 602
  <weblogic> element 336
  lack of DynamicConfigurator
    support 495
setDynamicAttribute() 494
setNewProperty
  used in <script> task 500
setNewProperty() 471
setProject() 483
<setproxy> task 602
  using before retrieving a WSDL
    file 359
setters
  for Ant task population 474
<signjar> task 153, 603
<sleep> task 168, 603
  during deployment 449

SMTP
  to send build failure
    notifications 509
SMTPAppender
  Log4j to send build failure
    email 507
SOAP. *See* web services
Software Configuration Management
  See SCM
<soscheckin> task 245, 603
<soscheckout> task 245, 604
<sosget> task 245, 604
<soslabel> task 245, 605
<sound> task 239–241, 605
SourceOffSite, tasks 245
SourceSafe, tasks 245
<splash> task 239–241, 606
SQL
  executing with Torque 250
<sql> task 252, 606
  creating database 351
SSH, deployment 442
StarTeam, tasks 245
<stcheckin> task 245, 607
<stcheckout> task 245, 607
<stlabel> task 245, 608
<stlist> task 608
Struts 18, 343
  code generation using
    XDoclet 268
  generation using XDoclet 260
  library management 198
  validating struts-config.xml 319
<style> task 609
  See <xslt>
  See <xslt> task
<stylebook> task 609
Styler 327
stylesheets
  transforming XML build log 328
<switch> task 255

T

Tag libraries 279
  creating 280
  TLD generation 282
Taglibs. *See* Tag libraries
<tar> task 158, 610
  attributes 159
tar files 158–160
  setting file permissions 158
<target> 26
  description attribute 44
  if/unless 77

targetFinished event 502
targets
  conditional 77
  default 25
  definition 6
  dependencies 6, 35
  deployment issues 440
  determining from deliverables 206
  listing 44
  naming conventions 216, 548
  sharing across build files 227
targetStarted event 502
Task
  API 470
  built-in or core 235
  custom 235
  defining. *See* <taskdef> task
  defining using a properties file 247
  definition 6, 26
  development
    See Ant tasks, developing
  introspection
    mechanism 474–482
  lifecycle 469–470
  optional 235
    See also optional tasks
  project reference 471
  sharing definitions 258
  subclass 483–485
  third-party 235
  types of 235
Task library, building 495–496
TaskAdapter 470
<taskdef> task 247–248, 610
  custom task classapth 478
  custom task development 469
  defining custom task library 496
  definitions generated by
    XDoclet 265
taskFinished event 502
taskStarted event 502
<telnet> task 610
  attributes 443
  deployment 453–455
  remote deployment 443–446
  running Ant remotely 453
  server prompts 453
  timeout attribute 443
  to shutdown server 444
<tempfile> task 610
testing
  custom Ant tasks 487
  in-container
    See Cactus

  planning 207
  using JUnit 85–110
  web applications with
    HttpUnit 300
  with main() 86
<testSpec> task 309
third-party task 235, 237
ThoughtWorks
  CruiseControl 388
Timestamp 75
  generating 58
  generating in build 299
  ISO 8601 75
To-do list
  generation with XDoclet 261
Tomcat
  4.0 deployment 456
  4.1 deployment 457
  deployment 456
  installing application 450
  management interface 175
  remote deployment 181
  securing management
    requests 457
  unloading application 449
Torque 19, 250–253
<touch> task 611
<translate> task 611
translatePath() 472
troubleshooting 527–531
  Ant not found 528
  ANT_HOME 529
  ANT_OPTS 530
  CLASSPATH 529
  JAVA_HOME 528
  JDK not installed 527
  missing task 529
  multiple Ant versions 528
  sealing violation 530
  stack overflow 527
<trycatch> task 256
<tstamp> task 58, 75–76, 611
  generating deployment
    timestamp 460
<typedef> task 611

U

Unix
  installing Ant 525–526
  line endings 144
  scheduling 388
<unjar> task 612
<untar> task 612
<unwar> task 612

<unzip> task 612
  expanding WAR files 287
<uptodate> task 612
  example 193
  for JUnit tests 106
  used with XDoclet 277
  using package mapper 106
  within <condition> 72
<uptodate> 72

V

<vajexport> task 612
<vajimport> task 613
<vajload> task 613
-verbose 41
verbosity
  controlling 42
-version 24, 41
VSS
  See Microsoft Visual SourceSafe
<vssadd> task 613
<vsscheckin> task 245, 613
<vsscheckout> task 245, 614
<vsscp> task 614
<vsscreate> task 614
<vssget> task 245, 615
<vsshistory> task 615
<vsslabel> task 245, 615

W

<waitfor> task 167, 616
  attributes 167
  deployment verification 461
<war> task 161, 616
  adding library dependencies 286
  deployment issues 441
  integrating tag libraries 286
  <zipfileset> nested 298
WAR files 160–161
  creating custom 440
  expanding 287
  structure 160
<war> task
  <zipfileset> 65
WAR, building
  See <war>
web development 278–316
  conditionally enabling servlets 293
  customizing deployed libraries 297
  customizing deployment
    descriptors 292
  customizing with XDoclet 294
  generating static content 297–299
  process 279–280

testing in-container
  See Cactus
testing with HttpUnit 300
web services
  adding to existing web
    application 367
  Adding web services to Java 357
  Axis 357
  calling a SOAP service from
    Ant 362
  creating a SOAP client
    application 357
  creating a SOAP client in C# 376
  creating a SOAP service with Axis
    and Ant 363
  creating SOAP proxy classes 359
  creating with Axis 364
  interoperability 376
  introducing SOAP 356
  invoking Ant as 383
  reviewing SOAP client
    creation 363
  running a C# client
    application 380
  Sun's Java Web Services
    Developer Pack 357
  Working with 355
  WSDL—Web Service Description
    Language 356
  See also Axis
web testing
  using WebTest 306
web.xml
  tag library definitions 284
  validating 319
  See also web development
WebDAV
  deployment 442
<webdoclet> task
  conditional deployment 451
  deployment issues 441
  including Axis servlets 367
WebLogic
  compiling JSP 292
  deployment using 458
  and <ejbjar> 340
  EJB tasks 336
  and <serverdeploy> 348, 443
  support in Middlegen 348
  XDoclet subtask 343
WebSphere
  and <ejbjar> 340
  XDoclet subtask 343
WebTest 306

Windows
  installing Ant 524–525
  line endings 144
  scheduling 387
Windows NT
  Telnet issues 443
Windows XP
  mounting WebDAV folder 442
<wljspc> task 292, 617
<wlrun> task 336, 617
<wlstop> task 336, 618
workflow engine 21
<wsdltodotnet> task
  importing WSDL into C# 378
  618

X

XDoclet 19, 260–277
  architecture 262–265
  best practices 276
  building task library 495
  custom code generation 267
  custom tag handler 274
  custom templates 265
  customizing web.xml 294
  dependency checking 276
  EJB build file example 351
  in EJB development 340–345
  EJB subtasks 341
  filtering classes processed 273
  future direction 275
  how it works 265
  installing 261
  merge points 284
  per-class generation 272
  property substitution 343
  and tag libraries 280
  tasks 263
  templates 264
  to-do list generation 192
  using Middlegen to start 345
XML
  accessing as Ant properties 331
  build log 327
  CDATA section 534
  comments 535
  DTD resolution 321–322
  encoding 534
  entity references 534
    in custom tasks 482
  manipulation in Ant 317–332
  parser issues 318
  primer 532–535
  resolving entities and DTDs 325

XML *(continued)*
  transformations, *See* <xslt>
  validation, *See* <xmlvalidate>
XML entity reference 189, 225
  sharing task definitions 258
XML Schema 250, 323, 532
XMLCatalog 325–327
XmlLogger 327
  output file 329
<xmlproperty> task 76, 331, 618
<xmlvalidate> task 319–321, 619
XP, *See* eXtreme Programming
X-Power 327

XSD, *See* XML Schema
XSL-FO 21, 327
<xslt> task 323–327, 619
  and Canoo WebTest 310
  transforming CVS
    change logs 246
XSLT, *See* <xslt> task

Z

<zip> task 620
  <zipfileset> element 154
  merging another Zip file 65

Zip files 154–158
  best practices 157
  creating binary distribution 154
  merging 157
  source distribution 156
Zip, *See* <zip> task
<zipfileset> 65, 325
  example in <war> 298
  within <zip> 154
<zipgroupfileset> 157

More Java titles from Manning

JMX in Action

BENJAMIN G. SULLINS AND
MARK B. WHIPPLE
ISBN 1930110561
360 pages, $39.95, Fall 2002

JSTL in Action

SHAWN BAYERN
ISBN 1930110529
480 pages, $39.95
Summer 2002

SCWCD Exam Study Kit:
Java Web Component
Developer Certification

HANUMANT DESHMUKH AND
JIGNESH MALAVIA
ISBN 1930110596
560 pages, includes CD ROM, $44.95
Summer 2002

Bitter Java

BRUCE A. TATE
ISBN 193011043X
368 pages,$44.95
Spring 2002

For ordering information visit www.manning.com

More Java titles from Manning

JDK 1.4 Tutorial

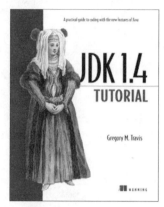

GREGORY M. TRAVIS
ISBN 1930110456
408 pages, $34.95, Spring 2002

Java 3D Programming

DANIEL SELMAN
ISBN 1930110359
400 pages, $49.95, Spring 2002

Instant Messaging in Java: The Jabber Protocols

IAIN SHIGEOKA
ISBN 1930110464
400 pages, $39.95
Spring 2002

Web Development with Java Server Pages, Second edition

DUANE FIELDS, MARK A. KOLB,
AND SHAWN BAYERN
ISBN 193011012X
800 pages, $44.95, November 2001

For ordering information visit www.manning.com